PREFACE

'THE Eastern Question has by degrees assumed such large proportions that no one can be surprised at the space it occupies in all public discussions whether of the tongue or of the pen.' So Lord Stratford de Redcliffe wrote to *The Times* on September 9, 1876. His words testified to a notorious fact. The fact has not become less notorious during the forty years since the words were written nor have the proportions assumed by the Eastern Question become less ample. In view of these facts it is the more surprising that English Historical Literature should still lack any systematic and continuous account of the origin and development of the Eastern Question.

Monographs exist in plenty on special aspects of the problem, and many general Histories of Europe contain useful chapters on the subject, but I do not know of any book in English which attempts the task which in the present work I have set before myself.

The main lines of this book were laid down many years ago; the subject has formed part of my academic teaching; for this purpose my material has been under constant revision, and some of it has been utilized for articles recently contributed to the *Edinburgh Review*, the *Fortnightly Review*, and the *Nineteenth Century and After*. To the proprietors and editors of these *Reviews* I am indebted for permission to reproduce portions of my articles, but none of them are reprinted *in extenso*. Elsewhere, in the course of my protracted journey,

I have come across traces of my own footsteps, indicating the route of previous historical excursions. In such cases I have not been careful to avoid them, and here and there I have incorporated whole paragraphs from earlier works, for I was long ago impressed by the warning that a man may say a thing once as he would have it said, but he cannot say it twice.

To each chapter I have suffixed a list of authorities which will I trust be found useful by students, by teachers, and by the 'general reader' who may desire further information on special topics which in a work like the present must needs be somewhat summarily dismissed. To stimulate such curiosity and to encourage more detailed research are among the main objects which I have had in view. But my primary purpose has been to provide for those who are in any degree charged with the responsibility for the solution of a most complex political problem an adequate basis of historical knowledge. A knowledge of the past is not in itself sufficient to solve the problems of the present ; but no solution is likely to be effective or enduring which is not based upon such knowledge. Least of all in the case of a problem which, like that of the Near East, includes numerous factors which are intelligible only in the light of past events, many of them remote, and most of them obscure.

Especially obscure are the facts of the political geography of the Balkans. My numerous maps are intended to elucidate them, and if they are found to fulfil their purpose at all adequately it is mainly owing to the kind help of my friend and colleague Mr. C. Grant Robertson, M.A., C.V.O., of All Souls College, and to the extraordinary patience and care bestowed upon their preparation by the Assistant Secretary to the

THE
EASTERN QUESTION

AN HISTORICAL STUDY

IN

EUROPEAN DIPLOMACY

BY

J. A. R. MARRIOTT

HON. FELLOW OF WORCESTER COLLEGE

FOURTH EDITION

OXFORD
AT THE CLARENDON PRESS
1940

OXFORD
UNIVERSITY PRESS
AMEN HOUSE, E.C. 4
London Edinburgh Glasgow New York
Toronto Melbourne Capetown Bombay
Calcutta Madras
HUMPHREY MILFORD
PUBLISHER TO THE
UNIVERSITY

33

FIRST EDITION, demy 8vo, 1917
SECOND EDITION, cr. 8vo, 1918
THIRD EDITION, 1925
REPRINTED, 1930

PRINTED IN GREAT BRITAIN

Delegates of the Press. But every student of historical geography will acknowledge the difficulty of the task. Among the maps will be found one on Balkan Ethnography which no one should consult without taking heed to Sir Charles Eliot's warning : ' every Ethnographic map of the Balkan Peninsula gives a different view of the arrangement of the populations.' In truth precision is unattainable, and the map must be accepted only as a rough indication of the distribution of races.

In the accomplishment of my task I have incurred many obligations to friends which it is a duty and a pleasure to acknowledge. Sir Arthur Evans kindly allowed me to consult him on one or two geographical points ; Dr. Holland Rose of Cambridge and Professor Alison Phillips of Dublin were good enough to reply in some detail to questions addressed to them, while to Dr. R. W. Macan, Master of University College, and to Mr. Grant Robertson I owe a debt which I find it difficult to acknowledge in terms which shall be at once adequate to my own sense of gratitude and not repugnant to them. Both these distinguished scholars have subjected my proof sheets to the most careful revision, and from both I have received invaluable suggestions. My obligations to writers who have covered parts of the same ground are, it is needless to add, exceedingly numerous, but I trust that they have been acknowledged in the foot-notes and bibliographies. For any unacknowledged or unwitting appropriation I crave pardon. To the modern school of French historians my debt is particularly heavy, and I desire to pay my respectful homage to the skill with which they combine massive erudition with a brilliance of exposition which none may hope to rival. Neither in French, however, nor in any other language have I come across any book which is identical in scope and purpose with my own, and though no one can be more conscious than myself both of the inadequacy of my equipment and the imperfection of my execution, yet I have no misgivings as to the importance or the timeliness of the task I have essayed. The author may have dared too much ; but the book itself was overdue.

J. A. R. MARRIOTT.

OXFORD,
Easter Eve (April 7), 1917.

NOTE TO SECOND EDITION

I SHOULD be grossly insensible to generosity if I failed to acknowledge with gratitude the kindly reception accorded to the first edition of this work, more particularly by those of my critics and confrères who are most competent to judge. To their appreciation I must attribute the fact that a second edition has been called for sooner than I dared to anticipate. I have also to thank many correspondents known and unknown who have favoured me with a list of *corrigenda*, mostly slips of the pen, or slight typographical errors. These, I need not say, have been corrected. This Second Edition has also enjoyed the advantage of a careful revision at the hands of two friends, who approached the task from widely different standpoints : the Right Hon. Austen Chamberlain, M.P., and the Rev. Dr. Margoliouth, Laudian Professor of Arabic in the University of Oxford. To both I desire to tender my grateful thanks for a substantial list of corrections ; but neither must be held responsible for any errors in which I may have decided to persist ; still less for any opinions to which I adhere.

The book was and is intended to close with the outbreak of the European War in 1914. In deference to the opinion of friends, I added to the first edition an epilogue, and I have in this edition, under similar pressure, brought the epilogue up to date. But the chapter is added merely for the convenience of readers ; obviously it can possess no historical value save as recording the rapid impression conveyed to a contemporary by passing events. Before the written word is in print the impression may be effaced and the assumed facts may have to be corrected. For such work the historian can accept no responsibility, though it is needless to add that in compiling the summary I have exercised all possible care. I should like, in this connexion, to acknowledge the help derived from that invaluable publication, *The Annual Register*, and from the spirited journalistic enterprise, *The New Europe*.

Substantial additions have been made to the bibliographies; in compiling them I have received from Mr. C. H. Firth, Regius Professor of Modern History, the help which no one is more competent and no one more ready to afford.

J. A. R. MARRIOTT.

Oxford,
June 24, 1918.

NOTE TO THIRD EDITION

At the request of my publishers I have added a Second Epilogue, containing a brief summary of events between 1917 and the Signature of the Treaty of Lausanne (1923).

I have to thank my friend the Rev. Dr. Margoliouth, Laudian Professor of Arabic, for his signal kindness in correcting the proofs of the Epilogue (Part II).

J. A. R. MARRIOTT.

House of Commons Library,
September 7, 1924.

NOTE TO FOURTH EDITION

A NEW edition of this book having been called for, it seemed advisable to the author and his publishers to add yet another epilogue, in order to bring the narrative up to date. That has been done; but no more than a bare narrative of events has been attempted. Even so, the task imposed on me, at rather short notice, in September of this year, has been rendered exceedingly difficult by enforced residence in a remote country district, where access to any great library, or even to his own, was denied to the author. Readers may, however, be glad to have even a brief summary of the more important events that have happened since the previous epilogue was written (1924). Apart from works included in the list of books appended to the epilogue, I have to acknowledge a particularly heavy debt to the special correspondents of *The Times*, and the *Daily Telegraph and Morning Post*, in Turkey, Greece, and the Balkans, and to many valuable articles contributed to those Journals. I hope that three visits which I have personally paid to the Near East since the publication of the last edition may also have helped me, and my readers, to a better understanding of 'that shifting, intractable, and interwoven tangle of conflicting interests, rival peoples, and antagonistic faiths' that is still, as John Morley said long ago, 'veiled under the easy name of the Eastern Question'.

J. A. R MARRIOTT.

December, 1939.

CONTENTS

PAGE

LIST OF MAPS

Introductory

The Problem of the Near East

'That shifting, intractable, and interwoven tangle of conflicting interests, rival peoples, and antagonistic faiths that is veiled under the easy name of the Eastern Question.'—JOHN MORLEY.

FROM time immemorial Europe has been confronted with an 'Eastern Question'. In its essence the problem is unchanging. It has arisen from the clash in the lands of South-Eastern Europe between the habits, ideas, and preconceptions of the West and those of the East. But although one in essence, the problem has assumed different aspects at different periods. In the dawn of authentic history it is represented by the contest between the Greeks and the Persians, the heroic struggle enshrined in the memory of Marathon, Thermopylae, and Salamis. To the Roman the 'Eastern Question' centred in his duel with the great Hellenistic monarchies. In the early Middle Ages the problem was represented by the struggle between the forces of Islam and those of Christianity. That struggle reached its climax, for the time being, in the great battle of Tours (732). The chivalry of Western Europe renewed the contest, some centuries later, in the Crusades. The motives which inspired that movement were curiously mixed, but essentially they afforded a further manifestation of the secular rivalry between Cross and Crescent; a contest between Crusaders and Infidels for possession of the lands hallowed to every Christian by their association with the life of Christ on earth.

With none of these earlier manifestations of an immemorial

antithesis is this book concerned. Its main purpose is to sketch the historical evolution of a problem which has baffled the ingenuity of European diplomatists, in a general sense, for more than five hundred years, more specifically and insistently for about a century. In the vocabulary of English diplomacy the *Eastern Question* was not included until the period of the Greek War of Independence (1821–9), though the phrase is said to be traceable at least as far back as the battle of Lepanto (1571). A definition of the ' Question ', at once authoritative and satisfactory, is hard to come by. Lord Morley, obviously appreciating the difficulty, once spoke of it, with characteristic felicity, as ' that shifting, intractable, and interwoven tangle of conflicting interests, rival peoples, and antagonistic faiths that is veiled under the easy name of the Eastern Question '. A brilliant French writer, M. Édouard Driault, has defined it as *Le problème de la ruine de la puissance politique de l'Islam.* But this definition seems unnecessarily broad. Dr. Miller, with more precision, has explained it thus : ' The Near Eastern Question may be defined as the problem of filling up the vacuum created by the gradual disappearance of the Turkish Empire from Europe.' But though this definition is un-exceptionable as far as it goes, our purpose seems to demand something at once more explicit and more explanatory. Putting aside the many difficult problems connected with the position of Ottoman power in Asia and Africa, the ' Eastern Question ' may be taken, for the purpose of the present survey, to include :

First and primarily : The part played by the Ottoman Turks in the history of Europe since they first crossed the Hellespont in the middle of the fourteenth century ;

Secondly : The position of the loosely designated Balkan States, which, like Greece, Serbia, Bulgaria, and Roumania, have gradually re-emerged as the waters of the Ottoman flood have subsided ; or, like Montenegro, were never really submerged ; or, like Bosnia, the Herzegovina, Transylvania, and the Bukovina, have been annexed by the Habsburgs ;

Thirdly : The problem of the Black Sea ; egress therefrom, ingress thereto ; the command of the Bosphorus and the Dardanelles, and, above all, the capital problem as to the possession of Constantinople ;

Fourthly : The position of Russia in Europe ; her natural impulse towards the Mediterranean ; her repeated attempts to secure permanent access to that sea by the narrow straits ; her relation to her co-religionists under the sway of the Sultan, more particularly to those of her own Slavonic nationality ;

Fifthly : The position of the Habsburg Empire, and in particular its anxiety for access to the Aegean, and its relations, on the one hand, with the Southern Slavs in the annexed provinces of Dalmatia, Bosnia, and the Herzegovina, as well as in the adjacent kingdoms of Serbia and Montenegro ; and, on the other hand, with the Roumans of Transylvania and the Bukovina ; and

Finally : The attitude of the European Powers in general, and of England in particular, towards all or any of the questions enumerated above.

The primary and most essential factor in the problem is then, the presence, embedded in the living flesh of Europe, of an alien substance. That substance is the Ottoman Turk. Akin to the European family neither in creed, in race, in language, in social customs, nor in political aptitudes and traditions, the Ottomans have for more than five hundred years presented to the other European Powers a problem, now tragic, now comic, now bordering almost on burlesque, but always baffling and paradoxical. The following pages, after sketching the settlement of this nomad people in Anatolia, will describe their momentous passage from the southern to the northern shore of the Hellespont ; their encampment on European soil ; their gradual conquest of the Balkan peninsula ; their overthrow of the great Serbian Empire ; their reduction of the kingdom of Bulgaria ; and finally, by a successful assault upon Constantinople, their annihilation of the last feeble remnant of the Roman Empire of the East.

From Constantinople we shall see the Ottomans advancing to the conquest of the whole of the Eastern basin of the Mediterranean : the Aegean islands, Syria, Egypt, and the northern coast of Africa. The zenith of their power was attained with remarkable rapidity. Before the end of the sixteenth century it was already passed. The seeds of decay were indeed sown, even if they were not yet discernible, during the reign of Suleiman the Magnificent (1520–66), a period generally accounted the noontide of Ottoman greatness and prosperity. Within five years of Suleiman's death the great naval disaster at Lepanto (1571) had revealed to an astonished world the obvious weakening of Ottoman morale and the waning of their power at sea.

Political decay was temporarily arrested during the following century. But for any success achieved by the Turks the Sultans were no longer personally responsible. Not one of the Sultans of the seventeenth century, nor for that matter of the eighteenth, left any impress upon the page of Ottoman history. The revival of Turkish prestige in the seventeenth century was due to a remarkable Albanian family, the Kiuprilis ; but that revival rested upon no substantial foundations, and its evanescent character was clearly manifested before the century had drawn to a close. The failure of the Moslems to take advantage of the distractions of their Christian enemies during the Thirty Years' War (1618–48) was in itself symptomatic of a loss of energy and initiative. Still more significant were the reverses sustained by Turkish arms. At the great battle of St. Gothard

(1664) Montecuculi proved that the Ottomans were no longer invincible on land, as Don John had demonstrated at Lepanto that they were no longer invincible by sea.

Twenty years later the Vizier, Kara Mustapha, did indeed carry the victorious arms of Turkey to the gates of Vienna. But the Polish King, John Sobieski, snatched from him the supreme prize; saved the Austrian capital; and relieved Europe from the nightmare by which it had long been oppressed.

From that moment (1683) the Turks ceased to be a menace to Christendom. The Habsburgs inflicted a series of crushing defeats upon them in the north; the Venetians conquered the Morea; while France was so deeply involved in Western Europe that she could do little to help the Power with whom she had so long been allied in the East. The Treaty of Carlo-witz, concluded in 1699 between the Habsburgs and the Turks, supplemented by that of Azov, dictated by Russia in 1702, afforded conclusive evidence that the tide had turned. For two and a half centuries the Ottomans had been the scourge of Christendom and had seriously threatened the security of the European polity. The menace was now dissipated for ever. John Sobieski's brilliant exploit was in this sense decisive. The advance of the Moslem was finally arrested, and the first phase of the Eastern Question had closed.

Only, however, to give place to another less alarming but more perplexing. Ever since the early years of the eighteenth century Europe has been haunted by the apprehension of the consequences likely to ensue upon the demise of the sick man, and the subsequent disposition of his heritage. For nearly two hundred years it was assumed that the inheritance would devolve upon one or more of the Great Powers. That the submerged nationalities of the Balkan peninsula would ever again be in a position to exercise any decisive influence upon the destinies of the lands they still peopled was an idea too remote from actualities to engage even the passing attention of diplomacy. From the days of Alberoni ingenious diplomatists in long succession have amused themselves by devising schemes for the partition of the Ottoman Empire, but none of these schemes paid any heed to the claims of the indigenous inhabitants. It would, indeed, have been remarkable if they had ; for from the fifteenth century to the nineteenth nothing was heard and little was known of Bulgar, Slav, Rouman, or Greek. The problem of the Near East concerned not the peoples of the Balkans, but the Powers of Europe, and among the Powers primarily Russia.

In its second phase (1702–1820) the Eastern Question might indeed be defined as the Relations of Russia and Turkey. The Habsburgs were frequently on the stage, but rarely in the leading rôle, and the part they played became more and more definitely subsidiary as the eighteenth century advanced. From the days of Peter the Great to those of Alexander I Europe, not indeed without spasmodic protests from France, acquiesced in the assumption that Russia might fairly claim a preponderant interest in the settlement of the Eastern Question. This acquiescence seems to a later generation the more remarkable in view of the fact that Russia herself had so lately made her entrance upon the stage of European politics. Perhaps, however, this fact in itself explains the acquiescence. Russia was already pushing towards the Black Sea before Western Europe recognized her existence. By 1774 her grip upon the inland sea was firmly established, and she was already looking to the possibilities of egress into the Mediterranean. The Treaty of Kainardji, concluded in that year, not only provided ample excuse for subsequent interference in the Balkans, but gave Russia the right of establishing a permanent embassy at Constantinople. The Treaties of Jassy (1792) and

Bucharest (1812) carried her two stages further towards her ultimate goal. But by this time new factors in the problem were beginning to operate.

France had never been unmindful of her interests in the Eastern Mediterranean. By the capitulations of 1535 Francis I had obtained from Suleiman the Magnificent considerable trading privileges in Egypt. D'Argenson, in 1738, published an elaborate plan for the construction of a canal through the Isthmus of Suez and for restoring, by the enterprise of French traders and the efforts of French administrators, political order and commercial prosperity in Egypt. In the negotiations between Catherine II and the Emperor Joseph for the partition of the Ottoman dominions the interests of France were recognized by the assignment of Egypt and Syria to the French monarch.

But it was Napoleon who first concentrated the attention of the French people on the high significance of the problem of the Near East. The acquisition of the Ionian Isles ; the expedition to Egypt and Syria ; the grandiose schemes for an attack on British India ; the agreement with the Tsar Alexander for a partition of the Ottoman Empire—all combined to stir the imagination alike of traders and diplomatists in France.

And not in France only. If Napoleon was a great educator of the French, still more was he an educator of the English. For some two hundred years English merchants had been keenly alive to the commercial value of the Levant. The politicians, however, were curiously but characteristically tardy in awakening to the fact that the development of events in the Ottoman Empire possessed any political significance for England. The statesmen of the eighteenth century observed with equal unconcern the decrepitude of the Turks and the advance of the Russians. The younger Pitt was the first and only one among them to display any interest in what, to his successors in Downing Street, became known as the *Eastern Question*. With a prescience peculiar to himself he perceived that England was supremely concerned in the ultimate solution of that problem. His earliest diplomatic achievement, the Triple Alliance of 1788, was designed largely, though not exclusively, to circumscribe Russian ambitions in the Near East. But his apprehensions were not shared by his contemporaries. Few English statesmen have commanded the confidence and the ear of the House of Commons as Pitt commanded them. Yet even Pitt failed to arouse attention to this subject, and when in 1790 he proposed a naval demonstration against Russia he suffered one of the few checks in his triumphant parliamentary career. The enemies of England were less slow to perceive where her vital interests lay. ' Really to conquer England,' said Napoleon, ' we must make ourselves masters of Egypt.'

Hence the importance attached by General Bonaparte, at the very outset of his political career, to the acquisition of the Ionian Isles. Corfu, Zante, and Cephalonia were, he declared in 1797, more important for France than the whole of Italy. They were the stepping-stones to Egypt ; Egypt was a stage on the high road to India. Hardly a generation had elapsed since Clive, strenuously seconded by the elder Pitt, had turned the French out of India. To Egypt, therefore, the thoughts of Frenchmen naturally turned,not only as affording a guarantee for the maintenance of French commercial interests in the Near East, but as a means of threatening the position so recently acquired by England in the Further East. These ideas constantly recur in the reports of French ambassadors at the Porte, and Talleyrand, on taking office, found, as he tells us, his official portfolio bulging with schemes for the conquest of Egypt.[1] Napoleon, therefore, in this as in other things,

[1] C. de Freycinet, *La Question d'Égypte*, p. 2.

was merely the heir and executor of the traditions of the *Ancien régime*. He brought, however, to the execution of these schemes a vigour which, of late years, the old monarchy had conspicuously lacked. But even Napoleon was only partially successful in arousing the attention of the English people to the importance of the Eastern Mediterranean. The decrepitude of the Turk, the advance of Russia, the ambitions of France were all regarded as the accentuation of a problem that was local rather than European.

Not until the events which followed upon the insurrection of the Greeks in 1821 did the English Foreign Office, still less did the English public, begin to take a sustained interest in the development of events in South-Eastern Europe.

The Greek Revolution was indeed sufficiently startling to arouse the attention even of the careless. For more than four hundred years the Greeks, like the Bulgarians and the Serbians, had been all but completely submerged under the Ottoman flood. To the outside world they had given no sign whatever that they retained the consciousness of national identity, still less that they cherished the idea of ever again achieving national unity. There had indeed been a rising in Serbia in 1804, and by the Treaty of Bucharest the Serbians had obtained from the Porte a small measure of internal autonomy, but all the strong places were garrisoned by Turks, and the step towards independence was of insignificant proportions. Besides, Europe was preoccupied with more important matters; Balkan affairs were of merely local interest.

The Greek rising was in a wholly different category. When Prince Alexander Hypsilanti unfurled the flag of Greek independence in Moldavia, still more when the insurrection spread to the Morea and the islands of the Aegean archipelago, even the dullards began to realize that a new force was manifesting itself in European politics, and that an old problem was entering upon a new phase. The Greek rising meant an appeal to the sentiment of nationality : Pan-hellenism—the achievement of Hellenic unity and the realization of Hellenic identity—was the motto inscribed upon their banner. Plainly, a new factor had entered into the complex problem of the Near East. But the nationality factor was not the only one disclosed to Europe by the Greek insurrection. Hitherto, the Eastern Question had meant the growth or the decline of Ottoman power ; a struggle between the Turks on the one hand and Austrians and Venetians on the other. More lately it had centred in the rivalry between the Sultan and the Tsar. Henceforward it was recognized, primarily through the action of Russia and the newly aroused sympathies of England, as an international question. The more cautious and more disinterested of European statesmen have persistently sought to ' isolate ' the politics of the Near East. They have almost consistently failed. The Greek insurrection struck a new note. It refused to be isolated. The Tsar Alexander, though deaf to Hypsilanti's appeal, had his own quarrel with Sultan Mahmud. There was, therefore, an obvious probability that two quarrels, distinct in their origin, would be confused, and that the Tsar would take advantage of the Greek insurrection to settle his own account with the Sultan.

To avoid this confusion of issues was the primary object of English diplomacy. Castlereagh and Canning were fully alive to the significance of the Hellenic movement, alike in its primary aspect and in its secondary reaction upon the general diplomatic situation. And behind the statesmen there was for the first time in England a strong public opinion in favour of determined action in the Near East. The sentiment to which Byron and other Philhellenist enthusiasts appealed with such effect was a curious compound of classicism, liberalism, and nationalism. A people who claimed affinity with the citizens of the States of ancient Hellas ; a people who were struggling for political freedom ; who relied upon the inspiring though elusive sentiment of nationality, made an irresistible appeal to the educated classes in England. Canning was in complete accord with the feelings of his countrymen. But he perceived, as few of them could, that the situation, unless dexterously handled, might lead to new and dangerous developments. Consequently, he spared no efforts to induce the Sultan to come to terms with the insurgent Greeks lest a worse thing should befall him at the hands of Russia.

The Porte was, as usual, deaf to good advice, and Canning then endeavoured, not without success, to secure an understanding with Russia, and to co-operate cordially with her and with France in a settlement of the affairs of South-Eastern Europe. That co-operation, in itself a phenomenon of high diplomatic significance, was in a fair way of achieving its object when Canning's premature death (1827) deprived the new and promising machinery of its mainspring. Owing to untimely scruples of the Duke of Wellington, England lost all the fruits of the astute and far-seeing diplomacy of Canning ; the effectiveness of the Concert of Europe was destroyed, and Russia was left free to deal as she would with the Porte and to dictate the terms of a Treaty, which, by the Duke's own admission, ' sounded the death-knell of the Ottoman Empire in Europe '. But, although the Treaty of Adrianople represented a brilliant success for Russian policy at Constantinople, Great Britain was able to exercise a decisive influence on the settlement of the Hellenic question. By the Treaty of London (1832) Greece was established as an independent kingdom, under the protection of Great Britain, Russia, and France.

The tale of the Sultan's embarrassments was not completed by the Treaties of Adrianople and London. The independence of Greece had not only made a serious inroad upon the integrity of the Ottoman Empire in Europe, but had precipitated a disastrous conflict with Russia. Worse still, the effort to avert the disruption of his Empire had induced the Sultan to seek the assistance of an over-mighty vassal. If there is anything in politics more dangerous than to confer a favour it is to accept one. Mehemet Ali, the brilliant Albanian adventurer, who had made himself Pasha of Egypt, would, but for the intervention of the Powers, have restored Greece to the Sultan. The island of Crete seemed to the vassal an inadequate reward for the service rendered to his Suzerain. Nor was the revelation of Ottoman weakness and incompetence lost upon him. He began to aspire to an independent rule in Egypt; to the pashalik of Syria; perhaps to the lordship of Constantinople itself. The attempt to realize these ambitions kept Europe in a state of almost continuous apprehension and unrest for ten years (1831–41), and opened another chapter in the history of the Eastern Question.

To save himself from Mehemet Ali the Sultan appealed to the Powers. Russia alone responded to the appeal, and as a reward for her services imposed upon the Porte the humiliating Treaty of Unkiar-Skelessi (1833). By the terms of that Treaty Russia became virtually mistress of the Bosphorus and the Dardanelles. The Tsar bound himself to render unlimited assistance to the Porte by land and sea, and in return the Sultan undertook to close the Straits to the ships of war of all nations, while permitting free egress to the Russian fleet. To all intents and purposes the Sultan had become the vassal of the Tsar.

Thus far England, as a whole, had betrayed little or no jealousy of the Russian advance towards the Mediterranean. Canning, though not unfriendly to Russia, had indeed repudiated, and with success, her claim to an exclusive or even a preponderant influence over Turkey. But by the Treaty of Unkiar-Skelessi that claim was virtually admitted. Russia had established a military protectorship over the European dominions of the Sultan.

The Treaty of Unkiar-Skelessi inaugurates yet another phase in the evolution of the Eastern Question. From that time down to the Treaty of Berlin (1878) the primary factor in the problem is found in the increasing mistrust and antagonism between Great Britain and Russia. Lord Palmerston, inheriting the diplomatic traditions of Pitt and Canning, deeply resented the establishment of a Russian protectorate over Turkey, and determined that, at the first opportunity, the Treaty in which it was embodied should be torn up. Torn up it was by the Treaties of London (1840 and 1841), under which the collective protectorate of the Western Powers was substituted for the exclusive protectorate of Russia. After 1841 the Russian claim was never successfully reasserted.

That Great Britain had a vital interest in the development of events in South-Eastern Europe was frankly acknowledged by Russia, and the Tsar Nicholas I made two distinct efforts to come to terms with Great Britain. The first was made in the course of the Tsar's visit to the Court of St. James's in 1844; the second occurred on the eve of the Crimean War, when the Tsar made specific though informal proposals to Sir Hamilton Seymour, then British Ambassador at St. Petersburg. Neither attempt bore fruit. The overtures were based upon the assumption that the dissolution of the Ottoman Empire was imminent, and that it was the duty, as well as the obvious interest, of the Powers most closely concerned to come to an understanding as to the disposition of the estate. British statesmen refused to admit the accuracy of the Tsar's diagnosis, and questioned the propriety of the treatment prescribed. The ' sick man ' had still, in their opinion, a fair chance of recovery, and to arrange, before his demise, for a partition of his inheritance, seemed to them beyond the bounds of diplomatic decency. Lord Palmerston, in particular, was at once profoundly mistrustful of the designs of Russia, and singularly hopeful as to the possibilities of redemption for the Ottoman Empire. The advances of the Tsar were, therefore, rather curtly declined.

However distasteful the Tsar's proposals may have been to the moral sense or the political prejudices of English statesmen, it cannot be denied that they were of high intrinsic significance. Had they found general acceptance—an extravagant assumption—the Crimean War would never have been fought ; Russia would have become virtually supreme in the Balkans and over the Straits, while England would have established herself in Egypt and Crete. The refusal of the Aberdeen Cabinet even to consider such suggestions formed one of the proximate causes of the Crimean War.

That war, for good or evil, registered a definite set-back to the policy of Russia in the Near East. It has, indeed, become fashionable to assume that, at any rate as regards the British Empire, the war was a blunder if not a crime. How far that assumption is correct is a question which will demand and receive attention later on. For the moment it is sufficient to observe that the Crimean War did at any rate give the Sultan an opportunity to put his house in order, had he desired to do so. For twenty years he was relieved of all anxiety on the side of Russia. The event proved that the Sultan's zeal for reform was in direct ratio to his anxiety for self-preservation. To relieve him from the one was to remove the only incentive to the other. Consequently, his achievements in the direction of internal reform fell far short of his professions.

Little or nothing was done to ameliorate the lot of the subject populations, and in the third quarter of the nineteenth century those populations began to take matters into their own hands. Crete, the ' Great Greek Island ', had been in a state of perpetual revolt ever since it had been replaced, in 1840, under the direct government of the Sultan. In 1875 the unrest spread to the peninsula. It was first manifested among the mountaineers of the Herzegovina ; thence it spread to their kinsmen in Bosnia, Serbia, and Montenegro. The insurrection among the Southern Slavs in the west found an echo among the Bulgars in the east. The Sultan then let loose his Bashi-Bazouks among the Bulgarian peasantry, and all Europe was made to ring with the tale of the atrocities which ensued. The Powers could not stand aside and let the Turk work his will upon his Christian subjects, but mutual jealousy prevented joint action, and in 1877 Russia was compelled to act alone.

An arduous but decisive campaign brought her within striking distance of Constantinople, and enabled her to dictate to the Porte the Treaty of San Stefano. The terms of that famous Treaty were highly displeasing, not only to Austria and Great Britain, but to the Greeks and Serbians, whose ambitions in Macedonia were frustrated by the creation of a Greater Bulgaria. Great Britain, therefore, demanded that the Treaty should be submitted to a European Congress. Russia, after considerable demur, assented. Bismarck undertook to act as the 'honest broker' between the parties, and terms were ultimately arranged under his presidency at Berlin. The Treaty of Berlin (1878) ushers in a fresh phase in the evolution of the Eastern Question.

It had already become clear that the ultimate solution of an historic problem would not be reached in disregard of the aspirations and claims of the indigenous inhabitants of the Balkan peninsula. The Slavs and Bulgars were indeed only in one degree more indigenous than the Turks themselves. Roumans, Albanians, and Greeks might claim by a more ancient title. But all alike had at any rate been established in the lan is they still continue to inhabit many years before the advent of the alien Asiatic power. For centuries, however, all, save the hillsmen of Albania and the Black Mountain, had been more or less completely submerged under the Ottoman flood. When the tide turned and the flood gave signs of receding, the ancient nationalities again emerged. The rebirth of Greece, Roumania, Serbia, and Bulgaria represents in itself one of the most remarkable and one of the most characteristic movements in the political history of the nineteenth century. Incidentally it introduced an entirely new factor, and one of the highest significance, into the already complex problem of the Near East. The principle of nationality is itself confessedly elusive. But whatever may be its essential ingredients we must admit that the principle has asserted itself with peculiar force in the Balkan peninsula. Nor have the peoples of Western Europe been slow to manifest their sympathy with this new and interesting development. The official attitude of Great Britain during the critical years 1875–8 might seem to have committed the English people to the cause of reaction and Turkish misgovernment. Whatever may have been the motives which inspired the policy of Lord Beaconsfield it is far from certain that, in effect, it did actually obstruct the development of the Balkan nationalities. Two of them, at any rate, have reason to cherish the memory of the statesman who tore up the Treaty of San Stefano. Had that Treaty been allowed to stand, both Greece and Serbia would have had to renounce their ambitions in Macedonia, while the enormous accessions of territory which it secured for Bulgaria might ultimately have proved, even to her, a doubtful political advantage.

Since 1878 the progress of the Balkan nations has been rapid, and with that progress the concluding portion of this book will be mainly concerned. It will also have to chronicle the appearance of yet another factor in the problem. At no time could the Habsburgs regard with unconcern the development of events in South-Eastern Europe, but between 1848 and 1878 they had much to engage their attention elsewhere. They played a shrewd and calculating game between 1853 and 1856, and not without success; but their conduct during the Crimean crisis was hotly resented in Great Britain, and it may perhaps account for the lack of sympathy with which the English people regarded the misfortunes of the Austrian Empire during the next ten years. Prussia, too, was busy elsewhere, and as long as Bismarck remained in power Prussia disclaimed any interest in the problem of the Near East.

Nothing differentiates more clearly the policy of the Emperor William II from that of Bismarck than the increasing activity of German diplomacy in the Balkans. The growing intimacy of the relations between Berlin and Vienna, still more between Berlin and Buda-Pesth, must in any case have led to this result. The virtual annexation of Bosnia and the Herzegovina to the Austrian Empire was Bismarck's acknowledgement of the obligations which in 1870 he had incurred to Habsburg neutrality. But the gift bestowed upon Austria caused the first serious breach in the good relations between Berlin and St. Petersburg. The wire between those capitals was never actually cut so long as Bismarck controlled the German Foreign Office; but his successor found himself compelled to choose between the friendship of Austria and that of Russia, and he deliberately preferred the former.

That choice inevitably involved a change in the attitude of Germany towards the Near Eastern Question. Austria made no secret of her ambition to secure access to the Aegean. Germany not only identified herself with this ambition, but she developed similar ambitions of her own. If Salonica was the obvious goal for Austrian activities, those of her ally might naturally be directed towards Constantinople, and from Constantinople onwards to Bagdad and Basra. From such grandiose designs Bismarck instinctively recoiled; but to the very differently constituted mind of William II their appeal was irresistible. Consequently, in the Near East as elsewhere, German diplomacy has followed since 1890 a perfectly consistent and undeviating path. In every conceivable way the Turk was to be caressed. Not even the massacre of the Armenian Christians was allowed to interrupt the growing intimacy between Berlin and Constantinople. The moment when the rest of the Powers shrank in horror from the perpetrator of those massacres was selected by the Kaiser to demonstrate his unalterable friendship for his new ally. From 1904 onwards the Triple Alliance was enlarged to include the Ottoman Turk. Not, indeed, without embarrassment to one of the original partners. Berlin was continually engaged in the delicate task of preventing a rupture between Rome and Vienna on questions connected with the Near East, and for the time her diplomacy succeeded. The Alliance was still further strained by the Turco-Italian War in 1911; but for three more years it remained nominally intact. Not until 1914 was it finally broken.

German policy in the Near East had in the meantime sustained more than one check. Depending, as it did, largely on a personal equation, the deposition of Abdul Hamid and the triumph of the 'Young Turks' threatened it with ruin. But the danger passed; the Young Turks proved no less amenable than Abdul Hamid to the influence of Berlin; Germany was again supreme at Constantinople. Even more serious was the formation, in 1912, of the Balkan League and its astonishing success in the field. All the arts known to German diplomacy were needed to avert disaster; but they did not fail. With consummate adroitness Serbia was pushed away from the Adriatic and compelled to turn southwards; the most extravagant demands of Greece were encouraged in Macedonia; Bulgaria was effectively estranged from its allies; a remnant of the Ottoman Power in Europe was salved; a German vassal still reigned at Constantinople.

One danger remained. Between Central Europe and its *Drang nach Südosten* there intervened Serbia; no longer the Serbia of 1878; no longer the client of Austria-Hungary; but a Serbia in which was reborn the ancient spirit of the Jugo-Slav race; a Serbia which believed itself destined to be the nucleus of a great Serbo-Croatian Empire; which should embrace all the lands in which their race was dominant: Croatia, Slavonia, Bosnia and the Herzegovina, Serbia, Montenegro, Dalmatia, with parts of Carniola, Carinthia, Istria, and Styria. The foundation of such an empire would mean not only the dismemberment of the Dual Monarchy, but the death-blow to the ambitions of Central Europe in the Near East. At all hazards, even at the hazard of a world-war, such a danger must be averted.

The Great War of 1914 was the outcome of this conviction. Once more had the Near East reacted upon the West; indeed upon the whole world. In order that Austria-Hungary might keep a road open to the Aegean; in order to prevent a change of gauge between Berlin and Basra, the world must be flung into the crucible: Belgium, peaceful and unoffending, must be ruthlessly devastated, given over to arson, pillage, and abomination of every description; Poland must pay the last of many penalties; some of the fairest fields and most prosperous cities of France must be laid waste; the vast resources of the British Empire must be strained to the uttermost; Canadians must pay the toll in Flanders; Australians and New Zealanders must make the last heroic sacrifice in Gallipoli; Englishmen must perish in the swamps cf the Euphrates;

Indians must line the trenches in France; women and babes must perish on land and sea; from London to Melbourne, from Cairo to the Cape, from Liverpool to Vancouver the whole Empire must fight for its life; the whole world must groan in pity and suffering.

If it be true that in its dealings with the Near East Western Europe has in the past exhibited a brutal and callous selfishness, the Near East is indeed avenged.

The end no man can see. But one thing is certain. The future will not be as the past, nor as the present. Yet in order to face the future fearlessly and to shape it aright nothing is more indispensable than a knowledge of the past. Nor can that knowledge safely be confined to the few who govern; it must be diffused among the many who control. To diffuse that knowledge is the purpose of the pages that follow.

2

Physics and Politics

'No other site in the world enjoys equal advantages nor perhaps ever will enjoy them.'—D. G. Hogarth (of Constantinople).

'It is the Empire of the world.'—Napoleon (on Constantinople).

'When the Turks threw themselves across the ancient paths in the fifteenth century A. D., a great necessity arose in Christendom for searching out new lines of approach to India. From that quest the history of modern commerce dates.'—Sir W. W. Hunter.

'By whichever way we approach the problems before us we are brought back to the unique importance of the position occupied by Belgrade. It is in several ways the most commanding of any European city.... Belgrade lies at the only available gateway on the road to Salonica and the Piraeus as well as to Constantinople.'—Sir Arthur Evans.

This book will be concerned, as the introductory pages should have made clear, primarily with Politics; with the history of the Near East as the home of man; as the cockpit of nations, and as the arena of international rivalries. But there is no region in the world where physical conditions have played a more dominating part in shaping the destinies of individual men or of those political aggregations which we know as Nations and States. This is demonstrably true whether we have regard to the region as a whole, or to that segment of it with which this book is more particularly concerned, the lands which the geographers of the last generation described as *Turkey in Europe,* but for which political changes have compelled us to seek a new name. The name generally given to that segment is *The Balkan Peninsula,* or simply *The Balkans.* In strictness the description applies only to the lands to the south of the great *Divide* formed by the Shar mountains and the Balkan range. It excludes, therefore, a great part of Serbia and the Southern Slav provinces, and the whole of Roumania. In the following pages *The Balkans* will, however, be used as synonymous with the *Turkey in Europe* of our forefathers.

Only a few words can be spared for the geographical significance of the general region of the Near East. Nor, indeed, is it necessary to labour a commonplace. A glance at a map of the world—more particularly of the known world of A. D. 1450—can hardly fail to carry conviction even to those who are not wont to cultivate the historical or geographical imagination. The lands which fringe the Eastern Mediterranean—roughly the region bounded on the west by the Adriatic and the island of Crete, to the north by the Danube, to the east by Asia Minor and Mesopotamia, and to the south by Syria and Egypt—have possessed a significance in world-history incomparably greater than any other. If it be objected that the definition excludes all the lands dominated by the Anglo-Saxon race it is sufficient to reply, first, that this statement refers to the past, not to the future; and, secondly, that indications are not wanting that, in the future, the region may play a part in determining the fate of world-empires hardly less important than that which it has played in the past.

Until the establishment of the Ottoman Empire the region thus defined formed the nerve-centre of the world's commerce. From time immemorial the trade between the East and the West has followed well-defined routes. The most ancient is the caravan route which, from the dawn of history down to the sixteenth century, was commanded by the Semites. From the Far East goods found their way to the head of the Persian Gulf, thence by caravan they ultimately reached the Syrian sea-board, and from Tyre and Sidon were distributed by the Phoenicians to the peoples of the West. Basra, Bagdad, and Damascus were the dominating stations on this trunk-line. The Mongol invasions of the thirteenth century gravely impaired the security of the Mesopotamia-Syria route, and proportionately increased the importance of the northern and southern routes. The former reached Europe by the Oxus, the Caspian, and the Black Sea, its outer gate being commanded, of course, by Constantinople; the latter came by way of the Indian Ocean, the Red Sea, and the valley of the Nile, debouching from 332 B. C. onwards at Alexandria.

Every one of these Mediterranean outlets, Constantinople, Alexandria, and the Syrian coast, passed into the hands of the Ottoman Turks between 1453 and 1516. One after another the great trade-routes were blocked by a Power, inimical to commerce, and still more inimical to those Christian nations for whose benefit intercourse between East and West was mainly carried on. It will, therefore, be readily understood that the Ottoman conquest of the Near East constitutes one of the decisive events in world-history. After that conquest the Western world found itself confronted by three alternatives: to forgo the profits and conveniences of its trade with

the East ; or to expel the Ottomans from the ' nodal-points ';
or to discover a new route to the East with the continuity of
which the Ottomans could not interfere. Europe preferred
the last. Hence the abnormal activity displayed at Cadiz,
Bristol, and above all at Lisbon, in the latter half of the fifteenth
century. Portugal, thanks to Prince Henry the Navigator, had
indeed long been a centre of maritime activity and scientific
research. It was fitting, therefore, that the first prize in the
quest for a new route to the East should fall to the Portuguese
explorers.

The rounding of the Cape of Good Hope by Vasco da Gama
in 1498 opened a sea-route to India which was successively
dominated by the Portuguese, the Dutch, and the English.
Columbus setting forth on a similar quest a few years earlier
had stumbled upon the West Indies, and had thus opened to
his Spanish patrons a path to Empire in South America. The
Cabots, sailing from Bristol, under the English flag, discovered
and explored the coast of North America. Plainly, then, the
geographical renaissance of the later fifteenth century was due
primarily, though not exclusively, to the advent of the Ottomans in South-Eastern Europe and the consequent blocking
of the old established trade-routes.

The opening of the new route to the East Indies, together
with the discovery of America and the West Indies, had a profound and far-reaching influence upon the European polity.
The centre of gravity, commercial, political, and intellectual,
rapidly shifted from the south-east of Europe to the north-
west ; from the cities on the Mediterranean littoral to those
on the Atlantic. Constantinople, Alexandria, Venice, Genoa,
and Marseilles were deprived, almost at one fell swoop, of the
economic and political pre-eminence which had for centuries
belonged to them. Four of the five cities have regained
a large measure of importance, and at least one of them may

be destined to pre-eminence in the near future ; but for four centuries the Mediterranean, which had been the greatest of commercial highways, was reduced almost to the position of a backwater. Commercial supremacy passed to the Atlantic. The *Thalassic* Age, to adopt the terminology rendered classical by Sir John Seeley, was superseded by the *Oceanic*. To Western Europe, as a whole, and to England in particular, these changes were of the highest possible significance ; but it is neither necessary, nor in this connexion pertinent, to elaborate a commonplace of historical generalization.

Towards the end of the nineteenth century the great enterprise of M. de Lesseps, the cutting of the Isthmus of Suez by a canal, restored in large measure the commercial significance of the Mediterranean. Hardly less important has been the influence exerted in the same direction by the political reorganization and the economic development of Egypt under Lord Cromer. Genoa and Marseilles have responded superbly to the new demands made upon them, Alexandria has regained much of its importance.

The twentieth century has witnessed the initiation of an enterprise which, if it be carried through to a successful issue, may possibly have consequences, political and economic, hardly inferior to those which have accrued from the cutting of the Suez Canal. Just as at the close of the fifteenth century the Western Powers were intent upon securing for the eastern trade a route beyond the control of the Ottomans, so at the present day *Mitteleuropa* is straining every nerve to obtain command of a great trunk-line which, undisturbed by the dominant sea-power of Great Britain, shall carry the commerce and the influence of the Teutonic Empires from the shores of the North Sea to the Persian Gulf. The Bagdad railway is not yet completed, nor is it by any means certain that if and when it is completed the control will be vested in Berlin or

Hamburg. But the mere initiation of the enterprise affords one more indication of the commanding geographical situation of the lands which still form part of the Ottoman Empire, and in particular the incomparable significance of Constantinople. The convergence of all the great trade-routes of the ancient and the mediaeval worlds upon the Eastern Mediterranean, the importance attached in the modern world to Egypt, Syria, Mesopotamia, and Constantinople, are conclusive proof of the propositions advanced in the opening paragraphs of this chapter. England would not be in Egypt to-day, the German Emperor would not have courted the Sultan Abdul Hamid and Enver Pasha, had not the Near East retained all the significance which in all previous ages of world-history has been conferred upon it by a geographical situation pre-eminently and perhaps uniquely advantageous.

Not less obvious is the influence which physics have exercised upon the history of the Balkan lands. Before this proposition can be accepted it is necessary to discriminate with some nicety the outstanding geographical features of this region. For the first impression is one of almost hopeless confusion.

The orographical relief is, indeed, singularly complex. At first sight the peninsula seems, with small exceptions, to be covered by a series of mountain ranges, subject to no law save that of caprice, starting from nowhere in particular, ending nowhere in particular, now running north and south, now east and west, with no obvious purpose or well-defined trend. Closer scrutiny corrects the first impression, though not fundamentally. Still, where all had seemed chaotic, certain features emerge : the lower Danube basin, the two valleys of the Maritza, the plain of Thessaly, the valley of the Mozawa, and the lower Vardar valley. These are the most obvious exceptions to the mountain ranges and the high uplands. Still closer observation reveals a gap between the southern end

THE BALKANS: PHYSICAL FEATURES

of the Dinaric Alps and the northern terminus of the mountains of Albania. This 'Albanian Gap', created by the Drin river and extending on the Adriatic coast from Scutari to Alessio or S. Juan di Medua, has already played a considerable political rôle, and may be destined to play a much larger one. It is, indeed, hardly too much to say that the whole political future of Serbia depends upon the economic potentialities of this break in the coastal mountains. Another feature, of hardly less significance to Serbia, is the passage-way between the western coastal mountain chains and the central upland, a passage which opens at the northern end into the great Hungarian plain, and at the southern into the lower Vardar valley, connecting, in fact, Belgrade and Salonica. 'Within this belt is concentrated', as a recent writer has admirably said, 'most of the drama and most of the tragedy of the peninsula.'[1]

A third feature which disentangles itself from the confused mountainous mass is the Rhodope upland, a fairly defined central earth-block of triangular shape, based upon Salonica and Constantinople, and stretching in a north-westerly direction towards an apex at Belgrade. Along the sides of this triangular upland run the main lines of communication, with their junction at Nish (see maps, pp. 34, 35).

The most pronounced features of the mountain system still remain to be summarily noted. The first is the prolongation of the Alpine chain which, starting between Nice and Genoa, forms the northern boundary of the great Lombard plain, then sweeping round the head of the Adriatic begins to run down its eastern shore, first as the Julian and then as the Dinaric Alps. There is a fairly wide gap north-east of Fiume, and a well-marked one, already referred to, where the Drin has forced its way to the sea. Otherwise the coastal range runs

[1] Newbigin, *Geographical Aspects of Balkan Problems*, p. 9.

almost continuously parallel with the shore, and, what is more important, generally close to it. These geographical facts are not without significance in relation to the claim put forward by Italy to the eastern shore of the Adriatic. The Venetian character of the Dalmatian cities is as indisputable as is the Slavonic blood of the vast majority of the inhabitants, and if it be true that a mountain range affords a more scientific frontier than a river bank or even a sea-coast line, geographical symmetry might seem to argue in favour of Italy's claim to the ancient Illyria and modern Dalmatia. But here, as elsewhere in the Balkans, ethnography conflicts sharply with geography, agreeing with it only so far as to assert that whoever ' the rightful claimant may be it is not the present occupant '. Once past the Bocche di Cattaro the coastal mountains recede from the sea-coast until they reach Valona. From Valona they have a south-westerly trend until, in the Pindus range, they form the spinal cord of Greece.

From the west-coastal mountains there runs almost to the Black Sea an horizontal range. It starts with the Shar mountains just south of the Albanian Gap ; and broken once or twice, notably by the Belgrade-Salonica gangway, it continues as the Balkan range almost due east, stopping short of Varna on the Black Sea coast. This forms the great central watershed of the peninsula. North of it all the rivers, such as the northern or white Drin, the Morava, the Isker, and the Vid, empty into the Danube ; south of it the Vardar, the Struma, and the great Maritza system all flow into the Aegean.

Finally, we have to note the position of the Carpathians. They belong, in a sense, rather to the Central European than to the Balkan system. But the Balkan range itself may almost as well be regarded as a continuation of the Carpathian folds as of the central watershed, and apart from this the Carpathians have a paradoxical significance of their own which cannot be ignored. In one sense they form an obvious and formidable barrier between the Hungarian plain and the basin of the lower Danube, which in its turn marks, from the Iron Gates almost to the Black Sea, the southern frontier of Roumania. But the physiographic frontier, in the case of the Danubian principalities, conflicts curiously with the ethnographic. If there are some nine million Roumanians dwelling to the east of the Carpathians, there are four million people of the same race to be found on the western side of the mountains. In this fact lies the core of the political problem of Roumania, a problem deliberately created, it would seem, by a capricious but obstinate geography.

Caprice is, indeed, the obtrusive characteristic of Balkan physiography. If anything could be more confusingly capricious than the orographical relief, it is the river system of the peninsula. Why does the Danube, after a prolonged, regular, orthodox, west to east course from Belgrade to beyond Silistria, take a sudden tilt due north as far as Galatz before it is content to empty itself into the Black Sea? Its only purpose seems to be the purely malicious one of involving Roumania and Bulgaria in disputes over the unattractive marshes of the Dobrudja. If the Danube had only persevered a little longer in its eastward course and reached the sea—as the railway line from Bucharest does—at the port of Constanza, there would be practically nothing to prevent unbroken amity between the Roumanians and their Bulgarian neighbours. But that again would be so contrary to every Balkanic principle and tradition that perhaps, after all, the Danube, under an outer cloak of perversity, is only attempting to preserve spiritual conformity with the circumstances of its political environment.

Further south, the Maritza plays us an almost identical trick with political results hardly less embarrassing. This great river drains the valley which intervenes between the Balkans and the Rhodope block of central uplands ; it maintains a south-easterly course from Philippopolis to Adrianople, and then, instead of continuing its orthodox course to the Black Sea, or even to the Sea of Marmora, it takes a sudden turn to the south and finally, by a course decidedly south-westerly, reaches the Aegean at Enos. The curious deflection of this great river system is due to the geological process known as ' river capture '. The sinking of land below what is now the surface of the Aegean Sea—a process the incompleteness of which is manifested by the existence of the Aegean archipelago—has increased the velocity and therefore the erosive power of the streams flowing southward to such a degree that the watershed has been thrust northward, and the Aegean streams have ' captured ' the head-waters of systems which did not originally belong to them. Geologically the Aegean has thus exerted a very powerful attractive force. The Maritza, the Mista, the Struma, to say nothing of the Vardar and the Vistritza, all flow into the Aegean. Politics have followed the lead of Physics. Men, like streams, have been attracted towards the Aegean littoral, and thus Macedonia has become the ' key to the history of the whole peninsula '.[1] Nowhere in the Balkans has physiography more obviously dictated the course of history than in this difficult and debatable region. Macedonia consists of a string of basins more or less connected by the threads of the Vardar and the Vistritza. But here, as in Roumelia, geography has made it much easier for the northern peoples to come south than for the southern peoples to go north.[2] Therein lies, perhaps, the primary cause of the outbreak of the Second Balkan War in 1913, though the monitions of nature were in that case powerfully assisted by the promptings of

[1] Newbigin, *op. cit.*, p. 10. On the whole subject of ' river capture ' cf. chap. v in the same illuminating work.

[2] Hogarth, *Nearer East*, pp. 170-1.

diplomacy. Apart, however, from this particular instance history shows the continuous attraction of the Aegean littoral for the several peoples of the peninsula.

Closely connected with the geological process to which reference has been made is the uncertainty of the watershed between the upper waters of the Vardar and those of the Morava. That physical phenomenon finds its political reflection in the position of the Southern Slavs. By which route will they ultimately obtain access to the sea ? By the Vardar valley to the Aegean or by the Albanian Gap to the Adriatic ? But for the malicious interposition of the Central European Powers the Serbians would, without question, be on the Adriatic to-day. Whether that or the Aegean is their 'natural' destiny is a point upon which nature has not very decisively pronounced. It is, however, worthy of note that there is no such 'pull' to the Adriatic as there is to the Aegean. To Italy the strategical value of the Dalmatian and Albanian coast is unquestionable. It has still to be demonstrated that it is for the Southern Slavs a 'natural' outlet either in a commercial or in a political sense. If the dictates of ethnography are to be accepted as final the award cannot be in doubt. The claim of the Southern Slavs is indisputable. But race is not the only factor of which account must be taken.

A conspectus of the physical features of the peninsula seems, indeed, to suggest the conclusion that the main structural lines are not horizontal but vertical. The general trend is north to south, not east to west nor west to east.[1] It would be unwise to lay exaggerated emphasis upon this physiographic tendency. To do so might supply a physical justification for the *Drang nach Südosten* of the Central European Empires. But it may not, on this account, be ignored. The conclusions suggested by the main lines of communication are indeed irresistible.

[1] Cf. Evans, *The Adriatic Slavs.*

In a country such as has been described above it would be ridiculous to look for elaborate means of communication. In the Balkans, at any rate, they will be looked for in vain. Neither by road nor rail is communication easy. The difficulties interposed by nature may be gauged by a comparison, extraordinarily suggestive, between the Roman road map and a modern railway map of the peninsula. A glance at the maps on pp. 34 and 35 will show that only in one respect is there any conspicuous divergence between the two. The primary purpose of the Roman roadmaker was to secure a direct line of communication between the old Rome on the Tiber and the new Rome on the Bosphorus. This purpose was achieved by the construction of the famous *Via Egnatia*, which, starting from Durazzo on the Adriatic, ran by way of Lake Ochrida to Monastir and thence to Salonica. From Salonica it ran parallel to, but at some little distance from, the Aegean littoral to Kavala, and thence down to the shore at Dedeagatch, from which point it made straight for Constantinople. A second trunk-road from Belgrade to Constantinople via Nish, Sofia, Philippopolis, and Adrianople—the precise route of the line now traversed by the Berlin to Constantinople express. A third, starting from Metkovitch, followed the stream of the Narenta, and thence ran up to Serajevo, and linked Serajevo with Salonica by way of Novi Bazar, the plain of Kossovo, and Uskub. Subsidiary roads connected Scutari with the Danube via Nish, and Monastir with the Danube via Sofia.

The modern lines of communication are, with one exception, far less systematic. Bucharest now is connected by different lines with the Roumanian port of Constanza, the Bulgarian port of Varna, with Sofia, and, via Philippopolis, with Constantinople. Otherwise, the advantage lay with the Roman roads. Besides the trunk-line already mentioned between Belgrade and Constantinople, a second connects Belgrade with Nish, Uskub, and Salonica, and a branch line runs from Salonica to Constantinople. But, with the exception of a line from Ragusa to Serajevo, there is not a single railway running westward from or eastward to the Adriatic. There is nothing to connect either Durazzo or Valona with Monastir and Salonica; nor Serajevo with anything to the south of it. The outbreak of the European War interrupted various projects for supplying the more obvious of these deficiencies, but many repairs will have to be effected before any large schemes of construction are likely to be resumed. Meanwhile, the main lines of communication remain much as the Romans left them. Now, as then, they are dictated by the triangular central upland which, based upon Constantinople and Salonica, reaches its apex at Belgrade. Now, as then, these three cities hold the keys of the peninsula.

The foregoing survey of the geographical features of the Balkans, summary as it has been, is sufficient to indicate the exceptional degree of influence which in this interesting region Physics has exercised upon Politics. In such a country it would be vain to expect the establishment of a strong centralized State, such as was possible in England, and still more obviously in France. Nor, in fact, has there ever been such a State in the Balkans. The Greek city States represent the antithesis of centralization, and neither Macedon nor Rome was foolish enough to attempt the impossible. The Ottoman Empire, though in a sense despotic, has never been a centralized despotism. Subsequent chapters will make it clear that in practice a very considerable amount of local autonomy was permitted to the conquered peoples even throughout the most oppressive periods of Ottoman dominion. Centralization is indeed prohibited by nature.

Even a closely knit federal State would seem to be outside

THE BALKANS
under the
Roman Empire
Roads

THE BALKANS
at the
Present Day
Railways ⎯⎯

the realm of possibilities for the Balkans. Nature points imperiously to a congeries of relatively small States, and the geographical presuppositions are re-enforced by the principle of ethnography. The present distribution of States and races is, on the whole, tolerably scientific. As usual, however, nature has done her political work in a slovenly fashion, and has left a number of very ragged edges. Or perhaps it would be more modest and more true to say that man has been too stupid to interpret with precision the monitions of nature. But wherever the blame lies, the fact remains that there are in the Balkans a good many intermediate or debatable districts, the political destiny of which cannot easily be determined. As we have already seen, nature has not made it quite clear whether she means Serbia to expand towards the Adriatic or towards the Aegean. Politically, the former alternative would be the less inconvenient, for it might untie one of the many knots in which the Macedonian problem is involved.

Of all the debatable areas Macedonia is the most conspicuous. If the Moslems are to evacuate it, upon whom is the inheritance to devolve ? Upon Greece, Serbia, or Bulgaria ? If upon all three, how will the lines of a satisfactory frontier be drawn ? That Bulgaria cannot be permanently content with the present arrangement is frankly admitted by the most prescient of Greek statesmen. But if Greece makes room for Bulgaria at Kavala, ought Serbia to keep Monastir ? Does not the road system of the Romans, however, suggest a connexion between Monastir and Durazzo ? Again, is not Salonica the obvious port of Belgrade ? Or possibly, *horresco referens*, of Buda-Pesth, or even of Berlin ? It is much easier to ask these questions than to answer them. And they are far from being exhaustive. They may serve as samples of the problems propounded by Physics to Politics in the Balkans.

Two conclusions would seem, however, to emerge with tolerable clearness, and there is some danger of our being compelled to accept a third. It will always be difficult to maintain in the Balkans a single centralized State; unless, therefore, the ingenuity of man can triumphantly overcome the dispositions of nature there will always be a congeries of relatively small States. Must we also conclude that these States will remain to all time in a condition of rivalry; is an armed peace the best that is to be hoped for in the Balkans? This question cannot in any case be disposed of summarily, and an attempt at a considered answer may conveniently be deferred to a later chapter. But this much may be said at once. It would be hazardous to draw conclusions either from the 'miracle' of 1912 or from the grotesquely disappointing sequel of 1913. Grossly exaggerated were the hopes founded upon the formation of the Balkan League; perversely pessimistic were the opposite conclusions derived from its melodramatic dissolution.

Two inferences seem to be justified by recent events. First, that the utmost degree of centralization which may be reasonably looked for in the Balkans is a somewhat loose confederation of the Christian States. Unification is prohibited alike by geography and by ethnography. Even federalism presupposes the existence of unifying forces which have not as yet manifested themselves in this region. Things being as they are, a *Staatenbund* would therefore be preferable to a *Bundesstaat*: Switzerland is a model more appropriate to the Balkans than Germany or the Australian Commonwealth; and the Switzerland ante 1848 rather than that of to-day. Secondly, even this measure of union is unattainable without a thorough territorial readjustment. No confederation, however loose in structure, could be expected to endure for six months, unless a fairly satisfactory settlement of outstanding difficulties can be previously effected. And that settlement must come from within. The Treaties of London and Bucharest (May and August, 1913) are a sufficient warning against the futility of European intervention in Balkan affairs. Even assuming complete disinterestedness and goodwill, the event is only too likely to defeat benevolent intentions; where, as at Bucharest, such an assumption is forbidden by notorious facts, intervention can issue only in disaster.

The above reflections suggest irresistibly a further conclusion. Physiography, as we have seen, denies to the Balkan lands any pre-eminent importance from the productive point of view. In this respect the Danubian principalities are the most favourably circumstanced among the States of the peninsula. The external commerce of Roumania is approximately equal to that of the rest of the States put together, and Roumanian oil and cereals have undoubtedly a great future in the European markets. But only on one condition—that the egress of Roumanian merchandise through the narrow straits is unimpeded. The future of Constantinople is therefore of vital consequence to Roumania. Bulgaria, with an Aegean sea-board, is obviously less interested, but only in one degree. Bulgaria, like Roumania, is giving evidence of improvement in the methods of cultivation by the exportation of cereals. Nor are the exports of Greece and Serbia insignificant, though Greece ministers chiefly to luxuries.

It is not, however, in its productive capacity that the economic importance of the Near East consists. That is to be sought in its general geographical situation regarded from the point of view of *Weltpolitik* and *Weltökonomie*. Throughout the ages this region has possessed an incomparable importance in relation to the commercial lines of communication. Temporarily diverted by the discovery of America and of the Cape route to India, commerce, always conservative in its instincts, has lately regained the accustomed paths. The Balkans, Egypt, Mesopotamia, are again to-day, what from the dawn of history they have been, objects of jealous desire to all economically minded peoples. Less from the point of view of occupation than of control; less for their intrinsic importance than as a means of access to other lands. Hence the concentration of international rivalries upon the lands which fringe the Eastern Mediterranean. That rivalry has not exhausted itself during the last twenty centuries; on the contrary, it seems possible that we may be about to witness its manifestation on a scale without precedent in the history of the world. Nor can there be any doubt that the lands which form part, or until recently did form part, of the Ottoman Empire will provide the arena. Enough has been already said on the importance of Egypt, Syria, and Constantinople as guarding the lines of communication, but we must not fail to notice that the geographical formation of the peninsula itself has rendered it exceptionally open to incursions. Unlike the Iberian peninsula, that of the Balkans is widest where it joins the European continent. Neither to the north-east nor to the north-west is there any natural line of separation, still less is there any substantial obstacle to the advance of a hostile incursion.[1] Over and over again has Roumania offered a convenient high road for the passage of invading hosts: Goths, Huns, Lombards, Avars, and Slavs traversed it in turn, though only the last tarried in Roumania itself. Between Bucharest and Constantinople there is no serious impediment, still less between Belgrade on the one hand and either the Aegean or the Bosphorus on the other.

Relatively small and weak as the States of the Balkans are, and must necessarily be, what hope is there of their being able to offer any effective resistance to similar incursions in the

[1] Cf. Newbigin, *op. cit.*, p. 15.

future ? There would seem to be none except in the adoption of safeguards similar to those which for more than a century have maintained inviolate the neutrality and independence of the Swiss Confederation : constitutional readjustment, neutralization under an international guarantee, and a confederate citizen army, well trained and well equipped, and prepared, if need be, to extort the respect of powerful neighbours. Before these conditions can be attained there will have to be a good deal of give and take among the Balkan States ; irreconcilable claims in Macedonia and elsewhere will have to be compromised. This will be no easy task, but it may perhaps be accomplished if once the contending parties can be convinced that there are only two other alternatives. Either the peninsula will, in the future as in the past, be the prey of any sufficiently powerful invader, or it will find protection by common subordination to an alien empire, drawing upon resources external to the peninsula, and imposing its will by irresistible military strength. These alternatives to a domestic accommodation are not attractive, but they are exhaustive. Physiography excludes a third.

For further reference : D. G. Hogarth, *The Near East* ; Miss Newbigin, *Geographical Aspects of the Balkan Problem* ; Sir W. W. Hunter, *History of British India*, vol. i ; E. Himly, *La formation territoriale* ; E. A. Freeman, *Historical Geography of Europe* ; Sir Arthur Evans, *The Adriatic Slavs and the Overland Route to Constantinople.*

3

The Advent of the Ottomans

Conquests in Europe

'Modern history begins under the stress of the Ottoman Conquest.'—
LORD ACTON.

'Il n'y a point de nation turque, mais seulement des conquérants campés
au milieu de populations hostiles ; les Turcs ne forment point un État, mais
une armée qui ne vaut que pour la conquête et tend à se dissoudre dès qu'elle
est contrainte de s'arrêter.'—ALBERT SOREL.

THE origins of the Turkish tribe, subsequently known as
the Osmanlis, Othmans or Ottomans, are shrouded in baffling
obscurity. The highly coloured pictures drawn by their own
historians are, by common consent, entirely untrustworthy.
But if little can be learnt authoritatively, perhaps it is because
there is little to learn. It is still more probable that we have
a good deal to unlearn. We are bidden, for example, to discard
the commonly accepted tradition of a westward migration on
an imposing scale ; of a great struggle between the Ottoman
and Seljukian Turks ; of the dramatic overthrow of the Seljuk
Empire ; of the establishment of a powerful Ottoman Empire
in Asia Minor and the advance of the conquerors upon South-
Eastern Europe. This book is not, however, a history of the
Ottomans, and the critical discussion of these and similar
questions must not therefore be permitted to detain us. Let
it suffice to say that the Ottomans emerge into the realm of
authentic history in the thirteenth century. The first reliable
mention of them is in the Seljuk Chronicle, where Ertogrul
appears as one of several Turkish chieftains in the employment
of the Seljuk Sultan. More legendary history represents the
Ottomans as first appearing as a band of nomads, warriors, and

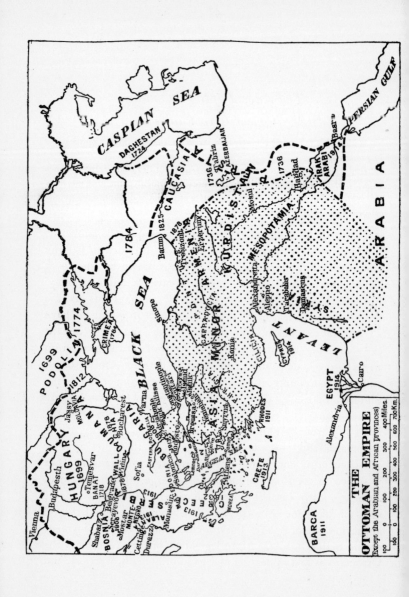

THE OTTOMAN EMPIRE

(Except the Arabian and African provinces)

herdsmen, flying from the highlands of Central Asia before the fierce onset of the Moguls. A picturesque but exceedingly doubtful story tells how Ertogrul found himself in a position to perform a signal service to Alaeddin, Sultan of the Seljukian Turks. The Seljuks had established a powerful empire in Asia Minor in the course of the eleventh and twelfth centuries, but by the thirteenth their power was manifestly in decay. To the Seljuk Empire there was no immediate successor. The story of its overthrow by the Ottomans cannot be accepted. All that we know is that Ertogrul and his small band of followers established themselves, towards the middle of the thirteenth century, in the north-western corner of Asia Minor, in the plain between Brusa and Nicaea, with a 'capital' at Yenishehr.

To Ertogrul there succeeded in 1288 his son Osman or Othman, from whom the tribe, destined to fame as the conquerors of Constantinople and inheritors of the Byzantine Empire, took their name. Osman extended his modest heritage partly at the expense of other Turkish Emirs but mainly at the expense of the Greek Empire in Asia Minor, and, upon the extinction of the Seljuk Empire, he assumed the title of Sultan (*circ.* 1300). In 1301 he won his first notable victory over the Greeks at Baphaeon, in the neighbourhood of Nicomedia, and during the next few years he pushed on towards the Black Sea, and thus hemmed in the strong Greek cities of Nicomedia, Brusa, and Nicaea. On his death-bed (1326) he learnt that Brusa had fallen to his son Orkhan, and though the great prize of Nicaea was denied to him, Osman died ' virtual lord of the Asiatic Greeks '.[1]

His son and successor Orkhan not only rounded off Osman's work in Asia Minor, but obtained a firm foothold upon the European shores of the Hellespont. Nicomedia, the ancient

[1] Hogarth, *Balkans*, p. 325.

capital of the Emperor Diocletian, fell to him in the first year of his reign. A few years later he crowned his victories over the Byzantine Empire in Asia Minor by the capture of Nicaea, the second city of the Empire. By this time the Eastern Empire was, as we shall see later, tottering to its fall, not only in Asia Minor but in Europe. Towards the middle of the fourteenth century the pitiful remnant of it was distracted by civil war between the Palaeologi and John Cantacuzenos, who in 1341 had crowned himself Emperor at Demotika. Both parties appealed to Sultan Orkhan for help. Orkhan went to the assistance of Cantacuzenos in 1345, and was rewarded by the hand of Theodora, daughter of Cantacuzenos and grand-daughter of the Bulgarian Tsar. This marriage may be re-garded as the first step towards the establishment of an Ottoman-Byzantine Empire in Europe. In 1349 Orkhan's assistance was again invoked by his father-in-law, to help in repelling the attacks of the Serbians, now at the zenith of their power, upon Macedonia. Orkhan's response was suspiciously prompt, and again a large body of Ottoman warriors feasted their eyes with a vision of the promised land.

Hitherto the Ottoman horsemen, once their mission was accomplished, had duly withdrawn to their home on the Asiatic shore. But we are now on the eve of one of the cardinal events in world-history. That event was in one sense only the natural sequel to those which immediately preceded it ; never-theless it definitely stands out as marking the opening of a new chapter. In 1353 Cantacuzenos once more appealed for the help of the Ottoman Sultan against the Serbians : accordingly, Orkhan sent over his son Suleiman Pasha, by whose aid the Serbians were defeated at Demotika and the Greeks recaptured the Thracian capital Adrianople. In acknowledgement of these signal services Suleiman Pasha received the fortress of Tzympe, and there the Ottomans effected their first lodgement

on European soil. Much to the chagrin of the rival emperors Gallipoli fell before the Ottoman assault in the following year (1354), and a few years later Demotika also was taken. By this time the breach between Orkhan and his father-in-law was complete, and henceforward the Osmanli horsemen fought in Europe no longer as auxiliaries but as principals. Suleiman Pasha was killed by a fall from his horse in 1358, and a year later his father followed him to the grave. But the grip which they had got upon the European shore of the Dardanelles was never afterwards relaxed.

Before proceeding to describe the wonderful achievements of Ottoman arms during the next hundred years it seems desirable to get some clear idea of the political conditions which prevailed in South-Eastern Europe.

The Eastern Empire

The Empire of the East, known indifferently as the Greek or Byzantine Empire, had by this time reached the last stage of emasculate decay. The life of the Roman Empire had been prolonged for more than a thousand years by the epoch-making resolution of the Emperor Constantine. But it was now ebbing fast. For three hundred years after Constantine's removal of the capital to Byzantium (330 A.D.) the Empire continued to be essentially Roman. With the reign of Heraclius (610–41) it became as definitely Greek. Under Leo III (the Isaurian, 716–41) Greek became the official language of the Empire, though its subjects still continued, until the advent of the Ottomans and beyond it, to style themselves *Romaioi*. Many hard things have been said of the Eastern Empire, but this at least should be remembered to its credit. For nearly a thousand years it held the gates of Europe against a series of assaults from the East, until in turn it was itself partly overwhelmed and partly absorbed by the Ottomans. Not that the Ottomans were the earliest of the Turkish tribes to threaten the Greek Empire. Towards the end of the eleventh century the Seljuks overran Asia Minor, drove the Emperor out of his Asiatic capital, Nicaea, and assumed the title of Sultans of Roum. The Emperors of the House of Comnenos pushed back the Seljuks from Nicaea to Iconium (Konia), but in the latter part of the twelfth century the Eastern Empire again showed symptoms of decrepitude, and at the opening of the thirteenth century it suffered an irreparable blow.

The fourth crusade (1200–4) has generally been accounted one of the blackest crimes in modern history.[1] The immediate result of it was to establish a Latin or Frankish Empire, under Baldwin, Count of Flanders, in Constantinople; more remotely it may be held responsible for the Ottoman conquest of South-Eastern Europe. It lasted little more than half a century (1204–61); but during those years the work of disintegration proceeded apace in the Balkan lands. The Slavonic kingdoms firmly established themselves in the northern parts. Boniface of Montferrat proclaimed himself King of Salonica. Greece proper was divided up into various Frankish principalities, while the Aegean islands passed, for the most part, under the flag of the maritime Republic of Venice. Meanwhile, the Greek Empire, dethroned at Constantinople, maintained itself, in somewhat precarious existence, at Nicaea. Not less precarious was the hold of the Latin Empire upon Constantinople. The latter was purely a military adventure. It never struck any roots into the soil, and in 1261 Michael Palaeologus, Emperor of Nicaea, had little difficulty in reconquering Constantinople from the Latins. The restored

---

[1] See e. g. Sir Richard Jebb, *Modern Greece*, p. 30; Sir Edwin Pears, *Conquest of Constantinople*; the famous chapters in Gibbon's *Decline and Fall*; and Milman's *Latin Christianity*.

Byzantine Empire survived for nearly two centuries, but its prestige had been fatally damaged, its vitality had been sapped, and it awaited certain dissolution at the hands of a more virile race. There can indeed be little doubt that only the advent of the Ottomans prevented Constantinople itself from falling into the hands of the Southern Slavs. The condition of the Byzantine Empire during this last period of its existence presents a curious analogy to that of the Ottoman Empire in the nineteenth. ' It is ', writes a penetrating critic, ' the story of an uninterrupted succession of bitter internal quarrels, of attacks by former vassals upon the immediate frontiers of its shrunken territory, of subtle undermining by hostile colonies of foreigners whose one thought was commercial gain, and of intermittent, and in almost all cases selfishly inspired, efforts of Western Europe to put off the fatal day.' [1]

Territorially, the Greek Empire had shrunk to the narrowest limits, little wider, in fact, than those to which the Ottoman Empire in Europe is reduced to-day. The Empire of Trebizond represented the remnant of its possessions in Asia, while in Europe, apart from Constantinople and Thrace, it held only the Macedonian coast with the city of Salonica and the Eastern Peloponnesus. Hungary, Transylvania, Wallachia, Croatia, and Bosnia owned the sway of Lewis the Great ; the Serbian Empire stretched from Belgrade to the Gulf of Corinth, from the Adriatic to the Aegean ; Bulgaria held what we know as Bulgaria proper and Eastern Roumelia ; Dalmatia, Corfu, Crete, and Euboea were in the hands of Venice ; the Knights of St. John were in possession of Rhodes, while the Franks still held the kingdom of Cyprus, the principality of Achaia, the Duchies of Athens, Naxos, and Cephalonia, not to speak of many of the Aegean islands. Little, therefore, was left to the successors of the Caesars in Constantinople.

[1] H. A. Gibbons, *op. cit.*, p. 36.

Illyrians and Thracians

When the Romans first made themselves masters of South-Eastern Europe they found three great races in possession : the Illyrians, the Thracians, and the Hellenes. The Illyrians, who had established the kingdom of Epirus in the fourth century B.C., were represented in the thirteenth century, as they are still, by the mountaineers of Albania. The Thracians, dominant during the Macedonian supremacy, mingled with Trajan's colonists in Dacia to form the people represented by the modern Roumanians. But neither of these aboriginal races would, perhaps, have preserved, through the ages, their identity but for the existence of the third race, the Greeks. It was the Greeks who, by their superiority to their Roman conquerors in all the elements of civilization, prevented the absorption of the other races by the Romans, and so contributed to that survival of separate nationalities which, from that day to this, has constituted one of the special peculiarities of Balkan politics. Of the Illyrians in Albania little need, in this place, be said, except that they have successfully resisted absorption by the Turks as they had previously resisted similar efforts on the part of Romans, Byzantines, and Slavs.

The Albanians have never contributed an important factor to the Balkan problem. Like the Slavs, but in even greater degree, ' they were devoid of cohesion and political sentiment, and have at no time been more than an aggregate of tribes, mostly occupied with internal quarrels,' [1] though, as we shall see, they have more than once produced a man of virile and commanding personality.

The Danubian Principalities

Far different has been the history of the Thracians in the Danubian principalities. That history is largely the outcome of geography. Their geographical situation, as was explained

[1] Eliot, *op. cit.*, p. 44.

in the preceding chapter, though suggesting a highway to westward-bound invaders, rendered them relatively immune from conquest, and, as a fact, they have never been actually submerged. Least of all by the Ottomans, who, as we shall see later, never made any serious or sustained attempt to absorb them into their Empire.

The modern Roumanians are commonly supposed to be descendants of the Roman colonists settled (*circ.* A. D. 101) by the Emperor Trajan in the province of Dacia for the protection of the Roman Empire against the northern barbarians. This account of their origin was disputed, however, by Dr. Freeman, who held that they represented ' not specially Dacians or Roman colonists in Dacia, but the great Thracian race generally, of which the Dacians were only a part '.[1] The question is not one which can be permitted to detain us. It must suffice for our present purpose to say that just as the Hungarians represent a great Magyar wedge thrust in between the Northern and the Southern Slavs, so do the Roumanians represent a Latin wedge, distinct and aloof from all their immediate neighbours, though not devoid, especially in language, of many traces of Slav influences. Towards the close of the third century (*circ.* A. D. 271) the Emperor Aurelian was compelled by barbarian inroads to abandon his distant colony, and to withdraw the Roman legions, but the colonists themselves retired into the fastnesses of the Carpathians, only to emerge again many centuries later, when the barbarian flood had at last subsided.

For nearly a thousand years, reckoning to the Tartar invasion of 1241, Dacia was nothing but a highway for successive tides of barbarian invaders, Goths, Huns, Lombards, Avars, and Slavs. But, except the last, none of the invaders left any permanent impress upon the land. Still, the successive tides

---

[1] E. A. Freeman, *Ottoman Power in Europe*, p. 51.

followed each other so quickly that the Daco-Romans themselves were completely submerged, and for a thousand years history loses sight of them.

But though submerged they were not dissipated. 'The possession of the regions on the Lower Danube', writes Traugott Tamm, 'passed from one nation to another, but none endangered the Roumanian nation as a national entity. " The water passes, the stones remain " ; the hordes of the migration period, detached from their native soil, disappeared as mist before the sun. But the Roman element bent their heads while the storm passed over them, clinging to the old places until the advent of happier days, when they were able to stand up and stretch their limbs.' [1] The southern portion of what is now Roumania emerged, towards the close of the thirteenth century, as the principality of Wallachia (or Muntenia, i. e. mountain-land) ; the northern, a century later, came to be known as the Principality of Moldavia. Both principalities were founded by immigrant Rouman nobles from Transylvania, and, as a consequence, Roumania has always been distinguished from the other Balkan provinces by the survival of a powerful native aristocracy. In Serbia the nobles were exterminated; in Bosnia they saved their property by the surrender of their faith; in Roumania alone did they retain both.

Such was the position of the Danubian principalities when the Ottomans began their career of conquest in South-Eastern Europe. The principalities had never been in a position, like their neighbours to the south and west of them, to aspire to a dominant place in Balkan politics. Nor were they, like those neighbours, exposed to the first and full fury of the Ottoman attack. Still, under its famous Voivode Mircaea the Great, Wallachia took part against the Ottomans in the great Slavonic

[1] Quoted by D. Mitrany, *The Balkans*, p. 256.

combinations, which were dissolved by the Turkish victories at Kossovo (1389) and Nicopolis (1396).

Early in the fifteenth century the Ottomans crossed the Danube, and in 1412 Wallachia was reduced to a state of vassaldom. But it was never wholly absorbed like Serbia, Bulgaria, Greece, Macedonia, and Thrace into the Ottoman Empire. Nor was Moldavia, which, for obvious geographical reasons, managed to maintain its independence for a hundred years longer than Wallachia. In 1475 Stephen the Great, Voivode of Moldavia, won a resounding victory over the Turkish army at Racova. In 1512, however, his son Bogdan, weakened by the attacks of Poland and Hungary, made a voluntary submission to the Ottomans. He agreed to pay tribute to the Sultan and to assist him in time of war, but Moldavia was to continue to elect its own prince, and no Turk was to be permitted to settle in the principality. These terms were confirmed, in 1536, by Suleiman the Magnificent, and formed the basis of the relations which subsisted between Constantinople and the two Danubian principalities down to the eighteenth century.

Bulgaria

South of the Danube and between that river and the Aegean lay the district known as Bulgaria. The Thraco-Illyrian race by which it was originally inhabited was conquered by the Slavs who, from the beginning of the sixth century onwards, inundated the peninsula. By the middle of the seventh century the Slav penetration of the Balkans was complete ; from the Danube to the Maritza, from the Adriatic to the Black Sea, the Slavs formed a solid mass, broken only by Albania and Southern Thrace ; Greeks held the Aegean coast and most of the towns—Athens, Corinth, Patras, Larissa, and Salonica : but even in the interior of the Morea there was a considerable infusion of Slavs. Upon the heels of the Slavs came the Bulgars. The latter belonged originally to a Turanian race, akin to the Avars, Huns, Magyars, and Finns. Coming like other Mongol races from Eastern Asia, they settled on the Volga, where the Greater or White Bulgaria continued to exist down to the sixteenth century. Thence they made various predatory inroads into the Balkan peninsula, in the latter part of the sixth and first half of the seventh century, and eventually in 679 subjugated the Slavs of Moesia and effected a definite and permanent settlement in the land between the Danube and the Balkan mountains. After their settlement, however, they were completely assimilated in language and in civilization to the conquered Slavs, and to-day they are commonly accounted a Slavonic people. Yet despite identity of speech, and despite a very large infusion of Slav blood, the Bulgar has developed a distinct national self-consciousness which has constantly come into conflict with that of the Southern Slavs.

The antagonism between these near neighbours has been accentuated in recent years by the establishment of an independent Bulgarian Exarchate. That exceedingly important step was taken in 1870, precisely one thousand years after the fateful decision by which the Bulgarian Church was placed under the Patriarch of Constantinople. Prince Boris of Bulgaria had been converted to Christianity in 865, but for the first few years it was uncertain whether the infant Bulgarian Church would adhere to Constantinople or to Rome. In 870, during the reign of the Emperor Basil I, the victory, pregnant with consequences for Bulgaria, was assured to Constantinople.

It was under Simeon the Great (893–927), the son of Boris, that Bulgaria attained to the position of a great Power.[1] Simeon himself adopted the style of ' Tsar and Autocrat of all Bulgars and Greeks ', and the territorial expansion of his kingdom,

[1] See map, p. 53.

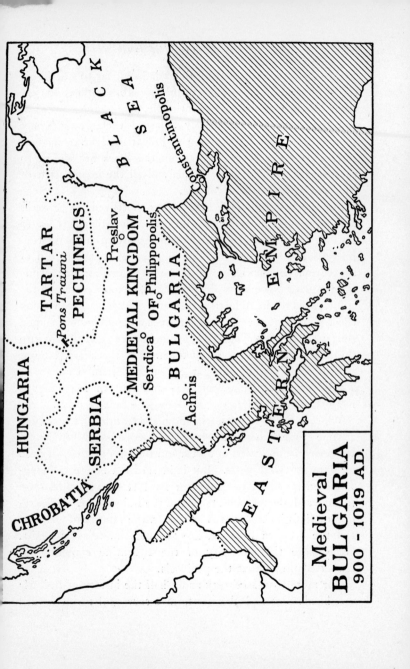

HUNGARIA

TARTAR

PECHINEGS

Pons Traiani

BLACK SEA

Preslav

CHROBATIA

SERBIA

MEDIEVAL KINGDOM

Serdica○ OF○Philippopolis

○ Achris

BULGARIA

Constantinopolis

EASTERN

EMPIRE

Medieval
BULGARIA
900 - 1019 A.D.

the widest as yet achieved by Bulgaria, went far to sustain his titular pretensions. The Byzantine emperors could command the allegiance only of Constantinople, Adrianople, Salonica, and the territory immediately adjacent thereto, and were compelled to pay tribute to the Bulgarian Tsar. Simeon's empire stretched at one time from the Black Sea almost to the Adriatic, and included Serbia and all the inland parts of Macedonia, Epirus, and Albania.

But the first Bulgarian Empire was shortlived. The Serbs reasserted their independence in 931 ; domestic feuds led to the partition of Bulgaria itself into Eastern and Western Bulgaria in 963 ; ecclesiastical schism, due to the spread of the curious Bogomil heresy, accentuated civil strife ; while the Emperor Nikephoros Phokas (963–9) renounced in 966 the tribute paid to the Bulgarian Tsar, and, shortsightedly invoking the assistance of the Russians, inflicted a crushing defeat upon Bulgaria. It was, indeed, easier to introduce the Russians into the Balkans than to get rid of them. But the latter feat was at length accomplished by the Emperor John Tzimisces— a brilliant Armenian adventurer—and Eastern Bulgaria was merged, for the time, into the Byzantine Empire (972).

Western Bulgaria, with its capital at Okhrida, and including at one time Thessaly, Macedonia, Albania, Montenegro, Herzegovina, and parts of Serbia and Bulgaria proper, survived for another thirty years. But it in turn fell before the long-sustained attack of the Emperor Basil II (976–1025), known to fame as Bulgaroktonos, ' slayer of the Bulgarians '. A succession of victories culminated in 1016 in the capture of Okhrida, and the Western Bulgaria, like the Eastern, ceased to exist. Once more the authority of the Byzantine emperor was reasserted throughout the peninsula.

For more than a century and a half the history of Bulgaria a blank. Its revival dates from a successful revolt headed in 1186 by John Asen—a Vlach shepherd—against the tyranny of the Emperor Isaac Angelus. The capital of this second or Vlacho-Bulgarian Empire was at Tirnovo where, in 1187, John Asen was crowned. It included, at one time, besides Bulgaria proper, most of Serbia, with parts of Thrace, Macedonia, Thessaly, and Epirus, but the murder of Michael Asen II in 1257 brought the Vlach dynasty and the Vlacho-Bulgarian Empire to an end. Most of its provinces had already been lost to it, and the remnant was held in vassaldom to Serbia. For the Serbs had by this time become the dominant power in the peninsula, and it was, as we have seen, to combat the insistent menace of this people that Cantacuzenos, in the middle of the fourteenth century, invoked the aid of the Ottomans. The place of the Southern Slavs in the Balkan polity of the fourteenth century must, therefore, be our next concern.

Serbia and the Southern Slavs

Of the coming of the Slavs into the Balkan Peninsula something has been already said. By the middle of the seventh century the peninsula had become predominantly Slavonic, and the lines of the chief Slav States had already been roughly defined. Of Bulgaria no more need be said. The other three were inhabited by Serbs, Croatians, and Slovenes respectively. The last occupied what we know as Carniola and Southern Carinthia ; the Croats held Croatia with parts of Bosnia, Herzegovina, and Dalmatia ; the Serbs held the remaining portions of the three last-named provinces together with Montenegro and practically everything which was assigned to Serbia by the Treaty of Bucharest (1913), i. e. Serbia proper, old Serbia, and the northern part of Macedonia. The Southern Slavs have always been more devoted to independence than to discipline, more conspicuous for valour than for organizing capacity. From the first they were, in a political sense, loosely

TARTAR EMPIRE

KINGDOM OF HUNGARY

MOLDAVIA

SLAVONIA

Aspalathon

Skopia

KINGDOM

WALLACHIA

KINGDOM OF BULGARS

BLACK SEA

Rausion
Dioclea
Dekatera

OF

Philippopolis

Constantinople

Antibaris

SERBIA
(C.1350)

Hadrianople

Ochrida

EASTERN EMPIRE

Castoria

Thasos

Thessalonica

Imbros

THESSALY

Lesbos

TURKS

Ionian Islands

D.Y. OF ATHENS

Negroponte

Chios

P. DOM OF ACHAIA

Athens

D.Y. OF NAXOS

Modon

Coron

Monembasia

Rhodes

Crete

Medieval
SERBIA
under
Stephen Dushan

knit, lacking in coherence or in the power of continuous combination. They were bound to the soil, not by serfdom, but by the affectionate ties of cultivating proprietors. Such governmental machinery as they devised was local rather than central ; they organized themselves in agricultural village-communities, and showed a marked aversion, in strong contrast with the Greeks, to city life. Originally they had neither kings, nor priests, nor even slaves, but settled down in free communities of peasant owners and organized their social and economic life on ' a system of family communism '.[1] Freedom-loving and brave, they had the defects of their qualities. Their lack of discipline, subordination, and political coherence, not less than the physical characteristics of their country, made it difficult to weld them into a powerful State, while their jealous devotion to the soil disposed them to local feuds of a peculiarly ferocious character.

Torn by internal dissensions the Serbs have always lacked, except towards the north, natural and definable frontiers. Still more unfortunate has been their lack of coast-line. They have never reached the Aegean, and only for a short period were they established on the Adriatic. The Greeks headed them off from the former ; the Venetians and Hungarians, after the fall of Rome, generally kept a jealous hold upon the latter.

The Serbs embraced Christianity towards the end of the ninth century, but in ecclesiastical as in political affairs the Southern Slavs found it difficult to agree ; for while the Serbs adhered to Constantinople the Croats acknowledged the authority of Rome. Temporal allegiance tended to follow the same direction. From the ninth century to the twelfth the Serbs were for the most part under the suzerainty of the Bulgarian or the Byzantine Empires ; the Croats were subject to Hungary or Venice.

[1] Eliot, *op. cit.*, p. 25.

The great period in the mediaeval history of Serbia extends from the middle of the twelfth to the close of the fourteenth century. Under the Nemanya dynasty (1168–1371) Serbia managed to compose, in some degree, her internal quarrels, and so gave herself, for the first time, a chance of attaining to a dominant position in Balkan politics. Stephen Nemanya, the first of the new line, succeeded in uniting most of the Serbian countries—Serbia proper, Montenegro, and Herzegovina, and though forced to make submission to the Emperor Manuel I Comnenus, he renewed his career of conquest on the latter's death, 1180, and when, in 1196, he resolved to abdicate, he handed over to his second son, Stephen Urosh (1196–1223), a kingdom tolerably homogeneous, and, in extent, indubitably imposing.

The new ruler was, on his accession, confronted by difficulties which have recurred with ominous regularity in every period of Serbian history. These difficulties arose from three main causes : dynastic disunion ; the jealousy of Bulgaria ; and the unremitting hostility of the Magyars of Hungary. The chagrin of an elder brother, passed over in the succession, was mollified by the tact of a younger brother, a monk, the famous St. Sava. The same tactful intermediation secured for the Serbian Church internal autonomy and independence of the Patriarchate of Constantinople. Against the jealousy of Bulgaria St. Sava was less successful, for the Bulgarians, seizing the opportunity of Serbian disunion, made themselves masters of a large part of Eastern Serbia, including the important towns of Belgrade, Nish, and Prizren. The hostility of Andrew II of Hungary had, for the time being, little definite result, but its existence supplies one of those constant factors which give something of unity and consistency to the confused annals of the Southern Slavs. If at any time there has been any special manifestation of national self-consciousness on the part of the Southern Slavs, Buda-Pesth has immediately responded by a marked exhibition of its unceasing vigilance and its ineradicable jealousy. Nor is it possible to deny that the antagonism between the two peoples is due to a direct conflict of interest. The Magyars have always striven to obstruct the progress of the Southern Slavs towards the Adriatic; the Serbians still block the access of the Magyars to the Aegean. Notwithstanding these initial difficulties the reign of Stephen Urosh was exceptionally prosperous. He himself was the first of Serbia's kings to receive the consecration of a solemn coronation, and so skilful was his diplomacy in playing off Rome against Constantinople, and Nicaea against both, that he secured the recognition of Serbian independence, both civil and ecclesiastical, not only from the Pope but from the Latin and Greek emperors.[1]

We must pass over with scant notice the century which elapsed between the death of Stephen Urosh (1223) and the accession of the most renowned of all Serbian rulers, Stephen Dushan (1331). Serbian annals have little else to record during this period but a monotonous tale of domestic quarrels and military expeditions, conducted with varying success, against immediate neighbours. A crushing defeat inflicted upon a combination of Greeks and Bulgars by Stephen VII [2] (1321–31) is perhaps worthy of record, since it prepared the way for the brilliant success achieved by his son. It should be noted also that by this time the Serbians had already come into contact with the Turks.

The reign of Stephen VIII, 'Dushan,' [3] demands more

[1] The Latin Empire was established at Constantinople in 1204, see *supra*, p. 46.

[2] It should be noted that the numeration of kings and the chronology of their reigns are alike uncertain.

[3] Dushan = the *strangler*, and according to one, but not the only, version Stephen VIII strangled his father.

detailed consideration, for it marks the meridian of Serbian history. Cut off at the early age of forty-six, perhaps by poison, he yet lived long enough to establish his fame both as lawgiver and conqueror. His code of laws published in 1349, not less than his encouragement of literature and his protection of the Church, has given to Dushan a place in the history of his own land analogous to that of King Alfred in our own. It is, however, as a mighty conqueror that his memory lives most vividly in Balkan history.

His first military success was achieved against the Emperor Andronicus III. He invaded Thessaly, defeated the forces of the emperor, and by a treaty dictated in 1340 Serbia was recognized as the dominant power in the peninsula. Bulgaria, the sister of whose king Dushan married, formally recognized his supremacy, and in 1345 Stephen was crowned at Uskub, which he made his capital, Tsar of the Serbs, Bulgars, and Greeks. So formidable was Dushan's position in South-Eastern Europe that in 1353 the Pope, Innocent VI, deemed it prudent in the interests of Western Christendom to incite Lewis, King of Hungary, to an attack upon the Serbian Tsar. The Magyars, as we have seen, were never backward in such enterprises ; but, in this case, their intervention recoiled upon their own heads. The city of Belgrade and the provinces of Bosnia and Herzegovina rewarded the victorious arms of Dushan. The extent of his empire was now enormous. It extended from the Save and Danube in the north almost to the Aegean in the south ; from the Adriatic in the west almost to the Lower Maritza in the east. It thus comprised Serbia, Montenegro, Albania, Southern Dalmatia, Bosnia and Herzegovina, Northern Macedonia, and a great part of Greece.

The South Slavonic lands of Croatia, Slavonia, and Northern Dalmatia were still outside the Serbian Empire, nor did it even include Salonica, still less the imperial city itself. Not that Constantinople was beyond the range of Dushan's ambition. The distracted condition of the Eastern Empire seemed indeed to invite an attack upon it. In the domestic dissensions which so grievously weakened the Byzantine emperors in their incipient duel with the Ottomans, Dushan espoused the side of the Empress Anna against Cantacuzenos, and with marked success. In 1351 Dushan organized a great crusade against the decadent Empire of Constantinople with the hope of re-establishing the imperial city as a barrier against the advancing power of the Ottomans.

Cantacuzenos, as we have seen, had not hesitated, again and again, to invoke the aid of Sultan Orkhan against the redoubtable Dushan. In 1353 the Serbians were defeated by the Ottomans at Demotika and Adrianople, and Thrace and parts of Macedonia were thus recovered for the Byzantine Empire. Dushan was great enough both as statesman and strategist to see that, if South-Eastern Europe was to be saved from the Asian menace, Constantinople itself must be held by a national Power, more virile than that of the decadent Byzantines. Under the circumstances that Power could be none other than Serbia. Advancing in 1355 to the accomplishment of this great enterprise, Stephen Dushan was suddenly and prematurely cut off. That poison should have been suspected was inevitable, and the suspicion may be justified.

The death of the Tsar Dushan may fitly close our prolonged parenthesis.

The object of that parenthesis has been to enable the reader to grasp the main features of the general political situation in the Balkans at the moment when a new Power intervened in European affairs. The close of it tempts to speculation. Is it idle to conjecture what might have happened had the Ottomans declined the invitation of Cantacuzenos and elected to remain an Asiatic Power ? What, under those circumstances, would have been the fate of South-Eastern Europe ? The Greek Empire, undeniably damaged in prestige by the Latin episode, had itself fallen into a state of decrepitude which forbad any possible hope of redemption. Could a suitable successor have been found among the other Balkan ' States ' ? The autochthonous Illyrians, now settled in Albania, might perhaps have kept a hold on their mountain fastnesses, but they could never have hoped to do more. The Daco-Roumans. representing the other indigenous race, were geographically too remote from any one of the three keys of the Balkans— Belgrade, Salonica, and Constantinople—to assume at this stage a leading rôle. The Greeks were politically successful only so long as they remained within sight and smell of the sea. The subjection of a hinterland has always seemed to be beyond their powers. By a process of exclusion we reach the Bulgarians and the Serbs, and judging from the experience of the recent past the future seemed to belong to one or other of these peoples, or still more certainly, if they could compose the differences which divided them, to both. Twice had the former attained to clear pre-eminence, if not to domination. But the empires of Simeon and Asen were matched if not surpassed by that of Stephen Dushan. And to Serbia came the ' psychological ' chance. Her supremacy in Balkan politics coincided with one of the great moments in human history. Tremendous issues hung in the balance when Stephen Dushan was suddenly smitten with mortal illness, as he was advancing on Constantinople ; when, from the Danube almost to the Aegean, from the Black Sea to the Adriatic, Serbian suzerainty was virtually unchallenged ; when the Ottomans were effecting their first lodgement on European soil.

The history of the Southern Slavs had already revealed congenital weaknesses ; it would be idle to pretend that more recent experience has proved that during the dark days of adversity and oblivion they have been entirely overcome. But whatever the explanation the fact remains that, in the middle of the fourteenth century, the Balkan Slavs had a chance such as comes to few peoples ; and they missed it. As a result the history of South-Eastern Europe belongs for the next five hundred years not to the Slavs, nor to the Greeks, but to their Ottoman masters.

Ottoman Conquests in Europe

To the story of the Ottomans we must, therefore, after a long but necessary diversion, return. It was against the Serbs, not against the Greeks, that the Ottoman arms in Europe were first directed—a point on which a recent historian has laid considerable emphasis. The result was to involve the Ottoman invaders ' in a tangle of Balkan affairs from which they only extricated themselves after forty years of incessant fighting '.[1] Nevertheless it was upon the Thracian Chersonese that the invaders first fastened. Cantacuzenos was not slow to perceive the blunder he had made. An appeal to Orkhan to quit his hold was met by a courteous but firm refusal. Whereupon the wretched emperor so far humiliated himself as to beg for the assistance of the Bulgars and Serbs. On their refusal his position in Constantinople became desperate. His subjects recalled John Palaeologus, and Cantacuzenos abdicated his uneasy throne and withdrew into a monastery (1354).

Four years later Sultan Orkhan, his son-in-law, died. The reign of his son, Murad I, was one of the most splendid in the annals of the Ottomans. It opened auspiciously with a long and successful campaign in Thrace (1360-1) which finally assured the foothold of his people on the soil of Europe. One after another the important strategic points in Thrace fell

[1] Hogarth, *The Balkans*, p. 327.

into their hands, until at last, by the capture of Adrianople and Philippopolis, they confined the Greek Empire to Constantinople. The Emperor, John V, bowed to the inevitable, recognized the Ottoman conquest of Thrace as definitive, and agreed to become the vassal of the Sultan (1363).

By this time the Christian States were awakening to the gravity of the situation, and in 1363 Lewis the Great of Hungary led a crusading expedition of Hungarians, Serbians, Bosnians, and Wallachians against the successful infidel. Very little, however, was achieved by the enterprise, which came to a disastrous, if not a disgraceful, end in a crushing defeat on the banks of the Maritza.

In 1366 Sultan Murad took a step of high significance; he established his capital at Adrianople, and, turning his back upon the imperial city, devoted himself for the remainder of his life and reign—twenty-three years—to the conquest of the Balkan Peninsula. Sisman of Bulgaria was, in 1379, reduced to vassaldom; the Serbs were decisively defeated at Taenarus, and the Nemanya dynasty came to an end. With the extinction of the dynasty to which Dushan had given distinction Serbia's brief day was over. Little hope now remained to the Byzantine emperor. Frantic appeals were once more addressed to the Christian princes; the emperor himself undertook a special pilgrimage to Rome, but no help was forthcoming from a distracted and divided Christendom, and in 1373 John V definitely accepted the suzerainty of the Ottoman conqueror; undertook to render him military service; and entrusted to his custody his son Manuel as a hostage for the punctual performance of his promises.

Meanwhile Murad made rapid progress in the subjugation of the peninsula: Eastern Macedonia, up to the Vardar river, was conquered in 1372; the rest of Macedonia was occupied in 1380; the Ottomans established themselves in Prilep and

Monastir, and, a few years later, in Okhrida. Murad then turned to complete the subjection of Bulgaria and Serbia. Sofia was taken in 1385, and a year later Nish also fell.

One last and desperate effort was now made by the Slavs to avert their impending doom. A great combination was formed between the Southern Slavs of Serbia and Bosnia, the Bulgars, the Vlachs, and the Albanians. On June 15, 1389, one of the most fateful battles in the history of the Near East was fought on the historic plain of Kossovo. The arms of the Ottoman were completely victorious, and the Slav confederacy was annihilated. The assassination of the Sultan Murad by a pretending Serbian traitor, Milosh Obilic, adds a touch of tragedy to sufficiently impressive history. But the tragedy did not affect the issue of the day. Murad's son, Bayezid, rallied his troops and pressed the victory home. Lazar, the last Serbian Tsar, was captured and executed, and his daughter, Despina, became the wife of the victorious Sultan. The memory of the battle of Kossovo Polye—the Field of Blackbirds—has been preserved in the ballad literature of a freedom-loving peasantry. Not until 1912 did the memory cease to rankle ; not until then was the defeat avenged, and the bitterness it had engendered even partially assuaged.

For five hundred years after Kossovo the Serbs never really rallied. Many of them took refuge in the mountains of Montenegro, and there maintained throughout the ages a brave fight for freedom ; many more migrated to Bosnia, and even to Hungary. But as an independent State Serbia was blotted out.

Four years after the overthrow of the Southern Slavs at Kossovo Bulgarian independence suffered a similar fate. The Turks had already taken Nikopolis in 1388, and in 1393 they destroyed the Bulgarian capital, Tirnovo. The Bulgarian Patriarch was sent into exile ; the Bulgarian Church was, for just five hundred years, reduced to dependence on the Greek Patriarchate at Byzantium ; the Bulgarian dynasty was extinguished, and the Bulgarian State was absorbed into the Empire of the Ottomans.

From the conquest of Bulgaria Bayezid turned to Hungary. He had already, in 1390, carried out a series of successful raids into that country ; he now aspired to more permanent conquest. Sigismund, who had succeeded to the throne of Hungary in 1387, was fully conscious of the impending peril. He made a strong appeal to the other Christian princes of Europe, and in 1394 Pope Boniface IX proclaimed a crusade. One hundred thousand Paladins, the flower of the chivalry of France and Germany, nobles not a few from England, Scotland, Flanders, and Lombardy, and a large body of the Knights of St. John responded to the papal call, and enlisted under the banner of Sigismund. In the battle of Nikopolis (1396) the forces of Christendom were overthrown by the Ottomans. The larger part of Sigismund's followers were slain or driven into the Danube to be drowned ; no fewer than four French Princes of the Blood and twenty sons of the highest nobility in France were among Bayezid's prisoners ; of the Knights of Rhodes only the Grand Master survived, while Sigismund himself escaped with difficulty down the river, and thence by sea returned to Hungary. After the battle a force of Turks invaded Hungary, destroyed the fortresses, and carried off sixteen thousand Styrians into captivity. The triumph of the Ottomans was complete.

The effort of Christendom was unfortunately premature. Could they have waited another six years, and then have struck hard when Bayezid was himself a prisoner in the hands of Tamerlane, the whole future course of European history might have been profoundly affected. When the chance did come in the first years of the fifteenth century, Christian

Europe was too hopelessly distracted by the Great Schism and other quarrels to take advantage of it.

After his victory at Nikopolis Bayezid turned southwards. Hitherto Greece proper had been spared ; but between 1397 and 1399 Bayezid conquered Thessaly, Phocis, Doris, Locris, part of Epirus, and Southern Albania. Thus the conquest of the Balkan Peninsula was all but complete. Athens and Salonica remained in Christian hands,[1] but the emperor himself retained nothing but the extreme south of the Morea and Constantinople.

Could even this remnant be saved ? At the end of the fourteenth century it seemed more than doubtful ; at the beginning of the fifteenth it appeared at least to be possible ; for the whole situation was temporarily transformed by the bursting over Western Asia of a storm which for some years had been gathering in the East.

Born in Bokhara in 1336, Timour ' the Tartar ' had in the latter half of the fourteenth century made himself master of a vast-stretching territory between the Indus and Asia Minor. From Samarkand to Khorasan, from Khorasan to the Caspian ; northwards from the Volga to the Don and the Dnieper ; southwards to Persia, Mesopotamia, Armenia, and Georgia— all acknowledged him as lord. In 1398 he invaded India, and was proclaimed Emperor of Hindustan ; then, westwards again, he made himself master of Bagdad, Aleppo, and Syria. Finally, in 1402, he challenged the Ottoman Sultan in Anatolia. With the Ottoman Empire in Asia this book is not primarily concerned ; but it is essential to remember that, coincidently with their ceaseless activity in Europe, the Ottomans had gradually built up, partly at the expense of the Greek emperors,

---

[1] Gibbons, *op. cit.*, p. 231, seems to have established his point that Salonica was not taken until 1430, and that Athens survived the capture of Constantinople ; but it is not certain.

partly at that of the Seljukian Turks, partly at that of smaller Turkish emirs, an imposing empire in Asia Minor.

At the beginning of the fifteenth century the whole of their hardly-won empire was threatened by the advent of the mighty conqueror Tamerlane. In 1402 Tamerlane inflicted a crushing defeat upon the Ottomans at Angora, and took the Sultan Bayezid prisoner. Later on he captured Brusa and Smyrna, and overran the greater part of Asia Minor. But then, instead of advancing into Europe, he again turned eastwards, and in 1405 he died. The cloud dispersed almost as quickly as it had gathered.

Sultan Bayezid died in captivity in 1403. The battle of Angora is memorable for the fact that it resulted not only in a crushing military defeat but in the capture of an Ottoman Sultan. Never had this happened before; never has it happened since. But apart from this, the defeat of Bayezid at Angora had curiously little significance. The remnant of the Byzantine Empire did, indeed, get a temporary respite; the imperial city was saved to it for half a century; and there ensued among the Ottomans a decade of confusion, civil war, and interregnum.

Yet during this period of confusion no attempt was made either by the Greek emperor or by the Slav peoples in the peninsula, or by interested competitors such as the Venetians or Genoese, or by Sigismund of Hungary, or by the Pope as representing Christendom, to repair the damage wrought in the last half century by the infidel. What is the explanation of this astounding neglect of a unique opportunity? Christendom had, it is true, plenty on its hands. The Great Schism rendered nugatory any action on the part of a Pope. Sigismund, too, was preoccupied. But the essential reasons must be sought elsewhere. It is clear, in the first place, that the Greek Empire was sunk beyond hope of redemption; secondly, that the

Balkan ' peoples ' were unready to take its place ; and finally, that the Ottoman Emperors, Orkhan, Murad, and Bayezid, had builded better than they knew. It is, indeed, a remarkable testimony to their statesmanship that the infant empire should have passed through the crisis after Angora practically unscathed. The ten years' anarchy was ended in 1413 by the recognition of Mohammed I. (1413-21) as sole Sultan, but his brief reign did little to repair the havoc. That task he bequeathed to his son.

For thirty years Murad II devoted his great energy and ability to its accomplishment. His first effort was directed against Constantinople ; but the great prize was snatched from his grasp, as all men then believed, by the miraculous apparition of the Virgin on the walls of the beleaguered city, or possibly by an urgent call from Asia Minor. To Asia Minor, at any rate, he went, and having effectually restored his authority there, he returned to Europe in 1424. The attack upon Constantinople was not resumed, but in 1430 Salonica was for the first time taken by the Ottomans, and Murad's victorious army advanced into Albania.

But the main work of Murad lay elsewhere. In 1440 he was confronted by a great confederacy in the north. The Turkish victory at Nikopolis owed not a little to the help of the Serbians, who, as a reward, were reinvested with Belgrade. In 1427, however, the lordship of the Serbians passed to George Brankovic, whereupon Murad immediately declared war, and Brankovic was compelled to surrender Nish to the Turks and Belgrade to the Magyars. But he built, lower down the Danube, the great fortress of Semendria, which remained, until the nineteenth century, the Serbian capital. Shortly afterwards the Ottomans were threatened by the rise of a great leader among the Magyars. Of all the foes whom the Turks encountered in their conquest of the Balkans, the most brilliant, perhaps, was John Corvinus Hunyadi, Voivode of Transylvania, and celebrated by Commines as ' le chevalier blanc des Valaques '. Under his banner Magyars, Czechs, Vlachs, and Serbians united in an attempt to stem the Ottoman tide. The first encounter between Hunyadi and the Turks was in 1442 at Hermannstadt in Transylvania, when he inflicted a crushing defeat upon the Ottoman general. An attempt to avenge this defeat ended in an even more decisive victory for the arms of Hunyadi. In the summer of 1443 Hunyadi again led an imposing host against the Ottomans. Crossing the Danube near Semendria, he marched up the valley of the Morava, and on November 3 defeated the Turks at Nish. He then took Sofia, forced the passage of the Balkans, and having won another great victory in the valley of the Maritza, found himself within striking distance of Constantinople.

Sultan Murad, beaten to his knees, begged for peace, which was solemnly concluded at Szegedin (July 12, 1444). There was to be a truce for ten years ; Serbia and Herzegovina were to be restored to George Brankovic in complete independence, and Wallachia was to pass under the suzerainty of Hungary. Ladislas, King of Hungary, swore upon the Gospels, the Sultan swore upon the Koran, that the terms should be faithfully observed.

Hardly was the ink dry upon the treaty when Ladislas, on yielding to the combined and perfidious persuasion of the Papal Legate, Cardinal John Cesarini, and the Greek Emperor, determined to break it. Hunyadi, bribed by a promise of the throne of Bulgaria, reluctantly consented, and on September 1 the Hungarian army marched into Wallachia, and in less than two months found themselves in front of Varna. The surrender of Varna, however, put a term to the triumph of the Hungarians.

Secure in the oath of a Christian, Sultan Murad had gone

into retirement after the Treaty of Szegedin, and had sent his army into Asia Minor. The news of the Hungarian advance recalled both the Sultan and his army. Transported from Asia by a heavily bribed Genoese fleet, the Turks reached Varna, and there on November 10, 1444, inflicted a crushing and merited defeat upon their foes. The King of Hungary, the Papal Legate, and two bishops paid for their perfidy with their lives upon the field of battle.

Hunyadi, however, escaped, and four years later he again led a great army across the Danube. The Turks met him on the historic field of Kossovo (October 17, 1448), and there, after three days battle, aided by the defection of George Brankovic, they won, for the second time, a decisive victory.

Thus was the infant empire of the Ottomans saved at last from one of the greatest dangers that ever threatened it. In the same year the Emperor John VIII died, and the rival claimants appealed to Sultan Murad, who designated Constantine as his successor. In 1451 Murad himself died, and was succeeded by his son, Mohammed II.

Mohammed, a young prince of one and twenty, lost no time in plunging into the task with the accomplishment of which his name will always be associated. Having hastily renewed all his father's engagements with Hungary, Serbia, Wallachia, the republics of Ragusa, Venice, and Genoa, he promptly declared war upon the Greek emperor and advanced to the siege of the imperial city. On May 29, 1453, Constantinople was carried by assault, and the last Greek emperor died fighting in the breach.

The last Greek emperor died, but his empire survived. It has been recently argued that modern critics have attached to the conquest of Constantinople an importance of which contemporaries were ignorant. The contention is partly true. Contemporaries, however, are not the best judges of the historical perspective of the events they witness. To the people of that day the capture of Constantinople was merely the inevitable climax of a long series of Ottoman victories on European soil. The Sultan was already sovereign of the Greek Empire ; the emperor was his vassal ; the taking of the imperial city was merely a question of time.

Nevertheless, the fall of Constantinople is in the true historical sense ' epoch marking '. Of its significance in an economic and commercial sense, and its relation to the geographical Renaissance, mention has been already made. Hardly less direct was its relation to the Humanistic Renaissance. Learning fled from the shores of the Bosphorus to the banks of the Arno. From Florence and Bologna and other Italian cities the light of the new learning spread to Paris and to Oxford. The Oxford lectures of John Colet, the *Novum Instrumentum* of Desiderius Erasmus, perhaps even Luther's historic protest at Wittenberg, may be ascribed, remotely perhaps but in no fanciful sense, to the Ottoman conquest of Constantinople. But most important of all its consequences, from our present standpoint, was the foundation of a new empire. That empire was not exclusively Turkish ; still less was it purely Byzantine. It was a fusion and combination of the two. The Ottomans were in truth not merely the conquerors of the Balkans but the heirs of the Graeco-Roman Empire of the East.

For further reference : H. A. Gibbons, *The Foundations of the Ottoman Empire* (with an elaborate bibliography for the period prior to 1403) ; E. A. Freeman, *The Ottoman Power in Europe* (London, 1877) ; S. Lane Poole, *Turkey* (1250–1880), (London, 1888) ; D. S. Margoliouth, *Mohammed and the Rise of Islam* (London, 1905) ; Sir W. Muir, *The Caliphate, its Rise, Decline, and Fall* (London, 1891) ; A. Wirth, *Geschichte der Türken* ; H. F. Tozer, *The Church and the Eastern Empire* (1888) ; L. von Ranke, *History of Servia* (Eng. trans. 1858) ; Lavisse et Rambaud, *Histoire Générale*, vol. iii (with excellent bibliography for this period) ; Sir W. M. Ramsay, *Historical*

Geography of Asia Minor (1890); W. Miller, *The Balkans* (1896), *The Latins in the Levant : a History of Frankish Greece* (1908); Vᵗᵉ A. de la Jonquière, *Histoire de l'Empire Ottoman*, 2 vols. (new ed. 1914); E. Creasy, *History of the Ottoman Turks*; J. von Hammer, *Gesch. des Osmanischen Reichs*, 10 vols.; Lord Eversley, *The Turkish Empire : its Growth and Decay* (London, 1917); E. Gibbon, *Decline and Fall of the Roman Empire*; J. H. Newman, *The Ottoman Turks*; J. W. Zinkeisen, *Gesch. des Osmanischen Reichs in Europa*, 7 vols. (vol. i); Sir E. Pears, *Destruction of the Greek Empire* (1903); C. Oman, *Byzantine Empire*; W. H. Hutton, *Constantinople*.

4

The Ottoman Empire : its Zenith 1453–1566

Suleiman the Magnificent

'The peculiarity of the Turks is at once apparent when we observe that their history is almost exclusively a catalogue of names and battles.'— *Odysseus* (Sir Charles Eliot).

'The failure of the Turks is due to Byzantinism. . . . The decadence of the Turk dates from the day when Constantinople was taken and not destroyed.'—'DIPLOMATIST,' *Nationalism and War in the Near East.*

THE events recorded in the preceding chapter demonstrated conclusively one fact of supreme significance : a new nation had definitely planted itself on European soil; the Osmanlis had come to stay.

Down to the capture of Constantinople some doubts upon this point might have lingered; after it there could be none. The Osmanlis were now plainly something more than brilliantly successful adventurers. The taking of Constantinople fundamentally altered their position. It is true that in its declining years the Byzantine Empire enjoyed, as it deserved, little prestige; yet the mere possession of the imperial city did confer upon its conquerors, altogether apart from questions of strategic or commercial advantage, a quasi-constitutional authority such as they could not otherwise have obtained.

And the Sultan Mohammed clearly recognized the significance of the change. Hitherto his followers had been merely an army of occupation in a conquered land. They have always been that and, according to one reading of their history, they have never been anything more. How far that reading is accurate the following pages will show; a point of more immediate significance is that after 1453 Sultan Mohammed initiated the attempt to devise a polity for the new nation.

To what extent could he rely upon the essential characteristics of his people? Many contradictory attributes have been predicated of the Ottoman Turks. They have been delineated by friends and by foes respectively as among the most amiable, and unquestionably the most detestable of mankind; but on one point all observers are agreed. The Turk never changes. What he was when he first effected a lodgement upon European soil, that he remains to-day. Essentially the Ottoman Turk has been from first to last a fighting man, a herdsman, and a nomad.

'In the perpetual struggle', writes one, 'between the herdsman and the tiller of the soil, which has been waged from remote ages on the continents of Europe and Asia, the advance of the Ottomans was a decisive victory for the children of the steppes. This feature of their conquest is of no less fundamental importance than its victory for Islam.'[1]

'The Turks', writes another, 'never outgrew their ancestral character of predacious nomads; they take much and give little.'[2]

Thus, to close observers, the Turks have always given the impression of transitoriness; of being strangers and sojourners in a land that is not their own. 'Here', they have seemed to

[1] J. B. Bury, ap. *C. M. H.*   [2] Eliot, *Turkey in Europe.*

say, ' we have no abiding city.' 'A band of nomadic warriors, we are here to-day ; we shall be gone to-morrow.'

But the sense of temporary occupation was not inconsistent with a rigid conservatism as long as the occupation might last. And in nothing have the Ottomans shown themselves more conservative than in fulfilment of the obligations which they inherited from their predecessors. No sooner were they masters of the imperial city than they made it plain to the world that they regarded themselves as the legitimate heirs of the Byzantine Empire. No Greek could have exhibited more zeal than Sultan Mohammed in resisting the encroachments, whether territorial or ecclesiastical, of the Latins. Venetians, Genoese, and Franks were alike made to realize that the Turk was at least as Greek as his predecessor in title. Most clearly was this manifested in his dealings with the Orthodox Church.

The Greek Church

Some of the more fanatical adherents of that Church had actually favoured the revolution by which a Turkish Sultan had replaced a Greek Basileus who was known to approve of reunion with Rome. They had their reward. At the moment when Constantinople was taken the patriarchal throne happened to be vacant. Within three days Sultan Mohammed had given orders that a new Patriarch should be elected and consecrated with all the accustomed rites. After his election the Patriarch was treated with the deepest personal respect, and received from the Sultan a solemn guarantee for all the rights and immunities of his Church ; in particular, there was to be complete freedom of worship for the Greek Christians. In every way the Orthodox Church was encouraged to look to the Sultan as its protector against the pretensions of the rival Rome. Thus the Patriarch became in effect the Pope of the Eastern Church. He was invested, indeed, with extraordinary privileges. After the conquest, as before, he was permitted to summon periodical synods, to hold ecclesiastical courts, and to enforce the sentences of the courts with spiritual penalties.-

Nor was the favour shown to the Greeks confined to ecclesiastics. On the contrary the Sultans developed among the Greek laymen a sort of administrative aristocracy. Known as Phanariotes from the *Phanar*, the particular quarter which they inhabited in Constantinople, these shrewd and serviceable Greeks were utilized by the Turks for the performance of duties for which the conquerors had neither liking nor aptitude. The Turk is curiously devoid of that sense which the ancient Greeks described as *political*. He desires neither to govern nor to be governed. He is a polemical not a ' political animal '. To conquer and to enjoy in ease the fruits of conquest has always been his ideal of life. With the dull details of administration he has never cared to concern himself. That was the work of ' slaves ', and as a fact, though none but a Moslem could in theory aspire to the highest administrative posts, the actual work of administration was confided to the Phanariotes. Whether this practice, in the long run, contributed either to the well-being of Christianity in the dominions of the Porte, or to the better government of the Greek population, is a moot point to which we may recur. For the moment it must suffice to say that while the Higher Clergy of the Orthodox Church became almost wholly dependent upon the State, the parish priests laboured with extraordinary devotion to keep alive among their flocks the flame of nationality even more perhaps than the tenets of Orthodoxy. To their efforts, maintained with remarkable perseverance throughout a period of four and a half centuries, the success of the Greek revival, in the early nineteenth century, was largely due.

The attitude of the Ottomans towards the Greek Christians

[1] Hutton, *Constantinople*, p. 156.

was inspired by a mixture of motives. It was due partly to an innate tendency towards toleration, and still more perhaps to invincible indolence. In view of the hideous massacres perpetrated by Abdul Hamid it is not easy to insist that religious toleration is one of the cardinal virtues of the Turk.[1] Yet the fact is incontestable. Although the Ottoman State was essentially theocratic in theory and in structure, although the sole basis of political classification was ecclesiastical, the Turk was one of the least intolerant of rulers. He was also one of the most indolent. So long as his material necessities were supplied by his subjects, the precise methods of local government and administration were matters of indifference to him. This had its good and its bad side. It often left the conquered peoples at the mercy of petty tyrants, but where the local circumstances were unfavourable to tyrannies it left the people very much to themselves. Hence that considerable measure of local autonomy which has frequently been noted as one of the many contradictory features of Ottoman government in Europe, and which largely contributed, when the time came, to the resuscitation of national self-consciousness among the conquered peoples.

The traits already delineated may perhaps account for another marked characteristic of Ottoman history. Whether it be due to pride or to indolence, to spiritual exclusiveness or to political indifference, the fact remains that the Turks have neither absorbed nor been absorbed by the conquered peoples ; still less have they permitted any assimilation among the conquered peoples. Mr. Freeman put this point, with characteristic emphasis, many years ago :

'The Turks, though they have been in some parts of Turkey

[1] Cf. a recent writer : 'The Osmanlis were the first nation in modern history to lay down the principle of religious freedom as the corner-stone in the building up of their nation.' Gibbons, *op. cit.*, and cf. an interesting note on the Armenian massacres, p. 74.

for five hundred years, have still never become the people of
the land, nor have they in any way become one with the
people of the land. They still remain as they were when they
first came in, a people of strangers bearing rule over the people
of the land, but in every way distinct from them.'

The original Ottoman invaders were relatively few in
numbers, and throughout the centuries they have continued
to be ' numerically inferior to the aggregate of their subjects '.
But for two considerations it is almost certain that like the
Teuton invaders of Gaul they would have been absorbed by
the peoples whom they conquered. The Teuton conquerors
of Gaul were pagans, the Turks, on the contrary, brought with
them a highly developed creed which virtually forbade assimilation. Under the strict injunctions of the Koran the infidel
must either embrace Islamism ; or suffer death ; or purchase,
by the payment of a tribute, a right to the enjoyment of life
and property. Only in Albania was there any general acceptance of the Moslem creed among the masses of the population.
In Bosnia, and to a less degree in Bulgaria, the larger landowners purchased immunity by conversion ; but, generally
speaking, the third of the alternatives enjoined by the Koran
was the one actually adopted. Christianity consequently
survived in most parts of the Turkish Empire. And the Turk,
as we have seen, shrewdly turned its survival to his own advantage. The second pertinent consideration is that the conquered
peoples were hopelessly divided amongst themselves. Before
the coming of the Turk, the Bulgarians, as we have seen, had
been constantly at the throats of the Serbians, and both at
those of the Greeks. This antagonism the Turk set himself
sedulously to cultivate, and with conspicuous success. As
a close and discriminating observer has justly said : ' they
have always done and still do all in their power to prevent the
obliteration of racial, linguistic, and ' religious differences ',

with the result that ' they have perpetuated and preserved, as in a museum, the strange medley which existed in South-Eastern Europe during the last years of the Byzantine Empire '.[1]

If the Turk was not, in the Aristotelian sense, a ' political animal ', still less was he an ' economic man '. He adhered faithfully to his primitive nomadic instincts. There is a proverbial saying in the East : *where the Turk plants his foot the grass never grows again.* To a nomad it is a matter of comparative indifference whether it does. He is a herdsman, not a tiller of the soil. Agriculture and commerce are alike beneath his notice, except, of course, as a source of revenue. Here, as in the lower ranks of the administrative hierarchy, the Greek could be pre-eminently useful to his new sovereign. Consequently the Greek traders in Constantinople, for example, and Salonica and Athens, were protected by a substantial tariff against foreign competition. In the sixteenth century the expulsion of the Moors from Grenada led to a considerable influx of Moors and Spanish Jews into Salonica, where they still predominate, and even into Constantinople. In them and also in the Armenians the Greeks found powerful competitors, both in finance and in commerce. For the governing Turks these matters had no interest except in so far as they affected the contributions to the imperial treasury. So long as that was full it mattered nothing to the Turks who were the contributors, or whence their wealth was derived.

Such were some of the outstanding characteristics of the

---

[1] Eliot, *op. cit.*, p. 16. Cf. Rambaud, ap. *Hist. Générale*, iv. 751 : ' L'assimilation, l'absorption de l'un des deux éléments par l'autre était impossible grâce à l'opposition du Koran à l'Évangile, du croissant à la croix. Plus d'une fois les Osmanlis ayant conscience de leur infériorité numérique s'inquiétèrent de cette situation grosse de périls pour l'avenir de leur puissance.'

people who in the fifteenth century established themselves permanently in South-Eastern Europe. But though they were permanently established by 1453, they had by no means reached the final limits of political ascendancy or of territorial conquest and expansion.

Mohammed's first anxiety after the taking of Constantinople was to complete the subjugation of the Southern Slavs. But so long as Hunyadi lived the latter did not lack an effective champion. Appealed to by George Brankovic of Serbia, Hunyadi, in 1454, came to the relief of Semendria, and then burnt Widdin to the ground. But in 1455 Mohammed captured Novoberda, and in the following year laid siege to Belgrade. Once more the Pope, Calixtus III, attempted to rouse Christendom against the Moslems. A considerable measure of enthusiasm was excited by the preaching of a Minorite brother, John of Capistrano, and in 1456 Hunyadi marched at the head of a great army to the relief of Belgrade. The frontier fortress was saved, and the Turks were routed with a loss of 50,000 men and 300 guns. But this was the last exploit of John Corvinus Hunyadi, who died in this same year (1456). Brankovic of Serbia died almost simultaneously.

The death of these two men shattered the last fragment of independence enjoyed by the Southern Slavs. Serbia was converted into a Turkish Pashalik, and was finally annexed to the Ottoman Empire in 1459 ; Bosnia shared its fate in 1463, and Herzegovina in 1465. For more than three centuries and a half the Southern Slavs disappear from the page of history.

Only in the region of the Black Mountain did a remnant of the race maintain their independence ; but until the nineteenth century the gallant resistance of Montenegro was devoid of political significance.

Almost the same is true of Albania, though in the middle of the fifteenth century the sombre story of the Albanian mountaineers was illuminated by the brief but brilliant episode of a famous adventurer known as Scanderbeg or Iskendar Bey. George Castriotis, 'the dragon of Albania', was brought up as a Moslem at the court of Murad II and served in the Ottoman army, but at the age of forty he was converted to Christianity, abjured his allegiance to the Sultan, and initiated, in his native mountains, a guerrilla warfare against the Turks. This war was maintained with extraordinary success during the remaining years of Scanderbeg's life (1443–67) ; one Turkish army after another was thrown into Albania only to be repelled by the indomitable courage of Scanderbeg and his compatriots, seconded by the inaccessible nature of their fastnesses. In 1461 Mohammed II came to terms with Scanderbeg, acknowledging the independence of Albania and the lordship of Castriotis over Albania and Epirus. A few years later, however, the struggle was renewed, but with no better success for the Turks. Castriotis died still unconquered in 1467, and after his death many of his followers migrated to Italy. Of the rest a large number embraced Mohammedanism ; not a few entered the service of the Porte ; and some, notably the Kiuprilis, rose to eminence in that service. But the country itself has never really been subdued by the foreigner, and only at rare intervals has it been united in submission to one of its own native chieftains. Geography has indeed prohibited both union and subjection ; both commercial and political development. Bands of brigands, with little or no mutual cohesion, have, throughout the centuries, maintained a precarious existence by preying on each other or on their neighbours. That the race has virility is proved by the men it has spasmodically thrown up—a Castriotis, a Kiuprili, an Ali Pasha of Janina, and, most notable of all, the famous soldier and statesman who played in the nineteenth century so great a part in the history of Egypt and indeed of Europe, Mehemet

Ali. But apart from individuals such as these, and the episodes connected with one or two of them, Albania from the end of the fifteenth century until the end of the nineteenth played no appreciable part in Balkan politics. In recent years European diplomacy has, for its own purposes, discovered an ' Albanian Question ', but it is not cynical to suggest that the discovery is due to the existence of two harbours on the Albanian coast, Durazzo and Valona. The significance of the discovery must engage attention at a later stage of our inquiry. For at least four centuries after the death of Scanderbeg, as a factor in the problem of the Near East, Albania may be ignored.

The Morea and Greece proper were, as we saw, distributed, at the time of the Ottoman invasion, among a number of principalities, Byzantine, Frankish, and Venetian. After the conquest of Constantinople these were gradually reduced to submission. The Florentine dynasty in Athens was finally expelled in 1456; Corinth capitulated in 1458; the two Palaeologi, whose rule in the Morea had long been a public scandal, were dethroned in 1459, and the Morea itself was finally annexed to the Ottoman Empire.

Aegina and some half-dozen coast towns, not to mention the great majority of the Aegean islands, still remained in the hands of the Venetians. Between the Turks and the Venetian Republic there was intermittent war for nearly twenty years. In 1463 Venice attempted to rouse Western Europe to a sense of the gravity of the Ottoman peril. But only with partial success. A league was formed between the Republic, the Pope, the Duke of Burgundy, and the King of Hungary, but though a considerable force assembled at Ancona it lacked organization, and Venice was left to fight the battle of Christendom alone. She fought bravely but without success. Argos was taken by the Turks in 1463, and in 1467 Euboea was attacked in force by land and sea. Its conquest, in the following year, was the death-blow to the Venetian Empire in the Near East. Joined by Pope Sixtus IV, by Naples, and by the Knights of St. John, Venice then attempted a diversion in Asia Minor. Their combined fleets attacked and captured Smyrna, and an attempt was made to incite Karamania to revolt against the Turks. But little was actually accomplished. Nearer home Scutari was held by the Venetians against repeated sieges, but in 1478 the Turks took Kroia, the Albanian fortresses, and thence advanced again upon Scutari. Deserted by her allies Venice then determined to treat, and in 1479 the Treaty of Constantinople was concluded. The Doge surrendered to the Turks Lemnos, Euboea, and Scutari, and agreed to pay an indemnity of 100,000 ducats and an annual tribute of 110,000. In return Venice was to have the privilege of a consular establishment in Constantinople, and to enjoy freedom of trade throughout the Ottoman dominions.

Meanwhile the Turks had been making rapid progress on both shores of the Black Sea. In 1461 Amastris, in the north of Anatolia, was taken from the Genoese; in the same year Sinope and Paphlagonia were captured from one of the Turkish emirs; and—greatest prize of all—Trebizond, the last refuge of the Greek emperors, fell into the hands of Mohammed. A few years afterwards the Emperor, David Comnenus, and all his kinsmen were strangled. Thus perished the last of the Roman emperors of the East. The Seljukian Empire survived that of Byzantium only a few years. In 1471 Karamania, the last Seljukian principality, was annexed by Mohammed, and two years later a terrific contest between Mohammed and Ouzoun Hassan, the Turcoman ruler of Persia and part of Armenia, ended in the decisive defeat of the latter. Thenceforward the Turks were undisputed masters of Anatolia. Finally, in 1475 Azov and the Crimea were conquered, and the Tartars accepted the suzerainty of the Sultan. This completed

Turkish supremacy on both shores of the Black Sea. Not until the latter part of the eighteenth century was it ever again questioned.

The career of Sultan Mohammed, now nearing its close, had been one of almost uninterrupted success. One last ambition which he cherished was destined to remain unfulfilled. He had already conquered most of the Aegean islands, Lemnos, Imbros, Thasos, and Samothrace; but the island of Rhodes was still held by the Knights Hospitallers. A great armament was accordingly dispatched from Constantinople in 1480 to effect its conquest, but after besieging it for two months the Turks were beaten off with heavy loss. Mohammed, nettled by this reverse, determined to take command of the next expedition in person, but just as it was starting the Sultan suddenly passed away (May 3, 1481). He well deserves the name by which in Turkish history he is distinguished; among a long line of brilliant soldiers he was pre-eminently 'the Conqueror'. A few outlying portions of the Byzantine Empire, each important in a strategic sense, were nevertheless denied to him: Belgrade in the north; Crete, Cyprus, and Rhodes in the south; but apart from these hardly an ambition of his life was unfulfilled, and to his successor he bequeathed an empire which extended from the Danube to the Euphrates.

That successor was destined to a more chequered fortune. One distinguished critic has held that the seeds of the decay of the Ottoman Empire began to be sown as early as the reign of Bayezid II. Be that as it may, his career was certainly less consistently successful than that of his predecessor. To begin with, the succession was not undisputed. His half-brother Djem proposed partition: that Bayezid should keep the European dominions, while Djem should rule Asiatic Turkey with Brusa as his capital. Bayezid declined the offer, and in one decisive battle, at Yenishehr, disposed of his brother's

pretensions. Supported by the Mamluke Sultan, with whom
he took refuge in Cairo, Djem had the temerity to repeat the
proposal, only to meet with an equally decided rebuff. Djem
then fled for refuge to the Knights of St. John, by whom he
was sent on to France, whence, six years later, he passed to
his final captivity at the Vatican. So long as he lived (until
1495) he was a source of some disquietude to Sultan Bayezid,
and a pawn of some potential value in the hands of the Christians, but the effective use they made of him was not great.

Of Bayezid's numerous wars the most important was that
with the Venetian Republic. The progress made by the
Venetians in the Aegean, more particularly the taking of
Cyprus, had seriously alarmed the Sultan. Further stimulated,
perhaps, by the Italian rivals of the Republic, he declared war
upon it in 1498. The Turkish fleet won a great victory at
Lepanto, but in the Morea, where most of the land fighting
was concentrated, the fortunes of war were very uncertain.
Hungary, the Papacy, and other Western Powers sent some
assistance to the Republic, and their combined fleet inflicted
a severe defeat upon the Turkish navy, raided the coast of
Asia Minor, and seized the island of Santa Maura. Bayezid,
therefore, concluded peace with Venice in 1502 and with
Hungary a year later. The Sultan recovered Santa Maura,
and retained all his conquests in the Morea, while Cephalonia
was retained by the Republic.

The next twenty years (1503–20) formed a period, as far as
Europe was concerned, of unusual tranquillity. The Turkish
Sultan was busy elsewhere. The rise of the Safawid dynasty
in Persia led to a struggle between Persia and the Ottomans ;
there was a war also, not too successful, with the Mamlukes ;
and, worst of all, Bayezid had serious trouble with his own
house. So serious, indeed, did it become that in 1512 Sultan
Bayezid was compelled by Selim, the youngest of his three

sons, to abdicate, and shortly after his abdication he died, probably by poison.

Entirely devoid of pity or scruples, the new Sultan began his reign by the murder of his two brothers and eight nephews. Still his reign, though brief, was brilliant. Perpetually at war, he never crossed swords with a Christian. But his wars and conquests in the East were on such an imposing scale that in less than eight years he nearly doubled the size of the Ottoman Empire.

Conquest of Northern Mesopotamia, Egypt, Syria, and Arabia

A three years' war with the Shah Ismail of Persia resulted in the acquisition of Northern Mesopotamia ; Egypt, Syria, and Arabia were successively conquered, and, to crown all, the Khalifate was transferred to the Ottoman Sultan, who became henceforward the protector of the Holy Places and the spiritual head of Mohammedanism throughout the world. The conquest of Egypt rendered the continued occupation of Rhodes by the Knights Hospitallers increasingly galling to the masters of Cairo and Constantinople. But to Selim, as to his grandfather, this prize was denied. Like Mohammed he was preparing for an expedition against the Knights when he was overtaken by death.

Few reigns in Ottoman history have been shorter ; none has been more crowded with notable events. Of these by far the most significant, apart from the territorial expansion of the empire, was the assumption of the Khalifate—significant but sinister. For, as an acute critic has said, ' it marked the supersession of the Byzantine or European ideal by the Asiatic in Osmanli policy, and introduced a phase of Ottoman history which has endured to our own time.' [1]

[1] Hogarth, *op. cit.*, p. 338.

The Khalifate and the Sultanate passed without dispute, thanks to the sanguinary precautions of Sultan Selim, to his only son Suleiman, known to European contemporaries as ' the Magnificent ', to his own people as the ' lawgiver '.

In the reign and person of Suleiman the history of his nation reaches its climax ; as warrior, as organizer, as legislator, as man he has had no superior, perhaps no equal, among the Ottoman Turks. Physically, morally, and intellectually Suleiman was richly endowed : a man of great strength and stature ; capable of enduring immense fatigue ; frank, generous, amiable in character ; indefatigably industrious ; a capable administrator, and no mean scholar. But despite his brilliant gifts, sedulously cultivated, the reign of Suleiman is, by general consent, taken to mark not only the zenith of Ottoman greatness, but the beginnings, though at first hardly discernible, of decline.

The opening of the reign was extraordinarily auspicious. His predecessor bequeathed to Suleiman a vast empire ; but in that empire there were two points of conspicuous weakness. In the north, the Turkish frontier was insecure so long as the great fortress of Belgrade remained in the hands of Hungary ; in the south, the presence of the Knights Hospitallers in Rhodes constituted a perpetual menace to the safety and continuity of communication between Cairo and Constantinople. Within two years of Suleiman's accession both these sources of weakness had been removed. Belgrade and Sabacz were conquered from Hungary in 1521 ; Rhodes at last fell before the Ottoman assault in 1522. The Knights found a temporary refuge in Crete, and in 1530 settled permanently in Malta. Belgrade remained continuously in the hands of the Ottomans until the end of the seventeenth century.

The acquisition of this great frontier fortress opened the way for the most conspicuous military achievement of the reign. With Belgrade in his hands Suleiman could safely embark upon a more ambitious enterprise, the conquest of Hungary itself.

That enterprise initiates a new phase in the history of the Ottoman Empire in Europe. The Turks had now been 'encamped' upon European soil for nearly two centuries; but though *in* Europe they were not *of* it. They were pariahs, with whom no respectable prince, except surreptitiously, would hold converse. The reign of Suleiman marks, in this respect, a notable change, a change mainly due to the new political conditions which were beginning to prevail in Western Europe. The States-system of modern Europe only came into being in the sixteenth century, and the first manifestation of the new system was the prolonged and embittered rivalry between the kingdom of France and the Habsburg Empire. The contest between Charles V and Francis I for the imperial crown (1519) brought that rivalry to a head. The success of Charles V opened a chapter which did not close until, at the beginning of the eighteenth century, Louis XIV put his grandson on the throne of Spain. The first bout of this prolonged contest ended with the utter defeat of Francis I in the battle of Pavia (1525). Pavia was a great day not only for the Habsburgs but for the Turks. Francis I had begun his reign with a fervent reaffirmation of the traditional policy of his house. Fresh from the glory achieved at Marignano he would lead a great crusade of all the powers of the West against the intruding Ottoman. That crusade was a main plank of his platform in the contest for the empire. He promised that if elected he would, within three years, either be in Constantinople or in his coffin. His failure to obtain the imperial crown somewhat tempered his crusading zeal, and after his humiliating defeat at Pavia, Francis, while yet a prisoner in the hands of his rivals, made overtures to the Ottoman Sultan. The alliance that ensued between Turkey and France was destined to supply one of the most important and one of the most continuous threads in the fabric of European diplomacy for more than three hundred years to come.

The overtures of a French king, even in captivity, could not fail to cause gratification at Constantinople, and the response was prompt. In April, 1526, the Sultan started from Constantinople at the head of a magnificent army of 100,000 men. Crossing the Danube he took Peterwardein in July, and on August 28, 1526, he met and defeated on the plain of Mohacz the flower of the Hungarian nobility. Lewis, the last Jagellon King of Hungary and Bohemia, the brother-in-law of Ferdinand of Austria, was drowned in his flight from the field. Nothing could now arrest the advance of Suleiman upon Buda, the Hungarian capital, which he occupied on September 10. But after a fortnight's stay he was recalled to Constantinople, leaving the fate of Hungary undecided. For the next two years Suleiman's energies were fully occupied with the affairs of his empire in Asia Minor.

Meanwhile, there was acute dissension in the two kingdoms where the Jagellons had ruled. To Bohemia, Ferdinand of Austria made good his claim, but in Hungary he encountered a serious rival in John Zapolya, the Voyvode of Transylvania. Favoured by Suleiman the latter was crowned king in 1526, but in 1527 he was driven back by Ferdinand into Transylvania. Both parties then appealed for help to the Ottoman Sultan. Accordingly, Suleiman again set out for Hungary in 1529, and in August of that year again found himself on the plain of Mohacz. There he was joined by Zapolya, and together they advanced on Buda. Buda offered little resistance, and Suleiman then determined to attack Vienna itself.

Exclusive of the Hungarian followers of Zapolya the Turkish army numbered 250,000 men, and had 300 guns. The garrison consisted of only 16,000 men, but they defended the city with splendid gallantry. In view of the menace to Christendom Lutherans and Catholics closed their ranks, and large reinforcements were soon on their way to the capital. After a fruitless siege of twenty-four days Suleiman, therefore, decided to retire (October 14).

The failure of the greatest of the Sultans to take Vienna, and his withdrawal in the autumn of 1529, mark an epoch in the history of the Eastern Question. A definite and, as it proved, a final term was put to the advance of the Ottomans towards Central Europe. The brave garrison of Vienna had rendered an incomparable service to Germany and to Christendom. Here at last was a barrier which even Suleiman could not pass.

Three times more at least did Suleiman lead expeditions into Hungary : in 1532, in 1541, and finally in the very last year of his reign and life, 1566. But never did he renew the attempt upon Vienna. The failure of 1529 was accepted as final.

It would be tedious to follow in detail the fortunes of Suleiman's Hungarian enterprises ; nor is it pertinent to the purpose of this book. The expedition of 1532 was on a very imposing scale. Suleiman left Constantinople at the head of a force of 200,000 men, and was joined at Belgrade by 100,000 Bosnians and 15,000 Tartars. But the Turkish host suffered a serious check at the little town of Güns, and after taking it Suleiman, instead of advancing on Vienna, contented himself with laying waste a great part of Styria and Lower Austria. Nothing of importance had been effected, and in June, 1533, a treaty—memorable as the first between the House of Austria and Turkey—was concluded.

The expedition of 1541 had more permanent results. Zapolya had died in July, 1540, and though Suleiman espoused the cause of his widow and infant son, the interests of the

Zapolya family were virtually set aside. What the Sultan now conquered he conquered for himself. Buda again fell into his hands in 1541, not to be surrendered for nearly a century and a half. Another expedition in 1543 confirmed the Turkish possession of Hungary and Transylvania which, except for a strip retained by Ferdinand, was definitely incorporated as the pashalik of Buda in the Ottoman Empire. The country was divided into twelve *sanjaks*, in each of which a regular administrative and financial system was established. Negotiations between the Habsburgs and the Turks continued for several years, but at last, in 1547, the former accepted the inevitable and a five years' armistice was concluded. Ferdinand then agreed to pay to the Porte an annual tribute of 30,000 ducats for the strip of Hungary which he was permitted to retain. The truce was imperfectly observed on both sides, and in 1551 the war was resumed. With short intervals of inactivity it continued, without essentially modifying the situation on either side, until 1562, when a treaty was concluded between the veteran antagonists. Ferdinand died two years afterwards (1564), but in 1566 war was renewed between his successor, the Emperor Maximilian II, and the Ottomans. It was in the course of this campaign, which he led in person, that the great Sultan Suleiman passed away.

The wars against the Habsburgs, extending with brief intervals from the first year of Suleiman's reign to the last, constitute the most important as well as the most continuous preoccupation of that monarch's career. But these wars did not stand alone, nor were the Sultan's activities confined to the Hungarian expeditions. Six campaigns at least did he undertake in person against the rival Mohammedan Power of Persia with the result that large portions of Armenia and Mesopotamia, including the city of Bagdad, were added to the Asiatic dominions of the Ottomans. Suleiman went indeed even further afield. Thanks to his omnipotence at sea he was able to effect a permanent occupation of Aden, which was strongly fortified, and to make his influence felt along the coasts of Arabia, Persia, and even North-Western India.

Ottoman Sea-power

Even more conspicuous was the superiority of Ottoman sea-power in the Mediterranean. Great as was the terror inspired in Europe by the military prowess of Suleiman, that inspired by the exploits of the Turkish navy was hardly less. For this reputation Suleiman was largely indebted to the genius of one of the most remarkable seamen of the sixteenth century. In that age of buccaneers Khaireddin Barbarossa fills a conspicuous place. He did not, like Frobisher or Drake, add to knowledge, but his seamanship was unquestioned, and to the Spaniards his name was hardly less terrible than that of Drake. Born in Mitylene after the conquest of that island by the Turks he was by birth an Ottoman subject. About the year 1516 he and his brother established themselves in Algiers, whence they carried on a perpetual and harassing contest with the naval forces of Spain. Recognized by Suleiman as Beyler Bey of Algiers, Barbarossa placed his services at the disposal of his suzerain, and in the year 1533 was appointed admiral in chief of the Ottoman navy, then at the zenith of its reputation.

About the same time he undertook a series of voyages, seven in all, from Algiers to the Andalusian coast, in the course of which he transported 70,000 Moors from Spain to Algiers. By this remarkable feat he not only consolidated his own corsair kingdom on the African coast, but rescued a large number of persecuted Moslems from the tender mercies of the Inquisition. In 1533 he was employed by the Sultan to drive off Andrea Doria, the famous Genoese sailor who commanded the imperial fleet in the Mediterranean. Doria had lately seized Coron, Patras, and other fortified coast-towns belonging to the Ottomans, and Barbarossa's intervention was as opportune, therefore, as it was effective. In 1534, at the head of a powerful and well-equipped fleet, Barbarossa attacked and plundered the coasts of Italy, and later in the year conquered Tunis and added it to his Algerian principality. But his triumph in Tunis was short-lived. Muley Hassan, the representative of the Arabian family who had ruled for centuries in Tunis, appealed to the Emperor Charles V. The latter, seriously alarmed by Barbarossa's activity in the Western Mediterranean, collected a large army and a powerful fleet, and in 1535 sailed from Barcelona for the Tunisian coast. He reconquered the principality, and having put the capital to the sack with a barbarity which no Turk could rival, he drove out Barbarossa and reinstated Muley Hassan.

In the same year, 1535, the war between the Habsburg Emperor and Francis I was renewed, and the latter turned for assistance to the Sultan Suleiman.

Franco-Ottoman Alliance

The treaty then concluded between the French monarch and the Ottoman Sultan is of the highest possible significance. It is indicative of the position to which the Turks had by now attained that even a French writer should describe the convention as ' less a treaty than a concession '.[1] The Sultan now extended throughout the Ottoman Empire the privileges accorded, in 1528, to the French in Egypt. Frenchmen were to enjoy complete freedom of trade and navigation in all Turkish ports, subject to a uniform duty of 5 per cent. ; no foreign vessel might sail in Turkish waters except under the French flag ; French traders were to be under the exclusive jurisdiction, both civil and criminal, of their own consuls, and

[1] Albin, *Les Grands Traités politiques*, p. 128.

the Turkish officials guaranteed the execution of all judgements in the consular courts ; French settlers in the Ottoman Empire were to enjoy peculiar privileges in respect of the transmission of property by will and even of intestate estates ; they were to have not only complete religious liberty for themselves, but also the custody of the Holy Places, and thus to exercise a species of protectorate over the Christian subjects of the Porte. The King of France, alone among the European sovereigns, was regarded and treated as an equal by the Sultan, being henceforward described in official documents as *Padishah*, instead of *Bey*.

The privileges thus accorded, in the Ottoman Empire, to France were not only extraordinarily valuable in themselves ; they established, on firm foundations, a diplomatic friendship which operated powerfully, in the sixteenth century, against the dominance of the Habsburgs, and for more than three hundred years continued to be an essential factor in French diplomacy.[1]

Its immediate significance was far from negligible. France was at war with the Habsburgs, with very brief intervals, from 1535 to 1559, and not until 1598 was peace finally concluded. Throughout the whole of that period, and indeed much beyond it, France could count upon the loyal co-operation of the Turks. It must, indeed, be confessed that the loyalty of the Turks to the alliance was a good deal more constant and continuous than that of the French. The latter were glad enough to take advantage of it whenever and for so long as it suited their purpose ; but they did not hesitate to come to terms with the adversaries of the Turk when their own interests dictated the step. Nevertheless, the alliance confirmed in 1535 forms a guiding thread in a tangled diplomatic skein.

[1] Cf. *infra*, chap. vi.

In that year war was resumed between Francis I and the emperor. Barbarossa, far from discouraged by the loss of Tunis, was ready to embarrass Charles V in the Mediterranean. Secure in the possession of Algiers he was still in a position to attack with effect, and in the space of a few months he plundered the island of Minorca, sacked the coasts of Apulia and Calabria, and recovered Coron. In 1537 Suleiman, in response to an appeal from France, declared war upon the Venetians, who were staunch in their alliance with the emperor. Sailing from Valona he laid siege to the island of Corfu, while Barbarossa seized the opportunity to conquer for his master most of the Aegean islands which still flew the flag of the Republic. In 1538 the Pope and King Ferdinand joined with the emperor and Venice in a Holy League against the Turks, and in the same year Francis I concluded with Charles V the Truce of Nice. The Venetians, however, found themselves ill-supported in their contest with the Turks by their Holy allies ; the Venetian fleet suffered a tremendous reverse at the hands of Barbarossa off Prevesa in September, 1538, and in 1539 negotiations were opened between the Republic and the Porte. A three months' truce was arranged, and in 1540 a definite peace was concluded. The Republic agreed to pay to the Sultan an indemnity of 300,000 ducats, and to surrender various points on the Dalmatian coast, and all claims to the recovery of the Aegean islands which had been captured by Barbarossa. The triumph of the Ottoman Sultan was complete.

Neither the conclusion of the Truce of Nice between the French king and the Habsburgs nor the definitive treaty between the Republic and the Porte was permitted to interrupt the contest between the Sultan Suleiman and the Emperor Charles V. Barbarossa's continued possession of Algiers was a perpetual menace to the Spanish and Italian dominions of the emperor. In 1541, therefore, Charles V fitted out another expedition with the object of finally expelling Barbarossa from his corsair kingdom. The expedition was a complete fiasco. Francis I renewed his contest with Charles V in 1542, and in the following year a French fleet, commanded by the Duc d'Enghien, combined with that of Barbarossa to effect a capture of the town of Nice which was sacked and burnt by the Ottomans. The accord between Barbarossa and the French was far from perfect, but the latter gave proof of their friendship by handing over the harbour of Toulon to their allies. But in 1544 Francis and Charles again made peace at Crespy, and again the Turks and the Habsburgs were left confronting each other both in the Mediterranean and on the Hungarian plain.

In 1546 Suleiman suffered a great loss by the death of his brilliant admiral, Barbarossa. The genius of the corsair had not merely added materially to the Empire of the Ottomans, but had secured for their navy in the Mediterranean, in the Red Sea, and in the Indian Ocean an ascendancy which it never again enjoyed. The death of Barbarossa, following closely upon the desertion of France, inclined Suleiman to peace with the emperor, and in 1547, as we have seen,[1] a five years' truce was concluded at Constantinople.

The death of Francis I in the same year was of much less consequence than that of Barbarossa, for the alliance between him and Suleiman was cemented and perhaps more consistently maintained by his son. In 1556, however, the Emperor Charles V, in view of his impending abdication, concluded with France the Truce of Vaucelles, and at the same time recommended his brother Ferdinand to come to terms with the Turks. The French king was at pains to explain to his Ottoman ally that the truce concluded with the emperor involved no weakening of his hereditary friendship, and Suleiman graciously accepted the assurance. The truce did not endure; in 1557

[1] Cf. *supra*, p. 91.

the French suffered a severe defeat at St. Quentin, and Henry II was more than ever anxious for the assistance of the Sultan ; and that in more than one form. He begged Suleiman to attack the Habsburgs in Hungary, to send an expedition to Naples, to maintain their fleet on a war footing, even throughout the winter months, in the Mediterranean, and, finally, to accommodate him with a considerable loan. As to the last, the Sultan replied, not without dignity, that ' the Ottomans were wont to succour their friends with their persons and not with their purses, since their religion forbade money loans to the enemies of their faith '. Naval assistance in the Mediterranean was, however, readily promised. As a fact, there had been no cessation of naval hostilities throughout all these years. Even the conclusion of the Peace of Prague between the Sultan and the Habsburgs did not interrupt them, for Spain was not included in the peace. Soon after his accession (1556) Philip II of Spain had endeavoured to rid himself of the perpetual embarrassment of the naval war ; but his effort was fruitless, and the contest in the Mediterranean dragged its wearisome length along. On both sides it was largely irregular and almost piratical in character ; sustained on the one hand by Torgoud, the successor of Barbarossa in Algiers, and on the other by the Knights of St. John.

The Knights, driven by Suleiman from Rhodes, had established themselves in Malta. The possession of that island is, and always has been, deemed essential to naval supremacy in the Mediterranean. Apart from the shelter it afforded to the buccaneering Knights it offered tempting advantages to the Turks in their contest with the Sovereign of Spain. In 1565 Suleiman determined to make a strenuous effort to capture the island. In the spring of that year, therefore, he dispatched from Constantinople a magnificent fleet, numbering not less than one hundred and ninety ships, with an army, on board, of 30,000 men, under the command of Mustapha Pasha. The fort of St. Elmo was taken but with very heavy loss to the Turks, and the Castles of St. Angelo and St. Michel resisted all their efforts. Again and again the assault was renewed, but after four months of fruitless fighting Mustapha, having lost two-thirds of his army, decided to abandon the attempt. What the Turks could not do in the sixteenth century no one else ventured to attempt, and the Knights were left undisturbed until the Napoleonic wars.

The great Sultan's course was now nearly run. It had been attended, in the main, with extraordinary success, yet the failure to take Malta was not the only shadow which fell over his declining years.

Like other men who present to the world an adamantine front, Suleiman was not proof against the cajolery of a fascinating woman. A Russian slave, named Khurrem, better known as Roxalana,[1] had in his early years acquired an extraordinary influence over her lord, who was persuaded to enfranchise her and to make her his wife. All the Sultana's efforts were then directed to securing the succession for her son, Prince Selim. An elder son, Prince Mustapha, born to the Sultan by another wife, had already shown extraordinary promise, and had won, among his father's subjects, a fatal measure of popularity. The intrigues of Roxalana turned that popularity to his destruction, and the prince was murdered in his father's presence. After Roxalana's death, which preceded that of the Sultan by eight years, her second son, Prince Bayezid, with his children, was murdered, at his father's instance, by the Persians. The purpose of all these sordid tragedies was to clear the succession for Roxalana's favourite son Selim, ' the Sot '.

It seems at first sight paradoxical that these revolting

[1] A corruption or emendation of La Rossa, the Russian woman.

murders should have been instigated by a sovereign famed, and justly famed, for magnanimity, generosity, kindliness, and courtesy. Yet the contradiction is not peculiar to great rulers, or even to great men. Suleiman, perhaps the most brilliant of the Ottoman Sultans, certainly one of the greatest among contemporary sovereigns, was as wax in the hands of the woman to whom he gave his heart. Whether that complaisance affected in any degree his policy or capacity as a ruler is open to question; but two things are certain: on the one hand that the Ottoman Empire attained, in the days of Suleiman, the zenith of splendour and the extreme limits of its territorial expansion; and, on the other, that the seeds of decay were already sown and were beginning, though as yet imperceptibly, to germinate.

Estimates of population are notoriously untrustworthy, but it seems probable that at a time when Henry VIII ruled over about 4,000,000 people the subjects of the Sultan Suleiman numbered 50,000,000. These included not less than twenty distinct races: Ottomans, Slavs, Greeks, Magyars, Roumans, Armenians, Arabs, Copts, and Jews, to mention only a few. The empire extended from Buda to Basra; from the Caspian to the Western Mediterranean; and embraced many lands in Europe, Asia, and Africa. To the north the walls of Azov guarded the frontiers of the Turkish Empire against Russia; to the south ' the rock of Aden secured their authority over the southern coast of Arabia, invested them with power in the Indian Ocean, and gave them the complete command of the Red Sea. . . . It was no vain boast of the Ottoman Sultan that he was the master of many kingdoms, the ruler of three continents, and the lord of two seas '.[1]

This vast-stretching empire was organized by Suleiman in twenty-one governments, which were subdivided into two

[1] Finlay, *History of Greece*, v, p. 6.

hundred and fifty sanjaks, each under its own *Bey*. Land
tenure and local government were alike assimilated to the
feudalism of the West; but it was feudalism devoid of its
disintegrating tendencies, for all power was ultimately concentrated in the Sultan, who was at once *Basileus* and Khalif,
Emperor and Pope.

The scope of this work does not permit of the discussion of
the details of domestic administration. It is concerned with
the Ottoman Empire only as a factor, though a very important
factor, in the problem of the Near East, as marking a stage
in the evolution of the Eastern Question. Yet there is one
domestic institution to which a passing reference must be made.

The Janissaries

Many things contributed to the astonishing success of the
early Ottomans and the rapid extension of their empire : the
hopeless decrepitude of the Greek Empire; the proverbial
lack of cohesion among the Slav peoples ; the jealousies and
antagonisms of the Western Powers ; the Babylonish captivity
at Avignon and the subsequent schism in the Papacy ; the
military prowess and shrewd statesmanship of many of the
earlier Sultans. But, after all, the main instrument in the
hands of the Sultan was his army, and in that army a unique
feature was the *corps d'élite*, the Janissaries.

As to the origin of this famous *corps* there has been much
controversy. It is, however, generally agreed [1] that the
beginnings of the institution must be ascribed to Alaeddin,
brother of Orkhan, and first vizier of the Ottomans, and
dated about the year 1326. But if Orkhan initiated, Murad I

[1] The latest authority on the early history of the Ottomans, Mr. Gibbons
(*op. cit.*, p. 118), dissents on this, as on many other points, from the hitherto
accepted view, and here as elsewhere gives reasons for his dissent.

perfected, the organization. Every four years [1] the agents of
the Sultan took toll of his Christian subjects ; one in five of
all the young boys, and always, of course, those who gave
most promise of physical and mental superiority, were taken
from their parents and homes, compelled to accept the Moslem
faith, and educated, under the strictest discipline, as the
soldier-slaves of the Sultan. Cut off from all human intercourse save that of the camp, without parents, wives, or
children, the Janissaries [2] formed a sort of military brother-
hood : half soldiers, half monks. Owing implicit obedience
to their master, inured to every form of toil and hardship
from earliest youth, well paid, well tended, they soon became
one of the most potent instruments in the hands of the Sultan.

Originally one thousand strong, the force increased rapidly,
and may have numbered 10,000 to 12,000 under Mohammed
the Conqueror, and anything between 12,000 and 20,000 in
Suleiman's day. It was recruited from all parts of the Ottoman
Empire in Europe, but mainly from Bosnia, Bulgaria, and
Albania. The child-tribute has been commonly regarded as
a peculiarly repulsive illustration of the cruelty and ingenuity
which characterized the rule of the Ottoman Turks. It is
far from certain that it was so regarded by the Christians
of the Empire. The privileges of the corps were so great,
and their prestige so high, that the honour may well have
outweighed the ignominy in many minds. There seems, at
any rate, to have been little need of compulsion, and one
distinguished authority has gone so far as to assert that the
Greek clergy 'tacitly acquiesced in the levy of tribute-children'.
Be this as it may, there can be no question as to the importance

---

[1] Or, as some say, every five. There is infinite variety, among authorities,
in regard to this and other details.

[2] The name is generally derived from *Yeni-Tscheri* = new or young
troops.

of the part played by this *corps* in the building up of the Ottoman Empire.

The institution of the Janissaries fulfilled a dual purpose. On the one hand, it provided the Sultan with a body of picked troops on whose loyalty and discipline he could implicitly rely. On the other, it represented a perpetual drain upon the young manhood of the peoples who obstinately refused to accept the creed of their conquerors. It may be that the extent of the debt which the earlier Sultans owed to the Janissaries has been exaggerated, no less than the resentment of those upon whom the tribute was levied. This, however, is certain, that the advance of the Ottomans synchronized with the period during which the corps was maintained in its pristine simplicity, and that the change in the position of the Janissaries coincided with the beginnings of the political decadence of the empire.

Early in his reign (1526) Suleiman was faced by a mutiny of the Janissaries. The mutiny was stamped out with salutary severity, but the hint was not lost upon the shrewd Sultan. He perceived that constant employment on war-service was absolutely essential to discipline ; nor did he fail to provide it. But the loyalty of the army was given not to a political institution but to a personal chief. Consequently, as the Sultan tended to withdraw from active service in the field and to yield to the seductions of the harem, the Janissaries manifested similar inclinations.

The whole position of the corps was revolutionized when, in 1566, its members were permitted to marry. The next step, an obvious one, was to admit their children to a body which thus in time became to a large extent hereditary. The hereditary principle soon led to exclusiveness. The Janissaries began to regard with jealousy the admission of the tribute-children, and after 1638 the tribute ceased to be levied.

A step, not less fatal to the original conception of a military order, was taken when members of the corps were allowed to engage in trade, and even to pay substitutes for the performance of their military duties. Throughout the seventeenth and eighteenth centuries this praetorian guard became more and more highly privileged ; more and more insolent in the exercise of power ; more and more the masters instead of the servants of the nominal sovereigns, who reigned on sufferance. At last, but not until the nineteenth century, there came to the throne a Sultan who was strong enough to deal with what had long been the most flagrant scandal and the most corroding weakness in a government which was rapidly dissolving into anarchy. In 1826 Sultan Mahmud exterminated the whole caste of the Janissaries and razed to the ground the quarter of Constantinople which they had appropriated. The treatment was drastic ; but no one could doubt that it was an indispensable preliminary to political reform.

But we anticipate events. The change in the position of the Janissaries was in part the cause, in part the consequence, of the general decrepitude in Ottoman administration. The general causes are not difficult to discern. The most important was the deterioration in personnel. In an autocracy everything depends on the efficiency of the autocrat. After Suleiman the Magnificent the Sultans exhibited symptoms of astonishingly rapid deterioration. Between the death of Suleiman (1566) and the accession of Mahmud II (1808) there was not a single man of mark among them. Few of them enjoyed any considerable length of days : there are twelve accessions in the seventeenth century as against six in the sixteenth. The deficiency of character among the seventeenth-century Sultans was to some extent supplied by the emergence of a remarkable Albanian family, the Kiuprilis, who provided the Porte with a succession of brilliant viziers ; but a great vizier is not the same thing in Turkey as a great Sultan, and even this resource was lacking in the eighteenth century.

The inefficiency of the dynasty was reflected in that of the armed forces of the Crown. The soldiers and sailors of the Crescent continued to fight, but they no longer conquered The only permanent conquests effected by the Porte after the death of Suleiman were those of Cyprus and Crete. Ceasing to advance the Turkish power rapidly receded. Victory in the field was as the breath of life to the Ottomans; success in arms was essential to the vigour of domestic administration.

So long as the Turks were a conquering race their government was not merely tolerable but positively good. There was no kingdom in Europe better administered in the sixteenth century than that of Suleiman. That great Sultan was, as we have seen, known to his own people as 'the legislator'; and his legislation was of the most enlightened character. Entirely based upon the Koran, Turkish law is not susceptible of expansion or reform; but there, as elsewhere, everything depends on interpretation and administration, and, under Suleiman, these left little to be desired. Nor did he fail of the appropriate reward. Taxation was light, but the revenue was prodigious, amounting, it is reckoned, to between 7,000,000 and 8,000,000 ducats, more than half of it being derived from Crown lands. Under Suleiman's successor corruption set in, and spread with fatal rapidity from the heart to the members. The taxes were farmed out to the Jews and Phanariote Greeks, with the inevitable consequences: the grinding oppression of the taxpayer and an habitually impoverished treasury.[1]

For one source of increasing weakness Suleiman himself may be held indirectly responsible. No autocracy could be expected permanently to sustain the burden of an empire

[1] Much new light has been thrown upon the working of the fiscal system by the *Corps de Droit Ottoman* (ed. 1906). Cf. in particular vol. v.

so extended as his. The more distant conquests meant a drain upon resources without any corresponding accession of strength. Even the incorporation of Hungary has not escaped criticism. It has been argued, and with some show of reason, that in a military sense the Porte would have been better without it. Economically, the Hungarian plain must always have been valuable, but strategically Belgrade is a better frontier fortress than Buda.

Still, when all criticisms have been weighed and all deductions effected, Suleiman was a great ruler, and his reign was incomparably the most brilliant epoch in the history of the Ottoman Empire. If, after his death, decay supervened with suggestive rapidity, we must not hastily assume that it could not have been arrested had competent successors been forthcoming. Subsequent chapters will show how little that condition was fulfilled.

For further reference see bibliography to chapter iii. Cf. also L. von Ranke, *The Ottoman and Spanish Empires in the Sixteenth and Seventeenth Centuries* (Eng. trans. 1854); J. de la Gravière, *Doria et Barberousse*; J. B. Zeller, *La Diplomatie française vers le milieu du xvie siècle*.

5

The Decadence of the Ottoman Empire
1566–1699

Contest with Venice and the Habsburgs

' My last judgement is that this Empire may stand, but never rise again.'— SIR THOMAS ROE (1628).

THUS far the main factor in the problem of the Near East has been the advent and progress of the Ottoman Turk. To an analysis of that factor the two preceding chapters have been devoted. We now enter upon a new period, which will disclose a considerable modification in the conditions of the problem. When the Sultan Suleiman passed away in 1566 the Ottoman Empire had already reached and passed its meridian. In the seventeenth century the symptoms of decay are manifest. Sultan succeeds Sultan, and, as one brief reign gives place to another, the decadence of the ruling race becomes more and more obvious. Anarchy reigns in the capital, and corruption spreads from Constantinople to the remotest corners of the empire. Lepanto has already announced that the Turks are no longer invincible at sea ; Montecuculi's great victory at St. Gothard, the failure to capture Vienna in 1683, Prince Eugène's victory at Zenta in 1697, combine to prove that the army is going the way of the navy. The Treaties of Carlowitz, Azov, and Passarowitz afford conclusive evidence that the Eastern Question has entered upon a new phase ; that the problem presented to Christendom will no longer be how to arrest the advance of the Ottoman, but how to provide for the succession to his inheritance.

The main interest of the period under review in the present chapter concentrates upon the prolonged duel between the Turks and the Habsburgs for supremacy in the valleys of the Danube and the Save. By the end of the period the issue of that duel is no longer in doubt. Hardly secondary is the interest attaching to the contest with the Venetian Republic. In the latter, fortune inclines now to this side now to that ; nor is this remarkable, for it is a struggle between combatants both of whom have passed their prime.

The most palpable symptom of Ottoman decadence is afforded by the deterioration in the personal character of the Sultans. Mustapha, the idiot son of Mohammed III, was declared incapable of reigning when in 1617 he succeeded to the throne. Excluding Mustapha no less than thirteen sovereigns occupied the throne between 1566 and 1718. Of these only two, Murad IV (1623–40) and Mustapha II (1695–1703) showed any anxiety to effect reform and to arrest the decrepitude of the empire. One out of the thirteen was murdered, three others were dethroned. Not one led an army to victory; most of them devoted all the time they could spare from the neglect of their duties to the pleasures of the harem. The son, for whom Roxalana had intrigued and Suleiman had murdered, was known as Selim 'the Sot' (1566–74). His son and successor, Murad III (1574–95), spent the twenty-one years of his reign in his harem. He began it by strangling his five brothers, and was otherwise remarkable only for the number of his children. Of the 103 who were born to him 47 survived him. As twenty of these were males, his successor, Mohammed III (1595–1603), had to better his father's example by the simultaneous slaughter of no less than nineteen brothers. The next Sultan, Ahmed I (1603–17), was a lad of fourteen when he succeeded, and died at the age of eight-and-twenty. His brother Mustapha was declared incapable of reigning owing to mental deficiency, and the throne accordingly passed to another minor, Othman II, whose brief reign of four years (1618–22) was only less disturbed than that of his successor, Mustapha I (1622–3), whose reign of fifteen months was the shortest and perhaps the worst in Ottoman history. His son, Murad IV (1623–40), was unspeakably cruel, but by no means devoid of ability, and he made a real effort to carry out much needed reform. But all the ground gained under Murad was lost under Ibrahim I, whose reign of eight years (1640–8) was brought to a close by a revolution in the capital and the violent death of the Sultan. His son, Mohammed IV (1648–87), was a child of six at the time of his father's murder. The anarchy which prevailed during the first years of the reign was unspeakable, but it was dissipated at last by the emergence (1656) of the Kiuprili ' dynasty ', who throughout the rest of the century provided the distracted empire with a succession of remarkable grand viziers.

The Kiuprilis might provide rulers, but they could not secure a succession of even tolerably efficient Sultans, and in the absence of the latter no permanent reform of Ottoman administration could be effected. Mohammed IV was dethroned in 1687, and was succeeded by two brothers, Suleiman II (1687–91), who at the age of forty-six emerged from his mother's harem to assume an unwelcome crown ; and Ahmed II (1691–5), who was a poet and a musician, and would have liked to be a monk. In 1695 the throne fell to Mohammed's son, Mustapha II, who in his reign of eight years (1695–1703) made a real effort to recall the virtues of the earlier Sultans, but was dethroned in 1703. The same fate befell his successor, Ahmed III, in 1730.

This tedious and catalogic enumeration will suffice to show that the student of the Eastern Question need not concern himself overmuch with the Ottoman Sultans of the seventeenth century. Until the accession of the Kiuprilis the internal history of the empire presents one monotonous vista of anarchy and decay. To follow it in detail would mean the repetition of features which become tiresomely familiar as one incompetent Sultan succeeds another. Fortunately, there is no reason for inflicting this tedium upon the reader.

The interest of the period, as already stated, centres in the contests between the Ottomans on the one hand, and, on the other, the Venetian Republic and the Habsburg Empire.

From the moment when the Ottoman Turks obtained command of the great trade-routes [1] the ultimate fate of Venice as a commercial power was sealed. She had already lost to the Turks many of her possessions on the mainland of the Peloponnese and in the Aegean archipelago, but the Republic

[1] See *supra*, chap. ii.

still carried her head proudly, and still held a position which was in many ways threatening to the Ottoman Empire. Planted in Dalmatia she headed off from the Adriatic the Turkish provinces of Bosnia and Herzegovina ; mistress of the Ionian isles she threatened the security of the coasts of the Morea ; while the continued possession of Crete and Cyprus not only rendered precarious the Ottoman hold on the Levant, but offered a convenient naval base to the Knights of St. John and the other Christian pirates who infested the Mediterranean.

One of the first exploits of the Sultan Suleiman was, as we have seen, the conquest of Rhodes ; one of the last was the capture of Chios (1566). A year later Naxos fell to his son Selim, who then proceeded to demand from Venice the cession of Cyprus.

The moment seemed favourable for the enterprise. The destruction by fire of her naval arsenal had just maimed the right hand of Venice (September, 1569), while the Sultan had freed his hands by concluding a truce with the Emperor Maximilian (1569) and completing (1570) the conquest of Yemen. The grand vizier, Mohammed Sököli, had lately conceived the idea of cutting a canal through the Isthmus of Suez and thus strengthening the strategical position of the empire. The outbreak of a revolt in Arabia deferred the execution of this interesting project and led to the conquest of Yemen. This accomplished, the Turks were free to turn their attention to Venice.

The Republic, gravely perturbed by the insolent demand for the cession of Cyprus, appealed to the Pope. Pius V promised to pay for the equipment of twelve galleys, sanctioned the levy of a tithe on the Venetian clergy, and appealed for help not only to the Christian princes but to the Persian Shah. The emperor's hands were tied by his recently concluded truce, but Philip II of Spain, Cosmo de Medici, Duke of Tuscany, and the States of Parma, Mantua, Lucca, Ferrara, and Genoa joined Venice and the Papacy in a Holy League against the Ottomans (1570). The command of the combined armada was entrusted to a brilliant young sailor, Don John of Austria, a natural son of the Emperor Charles V.

The two fleets, each with a large and well-equipped army on board, met near the entrance of the Gulf of Patras, and there, on the 7th of October, 1571, Don John fought and won the great battle of Lepanto. The battle was stubbornly contested, and the losses on both sides were enormous.[1] The victory of the Holy Allies resounded throughout the world; *Te Deums* were sung in every Christian capital; the Pope preached on the text, ' There was a man sent from God whose name was John '; but the actual fruits of a gigantic enterprise were negligible. The Turks, though hopelessly defeated in battle, retained command of the sea; a new and splendid fleet was rapidly built and equipped; the conquest of Cyprus was completed, and in May, 1573, Venice concluded peace with the Ottoman Empire. The terms of that peace reflected the issue of the campaign, not that of Don John's brilliant sea-fight. The Republic agreed to the cession of Cyprus; to the payment of a war indemnity of 300,000 ducats; to increase her tribute for the possession of Zante from 500 to 1,500 ducats, and to re-establish the *status quo ante* on the Dalmatian and Albanian coasts.

The terms were sufficiently humiliating to the victors at Lepanto. Yet the victory itself was by no means devoid of significance. Coming, as it did, so soon after the great days of Suleiman and Barbarossa, it was interpreted as a sign that the Turks were no longer invincible, and that their political decadence had set in. Nor was the interpretation wholly at fault.

[1] Among the wounded was Cervantes.

The truce concluded in 1569 between the Emperor Maximilian and the Turks lasted, *mirabile dictu*, for nearly a quarter of a century. But the truce between the rulers did not deprive the local chieftains on either side the artificial frontier from perpetual indulgence in the pastime of irregular war. Nominally, however, the truce was not broken till 1593. The breach of it was followed by thirteen years of war ; the Turks achieved one brilliant victory, but much of the fighting was of a desultory character, and the vassal rulers of Moldavia, Wallachia, and Transylvania allied themselves with the enemy of their suzerain ; the war went, on the whole, decidedly in favour of the Habsburgs ; it became clear that the Turks had reached the limits of expansion beyond the Danube. Peace was accordingly concluded, in 1606, at Sitvatorok. The Sultan renounced his suzerainty over Transylvania, and in exchange for a lump sum surrendered the annual tribute of 30,000 ducats which ever since 1547 the emperor had paid in respect of that portion of Hungary which he had then been permitted to retain. Thenceforward there was no question, on either side, of superiority. Sultan and emperor were on a footing of formal equality.

Fortunately for the Habsburgs, and indeed for Western Christendom, the half century which followed upon the Peace of Sitvatorok was, as we have seen, a period of anarchy and corruption in the Ottoman Empire. Were other proof lacking, sufficient evidence of the degeneracy of the Sultans would be found in their neglect to take advantage of the embarrassments of their chief opponent. From 1618 until 1648 the empire was in the throes of the Thirty Years' War ; the Habsburg dynasty did not finally emerge from the contest until 1659. In one sense, indeed, the fight did not cease until Louis XIV had ' erased ' the Pyrenees and put a Bourbon on the throne of Spain. The preoccupation of the Habsburgs ought to have been the opportunity of the Turk. Had the latter advanced from Buda to Vienna when the Habsburgs were engaged with the recalcitrant Calvinists of Germany; with Denmark, Sweden, or France, the Austrian capital could hardly have failed to fall to them. But the Turk let all the chances slip, and when, in 1648, the Treaties of Westphalia were concluded, the conditions of the secular contest were essentially altered.

The Thirty Years' War fatally weakened the Holy Roman Empire, but out of the welter the House of Austria emerged as a first-rate European Power. The Treaty of Westphalia, even more definitely than that of Prague (1866), marks the real beginning of the new orientation of Habsburg policy: the gravitation towards Buda-Pesth had begun. The Holy Roman Empire belonged essentially to the Western States-system; the interests of Austria-Hungary have drawn her irresistibly towards the East. This gravitation has necessarily accentuated the antagonism between the Habsburgs and the Ottomans, and the second half of the seventeenth century is largely occupied by a contest between them for supremacy in the Danube and the Save valleys.

Before we pass to the details of that contest it will conduce to lucidity if we dismiss briefly the subsidiary, but at times interdependent, war between the Turks and the Venetian Republic. So long as the latter retained Crete Ottoman supremacy in the Eastern Mediterranean lacked completeness. In 1645 the Sultan Ibrahim roused himself to the task of putting the coping stone upon the edifice. A pretext was soon found. In 1638 the Venetians, in pursuit of some Barbary pirates, had bombarded Valona on the Albanian coast. In 1644 a buccaneering raid was made by some galleys upon a valuable Turkish merchant fleet in the Levant. The successful assailants came, indeed, from Malta, but it sufficed that they found a refuge in a Cretan harbour. The disastrous failure, in 1565, of the last Turkish attack upon the Knights Hospitallers in Malta, had made the Sultan shy of renewing the attempt. The Venetian Republic seemed to be a less redoubtable enemy and Crete a more important prize. Against Crete, accordingly, the attack was delivered in 1645, and Candia was besieged. The town held out for just a quarter of a century, in the course of which the Venetian sailors managed to inflict more than one humiliation upon the Turks. The Ottoman fleet suffered an important reverse in the Aegean in 1649, and in 1656 Mocenigo, an intrepid Venetian admiral, won a great victory in the Dardanelles, captured Lemnos and Tenedos, and threatened Constantinople.

The Kiuprilis

The brilliant success of the Venetian fleet, combined with the degeneracy of the Sultans and the complete corruption of Ottoman administration, seemed to threaten the imminent dissolution of the Turkish Empire. The nadir of its fortunes was reached, however, in 1656, and in the same year there was initiated a remarkable revival. The revival was due to the stupendous energy and splendid ability of one man, Mohammed Kiuprili. To him the mother of the young Sultan turned, in the hour of the empire's deepest need. Belonging to an Albanian family which had long been resident in Constantinople, Mohammed Kiuprili was, in 1656, an old man of seventy, but he agreed to attempt the task demanded of him, on one condition. He stipulated that he should be invested with absolute authority. The condition was accepted, Kiuprili became grand vizier, and entered forthwith upon his work.

The strong hand upon the reins was felt at once, and the high-mettled steed immediately responded to it. The Janissaries were taught their place by the only method they could now appreciate—the simultaneous execution of 4,000 of their number; the administration was purged of the corrupting and enervating influences to which it had long been a prey; chaos gave way to order in the finances, and discipline was promptly restored in the army and navy.

In no sphere were the effects of the new régime more quickly manifested than in the prosecution of the war. Within twelve months the Venetian fleet was chased from the Dardanelles; the guardian islands, Lemnos and Tenedos, were recovered by the Turks; the operations against Crete were conducted with new vigour; and in 1658 the grand vizier undertook in person, despite his years, a punitive expedition against George Rákóczy II, the Voyvode of Transylvania. Rákóczy himself was deposed, and two years later was killed; Transylvania had to pay a large war indemnity and an increased tribute to the Porte.

Mohammed Kiuprili died in 1661, but was immediately succeeded by his son Ahmed, a man of a vigour and ability not inferior to his own. After an expedition into Hungary, to which reference will be made presently, Ahmed, in 1666, assumed personal control of the operations against Venice. In 1669 Louis XIV, in order to avenge an insult offered to the French ambassador in Constantinople, sent a force to the help of the Republic, but at last, after a siege which had dragged on, with intervals, for twenty-five years, Candia capitulated in 1669, and the whole island of Crete—except the three ports of Suda, Carabusa, and Spina-Lurga—passed into the hands of the Turks. The conquest of the great Greek island was doubly significant : it was the last notable conquest made in Europe by the Ottomans, and marked the final term of their advance; it marked also the complete absorption of the last important remnant of the Greek Empire. Not until 1913 did the Hellenes formally recover an island by which they have always set exceptional store.

The capitulation of Candia was immediately followed by the conclusion of peace between the Porte and the Republic. But, after the disaster to Turkish arms before Vienna in 1683, the Venetians again determined to try their fortunes against their old enemies. A Holy League, under the patronage of the Pope, was in 1684 formed against the infidel. Austria, Venice, Poland, and the Knights of Malta were the original confederates, and in 1686 they were joined by Russia. The Venetians invaded Bosnia and Albania, and a little later, under Francesco Morosini, they descended upon the Morea. Brilliant success attended the expedition; Athens itself was taken in September, 1687, and though it was restored by the Treaty of Carlowitz (1699), the whole of the Morea, except Corinth, together with the islands of Aegina and Santa Maura and a strip of the Dalmatian coast, were retained by the Republic.

Venetian rule in the Morea was not popular. The Venetians did something to improve education, and much of the lost trade between the Levant and Western Europe was, during the period of their occupation, recovered. But their domination was almost as alien as that of the Turks, and the Greeks gained little by the change of masters. When therefore the Turks, in 1714, declared war against the Venetians, they were able in some sort to pose as the liberators of the Morea. In places they were indubitably welcomed as such, and the progress of their arms was consequently rapid. But in 1716 Austria intervened in the war, and in 1718 the Porte was glad enough to conclude a peace by which she regained the Morea, though Venice retained her conquests in Dalmatia, Albania, and Herzegovina. If the Ottoman Empire was decadent, the Republic too had fallen from its high estate.

For the sake of lucidity we have anticipated the progress of events; we must now retrace our steps and follow the course of the struggle on the northern frontiers of the empire. For more than a century the Sultan had been direct sovereign of the greater part of Hungary, and had claimed a suzerainty, not always conceded, over Transylvania. By the middle of the seventeenth century it seemed possible that the latter principality, after many vicissitudes, might become hereditary in the house of Rákóczy. That possibility was dissipated, as we have seen, by the vigorous action of Mohammed Kiuprili. On the death of George Rákóczy II (1660), the Transylvanian nationalists elected John Kamínyi as Voyvode, while the Turks nominated a candidate of their own, Apafy. Kamínyi appealed to the Emperor Leopold, who sent a force under Montecuculi to his assistance. The succour did not, however, prove effective, and in 1662 Kamínyi was killed. Apafy, mistrustful of the disinterestedness of his patrons, sought, in his turn, help from the emperor. Meanwhile, Ahmed Kiuprili collected a force of 200,000 men, and in 1663 crossed the Danube at their head. He captured the strong fortress of Neuhäusel, ravaged Moravia, and threatened Vienna. Smarting under the diplomatic insult to which reference has been made, Louis XIV dispatched a force to the assistance of the emperor, and at St. Gothard, on the Raab, Montecuculi, commanding the imperial forces, inflicted, with the aid of the French, a decisive defeat upon Kiuprili.

St. Gothard was the most notable victory won by the arms of Christendom against those of Islam for three hundred years. But the emperor, instead of following it up, suddenly concluded a truce for twenty years with the Turks. The terms obtained by the latter, and embodied in the Treaty of Vasvar (1664), were unexpectedly favourable. The emperor agreed to pay an indemnity of 200,000 florins ; the Turks retained Grosswardein and Neuhäusel, and thus actually strengthened their position in Hungary, while their suzerainty over Transylvania was confirmed. The concession of such terms after such a victory as that of St. Gothard evoked resentment in some quarters, and astonishment in all. The explanation of the paradox must be sought in the repercussion of Western politics upon those of the East, and in the dynastic preoccupation of the Habsburg emperor. Philip IV of Spain was on his death-bed ; the succession to the widely distributed dominions of the Spanish crown was a matter of great uncertainty ; French help in Hungary, though acceptable at the moment, might well prove to have been too dearly purchased ; and it was intelligible that the emperor should desire to have his hands free from embarrassments in the East, in view of contingencies likely to arise in the West.

For the time being, however, his enemies were even more deeply involved than he was. The Venetian War was not ended until 1669, and three years later the Turks plunged into war with Poland.

The lawlessness of the border tribes to the north of the Euxine had already threatened to bring the Ottoman Empire into collision with the Russian Tsars. Towards the end of Ibrahim's reign (1640-8) the Tartars of the Crimea had pursued their Cossack enemies into Southern Russia and had brought away 3,000 prisoners. The Russians in turn advanced against Azov but were badly beaten, with the result that the Tartars sent 800 Muscovite heads as a trophy to Constantinople.

There were similar troubles on the side of Poland. In 1672 the Cossacks of the Ukraine, stirred to revolt by the insolence of the Polish nobles and the extortions of their Jewish agents, offered to place themselves under the suzerainty of the Sultan in return for assistance against their local oppressors. Ahmed Kiuprili, nothing loth, declared war upon Poland, and, accompanied by the Sultan, Mohammed IV, led a strong force to an assault upon Kaminiec, the great fortress on the Dniester, which strategically commanded Podolia. Kaminiec, though hitherto deemed impregnable, quickly yielded to the Turks, and the Polish King Michael hastily concluded with the Sultan a treaty, which involved the payment of an annual tribute and the surrender of Podolia and the Ukraine. The Polish Diet, however, refused to ratify the treaty, and entrusting the command of their forces to John Sobieski, they waged for four years an heroic struggle against the Ottomans. Thanks to the commanding character and the military genius of Sobieski, the Poles not only rallied their forces, but inflicted a crushing defeat upon the Turks at Khoczim (November, 1673). In 1674 the victorious general was elected to the Polish throne, and in the following year he again defeated the Turks at Lemberg. But despite this defeat the Turks steadily persisted and maintained their hold upon Podolia, and in 1676 both sides were glad to conclude the Peace of Zurawno. Under the terms of this treaty the Turks retained Kaminiec and the greater part of Podolia, together with a portion of the Ukraine, but agreed to forgo the tribute promised by King Michael.

The Peace of Zurawno may be regarded as a further triumph for Ahmed Kiuprili, but it was his last. In the same year he died, having substantially advanced the borders of the empire at the expense of Austria-Hungary, of Poland, and of Venice. He was succeeded, as grand vizier, by his brother-in-law, Kara Mustapha, who almost immediately found himself involved in war with Russia.

The war brought little credit to the new vizier, and nothing but disaster to his country. Kara Mustapha led a large army into the Ukraine, but he was driven back across the Danube by the Russians, and in 1681 the Porte was glad to conclude a peace by which the district of the Ukraine, obtained from

Poland in 1676, was ceded to Russia, and the two Powers mutually agreed that no fortifications should be raised between the Dniester and the Bug.

Kara Mustapha had more important work on hand. Lacking both character and ability he was nevertheless devoured by ambition. He determined to associate his name with the conquest of Vienna and the extension of the Ottoman Empire to the Rhine. The moment was not unfavourable to such a design. The attention of Western Europe was concentrated upon Louis XIV, who had now reached the zenith of his power. War had succeeded war and treaty had followed treaty, and from all France had extracted the maximum of advantage. By the Treaty of Westphalia, supplemented by that of the Pyrenees (1659), Louis XIV had gone some way towards realizing the dream of all patriotic Frenchmen, the attainment of *les limites naturelles* : the Rhine, the Alps, the Pyrenees, and the Ocean. France pushed her frontier to the Pyrenees and got a firm grip upon the middle Rhine ; Pinerolo guarded her frontier towards Savoy, and, on the north-east, a large part of Artois passed into her hands. Louis's marriage with Marie Thérèse, eldest daughter of Philip IV of Spain, opened out a still larger ambition. The War of Devolution gave him an impregnable frontier on the north-east, and ten years later, by the Treaty of Nimeguen (1678), he obtained the ' Free County ' of Burgundy, and made the Jura, for the first time, the eastern frontier of France. His next annexation was the great fortress of Strasburg (1681), and in 1683 he threatened Luxemburg.

The Habsburgs and Hungary

The emperor could not remain indifferent to these assaults upon the western frontiers of the empire ; but as Archduke of Austria and King of Hungary he had troubles nearer home.

The Turks were still, it must be remembered, in possession of by far the larger part of Hungary—the pashalik of Buda. In Austria-Hungary, moreover, there had long been much discontent with Habsburg rule. The Emperor Leopold, like his predecessors, was much under the influence of his Jesuit confessors, and his hand was heavy on the Hungarian Protestants, who looked with envy upon the lot of their brethren living under the tolerant rule of the Ottoman Turks.

Nor was religious persecution their only ground of complaint against the Habsburgs. The proud Magyar aristocracy denounced the Treaty of Vasvar as a craven betrayal of Hungarian interests on the part of a ruler by whom Hungary was regarded as a mere appendage to Austria. Their nationalist instincts were further offended by the attempt of the Emperor Leopold to administer his Hungarian kingdom through German officials responsible solely to Vienna. So bitter was the feeling that in 1666 a widespread conspiracy was formed under the nominal leadership of Francis Rákóczy, a son of the late Prince of Transylvania. The plot was betrayed to the Viennese Government. Louis XIV had lately concluded a secret agreement with the Emperor Leopold in regard to the Spanish succession, and hence was not, at the moment, disposed to help the Hungarian malcontents; above all, the Turks were busy in Crete. The movement, therefore, collapsed; Rákóczy was treated with contemptuous lenity, but the rest of the leaders were punished with pitiless severity, and the yoke of the Habsburgs was imposed with tenfold rigour upon what was now regarded as a conquered province. The office of Palatine was abolished; the administration was entrusted exclusively to German officials; the Hungarian aristocracy were exposed to every species of humiliation and crushed under a load of taxation; the Protestant pastors were sent to the galleys or driven into exile.

The reign of terror issued, in 1674, in a renewed revolt under the patriotic and devoted leadership of a Magyar aristocrat, Emmerich Tököli. The moment was propitious. The emperor was now at war with Louis XIV, who, in 1672, had launched his attack upon the United Provinces. Louis was, it is true, too much engaged on his own account to send help to the Hungarian nationalists, but he used his influence at Warsaw and Constantinople on their behalf. Not that either Poles or Turks engaged in fighting each other (1672–6) could at the moment do much for the Magyars. Kara Mustapha, however, promised that he would send help immediately his hands were free of the Polish War. But, as we have seen, that war was no sooner ended than the Turks were involved in war with Russia. The latter war ended, in its turn, in 1681, and at last Kara Mustapha was in a position to embark upon the larger designs which from the first he had entertained.

Promptly, the emperor attempted to conciliate the Hungarian nationalists. The administrative system was remodelled in accordance with their wishes; the governor-generalship was abolished; the German officials were withdrawn; the more oppressive taxes were repealed; the rights of citizenship were restored to the Protestants, both Calvinists and Lutherans, who were to enjoy liberty of conscience and of worship; the chief administrative offices were confided to natives; and the dignity of Palatine was revived in favour of Paul Esterhazy.

Concession could hardly have gone further, but the emperor's change of front was suspiciously coincident with the modification of the external situation. Emmerich Tököli refused to be beguiled into the acceptance of conditions so obviously inspired by prudential considerations. On the contrary, he entered into closer relations with the enemies of the emperor. He married the widow of Francis Rákóczy, and so strengthened his position on the side of Transylvania, and at the same time proclaimed himself Prince of Hungary under the suzerainty of the Sultan.

In 1682 Mohammed IV advanced to the support of his vassal. He led from Adrianople a magnificent army of 200,000, amply supplied with guns and siege trains. At Belgrade he surrendered the command to the grand vizier, who, having effected a junction with Tököli, advanced in 1683 towards Vienna.

John Sobieski

The Emperor Leopold, isolated by the diplomacy of Louis XIV in Western Europe, and even in the empire itself, turned for help to Poland, and, thanks to the king, not in vain. Sobieski undertook, notwithstanding an appeal from Louis XIV, to come with a force of 40,000 men to the rescue of the emperor and of Christendom.

Meanwhile Kara Mustapha was marching with leisurely confidence upon Vienna. The emperor and his court retired in haste to Passau, and Charles IV, Duke of Lorraine, the commander of the imperialist forces, having entrusted the defence of the capital to Count Stahremberg, withdrew to await the arrival of Sobieski and the Poles. Stahremberg proved equal to one of the heaviest responsibilities ever imposed upon an Austrian general. He burned the suburbs to the ground, and did his utmost to put the city itself into a posture of defence. The fortifications were in a most neglected condition ; the walls were in no state to resist an assault ; the garrison consisted of no more than 10,000 men ; while the defence was hampered by crowds of peasants who had fled for refuge to the city before the advance of the Ottomans.

Stahremberg, however, kept a stout heart, and inspired the garrison with his own grim determination. On July 14 the Ottoman host encamped before the walls, and proceeded to invest the city. The siege lasted for 60 days, and the beleaguered garrison was reduced to the last extremity. On September 5 Sobieski had joined the Duke of Lorraine, and had assumed command of their combined forces ; on the 9th a message reached him from Stahremberg that unless succour arrived immediately it would be too late ; on the 11th the relieving army took up its position on the Kahlenberg, the hill which overlooks the capital ; on the 12th it advanced to the attack upon the besiegers.

At the first charge of the Poles the Turks were seized with panic, and, before they could recover, Sobieski flung his whole force upon them. The great host was routed ; Vienna was saved ; 10,000 Turks were left dead upon the field ; 300 guns and an enormous amount of equipment and booty fell into the hands of the victors. Two days later the emperor returned to his capital to greet the saviour of Christendom.

Sobieski, however, started off at once in pursuit of the Turks, defeated them near Parkan in October, at Szecsen in November, and drove them out of Hungary. Kara Mustapha fled to Belgrade, and there on Christmas Day paid with his life the penalty of his failure.

The significance of that failure can hardly be exaggerated. Had Kara Mustapha's ability been equal to his ambition and superior to his greed, Vienna must have fallen to an assault. Had Vienna fallen, the Ottoman Empire might well have been extended to the Rhine. In view of the decadence of the Sultans and the corruption which had already eaten into the vitals of their empire, it is more than doubtful whether the advance could have been maintained ; there is, indeed, ground for the belief that even the absorption of Hungary was a task beyond their strength, and that the Danube formed their 'natural limit ' towards the north. But even the temporary occupation of Vienna, still more the annexation, however transitory, of lands wholly Teutonic in race and essentially ' western ' in their political connexions, could not have failed to administer a severe moral shock to Christendom. That shock was averted by the valour and intrepidity of Sobieski, the Pole. The ' most Christian King ', Louis XIV of France, so far from stirring a finger to save Christendom, regarded the advance of the Turks as a welcome military diversion; he exhausted all the unrivalled resources of French diplomacy to assure the success of their enterprise, and annihilate the only Power in Europe which seemed, at the moment, capable of circumscribing the ambition of the Bourbons.[1] It was five years later that the English Revolution gave to the Dutch stadholder the chance, which he did not neglect, of saving Europe from the domination of France.

Meanwhile, the war between the Habsburgs and the Turks continued for fifteen years after the raising of the siege of Vienna. Sobieski, having successfully accomplished the task which has won him imperishable fame, soon retired from the war. The French party reasserted itself at Warsaw; domestic difficulties, ever recurrent in Poland, demanded the personal intervention of the king, and in 1684 he surrendered the command of the imperialist forces to Charles of Lorraine. The formation of the Holy League, in that same year, gave to the war against the Turks something of the nature of a crusade, and volunteers flocked to the standard of the emperor from many countries besides those which actually joined the League.[2]

---

[1] Voltaire suggests (*Le Siècle de Louis XIV*, chap. xiv) that the French king was only waiting for the fall of Vienna to go to the assistance of the empire, and then, having posed as the saviour of Europe, to get the Dauphin elected king of the Romans. The idea may well have been present to Louis's mind.

[2] See *supra*, p. 115.

Led by Charles of Lorraine, by the Margrave Lewis of Baden, by the Elector of Bavaria, by Prince Eugène of Savoy, and other famous captains, the imperialists won a succession of significant victories against the Turks. They stormed the strong fortress of Neuhäusel, and drove Tököli and the Hungarian nationalists back into Transylvania in 1685, and in the following year they retook Buda, which for 145 years had formed the capital of Turkish Hungary. The Habsburg emperor, now master of the whole of Hungary, proceeded to deal with his rebellious subjects. A reign of terror ensued, and the embers of the insurrection were quenched in blood. Important modifications were introduced into the constitution. The Hungarian Crown, hitherto nominally elective, became hereditary in the House of Habsburg, and in 1687 the Austrian Archduke Joseph was crowned king.

In that same year the imperialist forces met the Turks on the historic field of Mohacz, and by a brilliant victory wiped out the memory of the defeat sustained at the hands of Suleiman the Magnificent 161 years before. The second battle of Mohacz was followed by the reduction and recovery of Croatia and Slavonia. This prolonged series of defeats in Hungary led to the outbreak of disaffection in Constantinople. The Janissaries demanded a victim, and in 1687, as we have seen, Sultan Mohammed IV was deposed. But the change of Sultans did not affect the fortunes of war. In 1688 the imperialists invaded Transylvania, and the ruling Prince Apafy exchanged the suzerainty of the Ottomans for that of the Habsburgs. Henceforward Transylvania became a vassal state under the crown of Hungary.

But a much more important triumph awaited Austrian arms. In September, 1688, the great fortress of Belgrade was stormed by the imperialists, and from Belgrade the conquering Teutons advanced into Serbia and captured Widdin and Nish.

Once more, however, the repercussion of Western politics was felt in the East, and, in 1688, the outbreak of the war of the League of Augsburg and the French invasion of the Palatinate, relieved the pressure upon the Turks. But this advantage was cancelled by the appearance of a new antagonist. In 1689 Peter the Great of Russia invaded the Crimea, and in 1696 captured the important fortress of Azov.[1] Meanwhile, for the Turks the situation was temporarily redeemed by the appointment as grand vizier of a third member of the famous Albanian family which had already done such splendid service for the State. Mustapha Kiuprili (III) was the brother of Ahmed; he was in office only two years (1689–91), but the effect of a strong hand at the helm was immediately manifested : the finances were put in order ; the administration was purified, and new vigour was imparted to the conduct of the war.

The death of Apafy, Prince of Transylvania (April, 1690), gave Mustapha a chance of which he was quick to avail himself. Master of Hungary, the Emperor Leopold was most anxious to absorb Transylvania as well, and to this end endeavoured to secure his own election as successor to Apafy. The separatist sentiment was, however, exceedingly persistent among the Roumans of Transylvania, and, with a view to encouraging it, the vizier nominated as voyvode Emmerich Tököli. With the aid of Turkish troops Tököli temporarily established himself in the principality, though his position was threatened by the advance of an imperialist army under Lewis, Margrave of Baden.

Meanwhile, Kiuprili himself marched into Serbia, retook Widdin and Nish, and advanced on Belgrade. That great fortress fell, partly as the result of an accidental explosion, into the hands of the Turks, who, in 1691, advanced into

[1] See, for further details, *infra*, p. 132.

Hungary. Recalled from Transylvania to meet this greater danger, Lewis of Baden threw himself upon the advancing Turks at Salan Kemen, and inflicted upon them a crushing defeat (August 19, 1691). 28,000 Turks were left dead upon the field, and 150 guns fell into the hands of the victors. The grand vizier himself was among the killed. With him perished the last hope of regeneration for the Ottoman Empire.

After the defeat and death of Kiuprili III, Tököli could no longer maintain his position in Transylvania, and the Diet came to terms with the emperor (December, 1691). Local privileges were to be respected, but the emperor was to become voyvode and to receive an annual tribute of 50,000 ducats. Transylvania thus virtually took its place as a province of the Habsburg Empire.

For the next few years the war languished. England and Holland tried to bring about peace in Eastern Europe, while Louis XIV, for reasons equally obvious, did his utmost to encourage the prolongation of the war. But in 1697 Louis XIV himself came to terms with his enemies in the Treaty of Ryswick, and thus the emperor was once more free to concentrate his attention upon the struggle in the Near East.

In 1697 Prince Eugène of Savoy assumed command of the imperialist forces, and on September 11 inflicted upon the Turks at Zenta on the Theiss the most crushing defeat their arms had sustained since their advent into Europe. The grand vizier and the flower of the Ottoman army, 20,000 in all, were left dead upon the field ; 10,000 men were wounded, and many trophies fell into the hands of the victors. Carlyle's comment on this famous victory is characteristic : ' Eugène's crowning feat ; breaking of the Grand Turk's back in this world ; who has staggered about less and less of a terror and outrage, more and more of a nuisance, growing unbearable, ever since that day.'

A fourth Kiuprili, who succeeded as grand vizier, made a gallant effort to redeem the situation ; he raised a fresh army and drove the Austrians back over the Save ; but the battle of Zenta was decisive, it could not be reversed, and on January 26, 1699, peace was concluded at Carlowitz

The terms were sufficiently humiliating for the Porte. The advantages secured by the Venetian Republic have already been enumerated. To the emperor the Turks were obliged to cede Transylvania, the whole of Hungary except the Banat of Temesvar, and the greater part of Slavonia and Croatia. Poland retained the Ukraine and Podolia, including the great fortress of Kaminiec. The peace with Russia was not actually signed until 1702, when she secured the fortress and district of Azov.

No such peace had ever before been concluded by the Turk. The tide had unmistakably begun to ebb. The principalities of Moldavia and Wallachia remained subject to the Sultan for a century and a half to come, but otherwise the boundary of the Ottoman Empire was fixed by the Drave, the Save, and the Danube. Never again was Europe threatened by the Power which for three centuries had been a perpetual menace to its security. Henceforward the nature of the problem was changed. The shrinkage of the Ottoman Empire created a vacuum in the Near East, and diplomacy abhors a vacuum. How was it to be filled ?

The succeeding chapters of this book will be largely concerned with the attempts of Europe to find an answer to that question.

For further reference cf. chapter iii ; and also L. Léger, *L'Autriche-Hongrie* ; Rambaud, *History of Russia* (Eng. trans.) ; Himly, *La formation territoriale* ; Freeman, *Historical Geography*.

6

The Eastern Question in the Eighteenth Century

Russia and Turkey, 1689–1792

' Pour la Russie toute la fameuse question d'Orient se résume dans ces mots : de quelle autorité dépendent les détroits du Bosphore et des Dardanelles ? Qui en est le détenteur ? '—SERGE GORIAINOW.

' Tout contribue à développer entre ces deux pays l'antagonisme et la haine. Les Russes ont reçu leur foi de Byzance, c'est leur métropole, et les Turcs la souillent de leur présence. Les Turcs oppriment les co-religionnaires des Russes, et chaque Russe considère comme une œuvre de foi la délivrance de ses frères. Les passions populaires s'accordent ici avec les conseils de la politique : c'est vers la mer Noire, vers le Danube, vers Constantinople que les souverains russes sont naturellement portés à s'étendre : délivrer et conquérir deviennent pour eux synonymes. Les tsars ont cette rare fortune que l'instinct national soutient leurs calculs d'ambition, et qu'ils peuvent retourner contre l'empire Ottoman ce fanatisme religieux qui a précipité les Turcs sur l'Europe et rendait naguère leurs invasions si formidables.'—ALBERT SOREL.

' L'introduction de la Russie sur la scène européenne dérangerait aussi le système politique du Nord et de l'Orient tel que l'avait composé la prudence de nos rois et de nos ministres.'—VANDAL.

§ 1. From the Treaty of Carlowitz to the Treaty of Belgrade, 1699–1739

THROUGHOUT the sixteenth and seventeenth centuries it was, as we have seen, the Habsburg emperors who, with the fitful aid of the Venetian Republic, bore the brunt of the struggle against the Turks. The prize for which they contended was domination in the Save and the Middle Danube valleys.

With the opening of the eighteenth century, just, indeed, before the close of the seventeenth, a new factor makes its appearance in the problem of the Near East. Russia comes more and more prominently forward as the protagonist. She challenges Turkish supremacy in the Black Sea, and begins to interest herself in the fate of her co-religionists in the Ottoman Empire. Connected with many of them by ties not merely of religion but of race, she stands forth as the champion of the Slav nationality no less than as the protector of the Greek Church. To her Constantinople is Tsargrad. She poses as the legitimate heir to the pretensions of the Byzantine emperors. But Constantinople is more than the imperial city. It is the sentinel and custodian of the straits. In alien hands it blocks the access of Russia to European waters. Without the command of the straits Russia can never become, in the full sense, a member of the European polity. Persistently, therefore, she looks towards the Bosphorus. Her ulterior object is to obtain unrestricted egress from the Black Sea into the Mediterranean. But a prior necessity is to get access to the shores of the Black Sea.

When Peter the Great, in 1689, took up the reins of government Russia had little claim to be regarded as a European Power. She had no access either to the Baltic or to the Black Sea. The former was a Swedish lake ; the latter was entirely surrounded by Turkish territory. With the opening of the ' window to the west ' this narrative is not concerned, though it is noteworthy that the prospect from St. Petersburg, like that from Azov, is a singularly contracted one, unless the tenant has the key of the outer door in his own pocket.

Russia and the Turks

Since 1453 there had been no attempt to force the door of the Euxine from either side. But the rapid rise of the Russian Empire in the seventeenth and eighteenth centuries rendered it certain that the attempt would not be indefinitely postponed. The first contact between the two Powers, which were destined to such acute rivalry in the Near East, dates from the year 1492, when the Tsar, Ivan III, protested against the treatment to which certain Russian merchants had been subjected by the Turks. The result of the protest was the opening of diplomatic relations between Moscow and Constantinople. The same Ivan, on his marriage with Sophia, niece of the Emperor Constantine XIII and the last princess of the Byzantine House, assumed the cognizance of the two-headed eagle, the symbol of the Eastern Empire. Already, it would seem, the ambitions of the Muscovite were directed towards the city and empire of Constantine. The reign of Ivan the Terrible (1533–84) is memorable for the first armed conflict between the Russians and the Turks. Sököli, the grand vizier of Selim the Sot, had conceived the idea of strengthening the strategical position of the Ottoman Empire in regard to that of Persia by cutting a canal to unite the Don with the Volga. A necessary preliminary was the occupation of Astrakhan. Not only was the attempt to seize that city successfully resisted by the Russian garrison, but a serious defeat was inflicted by the Muscovite forces upon another Turkish army near Azov (1575). Thus the Russians had drawn first blood, and Sököli's enterprise was abandoned.

Not for a century did the two Powers again come into direct conflict. In the meantime, however, they were frequently in indirect antagonism in connexion with the perpetual border warfare carried on by the Cossacks and the Tartars on the northern shores of the Black Sea. A raid of the Tartars into southern Muscovy would be followed by a Cossack attack upon Azov. The Sultan would disavow the action of his Tartar vassals; the Tsar would protest that he could not be held responsible for the lawlessness of the Cossacks, ' a horde of malefactors who had withdrawn as far as possible from the reach of their sovereign's power, in order to escape the punishment due to their crimes '. The protestations were on neither side wholly sincere ; but if they had been it would have made little difference to the conduct of the fierce tribesmen on the frontiers.

In 1677, as we have seen,[1] the relations between the Poles and the Cossacks of the Ukraine involved the outbreak of formal war between Russia and Turkey. A peace was patched up in 1681, but Russia joined the Holy League in 1686, and from that time until the conclusion of the Treaty of Carlowitz (1699) the two Powers were intermittently at war.

From the outset of his reign Peter the Great was firmly resolved to obtain access to the Black Sea. With that object he organized a great expedition against Azov in 1695. He himself led an army of 60,000 men against the fortress. Thrice did he attempt to storm it, and thrice was he repelled, but failures only stimulated him to further efforts. During the winter of 1695–6 25,000 labourers, headed by the Tsar himself, worked night and day on the building of a vast flotilla of vessels of light draught. In 1696 the attempt was renewed with fresh forces and with the assistance of this newly-built fleet, and on July 28 Azov surrendered. No sooner had the fortress passed into his hands than Peter proceeded to improve the fortifications, to enlarge the harbour, and to make all preparations for converting the conquered town into a great naval base. Two years later a Russian Tsar and an Ottoman Sultan were for the first time admitted to a European congress. By the treaty arranged at Carlowitz the Porte agreed to cede Azov and the district—about eighty miles in extent—which the Russians had conquered to the north of the Sea of Azov.

But ten years later the Turks turned the tables upon the Tsar. In 1709 the greatness of Sweden as a European power was destroyed at a single blow by the rash policy of Charles XII.

[1] *Supra*, p. 118.

Perhaps persuaded by the subtle diplomacy of Marlborough to turn his arms against the Tsar ; certainly lured by Mazeppa, the Cossack chieftain, to embroil himself in his quarrels, Charles XII led the army of Sweden to its destruction on the fateful field of Pultawa (July, 1709). After the annihilation of his army at Pultawa the Swedish king, accompanied by Mazeppa, took refuge in Turkey, and the Tsar's demand for their surrender was firmly refused by the Sultan. Urged to a renewal of the war with Russia by Charles XII, and still more persistently by his vassal, the Khan of the Crimean Tartars, Sultan Ahmed rather reluctantly consented, and in November, 1710, war was declared.

The Capitulation and Treaty of the Pruth (1711)

The Russian conquest of Azov, and the resounding victory over the Swedes at Pultawa, had created no small measure of unrest among the Christian subjects of the Ottoman Empire. The Slavs in the west, the Greeks in the south, and even the Latins in the north-east of the peninsula, began to look to the Tsar as a possible liberator, and the excitement among them was great when, in the summer of 1711, the Russian army crossed the Pruth. Peter, however, repeating the blunder which had led to the overthrow of the Swedish king at Pultawa, pushed on too far and too fast, found himself surrounded by a vastly superior force of Turks, and was compelled to sue ignominiously for peace. Despite the remonstrances of the Swedes and Tartars the Turkish vizier consented to treat, and on July 21, 1711, the terms of the capitulation were arranged. By this Treaty of the Pruth Azov and the adjacent territory were to be restored to the Ottomans ; the Tsar undertook to raze to the ground the fortress of Taganrog lately built on the Sea of Azov ; to destroy other fortifications and castles in the neighbourhood ; to surrender the guns and stores ; to withdraw his troops from the Cossacks, and not to interfere in the affairs of Poland or the Ukraine. The Russians were no longer to have an ambassador at Constantinople ; they were to give up all Moslem prisoners in their custody ; to afford Charles XII, the guest of the Ottoman Empire, free and safe passage to his own kingdom, and not to keep a fleet in the Black Sea. No surrender could have been more complete, but it is generally agreed that the vizier, either from weakness or something worse, made a fatal blunder in accepting it. Such an opportunity for annihilating the power of the Muscovite Tsar might never recur. Such was emphatically the opinion of contemporaries. The indignation of Charles XII knew no bounds, and he refused to leave the Ottoman dominions ; the vizier was deposed, and his two subordinate officers were executed, but thanks mainly to the mediation of English and Dutch envoys, a definitive peace, on terms corresponding to those of the capitulation, was finally concluded in 1713. Not for a quarter of a century did war break out again between Russia and Turkey.

The Turks, however, were at war again with the Venetian Republic in 1715. They had never acquiesced in the loss of the Morea, where Venetian rule, though favourable to commerce and education, did not prove popular among the mass of the people. In 1715, therefore, the Turks fell upon the Morea, with overwhelming forces, both by land and sea, and in the course of a few months the Venetians were expelled from the Morea and from all the islands of the Archipelago. The victors then prepared to follow up their success in the Adriatic ; but in 1716 Austria intervened, accused the Porte of a gross violation of the Treaty of Carlowitz, and concluded an alliance with the Republic. Prince Eugène won a great victory over the Turks at Peterwardein (August 13, 1716), and in November the city of Temesvar, the last fortress left to the Turks in Hungary, was compelled to surrender.

Prince Eugène's campaign against the Turks possessed political as well as military significance. Since the overthrow of the Slavs on the fatal field of Kossovo,[1] Serbia, as a political entity, had virtually been obliterated, but at the opening of this campaign Eugène appealed to the Serbians to seize the opportunity of throwing off the yoke of the Turks, and more than a thousand of them enlisted under his banners. Could they have looked into the future they might have shown less eagerness to help the Austrians to the possession of Belgrade.

The capture of that great fortress was the object and culmination of the campaign of 1717. The city was held by a garrison of 30,000 men, who for two months (June–August) resisted all the efforts of Eugène's besieging force. Early in August an army of 150,000 Turks marched to the relief of the beleaguered fortress, and Eugène was in turn besieged. On August 16, however, he attacked, and, with greatly inferior numbers, routed the relieving force. Two days later Belgrade surrendered.

The Porte now invoked the mediation of Great Britain and Holland. The emperor, anxious to have his hands free for dealing with a complicated situation in the West, consented to treat, and peace was signed at Passarowitz (July 21, 1718). The Sultan accepted terms from the emperor, but dictated them to Venice. The Republic had to acquiesce in the loss of the Morea and the Archipelago, and henceforward retained only the Ionian isles and a strip of the Albanian coast. Her sun was setting fast. For the Habsburgs, on the other hand, the Treaty of Passarowitz marks the zenith of territorial expansion in the Near East. By the acquisition of the Banat of Temesvar they completed the recovery of Hungary ; by the cession of Little Wallachia they made a serious inroad upon the Danubian principalities ; while

[1] *Supra*, p. 65.

by that of Belgrade, Semendria, a portion of Bosnia, and the greater part of Serbia they advanced towards both the Adriatic and the Aegean. It will not escape notice that the populations thus transferred from the Sultan to the emperor were not Ottomans, but, on the one hand, Roumanians, and on the other, Southern Slavs. The significance of that distinction was not, however, perceived at the time; it has, indeed, only recently been revealed.

A change of more immediate consequence to the Roumanians had been effected a few years before the Treaty of Passarowitz. Down to the year 1711 the Danubian principalities had, in accordance with an arrangement concluded with Suleiman the Magnificent,[1] been permitted to remain under the rule of native hospodars. The progress of Russia to the north of the Euxine, and the dubious attitude of one or more of these hospodars during the recent wars between Russia and Turkey, seemed to render desirable a strengthening of the tie between the principalities and the bureaucracy of Constantinople. The hospodarships were, therefore, put up to auction, and for 110 years were invariably knocked down to Phanariote Greeks. The tenure of each Phanariote was brief, for the more rapid the succession the greater the profit accruing to the Porte. Consequently each Phanariote had to make his hay while the sun shone, and it was made at the expense of the Roumanians.[2]

The capitulation of the Pruth was a humiliating, and for the time being a disastrous, set back to the advance of Russia. But its significance was merely episodical. Russia, notwithstanding the signature of a treaty of 'perpetual' peace with the Porte in 1720, never regarded it as anything more than the temporary adjustment of an embarrassing situation. Least

[1] In 1536.
[2] Between 1711 and 1821 there were 33 hospodars in Moldavia and 37 in Wallachia.

of all did she forgo for an instant her ambitions in regard to the Black Sea in general and Azov in particular. Nor were any of the outstanding difficulties between Russia and Turkey really settled. The Tartars of the Crimea, encouraged by the retrocession of Azov, were more persistent than ever in their incursions into South Russia; the quarrels between them and the Cossacks were unceasing and embittered; occasional co-operation between Russians and Turks against the Empire of Persia did nothing to adjust the differences between them in the Kuban district in Kabardia, and in the other disputed territories which lay between the Black Sea and the Caspian. Most insistent of all, however, was the problem of the Black Sea. It still remained a Turkish lake, and into this Turkish lake poured all the waters of the great Russian rivers, the Kuban, the Don, the Dnieper, the Bug, and the Dniester. These were and are the natural highways of Russia; so long as the Black Sea was a Turkish lake they were practically useless for purposes of trade. From the moment that Russia achieved something of political unity, from the moment she realized her economic potentialities, the question of access to the Black Sea, of free navigation on its waters, and free egress from them into the Mediterranean became not merely important but paramount. To have accepted as final the terms extorted in 1711 would have meant for Russia economic strangulation and political effacement. Without access to the Black Sea she could never become more than a second-class Power; without command of the narrow straits which stand sentinel over the outer door she can never fulfil her destiny as one of the leaders of world-civilization.

How far did the general diplomatic situation lend itself to the realization of Russian ambitions? Upon whom could she count as a steadfast ally? With whose enmity must she reckon?

For 200 years the permanent pivot of continental politics had been the antagonism between France and the House of Habsburg. In order to secure her own diplomatic interests France had cultivated close relations with Stockholm, with Warsaw, and, above all, with Constantinople. Nor were the ambitions of France exclusively political. Her commercial prosperity was derived mainly from the trade with the Levant, which was one of the by-products of the Franco-Turkish alliance.

The wars of Louis XIV, however flattering to French prestige, had imposed a terrible strain upon the economic resources of the country, and under Louis XV France was compelled to trust rather to diplomacy than to war for the maintenance of her pre-eminent position in Europe.[1] It was more than ever important for her to maintain her ascendancy at Constantinople. Originally an outcome of her rivalry with the Habsburgs, that ascendancy now involved her in prolonged antagonism to the ambitions of Russia. It was to France, then, that Turkey naturally looked for guidance and support, as did Poland and Sweden.

Between England and Russia there had as yet arisen no occasion of conflict, but England, if a friend, was a distant one. Prussia had hardly as yet attained the position of a second-class Power, though she was on the eve of attaining something more ; Austria, therefore, was the only great Power upon whose friendship Russia, in pursuit of her Near Eastern policy, could at all confidently rely. The Habsburgs had been fighting the Turks for two centuries ; the centre of gravity of their political system was still in Vienna ; the ideas of Pan-Slavism and Pan-Germanism were yet unborn ; the conflict between

[1] Not that France refrained from war. Far otherwise. But (i) the energies of France were largely diverted to India and North America ; and (ii) her arms were by no means so potent as under Louis XIV.

them was still in the distant future. To Austria, Russia now turned, and, in 1726, concluded with alliance which, with occasional and brief interruptior for more than a century, and proved of incomparable _____ to Russia.

Ten years later the long period of patient preparation, military and diplomatic, came to an end, and Russia plunged into war with Turkey. The trouble began, as it so often did, in Poland. In 1732 France offered her friendship to Russia on condition that the latter would support the candidature of Stanislaus Leczynski, the father-in-law of Louis XV. Osterman, the brilliant minister of the Tsarina Anne, declined the offer, and agreed to support the Saxon candidate, who afterwards became king as Augustus III. France then turned to Turkey, and reminded the Porte that it was by treaty bound to safeguard the independence of Poland, now menaced by the interference of Russia and Austria. The so-called War of the Polish Succession broke out in 1733. Two years later Russia declared war upon the Porte, and, in 1736, Azov was recaptured ; the whole of the Crimea was overrun by Russian troops, and Bagchaserai, the capital of the Tartar khan of the Crimea, was destroyed. The Russian triumph was complete, but it was purchased at enormous cost. Austria then offered her mediation, and Russia agreed to accept it—on terms. She demanded, as the price of peace, the whole of the territory encircling the Black Sea between the Caucasus and the Danube ; she required the Porte to acknowledge the independence of the frontier provinces of Moldavia and Wallachia under the suzerainty and protection of Russia ; and she insisted that Russian ships should be free to navigate the Black Sea and to pass into and from the Mediterranean through the narrow straits. Austria's disinterested friendship was to be rewarded by the acquisition of Novi-Bazar and a further slice of Wallachia.

The Porte naturally refused these exorbitant demands, and Austria consequently marched an army into Serbia and captured Nish. Encouraged by the Marquis de Villeneuve, the French ambassador at Constantinople, the Turks then took the offensive, marched down the Morava valley, captured Orsova, and besieged Belgrade. Outside Belgrade Villeneuve himself joined them, promptly opened direct negotiations with the Austrian general, Neipperg, and on September 1, 1739, the Treaty of Belgrade was signed.

Austria agreed to abandon all the acquisitions which had been secured to her in the last war by the brilliant strategy of Prince Eugène of Savoy. She restored Belgrade and Orsova and Sabacz to the Porte, and evacuated Serbia and Little Wallachia.

The news of the signature of this astonishing treaty came as a bitter surprise to Marshal Münnich, the commander of the Russian forces. The Russian part in the campaign had been as successful as that of Austria had been the reverse. The Russians had captured the great fortress of Oczakov in 1738, that of Choczim, on the Dniester, in 1739, and ten days after Austria had signed a separate peace at Belgrade they crossed the Pruth and entered the Moldavian capital. But, deserted by their ally, they had no option but to conclude a peace on the best terms they could. They recovered Azov, but only on condition that the fortifications were destroyed, and that the district immediately surrounding it should be cleared of all works ; they were to be allowed to trade on the Sea of Azov and the Black Sea, provided, however, that all their goods were carried in Turkish vessels.

The Treaties of Belgrade were a grievous disappointment to the Russians, a humiliation for Austria, a notable success for the Turks, but, above all, a brilliant triumph for the diplomacy of France. French historians may well exalt the skill of the Marquis de Villeneuve. It cannot be denied. They may well derive legitimate satisfaction from the testimony afforded by these treaties to the prestige of France, and to her controlling influence upon the politics of the Near East. But these things are insufficient, by themselves, to account for the astonishing surrender of Austria. The explanation is to be found in the consuming anxiety of the Emperor Charles VI, now nearing his end, to secure for his daughter, Maria Theresa, the succession to the hereditary dominions of his house, and for her husband the crown of the Holy Roman Empire. But whatever the explanation may be, the fact remains that the intervention of France had obtained for the Ottoman Empire a respite on the side of Russia, and a signal revenge upon Austria.

Cardinal Alberoni might mitigate the tedium of political exile by drafting schemes for the partition of the Ottoman Empire. But Montesquieu diagnosed the situation with a shrewder eye : ' L'Empire des Turcs est à présent à peu près dans le même degré de foiblesse où étoit autrement celui des Grecs ; mais il subsistera longtemps. Car si quelque prince que ce fût mettoit cet empire en péril en poursuivant ses conquêtes les trois puissances commerçantes de l'Europe connoissent trop leur affaires pour n'en pas prendre la défense sur-le-champ.' [1] As regards England, Montesquieu, writing in 1734, was considerably ahead of his time ; but his words made an obvious impression upon the younger Pitt, who referred to them in the House of Commons, when, in 1791, he vainly attempted to excite alarm on the subject of Russia's progress in South-Eastern Europe. There was no need to excite it among French statesmen. Jealousy of Russia's influence in the Near East had long since become one of the fixed motives of French diplomacy. France was definitely committed to the defence of the integrity and independence

[1] *Grandeur et Décadence des Romains*, chap. 23.

of the Ottoman Empire many years before that famous phrase
had ever been heard in England.

Nor are the reasons far to seek. Apart from the secular
rivalry between France and the Habsburgs; apart from all
questions of balance of power, France was vitally interested,
from commercial considerations, in the Near East. French
trade with the Levant was, for those times, on a most imposing
scale. 'En matière de commerce,' as a French historian has
put it, 'l'Orient nous rendait tous les services d'une vaste et
florissante colonie.'[1] The *Capitulations* originally conceded
to France by Suleiman in 1535[2] had been renewed in 1581,
1597, and 1604.

It was natural after the signal service rendered by Villeneuve
to the Ottoman Empire that the *Capitulations* should have
been re-enacted with special formality and particularity, and
should have been extended in several important directions.
Extraordinary and exclusive privileges were, in 1740, conferred
upon French traders in the Ottoman dominions, and special
rights were granted to Latin monks in the Holy Land, to
French pilgrims, and in general to Roman Catholics throughout the Turkish Empire.[3] It was to these *Capitulations* that
Napoleon III appealed when, on the eve of the Crimean War,
he attempted to reinstate Latin monks in the guardianship
of the Holy Places in Palestine.

§ 2. *From the Treaty of Belgrade to the Treaty of Kutschuk-Kainardji, 1739–74*

To France, then, the Ottoman Empire owed the new lease
of life which it obtained in 1739. The actual duration of the

---

[1] M. Vandal, ap. *Histoire Générale*, vii. 145.   [2] See *supra*, p. 93.
[3] The text will be found in Albin, *Les Grands Traités politiques*,
pp. 128 sqq.

lease was about thirty years, and it was the action of France which at the close of that period determined it.

During the interval the Porte was relieved of all pressure on the side either of Russia or of Austria-Hungary. Like the rest of the Great Powers they were preoccupied with other matters. Between 1740 and 1763 two great questions were in the balance : first, whether Austria or Prussia was to be the dominant power in Germany ; secondly, whether France or England was to be supreme in India and North America.

The death of Frederick William I of Prussia in May, 1740, followed in October by that of the Emperor Charles VI, opened a new chapter in German history—a chapter that was not finally closed until, in 1866, on the fateful field of König-grätz (Sadowa), the question of German hegemony was set at rest for ever. Almost simultaneously there opened in India and in America, between England and France, or rather, between England and the French and Spanish Bourbons, the war which was destined to determine the future of a great part of the world. Hardly was Frederick the Great seated on the Prussian throne when he snatched the Silesian duchies out of the hands of Maria Theresa. Great Britain supported Maria Theresa ; France was on the side of Frederick. The Peace of Aix-la-Chapelle (1748) left Frederick in possession of Silesia, while France and England restored the conquests they had respectively made in India and North America.

Between the conclusion of the so-called War of the Austrian Succession in 1748 and the renewal of war in 1756 there was a curious reversal of alliances. The rivalry of Austria and Prussia on the one hand, and of France and England on the other, remained unchanged and unabated. But Frederick reluctantly joined England on the question of the neutraliza-tion of Hanover, and thus France was compelled to accept the proffered friendship of Austria. The detachment of France from Prussia was a conspicuous triumph for the diplomacy of the Austrian minister, Kaunitz ; the wisdom of the change from the French point of view is much more questionable. It might have been argued that, on a long view, it could not be to the interest of France to contribute towards the aggrandizement of the Hohenzollern. But such an argument would, in 1756, have implied unusual prescience. The point which impressed itself upon contemporaries was that France surrendered in an instant the influence which for two hundred years she had exercised in Poland and at Constantinople. For friendship with Austria involved alliance with Russia.

The significance of this fact, obvious enough during the Seven Years' War, became much more startlingly apparent when, after 1763, the attention of the Eastern Powers was concentrated upon Poland. In 1762 one of the ablest rulers that ever sat upon a European throne succeeded to that of Russia. Catherine II did not lose a moment in picking up the threads of the ambitious foreign policy initiated by Peter the Great.

Catherine II

Marshal Münnich, the hero of the last Turkish War, used all his influence with the young Tsarina to induce her promptly to espouse the cause of the Greeks and Slavs in the Ottoman Empire. In the war of 1736 Münnich had assured the Tsarina Anne that Greeks, Slavs, and Roumanians alike looked to her not only as their protectress but as their legitimate sovereign ; he had begged to be allowed to take advantage of their enthusiasm for the Russian cause, and to carry the war to the gates of Constantinople. The signature of the Treaty of Belgrade had for the moment interrupted his plans, but he now urged the same policy upon Catherine II.

No scheme of foreign policy was too grandiose to command the assent of the Tsarina, but she thought it prudent to secure at least one trustworthy ally. France had been compelled, by her alliance with Austria, to surrender her interests at Warsaw and Constantinople. But the divergence from the traditional path of French policy was only temporary ; France, therefore, had to be reckoned as an opponent. Great Britain, though friendly enough to Russia, had already acquired the reputation of fickleness in diplomacy, and Catherine preferred a power whose interests were more definitely compatible, if not identical, with her own. That could not be said of Austria, and Catherine, therefore, turned to Frederick of Prussia.

The accession of the Tsar Peter III in 1762 had saved Frederick II at the most critical moment of the Seven Years' War, and, indeed, of his whole career. Catherine II was not at all unwilling to trade upon the good will acquired by her unfortunate husband. Prussia had no interests which could by any possibility conflict with her own in the Balkan peninsula, and their interests in Poland were, up to a point, identical.

Augustus III, the Saxon King of Poland, died on October 5, 1763, and it became immediately necessary to look out for a successor. A group of Polish patriots, led by the Czartoryskis, were anxious to seize the opportunity of effecting a radical reform of ' the most miserable constitution that ever enfeebled and demoralized a nation '. In particular they desired to make the crown hereditary, and to abolish the ridiculous privilege—the *liberum veto*—which permitted any single noble to veto legislation and obstruct reform. But the last thing desired either by Frederick or by Catherine was a reform of the Polish Constitution. They accordingly intervened to perpetuate the prevailing anarchy, and in April, 1764, agreed to procure the election to the Polish throne of Stanislas Poniatowski, a Polish nobleman of blemished reputation and irresolute character, and one of the discarded lovers of the Russian Empress. Stanislas was duly seated on the throne, and in 1768 a Diet, elected under the influence of a Russian army of occupation, declared the *liberum veto* and other intolerable abuses to be integral, essential, and irrevocable parts of the Polish Constitution, and placed that Constitution under the guarantee of Russia.

The Polish patriots made one more effort to escape from the toils of their ambitious neighbours, and formed the *Confederation of Bar*. The object of the Confederation was to put an end to Russian domination and to restore the supremacy of Roman Catholicism. Austria and France cordially supported the patriots. France, indeed, would gladly have done more, but crippled, both in a military and in a financial sense, by the prolonged and unsuccessful war with England, she was compelled to rely entirely upon diplomatic methods.

Choiseul had returned to power in 1766 eager for revenge upon England. As a preliminary to that revenge France must, however, recover her position upon the Continent, and for that purpose Choiseul tried to cement the recent alliance with Austria, and to renew the ancient ties of France with Sweden, Poland, and, above all, with the Ottoman Empire. To Vergennes, the French ambassador at Constantinople, he wrote : ' We must at all costs break the chain fastened upon the world by Russia. . . . The Ottoman Empire is the best instrument for doing it, and most interested in the success of the operation. True, the Turks are hopelessly degenerate, and the attempt will probably be fatal to them, but that does not concern us so long as we attain our objects.'

The immediate objects of French diplomacy were to rescue Poland from the grip of Catherine II and Frederick II, and to arrest the progress of Russian propaganda in the Balkans.

Catherine's pact with the King of Prussia (1764) had provided for common action at Constantinople with a view to averting Turkish intervention in Poland. The simplest way to effect this end was to keep the Turks busy at home. Accordingly, throughout the years 1765-7, Russian agents were constantly at work in Greece, Crete, Bosnia, and Montenegro. Both Greeks and Slavs were led to believe that the day of their deliverance was at hand ; that the ancient prophecy that ' the Turkish Empire would one day be destroyed by a fair-haired people ' was at last about to be fulfilled. Vergennes, on his part, lost no opportunity of emphasizing the significance of the ferment among the subject peoples, and of urging upon the Porte the necessity of a counter-attack.

A pretext was found in the violation of Turkish territory by Russian troops who had pursued some fugitive Poles into Tartary. Accordingly, in 1768, the Porte demanded that the Russian troops should immediately evacuate Poland. Russia hesitated to comply ; the Porte declared war (October 6), and, on the advice of Vergennes, issued a manifesto to the Powers. The Sultan, so it ran, had been compelled to take up arms against Russia in defence of the liberties of Poland, grievously compromised by the recent action of the Empress Catherine : ' she had forced upon the Poles a king who was neither of royal blood nor the elect of the people ; she had put to the sword all who had opposed her will and had pillaged and laid waste their possessions.' Turkey, in fact, stood forth as the guardian of international morality and the champion of small nationalities.

' War ', wrote Vergennes, ' is declared. I have done my master's bidding. I return the three millions furnished to me for my work. There was no need of the money.' [1] Thus, as Sorel pithily puts it : ' La France essaya de soutenir les confédérés catholiques avec les armes des Musulmans.'

The methods employed by France did not save Poland, and they brought destruction upon Turkey. The Turkish attack

[1] Sorel, *La Question d'Orient au dix-huitième Siècle*, chap. ii.

upon Russia served only to precipitate the partition of Poland. Catherine would much have preferred the maintenance of the *status quo* in Poland. Attacked on the flank by Turkey she was the more disposed to listen to the voice of the Prussian tempter. Frederick was profoundly impressed by the rapid development of Russia, and he dreaded in particular a renewal of that alliance between Russia, Austria, and France, which had so nearly proved fatal to Prussia in the Seven Years' War. How was he to retain the friendship of Russia ; to remove from Austria the temptation to fling herself into the arms of either Russia or of France, and at the same time avert the threatened annihilation of the Ottoman Empire ? Of these objects the last was not the least important in Frederick's eyes. It was, in his view, entirely opposed to the interests of Prussia that Turkey should be wiped out of the map of Europe, for circumstances might well render her a valuable counterpoise against the designs either of Russia or of Austria.[1] The problem was by no means simple, but the solution of it was found, for the time being, in the partition of Poland.

Early in 1769 that partition was informally suggested by Frederick to his ally at St. Petersburg. Almost simultaneously, Austria, alarmed by the outbreak of war between Russia and Turkey on her immediate frontier, deemed it prudent to reoccupy the county of Zips which had been mortgaged by Hungary to Poland in 1412. Maria Theresa was probably perfectly sincere when, two years later, she protested unalterable friendship for Poland, and repudiated the idea of partition. Nevertheless, the seizure of Zips had its place in the coil which was winding itself round the devoted kingdom. In 1772 the first partition was accomplished, and Maria Theresa accepted her share of the spoil.

Meanwhile, things were going badly for the Turks. In

[1] Frederick II, *Mémoires*, vi, p. 25, ap. Sorel, *op. cit.*, p. 49.

1769 a Turkish army was surprised on the Dniester, and fled in panic before the Russians, who then occupied Jassy and Bucharest.

In 1770, Catherine II, relying upon the reports of discontent among the subject populations in the Balkans, and particularly among the Greeks, made a determined effort to rouse them to insurrection against the Sultan. A Russian fleet, under the command of Admiral Elphinstone, formerly in the English service, issued from the Baltic and made its way round to the Mediterranean. Choiseul wished to arrest its progress, and in no other way could France have rendered so signal a service to her Turkish allies. But England firmly intimated to both France and Spain that any attempt to arrest the progress of the Russian fleet would be regarded as a *casus belli*, and it was permitted, therefore, to go on its way unmolested.

In the Mediterranean, Alexis Orloff, one of the murderers of Peter III, assumed the supreme command, and made a descent upon the coasts of the Morea. Great excitement was aroused among the Greeks in the Morea, and it extended to the Serbs and even to the Roumanians. The hour of their deliverance appeared to be at hand. But the Russian scheme miscarried. Orloff, with a small force, attacked Tripolitza, but was badly supported by the Greeks, and fell back before the Turks. The latter exacted a terrible vengeance from the unhappy Greeks, both in the Morea and in the islands of the Archipelago, and the Greeks, disillusioned and disappointed, cursed the fickle allies who had first roused them to rebellion and had then abandoned them to their fate.

Meanwhile Orloff, aided by some luck and still more by the English officers under his command, won a notable success at sea. He attacked the Turkish fleet near Chios, inflicted heavy losses upon them, and compelled them to take refuge in the harbour of Tchesmé. Elphinstone then suggested a brilliant manœuvre. The whole Turkish fleet, cooped up in harbour, was destroyed by a fireship, almost without another shot. Elphinstone was anxious to follow up the victory by an immediate attack upon Constantinople; but Orloff delayed, and though the English admiral took a few ships with him to the Dardanelles, no decisive operations could be attempted. Constantinople was quickly put in a posture of defence, and Orloff contented himself with the seizure of some of the islands in the Levant. But although the greater prize was denied to the English admiral, the appearance of a Russian fleet in the Mediterranean and the damage inflicted upon the Turkish navy created an immense sensation not merely in the Ottoman Empire but throughout the world. It seemed to presage the final overthrow of the power of the Turks.

Nor were the disasters at sea redeemed by success on land. The Crimea was conquered by Russia; the Turkish fortresses on the Dniester and the Danube fell one after another before the Russian assault; and before the end of 1771 Catherine was in undisputed occupation of Moldavia and Wallachia.

Meanwhile Austria, seriously alarmed by the rapid success of Russia, had, on July 6, 1771, signed a secret treaty with Turkey. If the Russians crossed the Danube Austria undertook to march an army to the assistance of the Sultan. An intimation to this effect was sent to St. Petersburg and Berlin. Frederick was gravely perturbed by the news. In two interviews with Joseph II in 1769 and 1770 at Neisse and Neustadt respectively he had brought the emperor over to his views on the Polish question. The whole scheme would be ruined if war were now to break out between Russia and Austria. But the partition itself, if promptly effected, seemed to offer a way out of the Balkan difficulty. Negotiations were hastily resumed, and in 1772 the partition was finally agreed upon. Catherine consented to surrender her conquests on the Pruth and the

Danube in return for a large slice of Poland ; Turkey was saved from disruption, and war between Russia and Austria was averted.

The Russo-Turkish War still dragged on, but although Catherine continued to win victories in the field, she was disposed towards peace by the outbreak of a formidable insurrection among the Cossacks of the Don, and in July, 1774, the Treaty of Kutschuk-Kainardji was signed.[1]

Treaty of Kutschuk-Kainardji, July 15, 1774

Of the many treaties concluded during the last two centuries between Russia and Turkey this is the most fundamental and the most far-reaching. A distinguished jurist has indeed asserted that all the great treaties executed by the two Powers during the next half century were but commentaries upon this text. Its provisions, therefore, demand close investigation. Apart from those of secondary or temporary importance three questions of pre-eminent significance are involved.

Russia restored to the Porte most of the territories she had recently occupied : Bessarabia, Moldavia, Wallachia, and the islands of the Archipelago ; but only, as we shall see, on condition of better treatment. For herself Russia was to retain Azov, Yenikale, and Kertsch, with the districts adjacent thereto ; also Kinburn at the mouth of the Dnieper, and, provided the assent of the Khan of Tartary could be obtained, the two Kabardas. By these acquisitions Russia obtained for the first time a firm grip upon the northern shore of the Black Sea ; she controlled the straits between the Sea of Azov and the Black Sea ; while the possession of the two Kabardas gave her a footing on the eastern shore. The Tartars to the east

[1] An admirable commentary upon this most important treaty, together with the full text, will be found in Holland's *Treaty Relations between Russia and Turkey*.

of the Bug were at the same time declared independent of the Porte, except in ecclesiastical matters—a further blow to the position of the Turks on the Euxine. Thus Turkish territory, instead of encircling the Black Sea, was henceforward to be bounded on the north-east by the river Bug. To develop her trade, Russia was to be allowed to establish consuls and vice-consuls wherever she might think fit; she was to have the right of free commercial navigation in the Black Sea; and the subjects of the Tsarina were to be allowed to trade in the Ottoman dominions ' by land as well as by water and upon the Danube in their ships . . . with all the same privileges and advantages as are enjoyed by the most friendly nations whom the Sublime Porte favours most in trade, such as the French and English. Reciprocal advantages were granted to Ottoman subjects in Russia '. (Art. xi.)

Not less significant was the diplomatic footing which Russia obtained in Constantinople. Henceforward Russia was to be represented at the Porte by a permanent Embassy; she was to have the right to erect, in addition to her minister's private chapel, ' a public church of the Greek ritual ', which was to be under the protection of the Russian minister. The Porte further agreed to permit Russian subjects, ' as well laymen as ecclesiastics ', to make pilgrimages to Jerusalem and other Holy Places, and the Sultan undertook ' to protect constantly the Christian religion and its churches '. The Porte also allowed ' the ministers of the imperial court of Russia to make, upon all occasions, representations as well in favour of the new church at Constantinople as on behalf of its officiating ministers, promising to take such representations into due consideration as being made by a confidential functionary of a neighbouring and sincerely friendly power '.

The clauses (Articles xii and xiv) in which these terms were embodied deserve the closest scrutiny, for upon them were founded the claims to a formal protectorate over the Greek Christians put forward by Russia on the eve of the Crimean War.[1] Lord Clarendon then declared that the interpretation which Russia sought to place upon these clauses was inadmissible. But however ambiguous, perhaps studiously ambiguous, they may have been, it cannot be denied that the provisions which defined the relations of Russia to the Greeks in Turkey registered a signal triumph for Russian diplomacy. Thugut, who was then Austrian minister at Constantinople, truly described the whole treaty as ' un modèle d'habileté de la part des diplomates russes, et un rare exemple d'imbécillité de la part des négociateurs turcs '.[2]

In regard to the territories lately occupied by Russia and now restored to the Ottoman Empire the stipulations were even more specific. The Danubian principalities, the islands of the Archipelago, and the provinces of Georgia and Mingrelia were restored only on condition of better government in general, and of particular privileges in regard to ' monetary taxes ', to diplomatic representation, and above all to religion. The Porte (Arts. xvi, xvii, and xxiii) definitely promised ' to obstruct in no manner whatsoever the free exercise of the Christian religion, and to interpose no obstacle to the erection of new Churches and to the repairing of old ones '.

From these stipulations Russian publicists have deduced, and not unnaturally, a general right of interference in the domestic concerns of the Ottoman Empire. ' De là,' as M. Sorel says, ' pour la Russie *l'obligation* de s'immiscer dans les affaires intérieures de la Turquie, chaque fois que les intérêts des chrétiens l'exige.' [3]

Such was the famous Treaty of Kutschuk-Kainardji : not the term but the real starting-point of Russian progress in the Near East.

[1] *Infra*, chap. x.   [2] Sorel, *op. cit.*, p. 263.   [3] *Op. cit.*, p. 262.

The next step toward the dismemberment of the Ottoman Empire was taken, however, not by Russia but by Austria. The Turks, declared Kaunitz, thoroughly deserved their misfortunes, as much by their feebleness in war as by their ' lack of confidence in those Powers which, like Austria, were disposed to help them out of their difficulties '. Austria's method of doing this was characteristic. She was far from satisfied with her share, though in point of population and extent of territory it was the giant's share, in the partition of Poland. Accordingly, directly after the conclusion of the Treaty of Kainardji, she helped herself to the Bukovina ; and the Turks were constrained to acquiesce. The formal treaty of cession was signed on May 7, 1775. Thus by a simple act of brigandage Austria obtained, in territory, far more than Russia had acquired by a prolonged and strenuous war. Nor did she gain only in territory. The acquisition of the Bukovina forged a fresh link in the chain of friendship between Vienna and St. Petersburg.

§ 3.   *Austro-Russian Alliance, 1775-92*

That friendship became even more intimate after the death, in 1780, of Maria Theresa. The Emperor Joseph II succumbed entirely to the seductive and dominating personality of the Tsarina Catherine, and cordially supported her ambitious policy in the Near East.

Catherine was, in respect of that policy, in direct apostolical succession to Peter the Great. It is a suspicious fact that the *Political Testament* of Peter the Great was first published in Paris at the moment when Napoleon, in preparation for his expedition to Moscow, was anxious to alienate sympathy from and excite alarm against the ' colossus of the north '. That famous document was probably an apocryphal forgery, but there can be no question that it accurately represented the trend and tradition of Russian policy in the eighteenth century.

Constantinople was clearly indicated as the goal of Russian ambition. The Turks were to be driven out of Europe by the help of Austria ; a good understanding was to be maintained with England ; and every effort was to be made to accelerate the dissolution of Persia and to secure the Indian trade. Whether inherited or original these were the principles which for nearly forty years inspired the policy of Peter the Great's most brilliant successor on the Russian throne.

To the realization of Catherine's dreams one thing was indispensable—the cordial support of the Habsburg emperor. One or two personal interviews sufficed to secure it, and in June, 1781, an agreement between the two sovereigns was embodied in private correspondence. A technical question of precedence alone prevented a more formal engagement. Catherine and Joseph were thus mutually pledged to support each other in the Near East.

In September, 1782, the Tsarina laid before her ally a specific plan for the complete reconstruction of the map of the Balkan peninsula, and the lands, seas, and islands adjacent thereto.

The governing presupposition of the whole scheme was the expulsion of the Ottoman Turks from all their European territories. Once the Turks were expelled, partition would not be difficult. The direct acquisitions of Russia were conceived on a moderate scale : she was to get only Oczakov and the territory, known as Lesser Tartary, which lay between the Bug and the Dniester, with the addition of a couple of the Aegean islands to be utilized as naval bases. Moldavia, including Bessarabia, and Wallachia were to be erected into the independent kingdom of Dacia, and a crown was in this way to be provided for Catherine's favourite and minister, Potemkin. Austria's share of the spoil was to consist of Serbia, Bosnia, Herzegovina, and Dalmatia, while Venice was to be compensated for the loss of Dalmatia by the acquisition of the

Morea, Cyprus, and Crete. Catherine did not apparently apprehend any opposition except from France, and that was to be averted by a timely offer of Egypt and Syria. The crowning feature of this wonderfully comprehensive scheme remains to be disclosed The Greek Empire, with Constantinople itself, Thrace, Macedonia, Bulgaria, northern Greece, and Albania was to be reserved for Catherine's second grandson. The boy, with sagacious prescience, had been christened Constantine ; he was always dressed in the Greek mode, surrounded by Greek nurses, and instructed in the tongue of his future subjects. That no detail might be lacking which foresight could devise, a medal had already been struck, on one side of which was a representation of the young prince's head, and on the other an allegorical device indicating the coming triumph of the Cross over the Crescent. Against the possible union of the Greek and Russian Empires the Tsarina was prepared to offer ample guarantees.

Catherine's proposals were not entirely to Joseph's liking. To a modern critic the most curious and significant feature of the scheme is the total lack of any recognition of the nationality principle ; the complete absence of any consideration for the likes and dislikes, the affinities and repulsions, of the peoples immediately concerned. That was, however, the way of the eighteenth century, and no criticism on that score was to be expected from the Habsburg emperor. Joseph's objection was of another kind. His own share was insufficient. He wanted not only Dalmatia but Istria, not only Serbia but Little Wallachia ; nor did it please him that the rest of the Danubian principalities should be torn from the Ottoman Empire only to pass into the control of Russia. But these were, relatively, details, and were not sufficient to cause a breach of the friendship existing between the august allies.

The grandiose scheme of 1782 was not destined to realization.

But in the following year Catherine resolved to put an end immediately to an embarrassing situation in the Crimea. By the Treaty of Kainardji the Porte had been deprived of its suzerainty over the Tartars in political affairs, though the Khalifal authority of the Sultan remained inviolate. Difficulties naturally arose from this contradictory arrangement, and in 1779 a *Convention explicative* defined the Turkish supremacy over the Tartars as purely spiritual. This virtually meant that political supremacy was transferred to Russia, and in 1783 Catherine resolved any remaining ambiguity by annexing the khanate of the Crimea. The administration of the new Russian province was confided to Potemkin, and, thanks to his energy, was rapidly transformed by Russian engineers and cultivators ; it began to bristle with fortresses and arsenals, and, according to some authorities, to yield a rich harvest of agricultural produce.[1]

In 1787 the Tsarina, accompanied by the Emperor Joseph, made a magnificent progress through her new dominions. She sailed down the Dnieper to Kherson, where she passed under a triumphal arch bearing the inscription, ' The Way to Byzantium ' ; she had the more solid satisfaction of witnessing, in company with her ally and the ambassadors of the Great Powers, the launch of three battleships from the newly constructed dockyard ; and then from Kherson she passed on to the Crimea, where she inspected Potemkin's crowning achievement, the new naval arsenal of Sebastopol. There was a touch of the theatrical, not to say the melodramatic, in the whole proceedings, but they did not lack real substance and significance.

It was not to be expected that the Porte would view with unconcern the rapid strides which Russia was making towards

---

[1] Zinkeisen (vi. 620, 621) draws a very different picture of the economic results of the Russian occupation.

supremacy in the Black Sea: the annexation of the Tartars; the fortification of the Crimea; the economic development of the southern provinces; above all, the striking progress of Russian sea-power. Sebastopol was within two days' sail of Constantinople; Varna, where Catherine had insisted upon establishing a consulate, was within 120 miles of it. Moreover, Russian agents had been busy of late in stirring up discontent among the Greeks, Slavs, and Roumanians; they had even extended their intrigues to Egypt. Sultan Abdul Hamid had, therefore, ample ground for disquietude.

Disquietude gave place to indignation when Catherine formulated her immediate demands. The Sultan was required to renounce his sovereignty over Georgia, to surrender Bessarabia to Russia, and to permit the establishment of hereditary governors in Moldavia and Wallachia. The cup of Abdul Hamid's anger was now full. He had already issued a manly manifesto to the true believers, calling attention to the treacherous advance of Russia, and in particular to the seizure of the Crimea in time of peace. He now demanded its immediate restoration, and followed up the demand by a declaration of war against Russia (August, 1787).

As to the wisdom of this move there are diversities of opinion among modern critics. Professor Lodge attributes the action of the Sultan to 'passion rather than policy'.[1] Dr. Holland Rose sees in it a 'skilful move',[2] in view of the reasonable probability that Prussia and Sweden would come to the assistance of the Porte. Catherine herself was deeply chagrined, and attributed the bold action of the Sultan to the perfidious encouragement of Pitt. For this suspicion there was not, as we shall see, a scintilla of justification.

Faithful to his alliance Joseph II declared war against the

---

[1] Ap. *Cambridge Modern History*, viii. 316.

[2] *Pitt and the National Revival*, p. 488.

Sultan in February, 1788, but the Austrians contributed little to the success of the campaign. Not that the Turks were making much of it. In October, 1788, Suvaroff, the Russian veteran, beat off with great loss a Turkish attack on Kinburn, the fortress which confronted Oczakov and commanded the estuary of the Dnieper and the Bug. Catherine, however, was on her side compelled to withdraw a considerable portion of her forces in order to repel the advance of Gustavus III of Sweden upon St. Petersburg. The Swedish attack, like that of the Turks, was set down by Catherine to English diplomacy. 'As Mr. Pitt', said the Tsarina, 'wishes to chase me from St. Petersburg, I hope he will allow me to take refuge at Constantinople.' There is no more ground for the one insinuation than for the other. Nevertheless, it cannot be denied that from the Turkish point of view the intervention of Gustavus was exceedingly opportune. It probably saved the Ottoman Empire from immediate annihilation.

Gustavus could not, however, secure the Turks from all damage. Before the close of the year 1788 Potemkin had made himself master of the great fortress of Oczakov and the surrounding district, and in 1789 the Austrians, after taking Belgrade and Semendria, made an incursion into Bosnia.

The Powers and the Eastern Question

The days were, however, drawing to a close when a war between the Ottoman Empire and its immediate neighbours could be regarded as a matter of concern only to the belligerents. It had never been so regarded by France, and the ablest ministers of the last period of the *Ancien Régime*, Choiseul, for example, and Vergennes, were entirely faithful to the traditions of French diplomacy in the Near East. Brandenburg-Prussia cannot be said to have had a diplomatic system before the eighteenth century, while England had so far been curiously unconcerned as to the development of events in Eastern Europe. But the period of acquiescence was nearly at an end. A new phase of the Eastern Question was clearly opening.

The Triple Alliance concluded, in 1788, between Great Britain, Prussia, and the United Provinces was not concerned primarily with the affairs of the Near East. But among its objects was that of holding in check the ambitious designs of Russia and Austria in that direction. Prussia, in particular, was anxious to use the machinery of the alliance for sustaining the resistance of the Turks to the aggressions of their neighbours. Not that Prussia's policy in the matter was free from ambiguity and vacillation. In May, 1789, the Prussian minister, Herzberg, propounded an ambitious project by which Prussia was to secure her heart's desire, Danzig and Thorn. Poland was to be compensated by the recovery of Galicia from Austria, while the latter was to be permitted to add Moldavia and Wallachia to Transylvania and the Bukovina.

Pitt, however, had not formed the Triple Alliance to further the ambitions of Prussia, but to save Belgium from France, and above all to preserve the peace of Europe. He frowned, therefore, upon proposals which were likely to provoke a general European war. He willingly combined with Prussia in bringing effective pressure to bear upon Denmark, when the latter, at the bidding of the Tsarina Catherine, attacked Gustavus III of Sweden. But only very gradually and reluctantly was he driven to the conviction that it was incumbent upon Great Britain to offer more direct resistance to the advance of Russia in South-Eastern Europe.

Hitherto England had not manifested any jealousy towards the remarkable progress of Russia. On the contrary, she had welcomed Russia's advent into the European polity : politically, as a possible counterpoise to the dangerous pre-eminence of

France; commercially, as an exporter of the raw materials required for naval construction, and as a considerable importer of English goods, and of 'colonial produce' carried to her ports in English bottoms. The elder Pitt was a strong advocate of a Russian alliance. 'I am quite a Russ,' he wrote to Shelburne in 1773; 'I trust the Ottoman will pull down the House of Bourbon in his fall.' In regard to Russia Fox inherited the views of Chatham. He was in office when Catherine annexed the Crimea and cordially approved of it, and, like Chatham, he would gladly have formed a close alliance with Russia and the northern powers.

The younger Pitt was the first English statesman to appreciate the real and intimate concern of Great Britain in the affairs of the Near East, and to perceive that those interests might be jeopardized by the dissolution of the Ottoman Empire, and the access of Russia to Constantinople. And the truth, as we have seen, dawned only gradually upon him. So late as 1790 he warned Herzberg that the armed mediation which Prussia proposed in the interests of the Porte was outside the scope of the Triple Alliance.[1] He did, however, go so far as to press Austria to come to terms with the Porte and so avoid the threatened rupture with Prussia.

Meanwhile, a combination of events disposed the belligerents to peace. In April, 1789, Abdul Hamid I died, and was succeeded by Selim III, a ruler of very different quality. The death of the Emperor Joseph (February 28, 1790) and the accession of his sagacious brother, Leopold, gave a new turn to Austrian policy. Above all, the development of the revolutionary movement in France was compelling the strained attention of every monarch and every government in Europe. In face of this new source of disturbance the emperor and the King of Prussia accommodated their differences, and in June,

[1] Rose, *op. cit.*, p. 521.

1790, concluded the Convention of Reichenbach. Prussia surrendered, for the moment, the hope of acquiring Danzig and Thorn. Leopold agreed to make peace with the Turks on the basis of the *status quo ante*.

Pitt now assumed a firmer tone towards Catherine II. In November, 1790, he demanded that she should surrender Oczakov, and in the following March the Cabinet agreed that an ultimatum should be dispatched to Russia in that sense. But subsequent debates, both in the House of Lords and in the Commons, showed that public opinion, as represented there, was not yet prepared for a reversal of the traditional policy which had hitherto governed the relations of Russia and England. On March 28 the king sent a message to both Houses recommending ' some further augmentation of his naval force ' in view of the failure of his ministers to ' effect a pacification between Russia and the Porte '. The ministers carried their reply in the Lords by 97 to 34, and in the Commons by 228 to 135. But although the ministerial majorities were substantial, the votes did not reflect either the temper of Parliament or the tone of the debate. Hardly a voice was raised in either House in favour of Pitt's proposed demonstration. Lord Fitzwilliam opposed it on the ground that ' no ill consequence was likely to arise from Russia's keeping in her hands Oczakov and Akerman '. Burke vehemently protested against a demonstration of friendship or support for ' a cruel and wasteful Empire ' and a nation of ' destructive savages '. Fox insisted that Russia was our ' natural ally ', that we had always looked to her to counterbalance the Bourbons, that we had encouraged her ' plans for raising her aggrandisement upon the ruins of the Turkish Empire ', that to oppose her progress in the Black Sea would be sheer madness, and that it would not hurt us if she emerged into the Mediterranean. Pitt urged that ' the interests which this country had in not suffering the Russians to make conquests on the coasts of the Black Sea were of the utmost importance ', but his reply as a whole was singularly unconvincing and even perfunctory.[1] In regard to the proposed armament Pitt wisely deferred to an unmistakable expression of public opinion, and promptly effected a somewhat humiliating but exceedingly prudent retreat. Catherine II had her way about Oczakov, without molestation from the English fleet. But it is pertinent to remark that though Oczakov is now merely an historical memory, Odessa is not.

In August, 1791, Austria concluded peace with the Porte at Sistova. Serbia was handed back to Turkey, and the *status quo ante* was restored. On January 9, 1792, a ' treaty of perpetual peace ' was signed by Russia and Turkey at Jassy. The Treaty of Kainardji, the *Convention Explicative* of 1779, and the Commercial Treaty of 1783 were confirmed ; the Porte recovered Moldavia, but again on condition that the stipulations contained in the preceding treaties were fulfilled ; the Russian frontier was advanced to the Dniester (Oczakov being thus transferred), and the Porte agreed to recognize the annexation of the Crimea.

The Treaty of Jassy brings to a close one of the most important phases in the history of the Eastern Question, and one of the lengthiest chapters in this book. When it opened Russia had hardly begun to play a part as a European Power ; the Black Sea was a Turkish lake. As it closes, Russia is firmly entrenched upon the shores of the Euxine, and is already

---

[1] Hansard, *Parliamentary History* (vol. xxix), for the debates which are supremely interesting in view of the subsequent policy of England. It is noteworthy that Pitt's speech on this occasion is not included in Hathaway's edition of his speeches, and from the critical point of view Hathaway was right. It is less remarkable that it should have been omitted from Mr. Coupland's recent edition of the *War Speeches*.

looking beyond them. Kherson and Sebastopol have been transformed into great naval arsenals; Kinburn and Oczakov, not to mention Taganrog, Azov, and the Kabardas, are secure in Russian keeping. To the north of the Euxine Turkish territory ends at the Dniester, and the border provinces between the Dniester and the Danube are retained only on sufferance. Upon the lands to the south of the Euxine the Turkish hold is already loosening. 'I came to Russia', said Catherine, 'a poor girl; Russia has dowered me richly, but I have paid her back with Azov, the Crimea, and the Ukraine' Proudly spoken, it was less than the truth.

For further reference see chapter iii; also Serge Goriainow, *Le Bosphore et les Dardanelles* (a valuable study in diplomacy with close reference to the documents); Cardinal Alberoni, *Scheme for reducing the Turkish Empire* (Eng. trans. 1736); A. Sorel, *La Question d'Orient au XVIIIe siècle*; T. E. Holland, *Treaty Relations of Russia and Turkey* (with texts of important treaties); W. E. H. Lecky, *History of England in the Eighteenth Century*; J. Holland Rose, *Pitt and the National Revival*; Paganel, *Histoire de Joseph II*; J. F. Bright, *Joseph II*; Vandal, *Louis XV et Elisabeth de Russie, Une ambassade française en Orient, La mission de Villeneuve*; R. Waliszewski, *Le roman d'une impératrice (Catherine II)*; A. Rambaud, *History of Russia*.

7

Napoleon and the Near Eastern Problem

'Really to ruin England we must make ourselves masters of Egypt.'— NAPOLEON to the Directory, Aug. 16, 1797.

'Egypt is the keystone of English ascendancy in the Indian Ocean.'— PAUL ROHRBACH (1912).

'Le personnage de Napoléon, en Orient comme ailleurs, domine les premières années du XIXe siècle ... certes il serait excessif d'affirmer que la question d'Orient fût le nœud de sa politique ... mais c'est précisément par l'Orient qu'il pensa atteindre son inabordable ennemie, et, par suite, il ne le quitta jamais des yeux; il y édifia ses combinaisons politiques les plus aventureuses sans doute, mais aussi les plus géniales. Il y porta ses vues dès ses premières victoires en Italie ; il y poursuivit les Anglais à travers l'ancien continent ; il y brisa sa fortune. C'est en ce sens qu'il put concevoir un moment l'idée de la domination universelle ; c'est bien à Constantinople qu'il plaça le centre du monde.'—Édouard Driault, *Question d'Orient.*

§ 1. *West and East, 1797–1807*

THE Treaty of Jassy closed one important chapter in the history of the Eastern Question. The next opens with the advent of Napoleon. By the year 1797 he had begun to arrive not only in a military but in a political sense. During the five years which elapsed between the Treaty of Jassy (1792) and that of Campo Formio the Eastern Question, as in this work we understand the term, was permitted to rest. This brief interval of repose was due to several causes, but chiefly to the fact that the year which saw the conclusion of the war between Russia and Turkey witnessed the opening of the struggle between the German Powers and the French Revolution.

Catherine's ambition in regard to Poland had been whetted rather than sated by the partition of 1772. But between 1772 and 1792 she was, as we have seen, busy elsewhere. Poland seized the opportunity to put what remained of its house in order—the last thing desired by Catherine. But in 1792 her chance came. She had been cudgelling her brains to urge the Courts of Vienna and Berlin to busy themselves with the affairs of France, so that she might have ' her own elbows free '. The German Courts played her game for her, and by the summer of 1792 her elbows were free. In 1793 the second partition of Poland was carried out. Prussia and Russia divided the spoil ; Austria got nothing. But in the third and final partition of 1795 Austria was admitted to a share. In the same year Prussia concluded peace with France at the expense of the empire ; two years later Austria followed suit.

Prussia had made her peace with the Directory. With

Austria the peace was negotiated directly by the young general who had commanded the French army in the great campaign of 1796–7. And General Bonaparte had already begun to comport himself as an independent conqueror. 'Do you suppose', said he to Miot de Mélito, 'that I have been winning victories in Italy to enhance the glory of the lawyers of the Directory—Barras and Carnot ? Do you suppose that I mean to establish the Republic more securely ? . . . The nation wants a chief, a supreme head covered with glory.' In Bonaparte's view they had not very far to look for him. Nor was the chief in any doubt as to his real antagonist. From the outset his eyes were fixed upon England, and upon England not merely or mainly as a unit in the European polity, but as a world-power, and above all as an Oriental power.

The Ionian Isles

Before the Treaty of Campo Formio was actually signed Bonaparte had written to the Directors (August 16, 1797) : ' Corfu, Zante, and Cephalonia are of more interest to us than all Italy.' ' Corfu and Zante ', he said to Talleyrand, ' make us masters both of the Adriatic and of the Levant. It is useless to try to maintain the Turkish Empire ; we shall see its downfall in our lifetime. The occupation of the Ionian Isles will put us in a position to support it or to secure a share of it for ourselves.' Amid the much more resounding advantages secured to France in 1797—Belgium, the Rhine frontier, and so on—little significance was attached to the acquisition of these islands. But Bonaparte was looking ahead. To him they were all important. Might they not serve as stepping-stones to Egypt ? To Choiseul Egypt had seemed the obvious compensation for the loss of the French Empire in India. Napoleon regarded the occupation of the first as a necessary preliminary to the recovery of the second. Volney, whose book, *Les Ruines*, had a powerful influence upon him, had written in 1788, ' Par l'Égypte nous toucherons à l'Inde ; nous rétablirons l'ancienne circulation par Suez, et nous ferons déserter la route du cap de Bonne-Espérance.'

Nor was Napoleon without warrant from his nominal masters. On October 23, 1797, the Directors had indited an elaborate dispatch commending to his consideration the position of Turkey, the interests of French commerce in the Levant, and indicating the importance they attached to the Ionian Isles and Malta.[1] The views of the Directors coincided with his own. It is safe to assume that if they had not done so they would not have found an agent in General Bonaparte. But alike to the Republicans and to the future emperor they came as a heritage from the *Ancien Régime*. French policy in the Near East has been, as we have repeatedly seen, singularly consistent. So far as Napoleon initiated a new departure, it was only in the boldness and originality with which he applied traditional principles to a new situation.

Egypt

In the summer of 1797 Napoleon had already made overtures to the Mainotes, the Greeks, and the Pashas of Janina, Scutari, and Bosnia. In regard to the Greeks of the Morea he was particularly solicitous. ' Be careful ', he wrote to General Gentili, whom he sent to occupy the Ionian Isles, ' in issuing your proclamations to make plenty of reference to the Greeks, to Athens, and Sparta.' He himself addressed the Mainotes as ' worthy descendants of the Spartans who alone among the ancient Greeks knew the secret of preserving political liberty '. But it was on Egypt that his attention was really concentrated, and on Egypt mainly as a means to the overthrow of the Empire

---

[1] Sorel, *L'Europe et la Révolution*, v. 253.

of England. Talleyrand represented his views to the Directory :
' Our war with this Power (England) represents the most
favourable opportunity for the invasion of Egypt. Threatened
by an imminent landing on her shores she will not desert her
coasts to prevent our enterprise (in Egypt). This further
offers us a possible chance of driving the English out of India
by sending thither 15,000 troops from Cairo via Suez.' [1]

It was, however, to the command of the Army of England
that Bonaparte was gazetted in November, 1797. He accepted
it not without an *arrière-pensée*. ' This little Europe ', he
said to Bourrienne, ' offers too contracted a field. One must
go to the East to gain power and greatness. Europe is a mere
mole-hill ; it is only in the East, where there are 600,000,000
of human beings, that there have ever been vast empires and
mighty revolutions. I am willing to inspect the northern coast
to see what can be done. But if, as I fear, the success of a
landing in England should appear doubtful, I shall make my
Army of England the Army of the East and go to Egypt.' [2]

A visit to the northern coast confirmed his view that the
blow against England should be struck in Egypt. The French
navy was not in a condition to attempt direct invasion. Besides,
he had his own career to consider. He must ' keep his glory
warm ', and that was not to be in Europe. He persuaded the
Directors to his views, and in April, 1798, he was nominated to
the command of the army of the East. His instructions,
drafted by himself, ordered him to take Malta and Egypt, cut
a channel through the Isthmus of Suez, and make France
mistress of the Red Sea, maintaining as far as possible good
relations with the Turks and their Sultan. But the supreme
object of the expedition was never to be lost sight of. ' You ',

---

[1] Jonquière, *L'Expédition d'Égypte*, i. 161 (cited by Fournier).

[2] I combine two separate conversations, both with Bourrienne, but, of
course, without altering the sense and merely for the sake of brevity.

he said to his troops as they embarked at Toulon, ' are a wing of the Army of England.'

The preparations for the expedition were made with a thoroughness which we have been too apt of late to associate with the Teutonic rather than the Latin genius. On Napoleon's staff were at least a dozen generals who subsequently attained renown ; but not generals only. Egypt was to be transformed under French rule ; the desert was to be made to blossom as the rose. To this end Napoleon took with him Berthollet, the great chemist, Monge, the mathematician, engineers, architects, archaeologists, and historians.

The expedition sailed from Toulon on May 19, 1798. Nelson had been closely watching the port, though quite ignorant of Napoleon's destination. But he was driven out to sea by a storm, and before he could get back the bird had flown. Meanwhile, Napoleon occupied Malta without resistance from the Knights of St. John (June 13) ; the French troops landed in Egypt on July 1 ; took Alexandria on the 2nd, fought and won the battle of the Pyramids on the 21st, and on the next day occupied Cairo. Three weeks had sufficed for the conquest of Lower Egypt. But Nelson and the English fleet, though successfully eluded during the voyage, were on Napoleon's track, and on the 1st of August they came up with the French fleet lying in Aboukir Bay, and, by a manœuvre conceived with great skill and executed with superb courage, they succeeded in completely annihilating it. Nelson's victory of the Nile rendered Napoleon's position in Egypt exceedingly precarious. Cut off from his base, deprived of the means of transport and supply, a lesser man would have deemed it desperate. Napoleon was only stimulated to fresh efforts.

The attack upon Egypt was, as we have seen, directed primarily against England. But the lord of Egypt was the Sultan, and to him the French conquest was both insulting and damaging. Encouraged by Nelson's success Sultan Selim plucked up courage to declare war upon France on September 1, and prepared to reconquer his lost province. Napoleon thereupon determined to take the offensive in Syria. He took by assault El Arish, Gaza, and Jaffa, laid siege to Acre (March, 1799), and on April 16 inflicted a crushing defeat upon the Turks at Mount Tabor.

Acre, thanks to the support of the English fleet under Sir Sydney Smith, sustained its reputation for impregnability; the sufferings of Napoleon's army were intense; their general, reluctantly resigning his dream of an advance through Asia Minor upon Constantinople, was compelled to withdraw to Egypt. Instead of conquering Constantinople, and from Constantinople taking his European enemies in the rear, he found himself obliged to defend his newly conquered province against the assault of its legitimate sovereign.

Convoyed by the English fleet a Turkish expedition reached Egypt in July, but Napoleon flung himself upon them and drove them headlong into the sea (July 25). This second battle of Aboukir firmly established Napoleon's supremacy in Egypt. But the victory, though militarily complete, was politically barren. News from France convinced Napoleon that the pear was at last ripe, and that it must be picked in Paris. Precisely a month after his victory over the Turks at Aboukir he embarked with great secrecy at Alexandria, leaving his army under the command of Kléber. The Mediterranean was carefully patrolled by the English fleet, but Napoleon managed to elude it, landed at Fréjus on October 9, and precisely a month later (18th Brumaire) effected the *coup d'état* which made him, at a single blow, master of France.

During Napoleon's absence in Egypt events had moved rapidly in Europe. Great Britain, Russia, Prussia, Naples, Portugal, and Turkey had united in a second coalition against

France. So long as Napoleon was away the war went in the main against France, but his return was signalized by the victories of Marengo (June) and Hohenlinden (December, 1800), and early in 1801 Austria was obliged to make peace.

Napoleon had already, without much difficulty, detached the Tsar of Russia[1] from the coalition. Alienated from England by the rigidity with which she interpreted the rules of International Law at sea, Paul I gladly came to terms with the First Consul, for whom he had suddenly conceived a fervent admiration. The bait dangled before the half-crazy brain of the Russian Tsar was a Franco-Russian expedition against British India.[2] A large force of Cossacks and Russian regulars were to march by way of Turkestan, Khiva, and Bokhara to the Upper Indus valley, while 35,000 French troops, under Masséna, were to descend the Danube, and, going by way of the Black Sea and the Caspian, were to make an attack on Persia, take Herat and Candahar, and then unite with the Russians on the Indus. The details of the scheme were worked out to an hour and a man; twenty days were to suffice for reaching the Black Sea; fifty-five more were to see them in Persia, and another forty-five in India. Towards the end of June, 1801, the joint attack would be delivered upon India. Towards the end of February, 1801, a large force of Cossacks did actually cross the Volga; but on March 24 the assassination of the Tsar Paul put an end to the scheme.

The projected expedition into Central Asia was not without its influence upon subsequent schemes entertained by Napoleon, but it did nothing to relieve the immediate situation in Egypt. Great Britain, by the taking of Malta (September, 1800), had made herself undisputed mistress of the Mediterranean,

---

[1] He succeeded Catherine in 1796.

[2] A French historian speaks of this scheme as 'une éclatante lumière jetée sur l'avenir', Driault, *op. cit.*, p. 78.

and she had also thrown a large army, including 10,000 Sepoys, into Egypt. Sir Ralph Abercromby won a great victory at Alexandria in March (1801) ; Cairo capitulated in June, and in September the French agreed to evacuate Egypt, which was forthwith restored to the Sultan. There was no longer any obstacle to the conclusion of peace, and in March, 1802, the definitive treaty was signed at Amiens. England undertook to restore Malta to the Knights, and the Ionian Isles were erected into a sort of federal republic under the joint protection of Turkey and Russia.

The truce secured to the two chief combatants by the Treaty of Amiens proved to be of short duration. Napoleon was angered, not unnaturally, by the refusal of England to evacuate Malta. England was ready to restore the island to its legitimate owners, but only when they could guarantee its security from Napoleon, against whom she had her own grievances. Among many others were the continued intrigues of Napoleon in Egypt and the Levant. In the autumn of 1802 he sent a Colonel Sebastiani on a commercial mission to the Near East. Sebastiani, who hardly disguised the political and military purpose of his journey, was, according to the French authorities, received with boundless enthusiasm in Tripoli, Alexandria, Cairo, and not less when he passed on to Acre, Smyrna, and the Ionian Isles.[1] On his return to France he presented a Report, which was published in the *Moniteur Officiel* for January 30, 1803. The publication gave deep offence in England, and well it might, for it discussed with complete frankness the military situation in the Near East ; it declared that, in view of the hostility between the Turks

[1] e. g. Driault, *op. cit.*, p. 82, but *contra*, see Fournier (*Napoléon*, i. 316), who declares, on the authority of Sebastiani himself, that the French mission, so far from being welcomed in Egypt, had been obliged to seek shelter from the mob in Cairo.

and the Mamlukes and the latter's sympathy with France, 6,000 French troops would suffice for the reconquest of Egypt, and it affirmed that the Ionian Isles only awaited a favourable moment to declare for France.

Sebastiani's *Report* had, before publication, been largely retouched, if not fundamentally altered, by Napoleon, and was published with the express purpose of goading England into a declaration of war. It succeeded, and in May, 1803, war was declared. Russia also, alarmed by the Sebastiani Report, strengthened her garrison in Corfu. Austria, moreover, discovered that Napoleon was again intriguing in the Morea, with the Senate of the little Republic of Ragusa, and with the Bishop of Montenegro, who had consented to hand over the Gulf of Cattaro to France.

Russia and the Balkans

The young Tsar Alexander, who, on the assassination of his father, had succeeded to the throne in 1801, was disposed to resort to the policy of the Empress Catherine in regard to Turkey. According to the Memories of Prince Adam Czartoryski, now Foreign Minister of Russia, 'the European territories of Turkey were to be divided into small States united among themselves into a federation, over which the Tsar would exercise a commanding influence. Should Austria's assent be necessary she was to be appeased by the acquisition of Turkish Croatia, part of Bosnia, and Wallachia, Belgrade, and Ragusa. Russia would have Moldavia, Cattaro, Corfu, and above all Constantinople and the Dardanelles.' [1]

Russia and Austria both joined the fresh coalition formed by Pitt in 1805, but their combined armies suffered a terrible reverse at Napoleon's hands at Austerlitz (December 2, 1805),

[1] Cited by Fournier, *op. cit.*, i. 347.

and before the close of the year Austria was compelled to conclude peace at Pressburg. The terms of the treaty were disastrous both to her pride and her territorial position. Napoleon took his reward in the Adriatic : Venetia, Istria (except the town of Trieste), and Dalmatia being annexed to the new kingdom of Italy. Talleyrand shrewdly advised the emperor to compensate Austria with the Danubian principalities and northern Bulgaria, and so interpose a stout barrier between Russia and Constantinople, and by that means turn the ambitions of Russia towards Asia, where she must needs come into collision with Great Britain. This suggestion anticipated by nearly a century the policy of Bismarck, but it is far from certain that Austria would have accepted the offer, even could Napoleon have been induced to make it.[1]

Austerlitz put Austria out of play for four years. But Frederick William III of Prussia chose this singularly unpropitious moment for breaking the neutrality which for ten shameful years Prussia had maintained. Prussia, therefore, was crushed at Jena and Auerstädt, and Napoleon occupied Berlin. Russia, however, still kept the field, while England had strengthened her command of the sea by the great victory off Cape Trafalgar.

Nelson's victory compelled Napoleon to play his last card—the continental blockade. England was still the enemy ; she could not be reached by an army from Boulogne ; she had proved herself irresistible at sea. What remained ? She must be brought to her knees by the destruction of her commerce. To this end every nation on the European Continent must be combined into his ' system ', and the whole of the coast from Archangel to the Crimea must be hermetically sealed against English shipping and English trade. Such was

[1] Lefebvre, *Hist. des Cabinets de l'Europe*, ii. 235, and Vandal, *Napoléon et Alexandre*, i. p. 9.

the meaning of the decree issued in November, 1806, by Napoleon from Berlin.

A month later the intrigues of Napoleon at Constantinople issued (December, 1806) in a declaration of war by the Porte upon England and Russia.

After the conclusion of the Treaty of Pressburg the place of the Ottoman Empire in the general scheme of Napoleonic policy becomes increasingly apparent. The annexations in the Adriatic were an essential part of a deliberate plan. ' The object of my policy ', he wrote in May, 1806, ' is a triple alliance between myself, the Porte, and Persia, indirectly aimed at Russia. The constant study of my ambassador should be to fling defiance at Russia. We must close the Bosphorus to the Russians.' [1]

The closing of the straits was, indeed, of high consequence to Napoleon's ambitions in the Adriatic, for Russia had taken advantage of her alliance with Turkey to send large Russian reinforcements to the Ionian Isles. She had also, to the indignation of the Turk and the chagrin of Napoleon, utilized the adjacent mainland of Albania as a recruiting ground for her garrison in the islands.

Russia and the Principalities

In the summer of 1806 Sebastiani was sent by Napoleon as ambassador extraordinary to Constantinople, charged with the special task of effecting a breach between Turkey on the one hand and Russia and Great Britain on the other. A hint of Russian intrigues in the principalities sufficed to persuade Sultan Selim, in direct violation of his treaty engagements with the Tsar, to depose the hospodars of Moldavia and Wallachia, Prince Morouzi and Prince Hypsilanti. To this insult the Tsar promptly responded by sending 35,000 men

[1] To Eugène Beauharnais, ap. Sorel, *op. cit.*, vii. 53–4.

across the Pruth, and before the end of the year the Russian army was in undisputed occupation of the principalities. The Sultan thereupon declared war on Russia. An English fleet under Admiral Duckworth then forced the Dardanelles, destroyed a Turkish squadron in the Sea of Marmora, and threatened Constantinople. The defences of the city were in a ruinous condition, and had an attack been delivered forthwith Constantinople would almost certainly have fallen. But Duckworth wasted precious days in negotiation; Constantinople was rapidly put into a state of defence by French engineers; the English fleet was compelled to withdraw from the Sea of Marmora, and, after sustaining considerable losses, repassed the Dardanelles on March 3, 1807.

To Napoleon Constantinople was not the term but the starting-point of adventure. He looked beyond Constantinople to Persia, and beyond Persia to the ultimate goal of India. The destruction of British Power in the Far East was fast becoming an obsession with the emperor.

A few weeks later General Mackenzie Fraser landed a force in Egypt and took Alexandria. But Egypt was now in the capable hands of Mehemet Ali, the Albanian adventurer, destined to play so prominent a part in later developments of the Eastern Question. The Sultan Selim had sent Mehemet Ali at the head of a force of Albanians to Egypt in order to bring back the Mamlukes to their allegiance. The latter consequently inclined towards the English invaders, but Mehemet Ali had the situation well in hand, and Fraser's intervention completely failed of its purpose.

Meanwhile, Napoleon was revolving larger schemes upon a more extended field. To him an alliance with Turkey was only a step towards Asiatic conquest. The call of the Far East was to a man of Napoleon's temperament irresistible. India, as he subsequently confessed, was now occupying more and more of his thoughts. England, as an insular State, might be impregnable, but her dominion in the Far East was continental. On the Continent there was nothing which a French army could not reach, and anything which a French army could reach it could conquer. But between Europe and India lay Persia. To Persia, therefore, he first turned his attention.

Ever since the Tsarina Catherine had conquered the Caucasus there had been intermittent war between Russia and Persia. The Shah was, therefore, only too ready to receive the advances of Napoleon. During the year 1806 no less than three French agents were sent to Teheran. 'Persia', wrote the emperor to Sebastiani, ' must be roused, and her forces directed against Georgia. Induce the Porte to order the Pasha of Erzeroum to march against this province with all his troops.' In April, 1807, a Persian envoy met the emperor in Poland, and the Treaty of Finkenstein was concluded. Napoleon promised to supply guns and gunners to the Shah, and to compel Russia to evacuate Georgia. The Shah on his part was to adhere to the continental system, to break off his relations with Great Britain, confiscate all British goods, exclude British shipping from his ports, stir up the Afghans against British India, afford free passage to a French army through Persia, and himself join in the attack against British Power in Asia.[1]

§ 2. *The Ottoman Empire and the Resurrection of Serbia*

For all these adventures, however, Constantinople was the starting-point. For the moment, therefore, the stability of the Ottoman Empire was a matter of considerable concern to Napoleon. How far could he depend upon it ?

The Sultan, Selim III (1789–1807), who, as we have seen,

[1] Fournier, *op. cit.*, i. 449; Driault, *La Politique orientale de Napoléon* (*passim*).

had come to the throne in the midst of the war with Russia and Austria, had made a real effort to carry out much needed reforms in his distracted empire. His success had not been equal to his zeal, and the situation had now become so grave that the Sultan could give little effective aid to his exacting ally. In Egypt the Mamlukes virtually repudiated the authority of their nominal sovereign, and were held in check only by the dangerous device of setting a poacher to watch the game. In Syria, Djezzar Pasha exercised his tyranny in virtual independence of the Sultan. The Wahhabites had conquered the Holy cities of Mecca and Medina in 1802 and were now masters of the whole of Arabia. Nearer home, the Suliotes and other tribes in northern Greece and Epirus were bound by the loosest of ties to Constantinople; Ali, Pasha of Janina, had carved out for himself an independent chieftainship in Albania; the Montenegrins had wrung from the Sultan an acknowledgement of the independence which they had always in practice enjoyed; while on the Danube, Passwan Oglou, one of the many Bosnian nobles who had accepted Mohammedanism, was already master of Widdin, Sofia, Nikopolis, and Plevna, and was dreaming of a revival of the Bulgarian Tsardom with Constantinople itself as his capital.

Most threatening of all was the position of affairs in Serbia. There, as in other provinces of the empire, the central government of Constantinople had ceased long since to exercise any real control over its nominal subordinates. The government of Serbia was in the hands of the Janissaries of Belgrade, who maintained their authority alike over the Moslem Spahis, or feudal landowners, and over the native peasantry by methods of revolting cruelty and tyranny.

Among the peasantry, however, the traditions of past greatness and independence, nurtured on popular ballads and encouraged by the Orthodox clergy, had somehow managed to survive through the long centuries of Ottoman oppression. The frequent change of masters, resulting from the wars of the eighteenth century, had tended to revive a spirit of hopefulness among the native Slavs. Whatever change war might bring to them could hardly be for the worse. At one time they looked with some expectation to Vienna. They were now turning, less unwarrantably, to their brothers in blood and creed, who were the subjects of the Russian Tsar.

Yet, in truth, the Serbians could count upon little effective assistance from any external Power. Fortunately, perhaps, they were compelled, by their geographical situation, to rely entirely upon themselves. Cut off, first by Venice and afterwards by Austria, from access to the Adriatic, they could obtain no help from the maritime Powers. Between themselves and their potential allies in Russia there interposed the Danubian principalities. Nor had they, like the Bosnians and Roumanians, any indigenous nobility to which they could look for leadership. Salvation, therefore, must come, if at all, from the peasantry. In the wars of the eighteenth century that peasantry had learnt to fight ; and when, in 1791, Serbia was restored to the Porte, the agents of the Sultan were quick to note the change in their demeanour. ' Neighbours, what have you made of our rayahs ? ' asked a Turkish Pasha of an Austrian official, when a regiment of native Serbs paraded before him. On the restoration of Turkish authority the Serbian troops were disbanded, but the lessons which the peasants had learned were not forgotten.[1]

The fact was proved in 1804. The Serbian rising of that year marks an epoch of incomparable significance in the history of the Eastern Question. For four hundred years the spirit of Slav nationality had been completely crushed under the heel of the Ottomans. That it had not been eradicated events

[1] Ranke, *Serbia*, p. 84.

were soon to prove. But its continued existence was little suspected. Still it was something that the Serbian peasants had learnt to fight. Napoleon had taught the same invaluable lesson to his Italian subjects. But the Serbians had not yet learnt to fight for an idea. The seed of the new idea came from the Revolution in France. It fell into the fertile soil of the Balkans : it fructified in the insurrection of 1804.

It is one of the paradoxes of which the recent history of the Near East is compact that this insurrection should have been directed in the first instance not against the Turkish Government, but against its rebellious servants the Janissaries of Belgrade. The tyranny of the latter was as intolerable to the Serbians as was their disloyalty to the Sultan and his officials. Selim accordingly determined to dislodge them.

Expelled from Belgrade the rebels joined forces with Passwan Oglou, and together they invaded Serbia. Responding to the appeal of the Turkish Pasha of Belgrade, the Serbians rose in defence of their country and repelled the invasion. Thereupon the Janissaries of Constantinople and the Moslem hierarchy compelled Sultan Selim to restore the Janissaries at Belgrade, and Serbia was virtually reoccupied by official Mohammedanism and given over to a reign of terror. The Sultan vainly endeavouring to restrain his agents only added fuel to the flames of vengeance by an obscure hint that unless they mended their ways ' soldiers should come among them of other nations and of another creed '. The Janissaries determined that the alien soldiers should not be Slavs.

To avert literal extermination the Serbs organized what was in truth the first national rising in the modern history of the Balkans, and elected as their Commander-in-Chief a peasant pig-merchant, George Petrovitch, or Kara (Black) George.

Kara George had served in the Serbian Volunteer Corps in the Austrian war of 1788–91, and now led the national insurrection with conspicuous courage and skill. So great was the success of the peasant army that in a very brief space of time the Janissaries were confined to Belgrade, and a few other fortresses. Unofficial Mohammedanism went to the assistance of the Janissaries, but the Pasha of Bosnia, acting upon instructions from Constantinople, put himself at the head of the Serbian nationalists. The strange combination of official Turk and Serb peasant again proved irresistible, and in the event the power of the Janissaries was annihilated.

Official Turkey had now to deal with its formidable allies. The latter refused to be disarmed, and in August, 1804, applied for help to Russia. The Tsar was sympathetic, but advised the Serbians to apply for redress, in the first instance, to their own sovereign. In 1805, accordingly, a mission was sent by the Serbians to Constantinople to demand that, in view of their recent exertions and sufferings, all arrears of tribute and taxes should be remitted, and that all the strong places in their land should be garrisoned by native troops.

Almost simultaneously the Sultan was confronted by a demand from Russia, now on the eve of war with France, that the Porte should enter into a strict offensive and defensive alliance with Russia, and that all its subjects professing the Orthodox faith should be placed under the formal protection of the Tsar.

Threatened on one side by the insurgent Janissaries, on a second by the Serbian *rayahs*, on a third by Russia, Sultan Selim found himself involved in the most serious crisis of a troublesome reign. He dealt with it in characteristic fashion by temporizing with the Russian envoy, while he attempted to crush the Serbians.

The Serbian nationalists, magnificently led by Kara George, defended themselves with energy against the Sultan's troops, and in the brilliant campaign of 1806 practically achieved their independence, without any external assistance whatsoever. At the end of the same year Turkey, as we have seen, was forced by Napoleon into war with Russia, and the Serbian forces united with those of Russia on the Danube ; in May, 1807, Sultan Selim was deposed by a palace revolution, and in July, 1808, both he and his successor, Mustapha IV, were killed, and there succeeded to the throne the only surviving male descendant of Othman, and one of the greatest of his successors, the Sultan known to history as Mahmud II.

The sequel of the Serbian insurrection may be briefly told. Fighting came to an end after the conclusion of the Treaty of Tilsit, and as soon as they ceased fighting the Turks, the Serbs began to fight each other. The Turks offered to Serbia an administration similar to that of the Danubian principalities.

The sudden death of Milan Obrenović, the leader of the Russophils, gave an occasion for the usual insinuations of foul play against Kara George, who led the Nationalists. This insinuation naturally intensified the bitterness between the two parties. Nor was this feeling diminished when the Pro-Russians procured the rejection of the Sultan's terms under which Serbia would have been placed on the same footing as the Danubian principalities. The terms procured at Bucharest (1812) were, as we shall see, decidedly less favourable.[1]

Nor were they observed. In 1813 the Turks, relieved from all fears of foreign intervention, reconquered the country, and administered it with such brutality that in 1815 a fresh insurrection broke out. Its leader, Milosh Obrenović, the half-brother of Milan, conducted it with a mixture of courage and craft to a successful issue. In 1817, however, Kara George, who had been interned in Hungary whither he had fled after the reconquest of his country, returned to Serbia. His presence was as unwelcome to Obrenovitch as it was to the Turks.

[1] *Infra*, p. 189.

They combined to procure his assassination (July 26, 1817), and his head was sent by Obrenović as a trophy to Constantinople. Such was the real beginning of the bitter blood-feud between the two dynasties, which have divided the allegiance of the Serbian people from that day until the consummation of the tragedy of 1903.

In November, 1817, a National Assembly was held at Belgrade, and, with the sulky assent of the Turks, Obrenović was elected hereditary prince of Serbia. A limited amount of local government was at the same time conceded to the province, though the sovereignty of the Sultan remained nominally unimpaired.

Treaty of Akerman (1826)

The Greek war of independence led to a further concession. By the convention of Akerman, concluded between Russia and the Porte in 1826, the latter recognized a Russian protectorate over Serbia, and at the same time conceded to the Serbians almost complete autonomy.

The terms agreed upon in 1826 were confirmed by the Treaty of Adrianople (1829), and by 1830 Serbia's autonomy was definitely achieved. Milosh Obrenović was recognized by the Porte as hereditary prince of a district (now the northern part of the modern kingdom) bounded by the rivers Dvina, Save, Danube, and Timok. No Turk was to be permitted to live in the principality, except in one or other of eight fortified towns which were still to be garrisoned by the Turks. The Serbs were to enjoy complete local autonomy, though remaining under the suzerainty of the Sultan to whom they were to continue to pay tribute. They were to be allowed to erect churches and schools, to trade freely, and to print books in the vernacular. In a word, but for the Turkish garrisons, they were to be free to work out their own salvation in their own way.

§ 3. *Napoleon and Alexander*

After this prolonged parenthesis it is time to resume the main thread of the story with which this chapter is concerned.

We left Napoleon in Poland conducting the war against Russia and Prussia, but finding time, in the midst of an arduous campaign, for the negotiation of a treaty which had as its ultimate object the annihilation of British power in India (April, 1807). The Treaty of Finkenstein was, indeed, no sooner signed than Napoleon dispatched to Teheran General Gardane to devise a detailed scheme for the invasion of India. But though primarily directed against Great Britain, the Franco-Persian alliance would serve if required against Russia as well.

From that point of view it proved to be otiose. On June 14 Napoleon brought the campaign in East Prussia to an end by a decisive victory over the Russians at Friedland (June 14, 1807). After that battle the Tsar applied for an armistice, which was readily granted, for Napoleon had already decided upon a *volte-face*. The real enemy was not Russia nor even Prussia. Prussia must incidentally be annihilated, but if Alexander was prepared to abandon his alliance with England, and to join forces with France, the two emperors might divide the world between them.

The Tsar was not indisposed to listen to the tempter; but before the conspirators met at Tilsit to arrange terms, the Prussian minister Hardenberg laid before the two emperors a scheme by which the attention of Napoleon might be diverted from the annihilation of his enemy Prussia to the spoliation of his ally, the Ottoman Sultan.

According to Hardenberg's scheme Russia was to get Wallachia, Moldavia, Bulgaria, and Roumelia, together with the city of Constantinople, the Bosphorus, and the Dardanelles; France was to have Greece and the islands of the Archipelago;

Austria to acquire Bosnia and Serbia ; a reconstituted Poland might go to the King of Saxony, who should in turn cede his own kingdom to Prussia. The idea was highly creditable alike to the courage and to the ingenuity of the Prussian statesman, and his plan had the merit of completeness. But Napoleon was in no mood to negotiate, on this or any other basis, with a defeated and despised foe. If Prussia were permitted to survive at all it must be on terms dictated by the conqueror.

In order to ensure complete secrecy the two emperors met in a floating pavilion which was moored in mid-stream in the Niemen. With most of the detailed questions discussed between them this narrative is not concerned ; enough to note that the emperors decreed that Prussia should be dismembered—but for the scruples of the Tsar it would have been completely wiped out ; the British Empire must be annihilated. The latter consummation was to be attained in two ways : by the ruin of English commerce through the enforcement of the continental blockade, and by an attack upon India. Napoleon had come to the conclusion that on the whole it was easier for him to transport an army from Paris to Delhi than from Boulogne to Folkestone. Never, in our whole history, has the significance of irresistible sea-power been more amply vindicated or more brilliantly illustrated. But the latter part of the scheme was still locked in the breast of Napoleon. Enough for the moment that an avaricious nation of shopkeepers should be compelled to concede the ' freedom of the seas ', and to share their commercial gains with equally deserving but less favoured peoples. For the annihilation of her two allies, Russia was to find her compensation in the acquisition of Finland and the partition of the Ottoman Empire.

According to the secret articles of the Treaty of Tilsit France was to have the Bocche di Cattaro, and it was further stipulated that, failing the conclusion of a peace between

Russia and the Porte within three months, Napoleon would join the Tsar in expelling the Turks from the whole of their European dominions except the city of Constantinople and the province of Roumelia.[1] How the provinces of European Turkey were to be apportioned was not specified, though it was taken for granted that Russia would retain Moldavia and Wallachia. But the Danubian principalities, even if their cession were procured by Napoleon—a large assumption—were an inadequate recompense for the desertion of allies ; and the Tsar intimated to Napoleon that he would not ultimately be satisfied with anything short of the possession of Constantinople. For Constantinople, as Alexander urged with unanswerable logic, was the ' key of his house '. The suggestion is said to have provoked from Napoleon an angry retort : ' Constantinople ! never ; that would mean the empire of the world.' The truth of the matter is that at Tilsit, as elsewhere, Napoleon had only one object in view : to engage Europe at large in his contest *à outrance* against Great Britain.

As for the Near East Napoleon's policy was palpably opportunist. The gradual publication of memoirs and documents has made it abundantly clear that Napoleon was merely amusing Alexander with hopes of rich spoils in South-Eastern Europe. For himself he had by no means made up his mind whether he would plump for the integrity of the Ottoman Empire or for its annihilation. His own preference was in favour of the former policy, a policy which, as we have seen, accorded with the unbroken traditions of monarchical France.[2] The latter accorded more precisely with the views of his ally, and Alexander was an important asset in his diplomatic balance-

---

[1] See A. Vandal, *Napoléon et Alexander Ier*, where the full text of the Treaty of Tilsit will be found in the Appendix to vol. i.

[2] Cf. Sorel, *L'Europe et la Révolution française*, vol. i, *passim*, and Bourgeois, *Manuel de la Politique étrangère*, vol. i.

sheet. For the English Foreign Office had lately passed into the vigorous hands of Canning, and English policy showed signs of unwonted promptitude and energy. Hardly was the ink dry on the Tilsit Treaty when the whole conspiracy was countermined by Great Britain's seizure of the Danish fleet and her prompt succour to Portugal and Spain. More than ever Napoleon was in need of his Russian ally. Grandiose schemes of policy in the East must therefore be dangled before the eyes of the Tsar. There was talk of a joint attack, French, Austrian, and Russian, upon Constantinople, which was to be the base of an expedition to India. The Tsar was prudent enough to wish to make sure of Constantinople before going further : the Ottoman Empire must first be disposed of : France might have Bosnia, Albania, and Greece ; Austria's share was to be Serbia and Roumelia, with possession of Salonica as a strategical and commercial base on the Aegean ; Russia was to have the Danubian principalities, Bulgaria, and Constantinople, with command of the Straits.

Napoleon and Alexander

Caulaincourt, who succeeded Savary as French ambassador at St. Petersburg in December, 1807, was entrusted by Napoleon with these delicate and protracted negotiations. He insisted that if Russia took Constantinople France must have the Dardanelles, but Alexander justly observed that Constantinople was important to Russia, only so far as it would give access to the Mediterranean. France was welcome to Egypt and Syria, but the key to the Straits must be in Russia's keeping.[1]

The whole of the negotiations between the Tilsit conspirators are of singular interest, both in themselves and in relation to the offer subsequently made by the Tsar Nicholas to Great Britain.[2] They are, moreover, strongly confirmatory

[1] Vandal, *op. cit.*, Appendix to vol. i.   [2] *Infra*, chap. x.

of the conclusion which M. Serge Goriainow, one of the most
eminent of Russian publicists, has deliberately reached : 'Pour
la Russie toute la fameuse question d'Orient se résume dans ces
mots : de quelle autorité dépendent les détroits du Bosphore
et des Dardanelles ; qui en est le détenteur.'[1]

But while the eyes of Russia were fixed upon the Near East
Napoleon preferred to avoid inconvenient details by pointing
to the rich prize which awaited bold enterprise in the further
East : Constantinople was the goal of the Tsar ; Napoleon's
supreme object was the humiliation of England.

Meanwhile, little came of the grandiloquent phrases and far-
reaching schemes with which the two emperors had amused
each other at Tilsit. Russia remained in occupation of the
principalities ; Napoleon resumed military control over the
Ionian Isles, where the joint rule of Russia and Turkey had
proved exceedingly unpopular. To the occupation of Corfu
in particular Napoleon attached immense importance : 'The
greatest misfortune that could happen to me ', he said, ' would
be the loss of Corfu.' Corfu he did manage to retain until
his abdication in 1814, but all the rest of the islands were
captured between 1809 and 1814 by the British fleet. During
those years Great Britain also occupied most of the islands off
the Dalmatian coast, and Lissa proved very valuable to her as
a naval base.

The two emperors met again at Erfurt in October, 1808.
Napoleon's reception of his ally lacked nothing of pomp and
magnificence ; but the relations between the august allies were
perceptibly cooler. The stern realities of the Peninsular campaign were already imparting more sober hues to Napoleon's
oriental dreams—all the larger schemes of partition were
consequently put aside. The Danubian principalities were,
however, guaranteed to the Tsar, who refused to evacuate

[1] *Le Bosphore et les Dardanelles*, p. 1.

them at the request of the Sultan. Accordingly, war was resumed between Russia and Turkey in 1809, and Russia, though by no means uniformly successful, took Silistria and other important fortresses from the Turks.

Relations between the Tsar and the Emperor of the French were, however, for reasons into which it is unnecessary to enter here,[1] growing more strained every day. Turkey, therefore, became an increasingly important pawn in the diplomatic game. Russia made repeated efforts in 1811 to conclude peace with Turkey on the basis of the cession of the principalities. But in vain. The accession of Sultan Mahmud II had infused a new vigour and decision into the counsels of the Porte. Napoleon then made a desperate effort to secure the alliance of the Sultan. If Turkey would join France and protect Napoleon's right flank in the projected advance against Russia, not only should the Danubian principalities be definitely and finally secured to her, but she should recover the Crimea, Tartary, and all the losses of the last half century. It is not wonderful that the Sultan, besieged by suitors for his favour, should have been able to perceive the cynical effrontery of these overtures, and should have firmly rejected them. The more firmly, perhaps, because England had threatened to force the Dardanelles and burn Constantinople if they were accepted. As a fact, however, Napoleon was too late. Sultan Mahmud had already come to terms with Alexander, and on May 28, 1812, the definitive treaty of peace was signed at Bucharest.

Previous treaties were specifically confirmed, but Russia obtained Bessarabia ; her boundary was ' henceforward to be the Pruth, to its entrance into the Danube, and, from that point, the left bank of the Danube down to its entrance into the Black Sea by the Kilia mouth '. The great islands were

[1] They will be found briefly summarized in the present writer's *Modern Europe*, chap. x.

to be left vacant. The Treaties of Kainardji and Jassy, in reference to the better government of the principalities, were to be duly observed, and for the first time the liberties of Serbia were made the subject of treaty obligations between Russia and Turkey.

Article VIII of the Treaty of Bucharest begins with the naïve recital that although 'it was impossible to doubt that the Porte, in accordance with its principles, will show gentleness and magnanimity towards the Serbians, as a people long subject and tributary to it', yet it seemed just 'in consideration of the share which the Serbians have taken in the war, to make a solemn agreement for their safety'. The Porte accordingly undertook, while continuing to garrison the fortresses, to allow the Serbians 'such liberties as are enjoyed by the islands of the Archipelago; and, as a token of its generosity, will leave to them the administration of their internal affairs'.[1] The Serbians, it may be added, considered these terms as vague and unsatisfactory, and resented what they regarded as a base desertion at the hands of their powerful protector, the Tsar.[2]

In the stirring and pregnant events of the next three years the problem of the Near East had no place. The disastrous expedition to Moscow, the war of German Liberation, the Hundred Days—none of these was concerned with the Orient. Yet the settlement effected at Vienna had an important influence upon the future evolution of the Eastern Question.

The many schemes and violent perturbations of the Napoleonic period left the Ottoman Empire, in a territorial sense, almost unscathed. Bessarabia had, indeed, been alienated to Russia, but this represented a loss not so much to the Turkey

---

[1] Holland, *op. cit.*, pp. 16, 17.

[2] Cf. Cunibert, *Essai historique sur les Révolutions et l'Indépendance de la Serbie*, cited by Creasy, *op. cit.*, p. 491.

of the present as to the Roumania of the future. For the rest, it was at the expense of Italy, or rather of Venice, that the neighbours of the Turk were enriched.

Austria recovered Trieste, Gradisca, and Gorizia, together with Istria, Carniola, and Carinthia, which took their place in the composite empire of the Habsburgs as the kingdom of Illyria. She acquired also Venetian Dalmatia and the ancient Slav republic of Ragusa, the islands appurtenant thereto, and the Bocche di Cattaro. The Ionian Isles were formed into 'The United States of the Ionian Islands, under the protectorate of Great Britain'. Had Great Britain known the things which belong unto her peace, she would never voluntarily have relaxed her hold upon islands, the strategical value of which was so clearly recognized by Napoleon. She also retained Malta, which greatly strengthened her naval hold upon the Mediterranean, and brought her, all unconscious, a step nearer to Egypt.

The net results of the wars, treaties, and negotiations of a quarter of a century appear disproportionately small. But it would be a fatal error to regard them as negligible.

The whole future of Austria, more particularly in relation to the Near East, was profoundly affected thereby. Crushed in the field again and again, Austria, nevertheless, emerged triumphant at the Peace. Her emperor had cleverly got rid of the troublesome appanage of the Netherlands, and in return had secured two compact and invaluable kingdoms in the south. King of Lombardo-Venetia, Lord of Trieste, King of Illyria, master of the ports of Venice, Trieste, Pola, and Fiume, not to mention the Dalmatian littoral, Ragusa, the Gulf of Cattaro, and the Adriatic archipelago, he found himself in a most commanding position as regards the Eastern Mediterranean and the Balkan Peninsula. On the other hand, his rival the Tsar was, save for the acquisition of Bessarabia, no nearer to Constantinople than he had been in 1792. The long war with Persia had, indeed, left the Tsar in possession of Georgia, Tiflis, and the coast of the Caspian up to the Araxes, and had greatly increased his influence at Teheran, but as regards the solution of the problem with which this work is concerned the advance of Russia was inconsiderable.

Infinitely the most important result of the period immediately under review was, however, one far too intangible to be registered in treaties or documents. Subsequent events make it abundantly clear that, whether as a direct consequence of the novel ideas disseminated by the French Revolution, whether in response to the principle of nationality so powerfully, if unconsciously, evoked by Napoleon, whether as a result of the general unrest, or from other causes too subtle for analysis, a new spirit had been awakened among the peoples of the Balkan Peninsula, so long inert and dumb beneath the yoke of the Ottoman Turk. It was stirring among the Latins of the Danubian principalities ; it was clearly manifested in the insurrection of Serbia ; above all, it was operating powerfully, though as yet silently, among the people destined, a few years later, to carve out of the European dominions of the Ottoman Sultan an independent commonwealth, and to add to the European polity a new sovereign State—the kingdom of the Hellenes.

With the making of the new State the next chapter will be concerned.

For further reference : Jonquière, *L'Expédition d'Égypte* ; A. Sorel, *Bonaparte et Hoche en* 1797 ; Driault, *La Question d'Orient, L'Europe et la Révolution française* ; Vandal, *Napoléon et Alexandre Ier* ; Fournier, *Life of Napoleon* ; Martens, *Recueil des traités de la Russie avec les Puissances étrangères* ; E. Driault, *La politique orientale de Napoléon* ; Tatistchef, *Alexandre Ier et Napoléon* ; H. W. V. Temperley, *History of Serbia* (1917) ; Brand, *Napoleon in Egypt.*

8

The Struggle for Hellenic Independence

'Did I possess their (the Athenians) command of language and their force of persuasion I should feel the highest satisfaction in employing them to incite our armies and our fleets to deliver Greece, the parent of eloquence, from the despotism of the Ottomans. But we ought besides to attempt what is I think of the greatest moment, to inflame the present Greeks with an ardent desire to emulate the virtue, the industry, the patience of their ancient progenitors.'—MILTON.

'It offers in detail a chequered picture of patriotism and corruption, desperate valour and weak irresolution, honour and treachery, resistance to the Turk and feud one with another. Its records are stained with many acts of cruelty. And yet who can doubt that it was on the whole a noble stroke, struck for freedom and for justice, by a people who, feeble in numbers and resources, were casting off the vile slough of servitude, who derived their strength from right, and whose worst acts were really in the main due to the masters, who had saddled them not only with a cruel, but with a most demoralizing, yoke?'—W. E. GLADSTONE, on the Greek War of Independence.

'As long as the literature and taste of the ancient Greeks continue to nurture scholars and inspire artists modern Greece must be an object of interest to cultivated minds.'—FINLAY.

'. . . England . . . sees that her true interests are inseparably connected with the independence of those nations who have shown themselves worthy of emancipation, and such is the case of Greece.'—LORD BYRON.

THE Emperor Napoleon was at once the heir of the French Revolution, and the product and agent of a powerful reaction against the principles which the Revolution had proclaimed. Of 'Liberty' he understood nothing; at 'Fraternity' he scoffed; 'Equality' he interpreted as 'equality of opportunity', the *carrière ouverte aux talents*. A chance was given not only to his subjects, but to two countries which he conquered, and to some which he did not.

The ferment of ideas caused by the outbreak of the Revolution, the political unrest which followed on the conquests of Napoleon, and on the perpetual rearrangements of the map of Europe, produced important consequences in the Near East. It is to the Balkan Peninsula that the political philosopher of to-day most frequently and most naturally turns for an illustration of the fashionable doctrine of nationality. Before 1789 the principle was unrecognized in those regions or elsewhere. In the great settlement of 1815 it was contemned or ignored. But in less than a decade after the Congress of Vienna it had inspired one of the most romantic episodes in the annals of the nineteenth century, and had presided over the birth of a new sovereign State.

The principle of nationality has defied definition and even analysis. Generally compounded of community of race, of language, of creed, of local contiguity, and historical tradition, it has not infrequently manifested itself in the absence or even the negation of many of these ingredients. But in the Hellenic revival, which by common consent constitutes one of the most conspicuous illustrations of the operation of the nationality principle, most of these elements may unquestionably be discerned.

In March, 1821, a bolt from the blue fell upon the diplomatic world. Many of the most illustrious members of that world happened, at the moment, to be in conference at Laibach, summoned thither by the Austrian minister, Prince Metternich, to discuss the best means of combating the spirit of revolution which had lately manifested itself in Spain, in Portugal, and in the Bourbon kingdom of the Two Sicilies.

In November, 1820, a formal protocol had been issued by the leading members of the Holy Alliance: Russia, Austria, and Prussia. The terms of this document are significant: ' States which have undergone a change of government due to revolution, the results of which threaten other States, *ipso facto* cease to be members of the European Alliance, and remain excluded from it until their situation gives guarantees for legal order and stability. . . . If, owing to such alterations, immediate danger threatens other States the Powers bind themselves to bring back the guilty State into the bosom of the great alliance.' To this protocol, Louis XVIII of France, in general terms, assented, but Lord Castlereagh warmly insisted that the principle on which the allies proposed to act was ' in direct repugnance to the fundamental laws of the United Kingdom '. Still stronger was his protest when the allies commissioned Austria to restore, by force of arms, Bourbon absolutism in Naples. ' We could neither share in nor approve, though we might not be called upon to resist, the intervention of one ally to put down internal disturbances in the dominions of another.' Castlereagh's protest, though consolatory to English liberalism, was quite ineffective as a restraint upon the Holy Allies.

Most disquieting, however, was the news which in the spring of 1821 reached the sovereigns and ministers in conference at Laibach. They learnt with alarm, that Prince Alexander Hypsilanti, the son of a Phanariote Greek, Hospodar successively of Moldavia and Wallachia, had placed himself at the head of an insurrectionary movement in Moldavia, and had unfurled the flag of Greek independence.

The *locale* for the initial rising was singularly ill chosen, yet not without intelligible reasons. The malcontent Greeks had, as we have seen, received frequent encouragement from St. Petersburg in the latter part of the eighteenth century. The Tsar Alexander was known to be a man of enlightened views, a firm believer in the principle of nationality, and pledged, in his own words, ' to restore to each nation the full and entire enjoyment of its rights and of its institutions '. So long ago as 1804 he had foreseen that the weakness of the

Ottoman Empire, ' the anarchy of its régime and the growing discontent of its Christian subjects ', must open a new phase in the history of the Eastern Question.[1] The Tsar's foreign minister, Count Giovanni Antonio Capo d'Istria, was by birth a Greek and a member of the *Philike Hetaireia*. Hypsilanti, the chosen leader of the insurrection, was his aide-de-camp. What more natural than that the Greeks should have looked for assistance to Russia, or that in order to obtain it the more effectually the initial rising should have been planned to take place in Moldavia ?

Nevertheless, the decision was a blunder. The Roumanians detested the Phanariote Greeks, whom they regarded as intrusive aliens and oppressors, and they neither felt nor displayed any enthusiasm for the Hellenic cause. Nor did it secure the anticipated assistance of the Tsar Alexander. Hypsilanti, after crossing the Pruth on March 6, issued a proclamation calling upon the people to rise against Ottoman tyranny, and declaring that his adventure was sanctioned and supported by ' a Great Power '.

The statement was entirely unwarranted. The Tsar, from the first, frowned sternly upon Hypsilanti's enterprise. His political confessor was now Prince Metternich ; under Metternich's influence Alexander, rapidly discarding the slough of liberalism, was easily persuaded that the rising of the Phanariote Greeks supplied only one more manifestation of the dangerous spirit which had already shown itself at Madrid, Lisbon, and Naples—the spirit which the Holy Allies were pledged to suppress.

Any doubts which might have existed as to the attitude of the Tsar were promptly dissipated. He issued a proclamation which disavowed all sympathy with Hypsilanti, ordered him

[1] Cf. Alexander's instructions to Novosiltsov (1804), ap. Phillips, *Confederation of Europe*, p. 35.

and his companions to repair to Russia immediately, and bade the rebels return at once to their allegiance to their legitimate ruler, the Sultan, as the only means of escaping the punishment which the Tsar would inflict upon all who persisted in aiding the revolt.

The firm attitude of Russia was fatal to the success of the rising in the Principalities. Hypsilanti himself betrayed a mixture of vanity, brutality, and incompetence; the Turks occupied Bucharest in force, and on June 19, 1821, inflicted a decisive defeat upon his forces at Dragashan, in Wallachia. Hypsilanti escaped into Hungary, where until 1827 he was, by Metternich's orders, imprisoned. He died a year later. Four days after the battle of Dragashan the Turks entered Jassy, and shortly afterwards the remnant of Hypsilanti's force was overwhelmed after a brief but heroic resistance at Skaleni.

The Moldavian rising was a mere flash in the pan: an enterprise unwisely conceived and unskilfully executed. Far otherwise was the movement in the Greek islands and in the Morea.

Causes of the Greek Insurrection

The outbreak has been described as a ' bolt from the blue '. So it appeared to the Holy Allies. In reality the motive forces which were behind it had been operating for a long time, and if any one had given serious heed to the Greeks a national revival among them might have been foreseen.

But the racial movement was obscured beneath an ecclesiastical designation. To the Turks the social and political differentia has always been not race but religion. Every one who was not a Moslem, unless he were an Armenian or a Jew, was a Greek. ' After the Ottoman conquest ', as Sir Charles Eliot has justly observed, ' the Greeks were not a local population, but a superior class of Christians forming a counterpart to the Turks. South-Eastern Europe was ruled by the Turks; but until this century its religion, education, commerce, and finance were in the hands of Greeks.' [1] Consequently, although the Greek Empire was annihilated and the Greek nation was submerged, the Greek population survived, and a large number of individual Greeks rose to positions of great influence under the Ottoman Empire.

The truth is, and too much emphasis can hardly be laid upon it, that the Turk is a great fighter, but not a great administrator : the dull details of routine government he has always preferred to leave in the hands of the ' inferior ' races. This fact must not be ignored when we seek the causes of the national revival among the Greeks and other Balkan peoples in the nineteenth century.

Largely as a result of this indifference the Greeks were permitted to enjoy, in practice if not in theory, a considerable amount of local autonomy. The unit of administration has, ever since classical days, been small ; and in the village communities of the interior and the commercial towns on the sea-board the Greeks, throughout the long centuries of Ottoman rule, preserved the memory, and to some extent retained the practice, of self-government. More particularly was this the case in the Greek islands of the Adriatic and the Aegean. These islands were inhabited by a race of shrewd traders and skilful mariners, and in them the national movement found its most devoted and most capable adherents.

The Turkish navy had always been manned to a large extent by Greeks, and most of the commerce of the empire was in the same hands. Among the Greeks the joint-stock principle had developed with great rapidity in the eighteenth century, and a large number of trading companies had been formed. To this development a powerful stimulus was given

[1] *Op. cit.*, p. 273.

by the victories of the Empress Catherine II, and the commercial advantages consequently conceded to Russia by the Porte. The provisions of the Treaty of Kainardji were supplemented in 1783 by a commercial convention under which the Greeks obtained the specific privilege of trading under the Russian flag. When, later on, the continental blockade and the British Orders in Council drove all shipping, save that of Turkey, from the sea, the Greeks were glad enough to resume the Turkish flag; and under the one flag or the other they not only amassed great fortunes, but practised the art of seamanship and cultivated the spirit of adventure.

Among the Greeks of the mainland the fighting spirit was maintained partly by the *Armatoli* and partly by the *Klephts*. The former were members of a local Christian *gendarmerie* officially recognized by the Turkish Pashas, and permitted to bear arms for the purpose of keeping in order their more unruly neighbours, and in particular the Klephts, from whose ranks, however, they were not infrequently recruited. The Klephts may fairly be described as brigands dignified by a tinge of political ambition. At their worst they were mere bands of robbers who periodically issued from their mountain fastnesses and preyed upon the more peaceable inhabitants. At their best they were outlaws of the Robin Hood type. In either case they habituated the people to the use of arms and maintained a spirit of rough independence among the Greek subjects of the Sultan.

From the opposite pole the Phanariote Greeks contributed to the same end. These Phanariotes have, as Sir Charles Eliot truly observes, 'fared ill at the hands of historians. They are detested by all whose sympathies lie with Slavs or Roumanians, and not overmuch loved by Philhellenes.'[1] Yet modern Greece owes to them a debt heavier than is generally

[1] *Op cit.*, p. 283.

acknowledged. Indolent in everything that does not pertain to war, the Turks, as we have previously noted, soon found it to their advantage to delegate the work of government to the Greeks of the capital, who were well-educated, supple, and shrewd. Employed, at first, mostly on humbler tasks, as clerks, interpreters, and so forth, the Greeks who generally inhabited that quarter of Constantinople assigned to the Patriarch and his satellites, known as the Phanar, rose rapidly to positions of great responsibility, and gradually came to fulfil the functions of a highly organized bureaucracy.

During the revival initiated by the Kiuprilis in the middle of the seventeenth century, a new office, the Dragoman of the Porte, was created in favour of a distinguished Phanariote, a Chiot named Panayoti; he was succeeded by a still more distinguished Greek, Alexander Mavrocordatos, with the result that the office which these men successively adorned became virtually a Ministry for Foreign Affairs. Henceforward, the foreign relations of the Ottoman Empire were mainly conducted by Greeks. Later on, a Dragoman of the Fleet or Secretary of the Admiralty was similarly appointed to assist the Capitan Pasha, a great official who was at once Lord High Admiral and Governor of the Archipelago. This second Dragoman, generally a Phanariote, was thus brought into close official relations with the intensely Greek communities in the Aegean islands.

Early in the eighteenth century the hospodarships of the Danubian principalities were, like other high offices, also entrusted to Greeks. These officials naturally secured the appointment of compatriots to the subordinate posts, and in this way the Greeks began to dominate the whole official hierarchy. That this hierarchy was inspired by any feelings of national self-consciousness it would be an affectation to suggest; still more that they maintained any close connexion, except as tax-gatherers, with their kinsmen in the Morea and the Archipelago. But although Gordon speaks of them derisively as ' a fictitious and servile noblesse ',[1] yet the large share of the Greeks in the actual administration was not without its influence upon the Hellenic revival.

Even more important was the position of the Orthodox Church. Nothing contributed more directly to the revival than the privileged relations between the Patriarch and the Sultan ; and, in another sphere, the singular devotion displayed, alike in a pastoral and a political capacity, by the lower clergy.

Reference has already been made to the policy adopted by the conqueror Mohammed II, and his successors, towards the Byzantine Church ; the result being that the Greek Patriarch of Constantinople was not only respected as the representative of the Orthodox Church, but was utilized by the Ottoman Sultans as the official channel of communication between them and the conquered Greeks. So much was this the case that Finlay describes the Patriarch as ' a kind of under-secretary to the grand vizier for the affairs of the orthodox Christians '.[2] From the point of view of Greek nationalism the peculiar position thus occupied by the Greek Patriarch may have had its drawbacks as well as its advantages. The continuous exertions of the parish priests were, on the other hand, wholly to the good. It was mainly owing to their devotion that through the long night of darkness there was maintained a flicker of the national spirit among the Greeks of the islands and the Morea. ' The parish priests ', writes Finlay, ' had an influence on the fate of Greece quite incommensurate with their social rank. The reverence of the peasantry for their Church was increased by the feeling that their own misfortunes were shared by the secular clergy.'

To the causes of revival enumerated above, many of them of

[1] *History of the Greek Revolution.*   [2] *Greek Revolution*, i. 21.

long standing, must be added two more which began to operate only towards the end of the eighteenth century. The first was a literary revival of the Greek language, and the second was the outbreak of the revolution in France. Spoken Greek began to diverge perceptibly from the literary language of classical days in the fourth century, but until the eighth classical Greek was generally understood. After the Slavonic inroads a large infusion of Slav words took place, and from the twelfth century onwards a literature sprang up in the vernacular. This vernacular was afterwards largely overlaid with Slav, Turkish, Albanian, and Italian words.[1]

The Venetian occupation (1684–1718) did nothing for the language, but a good deal for education, in the Morea, and may to some extent have contributed to the marked literary revival in the latter years of the eighteenth century. That revival was partly the product, and still more the cause, of the rising sense of national self-consciousness.

Two writers of the period call, in this connexion, for specific mention : Rhegas (1753–98) and Adamantios Koraes (1748–1833). The former, a Vlach, had studied in Paris, but his national songs sounded the first trumpet-note of the coming revolution. He was, however, more than a singer of songs. He was the founder of one of the secret societies out of which the *Hetaireia* subsequently developed, and he opened negotiations with other revolutionary spirits in various parts of the Balkans. Betrayed, when living in Hungary, to the Austrian police, he was handed over to the Turkish Government, and executed as a rebel at Belgrade in 1798. By the people, whose cause he served, he is commonly regarded as the proto-martyr of Greek independence. The great contribution made by Koraes to that cause consisted less in the political works of which he was the author than in his editions of the Greek

[1] *Modern Greece*, by R. C. Jebb, p. 46.

classics to which he prefixed prolegomena written in a purified and refined vernacular. These prolegomena served a twofold purpose : they provided a vehicle for thinly veiled political propaganda, and at the same time powerfully contributed to the movement for linguistic reform which, at the close of the eighteenth century, succeeded in purging the spoken language of the Greeks from many of the impurities with which it had been infected. The work of Koraes did more. ' It gave an impetus to the wave of Philhellenism which did so much to solve the practical question of the liberation of Greece from Ottoman misgovernment; and it supplied to the infant State, born after so much travail, a language and a tradition which linked it consciously with an inspiring past.' [1]

Not less inspiring to the Greeks was the example of revolutionary France. Under that example were founded a number of secret societies, the most famous of which was the *Philike Hetaireia*. This ' Association of Friends ' was founded at Odessa by four Greek merchants. The precise degree of significance to be attached to the influence of the *Hetaireia* has been very variously estimated,[2] but it certainly secured the adhesion of most of the leading Greeks, both at home and abroad, and is said by 1820 to have enrolled 200,000 members. Its object was the expulsion of the Turks from Europe and the re-establishment of the Greek Empire ; and, however questionable its methods, it indisputably gave coherence and unity of aim to a movement which, though powerful, was dispersed and hopelessly lacking in these qualities.

The immediate opportunity for the outbreak of the Greek insurrection was afforded by the extraordinary success attained by Ali Pasha of Janina, one of the many ambitious and discontented viceroys of the Sultan. Ali Pasha had taken advantage

[1] Alison Phillips, ap. *C. M. H.*, x. 174-5.
[2] e. g. by Finlay and Gordon respectively.

of the general unrest caused by the Napoleonic wars, and of the frequent changes in the hegemony of the Adriatic, to carve out for himself a principality, imposing in extent, and virtually independent of Constantinople, upon the Albanian sea-board. The hill tribes of Albania and northern Greece were gradually reduced to subjection, and in 1817 the position of Ali was so far recognized by the protectress of the Ionian Isles that Great Britain handed over to him the excellent harbour and town of Parga. The conduct of Lord Castlereagh in this, as in other matters, has been hotly canvassed, but the choice he had to make was not an easy one. The Pargiotes had voluntarily surrendered their town to us, and had sought British protection against a ruffianly adventurer. But the adventurer had rendered a considerable service to us in the Napoleonic wars, and the retention of a town, little valued for its own sake, might have led to embarrassments. So the ' Lion of Janina ' went from triumph to triumph.

Not until 1820 did Sultan Mahmud take action against his audacious viceroy. But, at last, a large force under Khurshid Pasha was dispatched from Constantinople, and after two years of successful evasion and resistance the ' Lion ' was trapped in Janina ; he was assassinated in the midst of a parley, and his head was sent as a trophy to the Sultan (Feb. 1822).

The Rising in the Morea, April, 1821

Meanwhile, encouraged by the preoccupation of the Porte, the Hetairists had initiated the disastrous insurrection in Moldavia, and, before the northern rising collapsed, had lighted in the Morea and the islands a torch which was not to be extinguished until a new nation had taken its place in the European polity.

The enthusiasm of Lord Byron, the knight errantry of Lord Cochrane, General Church, and other Philhellenist volunteers, cast over the ensuing war a glamour only partially deserved. Never, surely, did any movement display a more confused and perplexing medley of brutality and nobility, of conspicuous heroism and consummate cowardice, of pure-minded patriotism and sordid individualism, of self-sacrificing loyalty and time-serving treachery.

The initial uprising in the Morea was marked by terrible ferocity. It was avowedly a war of extermination. ' The Turk ', sang the Moreotes, ' shall live no longer, neither in the Morea, nor in the whole earth.' In the Morea the threat was almost literally fulfilled. In April, 1821, a general massacre of Moslems began. Out of 25,000 Ottomans hardly one was suffered to remain outside the walled towns into which all who escaped the massacre had hastily fled for refuge. Within a month the Turkish domination of the Morea was at an end.

Meanwhile the massacre of Turks in the Morea was promptly followed by reprisals wherever Christians could be taken at a disadvantage. In Constantinople itself Sultan Mahmud wrought a deed, the news of which startled and horrified Christendom. On the dawn of Easter Day (April 22, 1821) the Venerable Patriarch Gregorius was seized as he emerged from the celebration of mass, and, still clothed in his sacred vestments, he was hanged, and with him the Archbishops of Adrianople, Salonica, and Tirnovo. For three days the bodies hung outside the episcopal palace, and were then cut down and flung into the Bosphorus. The body of the Patriarch was picked up by a Greek trading ship and carried to Odessa, where it was interred with all the honour due to a martyr for the faith.

The murders in Constantinople gave the signal for a whole-sale massacre of Christians. In Thessaly, Macedonia, and Asia Minor, Christian Churches were pillaged, the men were put to the sword, and the women sold into slavery.

The Powers could not look on at these things unmoved.

Least of all Russia. Metternich regarded the Greek insurrection with unfeigned alarm. To him it was merely one more manifestation of the revolutionary temper which was infecting a great part of Southern Europe. He would have left the Greeks to their fate, and did his utmost to restrain his august ally. But Alexander was not only the head of the Holy Alliance; he was the protector of the Orthodox Church and the hereditary enemy of the Sultan. His subjects, moreover, were deeply moved by the insult to their faith and the unhappy plight of their co-religionists.

Apart from the question of Greek independence, and the outrages upon the highest ecclesiastics of the Greek Church, the Tsar had his own grievances against the Porte. The Turks had insulted Russian ships in the Bosphorus, and had continued to administer the principalities, not perhaps unwarrantably but in defiance of Treaty obligations, by martial law. Accordingly, though Alexander no less than Metternich ' discerned the revolutionary march in the troubles of the Peloponnese ', the Russian ambassador at Constantinople was instructed, in July, 1821, to present the following demands and to require an answer within eight days :

(i) that the Greek Churches, destroyed or plundered, should be immediately restored and rendered fit for the celebration of Divine worship ; (ii) that the Christian Religion should be restored to its prerogatives by granting it the same protection it formerly enjoyed, and by guaranteeing its inviolability for the future, to console Europe in some degree for the murder of the Patriarch ; (iii) that an equitable distinction should be made between the innocent and the guilty, and a prospect of peace held out to those Greeks who should hereafter submit within a given time ; and lastly (iv) that the Turkish Government should enable Russia, by virtue of existing treaties, to contribute to the pacification of the principalities of Wallachia and Moldavia.

The Porte was, at the same time, informed that immediate assent to these demands was ' the only means by which it would be able to avoid utter ruin '. The answer was not forthcoming within the specified time ; the Russian ambassador demanded his passports, quitted Constantinople on July 27, and a Russo-Turkish war seemed imminent.

The rest of the Powers were, however, in no mood for the renewal of war. The restored Bourbons in France were pre-occupied with the congenial task of restoring legitimism and autocracy in Spain. Metternich was supremely anxious to avert the reopening of the Eastern Question in its larger aspects. Berlin echoed the voice of Vienna.

Lord Castlereagh was not indifferent to the fate of the Greeks, but, like Metternich, was primarily concerned to avoid a European conflagration. To that end he joined Metternich in putting pressure upon the Sultan to induce him to agree quickly with his powerful adversary. Capo d'Istria would have been glad to serve the cause of his people by engaging his master in a war with the Turks, but Alexander did not wish to push matters to extremities. Pacific counsels there-fore prevailed. The Sultan was induced to yield a point and evacuate the principalities, and Metternich could congratulate himself upon having, for the time, averted war. In September, 1822, he met his allies at Verona in comparatively cheerful mood.

Meanwhile the Near East remained in a state of profound perturbation. The unrest was not appeased by the events of 1822. In February of that year the Albanian revolt was, as we have seen, extinguished, and thus the border provinces were preserved from Hetairist infection and secured to the Porte. Khurshid Pasha, fresh from his triumph over the Lion of Janina, then delivered his attack in force upon the insurgents of central Greece and the Morea. On July 16 a serious defeat was, owing partly to treachery and partly to mismanagement, inflicted upon a Greek force, and Mavrocordatos withdrew to the shelter of Missolonghi. Missolonghi stood a siege for two months and then beat off its assailants ; and before the end of the year the Greeks had recovered Athens, Nauplia, and Corinth.

The Greeks were equally successful at sea, but their mastery was not established before the Turks had perpetrated terrible atrocities in Chios. On April 22, 1822, precisely a year after the murder of the Greek Patriarch, the Turks landed a force of 15,000 men in Chios, and put to the sword the whole population—priests and peasants, women and children, save some thousands of young girls who were carried off into slavery. Including the latter the Turks claimed, in Chios alone, some 30,000 victims.

But their savage triumph was short-lived. The Greek fleet which, but for divided counsels, ought to have prevented the Turkish landing in Chios, presently appeared upon the scene and exacted a terrible though tardy vengeance. Employing a device familiar to the Greeks, Constantine Kanaris, their admiral, inflicted a crushing blow upon the Turks. On the night of June 18 he rammed, with a fireship, the Turkish admiral's flagship ; and it was blown up with the admiral and a thousand men on board. This bold and skilful stroke cleared the Levant. The rest of the Turkish navy fled in terror and took shelter in the Dardanelles. On sea as on land the Greek cause seemed destined to a victory, speedy and complete.

Meanwhile the Greeks had taken a step of considerable political significance. On January 1, 1822, a national assembly met in a wood near Epidaurus, solemnly proclaimed the independence of Greece, and promulgated a constitution. There was to be an executive council of five members under the presidency of Alexander Mavrocordatos, and a legislative assembly of fifty-nine members elected on a popular franchise and presided over by Demetrius, the brother of Alexander Hypsilanti. The formation of a new State, under a regularly constituted government, was thus officially announced to the world.

Great Britain and the Greeks

For some time the Powers made no response. But to Great Britain and other maritime Powers the situation was highly inconvenient, and, as the Greek navy asserted its supremacy in the Levant, became intolerable. The Greeks were still technically pirates. No redress for the outrages they committed could be obtained from Constantinople, nor under existing conditions could redress be sought from the provisional government in the Morea.

In August, 1822, the death of Lord Londonderry (Castlereagh) had opened the Foreign Office to George Canning. In regard to the Near East Canning accepted in principle the policy of his predecessor, but circumstances soon forced him to a much more active intervention than Castlereagh would have approved. In the first place, the injuries inflicted upon English commerce compelled him, on March 25, 1823, to recognize the Greeks as belligerents.

The rising tide of Philhellenism pushed him still further in the same direction. The enthusiasm aroused in England, as among other progressive peoples, for the cause of the Greek insurgents was extraordinary. It was due partly to reverence for the past, partly to hope for the future. The mere name of Hellenes, heard once more upon the lips of men after centuries of complete oblivion, thrilled the hearts of those who owed to Greek philosophy, Greek art, and Greek literature a debt larger than they could acknowledge or repay. But Philhellenist sentiment did not derive its sustenance solely from the memories of the past. In England the long reign of the Tory party was drawing to a close. The peace of 1815 had been followed not by plenty but by a period of profound depression in agriculture, finance, and trade. Distress led to an epidemic of disorder; disorder necessitated repression; repression stimulated the demand for reform. Liberalism not less than nationalism looked exultingly to Greece.

Of both sentiments Lord Byron was the most impassioned representative, and in July, 1823, he started from Italy for Greece. He tarried in Cephalonia during the autumn, and in January, 1824, landed at Missolonghi.

During the last twelve months the outlook for the Greek nationalists had darkened. Distracted by internal feuds, gravely hampered, despite a generous loan from English sympathizers, by lack of money, the Greeks had nevertheless managed until 1824 to hold their own against the Turks.

In January, 1824, however, Sultan Mahmud took a bold but desperate step. He summoned to his aid his powerful vassal Mehemet Ali of Egypt, the ' exterminator of infidels '. The reward of his assistance was to be the Pashalik of Crete, while his son [1] Ibrahim was to govern, in the Sultan's name, the reconquered Morea.

In the early spring of 1824 a great expedition was fitted out at Alexandria, and in April Ibrahim landed in Crete. The fortresses were captured and, by methods soon to be repeated on a larger scale in the Morea, the island was reduced to submission. Ibrahim next exterminated the population of Kasos, while his Turkish allies dealt in similar fashion with Psara. Had there been anything approaching to unity in the counsels of the Greeks, had there been any co-ordination between the ' government ', the soldiers and the sailors, Ibrahim might never have accomplished the short voyage

[1] By some authorities Ibrahim is described as his stepson. The point is not quite certain.

between Crete and the Morea. But thanks to the negligence of the Greek navy Ibrahim landed a large force at Modon in February, 1825, and secured Navarino as a naval base. Bravely as they fought, the Greek irregulars were no match for disciplined forces led by a skilled soldier. From Navarino Ibrahim advanced through the Morea 'harrying, devastating, and slaughtering in all directions'.

It seemed in 1825 as if no assistance, short of the official intervention of one or more great Powers, could avail to save the Greek cause. While the Egyptians attacked from the south-west, the Turks delivered their assault on the north-west. The two forces converged on Missolonghi where, on April 19, 1824, Byron had given the last proof of his devotion to the cause of Hellas.

In April, 1825, the Turks, under Reshid Pasha, invested the town by land and sea. Again and again the assault was delivered ; again and again it was repelled. Reshid himself was in danger of being cut off by the Greek fleet ; but in November the Turkish forces were reinforced by Ibrahim. The efforts of the Egyptians were as vain as those of the Turks ; the besiegers still repelled every assault. At last, after more than six months of siege, the assault was abandoned, and the combined force of the besiegers sat down to a blockade. The heroic defenders were starved out ; and in April, 1826, after a close investment of exactly a year, the whole population determined to make a sortie. On April 22 every man, woman, and child—not physically disabled—assembled at the gates prepared for the last desperate sally ; only the infirm were left behind. The vanguard cut their way through, and the gallant attempt seemed on the point of complete success, when, owing to a mistaken order, the force divided, part advanced, part retired ; some of the advancing party got through ; but the besiegers closed in upon the rest; hardly a man of them escaped;

most of them died sword in hand ; the small remnant set fire to the magazines and perished in the flames. Some three thousand women and children, the sole survivors of the siege, were carried off into slavery.

From Missolonghi the victors marched on Athens ; Athens in its turn was besieged, and on June 2, 1827, despite the efforts of the Greeks themselves, and despite the assistance of Lord Cochrane, General Church, and others, was compelled to surrender. The Greek cause seemed desperate. Unless help were forthcoming from outside, the whole movement must collapse. In despair the Greeks formally placed themselves under British protection, and begged that Great Britain would send them a king. It was, of course, impossible to accede to the request, and Canning, though he received the Greek deputies with cordiality, made it clear to them that England could not depart from her attitude of strict, though benevolent, neutrality. This negotiation took place at the close of 1825. Just about the same time an event happened which profoundly modified the whole European situation.

The Powers and the Greek Question

In December, 1825, the Tsar Alexander died suddenly in the Crimea, and after a short interval of uncertainty and confusion his brother Nicholas succeeded. Nicholas was a man entirely opposed in taste and temper to his predecessor. Alexander was a curious mixture of shrewdness and sentiment ; Nicholas had none of his brother's Western veneer, and cherished none of his illusions ; he was Russian to the core. For the Greeks he cared little ; but he was indisposed to allow the Porte to play fast and loose with Russia. The questions at issue between the two Courts were no nearer a satisfactory settlement than when, four years earlier, Russia had broken off diplomatic relations with Constantinople. The British ambassador to the Porte had done all in his power to bring about a settlement of the dispute; but he had no sooner, with infinite labour, secured an adjustment on one point than another had been raised.

On the accession of the new Tsar, Canning induced the Duke of Wellington to undertake a special mission to St. Petersburg. His object was twofold: to adjust, if possible, the outstanding difficulties between Russia and the Porte, and thus to avert the war, which at any moment in the last four years might have been regarded as imminent; and to arrive at a common understanding with Russia on the Greek Question.

For it was hardly possible that the great Powers could much longer hold aloof. Metternich, indeed, never wavered for an instant from the attitude which he had from the first assumed: the Greeks were rebels against legitimate authority, and must be left to their fate. Prussia still adhered to the policy of Austria. In France, however, the Philhellenist sentiment was not powerless; and in England and Russia it might at any moment get beyond the control of the respective governments. More particularly was this the case after Ibrahim's devastating conquest in the Morea. Ibrahim has been described as a 'savage'; and if he was not that, it must, at least, be admitted that his methods of warfare were exceedingly repugnant to Western ideas. Moreover, an ugly rumour had got abroad that Ibrahim had formed a plan to carry off into slavery all the Greeks whom he did not exterminate, and having made of the Morea a desert, to repeople it with submissive fellaheen. The Porte found it necessary to repudiate the report. But the report was more impressive than the repudiation. Nothing did so much to excite the sympathies of the Philhellenes in Western Europe, or to hasten the halting paces of diplomacy. Canning, indeed, regarded the rumour, first communicated to him by Prince Lieven, as incredible.

But towards the end of 1825 he had appointed to the Embassy at Constantinople his cousin, Stratford Canning; a man destined to fame as Lord Stratford de Redcliffe. The first Reports sent home by the new ambassador were a cautious confirmation of Prince Lieven's account. ' If the statements which had reached Mr. S. Canning were true, Ibrahim then acted on a system little short of extermination . . . and there was room to apprehend that many of his prisoners had been sent into Egypt as slaves, the children, it was asserted, being made to embrace the Mahommedan Faith.'

Stratford Canning was instructed to satisfy himself as to the facts, and, if they should correspond with the rumour, ' to declare in the most distinct terms to the Porte that Great Britain would not permit the execution of a system of depopulation'. More than that, a naval officer was to be dispatched from the Mediterranean fleet direct to Ibrahim, and to give ' the Pasha distinctly to understand that unless he should in a written document distinctly disavow or formally renounce . . . the intention of converting the Morea into a Barbary State, by transporting the population to Asia or Africa and replacing them by the population of those countries, effectual means would be taken to impede by the intervention of his Majesty's naval forces the accomplishment of so unwarrantable a project '.

Meanwhile the Duke of Wellington had, with some difficulty, brought the Tsar Nicholas into line with Canning's policy on the Greek Question; had secured his promise to ' co-operate with Great Britain to prevent the execution of the designs imputed to Ibrahim Pasha '; and on April 4, 1826, had concluded with him the Protocol of St. Petersburg.

By this treaty the two Powers, renouncing any ' augmentation of territory, any exclusive influence ', or any superior commercial advantages for themselves, agreed to offer their mediation to the Porte. Greece, though continuing to pay tribute to the Porte, was to become a virtually independent State, to be governed by authorities chosen by itself, and to enjoy ' entire liberty of conscience and commerce '. To prevent collisions in the future the Turks were to evacuate Greece, and the Greeks were to ' purchase the property of the Turks . . . on the Grecian continent or islands '.

This protocol must be regarded as a conspicuous personal triumph for Canning. And it went a long way to settle the Greek Question. But as to the outstanding questions between Turkey and Russia it did nothing : and on these the mind of the Tsar Nicholas was bent. Though professing his readiness to treat of the matter with Wellington, the Tsar had already (March 17, 1826) dispatched an ultimatum to the Porte. The ultimatum demanded the immediate evacuation of the principalities ; the abandonment of the appointment of the police ; and the instant dispatch of plenipotentiaries to the Russian frontier.

These demands the Porte was not in a position to refuse. A critical moment in the domestic history of the Ottoman Empire had indeed arrived. The marvellous expansion of that empire in the fifteenth and sixteenth centuries had been largely due to the Corps of Janissaries. The decay of the empire in the seventeenth and eighteenth centuries had been coincident with their deterioration. Of late years the whilom defenders of the empire had degenerated into oppressive and obstructive tyrants. Without their concurrence no real reforms could be effected, and that concurrence was invariably withheld.

To Mahmud II, the greatest of the Sultans since Suleiman the Magnificent, it seemed that the time had come to make a final choice ; either he must be content to see the authority of the Sultan crumble and the empire perish, or he must by one bold stroke destroy the jealous military oligarchy which had become as ineffective in the field as it was obscurantist and tyrannical in domestic affairs. His vassal Mehemet Ali had exterminated the Mamlukes of Egypt; Ibrahim Pasha had crushed the Wahhabites; why should Mahmud hesitate to strike down the Janissaries? They were not, it seemed, equal even to the task of subduing the infidel insurgents in Greece. That Moslems could still fight when armed and disciplined on a European model Ibrahim had clearly demonstrated in the Morea. Small wonder that the contrast between his own troops and those of his vassal was too galling to Mahmud's pride to be endured, or that he resolved to remove the principal obstruction in the path of reform.

A great Council of State decreed that, in order to subdue the infidels, the military system of the empire must be completely reorganized. The Janissaries were ordered to submit to a new discipline. They refused; and broke out into rebellion.

Their mutiny had been foreseen, and every preparation had been made to quell it. A force of 14,000 artillerymen, splendidly equipped with guns, with a corresponding force of infantry drawn from Asiatic Turkey, had been assembled in the neighbourhood of the capital. The command of the artillery was entrusted to Ibrahim, a general of known devotion to the person of the Sultan, and of unquenchable resolution. Ibrahim, or Kara Djehennum ('Black Hell') as he came, after the great day, to be called, had made all necessary dispositions for street fighting of a severe character. As the Janissaries advanced on the palace they were mown down by the gunners: they then fled to their own barracks, which were battered with shell-fire until the whole body of the Janissaries of Constantinople had perished in the blazing ruins of the Atmeidan.

The blow struck in Constantinople was repeated in every city of the empire where there existed a body of Janissaries.

Thus was the Sultan at last master in his own house and free to carry out the reforms indispensable to its preservation.

A comprehensive scheme of military reorganization was promptly initiated, and a great military critic has put on record his opinion that 'if Turkey had enjoyed ten years of peace after the destruction of the Janissaries, Sultan Mahmud's military reforms might in that time have gained some strength ; and, supported by an army on which he could depend, the Sultan might have carried out the needful reforms in the administration of his country, have infused new life into the dead branches of the Ottoman Empire, and made himself formidable to his neighbours '.[1]

'Ten years of peace.' The war with Greece still continued ; and, although Ibrahim's intervention had relieved the pressure on one side, it stimulated activity on the other. The new Tsar would brook no delay. The last day permitted for a reply to his ultimatum was October 7, and on that day the Convention of Akerman was signed. By that Convention the Sultan made, as we have already seen, large concessions in regard to Serbia and the Principalities, and in all things submitted to the will of the Tsar.

As regards Greece, on the other hand, the Porte, in the full tide of successful barbarity, showed no signs of accepting mediation unless backed by force. Greece had already formally applied for it. Accordingly, in September, 1826, Canning proposed to the Tsar common action to enforce mediation upon the Sultan. The two Powers agreed to intimate to the Sultan, if he remained obdurate, that 'they would look to Greece with an eye of favour, and with a disposition to seize the first occasion of recognizing as an independent State such portion of her territory as should have freed itself from Turkish dominion '.

[1] Moltke, p. 456, quoted by Creasy, *op. cit.*, p. 506.

Every effort was made to bring the other Powers into line; Metternich, however, left no stone unturned to frustrate Canning's policy, even to the extent of using backstairs influence to create mistrust between the Court and the Cabinet. Prussia followed Metternich's lead, but France concluded with Russia and Great Britain the Treaty of London (July, 1827).

The public articles of the treaty were substantially identical with the terms of the Protocol of St. Petersburg, in accordance with which an ' immediate armistice ' was to be offered to the belligerents. A secret article provided that the Porte should be plainly informed that the Powers intend to take ' immediate measures for an approximation with the Greeks '; and that if within one month ' the Porte do not accept the armistice . . . or if the Greeks refuse to execute it ' the High Contracting Powers should intimate to one or both parties that ' they intend to exert all the means which circumstances may suggest to their prudence to obtain the immediate effect of the armistice . . . by preventing all collision between the contending parties . . . without, however, taking any part in the hostilities between them '. It was further provided that ' instructions conformable to the provisions above set forth ' should be sent ' to the admirals commanding their squadrons in the seas of the Levant '.

This treaty may be regarded as the crown of Canning's policy in regard to the Eastern Question. The principles of that policy are clear; the Powers could not ignore the struggle of Greece for independence: ' a contest so ferocious (as Canning wrote to Lieven), leading to excesses of piracy and plunder, so intolerable to civilized Europe, justifies extraordinary intervention, and renders lawful any expedients short of positive hostility.' On the other hand, they could not consistently interfere by force; nor must the Russian Tsar be permitted to utilize the Greek struggle, for which he cared little, to attain objects for which he cared much. This policy is clearly reflected in the terms of the Treaty of London ; but its practical application was not free from difficulty and ambiguity. The Porte was notorious for sullen obstinacy. How were the 'high contracting parties', in the all too probable event of a refusal of an armistice by the Porte, to ' prevent all collision between the contending parties without taking any part in the hostilities ' ? Either the matter had not been clearly thought out, or there was a deliberate intention to leave the Gordian knot to be cut by the Executive Officers of the Powers, i. e. ' the admirals commanding their squadrons in the seas of the Levant '. Canning was obliged to move warily ; but that he himself contemplated the employment of force is clear from the Duke of Wellington's condemnation of the Treaty of London on the ground that ' it specified means of compulsion which were neither more nor less than measures of war '.

In August, 1827, the mediation of the three Powers was offered to the ' contending parties ', was accepted by the Greeks, and refused by the Porte.

The game now passed from the hands of diplomatists into those of sailors. The British fleet in the Levant was under the command of Sir Edward Codrington. Codrington received his instructions on August 7 ; but, not being a diplomatist, he found them difficult of interpretation. How was he ' to intercept all ships freighted with men and arms destined to act against the Greeks, whether coming from Turkey or the coast of Africa ', and, at the same time, prevent his measures from ' degenerating into hostilities ' ? In a word, was he, or was he not, to use force ? Such was the blunt question which he addressed to our ambassador at Constantinople. Stratford Canning's answer was unequivocal : ' the prevention of supplies is ultimately to be enforced, if necessary, and when all other means are exhausted, by cannon shot.'

Meanwhile large reinforcements from Egypt had reached Ibrahim who was still in the Morea ; and a squadron of Turkish and Egyptian ships was lying in Navarino Bay. Ibrahim was informed that not a single ship would be allowed to leave the harbour, and on making one or two attempts to sail he found that the admirals were determined to enforce their commands. Foiled in his attempt at naval operations, and instructed by the Porte to prosecute the war on land with all possible energy, Ibrahim proceeded to execute his orders with merciless severity. All who were found in arms were put to the sword, while the miserable survivors were to be starved into submission by the total destruction of every means of subsistence. ' It is supposed ', wrote one eye-witness, Captain Hamilton, ' that if Ibrahim remained in the Morea, more than a third of its inhabitants would die of absolute starvation.' Of these atrocities the allied admirals were all but eyewitnesses. ' Continual clouds of fire and smoke rising all round the Gulf of Coron bore frightful testimony to the devastation that was going on.' The admirals thereupon determined to ' put a stop to atrocities which exceed all that has hitherto taken place ', and for this purpose to sail into Navarino Bay, and there renew their remonstrances with Ibrahim. No hostilities were intended ' unless the Turks should begin '. The Turks, however, fired on a boat from the *Dartmouth* ; the *Dartmouth* and the French flagship replied ; the battle became general ; and before the sun went down on October 20 the Turco-Egyptian ships ' had disappeared, the Bay of Navarino was covered with their wrecks '.

The news of the battle of Navarino was received with amazement throughout Europe, and by the English Government with something like consternation. The sailors had indeed cut the Gordian knot tied by the diplomatists, but they got no thanks in England for doing it. Canning had died two months before the battle of Navarino (August 8), and Wellington, who, after five months' interval, succeeded to his place, made no secret of his dislike of Canning's policy. The Turk, with consummate impudence, described Navarino as a ' revolting outrage', and demanded compensation and apologies. Even Wellington was not prepared to go this length, but the king was made (January 29, 1828) to ' lament deeply ' that ' this conflict should have occurred with the naval forces of an ancient ally', and to express ' a confident hope that this untoward event will not be followed by further hostilities '.

The one anxiety of the new Government was to preserve the independence and integrity of the Ottoman Empire. No language could have been more nicely calculated to defeat this object. Turkey was, of course, encouraged to persist in her attitude towards Greece, and to renew her quarrel with Russia. Russia was permitted, and even compelled, to engage single-handed in war with the Turks. Thus all the fruits of years of diplomacy on Canning's part were carelessly dissipated in a few months by his successors.

Russo-Turkish War, 1828–9

Sultan Mahmud had meanwhile denounced the Convention of Akerman, and had declared a Holy War against the infidel (December 20, 1827). Russia, though with ample professions to the Powers of complete disinterestedness, accepted the challenge, and on April 26, 1828, the Tsar Nicholas formally declared war. In May, 1828, the Tsar himself took the field, crossed the Pruth at the head of an army of 150,000 men, and again occupied the principalities. About the same time the Russian fleet entered the Dardanelles.

Neither France nor England was quite happy about the action of the Tsar, nor disposed to confide the settlement of

Near Eastern affairs to his hands exclusively. Consequently, in July, 1828, while the Turks, to the amazement of Europe, were holding the Russians in the Balkans, the two Western Powers concluded a protocol, providing for immediate action against Ibrahim in the Morea. England, less jealous of France than France was of her, confided the execution of the protocol to France. Accordingly, at the end of August, a French force of 14,000 men under the command of General Maison reached the Gulf of Corinth. The English consul offered some objection to their landing, on the ground that Sir Pulteney Malcolm, the English admiral, was at that moment in Egypt, negotiating with Mehemet Ali for the withdrawal of the Egyptian forces from the Morea. Malcolm's mission was successful, and a convention was signed in Alexandria to that effect on August 6.

Meanwhile 14,000 French troops landed at Petalidi in the Gulf of Coron and arranged with Ibrahim for an immediate evacuation of the Morea. The good accord thus established between the French and the Egyptian Pasha was not, perhaps, without its influence on later events.[1] Ibrahim had, however, surrendered the fortresses, not to the French, but to the Turks. The latter quitted them on the summons of the French general ; Navarino, Coron, Patras, Tripolitza, and Modon were occupied by the French, virtually without resistance, and in a few days the Morea was entirely free of both Egyptian and Turkish forces.

A protocol concluded in London (November 16, 1828) placed the Morea and the islands under the protection of the Powers, and a further protocol (March 22, 1829) provided that Greece was to be an autonomous but tributary State, governed by a prince selected by the Powers, and that its frontier should run from the Gulf of Arta, on the west coast, to the Gulf of Volo on the east.

[1] See chap. ix.

Russia, meanwhile, was finding in the Porte a tougher antagonist than she had looked for. In the Caucasus, indeed, the Russians carried everything before them, but in Europe their progress in 1828 was very slow. Varna held them up for three months and Choumla for three more.

In 1829 Diebitsch was entrusted with the supreme command, and for the first time Russian troops crossed the Balkans. Leaning on his fleet, Diebitsch advanced with little resistance, by way of Burgas, upon Adrianople. Adrianople surrendered without firing a shot on August 14, and a month later the Treaty of Adrianople was signed.

In the long history of the Eastern Question the Treaty of Adrianople (September 14, 1829) is inferior only in importance to those of Kainardji and Berlin. Russia restored her conquests, except the 'Great Islands' of the Danube; but her title to Georgia and the other provinces of the Caucasus was acknowledged; all neutral vessels were to have free navigation in the Black Sea and on the Danube; practical autonomy was granted to the principalities of Moldavia and Wallachia under Russian protection; Russian traders in Turkey were to be under the exclusive jurisdiction of their own consuls, and, in regard to Greece, the Porte accepted the Treaty of London—thus virtually acknowledging Greek independence.

The actual settlement of the affairs of Greece was relegated to a conference in London, and by the Protocol of London (February 3, 1830) Greece was declared to be an independent and monarchical State under the guarantee of the three Powers. This arrangement was confirmed and enlarged by the subsequent Convention of London (May 7, 1832), by which the Powers further undertook jointly to guarantee a loan of 60,000,000 francs to the Greek kingdom.[1]

[1] The texts of these important documents will be found in Hertslet, *Map of Europe by Treaty*, vol. ii, pp. 841 and 893 sq.

It was comparatively easy for the protecting Powers to declare that Greece should be a monarchical State; it was more difficult to find a suitable monarch, and most difficult of all to educate the Greek people in that purely exotic and highly exacting form of government known as 'constitutional monarchy'. The Crown having been successively declined by Prince John of Saxony and, after a temporary acceptance, by Prince Leopold of Saxe-Coburg (afterwards King of the Belgians), was ultimately accepted by Prince Otto of Bavaria. Capo d'Istria, who, in March, 1827, had been recalled from voluntary exile in Switzerland, and had been elected President by a National Assembly in Greece, was assassinated in 1831, and the way was clear for the Bavarian princeling, who, at the age of seventeen, ascended the Greek throne on January 25, 1833.

The Treaties of Adrianople and London, and the accession of King Otto, mark the final achievement of Greek independence, and bring to a close one of the most significant chapters in the history of the Eastern Question. For the first time the principle of nationality had asserted itself in a fashion at once completely successful and striking to the historical imagination. For the first time the future of the Ottoman Empire was recognized as a matter of profound concern not merely to the Porte itself, to Russia and to Austria, but to Europe as a whole, and not least to Great Britain. For the first time an Ottoman Sultan of exceptional vigour and disposed to reform had been compelled to call to his aid an ambitious vassal, and despite that assistance to consent to terms of peace dictated by the Powers and involving the partial dismemberment of his European dominions. Plainly, Europe was face to face with all the perplexities, paradoxes, and contradictions which contribute to the tangle of the Eastern Question.

For further reference : T. Gordon, *History of the Greek Revolution*, 2 vols. (London, 1832) ; A. von Prokesch-Osten, *Geschichte des Abfalls der Griechen vom türkischen Reiche im Jahre 1821*, 6 vols. (Vienna, 1867) ; G. Finlay, *History of Greece*, 7 vols. (ed. Tozer) (Oxford, 1877) ; *The History of the Greek Revolution* (Edinburgh, 1861) ; G. Isambert, *L'Indépendance grecque et l'Europe* (Paris, 1900) ; W. A. Phillips, *The Greek War of Independence* (London, 1897) ; Lady Jane Bourchier, *Memoir of the Life of Admiral Sir Edward Codrington* (well documented) (London, 1875) ; W. E. Gladstone, *The Hellenic Factor in the Eastern Problem* (*Gleanings from Past Years*, Series iv, London, 1879) ; W. Miller, *The Ottoman Empire* (Cambridge, 1913) ; E. M. Church, *Sir Richard Church in Greece and Italy* (Edinburgh, 1895) ; L. Sargeant, *Greece in the Nineteenth Century* (London, 1897) ; Murray, *Handbook to Greece*.

9

The Powers and the Eastern Question, 1830–41

Mehemet Ali of Egypt

‘ L'Égypte vaut moins par elle-même que par sa situation. . . . Qui touche à l'Égypte touche à la Turquie. Qui soulève la question d'Égypte soulève la question d'Orient, dans toute son ampleur et avec toutes ses conséquences.'—C. DE FREYCINET, *La Question d'Égypte*.

IT is proverbially dangerous in public affairs to confer a favour ; it is even more dangerous to accept one. Never has there been a more apt illustration of this truth than that afforded by the curious phase of the Eastern Question which it is the purpose of this chapter to disclose.

Had it not been for the intervention of the Powers, Mehemet Ali of Egypt and Ibrahim Pasha would indubitably have rescued the Ottoman Empire from imminent dismemberment. Such a service it was difficult for the recipient to requite, and still more difficult to forgive. Mehemet Ali, on his part, was not disposed to underrate the obligations under which he had placed his suzerain, and the cession of Crete seemed to him a wholly inadequate reward. In the disgust thus engendered we have one of the clues to the intricacies of the period which intervened between the Treaty of Adrianople and the Treaty of London of 1841,

Recent events had, moreover, revealed the weakness, military, naval, and political, of the Ottoman Empire. If Greece, an integral part of his European dominions, could so easily be detached from the sceptre of the Sultan, why not other parts of the empire, connected with Constantinople by a looser tie ? Algiers, which still acknowledged the titular sovereignty of the Sultan, had been seized in 1830 by the French, who had proclaimed their purpose to deliver that promising land from the yoke of the Ottoman Sultan. If Algiers, why not other parts of Africa or of Asia ?

Mehemet Ali

The extraordinary success already achieved by Mehemet Ali might well inspire that brilliant barbarian—half an illiterate savage, half a consummate statesman, wholly a genius—with ambitions even more far reaching.

Born in 1769 at Kavala, a small seaport in eastern Macedonia, Mehemet Ali was, like Ali Pasha of Janina, by race an Albanian. The son of a peasant cultivator he was himself a small trader, but Napoleon's invasion of Egypt in 1798 gave him his chance of carving out a career for himself. It was not neglected. As second-in-command of a regiment of Albanian irregulars, he took part in the Turkish expedition to Egypt, which began and ended so disastrously with the battle of Aboukir. Driven into the sea with his comrades he was picked up by the gig of the English admiral, Sir Sydney Smith, and two years later (1801) he returned to Egypt in command of his regiment.

Mehemet Ali was greatly impressed by the military superiority of troops trained on European models, and still more impressed by the career open, in such times, to a man of genius like Napoleon or himself. After the successive evacuations of the French and English, Egypt was in a terrible condition of anarchy. The Mamluke Beys were as independent of their suzerain the Sultan as they were impotent to rule the Egyptians.

In the prevailing confusion Mehemet Ali saw his chance; he determined to stay in Egypt, and in 1805 was requested by the Sheiks of Cairo to become their Pasha. A little later the choice of the Sheiks was confirmed by the Sultan (July 9, 1805).

Nor was Mehemet Ali long in justifying it. The Sultan, in 1806, was forced by Napoleon to declare war upon the Third Coalition, and in 1807 England made the disastrous descent upon Egypt already described.[1] The moment was not ill chosen. The Pasha was preoccupied with domestic difficulties, but on receiving news that the English had taken Alexandria, and were advancing upon Rosetta, Mehemet Ali did not lose an hour. He hastily collected his forces, marched northwards, and flung back the English, who were besieging Rosetta, with terrible loss upon Alexandria. The attempt to take Rosetta was repeated with equally disastrous results, and in September the English force was withdrawn. All traces of this humiliating episode are now erased ; is the memory of it also eradicated ?

' Few who nowadays drive by the Ezbekieh garden are aware ', writes Sir Auckland Colvin, ' that the space which it covers was hideous less than a century ago with the heads of British soldiers.' [2]

Having repulsed the English attack, the new Pasha concentrated all his energies upon the accomplishment of his life-work in Egypt. That work owed much to French ideas and to French agents. Napoleon, when he went to Egypt in

---

[1] *Supra*, chap. vii.   [2] *Modern Egypt*, p. 4.

1798, was accompanied not only by great soldiers but by a brilliant staff of scientific experts, administrators, engineers, and financiers. Their work was less evanescent than that of their chief. And no none knew better how to appreciate the skill of subordinates than the 'illiterate savage' who, between 1805 and 1849, was the real ruler of Egypt. Still, though Mehemet Ali utilized the technical skill of French soldiers, sailors, engineers, financiers, jurists, and agriculturists, the work accomplished was his own, and bears in every detail the mark of a vigorous mind and a dominating personality.

There was no obscurity as to the objects which he meant to attain. The first was to make himself master of Egypt : to annihilate ruthlessly every competing force or authority in the land ; to concentrate in a single hand all the economic resources of the country, and to make of the army and navy an instrument perfectly fashioned for the accomplishment of the task to which it was destined.

The task was threefold : to make Egypt supreme over the adjacent lands, the Soudan and Arabia ; to render it virtually independent of the Sultan ; and to use it as a stepping-stone to the conquest of Syria, perhaps of Asia Minor, and possibly of the Ottoman Empire as a whole. Was not the vigour of the Osmanlis exhausted ; had not the time come to replace the house of Ottoman by a dynasty drawn from the virile races of Albania ? But the question as to the future of Constantinople was not immediate. Mehemet Ali was enough of a diplomatist to realize the international advantages which for the time being he enjoyed as a vassal of the Sultan. Slight as was the connexion which bound him to his suzerain, it sufficed to ward off many inconveniences which might otherwise have arisen from the mutual jealousies of the Powers. His successors in the government of Egypt have sometimes made use of the same fiction to their advantage.

His first business, then, was to reorganize the army and navy. A brilliant French officer, Colonel Sèves, better known as Suleiman Pasha, entirely reconstructed the Egyptian army : he introduced a new method of recruiting by which the army establishment was raised from 20,000 to 100,000 men ; he set up special schools of military instruction ; applied to Egyptian troops European discipline, and supplied them with arms and equipments of the most approved French pattern. The navy was similarly rebuilt by M. de Cérisy, a naval constructor imported from Toulon, while the armament was supplied and the sailors trained under the direction of a French engineer, M. Besson, of Rochefort. One fleet was stationed in the Mediterranean and another in the Red Sea, and at Alexandria a magnificent dockyard and arsenal were constructed.

Mehemet Ali applied himself not less vigorously and systematically to the work of economic reconstruction.

By an act of sheer confiscation the land was 'nationalized', the proprietors were expropriated, and Mehemet Ali himself became the sole owner of the soil of Egypt. Most of the principal products of the country were, in similar fashion, converted into State monopolies. New industries were established : under the scientific direction of M. Jumel cotton growing was developed in the Delta, and vast tracts of land yielded abundant crops of sugar, olives, and mulberries. Nor did raw products monopolize his attention. Factories were built, though with less remunerative results, and Egyptian youths were sent to western lands to extract from them the secrets of commercial and industrial success. The Mahmudiya Canal was constructed by the forced labour of the fellaheen to connect Alexandria with the Nile. During the accomplishment of this useful but laborious task 20,000 workmen are said to have perished of dysentery, but of human life Mehemet Ali was prodigal. Not that he neglected sanitary science. It was part of the equipment of a modernized State, and must, therefore, find its place in his scheme of reform. Thus Alexandria was rebuilt and provided with a new water supply. Similarly in regard to education. Mehemet Ali is said not to have been able to read or write,[1] but the modern State demanded education, Egypt, therefore, must have it. These things, as modern States have learnt to their cost, cannot be done without money, and the taxation imposed by Mehemet Ali was crushing. Combined with the system of State monopolies heavy taxation had the effect of raising prices to an almost incredible extent,[2] and the sufferings of the fellaheen were consequently intense. It is, indeed, true of many of Mehemet Ali's economic reforms that they were more productive of immediate advantages to the ruler than conducive to the ultimate prosperity of his people ; but not of all. Many works of permanent utility were carried out, and not until the British occupation did Egypt again enjoy an administration equally enterprising and enlightened.

Mehemet Ali's enterprise was, however, that of a savage despot. His dealing with the Mamlukes affords an illustration of his ruthless temper. The Mamlukes had raised him to power, but they were now in his way and must be destroyed. With every circumstance of treachery and cruelty the deed was accomplished in 1811 ; the Mamlukes were wiped out in a general massacre, and thus the last possible competitors for political ascendancy were removed from the adventurer's path.

In the same year Mehemet Ali launched his expedition against the Wahhabites of Arabia. At the request of his suzerain he dispatched Ibrahim in 1811 to bring these troublesome schismatics to submission. Several years were devoted

---

[1] Other authorities state that in middle life he taught himself to read.

[2] Colonel Campbell, who was sent to Egypt as Consul-General in 1833, put the increase as high as six to tenfold.

to the arduous task, but by 1818 it was accomplished : the Holy Cities of Mecca and Medina were recovered for the Sultan, and the remnant of the Wahhabites were driven into the desert.

In 1821 his son Ismail penetrated to the confluence of the Niles and conquered the Soudan. Kordofan was annexed in 1822, and in 1823 were laid the foundations of Khartoum. From 1824 to 1829, as was explained in the last chapter, the military energies of Mehemet Ali were concentrated upon Europe.

For the services then rendered to Sultan Mahmud, and for the still greater service which, but for the Powers, the Egyptian Pasha was prepared to render to his suzerain, the island of Crete was a recompense *pour rire*. To fulfil his promise in regard to the Morea was not within the Sultan's power ; in regard to Syria it was. And Syria, at least, Mehemet Ali was determined to have.

A pretext for invasion was found in the refusal of Abdullah Pasha of Acre to surrender the Egyptian ' rebels ' who had sought refuge with him. In November, 1831, a force variously estimated at 10,000 to 35,000 men was sent into Palestine under the command of the redoubtable Ibrahim. The great fortress of St. Jean d'Acre offered, as usual, an obstinate resistance, and, leaving a force to besiege it, Ibrahim occupied Jaffa, Gaza, and Jerusalem. On May 27, 1832, however, Acre was taken by storm, and on June 15 Damascus also was captured.

Ibrahim's progress naturally caused great alarm at Constantinople, but in reply to the remonstrances of the Sultan, Mehemet Ali protested his unbroken loyalty, and declared that the sole object of the expedition was to chastise the presumption of Abdullah Pasha who had ' insulted his beard whitened in the service of his sovereign '.[1] No one was deceived by these assurances, but there were those about Sultan Mahmud, and not his least sagacious counsellors, who urged him to come

[1] Hall, *England and the Orleans Monarchy*, p. 150.

to terms with his formidable vassal, and turn their combined arms against the infidel. Hatred of Mehemet Ali was, however, the master passion of Mahmud's declining years, and he decided, though not without hesitation, to send an army against him. In May, 1832, sentence of outlawry was pronounced against both Mehemet Ali and Ibrahim, and Hussein Pasha, the destroyer of the Janissaries, was appointed to command the Turkish troops.

On July 9 Ibrahim routed the advanced guard of the Turks in the valley of the Orontes, entered Aleppo, which had closed its gates upon Hussein Pasha on July 16, and on the 29th inflicted a decisive defeat upon Hussein himself in the Beilan Pass. The Turks were thrown back in complete confusion into the Taurus Mountains, and Asia Minor was open to Ibrahim.

A second army was then dispatched from Constantinople under Reshid Pasha ; it encountered Ibrahim at Konieh on December 21, and suffered at his hands a crushing reverse. Ibrahim advanced to Kutaya, and thence wrote to the Sultan asking permission to take up a still more threatening position at Brusa.

At this moment it looked as though Constantinople itself would soon be at his mercy. But now, as so often, Turkey found in its military weakness diplomatic strength. In the summer of 1832 the Sultan had appealed to the Powers. Only the Tsar Nicholas was prompt in the offer of assistance ; but to accept assistance from Russia alone was too risky a policy even in the hour of Turkey's extreme need. Yet where else was it to come from ? England and Austria were unreservedly anxious to maintain the integrity of the Ottoman Empire, and Prussia followed humbly in the wake of Metternich. England, however, was at the moment (1832) in the throes of a domestic revolution, and was still preoccupied with the affairs of Belgium. France had a traditional interest in Egypt, and in addition to this there had sprung up a curious but undeniable cult for Mehemet Ali, particularly among the Bonapartists, who regarded him as the disciple of Napoleon, almost as his apostolic successor in Egypt. Of all the Powers, therefore, Russia alone was at once anxious and able to go to the assistance of the Sultan in 1832. And not the most obtuse could be doubtful as to her motives.

The Sultan, accordingly, made a desperate attempt to secure the assistance of England. Stratford Canning, in Constantinople, strongly urged the English ministry to accede to the Sultan's request for a naval expedition to the Syrian coast. Lord Palmerston, however, was in an unusually cautious mood, and, though generally in complete sympathy with the views of Stratford Canning, was not, at the moment, willing to risk the breach with Russia and France, likely to arise from isolated action in the Levant.

Russia and Turkey

Russia, meanwhile, reiterated, with added *empressement*, her offers of assistance. In December, 1832, there arrived in Constantinople, simultaneously with the news of the disaster at Konieh, General Mouravieff on a special mission from the Tsar Nicholas. Mouravieff was charged to represent to the Sultan the fatal consequences likely to accrue to his empire from the phenomenal success of his Egyptian vassal, and to offer him a naval squadron for the protection of the capital. The Sultan still hesitated, however, to accept the offer, and Mouravieff, therefore, started off to Alexandria to attempt the intimidation of Mehemet Ali. The reasons for the Tsar's disquietude are not obscure.[1] Not Turkey alone was threatened

[1] They are fully set out in the instructions given to Mouravieff, which will be found in Serge Goriainow's valuable monograph, *Le Bosphore et les Dardanelles*, pp. 28–9.

by the advance of Ibrahim. The rights secured to Russia by a succession of treaties were also directly jeopardized. The substitution of a virile Albanian dynasty at Constantinople in place of the effete Osmanlis was the last thing desired by the Power which wished, naturally enough, to command the gate into the Mediterranean.

The most that Mouravieff could get out of Mehemet Ali was that Ibrahim should not, for the moment, advance beyond Kutaya.[1] The Sultan had, meanwhile, come to the conclusion that nothing but Russian aid could avert the ruin of his empire; he begged that not only a naval squadron might be sent to the Bosphorus, but that it might be followed by an army of 30,000 men.

Accordingly, on February 20, 1833, a powerful Russian squadron sailed into the Bosphorus and anchored before Constantinople. Its appearance seriously alarmed both France and Great Britain, who brought pressure upon the Sultan to procure its withdrawal. The Tsar, however, refused to withdraw until Ibrahim and his army had recrossed the Taurus Mountains.

Until his demands were conceded Mehemet Ali would issue no such orders to Ibrahim. Those demands included the cession of the whole of Syria, part of Mesopotamia, and the very important port and district of Adana. In March the Sultan agreed to the cession of Syria, Aleppo, and Damascus, but the Pasha stood out for his pound of flesh.

The arrival of a second Russian squadron in the Bosphorus and the landing of a Russian force at Scutari caused still further alarm to the Western Powers, and did not perhaps diminish that of the Sultan. A prolongation of the crisis seemed likely to result in the permanent establishment of

[1] 150 miles beyond Konieh, but 80 miles short of Brusa, Hall, *op. cit.*, p. 158.

Russia at Constantinople. France and England, therefore, applied further pressure both to Mehemet Ali and his suzerain. At last the latter yielded, and on April 8, 1833, there was concluded the Convention of Kutaya, by which Mehemet Ali's terms were conceded in full.

But the drama was not yet played out. Mehemet Ali had been bought off ; the debt to Russia remained to be discharged. So Russia took further security. On April 22 a third contingent of Russian troops arrived at Constantinople, and Russian engineers proceeded to strengthen the defences of the Bosphorus and the Dardanelles. Against what enemy ? On the heels of the third Russian contingent came Count Alexis Orloff to take up his appointment as ' Ambassador-Extraordinary to the Porte, and Commander-in-Chief of the Russian troops in the Ottoman Empire '.[1] At the end of April Count Orloff made a State entry into his new kingdom, and after two months of tiresome negotiations he received the title-deeds under the form of the Treaty of Unkiar-Skelessi (July 8, 1833).

This famous treaty marked the zenith of Russian influence at Constantinople. In effect, it placed the Ottoman Empire under the military protectorship of Russia. The six public articles simply reaffirmed, in platonic terms, the relations of peace and friendship between the two empires, though the

[1] The instructions given to Orloff are of supreme interest. They are now printed, *in extenso*, in Goriainow, *op. cit.*, p. 33 seq. Orloff was to (i) induce the Porte to confide absolutely in the support of Russia; (ii) combat French influence at Constantinople ; (iii) conciliate the support of Austria and neutralize the perpetual ill-will of England by making it clear that the sole object of Russian intervention was to preserve the Ottoman Empire ; (iv) reserve to Russia complete independence of action, and resist any proposal for collective intervention ; (v) keep the Russian forces at Constantinople until the conclusion of a definitive peace between Turkey and Mehemet Ali, and, above all, convince Mahmud that in the support of Russia lay his one hope of salvation.

Tsar of Russia pledged himself, should circumstances compel the Sultan to claim his help, to provide such military and naval assistance as the contracting parties should deem necessary. Reciprocal assistance was promised by the Sultan. The real significance of the treaty was contained in a secret article, which released the Sultan from any obligation to render assistance to Russia, save by closing the Dardanelles against the ships of war of any other Power. The precise meaning to be attributed to this stipulation was disputed at the time, and has been the subject of controversy ever since. But Count Nesselrode was clearly not guilty of an empty boast when he declared that the treaty ' legalized the armed intervention of Russia '. It did more. It guaranteed to Russia a free passage for her warships through the straits, and it closed the door into the Black Sea to every other Power. The day after the treaty was signed the Russian troops re-embarked, and the Russian navy sailed back to Sebastopol.

The conclusion of this treaty excited the liveliest apprehensions in England and France. In Lord Palmerston's view its terms were inconsistent with the Anglo-Turkish Treaty of 1809, by which ' the passage of ships of war through the straits is declared not allowable '.[1] The English fleet in the Levant, under the command of Sir Pulteney Malcolm, was reinforced and sent up, with a French squadron, to Besika Bay. England and France presented identical notes at St. Petersburg and Constantinople protesting against the proposed violation of the neutrality of the straits, and things looked like war between the maritimes and Russia.

None of the Powers, however, desired war. Metternich interposed his good offices, and the Tsar was induced to give a verbal assurance that he had no intention of enforcing the rights conferred upon him by the Treaty of Unkiar-Skelessi.

[1] Palmerston to Temple, Oct. 8, ap. Bulwer, *Life*, ii. 171.

For the moment the assurance was accepted, but Palmerston made up his mind that at the first convenient opportunity the treaty itself should be torn up.

In September a conference was held between the Tsar, the Austrian Emperor, and the Crown Prince of Prussia at Münchengrätz. Its outcome was a formal Convention (September 18, 1833) between Russia and Austria, by which the two Powers mutually undertook to oppose any extension of the authority of the Egyptian Pasha over the European provinces of the Ottoman Empire, and agreed that, should their efforts fail to maintain the integrity of that empire, they would act in the closest concert in regard to future dispositions. The second provision, as Goriainow [1] points out, was studiously vague : the first was precise. Sultan Mahmud nearly provoked a renewal of the troubles by shuffling about the cession of Adana, but eventually gave way, and by the beginning of 1834 the first phase of the Egyptian crisis was at an end.

The diplomatic fires were only smouldering. Sultan Mahmud was eager to be revenged upon his detested rival in Egypt, and in particular to recover Syria ; between England and France there was increasing suspicion and tension ; while the Tsar Nicholas made no secret of his dislike for the Orleanist Monarchy in France, and his contempt for the policy pursued by its ministers. By 1838 events seemed hastening towards a renewed war in the Near East. The Sultan had invoked the help of Prussia in the reorganization of his army, and Prussia had lent him the services of a young officer, destined to fame as the conqueror of Austria and France, Helmuth von Moltke. By the conclusion (August 19, 1838) of a commercial treaty with England, the Sultan not only drew closer the ties between that country and himself, but at the same time, with consummate adroitness, deprived Mehemet Ali of much of the

[1] *Op cit.*, p. 52.

advantage derived from his commercial monopolies, and still further widened the breach between Egypt and England.

Mehemet Ali was, on his side, chafing under the restrictions imposed upon him by the Convention of Kutaya, and was restrained from declaring his formal independence only by the pressure of the Powers. In Syria, however, his rule proved to be as unpopular as it was tyrannical, a fact which encouraged the Sultan in his resolution to delay his revenge no longer. The Powers did their utmost to dissuade him ; Moltke warned him that the army was not ready ; but Mahmud would listen to no counsels of prudence, and in the spring of 1839 the war for the reconquest of Syria began. The issue was disastrous. In April, 1839, a large Turkish force crossed the Euphrates, and on June 24 it was routed by Ibrahim near Nessib, on the Syrian frontier. Nearly 15,000 prisoners were taken, and almost the whole of the Turkish artillery and stores fell into his hands. His victory was complete and conclusive.

Before the news could reach Constantinople the old Sultan died (June 30), with rage in his heart and curses on his lips. He was succeeded by his son, Abdul Mejid, a youth of sixteen. Nothing could have been darker than the prospects of the new reign. Close upon the news of the disaster at Nessib came tidings of treachery in the fleet. The admiral, Ahmed Pasha, had carried off the Turkish fleet to Alexandria, and had surrendered it to Mehemet Ali.

The young Sultan promptly opened direct negotiations with the Egyptian Pasha. The latter demanded that the hereditary government of both Egypt and Syria should be secured to him, and the Sultan seemed disposed to acquiesce, when the Powers intervened.

On July 27, 1839, the Powers presented a collective note to the Porte, demanding the suspension of direct negotiations between the Sultan and the Pasha. To this the Sultan joyfully assented.

His assent only served to sow the seeds of discord between the members of the Concert. The soil was congenial. The government of Louis-Philippe was lavish in encouragements to Mehemet Ali. Firm alliance with the Egyptian adventurer seemed to open the prospect of a restoration of French prestige throughout the Near East. Strong in possession of Algeria, cordially united with Spain, France might even hope to convert the Mediterranean into a French lake ; and, by cutting a canal through the isthmus of Suez, might neutralize the advantages secured to England by the possession of Cape Colony.

England, however, had in 1839 taken the precaution to occupy Aden, and, with the rest of the Powers, was not minded to permit the break-up of the Ottoman Empire and the substitution of the rule of Mehemet Ali for that of a feeble youth at Constantinople. Hitherto England and France had acted in cordial co-operation in regard to the Near Eastern Question, and had to some extent succeeded in resisting the ambitions of Russia. The Tsar Nicholas now saw an opportunity of turning the tables upon the Western Powers, and in September, 1839, sent Baron Brunnow to London to make certain specific proposals to Lord Palmerston. The Treaty of Unkiar-Skelessi should be allowed to lapse ; the straits be closed to all ships of war ; Mehemet Ali should be restricted to the hereditary government of Egypt ; and Russia should go hand in hand with England towards a final solution of the Near Eastern problem.

Lord Palmerston was naturally attracted by the prospect, if only as a means of checking the ambitions of France. He was no more disposed to allow France to erect an exclusive protectorate over Egypt than he had been to see Russia supreme at Constantinople. Of Louis-Philippe he was at once contemptuous and mistrustful. His colleagues and his sovereign, on the other hand, were strongly averse to a rupture with France. Palmerston did not desire it ; neither did he fear it. 'It is evident', he writes to Bulwer, 'the French Government will not willingly take the slightest step of coercion against Mehemet Ali . . . anxious as we are to continue to go on with them, we are not at all prepared to stand still with them. They must therefore take this choice between three courses : either to go forward with us and honestly redeem the pledges they have given to us and to Europe ; or to stand aloof and shrink from a fulfilment of their own spontaneous declaration ; or lastly, to go right about and league themselves with Mehemet Ali, and employ force to prevent us, and those other Powers who may join us, from doing that which France herself is bound by every principle of honour and every enlightened consideration of her real interests, to assist us in doing, instead of preventing from being done.' [1]

As to the future of Turkey, Palmerston was far from pessimistic. 'All that we hear about the decay of the Turkish Empire, and its being a dead body or a sapless trunk, and so forth, is pure and unadulterated nonsense.' Given ten years of peace under European protection, coupled with internal reform, there seemed to him no reason why 'it should not become again a respectable Power'. For the moment two things were essential : Mehemet must be compelled 'to withdraw into his original shell of Egypt', and the protection afforded to Turkey must be European, not exclusively Russian. These were the key-notes of Palmerston's policy in the Near East. Negotiations between the Powers were protracted, but Palmerston had the satisfaction of seeing his views prevail.

France, however, was excluded from the settlement. In February, 1840, Thiers had come into power in France. Thiers had always asserted the claims of France to supreme influence in the Near East with peculiar vehemence, and

[1] September, 1839.

Palmerston soon convinced himself and the rest of the Powers that Thiers was playing exclusively for his own hand. The policy adopted by Russia in 1833, and so recently repudiated, was to be precisely repeated on the part of France.

In order to avert a European war a sharp lesson had to be administered to Thiers. If he were allowed to persist in his course in regard to Egypt, Russia would resume her claims over Constantinople. The ultimate result would, therefore, be 'the practical division of the Ottoman Empire into two separate and independent States, whereof one would be a dependency of France and the other a satellite of Russia'. Only by a threat of resignation did Palmerston bring his colleagues into agreement with himself, and on July 15, the four Powers—Russia, Prussia, Austria, and Great Britain—concluded with the Porte a 'convention for the pacification of the Levant'.

Under this Convention the Sultan agreed to confer upon Mehemet the hereditary Pashalik of Egypt, and, for his life, the administration of southern Syria, including the fortress of St. Jean d'Acre, with the title of Pasha of Acre. Failing Mehemet's acceptance within ten days, the latter part of the offer was to be withdrawn ; failing acceptance within twenty days, the whole offer. The rest of the contracting Powers, Great Britain, Russia, Austria, and Prussia, agreed to force their terms upon Mehemet ; to prevent sea-communication between Egypt and Syria, to defend Constantinople, and guarantee the integrity of the Ottoman Empire.[1]

It was, at the same time, expressly provided (Art. 4) that

---

[1] The full text of the Convention in French is printed in an appendix to Bulwer's *Life of Palmerston*, ii. 420–7 ; also (in English) in Holland's *European Concert in the Eastern Question*, pp. 90–7. The whole course of the preceding negotiations is described, with full references to the documents, in Goriainow, *op. cit.*, chap. x—of course, from the Russian point of view.

the naval protection of the straits against Mehemet Ali should
be regarded as an exceptional measure, ' adopted at the express
demand of the Sultan ', and it was agreed ' that such measure
should not derogate in any degree from the ancient rule of
the Ottoman Empire, in virtue of which it has in all times been
prohibited for ships of war of foreign Powers to enter the Straits
of the Dardanelles and of the Bosphorus '.

The Treaty of Unkiar-Skelessi was torn into shreds. Two
questions remained : would Mehemet Ali accept the terms to
be offered to him by the Sultan ? if not, could he count upon
the help of France in defying the will of Europe ?

The Quadruple Treaty aroused profound indignation in
France. For the best of reasons Palmerston had kept that
country in the dark as to its impending conclusion. Had
France known of it Mehemet Ali would undoubtedly have
been encouraged to thwart the will of Europe, and a general
war would have ensued.[1]

But Thiers was incensed no less at the substance of the
Convention than at the methods employed to secure it. The
Citizen King and his subjects had undeniably been bowed out
of the European Concert by Lord Palmerston. The will of
Europe was imposed explicitly upon Mehemet Ali ; implicitly
upon France. Thiers was all for defying the allied Powers.
Warlike preparations were pushed on apace ; the army and
fleet were strengthened, the fortification of Paris was begun,
and for a moment it seemed probable that a great European
conflagration would break out. Palmerston was quite unmoved.
He knew his man. He did not believe that Louis-Philippe was
' the man to run amuck, especially without any adequate
motive '.[2] Bulwer, therefore, was instructed to tell Thiers

---

[1] Palmerston's reasons are conclusively and exhaustively explained in a
letter to Hobhouse printed in the *English Historical Review* for January, 1903.

[2] To Bulwer, July 21, 1840.

' in the most friendly and inoffensive manner that if France throws down the gauntlet we shall not refuse to pick it up '.[1] Palmerston's confidence in his own judgement was not misplaced. His diagnosis of the situation was accurate. Louis-Philippe knew that a European war would complicate the domestic situation in France, and might imperil his dynasty. The fiery Thiers was permitted to resign in October and was replaced by Guizot, who was at once friendly to England and anxious to preserve peace in Europe.

The task was not an easy one. In the Levant things had been moving fast since the signature of the Quadrilateral treaty. As a precautionary measure the British Mediterranean squadron had been ordered to cut off all communication by sea between Egypt and Syria, and a portion of it, with some Austrian frigates, appeared off Beyrout on August 11, 1840. Ibrahim was now in a dangerous position, and Mehemet Ali, having virtually refused the terms required in the Convention of London, applied for protection to France. In September, therefore, the Sultan, with the approval of the four Powers, declared him to be deposed from all his governorships, and at the same time Sir Charles Napier bombarded and captured Beyrout, under the eyes of Ibrahim and the Egyptian army. Sidon was taken before the middle of October, and on November 3 the great fortress of St. Jean d'Acre, hitherto deemed impregnable, surrendered to Sir Charles Napier. Ibrahim himself had already been defeated by a force of British and Austrian marines, and Mehemet Ali at last realized that his hold upon Syria was gone for ever.

The British fleet then proceeded to Alexandria, and Mehemet Ali was compelled to yield to the will of the Powers. In return for the hereditary Pashalik of Egypt he agreed to surrender the Turkish fleet, which, since 1839, had been in his hands;

[1] To Bulwer, September 20, 1840.

R 2

to evacuate Syria, Arabia, and Crete; and to comply with the terms set forth in the Convention of London. The Porte, now relieved of all anxiety, hesitated to fulfil its part of the bargain. Palmerston was consequently obliged to apply pressure at Constantinople, and on June 1, 1841,[1] the Sultan issued a Firman by which, after an acknowledgement of the 'zeal and sagacity of Mehemet Ali', and a reference to the 'experience and knowledge which he had acquired in the affairs of Egypt', the government of Egypt, together with Nubia, Kordofan, Darfur, and Sennaar, was solemnly conferred upon him 'with the additional privilege of hereditary succession'.[2]

The Egyptian question was now settled. The European crisis was also successfully surmounted, thanks partly to the pacific disposition of Guizot and his bourgeois King, thanks even more to the incomparable self-confidence and undeviating firmness with which Lord Palmerston had conducted a series of difficult negotiations.

France was invited to re-enter the European Concert, and on July 13, 1841, a second Treaty of London was concluded between England, Russia, Austria, Prussia, and France. The Porte recovered Syria, Crete, and Arabia; Mehemet was confirmed in the hereditary Pashalik of Egypt under the suzerainty of the Sultan; and the Powers agreed that the Dardanelles and the Bosphorus should be closed to all foreign ships of war so long as the Turkish Empire was at peace. Palmerston's triumph was complete. The claim of Russia to a protectorate over Turkey, that of France to a protectorate over Egypt, was firmly repudiated; the Treaty of Unkiar-Skelessi was set aside; Turkey was rescued both from the

---

[1] To the terms of the original Firman of February 13 the Pasha had successfully objected.

[2] The full text of a remarkable and historic document will be found in Holland, *op. cit.*, pp. 110 sqq.

hostility of Mehemet Ali and from the friendship of Russia ; the will of Great Britain was made to prevail ; the peace of Europe was secured.

With the conclusion of the Treaty of London Mehemet Ali disappears from the political stage on which for five-and-thirty years he had played so conspicuous a part. He lived until 1849, but some years before his death his mind gave way, and the actual government of Egypt was vested in Ibrahim. Ibrahim, however, died before his father, in 1848, and on his death the Pashalik passed to his son Abbas I.

The country which Mehemet had recreated became, subject to the payment of an annual tribute to the Porte, completely autonomous in an administrative and economic sense. The Pasha was at liberty to conclude commercial, financial, and administrative conventions with foreign Powers ; he could, by consent, vary the terms of the ' capitulations ', raise loans, and set up any domestic institutions which seemed good to him. Yet the international position of Egypt was peculiar. Subject to an obligation to render military assistance when required to the suzerain, the Pasha was master of his own military establishment. With his African neighbours he could fight to his heart's content. He was prohibited from making war, without the Sultan's consent, upon any European Power ; but, obviously, no European Power could exact reparation, for any injury inflicted, from the Pasha, without a violation of international law, and offering a *casus belli* to the suzerain Power. The difficulties and contradictions involved in this situation were clearly revealed in the last decades of the nineteenth century, when Egypt again became the pivot of international politics.

A word seems to be required, before this chapter closes, as to the relations of the two Powers which, apart from the Ottoman Empire itself, were most intimately concerned in the events recorded in the preceding pages.

Russia and England

It was not until the outbreak of the Greek insurrection that Russia and Great Britain had come into contact in Near Eastern affairs. Canning laid down the principle that Russia must not be permitted to regard those affairs as her own exclusive concern. He, like his master Pitt, grasped the truth that Great Britain was not less interested than Russia, and much more interested than any other Great Power, in the fate of the Ottoman Empire. The Duke of Wellington, shocked by the ' untoward incident ' of Navarino, deserted Canning's principles and dissipated the hard-won fruits of his diplomacy. The Tsar profited by Wellington's blunder in 1829, and was tempted to an even bolder experiment in 1833.

But Canning's mantle had fallen, in even ampler folds, upon the shoulders of Palmerston. It was Palmerston, more definitely than Canning, who established the tradition that the actions of Russia in the Near East must be watched with ceaseless vigilance, not to say continuous jealousy. The lesson of Unkiar-Skelessi was always before his eyes. It revealed, as he thought, the true mind of Russia. Her real policy was not the annihilation of the Ottoman Empire, but its preservation in tutelage to herself. As a fact, Russian policy has throughout the nineteenth century halted between these two opinions.

As far back as 1802 Count Victor placed the two alternatives clearly before his master, Alexander I : on the one hand, the policy of partition ; on the other, the maintenance of a feeble power at Constantinople under a Russian protectorate.

This latter policy, as we have seen, attained the zenith of its success in the Treaty of Unkiar-Skelessi. But for the jealous vigilance of Palmerston the position then acquired by Russia might have been permanently consolidated. But if the lesson of 1833 sank deep into Palmerston's mind, so did that of 1840–1 make a profound impression upon the mind of the Tsar Nicholas.

The intellect of Nicholas may have been narrow, but it was singularly acute. He frankly recognized that England was hardly less interested than Russia in finding a satisfactory solution of the Near Eastern problem, and he endeavoured honestly, according to his lights, to assist her in the quest.

In the summer of 1844 the Tsar paid a visit to the English Court, and upon all with whom he came in contact his personality produced a pleasing impression. On public affairs, particularly those relating to the Eastern Question, he opened his mind freely to Lord Aberdeen, who was Foreign Secretary at the time, and to other statesmen in England, including the Prince Consort. The views expressed in conversation he was at pains to amplify and embody in a written memorandum. According to the account of it given by the Duke of Argyll, this singularly instructive document contained the following leading propositions : ' That the maintenance of Turkey in its existing territory and degree of independence is a great object of European policy. That in order to preserve that maintenance the Powers of Europe should abstain from making on the Porte demands conceived in a selfish interest, or from assuming towards it an attitude of exclusive dictation. That, in the event of the Porte giving to any one of the Powers just cause of complaint, that Power should be aided by the rest in its endeavours to have that cause removed. That all the Powers should urge on the Porte the duty of conciliating its Christian subjects, and should use all their influence, on the other hand, to keep those subjects to their allegiance. That, in the event of any unforeseen calamity befalling the Turkish Empire, Russia and England should agree together as to the course that should be pursued.' [1]

[1] *Autobiography of the eighth Duke of Argyll*, i. 443. The Duke gives a

' Nothing ', as the Duke justly says, ' could be more reasonable, nothing more friendly and even confidential towards us than this declaration of views and intentions of the Emperor of Russia.' The memorandum, so he tells us, remained in the Foreign Office, and ' was handed on by each minister to his successor ', and he adds an expression of his own strong conviction that ' if the Emperor Nicholas had abided by the assurances of this memorandum, the Crimean War would never have arisen '.[1] Be that as it may there can be no doubt that the personal relations established by the Tsar in 1844 with English statesmen, and particularly with Lord Aberdeen, who in 1852 became Prime Minister, did predispose them to anticipate with a confidence, which was perhaps excessive, a peaceful issue to the difficulties which then arose. On the other hand, the Tsar had drawn from his conversations in London an inference, even more fatally erroneous : that under no circumstances, so long as Lord Aberdeen controlled its destinies, would Great Britain draw the sword. In these mutual misunderstandings we have, perhaps, a warning against ' amateur ' diplomacy. That they were, in part, responsible for a most unhappy war cannot be denied.

With the antecedents and course of that war the next chapter will be concerned.

For reference : A. A. Paton, *A History of the Egyptian Revolution* (Trübner, 1863) ; C. de Freycinet, *La Question d'Égypte* (Paris, 1904) (presents the French point of view with admirable lucidity and ample reference to documents) ; Major John Hall, *England and the Orleans Monarchy* (Smith, Elder & Co., 1912 : a valuable monograph ; *bien documentée*) ; Serge Goriainow, *Le Bosphore et les Dardanelles* (written from the Russian documents by the Director of the Imperial Archives at St. Petersburg, and

vivid description of the Tsar. Cf. also *Queen Victoria's Letters*, ii. 13 -23, for the impression produced on the Court.

[1] *Autobiography of the eighth Duke of Argyll*, i. 444.

invaluable as presenting the Russian point of view); Dalling and Ashley, *Life of Lord Palmerston* (Bentley, 1870: vol. ii consists almost entirely of original letters and documents of first-rate importance); T. E. Holland, *European Concert in the Eastern Question* (Clarendon Press, 1885) (invaluable for texts); Hertslet, as before.

IO

The Crimean War

'Had it not been for the Crimean War and the policy subsequently adopted by Lord Beaconsfield's Government, the independence of the Balkan States would never have been achieved, and the Russians would now be in possession of Constantinople.'—LORD CROMER.

'A war to give a few wretched monks the key of a Grotto.'—THIERS.

'The only perfectly useless modern war that has been waged.'—SIR ROBERT MORIER.

'The Turkish Empire is a thing to be tolerated but not to be reconstructed: in such a cause . . . I will not allow a pistol to be fired.'—TSAR NICHOLAS.

AFTER twenty years of continuous storms (1822–41) Eastern Europe was permitted to enjoy a spell of unusual calm. It proved to be no more than an interlude between two periods of upheaval, but it lasted long enough (1841–52) to give the young Sultan, Abdul Mejid, an opportunity of putting his house in order.

Reforms in Turkey

The leader of the reform party was Reshid Pasha, who had been Turkish ambassador at the Court of St. James's, and had imbibed, during his residence in London, many ideas as to the nature of political progress in the West. His efforts to apply to his own country the lessons learnt in England were warmly encouraged by Sultan Mahmud and by his successor Abdul Mejid.

In 1839 all the grandees of the Ottoman Empire, viziers, ulemas, dignitaries secular and ecclesiastical, with the diplomatic corps were summoned to the place of Gülhanè; prayer was offered up; the omens were consulted; a salute of a hundred and one guns was fired, and then the young Sultan proclaimed, with all possible solemnity, the issue of a *Hattisherif*, an organic Charter of Liberties, sometimes known in history as the *Tanzimat*. The Sultan declared his fixed resolve to secure for the Ottoman Empire the benefits of a reformed administration : security of life, honour, and property was to be guaranteed to every subject; taxes were to be imposed and collected according to a fixed method ; military service was to be regulated; the administration of justice was to be reformed, and something in the nature of a representative, though not an elected, council to be instituted.

The announcement of this comprehensive programme marks an epoch of no little significance in the history of the Ottoman Empire. Nor was its execution delayed. A large scheme of military reform was initiated in 1843. The army, recruited in European fashion, was henceforth to be divided into two parts : the *Nizam*, or active army, in which men were to serve for five years ; and the *Redif*, or reserve, in which they were to serve for a further seven years.

Later on local government was reorganized, and a determined attempt was made to put a stop to the farming of the taxes and the gross abuses connected with that antiquated fiscal system. The market for negro-slaves was abolished, and the large profits accruing to the State therefrom were surrendered. Nor was education neglected. The ecclesiastical monopoly of education was restricted ; a medical school and a military academy were established, and a great impulse was given to technical training by the institution of schools of commerce, science, and art.

Finally, the Sultan declared that there should be no discrimination between the several creeds : Moslems, Jews, and Christians were all to regard themselves as equally under the protection of the sovereign, children of the same father.

Sentiments so enlightened, especially when translated, however tentatively, into action, could not fail to excite alarm and provoke opposition among the obscurantist elements of the Sultan's Empire. Nor did the reactionaries lack either numbers or influence. The ulemas denounced Reshid as a giaour ; declared that the Almighty would not fail to visit with his wrath such a blasphemous violation of the Koran ; that the *Hatti-sherif* was contrary to the fundamental law of the Ottoman Empire, and that the attempt to put Moslem and Christian on an equality, so far from allaying discontent, would promote unrest among the subject populations and encourage perpetual agitation.

The latter prediction seemed, indeed, likely to be justified. Concession served to whet the appetite for reform. The war of creeds blazed out more fiercely than ever, and each sect in turn applied to its external protector : the Orthodox to the Tsar ; the Catholics to France ; the few Protestants to England. The quarrels of the Greeks and Latins were, as we shall see, not the least important among the many contributory causes which issued in the great European conflagration known to history as the Crimean War.

Origins of the Crimean War

What Aristotle said of revolutions is true also of wars. The occasions may be trivial, the causes are always important. Emphatically was this the case with the Crimean War. It may be that the faggots were laid by the squabbles of the Greek and Latin monks in the Holy Land. Louis Napoleon may have applied the match to highly inflammable materials. The personalities of the Tsar Nicholas, of his ambassador Menschikoff, of Lord Stratford de Redcliffe, even, in another sense, of Lord Aberdeen, may have contributed to the outbreak. But to regard such things as the essential causes of the war implies a singularly superficial apprehension of the majestic and deliberate operation of historic forces. Kinglake wanted a villain for the central figure of his brilliant romance, and found him in the Emperor Napoleon. Much may be forgiven to a supreme artist, and something, as was hinted, to the disappointed suitor.[1] But scientific history is compelled to look further and deeper.

That Louis Napoleon was the immediate firebrand is indisputable. In 1850 he took up with great zeal the cause of the Roman Catholics in the Near East. In 1852 M. de Lavalette, the French ambassador at Constantinople, was instructed to insist upon the claims of the Latin monks to the guardianship of the Holy Places in Palestine. 'Stated in bare terms', writes Kinglake, ' the question was whether for the purpose of passing through the building into their Grotto, the Latin monks should have the key of the chief door of the Church of Bethlehem, and also one of the keys of each of the two doors of the sacred manger, and whether they should be at liberty to place in the sanctuary of the Nativity a silver star adorned with the arms of France.'[2] So stated, the question at issue seems puerile to the verge of criminal levity. But behind a question superficially trivial was the tradition of three hundred years of French diplomacy in the Levant. The privileged position bestowed upon France and its clients by Suleiman the Magnificent had, as we have seen, been specifically

---

[1] Kinglake is said to have been a suitor for the favours of Miss Howard, Napoleon's mistress : F. A. Simpson, *Rise of Louis Napoleon,* p. 162.

[2] *Invasion of the Crimea,* i. 46.

renewed and guaranteed by the more formal *Capitulations* of May 28, 1740.[1] Since 1740 the Latin monks had neglected their duties as custodians of the Holy Places, the Greeks had stepped into their shoes, with the tacit assent of France who had lost interest in the matter.

Louis Napoleon saw his chance. He was now on the brink of achieving his lifelong ambition. After two humiliating, but not futile, fiascoes [2] the ' man of destiny ' had come forward, at the precise psychological moment in 1848, and, declaring his name to be ' the symbol of order, nationality, and glory ', had announced his candidature for the Presidency of the Second Republic established on the collapse of the July Monarchy. In the contest which ensued, Lamartine, the hero of February, received less than 18,000 votes ; Cavaignac, who in the terrible ' days of June ' had saved the State, received less than a million and a half ; the unknown man, who bore the name of Napoleon, received 5,434,226. But Louis Napoleon had still to make good. He obtained a confirmation and prolongation of his Presidency by the *coup d'état* of December, 1851, and after a second *coup d'état* in December, 1852, he transformed the Presidency into an hereditary empire. He relied for support fundamentally upon the peasants of France, but more immediately on the two highly organized forces in France, the Church and the Army. The Bourgeois Monarchy had failed to touch the imagination of France. ' La France s'ennuie ', as Lamartine had sagaciously observed. Her prestige abroad had suffered severely from the conduct of foreign affairs under Louis-Philippe, particularly in that quarter as to which France was most sensitive—the Levant. Lord Palmerston had elbowed France out of the

---

[1] Articles 33–6 and 82 deal specifically with *Les Lieux saints*.

[2] At Strasburg (1836), at Boulogne (1840), the second followed by six years' imprisonment.

Concert in 1840, and had admitted her on sufferance in 1841.

Such a position was wholly inconsistent with the Napoleonic interpretation of ' la gloire '. That interpretation the new emperor was determined to revive. The traditions of French diplomacy dictated the direction. Nor was a personal motive lacking. With studied contempt Nicholas had refused to accord the successful conspirator the courtesy which prevailed between crowned heads : he had addressed him not as ' frère ' but as ' bon ami '. The Greek monks at Bethlehem and Jerusalem were to pay for the affront put by the Tsar upon the protector of the Latins.

But if the prestige of France had suffered at the hands of Lord Palmerston, not less had that of Russia. Ever since the days of Peter the Great, Russia had set before herself two supreme objects : a virtual protectorate over the Christian subjects of the Sultan ; and the domination of the Bosphorus and the Dardanelles. These objects had been practically attained when the Sultan, in 1833, signed the Treaty of Unkiar-Skelessi. That treaty Lord Palmerston had torn up.

For Great Britain, though tardy in realizing the significance of the Near Eastern Question to herself, was now deeply impressed with a sense of the danger to be apprehended whether from a French protectorate over Egypt or from a Russian protectorate over Turkey. To repudiate the exclusive pretensions of both Russia and France was, therefore, the key-note of English foreign policy throughout three-quarters of the nineteenth century.

Not that England asserted any exclusive claims on her own behalf. On the contrary, the principle to which she firmly adhered was that the problem of the Near East could be solved only by the Powers in Concert. That concert she has honestly endeavoured to maintain, and in maintaining it she has, to a large extent unconsciously, given room and opportunity for the growth of a new and vitalizing principle, the principle of nationality.

In this diagnosis of the situation the modern reader will detect, or imagine that he has detected, a palpable omission. What, he will ask, was the attitude of the German Powers, Austria and Prussia, and of Italy ? Austria was deeply interested, but preoccupied. The Habsburg dominions, German, Magyar, Bohemian, and Italian, had barely emerged from the crisis of 1848–9 : the crisis which had displaced Metternich, and threatened with disruption the empire which he had so long governed. Only the intervention of the Tsar Nicholas had preserved Hungary to the Habsburgs, and though gratitude, as events were soon to prove, is not the most conspicuous attribute of the Austrian House, the policy of the young emperor was at the moment in complete accord with that of his preserver.[1] Prussia had played no independent part in Eastern affairs since Metternich's accession to power. Italy had not yet come into being. But, as we shall see, the man destined to create it was no sooner in power than he firmly asserted that the Italy of the future had a vital interest in the solution of the Near Eastern Problem. For the moment, however, the game was in the hands of the Tsar Nicholas, Napoleon, and Great Britain.

The demands made, on behalf of the Latin monks, by Napoleon were supported by the other Roman Catholic powers : Austria, Spain, Sardinia, Portugal, Belgium, and Naples ; and after some delay they were, in substance, conceded by the Sultan. The concession roused bitter resentment in the mind of the Tsar Nicholas, who demanded, from the Porte, its immediate rescission. Thus the Porte found itself,

[1] ' When I speak of Russia I speak of Austria as well ' : Tsar Nicholas to Sir G. H. Seymour. *Eastern Papers*, Part V, 1854.

not for the first time, between the upper and the nether millstone; and, in order to escape from that embarrassing situation, the Sultan played an old diplomatic trick. His decision on the points at issue was embodied in a letter to the French chargé d'affaires, and in a Firman addressed to the Greek patriarch at Jerusalem. The language of the two documents was not identical: the letter laid stress upon the substantial concessions to France; the Firman dwelt upon the claims denied. In the upshot France was satisfied, Russia was not.

Accordingly, in March, 1853, the Tsar dispatched to Constantinople Prince Menschikoff, a rough and overbearing soldier, who was charged not only to obtain full satisfaction in regard to the Holy Places, but to demand from the Sultan a virtual acknowledgement, embodied in a formal treaty, of the Tsar's protectorate over all the Orthodox subjects of the Porte. On the question of the Holy Places the Tsar had a strong case; his claim to a protectorate over the Greek Church in Turkey was, on the contrary, an extravagant extension of the vague and indefinite engagements contained in the Treaty of Kainardji, and in subsequent conventions concluded between Russia and the Ottoman Empire.

This demand appeared to the British Government to be wholly inadmissible.

'No sovereign,' wrote Lord Clarendon, 'having a proper regard for his own dignity and independence, could admit proposals so undefined as those of Prince Menschikoff, and by treaty confer upon another and more powerful sovereign a right of protection over a large portion of his own subjects. However well disguised it may be, yet the fact is that under the vague language of the proposed Sened a perpetual right to interfere in the internal affairs of Turkey would be conferred upon Russia, for governed as the Greek subjects of the Porte are by their ecclesiastical authorities, and looking as these latter would in all things do for protection to Russia, it follows that 14,000,000 of Greeks would henceforth regard the emperor as their supreme protector, and their allegiance to the Sultan would be little more than nominal, while his own independence would dwindle into vassalage.' [1]

Inadmissible in substance, the Russian demand was urged upon the Sultan by Prince Menschikoff with insufferable insolence. But by this time Menschikoff himself had to reckon with an antagonist in whose skilful hands the blustering Russian was a mere child. On April 5 Lord Stratford de Redcliffe returned to Constantinople, and the whole diplomatic situation quickly underwent a complete transformation.[2]

The Tsar Nicholas had always, as we have seen, been anxious to maintain a cordial understanding with England in regard to the Eastern Question, and early in the spring of 1853 he had a series of interviews with Sir Hamilton Seymour, then British ambassador at St. Petersburg. During these interviews he discussed, in the most friendly manner, the relations of their respective countries in the Near East. Recalling his personal friendship with the head of the new ministry, Lord Aberdeen, he insisted that the interests of England and Russia were ' upon almost all questions the same ', and expressed his confidence that the two countries would continue to be on ' terms of close amity '. ' Turkey ', he continued, ' is in a critical state . . . the country itself seems to be falling to pieces . . . we have on our hands a sick man—a very sick man : it will be, I tell you frankly, a great misfortune if, one of these days, he should slip away from us before all necessary arrangements

[1] Lord Clarendon to Lord Stratford, May 31, 1853.

[2] For the relations between the home Government and the ambassador in Constantinople during these critical months see Maxwell's *Life of Lord Clarendon*, vol. ii, chap. xiii.

were made.' In the Tsar's view it was therefore ' very important that England and Russia should come to a perfectly good
understanding on these affairs, and that neither should take
any decisive step of which the other is not apprised '. The Tsar
further asserted that he had entirely abandoned ' the plans
and dreams ' of the Empress Catherine, but frankly admitted
that he had obligations in regard to the Christian subjects
of the Porte which treaties and national sentiment alike
compelled him to fulfil.[1] In his view, however, the governing
fact of the situation was that the Turk was in a state of hopeless
decrepitude. ' He may suddenly die upon our hands : we
cannot resuscitate what is dead ; if the Turkish Empire falls,
it falls to rise no more ; and I put it to you, therefore, whether
it is not better to provide beforehand for a contingency than
to incur the chaos, confusion, and certainty of a European
war, all of which must attend the catastrophe, if it should
occur unexpectedly and before some ulterior system has been
sketched.' England and Russia must settle the matter. But
neither England nor any other Great Power must have Constantinople. Nor would Russia take it permanently ; temporarily she might have to occupy it *en dépositaire* but not
en propriétaire. For the rest, the principalities might continue
to be an independent State under Russian protection ; Serbia
and Bulgaria might receive a similar form of government. To
counterbalance these indirect advantages to Russia, England
might annex Egypt and Crete. On one further point the
Tsar was particularly insistent : ' I never will permit ', he said,
' an attempt at the reconstruction of a Byzantine Empire, or
such an extension of Greece as would render her a powerful
State : still less will I permit the breaking up of Turkey into
little Republican asylums for the Kossuths and Mazzinis and
other revolutionists of Europe ; rather than submit to any of

[1] *Eastern Papers*, Part V (122 of 1854).

these arrangements I would go to war, and as long as I have a man or a musket left would carry it on.'

The English ministers, who had been captivated by the personality of the Tsar in 1844, were aghast at the coolness and candour of the specific proposals which were submitted to them in 1853 through the ordinary diplomatic channels. They refused to admit that the dissolution of the sick man was imminent ; they repudiated with some heat the idea of a possible partition of his inheritance ; they pointed out, with unanswerable force, that ' an agreement in such a case tends very surely to hasten the contingency for which it is intended to provide ; they urged the Tsar to act with forbearance towards the Porte ; they objected to an agreement concluded behind the back of Austria and France ; and, finally, they declined, courteously but very firmly, to entertain the proposals of the Tsar '.[1]

Those proposals were in form almost brutally candid, but there is no reason to doubt that they were put forward with a genuine desire to find a solution for a hitherto insoluble problem. Nor was the Tsar's diagnosis of the case substantially inaccurate. It is tempting to speculate as to what would have happened had the Tsar's advances been accepted by the English Government; but the temptation must be resisted. That they were refused was due largely to the mistrust inspired among ministers by the Treaty of Unkiar-Skelessi, much more to the popular detestation of Russia aroused by her treatment of the Poles, and most of all to the part played by the Tsar in the suppression of the Hungarian insurrection in 1849. Conversely, the Sultan was high in popular favour owing to the asylum he had chivalrously afforded to Louis Kossuth and other Hungarian refugees.

[1] The correspondence briefly summarized above may be read *in extenso* in *Eastern Papers*, Part V (122 of 1854).

Still, none of these reasons, though potent in their appeal to popular passions, can in the dry light of historical retrospect be regarded as an adequate justification of a great European war.

Into that war, however, the Powers were now rapidly ' drifting '. The expression was Lord Aberdeen's, and to him and to several of his colleagues it was undeniably appropriate. To one Englishman it was not. Lord Stratford at Constantinople knew precisely where he was going, and where he intended to go. He was persuaded that there could be no real settlement in the Near East until the pretensions of Russia had been publicly repudiated and until the Tsar had sustained an unmistakable defeat either in diplomacy or in war. If without war so much the better, but by war if necessary.

Lord Stratford's first task was to persuade Menschikoff to separate the question of the Holy Places from that of a general Russian protectorate over the Greek Christians. This important object was attained with consummate adroitness, and Stratford then induced the Porte to give satisfaction to Russia on the former point. Before the end of April the dispute as to the Holy Places was settled. But the concession made by the Porte effected no improvement in the diplomatic situation. On the contrary, as the Porte became more conciliatory, Menschikoff became more menacing. But he was now on weaker ground, on to which he had been lured by Lord Stratford's astuteness. The latter advised the Porte to refuse the protectorate claimed by Russia, and on May 22, 1853, Menschikoff and the staff of the Russian Embassy quitted Constantinople. A week later the Porte addressed to the Powers a Note announcing that ' the question of the Holy Places had terminated in a manner satisfactory to all parties ; that nevertheless the Prince Menschikoff, not satisfied with that, had demanded from the Porte a treaty to guarantee the rights and privileges of all kinds accorded by the Sultan to his Greek subjects '. ' However great ', it continued, ' may be the desire of the Porte to preserve the most amicable relations with Russia, she can never engage herself by such a guarantee towards a foreign Government, either concluding with it a treaty or signing a simple official Note, without compromising gravely her independence and the most fundamental rights of the Sultan over his own subjects.' Despite all this the Porte, though bound to take measures of self-defence, did not abandon hopes of peace.

The hopes became fainter day by day. A large Russian army under Prince Gortschakoff had been mobilized in Bessarabia during the spring ; on July 21 it crossed the Pruth and occupied the principalities. Russia thereupon announced to the Powers that the occupation was not intended as an act of war, but as a ' material guarantee ' for the concession of her just demands. But while condescending to offer this explanation, the Tsar was not greatly concerned as to the attitude of the Western Powers. He was confident that, if war really threatened, Austria and Prussia would send an army to the Rhine and keep France quiet. His confidence was misplaced. Austria, forgetful of the debt she had recently incurred to the Tsar, was more jealous of Russia than of France, and more ready, therefore, to mobilize upon the Danube than upon the Rhine. Moreover, on the news of the impending occupation of the principalities, the combined fleets of England and France had been sent into Besika Bay, and Palmerston believed that the only chance of now convincing Russia that we were in earnest and thus averting war would be to order them up to the Bosphorus and, if necessary, into the Black Sea. But Aberdeen still hung back, and the Sultan was advised, ' in order to exhaust all the resources of patience ', not to resist the Russian invasion by force.

The Vienna Note, July 31

Meanwhile, Austria, though unwilling to fight, was anxious to avert the all but inevitable war. Accordingly, the representatives of England, France, Austria, and Prussia met at Vienna in July and agreed upon a ' Note ' which it was hoped might satisfy both Russia and Turkey. The Note simply reaffirmed the adherence of the Porte to ' the letter and spirit of the Treaties of Kainardji and Adrianople relative to the protection of the Christian religion '. The Note was accepted by Russia, though not, as subsequently appeared, in the sense intended by the mediators. Turkey, like Russia, perceiving its ambiguities, insisted on amending it. For the words above quoted the Porte proposed to read : ' To the stipulations of the Treaty of Kainardji, confirmed by that of Adrianople, relative to the protection *by the Sublime Porte* of the Christian religion.' To a superficial view the amendment may appear a strangely inadequate reason for provoking a European war. But the addition of the words ' by the Sublime Porte ' had revealed, in succinct epitome, the whole question at issue between Russia and Turkey. Did the Treaty of Kainardji give to Russia a general protectorate over the Orthodox subjects of the Sultan ? Since Russia claimed that it did, the Vienna Note was sufficient for her purpose. The diplomatists at Vienna were simple enough to imagine that they had discovered a formula which might, by studied ambiguity, postpone or even avert war. Lord Stratford, however, was quick to perceive the ambiguity, and by the addition of four words, seemingly unimportant, brought Russia out into the open. These words implicitly repudiated the Russian claim to a general protectorate over the Greek Christians. The latter were to be protected not by the Tsar but by the Sultan. Russia promptly refused to accept the amendment ; Lord Stratford encouraged the

Sultan to insist upon it. 'No man', wrote the editor of the *Edinburgh Review*, 'ever took upon himself a larger amount of responsibility than Lord Stratford when he virtually overruled the decision of the four Powers, including his own Government, and acquiesced in—not to say caused—the rejection of the Vienna Note by the Porte after it had been accepted by Russia. The interpretation afterwards put upon that Note by Count Nesselrode showed that he was right ; but, nevertheless, that was the point on which the question of peace and war turned. . . . Russia had formed the design to extort from Turkey, in one form or another, a right of protection over the Christians. She never abandoned that design. She thought she could enforce it. The Western Powers interposed, and the strife began.' [1]

Russo-Turkish War

On October 5 the Porte demanded from Russia the evacuation of the principalities within fifteen days, and on October 23 Turkey declared war. The British fleet had already been ordered up to the Bosphorus—an order of which Russia had some cause to complain as an infraction of the Treaty of 1841.[2] Nevertheless, Russia and the Western Powers still remained at peace, and the Tsar declared that, despite the Turkish declaration of war, he would not take the offensive in the principalities. The Turks, however, attacked vigorously on the Danube, and on November 30 the Russian Black Sea fleet

[1] *Edinburgh Review*, April, 1863, p. 331. Special importance attaches to this article. Written primarily as a review of the two first volumes of Kinglake by the then editor, Henry Reeve, it was carefully revised by Lord Clarendon himself, and may be taken as an authoritative *apologia* for the policy pursued by the Aberdeen Cabinet.

[2] The Russian point of view on this important question is put with great elaboration and detailed reference to the documents in Goriainow, *op. cit.*, pp. 94 sqq.

retaliated by the entire destruction of a Turkish squadron in the Bay of Sinope.

The 'massacre of Sinope' aroused immense indignation in England and France, and must be regarded as the immediate prelude to the European War. 'I have been', wrote Sir James Graham, 'one of the most strenuous advocates of peace with Russia until the last moment; but the Sinope attack and recent events have changed entirely the aspect of affairs. I am afraid that a rupture with Russia is inevitable.'[1]

The Cabinet decided that in consequence of the 'massacre' of Sinope the allied fleets must enter the Black Sea. On January 4, 1854, this momentous order was executed, and it was announced that the English and French admirals had instructions to 'invite' all Russian ships in the Black Sea to withdraw into harbour. Even yet the Western Powers were not at war, and on February 22 Austria, always anxious about the presence of Russian troops in the principalities, but not too straightforward in her diplomacy, intimated that if the Western Powers would present an ultimatum, demanding the evacuation of Moldavia and Wallachia before a given date, she would support them. England and France promptly acted on this suggestion, and on February 27 Lord Clarendon informed Count Nesselrode that Great Britain, having exhausted all the efforts of negotiation, was compelled to call upon Russia 'to restrict within purely diplomatic limits the discussion in which she has for some time been engaged with the Sublime Porte', and by return messenger to 'agree to the complete evacuation of the Provinces of Moldavia and Wallachia by the 30th of April'.

Russia refused this ultimatum on March 19, and on the 27th and 28th the Western Powers declared war. It was then made manifest that Austria's promised support was only diplo-

[1] Parker, *Life of Graham*, ii. 226.

matic ; Prussia—to the great indignation of Queen Victoria—
followed Austria's lead ;[1] the concert on which so much
depended was broken, and England and France were left alone
to sustain an exceptionally arduous struggle.

Can the Crimean War be justified before the tribunal of
impartial history ? Retrospective criticism has tended to the
view that the war, if not a crime, was at least a blunder, and
that it ought to have been and might have been avoided.
Sir Robert Morier, writing in 1870, perhaps expressed the
current opinion when he described it as ' the only perfectly
useless modern war that has been waged '.[2] Lord Salisbury,
some twenty years later, enshrined in classical phrase the
opinion that ' England put her money on the wrong horse '.
The Duke of Argyll, on the contrary, writing at the close of
the century, confessed himself though one of the Cabinet
responsible for the war ' to this day wholly unrepentant '.[3]
More recently Lord Cromer has reaffirmed his conviction that
' had it not been for the Crimean War and the policy subsequently pursued by Lord Beaconsfield the independence of
the Balkan States would never have been achieved, and the
Russians would now be in possession of Constantinople '.[4]
Kinglake has popularized the idea that England was an innocent
tool in the hands of an unscrupulous adventurer, anxious to
establish a throne unrighteously attained, by a brilliant war
causelessly provoked. But to suggest that either Stratford or
Aberdeen was the dupe of Napoleon's ambition is grotesquely
inaccurate.

Popular passions had, as we have seen, been aroused by

---

[1] See the remarkable letters of Queen Victoria to the King of Prussia in
March and June, 1854, *Q. V. L.* iii. 21, 39.

[2] *Memoirs and Letters of Sir Robert Morier*, by his daughter, Mrs. Wemyss,
ii. 215.

[3] *Our Responsibilities for Turkey* (1896), p. 10.   [4] *Essays*, p. 275.

recent events against the Russian Tsar. More reflective opinion inclined to the view that the time had come for a sustained effort to repel the secular ambition of his people. The bias of Russian policy during the last century and a half was unmistakable. From the Treaty of Azov to that of Unkiar-Skelessi the advance had been stealthy but continuous. Was the dissolution of the sick man to be hastened now to satisfy the impatient avarice of the heir presumptive ? Was the Tsar to be allowed to convert the Black Sea into a Russian lake, and to establish an exclusive and dangerous domination in the eastern waters of the Mediterranean ? Was Europe in general, and England in particular, prepared to permit Russia to force upon the Porte a ' diplomatic engagement which would have made her the sole protector of the Christian subjects of the Porte, and therefore the sole arbiter of the fate of Turkey ' ? [1] Rightly or wrongly England came, slowly but steadily, to the conviction that the matter was one of vital concern to Europe at large and to herself in particular ; that the Tsar was determined to assert his claims by force, and that only by force could they be repelled. Of this conviction the Crimean War was the logical and inevitable result.

The Crimean War (1854-6)

To the conduct of that war we must now turn. Early in 1854 a British fleet was sent to the Baltic, under the command of Sir Charles Napier, but though it captured Bomarsund the results of the expedition were disappointingly meagre, and contributed little to the ultimate issue of the war. On April 5 a British force under Lord Raglan, who had served both in the field and at the Horse Guards under the Duke of Wellington, landed at Gallipoli. It was preceded by a French army

[1] Argyll, *op. cit.*, p. 10.

under Marshal Saint-Arnaud, the fellow conspirator of Napoleon III in the first *coup d'état*.

The Russians had already crossed the Danube (March 23) and had besieged Silistria. The prolonged defence of this weakly fortified town was due largely to two English volunteers, Captain Butler and Lieutenant Nasmyth, and in order to support it the allied army moved up from Gallipoli to Varna. There on May 19 a conference was held between Raglan, Saint-Arnaud, and Omar Pasha. On June 23, however, the Russians raised the siege of Silistria, and in July they commenced the evacuation of the principalities. Their withdrawal was due partly to the arrival of the allies on the Black Sea littoral ; partly, perhaps, to the hope of luring them on to a second Moscow expedition ; but most of all to the pressure of Austria, who, with the support of Prussia, had called upon the Tsar to evacuate the principalities. As soon as that had been effected the principalities were occupied, under an arrangement with the Porte, by an Austrian army. That occupation, though perhaps dictated in the first instance by jealousy of Russia, proved in the long run of incomparable advantage to her.

By the end of the first week in August there was no longer a Russian soldier to the west of the Pruth ; the ostensible and immediate object of the European intervention might seem, therefore, to have been attained. But the allies had already reached the momentous decision (June) to ' strike at the very heart of Russian power in the East—and that heart is at Sebastopol '.[1] On July 22 Lord Clarendon stated explicitly that they would no longer be satisfied by the restoration of the *Status quo ante bellum.* They must at least secure guarantees on four points :

1. Russia must be deprived of the Treaty Rights in virtue of which she had occupied the principalities ;

[1] *The Times,* June 24, 1854.

2. Turkey must be guarded against attack from the Russian navy in the Black Sea ;

3. The navigation of the Danube must, in the interests of European commerce, be secured against the obstruction caused by Russia's ' uncontrolled possession of the principal mouth of the Danube ' ; and

4. The stipulations of the Treaty of Kainardji relative to the protection of the Christians must be amended, since that treaty ' has become by a wrongful interpretation the principal cause of the present struggle '.[1]

Lord Clarendon's dispatch is of importance as defining at once the causes and the objects of the Crimean War.

On September 14, 1854, the allied army, more than 50,000 strong, disembarked in the Bay of Eupatoria to the north of Sebastopol. On the 19th the march towards Sebastopol began. On the 20th Menschikoff, in command of 40,000 troops, tried to stop the advance of the allies on the Alma— a stream about fifteen miles north of Sebastopol. After three hours of severe fighting the Russians were routed. The allies, though victorious, suffered heavily. But Raglan, despite the lack of transport and the ravages of cholera, wanted to make an immediate assault upon Sebastopol. Had his advice been taken Sebastopol would almost infallibly have fallen. But Saint-Arnaud, in the grip of a mortal disease, vetoed the suggestion, and it was decided to march round the head of the harbour and approach Sebastopol from the south. This difficult operation was effected without resistance from Menschikoff, who had withdrawn his main army into the interior, leaving the fortress under-garrisoned, and on the 26th Raglan occupied the harbour of Balaclava. Again Raglan

---

[1] Lord Clarendon to Lord Westmorland, Ambassador at Vienna, July 22, 1854.—*Eastern Papers.*

wanted to assault, this time from the south, and was strongly seconded by Admiral Sir Edmund Lyons, who was commanding the fleet. Saint-Arnaud was now dying on board ship,[1] and the command of the French force devolved upon General Canrobert, a man of great personal bravery, but devoid of the moral courage essential for high command. Canrobert was not less strongly opposed than Saint-Arnaud to the idea of assault, and the allied forces, therefore, encamped to the south of the fortress, and made slow preparations for a regular siege.

The hesitation of the allies gave the defenders of Sebastopol a chance which they seized with consummate adroitness and skill. They cleared the Russian ships of guns and men : sank some of the largest ships at the entrance to the harbour— thus rendering the allied fleets comparatively useless—and mounted the guns on shore ; Colonel von Todleben, the great engineer, and Admiral Korniloff worked with such energy and enthusiasm that the town was rapidly placed in a posture of defence. On October 17 the bombardment began. The experience of the first day was sufficient to prove the inadequacy of the preparations for a siege. In order to arm three batteries the English Commander had to dismantle ships and employ seamen.

But no perceptible effect was produced upon the fortress, and on October 25 the allies were unpleasantly reminded of the dangers to which their position was exposed by Menschikoff's strategy. Reinforced from home, Menschikoff, at the head of 30,000 men, re-entered Sebastopol, while a large detachment under General Liprandi delivered from outside an attack on the position of the allies, hoping to catch them between two fires and drive them out of Balaclava.

The familiar story of the battle of Balaclava may not be retold ; enough to say that the enemy, though repulsed in their attack upon Balaclava, retained their position on the

[1] He died on September 29.

heights above, and the besiegers were now, in fact, besieged, and ten days later were made to realize the fact.

For a regular investment of Sebastopol the allied forces were hopelessly insufficient: for a bombardment the navy had been rendered useless by Menschikoff's ingenious device, and the army by itself could make little impression on a fortress which six weeks before might have been taken by assault, but was rendered every day more proof against a siege by the greatest engineer of his day. All that the allies could do was to await the arrival of reinforcements, and meanwhile hold their position on the bay of Balaclava and the ridges above it. From that position Menschikoff was determined to dislodge them. The attempt, known as the battle of Inkerman, was made on November 5, with the result that the Russians were compelled to retire with the loss of 10,000 men. Now, if ever, was the moment to storm the fortress. Raglan was in favour of it; Canrobert, however, again refused to concur; and the opportunity of dealing a really effective blow at Menschikoff's army was lost.

On November 14 a terrible disaster befell the allies. A fierce hurricane, accompanied with storms of rain and snow, sprang up, swept down the tents on shore, and destroyed much of the shipping in the roads. *The Prince*, a new steamer of 2,700 tons, was driven on the rocks and thirty other ships foundered in the gale. Stores to the value of £2,000,000 were lost, and the men were deprived of all that might have rendered tolerable the cruel Crimean winter.

The gale was the real beginning of the sufferings which have made the ' Crimean Winter ' a byword in the history of military administration. For many weary months the condition of the British force before Sebastopol was deplorable. After the great fight of Inkerman (November 5) there were no operations on a large scale in the field until the middle of February.

Nevertheless, the intermission of fighting brought no cessation of toil or suffering to the unhappy soldiers.

While the soldiers were thus toiling and suffering in the trenches, the diplomatists were busy at Vienna. Austria, whose policy during this phase of the Eastern Question was consistently subtle, had set negotiations on foot towards the end of 1854, and on December 28 the allied Powers, in conjunction with Austria, presented to the Russian Plenipotentiary a Memorandum embodying the 'Four Points'. They were as follows:

1. The exclusive protectorate exercised by Russia over Moldavia, Wallachia, and Serbia was to cease, and the privileges accorded by the Sultan to the principalities were henceforward to be guaranteed collectively by the five Powers;
2. The navigation of the Danube was to be free;
3. The preponderance of Russia in the Black Sea was to be terminated; and
4. Russia was to renounce all pretensions to a protectorate over the Christian subjects of the Porte; and the five Powers were to co-operate in obtaining from the Sultan the confirmation and observance of the religious privileges of all the various Christian communities without infringing his dignity or the independence of his Crown.

The Conference formally opened on March 15, 1855, but before that date arrived two events had occurred, each, in its way, of profound significance. The first was the intervention of Sardinia; the second the death of the Tsar Nicholas.

On January 26, 1855, Count Cavour appended his signature to a Convention with Great Britain and France, promising the adherence of Sardinia to the alliance. Of good omen for the Western Powers, this step was incomparably the most momentous in the diplomatic history of modern Italy. On the face of it the resolution to take part in the war was at once cynical and foolhardy. What part or lot had the little sub-Alpine kingdom in the quarrel between Russia and the Western Powers ? To Cavour the mere question seemed to imply ' a surrender of our hopes of the future '. Accordingly, despite bitter opposition at home, 18,000 Italians were by the end of April on their way to the Crimea, under the command of General Alfonso La Marmora. ' You have the future of the country in your haversacks.' Such was Cavour's parting injunction to the troops. The response came from a soldier in the trenches, ' Out of this mud Italy will be made '. It was.

The adhesion of Sardinia came as a timely encouragement to the allies. To all those who were longing and working for peace, the death of the Tsar Nicholas seemed of still happier augury. Nicholas was unquestionably the prime author of the war ; he had sustained it with unflagging energy, and he was bitterly disappointed at his failure to bring it to a rapid and brilliant termination. What Russian arms failed to accomplish at the Alma, at Balaclava, and at Inkerman, ' Generals January and February ' might be trusted to achieve. But, as *Punch* felicitously pointed out, ' General February turned traitor '. The Tsar was attacked by influenza, to which on March 2, 1855, he succumbed. The news of his death evoked profound emotion throughout Europe, more particularly at Vienna, where the Conference was in progress.

The accession of the new Tsar, Alexander II, did not, however, render the Russian Plenipotentiaries more pliable. The real crux lay in the proposed limitation of Russian naval preponderance in the Black Sea. To that point Palmerston in particular attached the greatest importance, and on it the negotiations, at the end of April, broke down.[1]

[1] The history of these negotiations may be followed in minute detail in Goriainow, *op. cit.*, chap. xi.

Notwithstanding the failure of the diplomatists at Vienna, the war was nearing its end. Still, there was a great deal of hard fighting round Sebastopol during the spring and summer of 1855. On February 17 a Russian force, 40,000 strong, made a determined effort to take Eupatoria by storm, but was gallantly repulsed by the Turks under Omar Pasha, supported by a French detachment and by five men-of-war in the road-stead. After four hours' continuous fighting, the Russians retired with considerable loss. In March the Russians advanced the defensive works of Sebastopol into the allied lines by the seizure and fortification of a knoll known as the *Mamelon Vert*, and by the construction of a number of rifle pits. Desperate efforts were made by the allies to dislodge them from these advanced points, but without avail.

Towards the end of May, however, the allies planned and executed a diversion at the south-eastern extremity of the Crimea. A combined fleet, under Sir Edmund Lyons and Admiral Bruat, with a considerable force of English, French, and Turkish troops left Sebastopol on May 22, and three days later captured Kertsch and made themselves complete masters of the Straits of Yenikale, which lead from the Black Sea into the Sea of Azov. This expedition, brilliantly successful both in conception and execution, contributed in no slight degree to the general purpose of the campaign. The stores destroyed at Kertsch were computed to amount to nearly four months' rations for 100,000 men—a very serious loss for the Russian army in the Crimea.

On May 16 Canrobert asked to be relieved of his command, and was succeeded by General Pélissier, who was not only a great soldier, but was possessed of the moral courage which Canrobert lacked. He soon infused fresh vigour into the operations before Sebastopol. On June 18 a tremendous assault was delivered by the allies upon the Russian position ;

the French directed their attack upon the Malakoff, the English upon the Redan, two formidable outworks on the east of the fortress. Both attacks were repulsed by the Russians with heavy loss. The failure of the attack upon the Redan was a bitter disappointment to Lord Raglan, who, enervated by anxiety and worn out by ceaseless toil, was carried off by cholera on June 28. A braver soldier and a more gallant gentleman never breathed. The continuance of the French alliance was the best tribute to the extraordinary tact with which for two years he had eased the friction incidental to a difficult situation ; the fall of the great fortress was the posthumous reward of his persistency and courage. General James Simpson succeeded to the command, and reaped where Raglan had sown.

Slowly but surely the allied armies pushed forward their lines towards the Russian fortifications. Once more the covering army, under the command of Prince Michael Gortschakoff, made a desperate and gallant effort to raise the siege. On the night of August 15–16 the Russians descended from the Mackenzie Heights upon the Tchernaya river, where the Sardinian contingent, under General La Marmora, got their first real chance. Nor did they miss it. Fighting with the utmost gallantry they contributed in no small degree to the decisive repulse of the Russian army. Thus were Cavour's calculations precisely fulfilled. In the waters of the Tchernaya the stain of Novara was wiped out for ever ; out of the mud of the Crimean trenches was modern Italy built up. Henceforward Cavour could speak with his enemies in the gate. The victory of the allies at the Tchernaya shattered the last hopes of the besieged from the army in the field. For three weeks the allies kept up a continuous and terribly destructive fire upon the devoted fortress, and on September 8 the attack which had been foiled in June was renewed. The British, with a force miserably inadequate, again attacked the Redan and were again with great loss repulsed, but the Malakoff—the real key of the position—was already in the hands of their allies.

The storming of the Malakoff cost the French 7,500 in killed and wounded, including fifteen generals, but it preluded the fall of Sebastopol. Within a few hours the Russians blew up the magazines, withdrew across the harbour to the north, and on September 9, after a siege of 349 days, the allies occupied the burning ruins of the fortress that had been. The Russian garrison was unwisely permitted to make good its retreat, and thus the fall of Sebastopol did not bring the war to an immediate conclusion.

On November 28 General Fenwick Williams was compelled to surrender the fortress of Kars. He had been sent to reorganize the Turkish forces in Armenia, and with a small Turkish garrison had been holding Kars for nearly six months against overwhelming odds. It was an heroic defence, and it won for Fenwick Williams undying fame. A Turkish force had been dispatched too tardily to the relief of Kars, and before it arrived the little garrison was starved out. General Mouravieff's success at Kars was a slight set-off against the surrender of Sebastopol, and predisposed the mind of the Tsar Alexander to peace.

Treaty of Paris, March 30, 1856

The Emperor Napoleon was even more anxious for it. He had got all he could out of the war; the French army had gained fresh lustre from its concluding passages; the English army had not. Napoleon's restless mind was already busy with the future disposition of Europe. He was looking towards Russia and towards Italy; for England he had no further use. Cavour too had got all he wanted. The main obstacle to peace was Lord Palmerston. He was gravely mistrustful of France, and still more so of Austria. And he had reason. The part played by Austria was crafty, selfish, and even treacherous. Her interest was concentrated upon the Principalities. She had induced England and France to pick the chestnuts out of the fire for her there. Russia having been induced to withdraw from the Principalities, not by the threats of Austria, but by the action of England and France, Austria had promptly occupied them, and had thus enabled Russia to concentrate her efforts upon the Crimea. Finally, as soon as there was a chance of peace, Austria spared no effort to detach Napoleon from the English alliance. In this she nearly succeeded ; but on January 16, 1856, the Tsar (at the instance of his brother-in-law the King of Prussia) accepted as a basis of negotiation the ‘ Four Points ’,[1] including a stipulation for the neutralization of the Black Sea ; on February 1 a protocol embodying these terms was concluded by the representatives of the five Powers at Vienna, and the definitive Peace was signed at Paris on March 30, 1856. The main terms were as follows :

1. The Sublime Porte was formally admitted, on the invitation of the six Powers (including the King of Sardinia), to ‘ participate in the public law and concert of Europe ’, and the Powers engaged severally to respect, and collectively to guarantee ‘ the independence and the territorial integrity of the Ottoman Empire ’.

2. The Sultan, ‘ in his constant solicitude for the welfare of his subjects ’, announced to the Powers his intention to ameliorate their condition ‘ without distinction of creed or race ’ ; but the Powers, while recognizing ‘the high value of this communication’, expressly repudiated the ‘ right to interfere, either collectively or separately’, in the internal affairs of Turkey.

[1] Cf. *supra*, p. 271.

3. The Black Sea was neutralized, its waters and ports were to be open to the mercantile marine of every nation, but permanently ' interdicted to the flag of war ' ; and there were to be no arsenals, either Russian or Turkish, on its coasts.

4. Kars was to be restored to the Turks, and the Crimea to Russia.

5. The navigation of the Danube was to be open on equal terms to the ships of all nations, under the control of an international commission.

6. Southern Bessarabia was to be ceded by Russia to Moldavia. The Principalities of Moldavia and Wallachia were to remain under the suzerainty of the Porte ; Russia renounced her exclusive protectorate over them, and the contracting Powers collectively guaranteed their privileges. They were to enjoy ' an independent and national administration with full liberty of worship, legislation, and commerce, and were to have ' a national armed force '. In each province a national Convention was to be held ' to decide the definitive organization of the Principalities '.

7. The liberties of Serbia were to be similarly guaranteed.

To the main Treaty of Paris there were annexed three Conventions of the same date. With one between England, France, and Russia respecting the Aland Islands we are not here concerned. A second, concluded between the six Powers on the one part and the Sultan on the other part, reaffirmed in the most specific manner the ancient rule of the Ottoman Empire according to which the Straits of the Dardanelles and of the Bosphorus are closed to foreign ships of war, so long as the Porte is at peace. A third, concluded between the Tsar and the Sultan, defined the force and number of light vessels of war which under Art. xiv of the main treaty they were authorized to maintain in the Black Sea, notwithstanding the neutralization of its waters and its ports, for the service of their coasts.

Under a separate treaty, concluded on April 15, Great Britain, Austria, and France agreed to guarantee, jointly and severally, the independence and the integrity of the Ottoman Empire ; they pledged themselves to regard any infraction as a *casus belli*, and undertook to come to an understanding with the Sultan and with each other as to the measures necessary for rendering their guarantee effectual.

By an Addendum to the Treaty, known as the Declaration of Paris, it was agreed to abolish privateering, and to proclaim as permanently accepted principles of maritime war the concessions in favour of neutrals made during the recent war by England and France : (1) a neutral flag was to cover an enemy's goods, except contraband of war ; (2) neutral merchandise, except contraband, was not to be seized under an enemy's flag ; and (3) a blockade must be ' effective ', i. e. maintained by an adequate naval force. Such were the terms of the treaty which crowned the conclusion of the Crimean War.

What had the war achieved ? In reference to one of the most difficult and most interesting of the questions which the war had forced to the front, the future of the Principalities, nothing need now be said, as the subject will be considered in detail in the next chapter. So acute was the controversy on this point during the negotiations at Vienna and Paris that it was ultimately agreed that only the general principles of the settlement should be laid down in the formal treaty, and that their application should be left to be determined in a subsequent convention.

Of the other results of the war the most obvious was the new lease of life secured to the Ottoman Empire. The Sultan was to have his chance, free from all interference, friendly or otherwise, from his powerful neighbour, to put his house in order. He could enter upon his task with renewed self-respect, for was he not at last admitted to the most polite society of Europe ? And his subjects should realize the spontaneity of his beneficence ; if he chose to persecute, it was his affair : the Powers had expressly repudiated the right of interference ; equally, if he chose to extend civil or religious liberty, the extension was the outcome of his own loving-kindness towards his people. Such was the formal position secured to the Ottoman Empire by the Treaty of Paris. Yet the Sultan, if he were wise, could not fail to observe that the guarantee of independence and integrity vouchsafed to him by the Powers imposed upon them a corresponding obligation. Morally, if not legally, they were bound to see to it that the Porte behaved in accordance with the unwritten rules of polite society. In repudiating the exclusive protectorship of Russia they assumed a responsibility for the good government of the Christian subjects of the Porte which the Sultan could ignore only at his peril. On this point much will, unfortunately, have to be said later on.

To Russia the Treaty of Paris involved, for the time being, a bitter disappointment, if not a profound humiliation. For a century and a half she had pursued with singular consistency three main objects : to establish her naval and commercial supremacy on the waters and coasts of the Black Sea ; to secure a free outlet to the Mediterranean ; and to obtain from the Porte an acknowledgement of her position as champion of the liberties, political and ecclesiastical, of the Christian subjects of the Sultan. At times there had floated before the eyes of Russian rulers, notably those of the Tsarina Catherine, dreams even more ambitious. The Treaty of Paris not only dissipated completely all ideas of partition, but involved a disastrous set-back to those more sober and prosaic aims which had inspired Russian policy from the days of Peter the Great to those of Alexander II.

The Black Sea Question

The neutralization of the Black Sea was of special concern to England, as the leading Naval Power of the world. To the growth of the naval power of Russia, England, as we have seen, had become, in recent years, increasingly sensitive. The prolonged siege of Sebastopol had naturally made a profound impression upon the public mind. To allow Russia, in the complete security afforded by the closing of the straits, to build up a great naval force, and to convert the shores of the Black Sea into a great arsenal, seemed sheer madness to the Power which had large interests in the Near East and was paramount in the Far East.

Regarded from the Russian point of view the neutralization of the Black Sea was an insolent and intolerable interference in the domestic concerns of the Russian Empire, an attempt, inspired by petty jealousy, to arrest her natural and inevitable development. It was, therefore, absolutely certain that Russia would seize the first favourable opportunity to get rid of the shackles imposed upon her by the Treaty of Paris.

The opportunity came with the outbreak, in 1870, of the Franco-German War. Bismarck owed Russia a very heavy debt; the time had come to discharge it. Not that the obligations were all on one side. In the Crimean War the neutrality of Prussia was, as we have seen, more than benevolent towards Russia. During the Polish insurrection of 1863 Bismarck performed a signal service to the Tsar. For he not only kept a strict guard upon the western frontier of Russian Poland, but warded off the possible interference of Austria and the Western Powers. Bismarck's assistance, however, was never given without precise calculation. Each move in the great diplomatic game which he played during the next eight years was already in his mind, and in the course of that game Russia would be able to repay very amply any obligations incurred in 1863. Nor was Bismarck disappointed in the issue. The success of his policy in regard to the Danish Duchies in 1864, in regard to Austria and the Germanic Confederation in 1866, not least in regard to France in 1870, depended very largely upon the diplomatic goodwill of the Tsar, Alexander II. In 1864 Russia not only allowed the Treaty of London to be broken by Prussia, but declared herself ready to forgo her own claims upon Holstein and Oldenburg. In 1866 she avowedly regarded Prussia as 'the avenging instrument of Russian wrath' upon an ungrateful Austria. In 1870 it was Russia who kept Austria quiet while Bismarck worked his will upon France.

Such services demanded substantial requital. The means were ready to hand. In October, 1870, Prince Gortschakoff addressed to the Powers a circular denouncing on behalf of Russia the Black Sea clauses of the Treaty of Paris (1856), and declaring that the Tsar proposed to resume his 'sovereign rights' in the Black Sea. The step, if not actually suggested, was certainly approved beforehand by Bismarck. In justification of the action of Russia Gortschakoff cynically referred to the 'infringements to which most European transactions have been latterly exposed, and in the face of which it would be difficult to maintain that the written law . . . retains the moral validity which it may have possessed at other times'. In plain English the Tsar saw no reason why he should observe treaties when other people broke them.

The Russian circular evoked strong opposition both in England and in Austria. Lord Granville expressed the 'deep regret' of his Government at 'an arbitrary repudiation of a solemn engagement', and declared that England 'could not possibly give her sanction '. Count Beust, the Austrian minister, expressed himself as 'painfully affected' by the behaviour of the Tsar, and found it 'impossible to conceal his extreme astonishment thereat '.

But Gortschakoff went on his way unheeding. Bismarck was behind him, and Bismarck was confident that though England might bark she would not bite.

He had reason for his confidence. Plainly there were but two courses open to Great Britain : either to acquiesce in the bold and cynical action of the Tsar, or, without allies, to fight him. To declare war upon Russia, at this juncture, would be to provoke the Armageddon which England was using all her endeavours to avert. Was the game worth the candle ? Lord Derby declared that ' he would fight for the neutrality of Egypt, but not for the neutrality of the Black Sea '.[1] And he expressed the general opinion on the subject. In face of that opinion Lord Granville had no option but to extricate his country from a disagreeable situation with as little loss of prestige as possible. Accordingly, Bismarck was induced to invite the Great Powers to a conference to discuss the questions raised by Prince Gortschakoff's circular. Great Britain assented on condition that the conference met not at St. Petersburg but in London, and that it should not assume ' any portion of the Treaty to have been abrogated by the discretion of a single Power '. This assumption may be regarded as solemn farce ; the conclusion was foregone ; but Lord Granville was wisely attempting to put the best face upon an episode somewhat discreditable to all parties. The conference met in London in December, 1870, and Lord Granville got all the satisfaction he could out of a solemn protocol, declaring it to be ' an essential principle of the law of nations that no Power can liberate itself from the engagements of a Treaty . . . unless

[1] Odo Russell to Granville, ap. Fitzmaurice, ii. 72.

with the consent of the contracting Powers by means of an amicable arrangement '. For the rest, Russia got what she wanted.[1]

By the Treaty of London (March 13, 1871) the Black Sea clauses (Arts. xi, xiii, and xiv) of the Treaty of Paris were abrogated ; but the Black Sea was to remain open to the mercantile marine of all nations as heretofore ; at the same time the closing of the straits was confirmed with the additional proviso that the Sultan was empowered to open them in time of peace to the warships of friendly and allied Powers, if necessary, in order to secure the execution of the stipulations of the Treaty of Paris.

That English prestige suffered severely from the emasculation of that treaty can hardly be denied. To the Black Sea clauses she had attached great importance ; from a selfish point of view she had little else to show for a heavy expenditure in men and money.

France had not much more. But though France gained little by the Crimean War, Napoleon gained much. In 1853 his position in Europe was far from assured ; the Crimean War established it ; and until the advent of Bismarck his influence upon the Continent was almost overwhelming. The war gained him, paradoxically, the friendship of Russia : the peace lost him the confidence of England.

The greatest gainer by the war, excepting the Porte, was Italy. Cavour's prudent calculations were precisely fulfilled. He took his place, despite the angry protest of Austria, at the Council Board in Paris, as the representative not merely of Sardinia but of Italy. In the name of Italy he denounced the misgovernment of the two Sicilies ; for Italy he conciliated the sympathy of Great Britain and the active assistance of

[1] Cf. Holland, *European Concert in the Eastern Question* (with texts in full), p. 272.

Napoleon. The intervention of Sardinia in the Crimean War gave to her a place in the Concert of Europe, and gave to her the right as well as the opportunity to champion the cause of Italian liberation. At the Congress of Paris Cavour and the Emperor Napoleon came to an understanding; it was sealed two years later by the pact of Plombières, it bore fruit in the war of 1859.

The Crimean War was, then, supremely significant in relation to the fortunes of more than one of the nations of modern Europe. A keen student of affairs has expressed his conviction that if the war had not been fought ' the two subsequent decades of the century would not have seen the formation of a United Italy and a United Germany, and all its consequences'.[1] But it is as an epoch in the evolution of the Eastern Question that it must in these pages be considered. Some of its consequences, in that connexion, were palpable even to contemporaries. To these attention has already been drawn. Other consequences neither were, nor could have been, perceived by the men of that day. And these were the more enduring. Subsequent chapters will disclose them.

Works for further reference. For documents : *Eastern Papers*, presented to Parliament, 1854–6. For texts : T. E. Holland, *European Concert in the Eastern Question* ; Serge Goriainow (as before) ; Rambaud, *History of Russia* (trans.) ; Sir Herbert Maxwell, *Life and Letters of the Fourth Earl of Clarendon* ; Duke of Argyll, *Autobiography* ; Ashley, *Life of Lord Palmerston* ; Martin, *Life of Prince Consort* ; *Letters of Queen Victoria* (ed. Lord Esher and A. C. Benson) ; Morley, *Life of Gladstone* ; Parker, *Life of Sir James Graham* ; Lane Poole, *Life of Lord Stratford de Redcliffe* ; P. de la Gorce, *Histoire du Second Empire* ; É. Ollivier, *L'Empire Libéral* ; Debidour, *Histoire diplomatique* ; Kinglake, *Invasion of the Crimea* ; Sir E. B. Hamley, *The War in the Crimea* ; Sir E. Wood, *The Crimea in 1854 and 1894*. For the Sardinian intervention : Thayer, *Life of Cavour*, and Bolton King, *History of Italian Unity*.

[1] Lord Fitzmaurice, *Life of the Second Earl Granville*, i. 99.

II

The Making of Roumania

'Un îlot latin au milieu de l'océan slave et finnois qui l'environne.'—
Baron Jean de Witte.

'La Roumanie est latine d'origine et d'aspirations : elle a constamment
mis son orgueil à le dire et à le répéter. . . . Nous ne sommes ni Slaves,
ni Germains, ni Turcs ; nous sommes Roumains.'—Alexander Sturdza.

'La Dacie devint comme une Italie nouvelle. Ces Italiens du Danube
et des Carpathes ont conservé dans l'histoire le nom des Romains qui
leur donnèrent leur sang, leur langue, leur civilisation ; ils s'appellent les
Roumains et leur pays la Roumanie.'—G. Lacour-Gayet.

The Crimean War was fought ostensibly to maintain the
independence and integrity of the Ottoman Empire. That
principle received its consecration in the Treaty of Paris. The
supreme purpose which inspired the Western Powers in their
joint enterprise was to repudiate the claims of Russia to an
exclusive protectorate over the Christian subjects of the Porte,
and to arrest her progress in the Black Sea and the narrow
straits. That purpose was apparently achieved in 1856.

But contemporaries were as usual slow to apprehend the
things which really belonged unto their peace. Beneath the
surface of Balkan politics there were fires smouldering, forces
silently at work, which, in the middle of the nineteenth century,
few people could have perceived. Meanwhile the soldiers and
diplomatists were working better than they knew. They set
out to repel Russia and to save Turkey. What they really
saved was not the effete rule of the Ottoman Sultan, but the
future of nations which were not yet reborn.

Of these the first to come to the birth was that which we
know as the Kingdom of Roumania, but which figures in the
Treaty of Paris as the Principalities of Wallachia and Moldavia.
The diplomatists at Paris were, however, content to lay down

certain broad principles embodied in Articles xx to xxvii of the treaty, leaving it to a Special Commission at Bucharest to ' investigate the present state of the principalities and to propose bases for their future organization '. A Divan *ad hoc* was also to be convoked in each of the two provinces to express the wishes of the people in regard to the definitive organization of the principalities. The results of this somewhat startling recognition of the right of a people to a voice in its own political destiny will be in due course recounted. It seems, in the meantime, desirable to preface the story of the making of the modern State of Roumania by a rapid sketch of the previous history of the principalities.

The Roumanians occupy, in more ways than one, a unique place among the Balkan peoples. A Latin people, surrounded by Slavs and Magyars, they were never really absorbed, like the Serbs, Bulgars, and Greeks, into the Ottoman Empire. About the year A. D. 101 Trajan, as we have seen, organized the province of Dacia, and a province of the Roman Empire it remained until the close of the third century. About the year 271 the Roman legions were withdrawn, and the colonists, in order to avoid the barbarian inroads, fled into the Carpathians. For the next thousand years Dacia was merely a highway for successive hosts of barbarian invaders. But they came and went, and none of them, except the Slavs, left any permanent impress upon land or people. As the barbarian flood subsided, the Daco-Roumans emerged from their mountain fastnesses, and towards the close of the thirteenth century established the Principality of Wallachia, and a century later that of Moldavia. The former was reduced to vassaldom by the Turks in 1412, the latter in 1512 ; but neither principality ever wholly lost the sense or the symbols of independence. Both paid tribute to the Sultan, but down to the eighteenth century they continued to elect their own rulers.

Towards the close of the sixteenth century there occurred a brilliant interlude in the somewhat sombre history of the principalities. In the year 1593 Michael the Brave became Voyvode of Wallachia, and inaugurated his brief but brilliant reign by flinging down a challenge to the Ottomans, then hardly past the meridian of their fame. Engaged in their prolonged contest with the Habsburg Emperors, the Turks quickly realized the importance of Michael's defection, and turned aside from the Hungarian campaign to inflict upon their revolted vassal the punishment due for so daring a defiance of their suzerainty. But Michael's forces, though hopelessly outnumbered, won at Kalougareni a decisive victory over the Ottoman army under Sinan Pasha (August 13, 1595). Strengthened by reinforcements from Transylvania and Moldavia, the victor pursued his advantage with such effect as to drive the Turks in headlong rout across the Danube. At a single stroke the independence of Wallachia was temporarily achieved.

Victorious over the Turks, Michael then turned to the higher task of reuniting under one crown the whole Roumanian people. This also he achieved with singular success. Sigismund Báthory, Voyvode of Transylvania, suddenly resigned his crown to the Emperor Rudolph, and transferred to the latter such rights as he supposed himself to possess over Wallachia. Michael nominally accepted the suzerainty of the emperor, but the turn of events then gave him the opportunity of conquering Transylvania for himself. He eagerly embraced it, inflicted a crushing defeat upon a rival claimant at Schellenburg (October 28, 1599), and established himself as Voyvode of Transylvania. He then turned his attention to Moldavia. That also was reduced to submission, and thus for a brief space the whole Roumanian people were united under Michael ' the Brave '. It would be affectation to suggest that this achievement was regarded, at the time, as a triumph of the nationality principle. That principle had not yet emerged as a political force, and the sentiments of the Roumanians in Transylvania and Moldavia were entirely opposed to the rule of Michael. The significance of his achievement was wholly proleptic. Michael's reputation as a ' Latin hero ' really results from the revival of national self-consciousness in the nineteenth century. The Roumans of Transylvania and Moldavia regarded him, in his own day, as a meddlesome usurper. The Roumanians of to-day look to him as the national hero, who, for a brief space, realized the unity of the Roumanian people. What Roumania was under Michael the Brave, the Greater Roumania may be again. Michael's, therefore, is the name with which to conjure among the Roumanian irredentists. The temporary union of the various Rouman provinces was, however, dissolved by the assassination of Michael in 1601, and with him died all hopes of unity or even of independence for more than two centuries.

The fortunes of the principalities touched the nadir in the eighteenth century. Suleiman the Magnificent had, in 1536, concluded an arrangement, by which the election of the ruling princes was left to the principalities themselves. But in 1711 even this remnant of independence was extinguished. The hospodarships of the two principalities were put up by the Porte to auction and were invariably knocked down to Phanariote Greeks. For one hundred and ten years, therefore (1711–1821), Moldavia and Wallachia were ruled by a rapid succession of Greek bureaucrats. The more rapid the succession the better for the Turks. Consequently, each hospodar, knowing that his tenure would be brief,[1] had perforce to make hay while the sun shone, and the system was, as M. Xénopol has said, neither more nor less than ' organized brigandage '.

[1] In 110 years there were thirty-seven hospodars in Wallachia and thirty-three in Moldavia. Cf. Seignobos, *Political History of Europe*, ii. 640.

Meanwhile, paradoxical as it may appear, the prospects of Roumania suffered from the weakening of Ottoman power and the disintegration of the Ottoman Empire. By the Treaty of Carlowitz the Turks were compelled, as we saw, to cede to the Habsburgs the whole of Hungary, except the Banat of Temesvar, together with the Roumanian Duchy of Transylvania. By the Treaty of Passarowitz (1718) the recovery of Hungary was completed by the cession of the Banat of Temesvar, while at the same time the Habsburgs acquired the whole of the territory known as Little Wallachia, that is the portion of the principality bounded by the river Aluta. The latter acquisition proved to be only temporary, for the Turks recovered it by the Treaty of Belgrade in 1739. In 1775, however, the Habsburgs claimed and obtained from the Turks the Bukovina. The Moldavian boyards energetically protested to the Porte against the cession of a district which was not merely an integral part of the principality but contained their ancient capital, the mausoleum of their kings, and other historical monuments and associations. The Porte, despite a strong hint that the Moldavians might find it to their interest to seek protection elsewhere, declined to reconsider its bargain with the emperor.

Russia and the Principalities

Had the Moldavians carried out their threat, they would not have had to go far to find their new protector. Russia had begun, from the days of Peter the Great, to interest herself in the affairs of the Danubian principalities. That interest was not ethnographical, but partly geographical and partly ecclesiastical. The appearance of Russia as a Black Sea Power raised an entirely new problem for the Roumanian peoples, while the geographical situation of the principalities suggested to the Russian strategists questions of the highest significance.

Russia had temporarily occupied Moldavia during her war with the Turks, 1736–9, and both principalities were occupied during the war which was ended by the Treaty of Kainardji in 1774.

By that treaty, as we saw, Russia restored the principalities to the Porte, but only on condition of better government; and she formally reserved to herself the right of remonstrance if that condition was not observed. Five years later a *Convention explicative* (1779) stipulated that the tribute payable by the principalities to the Porte should be 'imposed with moderation and humanity'; a Russian consulate was, against the wishes of the Sultan, established at Bucharest, while the Prussian consul at Jassy complained of the activity of the Russian agents in Moldavia.[1] Clearly the policy of peaceful penetration had begun.

The principalities occupied a noticeable place in the agreement concluded between the Tsarina Catherine II and the Emperor Joseph II in 1781. The two sovereigns then decided that the time had arrived for the complete annihilation of Ottoman power in Europe, and for the partition of the dominions of the Sultan. Wallachia and Moldavia, including Bessarabia, were to be erected into a new kingdom of Dacia, and the crown was to be conferred upon Catherine's favourite and minister, Count Potemkin. The grandiose scheme, of which this was only one, though by no means the least interesting feature, was not destined to materialize. Six years later, however, Catherine and Joseph II were again at war with the Porte, and when, in 1792, peace was concluded at Jassy, the Russian frontier was advanced to the Dniester, the Tsarina acquired the great fortress of Oczakov with the surrounding districts, while Moldavia was restored to the Sultan, but

[1] Miller, *Ottoman Empire*, p. 8; but Zinkeisen (vi. 523) states that there was no Prussian consul at Jassy until 1786.

only on condition that the Porte fulfilled the stipulations of the Treaty of Kutschuk-Kainardji and the *Convention explicative*.

Napoleon and the Principalities

During the Napoleonic wars the principalities were regarded merely as a pawn in the game of diplomacy and of war. Thus in the war of the Second Coalition the Porte found itself in temporary alliance with Russia against France. Russia improved the occasion to obtain for her clients an important concession, and for herself a still stronger position as protectress. The Sultan agreed, in 1802, that henceforward the hospodars should hold office for a fixed term of seven years instead of at the good pleasure of the Porte, and that they should not be deposed without the assent of the Tsar. When, in 1806, Napoleon compelled the Sultan to declare war upon Russia, the latter retorted by an immediate invasion of the principalities. Before twelve months were over Napoleon had decided upon a new move in the diplomatic game, and agreed at Tilsit to divide the world with the Tsar Alexander. The Tsar's share was to include the Danubian principalities. But the Tilsit concessions were never carried out, and in 1812 the Tsar, anxious to secure his left flank, agreed to evacuate the principalities, and to accept from the Porte in full settlement of all immediate claims the province of Bessarabia. This arrangement, reached through the mediation of England, was embodied in the Treaty of Bucharest.

The Treaty of Bucharest was, for the Turks, a colossal blunder; to the Moldavians it involved a painful sacrifice. Nor did it tend to assuage the bitter memory which the period of Russian occupation had implanted in the minds of the Roumanians. Though the Russians had come as ' liberators ' there is no period in the history of their country to which the Roumanians look back with greater bitterness. More particularly do they resent the fact that by the dismemberment of Moldavia a population which now numbers two million Roumanians exchanged autonomy under the Sultan for absorption in the Empire of the Tsar.

At the general settlement in 1815 the Porte made desperate efforts to recover Bessarabia ; but Alexander was not likely to forgo the only, and as he might reasonably think the wholly inadequate, fruits of Russian diplomacy in the Near East, and Bessarabia remained in his hands.

The next scene in the drama of Roumanian history opens on the Greek revolution of 1821. The selection of the principalities for the initial rising, though intelligible, was, as we saw, singularly unfortunate. The Roumanian nationalists detested the Phanariote Greeks, and neither felt nor displayed any enthusiasm for the Hellenic cause. Still, Hypsilanti's insurrection had one important result. It led immediately to the extinction of Phanariote rule in the principalities. Greek hospodars were no longer acceptable to the Porte, and from 1822 onwards the hospodars of both principalities were selected from the native nobility.

To the Roumanians, however, the change brought little advantage. It signified only a transference from one alien master to another. From 1822, until the outbreak of the Crimean War, the Russians enjoyed a virtual protectorate over the principalities. The Convention of Akerman guaranteed to them all their privileges ' under the guardianship of the Cabinet of St. Petersburg '. The hospodars were to be elected for a term of seven years by the native boyards, and were not to be deposed by the Sultan without previous notice to Russia. The Treaty of Adrianople (1829) provided for the complete evacuation of the principalities by the Turks and conferred upon them practical autonomy. They were to pay tribute, at a slightly enhanced rate, to the Porte, but were to be free from all requisitions for corn, corvées, and the like. No Moslems were henceforward to reside there, and those who owned real property were to sell it within eighteen months. The hospodars were to hold office for life. Finally, the Turks undertook not to retain any fortresses on the left bank of the Danube, and to sanction the administrative regulations made during the Russian occupation. These regulations were embodied in a *Règlement organique* (1831) which the Russians bequeathed as a parting gift to the inhabitants when, in 1834, their occupation determined.

In some respects the Russian administration of the principalities had been excellent, but the material benefits which it conferred upon them were insufficient to counterbalance the loss of independence. Nor did Russian interference end with their formal evacuation. So bitter was the anti-Russian feeling that in 1848 the people of the principalities appealed to their nominal suzerain, the Sultan, to deliver them from their ' liberators ', and raised the standard of a national insurrection.

For Europe at large the year 1848 was essentially the ' year of revolution ' ; and nowhere did the fire burn more fiercely than in the heterogeneous empire which owned the Habsburgs as lords. Germans, Czechs, Magyars, Italians were all in revolt. But, while the Magyars of Hungary were in revolt against Vienna, they had themselves to confront a separatist movement within the borders which they regarded as their own. The feeling of Magyar against German was not more intense than the feeling of the Roumans of Transylvania against the Magyar. The nationalist fever had got into the blood of Europe, and, while the Transylvanian Roumans rose against Buda-Pesth, the Cis-Carpathian Roumans attempted once for all to throw off the yoke of St. Petersburg. Neither movement achieved any large measure of success. The Tsar Nicholas, as we have seen in another connexion, went to the assistance of the young

Emperor Francis Joseph and crushed the insurrections in Hungary and Transylvania, and, at the same time, in collusion with the Sultan, suppressed, without difficulty, the rising in the principalities. Ostensibly, the only result of the movement was the Convention of Balta Liman.

Under that Convention, concluded between the Sultan and the Tsar in May, 1849, the principalities were deprived of many of the privileges which they had previously enjoyed. The tenure of the hospodars was again limited to seven years; the representative assemblies were abolished, and they were replaced by Divans, nominated by the princes.

Here, as in Italy and elsewhere, the 'year of revolution' had come and gone, and to all outward seeming had left things worse than before. Not so, in reality. Good seed had been planted; the attempt to reap prematurely had failed; within a decade it was to fructify, and before the century closed was to yield an abundant harvest.

France and Roumania

The growth was native, but the culture was French. Ineffective as the movement of 1848 was, its inspiration was due to self-conscious nationalism. The nationalist spirit was fostered in part by the spread of education at home, not less by the historical and juristic studies pursued then, as now, by the young nobles in Paris.

For to the French the Roumans have persistently looked as the nearest of their blood relations; their natural allies in the secular struggle against Islamism on the one side and Pan-Slavism on the other. Nor can the modern history of Roumania be rightly apprehended unless this fact and all its many implications be kept steadily in view.

Modern Roumania is 'un îlot latin au milieu de l'océan

slave et finnois qui l'environne '.[1] Roumanian historians love
to recall the Roman origin of their race.[2] But the primary
debt, intellectual and political, acknowledged and emphasized
by the modern Roumanain, is not to Italy but to France.
' Nous sommes Roumains,' writes M. Alexander Sturdza,
the honoured bearer of an honoured Roumanian name,
' c'est-à-dire Latins ; et parlant ethniquement apparentés
à la France. La Roumanie moderne poursuit la réalisation
d'une œuvre éminemment nationale, mais elle aime sa sœur
aînée, sa bienfaitrice, la France.'

The debt warmly acknowledged in Roumania is proudly
claimed in France : ' C'est sous notre influence que la nation
roumaine s'est formée et a grandi ; ce sont les travaux de
nos écrivains, de nos historiens, qui ont révélé sa véritable
origine alors ignorée en Europe.' [3]

From France, then, came the spark which fired the insurrection of 1848. The flame, for the moment, flickered out, but
the fire was smouldering. It broke into flame again after the
Crimean War. That war marks an epoch of great significance
in the history of modern Roumania. On the first hint of
trouble with Turkey the Tsar, as we have seen, sent a force,
as usual, to occupy the principalities. But after their failure

[1] De Witte, *op. cit.*, p. 2.

[2] Cf. for example the speech of the Roumanian historian, V. A. Urechia,
in Rome: ' Nous sommes ici pour dire à tout le monde que Rome est notre
mère ' (cited by Mavrodin).

[3] de Witte, *Quinze ans d'histoire*, p. 8. Cf. also M. Georges Lacour-Gayet's
words : ' La France est certainement le pays, en dehors de la Roumanie, où
les questions roumaines provoquent le plus de sympathie, où les intérêts
roumains sont le mieux sentis et le mieux compris '—ap. C. D. Mavrodin,
La Roumanie contemporaine (p. x) ; and cf. also the elaborate studies of
M. P. Éliade, *L'Influence française sur l'esprit public en Roumanie* (Paris,
1898) ; and *Histoire de l'esprit public en Roumanie au XIXe siècle* (Paris,
1905).

to take Silistria (June, 1854) the Russians retired across the Pruth, and Austria occupied the principalities ; the Emperor Francis Joseph having pledged himself to protect them during the war, and to restore them to the Sultan on the conclusion of peace.

When the terms of that peace came to be considered at Vienna, and afterwards in Paris, the future position of Moldavia and Wallachia proved to be a subject of acute controversy between the Powers. The question of frontiers was the least of the difficulties, and was settled by the restoration of the southern portion of Bessarabia to Moldavia. Three other points were quickly decided : the Russian protectorate was to be abolished ; the suzerainty of the Sultan to be maintained ; the principalities themselves were to be virtually independent. The Emperor Napoleon had, indeed, originally suggested that they should be handed over to Austria, in return for the cession of Lombardy and Venetia to Sardinia. This characteristic but over-ingenious scheme found no favour in any quarter ; Austria had no mind for the bargain ; Russia naturally opposed the idea ; while the provinces themselves saw no advantage in getting rid of the Russians and the Turks in order to fall into the hands of the Habsburgs. They ardently hoped to achieve not merely independence but union.

The former was virtually conceded in the Treaty of Paris, by which the Porte engaged to preserve to the principalities ' an independent and national administration as well as full liberty of worship, of legislation, of commerce, and of navigation '.[1] The question as to the form of government was postponed, and in order to ascertain the wishes of the inhabitants the Sultan undertook ' to convoke immediately, in each of the two provinces, a Divan *ad hoc*, composed in such a manner as to represent most closely the interests of all classes of society '.[2]

[1] Article xxiii. [2] Article xxiv.

As to the wishes of the inhabitants there could be little doubt, and in Napoleon, the champion of nationality, the Roumanians found a cordial supporter. Napoleon brought Russia round to his views. Austria, on the other hand, obstinate in her adherence to the policy *Divide et Impera*, and justly fearful of the operation of the nationality principle among her own subjects—particularly among the Roumans of Transylvania and the Bukovina—offered a strenuous opposition. The Porte was naturally on the side of Austria, while the English Government, though not without considerable hesitation, eventually threw the weight of its influence into the same scale, on the ground that having fought to maintain the integrity of the Ottoman Empire, it could not logically support a project for its dismemberment. Persigny, the French ambassador in London, thought the *entente* with England much more important than the future of the principalities, and made no secret of his opinions.[1] Thouvenel, who represented France at Constantinople, was no less solicitous as to the maintenance of French influence over the Sultan, but behaved with greater discretion than his colleague in London.[2]

Under these circumstances much would obviously turn upon the views expressed by the Divans *ad hoc*. The elections were so manipulated by the provisional governors appointed by the Porte as to obtain the result desired by the Sultan. The scandal was so glaring that Thouvenel, supported by the ambassadors of Russia, Prussia, and Sardinia, entered an immediate protest, and, under the threat of a diplomatic rupture, compelled the Porte to cancel the results and hold the elections afresh.

Against this interference on the part of France and Russia

[1] Ollivier, *L'Empire Libéral*, iii. 411.
[2] Cf. Louis Thouvenel, *Trois Ans de la Question d'Orient* (1856-9), containing a number of important documents.

the English Government hotly protested. Lord Palmerston and Lord Clarendon were now deeply committed to the formula of 'the integrity of the Ottoman Empire'; still more deeply was Lord Stratford de Redcliffe concerned to maintain it. All three were profoundly suspicious of the good faith of Napoleon III, and gravely disquieted by his obvious *rapprochement* with Russia.

In August, 1857, however, the French Emperor, accompanied by the Empress and by his Foreign Minister, Count Walewski, paid a visit to the English Court at Osborne. The question of the principalities was exhaustively discussed, and Napoleon urged very strongly that their ' union, by rendering those countries contented, and particularly if well governed by a European prince, would form an effectual barrier against Russia, whilst the present disjointed and unsatisfactory condition of those countries would make them always turn towards Russia. The union was, therefore, in the interest of Turkey '.[1] As to the last point there may be a difference of opinion, but few people will now be found to deny that in his main contention the Emperor Napoleon was right, and the English statesmen wrong. Among the latter there were, however, one or two notable exceptions. The most notable was Mr. Gladstone, who, for once in his life, found himself in cordial agreement with Napoleon III, being drawn to the emperor's views by his warm sympathy with the nationality principle. He was not in office during the height of the crisis, but in May, 1858, he urged with characteristic vehemence that England ought to support the declared wish of the people of Wallachia and Moldavia. ' Surely the best resistance to be offered to Russia ', he said, ' is by the strength and freedom of those countries

---

[1] A record of this most important conversation, from the pen of the Prince Consort himself, will be found in Martin's *Life of the Prince Consort*, vol. iv, pp. 99 sq.

that will have to resist her. You want to place a living barrier between Russia and Turkey. There is no barrier like the breast of freemen.'[1] Mr. Gladstone carried with him into the division lobby not only Lord John Russell, but Lord Robert Cecil. They were unable, however, to prevail against the official view.

Meanwhile the diplomatic situation had become so grave as to threaten a renewal of war in the Near East. Napoleon III stoutly maintained his own views, and was supported by Russia, Prussia, and Sardinia. If war did not actually break out it was due partly to the sincere desire of the emperor to avoid any breach in the good relations between the English Court and his own ; partly to the natural reluctance of Russia and England again to draw the swords so lately sheathed; partly to English pre-occupation with the Sepoy mutiny in India ; but, above all, to the adroitness and tenacity of the principalities themselves.

Fresh elections having been held, the Divans *ad hoc* met in Jassy and Bucharest respectively (October, 1857). The Moldavian Assembly by 80 votes to 2, the Wallachian Assembly without a dissentient voice, declared in favour of the ' union of the Principalities in a single neutral and autonomous State, subject to the suzerainty of the Sultan, and under the hereditary and constitutional government of a foreign prince '.

What were the Powers to do ? Again they met in conference (May–August, 1858), and after nearly six months' deliberation resolved that the two principalities must remain politically separate : that each should have its own parliament and its own prince, to be elected by itself, but that affairs common to both should be entrusted to a joint commission of sixteen members, consisting of deputies from each parliament.

This arrangement was both intrinsically clumsy and grossly

[1] Morley's *Gladstone*, ii. 4.

insulting to the national sentiment of the Roumanians, who, with courage and ingenuity, resolved to cut the Gordian knot for themselves.

Alexander Couza

The National Assemblies duly met in the two capitals, and both unanimously elected as their prince the same man, a native noble, Colonel Alexander Couza (January and February, 1859).

This flagrant defiance of the will of Europe caused considerable commotion in the Chancelleries; but the Powers eventually had the good sense to accept the accomplished fact; and on December 23, 1861, the union of the principalities was formally proclaimed. The new-born State was christened Roumania; and an agreement was reached, not without heart-burnings at Jassy, that the capital should be Bucharest.

The united principalities did not provide a bed of roses for the prince of their choice; his brief reign sufficed to demonstrate the wisdom of the Roumanian leaders, who had, from the first, expressed a strong preference for a foreign hereditary dynasty. 'The accession to the throne of princes chosen from amongst us has', they declared, 'been a constant pretext for foreign interference, and the throne has been the cause of unending feud among the great families of this country.' Their misgivings were justified by the event.

Couza, though not conspicuous for domestic virtues, was a man of enlightened views, and anxiously desired to improve the social and economic condition of his people. Between 1862 and 1865 he carried through, despite much opposition from the 'feudal' party, a series of far-reaching reforms, mainly concerned with education and the agrarian problem.

The condition of education in Roumania was, indeed, deplorable, but Couza made a serious effort to improve it.

He founded two universities, one at Jassy and one at Bucharest ; he established a number of secondary and technical schools, all of them free, and elementary education was made not only gratuitous but nominally compulsory.[1] Despite this fact the percentage of illiterates in Roumania is still very large.[2]

Couza then tackled the land question. His first step was the secularization of monastic property. Not less than one-fifth of the land of the country had passed into the hands of the monks, who, to ensure themselves against spoliation, had affiliated their houses to the monasteries of Roumelia, Mount Athos, and Mount Sinai, and to the Patriarchies of Alexandria, Antioch, and Jerusalem. The device did not avail against the reforming zeal of Couza, who set aside over 27 million francs for the compensation of the patrons, but dissolved the monasteries, turned the abbots and monks adrift, seized their property for national purposes, and converted the houses themselves into hospitals and jails (1863).

The problem which confronted Couza was similar to that which, in the first years of the century, Stein and Hardenberg had faced and solved in Prussia. Roumanian feudalism was, in some respects, *sui generis*, but there, as elsewhere, the essential difficulty in modernizing a feudal land system was how, while respecting the vested interests of the 'lord' and the peasant owner respectively, to get rid of the legal and economic incubus of dual ownership.

Couza solved the problem, *mutatis mutandis*, much as it had been solved in Prussia. He abolished all dues, both in labour and kind, in return for an indemnity advanced to the lords by the State, to be repaid, in instalments, to the latter by the peasants ; and he handed over one-third of the land

---

[1] Since 1893, thanks to M. Take Jonescu, compulsion has been more than nominal.

[2] Some authorities say sixty per cent. of people over seven.

in unshackled proprietorship to the peasants, leaving two-thirds in possession of the lords. That the compromise did not satisfy the peasants is proved by the fact that although some readjustment of the terms was effected in 1881, and again in 1889, the last thirty years have witnessed no less than five insurrections among the Roumanian peasantry.

The path of the reformer is never easy, and in order to overcome the opposition of the feudal and military parties, Couza was compelled, on May 2, 1864, to carry out a *coup d'état*. The army was employed to evict the deputies, and the prince demanded a plebiscite from his people for or against the policy which he propounded. The sole initiative in legislation was to belong to the prince; a Senate, nominated by him, was to be superadded to the Chamber, and the latter was to be elected by universal suffrage. The plebiscite gave the prince 682,621 votes against 1,307. Couza's action, compounded of Cromwellianism and Bonapartism, subsequently received the sanction of the Powers.

Couza was now supreme, and the *coup d'état* was followed, appropriately enough, by the application of the Napoleonic codes—civil, criminal, and commercial—with slight modifications, to Roumania. That the *coup d'état* and its immediate results were generally approved by the people there can be no doubt, but the prince was assailed from many quarters: by the 'reds' who represented him as a pro-Russian dangerous to the peace of Europe; by the 'whites' who disliked his reforming activities; by the constitutionalists who denounced him as a bastard Bonaparte. Discontent reached a climax in August, 1865, when, during the prince's absence at Ems, a counter *coup d'état* was attempted at Bucharest. The Vienna *Fremdenblatt* (August 5, 1865) detected in this *coup d'état* the first signs of a revolutionary movement which would presently engulf not Roumania only, but Bosnia, Bulgaria, and Serbia as well.[1] Couza hurried back to Roumania, but the movement against him rapidly gathered force ; an association, comprising influential men from all parties, was formed with the object of substituting for him a foreign prince, and M. Jean Bratiano was sent abroad to find a suitable candidate. In Paris Couza was denounced as a Russian agent ; in St. Petersburg as the tool of Napoleon III.

Meanwhile, in February, 1866, the revolution had been quietly effected at Bucharest. Couza was deposed and deported, and a provisional government proclaimed as his successor Prince Philip of Flanders.[2] This prince was promptly elected by the chambers, and their choice was ratified by plebiscite. Hardly a voice was raised for Couza ; not a drop of blood was shed on his behalf ; he passed silently out of the land for which he had dared much, and seven years later he died in exile.

Prince Carol of Hohenzollern-Sigmaringen (1866–1914)

Prince Philip of Flanders promptly declined the proffered crown, which was thereupon offered to Prince Carol, the second son of the Prince of Hohenzollern-Sigmaringen, the elder and Catholic branch of the family ruling at Berlin.

A cousin of the King of Prussia, Prince Carol was, through his grandmother, connected with the Bonapartes.[3] The Emperor Napoleon was sounded as to his candidature through his intimate friend, Madame Hortense Cornu, and approved it. King William of Prussia, dutifully consulted by his kinsman, was more doubtful ; but Bismarck, who was just about to plunge into war with Austria, perceived the advantage of

---

[1] Damé, *La Roumanie contemporaine*, p. 146.

[2] Father of King Albert of Belgium.

[3] His maternal grandmother was Stéphanie de Beauharnais, adopted daughter of Napoleon I, and his paternal grandmother was a Murat.

having a Hohenzollern at Bucharest, and urged the prince to accept the offer, ' if only for the sake of a piquant adventure '. The prince himself, if rumour be true, had never heard of Roumania when the offer reached him, but he took down an atlas, and, finding that a straight line drawn from London to Bombay passed through Roumania, exclaimed : ' That is a country with a future ', and promptly decided to accept the crown.[1]

The provisional offer was conveyed to him by John Bratiano on March 30 ; a plebiscite taken in April confirmed it ; and on May 22 the prince, having travelled in disguise to the frontier, made his formal entry into Bucharest.

A congress of the Powers at Paris had pronounced by four votes to three against the candidature of the Prince, but, like the Sultan himself, they ultimately accepted the accomplished fact, and a Hohenzollern prince, a Prussian dragoon, reigned over the principalities.

The outstanding features of his long, and, on the whole, prosperous, reign can here be indicated only in summary.

His first act was to summon a constituent assembly, which drafted, on the Belgian model, a very liberal Constitution. Accepted in 1866, and considerably amended in 1879 and 1884, that Constitution is still in force. Like its prototype, it is exceedingly meticulous, consisting of no less than 133 clauses. Alone among the Balkan States may Roumania be said to possess a monarchy which is genuinely ' constitutional ' in the narrow English sense. The person of the king is, by article 92, inviolable ; his ministers are responsible, no act of the crown being valid unless signed by a responsible minister. Subject to this responsibility the crown enjoys the rights, and has to perform the duties, usually vested in the executive

[1] Carmen Sylva, wife of King Carol, tells the story (De Witte, *op. cit.*, p. 7).

of a Constitutional State.[1] The cabinet consists of nine members, who are responsible to the legislature. The latter is bi-cameral in form, but both chambers are elective. In each case, however, the election is indirect, the elections being made through electoral colleges, composed of the taxpayers, who are divided into three colleges, according to the amount of taxes paid. The franchise is, however, higher in the case of the senatorial electors than in that of electors to the popular chamber. The Senate consists of 120 members, who must be at least forty years of age and possess an income of £376 a year, and their term of office is for eight years. It enjoys a position not only of dignity but real power. The Chamber of Deputies consists of 183 members, who are elected for four years and must be at least five-and-twenty years of age.[2]

The Church has not played a part in the national evolution of Roumania at all comparable to that which it played in Greece. And for a simple reason. Greek in its allegiance, the Church finds itself an alien institution among a Latin people. The people have always associated it, therefore, with foreign influences : with the Phanariote domination of the eighteenth century ; with the Church of their Russian 'protectors' in the first half of the nineteenth. Nevertheless, it was at once a symptom and a result of reviving national self-consciousness that the Roumanian Church should, in 1865, have declared its independence of the Greek Patriarchate of Constantinople. Since that time the Church has been virtually autocephalous, though its independence was not officially recognized by the Greek Patriarch until 1885.

---

[1] The reality of the constitutional limitations upon the personal will of the sovereign was strikingly manifested, to the great advantage of the *Entente*, on the outbreak of the present war (1914).

[2] The full text of the Constitution will be found in Damé, *La Roumanie contemporaine*, Appendice, pp. 425 sq.

From a social and economic standpoint the reign of Prince Carol in Roumania has synchronized with the transformation of a mediaeval into a modern State. One or two illustrations must suffice. In 1866 there did not exist a single railway in the State; in 1910 there were 3,690 kilometres of railways. The export of cereals, which, in 1866, was less than half a million tons, amounted, in 1913, to 1,320,235. Of petrol, the production at the earlier date was 5,915 tons; at the later about two million. A budget of 56 million francs sufficed for the country in 1866; it now exceeds 500 millions. In the war of 1877–8 the army numbered 40,000, and Roumania possessed not a single man-of-war; the army now numbers more than a million, and there is an embryo fleet of thirty-one ships. Unlike most of the Balkan States, Roumania possesses a powerful native aristocracy, but out of a population of seven and a half millions over one million are proprietors, and most of the peasants own the land they cultivate. Industry develops apace, but agriculture is still the main occupation of the people, only twenty per cent. of whom dwell in towns. The natality is said to be, next to that of Russia, the highest in Europe. The external trade of the country—consisting mainly in the export of oil and cereals—is now about fifty millions, and exceeds that of all the other Balkan States together; but most of it is with the Central Empires. The imports from the United Kingdom are less than two millions; from Germany and Austria-Hungary they are over thirteen.

The last figures indicate, eloquently enough, the new orientation of Roumanian policy. More and more since the accession of Prince Carol was this Latin State drawn into the orbit of the Central-European Empires. Not unnaturally. 'Bien que je sois aujourd'hui prince de Roumanie,' so ran a telegram from Prince Carol to King William of Prussia in 1869, 'je suis et je reste toujours un Hohenzollern.' The prince's marriage, in the same year, with the Princess Elizabeth of Wied, known to the world as the gifted Carmen Sylva, did nothing to diminish the force of his Teutonic sympathies.

The Franco-German War revealed a serious cleavage of opinion between the prince and his subjects. When the war broke out the prince wrote to King William to express his disappointment at not being able to 'follow his beloved Sovereign on to the field of battle, and at being compelled to the most rigorous reserve among a people whose sympathies were on the side of France'. The prince was not mistaken. It is true that since 1866 French influence at Bucharest had been waning, but from the hearts of the Roumanian people nothing could eradicate the sentiment of kinship with the people of France.

The position of a German prince at Bucharest, particularly when that prince's brother had been made the stalking-horse for the enmity between Germany and France, could not, during the war of 1870, have been otherwise than difficult. In August, 1870, a serious *émeute* broke out at Ploïesti, a town about 60 kilometres north of Bucharest ; the 'Prussian prince' was denounced, and a republic proclaimed. The army remained loyal, and the insurrection was suppressed without difficulty, but it served to strengthen the disposition of the prince to abandon a thankless task. 'A German prince', so his father wrote to him on September 29, 'is made of stuff too precious to be wasted on such a useless job.' Financial complications, bitter discussions in parliament, insulting innuendos against the personal integrity of the prince, all tended to disgust Prince Carol with his position ; and in December, 1870, he appealed to the Powers to take into their consideration a revision of the Treaty of 1856.

The appeal came to nothing, and after the decisive victory of the Germans the excitement in Roumania tended to subside.

Only to be aroused, before long, and more acutely, over affairs nearer home. Already might be heard the distant rumblings of the storm, which, in 1875, was to burst over the Balkans. From Montenegro, Bosnia, Herzegovina, Bulgaria, and Serbia came news which presaged the advent of a critical time for all the States and peoples actually or nominally subject to the Ottoman Sultan. Plainly it was not a moment to think of abdication, least of all for the prince who regarded himself as ' the extreme advance guard of civilization, the sentinel posted on the frontier of the East '.[1]

The part played by Roumania in the great drama of 1875–8 ; the achievement of its independence (1878) ; its accession to the rank of a kingdom (1881) ; and its increasing inclination towards the Central European system, must receive notice in subsequent chapters.

By the close of the first decade of Prince Carol's reign the modern State of Roumania was fairly established. During the next few years the attention of the world was rivetted upon other parts of the Ottoman Empire in Europe. On the eve of the great events of 1875 it may be well, therefore, to pause and examine the condition of the other peoples of the Balkans.

For further reference : A. D. Xénopol, *Histoire des Roumains*, and other works (translated into French from the Roumanian) (Paris, 1896); P. Éliade, *Histoire de l'esprit public en Roumanie au XIXe siècle* (Paris, 1905), and *L'Influence française sur l'esprit public en Roumanie* (Paris, 1898) ; F. Damé, *Histoire de la Roumanie contemporaine, 1822–1900* (Paris, 1900); B^{on}. Jehan de Witte, *Quinze ans d'histoire, 1866–81* (Paris, 1905); C. D. Mavrodin, *La Roumanie contemporaine* (Paris, 1915); G. G. Giurgea, *Données politiques et économiques sur la Roumanie moderne* (Bucharest, 1913); R. W. Seton Watson, *Roumania and the Great War* (Constable & Co., 1915); D. Mitrany, *Roumania*, in *The Balkans* (Clarendon Press, 1915); *Encyc. Brit.* (11th edition), art. *Roumania* ; E. Pittard, *La Roumanie* (1917).

[1] Prince Carol to Bismarck in 1871.

12

The Balkan Insurrections

The Southern Slavs—The Russo-Turkish War—The Powers and the Eastern Question, 1856–78

' The Christian East has had enough of Turkish misrule. . . . High diplomacy will never solve the Eastern Question ; it can be solved only in the East, in the theatre of war, with the co-operation of the peoples directly concerned.'—Prince Carol of Roumania.

' That Turkey is weak, fanatical, and misgoverned no one can honestly deny. . . . The chief Powers of Christendom have all more or less an interest in the fortunes of an Empire which from being systematically aggressive has become a tottering and untoward neighbour.'—Lord Stratford de Redcliffe (1875).

Paradox is the eternal commonplace of the Eastern Question. But even in the Near East paradox was never more triumphant than in the settlement which concluded the Crimean War. The Powers, as we have seen, expressly repudiated the right of interference, individual or collective, in the internal concerns of the Ottoman Empire. Yet the Treaty of Paris marks indisputably the point at which Turkey finally passed into a state of tutelage to the European Concert.

A fortnight after the signature of the general Treaty (March 30) a separate Treaty was, it will be remembered, concluded between Great Britain, France, and Austria guaranteeing ' jointly and severally the independence and the integrity ' of the Ottoman Empire (April 15, 1856). That guarantee imposed upon the Powers concerned a moral if not a legal responsibility of the gravest kind.

But this Treaty did not stand alone. At the moment when the Powers were negotiating their Treaties in Paris a conference was taking place in the British Embassy at Constantinople between the Turkish ministers and the representatives of the Powers. The outcome of that conference was a charter of liberties which, as Lord Stratford de Redcliffe said, ' was made part of the general pacification under an agreement that its insertion in the Treaty should not be made a pretext for the interference of any foreign Power in the internal affairs of Turkey '.[1] The *Firman* of the Sultan was expressly described as ' emanating spontaneously from his sovereign will '; it was, however, 'communicated' to the contracting parties, and by them was ' annexed ' to the Treaty of Paris. Still, Turkey was to be entrusted with the fulfilment of her own promises.

Such was the paradoxical yet not unintelligible position in which matters were left by the Crimean War. The object of that war was, in the Prince Consort's words, ' the cancelling of all previous Russian treaties and the substitution of a European Protectorate of the Christians, or rather of European protection for a Russian Protectorate '.[2] That object was achieved. Plainly, however, there was a corollary. ' The Cabinet of Lord Aberdeen, while actively defending the independence of Turkey, felt that in objecting to the separate interference of Russia they were bound to obtain some guarantee for the security of the subjects of the Porte professing the Christian faith.' [3] Thus, at a later date, Lord Russell. How far did the Turks fulfil their own promises ? How far did the ' guarantee ' obtained by the Powers prove effective for its purpose ? It is the main purpose of this chapter to answer these questions.

While the Powers were concluding peace in Paris, the Sultan Abdul Mejid issued on February 18, 1856, a second

---

[1] *The Eastern Question*, p. 14.   [2] Martin, *Life*, iii. 92.

[3] *Turkey*, xvii, 1877, No. 148, p. 115, quoted by Duke of Argyll, *Eastern Question*, i, p. 34.

edition of the Tanzimat of Gülhané. Except in regard to military reform, the famous Tanzimat had remained a dead letter. The Christians, so far from obtaining the promised equality before the law, found themselves still treated as a despised and conquered people. Their word was not accepted in the courts; they were exposed to the extortions of every Moslem official, high or low; life, honour, fortune was still at the mercy of the dominant race. But all this was now to be reformed. The Hatti-Humayoun of 1856 guaranteed to every subject of the Porte, without distinction of creed or class, personal liberty; equality before the law; complete religious freedom; eligibility for office civil and military; equality of taxation; equal representation in the communal and provincial councils and in the supreme Council of Justice; and complete security of property.[1] On paper nothing could have been more satisfactory. But practically nothing came of it.

In 1861 Sultan Abdul Mejid at last drank himself to death, and was succeeded by Abdul Aziz. At this fateful moment in its history, when the Western Powers had secured to it—on conditions—a reprieve, when its life depended upon a radical reform not merely of law but of administration, the Ottoman Empire was entrusted to the care of an amiable and well-intentioned but half-insane ruler. Abdul Aziz was sincerely minded to follow the prudent monitions of the Powers; he did something to modernize and secularize the administration of the State; to initiate useful public works; to improve means of communication; to exploit the natural resources of his empire; and to found a system of education, primary and secondary, free from ecclesiastical control and open to pupils of every creed. He set up a High Court of Justice, composed in equal numbers of Christians and Moslems, and in 1868 he crowned the administrative edifice by establishing

---

[1] The full text is printed in Holland, *European Concert*, pp. 329 sq.

a Council of State. The council was to have legislative as well as administrative functions; it was to consist of Christians as well as Moslems, and, best of all, was to have as its first president Midhat Pasha, a statesman of enlightened views and strong character.

It was all to no purpose. The Ottoman Empire was and always had been a theocracy. It is impossible to secularize a theocracy: to reform law which rests upon an unchangeable religious sanction; or to secure good and equal government for men whose life, honour, and property were at the mercy of local officials, when those officials were in a few cases only at once honest and capable, in most cases were neither, and in all cases were beyond the reach or control of the energetic and well-intentioned reformers at Stamboul.

Here lay the root of the difficulty. To overcome it there was needed a man of exceptional strength of character, who was free to act without reference to the advice of more or less interested monitors; above all, a man who could rule, with a stern hand, his own political household.

Abdul Aziz had no such qualifications, and as his reign went on he plunged deeper and deeper into the grossest forms of personal extravagance. His incessant demands for money and more money afforded an excuse for the rapacity of subordinates, and even the best of the provincial Pashas were compelled to tighten the financial screw upon the peoples committed to their charge.

Nor were those peoples in a mood to submit to the exactions of the Turkish Pashas. A new spirit was beginning to stir the ' dry bones ' in the Balkan valleys. It was excited partly by the movement in the principalities; partly by the reforming movement at Constantinople; partly by the deliberate Pan-Slavist propaganda of Russian agents, and not least by the memory of the Napoleonic rule in the ' Illyrian provinces '.

Among the makers of United Germany and United Italy the first Napoleon already occupies a conspicuous place. It may be that he is destined to a place not less conspicuous among the makers of the future Jugo-Slav Empire. This at least is certain, that the Jugo-Slavs of to-day look back to the time, 1809–14, when, under the name of 'The Illyrian Provinces', Dalmatia, Istria, Trieste, Gorizia, Carinthia, Carniola, and part of Croatia were united under Napoleon's auspices, as the happiest and most fruitful period in the modern history of their race. The mere fact of union, though transitory and achieved under an alien ruler, was in itself an inspiration for the future, after the oppression and disunion of centuries ; and the rule though alien was enlightened. In particular, the modern Jugo-Slavs recall with gratitude the fact that Napoleon reintroduced their native tongue both as the medium of education and as the official language of the Illyrian State. Between 1830 and 1840 there was a renaissance of this 'Illyrian' spirit, which was, however, sternly repressed by the Austrian administrators.

Serbia

Of the Southern-Slav movement Serbia was, throughout the nineteenth century, the most conspicuous and powerful champion. After a quarter of a century of struggle and vicissitude Serbia had, as we saw, become by 1829 an autonomous principality under the suzerainty of the Sultan, though the Turks continued to garrison the eight principal fortresses.

But only the first steps had been taken along the path of national regeneration. An immense task still awaited the Serbian people. They had, in the first place, to remake Serbia, in a territorial sense. What Serbia had been in the days of her greatness we have already seen. What she had been in the past she aspired again to be. The Serbia of 1830 included a very small portion of her ancient territory. The Turks were still in possession not only of Bosnia and the Herzegovina, but of the Sanjak of Novi-Bazar and the district of northern Macedonia known as Old Serbia. To reunite with herself these territories was, and is, the minimum of Serbian aspirations.

In the second place, she had to work out her own constitutional salvation; to compose, if possible, the dynastic antagonisms which seemed so curiously at variance with the genius of a Peasant-State; to devise an appropriate form of government, and to get rid of the last traces of Turkish sovereignty.

She had, lastly, and above all, to prepare herself by social, educational, and economic reform for the great part which she believed herself to be destined to play as the liberator of the Southern Slavs, who were still under the heel of Habsburg and Turk, and as the centre and pivot of that Greater Serbia, the Jugo-Slav Empire, which is still in the future.

The period between 1830 and 1875 was largely occupied by dynastic alternations between the Obrenovićs and the Karageorgevićs which it would serve no useful purpose to follow in detail. The quarrel between the two families was not indeed really composed until the extinction of the former dynasty by the brutal though not undeserved assassination of King Alexander and his ill-omened consort Draga in 1903. Nothing could have been more disastrous for the infant State : not only was internal development seriously hampered, but, to an outside world ignorant of Serbia's great past, the impression was inevitably conveyed that the Serbia of the present consisted of half-civilized swineherds ; and that it was perhaps unfortunate that these swineherds should have escaped from the control of the Ottoman Empire which had alone understood the best way of dealing with unruly savages. How false that impression was it has required a political martyrdom to prove to the world.

Apart from almost perpetual squabbles between the turbulent peasantry and their elected rulers, and between the rival chiefs, there are only two events, in the period between the attainment of autonomy (1829) and the outbreak of the Balkan insurrections (1875), which call for special mention.

The first is the achievement, in 1831, of ecclesiastical independence ; the second is the evacuation of the Serbian fortresses by the Turks in 1867.

As in Greece, so also in Serbia, the Orthodox Church has been throughout the ages the nursing mother of national independence. Founded and organized by St. Sava, the son of King Nemanja, the Serbian Church has been at once Orthodox and national. 'If the father (King Nemanja) endowed the Serbian State with a body, the son (St. Sava) gave it ', as Father Nicholas Velimirović has eloquently and truly said, ' a soul. And later on, when the body of the Serbian State was destroyed by the Turkish invasion, the soul lived on through the centuries, and suffered, and nothing remained unconquered in this soul but her faith, and the tradition of the freedom of the past. The monasteries were centres of trust and hope. The priests were the guides of the people, upholding and comforting them. The Patriarchs of Ipek were in truth patriarchs of the people, and, like the patriarchs of old, true representatives of the people and their protectors.' [1]

The first act of the great Stephen Dushan had been, as we saw, to summon an Ecclesiastical Council and to proclaim the Serbian Church a Patriarchate with its ecclesiastical capital at Ipek in Montenegro (1345). After the Ottoman conquest the Patriarchate of Ipek was abolished ; the Serbian Church lost its independence ; was subordinated to the Greco-Bulgar Archbishopric of Ochrida, and, for some two centuries, fell completely under the control of the Greeks. But in 1557

[1] *Religion and Nationality in Serbia*, p. 7.

the Patriarchate of Ipek was revived. 'The revival of this centre of national life was momentous ; through its agency the Serbian monasteries were restored, ecclesiastical books printed, and, more fortunate than the Bulgarian national Church, which remained under Greek management, it was able to focus the national enthusiasms and aspirations and keep alive with hope the flame of nationality among those Serbs who had not emigrated.' [1]

Serbia suffered terribly at the hands of both Turks and Austrians during the wars of the seventeenth and eighteenth centuries, and in 1766 the Patriarchate of Ipek was finally abolished and the Serbian Church acknowledged the supremacy of the Greek Patriarch of Constantinople.

With the revival of national self-consciousness in the nineteenth century came a renewed desire for ecclesiastical independence, and in 1831 Prince Miloš finally broke the chain which still bound the Serbian Church to the Patriarchate of Constantinople. Thus, at last, after many vicissitudes, Serbia obtained a national Church with a Metropolitan at Belgrade.

The year 1867 witnessed the completion of another stage on the long and toilsome journey towards national independence. The position of Serbia during the second quarter of the nineteenth century was more than usually paradoxical. Still subject to the sovereignty of the Sultan, she was really under the protectorship of Russia. But the Sultan possessed a tangible symbol of authority in the continued military occupation of the fortresses. Nor were the garrisons withdrawn even after the Crimean War. In that war Serbia took no part. The people inclined towards the Russian side, but the prince (Alexander Karageorgević) was under considerable obligations both to Turkey and to Austria. Nor could the prince forget the encouragement which Serbia had obtained

[1] Forbes, *Serbia*, in *The Balkans*, p. 104.

from Lord Palmerston, who, for the first time, had sent a British consul to Belgrade in 1837, nor the support given to himself in 1843 by Lord Stratford de Redcliffe. By the Treaty of Paris, Serbia, like the principalities, was tacitly excepted from the protectorate of Russia; she was to continue to enjoy an 'independent and national administration, as well as full liberty of worship, of legislation, of commerce and navigation', and her rights and immunities were 'placed thenceforth under the collective guarantee of the contracting powers'. An *émeute* at Belgrade in 1862 led to the withdrawal of the civilian Turkish population, and in 1867 Prince Michael Obrenović III had the satisfaction of bringing about the final evacuation of the fortresses. Michael persuaded the Sultan that a grateful Serbia would be a far more effective barrier against an Austrian attack than a few isolated Turkish garrisons on the Danube and the Save; he persuaded Austria that a Serbian Belgrade would prove more neighbourly than a Turkish outpost; France, Russia, and Great Britain supported him; the Porte gave way; in May, 1867, the Turks finally evacuated Serbia, and Belgrade became, for the first time for many centuries, not merely the Serbian capital, but a Serbian city.

Independence was now virtually achieved, but the nominal suzerainty of the Sultan was not actually extinguished until the Turkish Empire had been broken by the Balkan insurrection of 1875 and the Russian War. To these events we must now turn.

But for the foolish and brutal murder of Prince Michael in 1868 the great national uprisings of 1875 would have started more obviously under the leadership of Serbia. That brilliant ruler had worked out an elaborate combination not only with the Southern Slavs of Montenegro, Bosnia, and the Herzegovina, but with the nationalist leaders in Croatia, with a Bulgarian patriotic society, and even with Greece. The Serbians have paid dearly for the dastardly crime, not the first

last of its kind, perpetrated in 1868. Had that crime
en place, the events of 1912–13 might possibly have been
ted by a whole generation ; Serbia might have placed
herself at the head of a great Southern-Slav Empire, while
Austria was still reeling under the shock of Sadowa, when
the German Empire had not yet come to the birth, when
Bosnia and Herzegovina were still ' Turkish', and when
Bulgarian aspirations were not yet formulated in opposition
to those of the Southern Slavs. The crime of 1868 robbed
Serbia of a chance which, in its original form, can never recur.

Bosnia and the Herzegovina

It was not Serbia then, but the Slav inhabitants of one
remote village in the Herzegovina who, in the summer of 1875,
gave the signal for the outbreak of an insurrection which
quickly involved the whole of the Slav States in the Ottoman
Empire ; which, before it was quelled, led to another war
between Russia and Turkey, and all but eventuated in a great
European conflagration.

The primary causes of the original rising in Bosnia and the
Herzegovina were not so much political as social and economic ;
they acquired strength less from the spirit of nationality than
from the unbearable nature of the fiscal burdens imposed upon
the peasantry by Turkish officials and native landowners.

Bosnia and the Herzegovina presented in several respects
a striking contrast to Serbia. It was against the powerful
Empire of Serbia that the attack of the Ottoman Turks was
first directed after their advent into Europe. Bosnia, more
remote and more obscure, managed to retain until 1463
independence. The Herzegovina until 1482. But when once
conquered they were more completely absorbed into the
Ottoman system than ever Serbia was. For another reason
these provinces became more ' Turkish ' than any other part

of the Balkan peninsula except perhaps Bulgaria and the provinces immediately adjacent to Constantinople. Bosnia was a land of large landowners who, to save their property, abandoned their faith and embraced Mohammedanism, not only with discretion, but with zeal.

Nor was the Slav peasantry ecclesiastically homogeneous. The majority adhered to the Orthodox Church, but mingled with them was a very strong body of Roman Catholics, who leaned upon the Roman Catholic Slavs of Croatia just as naturally as the Orthodox Bosnians looked to the Serbs. The aristocracy, who were exceptionally powerful in Bosnia, were Moslems to a man, and acknowledged in the Sultan not merely their political but their spiritual lord : sovereign and caliph in one. The Bosnian Moslems were indeed in every way ' more Turkish than the Turks ', and in no quarter did the reforming party in Constantinople encounter more bitter or more sustained opposition than from the feudal renegades in Bosnia. The suppression of the Janissaries and the other reforms attempted by Sultan Mahmud led to open revolt, and the policy embodied in the Tanzimat and the Hatti-Humayoun of 1856 was viewed with the utmost disfavour.

It is not difficult, therefore, to understand why the condition of the Christian peasantry in these provinces should have been even less tolerable than elsewhere. Exposed on the one hand to the unregulated rapacity of the Ottoman tax-farmer ; ground down on the other by the labour services and burdensome dues demanded by their native feudal lords ; the wretched peasants found themselves between the hammer and the anvil.

But there were other ingredients in the restlessness of the Balkan Slavs which are less easy to discriminate. Ever since the Crimean War missionaries of the new gospel of Pan-Slavism—mostly Russians—had been engaged in an unceasing propaganda among the peoples of their own faith and their own blood. In 1867 a great Pan-Slavist congress was held, under the thin disguise of a scientific meeting, at Moscow. It issued in the formation of a central Pan-Slavist committee with its head-quarters at Moscow, and a sub-committee sitting at Bucharest ; books and pamphlets were circulated in the Balkans, young Slavs flocked to Russian universities, just as the Roumanian youths flocked to Paris ; Serbia, Montenegro, Bosnia, and Bulgaria were honeycombed with secret societies.

Nor did the movement lack official support. Behind the popular propaganda were the forces of high diplomacy. Every Russian consul in the peninsula was a Pan-Slavist, and General Ignatieff, an enthusiast in the same cause, was appointed ambassador at Constantinople.

How far, at the precise moment of the outbreak, the incitement came from outside, how far it was a spontaneous explosion against political wrongs and fiscal oppression which had become intolerable, it is impossible to say. That both ingredients were present is beyond dispute ; their proportions cannot, with accuracy, be determined.

In July, 1875, the peasants of the Herzegovina suddenly refused to pay their taxes or to perform their accustomed labour services, and, when confronted by a Turkish force, inflicted upon it a decisive defeat (July 24). Sympathizers flocked to their assistance from Serbia, Montenegro, and Dalmatia, and things began to look ugly when the consuls of the Powers intervened with an attempt to mediate between the Ottoman Government and its discontented subjects.

For years past the British Government had been made aware by the reports of its consuls of the appalling condition of the Turkish provinces. As early as 1860 Mr. Holmes, the British consul in Bosnia, had warned the Foreign Office that ' the conduct of the Turkish authorities in these provinces had been sufficient, in conjunction with foreign agitation, to bring

Bosnia to the very verge of rebellion, whilst the Herzegovina was in a state of war '.[1] From Monastir, Janina, and other parts came stories of almost inconceivable misgovernment, obscurantism, and tyranny: another batch of reports, containing further evidence, was laid before Parliament in 1867.[2] In 1871 Mr. Holmes referred to ' the open bribery and corruption, the invariable and unjust favour shown to Mussulmans in all cases between Turks and Christians ' which was characteristic ' of what is called justice ' throughout the Ottoman Empire. ' I do not hesitate to say ', he wrote in April, that ' of all cases of justice, whether between Mussulmans alone, or Turks and Christians, ninety out of a hundred are settled by bribery alone.' These reports testify not only to the abuses of Turkish misgovernment, but to foreign interference. Thus in 1873 Mr. Holmes reported that Austrian and Russian agents were ' equally working to create difficulties '.[3]

Nor had the British Government neglected to warn the Porte of the inevitable outcome of the policy it was pursuing. Thus in 1861 Lord Russell, referring to the recent massacres in Syria, solemnly warned the Sultan that while Great Britain would resist ' a wanton violation of the rights or an unprovoked invasion of the territory of the Porte by any European sovereign ', yet ' the public opinion of Europe would not approve of a protection accorded to the Porte in order to prevent the signal punishment of a Government ' which should permit such atrocities to continue.[4] Similarly, in 1870, Lord Granville instructed Sir Henry Elliot to impress upon Turkey ' that her real safety will depend upon the spirit and feelings of the populations over which she rules '.

[1] *Reports on Condition of Christians in Turkey*, 1860, presented to Parliament, 1861, p. 73 and *passim*.

[2] *Reports*, 1867.   [3] *Turkey*, xvi, 1877, No. 21.

[4] *Turkey*, xvii, 1877, No. 73.

It is, however, unnecessary to multiply quotations. Writ large over the Papers presented at intervals to Parliament will be found overwhelming testimony, on the one hand, to Turkish misgovernment; on the other to the Pan-Slavist agitation; and, above all, to the reiterated but unheeded warnings addressed to the Ottoman Government.

In September, 1875, the insurgents themselves laid before the European consuls in Bosnia a statement of their case and an appeal for sympathy if not for help. They demanded freedom for their religion; the right to give evidence in the courts; the formation of a local Christian militia, and reforms in the imposition and collection of taxation; they declared that they would die rather than continue to suffer such slavery; they begged that the Powers would at least not obstruct their enterprise or assist their oppressors; and they concluded by suggesting alternative remedies: either (1) 'a corner of land' in some Christian state to which they might emigrate *en masse*; or (2) the formation of Bosnia and the Herzegovina into an autonomous state 'tributary to the Sultan with some Christian prince from somewhere, but never from here'; or (3), as a minimum, a temporary foreign occupation.

In an Iradé published on October 2 the Porte promised prompt and general reform; but nevertheless the insurrection deepened and spread. In a Firman issued on December 12 the Sultan offered the immediate establishment of local elective councils, in which the Christians were to take part; and a local gendarmerie. The reply of the insurgents took the form of further defeats inflicted on the Turkish troops.

The Powers could no longer refrain from interference, and their action was hastened by financial considerations.

It is one of the salutary paradoxes incidental to misgovernment that it is as ruinous to the sovereign as it is hurtful to the subject. The inherent extravagance of a bad system had combined with the peculation of officials to bring disaster upon Turkey, and on October 7, 1875, the Sultan was compelled to inform his creditors that he could not pay the full interest on the debt. Partial repudiation complicated an international situation already sufficiently embarrassing. Accordingly, the Sovereigns of Germany, Russia, and Austria took counsel together, and on December 30, 1875, the Austrian Chancellor, Count Andrassy, issued from Buda-Pesth the Note which bears his name.

The Andrassy Note professed the anxiety of the Powers to curtail the area of the insurrection and to maintain the peace of Europe; it drew attention to the failure of the Porte to carry out reforms long overdue, and it insisted that pressure must be put upon the Sultan effectually to redeem his promises. In particular he must be pressed to grant complete religious liberty; to abolish tax-farming; to apply the direct taxes, locally levied in Bosnia and Herzegovina, to the local needs of those provinces; to improve the condition of the rural population by multiplying peasant owners; and, above all, to appoint a special commission, composed in equal numbers of Mussulmans and Christians, to control the execution not only of the reforms now proposed by the Powers, but also of those spontaneously promised by the Sultan in the Iradé of October 2 and the Firman of December 12. Finally, the three emperors required that the Sultan should, by a signed Convention, pledge himself to a prompt and effectual execution of the reforms; in default of which the Powers could not undertake to continue their efforts to restrain and pacify the insurgents.[1] To this Note the British Government gave a general adhesion, though they pointed out that the Sultan had during the last few months promised to carry out the more important of the reforms indicated therein.

[1] The full text of the Andrassy Note will be found in Hertslet, *Map of Europe by Treaty*, vol. iv, pp. 2418–29.

The Note was presented to the Porte at the end of January, 1876; and the Sultan, with almost suspicious promptitude, accepted four out of the five points; the exception being the application of the direct taxes to local objects.

The friendly efforts of the diplomatists were foiled, however, by the attitude of the insurgents. The latter refused, not unnaturally, to be satisfied with mere assurances, or to lay down their arms without substantial guarantees. The Sultan on his side insisted, again not without reason, that it was impossible to initiate a scheme of reform while the provinces were actually in armed rebellion. Meanwhile the mischief was spreading. Bosnia threw in its lot with the Herzegovina; Serbia, Montenegro, and Bulgaria were preparing to do the same when, at the beginning of May, a fanatical Mohammedan outbreak at Salonica led to the murder of the French and German consuls. Drastic measures were obviously necessary if a great European conflagration was to be avoided.

On May 11 the Austrian and Russian Chancellors were in conference with Prince Bismarck at Berlin, and determined to make further and more peremptory demands upon the Sultan. There was to be an immediate armistice of two months' duration, during which certain measures of pacification and repatriation were to be executed under the superintendence of the delegates of the Powers. A mixed Commission, composed of natives faithfully representing the two creeds of the country and presided over by a native Christian, was to be appointed in Bosnia and the Herzegovina; and the insurgents were to be permitted to remain under arms until the reforms promised by the Sultan in October and December, 1875, had been carried into effect. If by the expiry of the armistice the object of the Powers had not been attained, diplomatic action would have to be reinforced.

France and Italy assented to the Note, but the British

Government regarded the terms as unduly peremptory; they resented, very naturally, the independent action of the three imperial Powers; they declined on May 19 to be a party to the Memorandum; and on the 24th ordered the fleet to anchor in Besika Bay. Accordingly, the proposed intervention was abandoned. The Moslem patriots replied in characteristic fashion to Christian menaces. On May 29 they deposed the Sultan Abdul Aziz as too feeble for their purposes, and on June 4 he was *suicidé*; his insane successor, Murad V, reigned only three months, being in turn (August 31) deposed to make room for his brother, Abdul Hamid, the cleverest Sultan Islam had known since the sixteenth century.

Mr. Disraeli's refusal to assent to the Berlin Memorandum created profound perturbation abroad, and evoked a storm of criticism at home. There can be no question that the European Concert, whatever it was worth, was broken by the action of Great Britain. If the latter had joined the other Powers, irresistible pressure would have been put upon the Porte, and some terrible atrocities might have been averted. On the other hand, it is indisputable that the Imperial Chancellors were guilty, to say the least, of grave discourtesy towards Great Britain; nor can it be denied that, assuming a sincere desire for the preservation of peace, they committed an inexcusable blunder in not inviting the co-operation of England before they formulated the demands contained in the Berlin Memorandum.

Events were in the meantime moving rapidly in the Balkans. On June 30, 1876, Serbia formally declared war upon the Porte; Prince Milan being stimulated to action partly by irresistible pressure from his own people, and partly by fear of Peter Karageorgević, the representative of the rival dynasty. One day later Prince Nicholas of Montenegro followed his example.

Montenegro

The tiny principality which thus came into the forefront of Balkan politics has not hitherto claimed much space in this narrative. Serbs of the purest blood and subjects of the great Serbian Empire, the inhabitants of the Black Mountain had, on the dissolution of Dushan's Empire, proclaimed their autonomy. During the sixteenth and seventeenth centuries the Black Mountain was technically included in the Turkish province of Scutari, but the inhabitants, secure in fastnesses almost inaccessible, continued to be ruled by their Prince-Bishops, and never acknowledged the authority of the Ottoman Sultan.

In the eighteenth century they came forward as the champions of the Slav nationality; they received cordial encouragement from Russia, and played some part in the Turkish wars of the Empress Catherine. When, by the Treaty of Pressburg, Napoleon seized Dalmatia, the Montenegrins, with the support of the Tsar Alexander, occupied the splendid harbour known as the Bocche di Cattaro, and refused to evacuate it. The Bocche di Cattaro had belonged to them until the Treaty of Carlowitz (1699). That treaty had assigned the harbour to Venice, from whom in 1797 it was transferred to Austria. At Tilsit, however, Napoleon claimed it from Alexander, who deserted the Montenegrin cause. Half a century later the championship of that cause was assumed by Austria. Bishops of the Orthodox Church being celibate, the succession in Montenegro had always been collateral. But in 1851, on the death of the Prince-Bishop Peter II, his nephew and successor, Danilo, proposed to marry and to secularize the principality. With the approval of the Tsar and the assistance of Austria this change, though not without a war with the Turks, was effected in 1852. Nowhere in the Balkans did the flame of

Slav nationality, frequently revived by contests with the Turks, burn more pure, and the intervention of the little principality in 1876 was therefore according to expectation.

Bulgaria

Nor was the unrest confined to Slavs of the purest blood. It spread even to Bulgaria, which of all the Balkan provinces had been most completely absorbed into the Ottoman system. For that reason we have heard nothing of Bulgaria since the last vestiges of its independence were crushed out by the Ottoman victories in the closing years of the fourteenth century.[1]

During the great days of the Ottoman Empire the lot of the Bulgarians, as of other conquered peoples in the peninsula, was far from intolerable. As in Bosnia, many of the nobles embraced Mohammedanism, but the mass of the people adhered to their own creed, and, provided the tribute of children and money was punctually forthcoming, the Turks did not interfere with the exercise of Orthodox rites, nor with the ecclesiastical jurisdiction of the Orthodox priests. Some of the towns were permitted to retain their municipal privileges; a considerable measure of autonomy was conceded to the province at large; and the natives were allowed the free use of their own language.

Here, as elsewhere, the condition of the subject people deteriorated as the rule of the Ottoman Government became enfeebled. The Bulgarians suffered much from the passage of the Ottoman armies as they marched north against the Austrians, and later from that of the Russians when they began to threaten or to defend Constantinople. To Russia, however, Bulgaria began to look towards the end of the eighteenth century for protection. The stipulations for the better

---

[1] *Supra*, chap. iii.

government of the principalities and the islands contained in the Treaty of Kainardji; the presence of a Russian ambassador at Constantinople; the privileges conceded, on Russia's demand, to the Christians, all tended in the same direction.

In Bulgaria, as in Serbia, the Ottoman Sultan was not the only nor perhaps the most formidable foe to the spirit of independence and the sense of nationality. By the Sultan's side in Constantinople was the Greek Patriarch. Politically, Bulgaria was conquered and absorbed by the Turks; socially and ecclesiastically, it was permeated by the Phanariote Greeks. The methods employed by the latter were parallel to, but even more thorough than, those which, as we have seen, were employed in Serbia: the independent Patriarchate of Tirnovo was in 1777 suppressed; all the higher ecclesiastical offices were monopolized by Phanariotes; the parish clergy, even the schoolmasters, were Greek, and Greek became not only the language of 'society' but the sole medium of instruction in the schools of the people.[1] The first step towards a revival of Bulgarian nationality was therefore a restoration of ecclesiastical independence. The Porte promised to make certain concessions—the appointment of native bishops and the use of the native tongue in schools and churches—in 1856. But nothing was done, and in 1860 the Bulgarians refused any longer to recognize the Patriarch of Constantinople. Not for ten years did the Porte give way, but in 1870 it agreed to the establishment of a separate Bulgarian Exarchate at Constantinople, with jurisdiction not only over Bulgarians in Bulgaria proper, but over those of Macedonia, and indeed over any community (*millet*) of Bulgarians in any part of the empire.

The demand for a Bulgarian Exarchate was symptomatic.

---

[1] 'Even forty years ago', wrote Sir Charles Eliot in 1896, 'the name Bulgarian was almost unknown, and every educated person coming from that country called himself a Greek as a matter of course' (*op. cit.*, p. 314).

The spirit which was moving the purer Slavs of Serbia, Montenegro, Bosnia, and the Herzegovina was not leaving the Bulgar-Slavs untouched. Nor were they less moved by the Pan-Slavist impulse from without. The Bulgarians, more even than the Serbs, were roused to a remembrance of their ancient greatness by the tramp of foreign soldiers in the peninsula. The march of the Russians upon Adrianople in 1828 naturally caused considerable excitement even among the phlegmatic peasants of Bulgaria ; the presence of the allied armies at Varna in 1854 evoked emotions of a different but hardly less exciting character. At least these were signs of impending changes. Clearly, things were not going to be in the Balkans as for five hundred years they had been.

Nevertheless, it was not until May, 1876, that the name Bulgarian first became familiar on the lips of men. On the first day of the month, some of the Bulgarian Christians, imitating the peasants of Herzegovina, defied the orders of the Turkish officials, and put one hundred of them to death. The Herzegovina was relatively remote, but now the spirit of insubordination seemed to be infecting the heart of the empire. The Porte, already engaged in war with Serbia and Montenegro, was terrified at the idea of an attack upon the right flank of its army, and determined upon a prompt and terrible suppression of the Bulgarian revolt. A force of 18,000 regulars was marched into Bulgaria, and hordes of irregulars, Bashi-Bazouks, and Circassians were let loose to wreak the vengeance of the Sultan upon a peasantry unprepared for resistance and mostly unarmed. Whole villages were wiped out, and in the town of Batak only 2,000 out of 7,000 inhabitants escaped massacre.

On June 23 a London newspaper published the first account of the horrors alleged to have been perpetrated by the Turks in Bulgaria. How much of exaggeration there was in the tale of atrocities with which England and the world soon rang it was and is impossible to say. But something much less than the ascertained facts would be sufficient to account for the profound emotion which moved the whole Christian world. In July Mr. Walter Baring was sent by the British Government to Adrianople to ascertain, if possible, the truth. After careful investigation he came to the conclusion that in the initial outbreak 136 Moslems had been murdered, while, in the subsequent massacres, 'not fewer than 12,000 Christians' perished.[1] His final report was not issued until September, but preliminary reports so far substantiated the accounts which had been published in the English Press as to move the conscience of England to its depths. In a dispatch [2] to Sir Henry Elliot, British Ambassador to the Porte, Lord Derby gave expression, in language not the less strong by reason of its restraint, to the feelings of indignation aroused in England by the accounts of the Bulgarian atrocities, and instructed him to demand from the Sultan prompt and effective reparation for the victims.

But a voice more powerful than that of Lord Derby was already making articulate the feelings of his countrymen. To Mr. Gladstone the tale of atrocities made an irresistible appeal. A pamphlet, published on September 6, was circulated by tens of thousands.[3] With voice and pen he vehemently demanded that the Turks should be cleared out 'bag and baggage . . . from the province they have desolated and profaned'.

Meanwhile another complication had arisen. At the end of June Serbia and Montenegro, as we have seen, had declared war upon the Porte. How far would that conflict extend? Could it be confined within the original limits? These

---

[1] M. Driault (*op. cit.*, p. 214) puts the number much higher: 25,000–30,000.

[2] September 21, 1876.

[3] *The Bulgarian Horrors and the Question of the East.*

were the serious questions with which diplomacy was now confronted. The Serbian army consisted largely of Russian volunteers and was commanded by a Russian general. How long would it be before the Russian Government became a party to the quarrel? The Serbian army, even reinforced by the volunteers, could offer but a feeble resistance to the Turk, and in August Prince Milan, acting on a hint from England, asked for the mediation of the Powers.[1] England, thereupon, urged the Sultan to come to terms with Serbia and Montenegro, lest a worse thing should befall him. The Sultan declined an armistice, but formulated his terms, and intimated that if the Powers approved them he would grant an immediate suspension of hostilities. But to Lord Derby's chagrin Serbia would accept nothing less than an armistice, and, after six weeks' suspension, hostilities recommenced. Nevertheless, the English Government was untiring in its efforts to promote a pacification, and suggested to the Powers some heads of proposals (September 21): the *status quo* in Serbia and Montenegro ; local or administrative autonomy for Bosnia and Herzegovina ; guarantees against maladministration in Bulgaria, and a comprehensive scheme of reform, all to be embodied in a protocol concluded between the Porte and the Powers. Russia then proposed (September 26) that, in the event of a refusal from Turkey, the allied fleets should enter the Bosphorus, that Bosnia should be temporarily occupied by Austria, and Bulgaria by Russia. Turkey, thereupon, renewed her dilatory tactics, but Russia's patience was almost exhausted ; General Ignatieff arrived at Constantinople, on a special mission from the Tsar, on October 15, and on the 30th presented his ultimatum. If an armistice were not concluded with Serbia within forty-eight hours, the Russian Embassy was to be immediately withdrawn. On November 2

[1] *Turkey*, 1877 (No. 1), p. 380.

the Porte gave way ; Serbia was saved ; a breathing space was permitted to the operations of diplomacy.

The interval was utilized by the meeting of a Conference of the Powers at Constantinople (December 23). The Powers agreed to the terms suggested by Lord Derby in September, but the Porte was obdurate. Profuse in professions and promises of reform, the Porte, with delicious irony, selected this moment for the promulgation of a brand-new and full-blown parliamentary constitution, but it stubbornly refused to allow Europe to superintend the execution of the reforms.[1] There was to be a Legislative Body of two Houses : a nominated Senate and an elected Chamber of Deputies ; a responsible Executive ; freedom of meeting and of the press ; an irremovable judiciary and compulsory education.[2] But though the Sultan was prodigal in the concession of reforms, on paper, no one but himself should have a hand in executing them. On this point he was inexorable. Thereupon General Ignatieff, refusing to take further part in a solemn farce, withdrew from the Conference. The Tsar had already (November 10) announced his intention to proceed single-handed if the Porte refused the demands of the Powers, his army was already mobilized on the Pruth, and war appeared imminent.

The diplomatists, however, made one more effort to avert it. Their demands were reduced to a minimum : putting aside an extension of territory for Serbia or Montenegro, they insisted upon the concession of autonomy to Bosnia, to the Herzegovina, and to Bulgaria, under the control of an international commission. On January 20 the Sultan categorically

---

[1] A draft of the constitution itself had been submitted to Sir Henry Elliot some twelve months before this date. Cf. *Life of Midhat Pasha*, by his son Ali Haydar Midhat Bey (c.v.).

[2] The first Turkish Parliament was opened with due ceremony on March 19, 1877.

refused, and on the 21st the Conference broke up. Great Britain, nevertheless, persisted in her efforts to preserve peace, and on March 31, 1877, the Powers signed in London a protocol proposed by Count Schouvaloff. Taking cognizance of the Turkish promises of reform, the Powers declared their intention of watching carefully ' the manner in which the promises of the Ottoman Government are carried into effect '. If, however, the condition of the Christian subjects of the Porte should again lead to a ' return of the complications which periodically disturb the peace of the East, they think it right to declare that such a state of things would be incompatible with their interests and those of Europe in general '. The Turk, in high dudgeon, rejected the London Protocol (April 10), and on April 24 the Tsar, having secured the friendly neutrality of Austria,[1] declared war.

Russia had behaved, in face of prolonged provocation, with commendable patience and restraint, and had shown a genuine desire to maintain the European Concert. The Turk had exhibited throughout his usual mixture of shrewdness and obstinacy. It is difficult to believe that he would have maintained his obstinate front but for expectations based upon the supposed goodwill of the British Government. The language of the Prime Minister [2] and the Foreign Secretary had unquestionably given him some encouragement. So much so that before the break-up of the Conference Lord Salisbury telegraphed [3] to Lord Derby from Constantinople : ' The Grand Vizier believes that he can count upon the assistance of Lord Derby and Lord Beaconsfield.' The Turk, it is true,

---

[1] By the Agreement of Reichstadt (July 8, 1876), confirmed by definite treaty January 15, 1877. The terms of the Austro-Russian agreement have never been authoritatively revealed : cf. Rose, *Development of European Nations*, p. 180.

[2] e. g. at the Guildhall on November 9.   [3] January 8, 1877.

is an adept at diplomatic 'bluff', and 'assistance' went beyond the facts. But this much is certain. If the English Cabinet had, even in January, 1877, frankly and unambiguously gone hand in hand with Russia there would have been no war.

Russo-Turkish War

The armistice arranged in November between Turkey and Serbia had been further prolonged on December 28, and on February 27 peace was concluded at Constantinople. But on June 12, Montenegro, encouraged by the action of Russia, recommenced hostilities, and on June 22 the Russian army effected the passage of the Danube.

No other way towards Constantinople was open to them, for the Russian navy had not yet had time since 1871 to regain the position in the Black Sea denied to it in 1856. The co-operation of Roumania was, therefore, indispensable, and this had been secured by a convention concluded on April 16, by which, in return for a free passage for his troops through the principalities, the Tsar engaged to 'maintain and defend the actual integrity of Roumania'. The Roumanian army held the right flank for Russia, but an offer of more active co-operation was declined with some hauteur by the Tsar. From the Danube the Russians pushed on slowly but success-fully until their advanced guard suffered a serious check before Plevna on July 30. On the following day Osman Pasha, strongly entrenched at Plevna, inflicted a very serious reverse upon them.

Instead of carrying Plevna by storm they were compelled to besiege it, and the task proved to be a tough one. In chastened mood the Tsar accepted, in August, the con-temned offer of Prince Carol, who was appointed to the supreme command of the Russo-Roumanian army. For five months Osman held 120,000 Russians and Roumanians at bay, inflicting meantime very heavy losses upon them, but at last his resistance was worn down, and on December 10 the remnant of the gallant garrison—some 40,000 half-starved men—· were ·compelled to surrender.

Four days later Serbia, for the second time, declared war upon the Porte, and recaptured Prisrend, the ancient capital of the kingdom. The Russians, meanwhile, were pushing the Turks back towards Constantinople ; they occupied Sofia on January 5, and Adrianople on the 20th. In the Caucasus their success was not less complete ; the great fortress of Kars had fallen on November 18 ; the Turkish Empire seemed to lie at their mercy, and in March Russia dictated to the Porte the Treaty of San Stefano.

A basis of agreement had already been reached at Adrianople (January 31) ; the terms were now embodied in a treaty signed, on March 3, at San Stefano, a village not far from Constantinople. Montenegro, enlarged by the acquisition of some strips of Bosnia and the Adriatic port of Antivari, was to be recognized definitely as independent of the Porte ; so also was Serbia, which was to acquire the districts of Nish and Mitrovitza ; the reforms recommended to the Porte at the Conference of Constantinople were to be immediately introduced into Bosnia and the Herzegovina, and to be executed under the joint control of Russia and Austria ; the fortresses on the Danube were to be razed ; reforms were to be granted to the Armenians ; Russia was to acquire, in lieu of the greater part of the money indemnity which she claimed, Batoum, Kars, and other territory in Asia, and part of the Dobrudja, which was to be exchanged with Roumania (whose independence was recognized by the Porte) for the strip of Bessarabia retroceded in 1856. The most striking feature of the treaty was the creation of a greater Bulgaria, which was to be constituted an autonomous tributary principality with a Christian government and a national militia, and was to extend from the Danube to the Aegean, nearly as far south as Midia (on the Black Sea) and Adrianople, and to include, on the west, the district round Monastir but not Salonica.[1] The Ottoman Empire in Europe was practically annihilated. The proposed aggrandizement of Bulgaria aroused grave concern in the other Balkan States. How was this treaty regarded by Europe in general and in particular by Great Britain ?

Great Britain and the Eastern Question

Lord Beaconsfield had come into power in 1874 with the deliberate purpose of giving to English foreign policy the new orientation imperatively demanded by the new conditions of the world.

' You have ', he said, ' a new world, new influences at work, new and unknown objects and dangers with which to cope. . . . The relations of England to Europe are not the same as they were in the days of Lord Chatham or Frederick the Great. The Queen of England has become the Sovereign of the most powerful of Oriental States. On the other side of the globe there are now establishments belonging to her, teeming with wealth and population. . . . These are vast and novel elements in the distribution of power. . . . What our duty is at this critical moment is to maintain the Empire of England.'

The first indication given to the world of the ' new Imperialism ' was the purchase of the Khedive's shares in the Suez Canal. On the 25th of November, 1875, the world was startled by the news that the British Government had purchased from the Khedive for the sum of four million sterling his 176,000 shares in the Suez Canal.[2] The success of this

---

[1] See *Turkey Papers*, No. 22 (1878); Holland, *European Concert*, pp. 335 sq.

[2] The total shares were 400,000. The idea of the purchase was said to

transaction, as a financial speculation, has long since been brilliantly demonstrated. As a political move, it marks a new departure of the highest significance. England, as preceding pages have shown, had been curiously blind to her interests in the Eastern Mediterranean ; Disraeli, by a brilliant *coup*, opened her eyes. But to him the purchase of the Canal shares was no isolated speculation, but only the first move in a coherent and preconcerted plan.

His next move had a twofold object. During the winter of 1875–6 the Prince of Wales had undertaken an extended tour in India. The visit, which was without precedent in the history of the empire, proved an eminent success, and prepared the way for a still more important departure. ' You can only act upon the opinion of Eastern nations through their imagination.' So Disraeli had spoken at the time of the Mutiny, and in Opposition. As first Minister of the Crown he gave effect to his convictions ; and touched the imagination not only of India but of the world by making his sovereign Empress of India. A magnificent Durbar was held at Delhi in the closing days of the year 1876, and on January 1, 1877, a series of celebrations culminated in the proclamation of Queen Victoria as Empress of India in the presence of sixty-three ruling Chiefs, and amid the acclamations of the most brilliant assemblage ever brought together in British India.

The purchase of the Canal shares, the assumption of the Imperial Crown of India, were parts of a coherent whole. Disraeli's attitude towards the complex problems, roused into fresh life by events in the Near East, was determined by precisely the same considerations. He never forgot that the queen was the ruler of Mohammedans as well as Christians,

have been suggested by Mr. Frederick Greenwood, a distinguished London journalist. See *The Times*, December 27, 1905, and January 13, 1906. But there are now other claimants to the distinction.

of Asiatics, Africans, Australians, and Americans as well as Europeans. It was therefore with the eyes of an oriental, no less than of an occidental, statesman that he watched the development of events in the Near East. Those events caused, as we have seen, grave disquietude in Great Britain. Before the Russian armies had crossed the Danube the Tsar undertook to respect English interests in Egypt and in the Canal, and not to occupy Constantinople or the Straits (June 8, 1877), but the Russian victories in the closing months of 1877 excited in England some alarm as to the precise fulfilment of his promises. Accordingly, in January, 1878, Lord Derby, then Foreign Secretary, deemed it at once friendly and prudent to remind the Tsar of his promise, and to warn him that any treaty concluded between Russia and Turkey which might affect the engagements of 1856 and 1871 ' would not be valid without the assent of the Powers who were parties to those Treaties.' (January 14).

In order to emphasize the gravity of the warning, the Fleet, which had been at Besika Bay, was ordered to pass the Dardanelles (January 23), and the Government asked Parliament for a vote of credit of £6,000,000.

In moving the vote on January 28, the Chancellor of the Exchequer (Sir S. Northcote) made public the terms demanded by Russia, which, in addition to the points subsequently embodied in the Treaty of San Stefano, included ' an ulterior understanding for safeguarding the rights and interests of Russia in the Straits '. This was the point in regard to which Russia had already been warned by Lord Derby, and the situation became critical in the extreme. In the preliminary terms concluded between the combatants on January 31 this stipulation disappeared ; but, in consequence of excited telegrams from Mr. Layard, the British ambassador in Constantinople, the Cabinet decided (February 7) to send a detachment of the Fleet into the Sea of Marmora for the protection of British subjects in Constantinople. Russia retorted that if British ships sailed up the Straits Russian troops would enter Constantinople for the purpose of similarly protecting the lives of Christians of every race. But the Sultan, equally afraid of friends and foes, begged the English fleet to retire, and it returned accordingly to Besika Bay.

The extreme tension was thus for the moment relaxed. The Austrian Government was already moving in the matter of a European Congress, and on March 4 Lord Derby informed Count Beust that Great Britain agreed to the suggestion, provided it were clearly understood that ' all questions dealt with in the Treaty of Peace between Russia and Turkey should be considered as subjects to be discussed in the Congress'. This had been throughout ' the keynote of our policy ', ' the diapason of our diplomacy '.[1] With regard to the Treaty of San Stefano the language of Lord Beaconsfield was emphatic : ' it abolishes the dominion of the Ottoman Empire in Europe ; it creates a large State which, under the name of Bulgaria, is inhabited by many races not Bulgarian . . . all the European dominions of the Ottoman Porte are . . . put under the administration of Russia . . . the effect of all the stipulations combined will be to make the Black Sea as much a Russian lake as the Caspian.'[2] Whether this description was exaggerated or no, there can be no question that, in every clause, the treaty was a ' deviation' from those of 1856 and 1871, and as such required the assent of the signatory Powers.

To the demand that the treaty in its entirety should be submitted to a congress Russia demurred. Great Britain insisted. Again peace hung in the balance. Apart from the dispute between England and Russia there was a great deal of

[1] Lord Beaconsfield in the House of Lords, April 8, 1878, *Speeches*, ii. 163.
[2] Ibid., p. 170.

inflammable material about, to which a spark would set light. Greece, Serbia, and, above all, Roumania, who with incredible tactlessness and base ingratitude had been excluded from the peace negotiations, were all gravely dissatisfied with the terms of the Treaty of San Stefano. Greece had indeed actually invaded Thessaly at the beginning of February, and only consented to abstain from further hostilities upon the assurance of the Powers that her claims should have favourable consideration in the definitive Treaty of Peace.

Lord Beaconsfield, however, was ready with his next move, and at this supremely critical moment he made it. On April 17 it was announced that he had ordered 7,000 Indian troops to embark for Malta. The *coup* was denounced as ' sensational ', un-English, unconstitutional,[1] even illegal.[2] That it was dramatic none can gainsay ; but it was consonant with the whole trend of Lord Beaconsfield's policy : if it alarmed England it impressed Europe, and there can be no question that it made for peace.

The operation of other forces was tending in the same direction. The terms of settlement proposed by Russia were not less distasteful to Austria than to England. An Austrian army was mobilized on the Russian flank in the Carpathians, and on February 4 the Emperor Francis Joseph demanded that the terms of peace should be referred to a Congress at Vienna. Austria might well take a firm line, for behind Austria was Germany.

Bismarck had made up his mind. He would fain have preserved in its integrity the *Dreikaiserbund* of 1872 ; he was under deep obligations to Russia, and was only too glad to assist and even to stimulate her ambitions so long as they conflicted only with those of Great Britain or France. But when it came to a possible conflict between Russia and Germany

---

[1] e. g. by Mr. Gladstone.   [2] e. g. by Lord Selborne.

matters were different. It was true that Russia had protected Prussia's right flank in 1864, and her left flank in 1866, and —highest service of all—had 'contained' Austria in 1870. The Tsar thought, not unnaturally, that in the spring of 1878 the time had arrived for a repayment of the debt, and requested Bismarck to contain Austria. Bismarck was still anxious to 'keep open the wire between Berlin and St. Petersburg', provided it was not at the expense of that between Berlin and Vienna. He replied, therefore, to the Tsar that Germany must keep watch on the Rhine, and could not spare troops to contain Austria as well. The excuse was transparent. Bismarck had, in fact, decided to give Austria a free hand in the Balkans, and even to push her along the road towards Salonica. His attitude was regarded in Russia as a great betrayal, a dishonourable repudiation of an acknowledged debt. It is not, however, too much to say that it averted a European conflagration. The Tsar decided not to fight Austria and England, but, instead, to accept the invitation to a Congress at Berlin.

The Treaty of Berlin

On May 30 Lord Salisbury and Count Schouvaloff came to an agreement upon the main points at issue, and on June 13 the Congress opened at Berlin. Prince Bismarck presided, and filled his chosen rôle of 'the honest broker', but it was Lord Beaconsfield whose personality dominated the Congress. 'Der alte Jude, das ist der Mann' was Bismarck's shrewd summary of the situation.

Little time was spent in discussion; the treaty was signed on July 13. Russia's sole acquisition in Europe was the strip of Bessarabia which had been retroceded to Roumania in 1856 and was now, by an act of grave impolicy and base ingratitude, snatched away from her by the Tsar. In Asia she retained Batoum, Ardahan, and Kars. Bosnia and the Herzegovina were handed over for an undefined term to Austria, who was also to be allowed to occupy for military, but not administrative, purposes the Sanjak of Novi Bazar. England, under a separate Convention concluded with Turkey on June 4, was to occupy and administer the island of Cyprus, so long as Russia retained Kars and Batoum. Turkey was to receive the surplus revenues of the island, to carry out reforms in her Asiatic dominions, and to be protected in the possession of them by Great Britain. France sought for authority to occupy Tunis in the future; Italy hinted at claims upon Albania and Tripoli. Germany asked for nothing, but was more than compensated for her modesty by securing the gratitude and friendship of the Sultan. Never did Bismarck make a better investment.

Greece, with no false modesty, claimed the cession of Crete, Thessaly, Epirus, and a part of Macedonia, but for the moment got nothing. Roumania was ill compensated for the loss of southern Bessarabia by the acquisition of part of the Dobrudja, but secured complete independence from the Porte, as did Serbia and Montenegro, who received most of the districts promised to them at San Stefano.

Bulgaria did not. And herein lay the essential difference between the Treaty of Berlin and that of San Stefano.

' Bulgaria ', as defined at Berlin, was not more than a third of the Bulgaria mapped out at San Stefano. It was to consist of a relatively narrow strip between the Danube and the Balkans, and to be an independent State under Turkish suzerainty. South of it there was to be a province, Eastern Roumelia, which was to be restored to the Sultan, who agreed to place it under a Christian governor approved by the Powers. By this change the Sultan recovered 2,500,000 of population and 30,000 square miles of territory; Bulgaria was cut off from the Aegean : Macedonia remained intact.

Such were the main provisions of the famous Treaty of Berlin. They were criticized at the time, and from several points of view, with great acerbity. Lord Beaconsfield's claim that he had brought back to England 'Peace with Honour', though conceded by the mass of his fellow countrymen, evoked some derision among them. His statement that he had 'consolidated' the Ottoman Empire was received with polite scepticism both at home and abroad, a scepticism to some extent justified by the Cyprus Convention, to say nothing of the cession of Bosnia and the Herzegovina. With some inconsistency, however, he was simultaneously assailed for having replaced under the withering tyranny of the Sultan a Christian population which Russia had emancipated. The charge is, on the face of it, difficult to rebut. But it does not lie in the mouths of the Philhellenists and Philo-Serbs to make it. Had the Treaty of San Stefano been permitted to stand, the ambitions both of Serbia and Greece would have been seriously circumscribed. It was not, indeed, of Serbia, or Greece, still less of Roumania, that Lord Beaconsfield was thinking at Berlin. The motive of his policy was that which had inspired Lord Palmerston and Mr. Canning. He definitely repudiated the claim of Russia to dictate by her sole voice and in her own interests the solution of a secular problem. It is only fair to Russia to say that if at the time of the Berlin Memorandum Lord Beaconsfield had been at more pains to preserve the Concert of the Powers, the claim might never have been preferred. Once preferred it could not be admitted.

For a final judgement on the events recorded in this chapter the time has not yet arrived. During the generation which has followed the Congress of Berlin opinion has swung backwards and forwards, and the pendulum is not, even now, at rest. This much, however, may with confidence be affirmed : the diplomatists at Berlin were working better than they knew. The settlement outlined at San Stefano was both hasty and premature. That it should be submitted to the collective judgement of the Powers was only reasonable. Lord Beaconsfield must at least have the credit of having secured for it that further scrutiny

Two of the Balkan States owe little gratitude to his memory. At San Stefano Roumania had been treated by Russia with discourtesy and ingratitude. At Berlin it was treated no better. Both Germany and England, to say nothing of France, might have been expected to extend towards the principality something more than sympathy. But Bismarck, indifferent to the dynastic ties which united Prussia and Roumania, was not sorry to see Russia neglecting a golden opportunity for binding Roumania in gratitude to herself. A Roumania alienated from Russia would be the less likely to quarrel with the Dual Monarchy and to press her claims to the inclusion of the unredeemed Roumanians in Transylvania and the Bukovina. Lord Beaconsfield professed much Platonic sympathy for the disappointment of their wishes in regard to Bessarabia, but frankly confessed that he could not turn aside from the pursuit of the larger issues to befriend a State in whose fortunes Great Britain was not directly interested. It was a gross blunder, the consequences of which are not yet exhausted. The Roumanian envoys left Berlin not only empty-handed, but deeply impressed by the cynicism of high diplomacy, and bitterly chagrined by the ingratitude of Russia and the indifference of Europe.

The sentiments of Bulgaria were not dissimilar. Against Russia she had no cause of complaint ; but in her view Germany and Great Britain had conspired to dash from her lips the cup proffered her by the Tsar. San Stefano had gone beyond the equities of the case, and had imperilled other interests not less important than those of Bulgaria. Berlin fell short of them. The barrier interposed between the Bulgarians of the new principality and those of Eastern Roumelia was not merely inequitable but manifestly absurd. Nor did it endure. The making of modern Bulgaria demands, however, and will receive, more detailed attention.

So also with the position of the Southern Slavs, to whom the settlement of 1878 was profoundly disquieting. Serbia gained some territory, but it was really at the expense of Bulgaria ; the Sanjak of Novi Bazar, garrisoned by Austria, but still governed by the Turks, severed the Serbs of Serbia from their brethren in Montenegro, while the Austrian occupation of Bosnia and the Herzegovina brought the Habsburgs into the heart of Balkan affairs and made a tremendous breach in the solidarity of the Jugo-Slav race.

The Treaty of Berlin is generally regarded as a great landmark in the history of the Eastern Question. In some respects it is ; but its most important features were not those with which its authors were best pleased or most concerned. They were preoccupied by the relations between the Sultan and the Tsar, and by the interest of Europe in defining those relations. The enduring significance of the treaty is to be found elsewhere : not in the remnant of the Ottoman Empire snatched from the brink of destruction by Lord Beaconsfield, but in the new nations which were arising upon the ruins of that empire—nations which may look back to the 13th of July, 1878, if not as their birthday, at least as the date on which their charters of emancipation were signed and sealed.

For further reference : the Papers laid before Parliament in 1861, 1867, 1877, and 1878, and referred to in the footnotes, are of great importance. They are usefully summarized by the Duke of Argyll in *The Eastern Question* (2 vols.). Lord Stratford de Redcliffe's *Eastern Question*, containing his letters to *The Times* in 1876–8 and other papers, has great contemporary interest. Holland and Hertslet are, as before, invaluable for the texts of treaties.

For relations of Russia and Germany : T. Klaczko, *The Two Chancellors*

(Gortschakoff and Bismarck); Busch, *Our Chancellor*; and Bismarck's *Reminiscences*.

On the Balkan movement: Marquis of Bath, *Observations on Bulgarian Affairs*, 1880; Duke of Argyll, as above; *The Balkans* (Clarendon Press, 1915); A. J. Evans, *Through Bosnia and Herzegovina on Foot* (1876); W. D. Gladstone, *Bulgarian Horrors and the Question of the East* (London, 1876); Iovanóvitz, *Les Serbes et la Mission de la Serbie dans l'Europe d'Orient* (Paris, 1876); A. Gallenga, *Two Years of the Eastern Question*, 2 vols. (London, 1877); Hanotaux, *Contemporary France*.

For English policy: Lord Fitzmaurice, *Life of Lord Granville*; Lord Newton, *Life of Lord Lyons*; Morley, *Gladstone*; Holland, *Duke of Devonshire*; Marriott, *England since Waterloo*; Paul, *Modern England*. The concluding volume of Monypenny and Buckle's *Disraeli* ought in this connexion to be of supreme interest.

Generally: Débidour, *Histoire diplomatique*; Driault, *La Question d'Orient*.

13

The Balkan States, 1878–98

The Making of Bulgaria—Modern Greece (1832–98)—The Cretan Problem

' These newly emancipated races want to breathe free air and not through Russian nostrils.'—SIR WILLIAM WHITE (1885).

' A Bulgaria, friendly to the Porte, and jealous of foreign influence, would be a far surer bulwark against foreign aggression than two Bulgarias, severed in administration, but united in considering the Porte as the only obstacle to their national development.'—LORD SALISBURY (December 23, 1885).

' It is next to impossible that the Powers of Christendom can permit the Turk, however triumphant, to cast his yoke again over the necks of any emancipated Provincials. . . . There is much reason to think that a chain of autonomous States, though still, perhaps, tributary to the Sultan, might be extended from the Black Sea to the Adriatic with advantage to that potentate himself. But, at all events, the very idea of reinstating any amount of Turkish misgovernment in places once cleared of it is simply revolting.'—LORD STRATFORD DE REDCLIFFE.

'Greece wants something more than the rules of political procedure that are embodied in written constitutions in order to infuse better moral principles among her people whose social system has been corrupted by long ages of national servitude ... until the people undergo a moral change as well as the government, national progress must be slow, and the surest pledges for the enjoyment of true liberty will be wanting.'—Dr. GEORGE FINLAY.

'Crete is an unexplored paradise in ruins, a political volcano in chronic activity, a theatre on the boards of which rapine, arson, murder, and all manner of diabolical crimes are daily rehearsed for the peace, if not the delectation, of the Great Powers of peace-loving Christendom. Truly this is far and away the most grotesque political spectacle of the nineteenth century.'—E. J. DILLON.

To pass from the Congress of Berlin to the early struggles of the reborn Balkan States means more than a change of temperature and environment. It involves an abrupt transition from drab prose to highly coloured romance; from a problem play to transpontine melodrama; from the traditional methods of nineteenth-century diplomacy to those of primitive political society. Transported to the Balkans we are in the midst of *bouleversements* and vicissitudes, political and personal; sudden elevations; sudden falls; democratic constitutions and autocratic *coups d'état*; plotting and counter-plotting; the hero of yesterday, the villain of to-day, and again the hero of to-morrow; abductions, abdications, and assassinations; the formation and dissolution of parties; a strange medley of chivalry and baseness; of tragedy and comedy; of obscurantism and progress.

The Treaty of Berlin meant the end of 'Turkey in Europe' as the term had been understood by geographers for the last four hundred years. The place of the provinces of the Ottoman Empire is now taken by independent, or virtually independent, States: Greece, Roumania, Serbia, Montenegro, and Bulgaria. But although the Ottoman Empire is broken and crippled, the new States are by no means fully fashioned. The garment woven at Berlin had many ragged edges. Greece got nothing at the moment, and had to wait three years before even a portion of her claims upon Thessaly and Epirus were conceded; Crete remained in Turkish hands for another generation. Serbia was profoundly dissatisfied and with reason : the arrangement proposed at San Stefano would have divided the Sanjak of Novi-Bazar between herself and the sister State of Montenegro, thus bringing the two Slav States into immediate contact, and giving Serbia indirect access, through Montenegro, to the Adriatic. The crafty restoration of the Sanjak to Turkey; the retention of the great harbour of the Bocche di Cattaro by Austria, and the Austrian occupation of Bosnia and the Herzegovina inflicted a series of terrible blows upon the aspirations of the Southern Slavs, and kept open sores which might have been healed. The Habsburgs were, however, far too clever to allow their hopes of access to the Aegean to be frustrated by the interposition of a compact Jugo-Slav State, whether that State was unitary or federal. The disappointment of Serbia was the immediate disappointment of Montenegro, and ultimately the disappointment of Bosnia and the Herzegovina.

Of the cruel blow to the legitimate hopes of Roumania enough, for the moment, was said in the last chapter. But the fatal character of the blunder then committed by Russia, without protest, be it added, from any of the Powers, cannot be too strongly emphasized. Most significant of all, however, was the partition of the proposed Bulgaria. That partition not only served to keep the Balkans in ferment for the next thirty years, but introduced into European diplomacy, or at least into its vocabulary, a new problem, that of ' Macedonia '. Whether Serbia and Greece would or could have acquiesced in the San Stefano settlement is a question which must be reserved for subsequent discussion ; but it is obvious that if

Lord Beaconsfield had not torn that treaty into shreds the Macedonian problem would never have emerged in the shape with which the present generation is familiar. The Greater Bulgaria might ultimately have raised as many problems as it solved ; but those problems would have been approached from a different angle and might have been solved with less friction and more satisfactory results.

Bulgaria

As things were, it was upon the fortunes of Bulgaria that the attention not merely of the Balkans but of Europe at large was concentrated during the twenty years succeeding the Congress of Berlin. To the affairs of Bulgaria a large section of this chapter must, therefore, be devoted.

In 1878 the Russian army was in occupation of the principality which Russian diplomacy proposed to create. The plans of the future edifice had been, it is true, profoundly modified at Berlin, but the task of executing them was committed to Russia.

The first business was to provide the new principality with a constitution. According to the Treaty of Berlin the ' Organic Law of the Principality ' was to be drawn up ' before the election of the Prince ' by an assembly of notables of Bulgaria convoked at Tirnovo ; particular regard was to be paid to the rights and interests of the Turkish, Roumanian, Greek, or other populations, where these were intermixed with Bulgarians, and there was to be absolute equality between different religious creeds and confessions.

Until the completion of the Organic Law the principality was provisionally administered by a Russian Commissary, assisted by a Turkish Commissary and Consuls delegated *ad hoc* by the Powers. The Constituent Assembly, elected in December 1878, met on February 26, 1879, and duly drafted an Organic Law which was adopted on April 28. Mainly the work of the first ruler of the independent Bulgaria, Petko Karaveloff,[1] this Law was amended in 1893 and again in 1911, but neither in its original nor amended form has it worked satisfactorily. It was said of modern Italy, perhaps with truth, that she was made too quickly. The saying is certainly true of Bulgaria. Her young men and old men were alike in a hurry. Without any training whatever in the most difficult of all political arts, that of self-government, Bulgaria adopted a form of constitution which presupposed a long political apprenticeship. Karaveloff was a sincere patriot, but he belonged to the worst type of academic radicals. The constitution reflected, in every clause, the work of the *doctrinaire*.

The Legislature was to consist of a Single Chamber, the Sobranje or National Assembly; any man over thirty years of age who could read and write, unless he were a clergyman, a soldier on active service, or had been deprived of civil rights, was eligible for election to it; all members were to be paid; the Assembly was to be elected on the basis of universal manhood suffrage, and each electoral district was to consist of 20,000 voters who were to return one member; unless dissolved by the prince (now the king) the Assembly was to sit for four years. Questions concerning the acquisition or cession of territory, a vacancy of the crown, regencies and constitutional revision were to be reserved from the competence of the ordinary Sobranje and to be referred to a Grand Sobranje, elected in the same manner by the same people but in double strength. The Executive was entrusted to a Council of eight ministers, to be nominated by the prince (king), but responsible to the Assembly.[2]

---

[1] For an admirable portrait see Laveleye, *The Balkan Peninsula*, pp. 259 sq.

[2] For convenience the subsequent amendments are incorporated.

Had this constitution been the outcome of a slow political evolution there would have been little to be said against it. Imposed upon a people totally inexperienced, it proved, as the sequel will show, unworkable.

Having drafted the Organic Law, the Assembly proceeded to the election of a prince. The Treaty of Berlin had provided that he was to be 'freely elected by the population, and confirmed by the Porte with the assent of the Powers, but no member of the reigning dynasty of a Great Power was to be eligible. The Tsar recommended and the Assembly elected (April 29, 1879) Prince Alexander of Battenberg, a scion, by a morganatic marriage, of the House of Darmstadt, a nephew by marriage of the Tsar, and an officer in the Prussian army.

Born in 1857 Prince Alexander was at this time a young man of twenty-two, of fine presence, and with plenty of character and brains. A close observer described him as ' a wise statesman, a brave soldier, a remarkable man in every respect '.[1] The description was perhaps partial, but the choice was unquestionably a good one, and if Prince Alexander had had a fair chance he would probably have done a great work for his adopted country. He was, however, hampered from the outset on the one hand by the jealousy and arrogance of the Russian officials by whom he was at first surrounded, and on the other by the opposition of the Sobranje, which was elected under the ridiculous provisions of the Organic Law.

Out of 170 members elected to the first Sobranje in 1879 not more than thirty were supporters of the ministers appointed by the prince, and after a session which lasted only ten days it was dissolved. A second Sobranje, elected in 1880, was even less favourable to the prince and his ministers. The appointment of a new ministry, under the Russophil radicals

[1] Major A. von Huhn, *The Struggle of the Bulgarians for National Independence* (1886), p. 6.

Zankoff and Karaveloff, temporarily eased the situation, but in May, 1881, the prince suspended the Organic Law, and in July a new Assembly ratified his *coup d'état* and conferred upon him extraordinary powers for a period of seven years. In September, 1883, however, the prince was compelled by pressure from St. Petersburg to re-establish the abrogated constitution. The new Tsar, Alexander III,[1] was much less friendly than his father to the Prince of Bulgaria, and from this time onwards there was more or less avowed hostility between St. Petersburg and Sofia.

That hostility accounts in part for the attitude of Russia towards the union of the two Bulgarias, so soon to be accomplished. Of all the provisions of the Treaty of Berlin, the one which was most obviously artificial was the severance of the Bulgarians to the south of the Balkans from their brethren to the north of them. Of the two provinces the southern was the purer Bulgarian. In the northern was a large sprinkling of Moslems, Greeks, and Wallachs. The southern was far more homogeneous in race. Ethnographically, therefore, the partition was absurd. Yet the policy of Russia under Alexander III went, as the sequel shows, some way to justify the suspicions of Lord Beaconsfield.

No less than ten articles of the Treaty of Berlin were devoted to the future organization of Eastern Roumelia, but these provisions proved to be so purely temporary that they need not detain us. Hardly was the ink on the treaty dry before the Russian agents, in both provinces, began to encourage the popular demand for reunion. More particularly among the Bulgarians of ' Eastern Roumelia '. By the formation of ' athletic societies ', the encouragement of national sports, and other methods common to the stimulation of nationalist movements, the youth of Eastern Roumelia were accustomed

---

[1] Succeeded in 1881 on the assassination of Tsar Alexander II.

to the idea of association and discipline. By the year 1885, 40,000 of them were trained in the use of arms. When Sultan Hamid protested against these proceedings he was reminded that the Turkish indemnity to Russia was not yet paid.

Meanwhile, in the northern province, the unionist movement was making rapid progress, under the powerful leadership of Karaveloff, who was now Prime Minister, and of Stephen Stambuloff, who, in 1884, had become President of the Sobranje.

Among the makers of modern Bulgaria this remarkable man holds, beyond dispute, the highest place. The son of an innkeeper, Stephen Stambuloff was born at Tirnovo in 1854. Educated at Odessa, he was powerfully attracted towards the views of the nihilist party, but the consuming passion of his life was not Russian nihilism but Bulgarian nationalism. On his return from Odessa he plunged into the turbid waters of Bulgarian politics, and, on his election to the Sobranje, was almost immediately appointed President of the Assembly. He ardently supported the movement for the union of the Bulgarias, and from the abdication of Prince Alexander to the days of his own dismissal by Prince Ferdinand he exercised an authority which was virtually dictatorial.[1]

On September 18, 1885, Gavril Pasha, the Turkish Governor-General at Philippopolis, was informed that his services were no longer required, and he was conducted, with some contumely, out of the province. Resistance there could be none, for the Bulgarians were unanimous. Not so the Powers. What was their attitude ? An answer to this question lands us once more in the realm of political paradox. To say that Russia frowned upon the enterprise thus launched at Philippopolis would be a ludicrous understatement. The attitude of Russia demands, however, and will repay, closer consideration.

[1] For Stambuloff's career cf. A. H. Beaman, *M. Stambuloff* (London, 1895).

To the union of the two Bulgarias the Tsar was not, and could not be, in principle, opposed. Seven short years had passed since the Treaty of San Stefano was drafted. But the circumstances were radically different. In the spring of 1878 a victorious Russian army had just pierced the Balkans, and could, at any moment, thunder at the gates of Constantinople. Russia was virtually in occupation of all the country between the Danube and the Bosphorus. She could dictate the destinies of the Bulgarians.

It was otherwise in 1885. The Bulgarians had found themselves. They had not learnt the art of parliamentary government, but what was more important they knew the meaning of 'nationality'. The arrogance of Russian officials towards the Bulgarian peasants had, in the course of seven years, gone far to obliterate from their minds the remembrance of the mighty services rendered by their liberators in 1877. Neither 'the Battenberg', as Prince Alexander was contemptuously known at St. Petersburg, nor the quondam nihilist, Stambuloff, was inclined to be the pliant instrument of Russian influence in the principality.

The Tsar was not ill-disposed towards the union, provided it was effected on his own terms, on terms which would have brought the Bulgarians to heel. And the first indispensable condition was that Prince Alexander should yield his place to a Russian nominee. 'You remember', were the orders issued by the Foreign Office to the Russian Consul-General at Rustchuk, 'that the union [of the two Bulgarias] must not take place until after the abdication of Prince Alexander.'[1] In other words, Russia was willing to see a Greater Bulgaria come into existence, but it must be as a Russian protectorate, not as a State, independent alike of the Sultan and the Tsar.

[1] Quoted by Rose (*op. cit.*, p. 262), whose masterly analysis of the evidence should be consulted.

Did not the contention of the Tsar afford some posthumous justification for the misgivings of Lord Beaconsfield in 1878 ? Plainly, there are two alternative answers to this question. It may be urged, on the one hand, that Lord Beaconsfield would have done well to exhibit a more robust faith in Bulgarian nationality ; on the other, that in 1878 the ambition of Russia was much more obvious than the independence of Bulgaria. Those Englishmen, who in 1878 favoured the creation of the Greater Bulgaria, were actuated much more by detestation of the Turk whom they did know, than love for the Bulgarian whom they did not know. They felt, with Lord Stratford de Redcliffe, that ' the very idea of reinstating any amount of Turkish misgovernment in places once cleared of it is simply revolting '.

The policy of England in 1885 was inspired by a different motive. ' If you can help to build up these peoples into a bulwark of independent States and thus screen the " sick man " from the fury of the northern blast, for God's sake do it.' Thus wrote Sir Robert Morier from St. Petersburg to Sir William White in Constantinople at the height of the Bulgarian crisis in December, 1885. Bulgaria, it will be observed, was to come into being not as the cat's-paw of Russia, but as a barrier against her advance towards Constantinople. Could any one have foreseen such a possibility in 1878 ? It was too much to expect. But Lord Beaconsfield's colleague at Berlin was now a complete convert to the views of our ablest representatives abroad. 'A Bulgaria, friendly to the Porte', said Lord Salisbury in December, 1885, ' and jealous of foreign influence, would be a far surer bulwark against foreign aggression than two Bulgarias, severed in administration, but united in considering the Porte as the only obstacle to their national development.' [1]

[1] *ap.* Rose, *op. cit.*, p. 273.

Prince Alexander, without reference to the Powers, had already taken the plunge. He showed a moment's hesitation when the patriots of Philippopolis came to offer him the crown, but Stambuloff told him bluntly that there were only two paths open to him : 'the one to Philippopolis and as far beyond as God may lead ; the other to Darmstadt.' The prince's choice was soon made, and on September 20 he announced his acceptance of the throne of united Bulgaria.

Serbo-Bulgarian War, November, 1885

Before his action could be ratified or repudiated by his suzerain or the Powers, Bulgaria was threatened with a new danger. If Russia began to see in a united Bulgaria a barrier in her advance towards the straits, Austria had no mind to see the multiplication of barriers between Buda-Pesth and Salonica.

On November 14 King Milan of Serbia, who, in 1882, had followed the example of Prince Carol of Roumania and assumed a royal crown, suddenly seized an obviously frivolous pretext to declare war upon Bulgaria.

Whether Austria actually instigated the attack it is at present impossible to say. Apart from Habsburg intrigues King Milan had his own reasons. Despite the new crown, his own position was none too secure. An attempt upon his life in Belgrade indicated the fact that his enemies were alert : a marriage between Prince Peter Karageorgević and a daughter of Prince Nicholas had lately strengthened the rival dynasty ; there were unsettled boundary questions and tariff questions between Serbia and Bulgaria ; above all, the idea of a Balkan 'Balance of Power' was germinating. If Bulgaria was to be doubled in size, and more than doubled, Greece and Serbia, to say nothing of Roumania, would look for compensations. Serbia was the first actively to intervene.

King Milan left his capital for the front amid enthusiastic cheers for ' the King of Serbia and Macedonia '. On November 14 the march towards Sofia began.

The chance to stab a friend and rival in the back was too tempting for a Balkan kinglet to refuse. The question of the union of the two Bulgarias, though answered with emphasis by the Bulgarian people, still hung in the diplomatic balance ; the Bulgarian army, thanks to the action of the Tsar in the withdrawal of his Russian officers, was left at a critical moment without instructors ; such officers as remained to it were raw and inexperienced ; the prince's own position was exceedingly precarious.

But his peasant subjects rallied superbly to his support ; Bulgarians from Macedonia flocked to the assistance of their kinsmen, and in a three days' battle at Slivnitza (November 17–19) they inflicted a decisive defeat upon the Serbians. The young Bulgarian army, emerging triumphant from its 'baptism of fire' at Slivnitza, promptly took the offensive and marched on Pirot, which was captured on November 27. The Serbian army seemed, to a close and competent observer,[1] to lie at their mercy ; but the short though significant war was over.

On November 28 Count Khevenhüller, the Austrian minister at Belgrade, arrived at Pirot, and imposed a truce upon Prince Alexander. The Bulgarians, flushed with victory, already dreaming of the absorption of Serbia into a Greater Bulgaria, were bluntly informed that if they advanced from Pirot they would find themselves ' face to face no longer with Serbian but with Austrian troops '.

Serbia was saved : but so also was the union of the Bulgarias.

---

[1] Major A. von Huhn, whose work, *The Struggle of the Bulgarians for National Independence*, translated from the German (Murray, 1886), contains much the best account known to me of these events.

The Battle of Slivnitza had decided that question. A peace signed at Bucharest (March 3, 1886) restored the *status quo ante* as between Bulgaria and Serbia ; but the larger question had been settled at Constantinople. A conference of the Powers had met on November 5, and Great Britain had taken the lead in urging the Sultan to acquiesce in the alienation of Eastern Roumelia.

To the diplomatic reasons, already detailed, for the attitude of Great Britain was now added a dynastic one. On July 23, 1885, Princess Beatrice, the youngest daughter and constant companion of Queen Victoria, had become the wife of Prince Henry of Battenberg, the youngest brother of the Prince of Bulgaria. Queen Victoria's interest in the Battenberg family was not confined to her own son-in-law. His eldest brother, Prince Louis, a distinguished officer in the English navy, had, in 1884, married the queen's granddaughter, Princess Victoria of Hesse, the eldest daughter of the Princess Alice, and in 1888 the queen interested herself keenly in a proposed marriage between another granddaughter, Princess Victoria of Prussia, and Prince Alexander. Before this time, however, much had happened to the prince and his people.

At Constantinople the will of Great Britain prevailed, and early in 1886 Sultan Abdul Hamid formally recognized the union of the two Bulgarias, and appointed Prince Alexander to be ' Governor-General of Eastern Roumelia '.

He was not destined to enjoy his new honour long. On his return from Pirot to Sofia he received an enthusiastic welcome from his subjects. Their enthusiasm intensified the chagrin of Russia, and in August, 1886, the Tsar carried out his counter-stroke. Implacable in enmity against his cousin, he determined to dethrone him by force. On the night of August 21 a band of Russian officers burst into the palace at Sofia, compelled the prince to sign an abdication, and carried him off a prisoner to

Reni, near Galatz, in Russian territory. Thence he was dispatched under escort to Lemberg. But the Russian party in Bulgaria gained little by this melodramatic *coup*.

A provisional government was hastily set up at Sofia under Stambuloff, and their first act was to recall their kidnapped prince (August 29). On September 3 Prince Alexander re-entered his capital amid the enthusiastic plaudits of his people. But by his own act he had already rendered his position untenable.

On his arrival at Rustchuk he had been welcomed by the Consul-General for Russia, and in gratitude for this friendly act he was foolish enough, perhaps under the stress of the conflicting emotions produced by recent experiences, to send to the Tsar a telegram, which concluded with these words : ' Russia having given me my Crown I am ready to give it back into the hands of its Sovereign.' The Tsar promptly took advantage of this amazing indiscretion, and refused curtly to approve his restoration. The prince, in despair of overcoming the antipathy of his cousin, and genuinely anxious to do the best he could for his distracted country, at once announced his abdication, and on September 7 he left Bulgaria for ever.[1]

Prince Alexander had presided with dignity and some measure of success over the birth-throes of a nation ; he left it, as he believed, for its good ; primarily, in order not to obstruct a *rapprochement* between Bulgaria and its ' natural ' protector.

Before leaving Prince Alexander appointed a regency, consisting of Stambuloff, Karaveloff, and Nikeforoff, to whom the Tsar sent as 'adviser' General Kaulbars. Having done his best to raise the country against the regents, and failed ignominiously, Kaulbars was, however, recalled. The Government

---

[1] He retired into private life, and, after the failure of Queen Victoria to obtain for him the hand of Princess Victoria, married an opera singer, and died in 1893.

and the people alike refused to be browbeaten by the Russian agent. A Sobranje containing no less than 470 supporters of the regency against thirty Russophils was returned; it conferred a virtual dictatorship upon Stambuloff, and elected Prince Waldemar of Denmark. The latter, acting under family pressure exerted by the Tsar, declined the offer, and again Bulgaria had to look for a ruler. For the time being Stambuloff more than filled the place, but in July, 1887, after Bulgarian delegates had searched the European Courts for a candidate, the Sobranje, refusing the Tsar's nominee, the Prince of Mingrelia, elected Prince Ferdinand of Saxe-Coburg-Gotha, a son of Princess Clémentine of Orleans, and a grandson, therefore, of King Louis Philippe. Prince Ferdinand, who was a young [1] and ambitious man, accepted the offer, and ascended the throne on August 14, 1887. Russia refused to recognize him, but, strong in the support of Bismarck and the Emperor Francis Joseph, in whose army he had served, the young prince defied the opposition of the Tsar and reaped his reward.

For the next seven years Bulgaria was ruled by Stephen Stambuloff. Prince Ferdinand wisely took time to feel his way, and thus escaped much of the odium which no statesman worthy of the name could, during those difficult years, have avoided.

A double task awaited Stambuloff: on the one hand to emancipate his country from foreign tutelage; on the other to introduce internal order and discipline, and lay the foundations, as yet non-existent, of a modern civilized State. In both directions he succeeded beyond expectation, but not by 'rose water' [2] methods. The situation demanded strength rather than finesse, and it cannot be denied that Stambuloff

[1] Born in 1861.

[2] The phrase, of course, is Carlyle's, and used by him in reference to Cromwell's work in Ireland.

was compelled to have recourse to weapons which excited just resentment and even indignation.[1] All through he had to fight for his political life, and more than once escaped actual assassination by a hair's-breadth, but he carried things through with a strong hand, to the infinite advantage of his country and his prince. He has been called the Bismarck of the Balkans; but he lacked the finesse which that supreme diplomatist concealed under an affectation of bluntness; in some respects he was Cromwellian rather than Bismarckian; but essentially he was himself: a rough, coarse-grained peasant, of indomitable will, strong passions, and burning patriotism. Involved in domestic trouble in May, 1894, he sent in his resignation, little suspecting that it would be accepted. To his intense chagrin it was. Prince Ferdinand himself succeeded to the vacant place.

Stambuloff bitterly resented his dismissal, and took no pains to hide the fact; it was, therefore, something of a relief to all parties when, in July, 1895, the fallen statesman was finally removed from the scene by assassination.

The people he had served so truly were stricken with grief at the news of the dastardly crime; but Prince Ferdinand was at last master in his own house.

The first use he made of his freedom was to effect a reconciliation with Russia. The death of Alexander III in 1894 rendered the task easier. Ferdinand himself had married, in 1893, Princess Marie of the house of Bourbon-Parma, and when, in 1896, an heir was born to them, the young crown prince was baptized according to the rites of the Orthodox Church, and the Tsar Nicholas II acted as godfather. Two years later the reconciliation was sealed by a State visit paid by the Prince and Princess of Bulgaria to Peterhof.

[1] A notable example was the high-handed execution of a Major Panitza in 1890.

Meanwhile, Ferdinand's international position was regularized when, in March, 1896, he was recognized by the Sultan as Prince of Bulgaria and Governor-General of Eastern Roumelia. His mother, the Princess Clémentine, who was at once exceedingly clever and exceedingly wealthy, devoted herself untiringly to the task of improving the dynastic and political position of her son. And not in vain. The development of Bulgaria, alike in European prestige, in political stability, and in all the economic and industrial appurtenances of a modernized society, was astonishingly rapid. Leaving it in this promising position we must turn our attention to other parts of the peninsula, or rather of the Ottoman dominions.

Armenian Massacres

From 1894 to 1897 interest in the Eastern Question was mainly concentrated upon the unhappy relations between the Sultan Abdul Hamid and the Armenian Christians. But this painful subject can be dealt with more conveniently in another connexion.[1]

Early in the year 1897 the outbreak of an insurrection in Crete—the ' Great Greek Island ' as the Greeks loved to call it—and the excitement caused thereby among the Greeks of the mainland once more brought into prominence the Hellenic factor in the Near Eastern problem.

In order to pick up the threads of the Hellenic question, it will be necessary to cast a brief retrospective glance upon Greek affairs since the formal achievement of independence in 1832.[2]

The protecting Powers, it will be remembered, had provided the new kingdom with a king in the person of a young German princeling, Otto of Bavaria.

[1] *Infra*, p. 395.   [2] *Supra*, p. 223.

The Reign of Otto (1833–62)

The task committed to him would have tried the skill of the most accomplished and experienced statesman ; Otto was a lad of seventeen, of indifferent natural capacity, devoid of any special aptitude for government, and entirely ignorant of the country and people whose fortunes were committed to his charge.

Manifold difficulties confronted him at the outset of his reign, and most of them dogged his footsteps until its inglorious ending. His tender years necessitated a Regency, which was committed, perhaps, inevitably to Bavarians, and by Bavarians he was surrounded for the first ten years of his reign. An ex-minister of Bavaria, Count von Armansperg ; General von Heideck, a typical German soldier ; Dr. Maurer, a distinguished jurist—this was the incongruous triumvirate who were to rule the young kingdom in the young king's name. Less distinguished men might have bungled things less badly ; they could hardly have bungled them worse.

A second difficulty arose from the niggardly and stupid fashion in which the northern frontiers were defined by the Treaty of London (1832). The line was then drawn from the Gulf of Arta on the west to the Gulf of Volo on the east. Beyond that line, in Epirus, Thessaly, and Macedonia, were a large number of Greeks who, ardently desiring reunion with their brethren in the kingdom, still remained subject to the rule of the Sultan. For half a century nothing whatever was done by the Powers to remedy the sense of wrong which poisoned the minds of patriotic Greeks on both sides of the purely artificial frontier.

On the outbreak of the Crimean War the Greeks were anxious, not unnaturally, to take advantage of the preoccupation of the Turks and to acquire the long-coveted provinces of Epirus and Thessaly. Early in 1854 a large though ill-disciplined force of Greeks burst into the provinces; but the invasion was repelled by the Turks; the Western allies occupied the Piraeus from May, 1854, until February, 1857; and King Otto was coerced into a highly distasteful neutrality. The only results of the ill-advised and inopportune invasion of Turkish territory were, therefore, the alienation of the best friends of Greece; an increase of her financial embarrassments; and, worst of all, a damaging blow to her prestige and self-respect. At the Peace of Paris Greece got nothing.

The Russo-Turkish War of 1877–8 was, in a territorial sense, more productive. Though not immediately. In the war itself Greece had taken no part. There was a strong party in Greece which believed that the moment had come for taking by force of arms the great prize—Thessaly and Epirus—denied to her by diplomacy in 1856. But Trikoupis, who was Foreign Minister, unwisely preferred to trust to diplomacy and, in particular, to the goodwill of Great Britain, who, as in 1854, strongly opposed the intervention of Greece. Popular insurrections broke out in Thessaly and Epirus as well as in Crete, but the peace between Greece and Turkey remained technically unbroken until February 2, 1878, when, at the acutest moment of the European crisis, Greece declared war upon the Porte. This most inopportune and not very courageous demonstration was at once suppressed by the Powers, and Greece acquiesced. Consequently Greece went to the Congress of Berlin as an outside suppliant, and, as might have been expected, came away empty-handed. Lord Beaconsfield, jealous for the integrity of the Ottoman dominions, suggested that Greece was 'a country with a future, who could afford to wait'. Mr. Gladstone, an ardent Philhellene, scathingly contrasted the fate of Greece with that of the Balkan States which, relying upon Russia, had made war upon the Turk and had reaped their appropriate reward. Greece, who had kept her sword in the scabbard and had relied upon English benevolence, got nothing more than a passing sneer from Lord Beaconsfield. The Congress of Berlin did indeed invite the Sultan to grant to Greece such a rectification of frontiers as would include Janina and Larissa in Greek territory, but the Sultan, not unnaturally, ignored the invitation.

Two years later (1880), when Mr. Gladstone himself had come into office, the Powers suggested to the Porte the cession of Thessaly and Epirus, and at last, in 1881, the tact and firmness of Mr. Goschen wrung from the unwilling Sultan one-third of the latter province and the greater part of the former. Macedonia was still left, fortunately for Greece, under the heel of the Sultan. Lord Beaconsfield did not exhibit much positive benevolence towards Greece, but negatively she, like Serbia, owes him a considerable debt. If he had not torn up the Treaty of San Stefano Bulgaria would have obtained a commanding position in Macedonia, Serbia would never have got Uskub and Monastir, Greece would still be sighing for Kavala and perhaps for Salonica.

Nearly twenty years earlier the Hellenic kingdom had been enriched by a gift even more romantic and hardly less prized than that of Thessaly and Epirus.

Ever since the Greek War of Independence the inhabitants of the seven islands of the Ionian archipelago—Corfu, Zante, Paxo, Ithaca, Cephalonia, Santa Maura, and Cerigo—had been restless under the British protectorate. To that protectorate they had, as we have seen, been confided after many vicissitudes by the Congress of Vienna (1815). But the arrangement did not work smoothly, and in 1858 Bulwer Lytton, then at the Colonial Office, persuaded Mr. Gladstone to undertake a special mission and to investigate the grievances of the islanders. The system of administration was such that, as Gladstone himself said, 'not Cherubim and Seraphim could work it'. The High Commissioner Extraordinary had a mixed reception in the islands, but everywhere he found one sentiment prevailing among the inhabitants, an ardent wish for immediate union with the Greek kingdom. To this step he was himself at the outset strongly opposed, believing that the surrender of the protectorate by England 'would be nothing less than a crime against the safety of Europe as connected with the state and course of the Eastern Question'. As a substitute he offered the islands constitutional reform, which they did not want. Within four years Mr. Gladstone had changed his mind; Lord Palmerston came round to the same opinion, and in the Queen's Speech of February, 1863, the offer of the islands to Greece was publicly announced. The National Assembly of the Hellenes gratefully accepted the gift on March 20, and the protocol concluded at London on June 5 contained a provision for the cession of the islands to Greece.

The cession of the Ionian Isles was in the nature of a christening present for the young Danish prince whom the Powers simultaneously presented to the Greeks. For by this time the rule of King Otto had reached its term.

To follow in detail the course of events which culminated in his enforced abdication would be both tedious and, in the present connexion, impertinent. One or two outstanding causes must, however, be noted. The tactlessness of the Bavarian advisers of the king; the intrigues of innumerable parties which rapidly evolved during and after the War of Independence; discontent among the disbanded irregulars who had fought in the war; unrest among a people who found themselves under a highly centralized German bureaucracy deprived of that communal autonomy which they had enjoyed under the Turks, all contributed to the unpopularity of the unfortunate king. His creed was another stumbling-block.

The attempt of a Roman Catholic to rule a people who owed their political emancipation in large measure to Orthodox priests must, in any case, have led to some friction. It led to much more when the domestic relations between Crown and Church were complicated by the withdrawal of the Greek Church of the kingdom from the jurisdiction of the Patriarch of Constantinople.

We have already noted the significance of the movements towards ecclesiastical independence in Serbia and Bulgaria. In those cases ecclesiastical preceded the achievement of political independence. In Greece political emancipation came first. Consequently, the delicate task of adjusting relations with the Greek Patriarch of Constantinople fell to a German and a Roman Catholic. The Orthodox Church in Greece renounced obedience in 1833, and the renunciation was accompanied by a measure of domestic reorganization, by a reduction in the numbers of the episcopate, and by the dissolution of all the smaller monasteries. These measures excited considerable opposition in Greece, and not until 1850 did the Church of the kingdom obtain formal recognition of its independence from the Patriarch.

In 1837 King Otto came of age, and immediately assumed the reins of power. For a brief moment the hope was entertained that he might prove to his people that the blunders which had thus far characterized his reign were those of his Bavarian ministers, not his own. They were; but unfortunately his own were worse. Otto, as Finlay pithily remarked, was neither ' respected, obeyed, feared, nor loved '.[1] The evils of the regency were if anything accentuated : a centralized administration of foreign type proved powerless to perform the elementary functions of government ; brigandage, ' an ineradicable institution '[2] in Greece, grew steadily more and

[1] Finlay, vii. 168. [2] Lewis Sergeant, *New Greece*, p. 104.

more intolerable ; extravagant expenditure without appreciably beneficent results, but involving oppressive taxation, led ultimately to financial repudiation ; the press was gagged ; the promised constitution was unaccountably withheld ; worst of all, from the Greek point of view, the destruction of local self-government denied to the people those opportunities for discussion and debate so warmly cherished by every typical Greek and regarded as the only tolerable alternative to the other national sport—guerrilla warfare. Denied the former, the Greeks resumed the latter ; and early in 1843 armed insurrection in epidemic form broke out in many parts of the country. But though armed, the insurrection of 1843 was bloodless. King Otto yielded at once to the demands of the insurgents, dismissed his Bavarian ministers, and agreed to accept a democratic constitution, with a bi-cameral legislature and a responsible executive.[1]

The concession was popular ; but it soon became evident that constitutional reform would not provide a permanent solution of the difficulties by which King Otto was confronted. The politicians amused themselves with a burlesque of parliamentary government ; parties innumerable were formed, but the ' English ', the ' French ', and the ' Russian ' parties were the only ones which had any correspondence with the realities of political affairs ; debates interminable took place in ' Senate ' and ' Chamber ' ; ministries, in rapid succession, were called to office and dismissed ; the forms of a representative democracy were all carefully reproduced. There was no reality behind them. Unless indeed he were aiming at a *reductio ad absurdum* King Otto had begun at the wrong end. His people had asked for a ' constitution ' based upon the rights

[1] The text of this constitution, together with a detailed account of the revolution, will be found in *British and Foreign State Papers*, 1843-4, vol. xxxii, pp. 938 sq.

of man, and other purely exotic ideas. What they wanted was a development of indigenous local democracies. But this was precisely what they did not get. Otto was by no means entirely to blame. The Powers—England and France in particular—must bear a very large share of responsibility. It was the era of doctrinaire liberalism in the West. The same principles must be exported to the Near East. The Greeks were essentially democrats ; but in the Swiss sense, not the French, still less the English.

If Otto had had the sense to build up a constitution from below instead of imposing it, in German method, from above, he might have led his people—as difficult a people as ever a man had to lead—along the first halting steps on the path towards real self-government. It was in truth not to be expected of the king. But it was, in a constitutional sense, the only possible chance for his infant kingdom.

Otto's constitutional experiment lasted for nearly twenty years, but there is nothing to be gained from a detailed account of its vicissitudes. All that need here be said is that Otto, in his domestic policy, lamentably failed to achieve the impossible.

In the domain of foreign relations the one really important episode of the reign was the raid into Epirus and Thessaly at the opening of the Crimean War. To this episode reference has already been made. Another incident, which at the time (1849) caused even more friction with England, was that associated with the name of Dom Pacifico. Two British subjects, Dr. George Finlay, the eminent historian, and Dom Pacifico, a Portuguese Jew born in Gibraltar, had suffered unquestionable wrong at the hands of the Greek Government. Dr. Finlay had tried in vain to recover damages for the loss of land illegally taken from him ; Dom Pacifico for the value of property destroyed by a mob with the connivance of the police. Dom Pacifico's own record was none of the best, but equally with Dr. Finlay he was a British subject, and for Lord Palmerston, who was then at the Foreign Office, that was enough. Redress was insolently denied not merely to the sufferers, but to the British minister. Lord Palmerston, therefore, instructed the British Admiral ' to take Athens on his way back from the Dardanelles'. Russia resented the pressure thus put upon King Otto, the *enfant gâté de l'absolutisme* ; the French President sulked, offended by the refusal of his offer of mediation, and withdrew his ambassador, Drouyn de Lhuys, from London. But Palmerston went on his way unheeding, and quickly achieved the desired end. The point at issue was trivial ; the whole incident was intrinsically unimportant except as illustrative of the stupidity displayed by King Otto and his ministers in their relations with other countries no less than with the Greek people.

By the year 1862 the patience of the Greeks, never their most conspicuous characteristic, was worn out, and they determined to get rid of their Bavarian king. The question of the succession to the throne brought matters to a crisis. The king and queen were childless, and no collateral member of the Bavarian House had qualified for the succession, according to the terms of the constitution, by embracing the Orthodox faith. Queen Amalia, an Oldenburg princess, was suspected of ambitious designs on her own account. The Greeks preferred to look elsewhere.

In February, 1862, a military revolt broke out at Nauplia ; the insurrection spread rapidly ; the king and queen found themselves excluded from their own capital ; in October, 1862, they embarked on an English gunboat, and from the Bay of Salamis the king issued a proclamation announcing that ' he had quitted Greece for a time in order to avoid plunging the country in civil war '.

They never returned. King Otto died in Germany in 1867 ;

meanwhile the Greek people had proceeded to the election by plebiscite of a successor.

The protecting Powers acknowledged the right of the Greeks to decide the matter for themselves, but reiterated their resolution not to permit a scion of the reigning house of any of the great European Powers to accept the throne.

The Greeks, however, were perversely determined, and elected Prince Alfred, the second son of Queen Victoria. On a plebiscite, Prince Alfred obtained 230,016 votes; the next candidate, the Duke of Leuchtenberg, got 2,400, Prince William George of Denmark was at the bottom of a long list with 6.

Prince Alfred, despite the warning of the Powers that both he and the Duke of Leuchtenberg were disqualified, was accordingly proclaimed king by the National Assembly (February 3, 1863).

The Powers, however, adhered to their resolution,[1] and England was entrusted with the invidious task of providing the Greeks with a 'constitutional' king. For some months the crown was hawked round the minor Courts of Europe. It was first offered to and refused by a Coburg prince, Ferdinand, the Ex-King-Consort of Portugal, and then, in succession, by two other Coburg princes.

King George of Greece (1863—1913)

The Greeks, in the meantime, being foiled in their attempt to obtain the services of an English Prince, tried to get an English statesman as their king. The offer of the crown was actually made to and declined by Lord Stanley, and Mr. Gladstone's name was also mentioned, much to his own amusement,

---

[1] Cf. Joint Note of December 15, 1862 (*State Papers*, vol. lviii, p. 1107), and translation *ap.* Hertslet, vol. iii, p. 2073.

in the same connexion.[1] Ultimately, however, Great Britain secured for the Greeks the services of Prince William George of Denmark, who, in 1863, ascended the throne as King George I.

The disappointment of the Greeks was, as we have seen, mitigated by the cession of the Ionian Isles, a transaction which was tactfully included in the same protocol (London, June 5, 1863) which provided for the nomination of the Danish prince to the crown.

The definitive treaty was concluded between Great Britain, France, and Russia of the one part, and Denmark of the other part, on July 13, and its terms deserve attention. Article III runs as follows : ' Greece, under the Sovereignty of Prince William of Denmark and the guarantee of the three courts, forms a Monarchical, Independent and Constitutional State.'

The precise connotation of the last epithet, ' Constitutional ', was, and is, a matter of dispute. If the epithet implied anything more than a promise that the constitution should be embodied in a written document (*Statuto*), its implications must have varied considerably in the minds of the three protecting Powers—Great Britain, Imperial France, and Autocratic Russia.

King George, like his predecessor, was at the time of his accession a youth of seventeen, and promptly proceeded to fulfil the promise of his sponsors. A National Assembly was summoned, and the king urged upon it the importance of completing without delay the revision of the constitution. By the end of October, 1864, the work was accomplished ; on

---

[1] ' Though I do love the country and never laughed at anything else in connexion with it before, yet the seeing my own name, which was never meant to carry a title of any kind, placed in juxtaposition with that particular idea made me give way.' Mr. Gladstone to a friend, *ap.* Morley, *Life,* i. 620.

November 28 the king took the oath to the constitution, and the Constituent Assembly was dissolved.

The constitution thus inaugurated was frankly democratic. The Senate, established in 1843, was abolished, and legislative power was vested in a single chamber with an absolute veto reserved to the crown. The Boulé, as it is called, was to consist of not less than 150 deputies apportioned to the several provinces according to population. The deputies were to be elected for four years by direct and universal suffrage, and to receive payment for their services. Half the members, plus one, were required to form a quorum. A special procedure was ordained for constitutional revision. Ministers were to be responsible to the Chamber, but the means of asserting their responsibility were not defined until 1876. There was to be a Cabinet of seven nominated by the king, not necessarily from among members of the Boulé. All ministers might speak in the Boulé, but could not vote unless they were members of it.[1]

Such were the main features of the constitution which continued practically unchanged down to 1911. In the latter year, the Council of State, a probouleutic body, was revived; soldiers were declared ineligible for seats in the Boulé; the quorum of the Boulé was reduced to one-third; and elementary education was made both compulsory and gratuitous. If parliamentary government has not hitherto proved a conspicuous success in Greece, it has not been for lack of meticulous constitutional definition. But the truth is that this particular form of polity postulates conditions which are not found in combination nearly so often as most Englishmen and some foreigners imagine. It demands, in the first place, a long and laborious apprenticeship in the art of self-government among the people; it demands in the elected representatives, as Cromwell perceived, substantial unanimity as regards the 'fundamentals' of government; it demands in the sovereign (if the polity be of the constitutional-monarchical type)

---

[1] For details cf. Demombynes, *Les Constitutions Européennes*, vol. i, pp. 801 sq. The full text of the constitution of 1864 is printed in Appendix V to Finlay, *op. cit.*, vol. vii.

consummate tact and considerable political experience and education. It must frankly be admitted that these prerequisites have not invariably been forthcoming in the modern Hellenic State, and that the parliamentary constitution has been subjected, at not infrequent intervals, to a strain to which it is manifestly unequal.

The Problem of Crete

With the establishment of the constitution of 1864 we may leave, for a time, the domestic politics of Greece and turn to the most pressing of its external problems.

Among these none appealed with such force to the mass of the Greek people as the condition of their brethren, still under Turkish rule, in the 'Great Greek Island'. Crete, more definitely even than the Peloponnesus, presents the quintessence of Hellenism. The Cretans, as a Greek writer has said, ' are as pure Greeks as exist to-day ',[1] and many of the foremost statesmen of the kingdom, including M. Venizelos himself, were born and bred in the island, and in the island served their political apprenticeship.

Crete was actually the last of the territorial acquisitions of the Ottoman Empire in Europe. Not until 1669 was it surrendered by the Republic of Venice to the Sultan. From the day of that surrender down to its virtual union with the Greek kingdom in October, 1912, Crete was the scene of perpetual revolts against Turkish tyranny. It was handed over by the Sultan to Mehemet Ali in 1830 as a reward for his services to his suzerain in the War of Independence, and for the next ten years it formed part of the Pashalik of Egypt. Under Mehemet Ali it enjoyed a species of local autonomy, but in 1840 it was restored by the Treaty of London to the Porte.

[1] D. J. Cassavetti, *Hellas and the Balkan Wars* (1914), p. 4.

The biographer of M. Venizelos has counted no less than fourteen insurrections in the island since the year 1830.[1] To follow them in detail would be tedious ; they were mostly of one pattern ; and all were promoted with the same ultimate object, that of securing reunion with the Greeks of the mainland.

The domestic grievances of the Cretans were practically the same as those with which we have become familiar among other subject peoples in the Ottoman Empire : extortionate and irregular taxation ; unequal treatment of Christians and Moslems ; denial of justice in the courts ; the refusal to carry out the promises contained in the Tanzimat and the Hatti-Humayoun, and so forth. In 1866 the islanders broke into open revolt, convoked a General Assembly at Sphakia, declared their independence of the Ottoman Empire, and proclaimed their union with the Hellenic kingdom (September 2). This declaration represented the Cretan reply to an offer made to them by the Sultan of reunion with the Pashalik of Egypt. The offer was indignantly repudiated, and from 1866 to 1868 the island was in a state of continuous revolt. The Turks were seriously embarrassed, and suppressed the revolt after three years' fighting with considerable difficulty, and only by the assistance of Egyptian troops.

In order to appease his troublesome subjects, whom he would gladly have handed over to the Khedive Ismail of Egypt, and to avoid, if possible, the expense and vexation of perpetual reconquests, the Sultan, in 1868, conceded a series of reforms which were embodied in the *Organic Statute*.

The Governor-General was henceforward to be assisted by two assessors, of whom one was to be a Christian ; similarly, the governor of each of the ten provinces into which the island was now divided was, if a Moslem, to have a Christian

[1] Kerofilas, *Eleftherios Venizelos*, p. 47.

assessor, or, if a Christian, a Moslem assessor; there was to be a central administrative council to advise the governor, and a similar local council in each province; the island as a whole was to have an elective general assembly; mixed tribunals were to be set up, and precautions were to be taken against religious persecution and oppressive taxation.

The new constitution proved entirely unworkable; it satisfied neither the privileged Moslem minority nor the Christian majority, and in 1876 large modifications were demanded by the islanders. The outbreak of the Russo-Turkish War in 1877 caused great excitement in Crete as in other Greek provinces still subject to the Sultan; a committee was formed to promote the complete autonomy of Crete, and, on the refusal of the Porte to grant their demands, an appeal was made to the Powers. From the Congress of Berlin the Cretans got nothing, except a promise that the Organic Law should be strictly enforced and even enlarged; but they had had enough of promises, and in despair they asked to be placed under the protectorate of Great Britain.

This privilege was denied to them, but by the good offices of the British Consul, Mr. Sandwith, a considerable amendment of the Organic Statute was secured from the Porte and was embodied in a pact which took its name from the suburb of Canea in which the consuls resided. The Judiciary was made nominally independent of the Executive; there was to be a General Assembly, consisting of forty-nine Christians and thirty-one Moslems; natives were to have the preference for official appointments, and the official language, both in the assembly and in the courts, was to be Greek; the revenue was to be reorganized so as to provide a surplus for the promotion of much-needed public works; the issue of paper money was prohibited, and the press was to be free. For the moment the Cretans were satisfied, or rather were content to await a more favourable time for the achievement of their ultimate ambition.

The Crisis of 1886-9

The success of the Philippopolis revolution[1] aroused among the Greeks, as among the Southern Slavs, much heartburning and excitement. Serbia the naval Powers have never been able either to coerce or to assist. Greece is more—or less—fortunately situated. In 1882 there had come into power Charilaos Trikoupis, one of the two great statesmen whom modern Greece has produced. With brief intervals Trikoupis remained at the head of affairs until 1895.[2] Trikoupis had served a long apprenticeship to diplomacy in England, and had naturally seen much of English public life when, in an administrative sense, that life was perhaps at its best. No man was better qualified to introduce into the politics of his own country the qualities so sadly lacking : financial honesty and economy, with a high sense of public duty. In the years between 1882 and 1894 he did much to improve the financial and social condition of Greece ; order was introduced into the public service, and foreign capital, desperately needed for the development of the material resources of the country, was slowly but steadily attracted.

The crisis of 1885-6 unfortunately coincided, however, with one of the brief intervals of power enjoyed by his rival Theodore Delyannis. Delyannis, oblivious of the paramount necessity of husbanding the resources of Greece, came in on the cry of a spirited foreign policy. Bulgaria had acquired Eastern Roumelia ; Serbia was making a bid—though an unsuccessful one—for an equivalent ; Greece could not afford to be left behind. The army and fleet were mobilized, and

---

[1] *Supra*, p. 353.

[2] He was at the Greek Legation in London, 1852–63.

several collisions occurred between Turkish and Greek forces on the frontier.

But the Powers, strongly adverse to a reopening of the Eastern Question on a large scale, called upon Greece to disarm. When Greece declined, the Powers, despite the refusal of France to co-operate, established a blockade. The excitement on the mainland spread to Crete, where the Christians proclaimed their union with the kingdom. Thanks, however, to the presence of the European fleets, things went no further. Delyannis was forced to resign; Trikoupis came back to power, and did his best to restore order at home and confidence abroad. In 1889, at the instance of the Porte, he persuaded the Cretans to acquiesce in the Turkish occupation of certain fortified places in the island, an act of complaisance characteristically rewarded by an abrogation of the Pact of Halépa. This gross breach of faith on the part of the Sultan not only evoked the liveliest indignation in the island, but fatally undermined the position of Trikoupis in the kingdom. In October, 1890, Delyannis came back to power, only, however, to give way again in 1892 to Trikoupis, who was recalled by the king, in the hope of averting national bankruptcy. Even he proved unequal to the task without recourse to a scaling down of interest on the debt, and when he ultimately resigned in 1895 Greece appeared to be plunging headlong towards financial ruin.[1]

A crisis of another kind was, however, rapidly maturing. Temporarily gratified, in 1894, by the appointment of a Christian governor, the Cretans were greatly incensed by his recall in 1895. The bad faith of the Porte in financial and other matters intensified the excitement, which was further stimulated by the rapid growth of the nationalist movement both in the island and in the kingdom.

[1] Trikoupis died in 1896.

Of this movement there were many manifestations. Not the least significant was the foundation, in 1894, of a secret society known as the *Ethniké Hetaireia* (National Society). Its objects were to stiffen the back of the Government in regard to the nationalist movement, both on the mainland and in the islands ; to repudiate international intervention which in 1854, in 1878, and in 1886 had, as the young patriots imagined, denied to Greece its reasonable share in the spoils of the Ottoman Empire ; to improve the military organization of the kingdom; to stimulate the 'Greek' movement in Macedonia, and thus avert absorption by Bulgaria ; and, not least, to promote reunion between the Greeks of the island and the kingdom.

Cretan Insurrection (1896–7)

In the spring of 1896 the islanders were again in arms. Civil war broke out between Moslems and Christians in Canea, and the Powers, to prevent the spread of disturbances, put pressure upon the Sultan to make concessions. The latter accordingly agreed to renew the Pact of Halépa, to grant an amnesty, to summon a National Assembly, and to appoint a Christian governor. On September 4 George Berovic, who had been ' Prince of Samos ', was appointed to the post. But neither Moslems nor Christians took the Sultan's promises seriously, and in February, 1897, war again broke out at Canea, and the Christians again proclaimed union with Greece.

No power on earth could now have prevented the Greek patriots from going to the assistance of the islanders. Prince George, the king's second son, was accordingly sent (February 10) with a torpedo-boat flotilla to intercept Turkish reinforcements, and three days later an army was landed under Colonel Vassos. The admirals of the Powers then occupied Canea with an international landing party, and compelled the insurgents to desist from further fighting.

Meanwhile diplomacy got to work, and, on March 2, presented identical notes at Athens and Constantinople. Greece was to withdraw her army and navy; the Turks were not to be allowed to send reinforcements to the island; Crete was (1) not at the moment to be annexed to Greece; (2) 'in no circumstances to revert to the rule of the Sultan'; and (3) to enjoy autonomy under the suzerainty of the Porte. To the ears of the Greeks these proposals had a painfully familiar sound. The Greek Government refused to abandon the Christian Cretans to their Moslem enemies, or to withdraw their forces until the islanders had been allowed to decide for themselves, by plebiscite, the future of their own land. The insurgents themselves declined to lay down their arms. The admirals accordingly established a blockade of the island (March 20) and bombarded the Christian insurgents at Malaxa,[1] occupied the ports, and issued a formal declaration to the effect that henceforward the island was under European protection, and that its autonomy was assured.

Interest then shifted to the mainland. The young patriots leagued in the *Ethniké Hetaireia* believed that the moment for decisive action had come. King George yielded, in words, to the warlike sentiment of his people, believing, it was said, that the Powers would intervene, as they had intervened in 1854, in 1878, and in 1886, to prevent war.[2] But if the Greek hot-heads wanted war, the Sultan was prepared for it, and his august ally at Berlin urged him to put to the test the new weapon which Germany had forged for him, and, once for all, teach the insolent Greeks their place.

'Greek' irregulars were already pouring over the frontiers of Thessaly, and accordingly, on April 17, the Sultan declared

[1] For details cf. Dr. E. J. Dillon's article 'Crete and the Cretans' in the *Fortnightly Review* for June, 1897.

[2] Miller, *Ottoman Empire*, p. 435.

war. The 'Thirty Days' War' ensued. It was all over before
the end of May. Greece was quite isolated. Russia had
warned her friends in the Balkans that there must be no
intervention. The European admirals policed the Levant.
The Greeks made no use of their superior sea-power, and on
land they were quickly pushed back over their own frontiers.
The Turkish army under Edhem Pasha occupied Larissa,
and won two decisive victories at Pharsalos and Domokos.
So disorganized were the Greek forces that Athens became
alarmed for its own safety, and turned savagely upon the king.
The Powers, however, having no mind to embark, for the
third time, upon the tedious task of providing the Greeks
with a king, imposed an armistice upon the combatants
(May 20). The definitive peace was signed in December.

The war was nothing less than disastrous to Greece : it
discredited the dynasty ; it involved the retrocession of a strip
of Thessaly ; and it imposed upon a State, already on the verge
of bankruptcy, the burden of a considerable war indemnity.
Nor was Greece spared the further humiliation of International
Control, exercised by means of a mixed Commission, over her
external finance. On the other hand, Crete obtained final,
though not formal, emancipation.

With the Cretan imbroglio the Powers had still to deal.
They dealt with it not the less effectually because they had
ceased to be unanimous. For reasons which the next chapter
will disclose, Germany and Austria-Hungary retired from the
Concert, and withdrew their ships from the naval blockade.
Great Britain, France, Russia, and Italy went forward and
completed the task. There were many factors in a difficult
problem : the antagonism of Christian and Moslem in the
island itself ; the wider rivalry of which Crete was the microcosm between Hellenes and Ottomans ; the mutual suspicions
of the Great Powers. At the very moment when the English

and French admirals were co-operating cordially in Crete, the two nations were brought to the brink of war by the Fashoda incident.[1] But all the difficulties were by patience overcome. Each of the four Powers occupied a coast-town ; the English holding Candia, and Canea being held by a joint force. In these towns the Moslems were concentrated, while the open country was left to the Christians. Colonel Vassos and the Greek troops had already withdrawn, and a characteristic incident presently led to a demand for the recall of the Turks. On September 18 the Moslems in Candia, having burnt the British vice-consul in his own house, proceeded to massacre all the Christians they could reach. The Porte was thereupon required to recall all its troops and all its civil officials, and by the end of November the last of the Turks had left the island. The admirals were now in sole and supreme control. But on November 26 the four Powers invited Prince George of Greece to act as their High Commissioner in Crete for a period originally of three years, but subsequently prolonged to eight. This ingenious arrangement was accepted by Greece, and on December 21, 1898, the prince landed at Suda Bay. Before the end of the year the naval squadrons withdrew, though the troops remained to police the island.

In April, 1899, a Constituent Assembly was summoned, and approved a new constitution on liberal lines. That constitution had been drafted by a young Cretan lawyer, destined to fill a conspicuous place not merely in Greek but in European politics, M. Eleftherios Venizelos. Thanks mainly to him Crete for the first time enjoyed real self-government. Owing to the international occupation, which was prolonged only long enough to restore order in the island, the experiment

---

[1] Kitchener won his victory at Omdurman on September 2, 1898, and occupied Khartoum on the 4th. Major Marchand planted the French flag at Fashoda on the Upper Nile on July 12 of the same year.

started under the happiest auspices. Unfortunately, however, friction soon developed between the prince and M. Venizelos. The latter retired from the Council, and when in 1905 a revolution broke out the leadership of the movement was by general consent confided to him.

The sole object of the rising was to hasten the day of reunion with the kingdom. By the Greeks of the island the appointment of Prince George as High Commissioner had been interpreted, not unnaturally, as a sign that the Powers had made up their minds to union, and only desired that it should be brought about with the least possible offence to the Sultan, and without raising difficult questions elsewhere. The High Commissioner-ship of a royal prince was in fact accepted as a step to union.

But years passed, nothing was done; the term of the prince's appointment was prolonged, and at last in August, 1904, the prince was formally requested to 'inform the Great Powers of the firm resolution of Crete, and urging them not to postpone its union with Greece'. No action followed, and in 1905 the islanders, led by M. Venizelos, attempted to take the matter into their own hands, and proclaimed the union of Crete with the Hellenic kingdom. The Powers, thereupon, again intervened; Prince George resigned; the king, by permission of the Powers, nominated M. Zaimis to succeed him, and for the next three years the island was policed by an international military force. The exciting events of 1908 : the proclamation of Bulgarian independence; the 'Young Turks'' revolution at Constantinople; above all, the annexation of Bosnia and the Herzegovina by Austria, produced an uncontrollable outburst of feeling in Crete, and again the islanders demanded annexation to Greece. A provisional government was set up with M. Venizelos as Minister of Justice and Foreign Affairs. The Powers, while refusing formally to recognize the provisional government, entered into administrative

relations with it. If, at this crisis, Greece had acted with
courage and promptitude, the Cretan problem would probably
have been solved there and then; but in fear of the Turk
on the one hand, and on the other of the Powers, the Greeks
allowed the favourable opportunity to slip. Not until the
whilom rebel M. Venizelos had become Prime Minister of
the kingdom was the union actually achieved. The recital of
the events which led to that long and ardently desired consummation must, however, be deferred. In the meantime there
had entered into the problem of the Near East a new factor
which must be subjected to close analysis. That analysis will
occupy the next chapter.

The best authorities are the Papers presented to Parliament under the
head of ' Bulgaria ' and ' Turkey '.

For further reference: Dr. J. Holland Rose's masterly essay on *The
Making of Bulgaria* (*The Development of the European Nations*, chap. x);
E. Dicey, *The Peasant State*; A. H. Beaman, *Life of Stambuloff*; J. Samuel-
son, *Bulgaria Past and Present* (1888); Major A. von Huhn, *The Struggle of
the Bulgarians for National Independence* (Eng. trans., 1886), *The Kidnapping
of Prince Alexander* (1887); Marquis of Bath, *Observations on Bulgarian
Affairs* (1880); A. G. Drandar, *Cinq Ans de Règne de Prince Alexandre de
Battenberg en Bulgarie* (Paris, 1884); E. de Laveleye, *The Balkan Peninsula*; *Encyclopedia Britannica* (11th edition); V. Bérard, *Les Affaires de
Crète*; Kolmar Fr. von der Goltz, *Der Thessalische Krieg und die Türkische
Armee* (Berlin, 1898); D. J. Cassavetti, *Hellas and the Balkan Wars* (1914);
Dr. C. Kerofilas, *Eleftherios Venizelos* (1915); Victor Bérard, *La Turquie
et l'Hellénisme contemporain* (1904); G. Isambert, *L'Indépendance grecque
et l'Europe* (Paris, 1900); R. W. Seton Watson, *The Rise of Nationality
in the Balkans* (1917).

14

A New Factor in the Problem

German Policy in the Near East, 1888–1908

'The attempt to dominate the East forms the keystone of German *Weltpolitik*.'—G. W. PROTHERO.

'Ce qui modifie l'évolution de la question d'Orient, ce qui bouleverse complètement les données du problème et par conséquent sa solution possible, c'est la position nouvelle prise par l'Allemagne dans l'Empire ottoman. . . . Hier, l'influence de l'empereur allemand à Constantinople n'était rien, aujourd'hui elle est tout ; silencieusement ou avec éclat, elle joue un rôle prépondérant dans tout ce qui se fait en Turquie.'— ANDRÉ CHÉRADAME (1903).

'I never take the trouble even to open the mail bag from Constantinople.' 'The whole of the Balkans is not worth the bones of a single Pomeranian grenadier.'—PRINCE BISMARCK.

'The 300,000,000 Mohammedans who, dwelling dispersed throughout the East, reverence in H.M. the Sultan Abdul Hamid their Khalif, may rest assured that at all times the German Emperor will be their friend.'— Speech of the GERMAN EMPEROR at Damascus in 1898.

'We have carefully cultivated good relations with Turkey. . . . These relations are not of a sentimental nature. . . . For many a year Turkey was a useful and important link in the chain of our political relations.'—PRINCE BERNHARD VON BÜLOW.

'La politique utilitaire de l'Allemagne, si odieuse soit-elle au sentiment européen, est au moins une politique ; elle gagne à l'empereur Guillaume les sympathies du monde musulman, ouvre les voies au commerce et impose un certain respect. . . . L'Orient ne respecte que la force.'—GAULIS.

ON November 1, 1889, the German imperial yacht, the *Hohenzollern*, steamed through the Dardanelles with the Emperor William II and his Empress on board. They were on their way to pay their first ceremonial visit to a European capital and a European sovereign.[1] The capital selected for

[1] The emperor and empress had recently attended the marriage at Athens of the Ex-King and Queen of Greece.

this distinguished honour was Constantinople ; the ruler was the Sultan Abdul Hamid.

It was precisely seven hundred years, as the German colony in Constantinople reminded their sovereign, since a German emperor had first set foot in the imperial city. But Frederick Barbarossa had come sword in hand ; the Emperor William came as the apostle of peace ; as the harbinger of economic penetration ; almost, as was observed at the time, in the guise of a commercial traveller. The reception accorded to him in Constantinople was in every way worthy of a unique occasion ; he and his empress were the recipients not only of the grossest flattery but of superb and costly gifts. But such attentions were not bestowed without the hope of reward. Sultan Abdul Hamid was one of the shrewdest diplomatists that ever ruled the Ottoman Empire. He was well aware that the State visit of the emperor and empress to Constantinople meant the introduction of a new factor into an immemorial problem. ' The East is waiting for a man.' So spake the Emperor William ten years later. His advent was foreshadowed in 1889. Rarely has a ceremonial visit been productive of consequences more important.

The ostentatious advances thus made by the Emperor William to Abdul Hamid marked an entirely new departure in Hohenzollern policy. Until the conclusion of the alliance with Holland and Great Britain in 1788 the Eastern Question had never come into the regular orbit of Prussian diplomacy.[1] Nor can it be pretended that solicitude for the fortunes of the Ottoman Turks had much weight in bringing Frederick William II into the triple alliance. Just before the meeting of the emperors at Tilsit, Hardenberg, the Prussian minister, did, as we have seen, amuse himself by adding one more to

[1] As far back as 1770 the Divan invoked the mediation of Frederick the Great. Carlyle, *Frederick*, vol. x, bk. xxi, p. 24.

the many schemes for the partition of the Ottoman Empire. But Hardenberg was clutching at straws to avert disaster nearer home. From the Congress of Vienna down to the advent of Bismarck, Berlin took its orders as to foreign policy from Vienna.[1] No Prussian diplomatist was at all a match for Metternich or Schwarzenberg.

During the first ten years of his official career Bismarck was far too much occupied in fighting Denmark, Austria, the Germanic Confederation, and France to pay much heed to the Eastern Question, even had the question been acute. But, as a fact, the years between 1861 and 1871 coincided with one of the rare periods of its comparative quiescence. Yet Bismarck lost no opportunity of turning the Near East to account as a convenient arena in which to reward the services of friends or to assuage the disappointment of temporary opponents without expense to Prussian pockets or detriment to Prussian interests.

Two illustrations of this policy will suffice. In 1866 Bismarck not only turned Austria out of Germany, but, in order to secure the assistance of Victor Emmanuel, he deprived the Habsburgs of the last remnant of their heritage in Italy. He had, however, no desire to see Austria unnecessarily humiliated, still less permanently disabled. Provided it were clearly understood that henceforward she had no part or lot in German affairs, Austria might regard him as a friend and ally.

Two results ensued. The new frontier of Italy was drawn with a most niggardly hand. The assistance rendered by the Italian forces on land and sea during the Seven Weeks' War had not indeed been such as to entitle her to an ounce more than the promised pound of flesh. And Bismarck, though

---

[1] If the *Zollverein* is deemed to belong to foreign policy one exception to this rule would have to be admitted ; but the *Zollverein* was primarily a domestic measure.

true to the letter of his bond, took good care that the weight was not exceeded. On the contrary, ' Venetia ' was interpreted in the narrowest possible sense. The northern frontier of Italy was defined in such a way as to deprive Italy of a compact mass of 370,000 Italians ; to exclude the industrial products of these Italian people from their natural market in north Italy ; and to thrust into the heart of an Italian province the military outpost of an unfriendly neighbour. From the boundary definition of 1866 has arisen the Trentino problem of to-day.

But that was not the only, nor, from our present standpoint, the most important, feature of the readjustment of 1866.

The Adriatic Problem

Italian though the Trentini are in race, in language, and in sympathies, the Trentino had never formed part of the kingdom of Italy, except for five years (1809–14), when it was annexed to his Italian kingdom by Napoleon. Nor was it ever politically united to Venetia except during the periods 1797–1805 and 1815–66, when Venice itself was under Habsburg rule. The same is true of Trieste. But it was otherwise with the Venetian provinces to the east of the Adriatic, Istria and Dalmatia, which Austria also retained in 1866. For four centuries at least the Venetian commonwealth had been dominant on the eastern coast of the Adriatic, and ardent Italians to-day base their claims upon an even earlier title. But be that as it may, a great opportunity was lost by Italy in 1866. Had Venice been wrung from Austria by Italy's strong right arm, instead of being accepted from Bismarck as the price of a diplomatic bargain, and in spite of a dubious success on land and a disastrous defeat at sea, there might be no 'Adriatic Problem ' to-day.

To Trieste and Fiume Italy cannot advance any historical

claim, and however strong her strategic or political claims may be they do not concern our present theme. What is important in this connexion is the problem of the Dalmatian coast. To its possession there are two claimants who can advance strong arguments, historical, racial, strategical, and commercial, in support of their respective claims : Italy and the Southern Slavs. If Bismarck had really been animated in 1866 by friendly feelings towards Italy, he would unquestionably have insisted, without any nice regard for ethnography, upon the transference to the Italian kingdom of the whole of the Venetian inheritance, including Istria and Dalmatia.

Bismarck, however, was concerned much less with the future of Italy than with the future of Austria-Hungary, and he deliberately encouraged the *Drang nach Osten*, which, from 1866 onwards, became a marked feature of Habsburg policy. Istria and Dalmatia, therefore, were retained by Austria. Thus did Bismarck conciliate a temporary enemy and a potential ally.

Four years later he took the opportunity of rewarding the services of a most constant friend. The Black Sea clauses of the Treaty of Paris were, as we have seen, torn up in favour of Russia. That transaction was not, of course, inspired entirely by benevolence towards Russia. Bismarck's supreme object was to keep Russia at arm's length from France, and, what was at the moment more important, from England. Nothing was more likely to conduce to this end than to encourage the pretensions of Russia in the Near East, and, indeed, in the Further East. The Black Sea served his purpose in 1870 ; the ' Penjdeh incident ' was similarly utilized in 1885.

Another critical situation arose in 1877. Since 1872 the *Dreikaiserbund* had formed the pivot of Bismarck's foreign policy. But the interests of two out of the three emperors were now in sharp conflict in the Balkans. It is true that in July, 1876, the Emperors of Russia and Austria had met at

Reichstadt, and that the Emperor Francis Joseph had agreed
to give the Tsar a free hand in the Balkans on condition that
Bosnia and the Herzegovina were guaranteed to Austria. But
by 1878 Russia was in occupation of Bulgaria and Roumelia,
and in less complaisant mood than in 1876; an immense
impulse had been given to the idea of Pan-Slavism by recent
events; the Southern Slavs were beginning to dream of the
possibility of a Jugo-Slav empire in the west of the peninsula.
Bosnia and the Herzegovina might easily slip, under the new
circumstances, from Austria's grip; the *Drang nach Osten*
might receive a serious set-back; the road to the Aegean
might be finally barred; even access to the Adriatic might
be endangered. Thus Bismarck had virtually to choose between
his two friends. At the Berlin Congress he played, as we saw,
the rôle of the ' honest broker '. For aught he cared Russia
might go to Constantinople, a move which would have the
advantage of embroiling her with England; but Austria
must have Bosnia and the Herzegovina. Austria got them,
and the road to Salonica was kept open.

Apart from any sinister design on the part of a *Mitteleuropa*
party in Germany or Austria-Hungary there was a great deal
to be said for the arrangement. Not least from the English
point of view. To the England of 1878 Russia was the enemy,
Pan-Slavism the bugbear. An Austrian wedge thrust into the
heart of the incipient States under Russian protection was, as
Lord Beaconsfield thought, distinctly advantageous to equili-
brium in the Near East. To the fate of the Balkan peoples,
as has been shown above, Lord Beaconsfield was indifferent.
Even from a selfish point of view it is now possible to view
the matter in a clearer light. We can perceive that ' the
occupation of Bosnia and Herzegovina . . . was the prelude to
the attempted strangulation of Serbian nationality ' ; [1] and we

[1] Professor Ch. Andler, *Pan-Germanism*—a brilliant summary.

can see also that the strangulation of that nationality was an essential preliminary to the realization of Central European ambitions in the Balkan Peninsula.

In the future of the Christian subjects of the Ottoman Empire Bismarck took as little interest as Lord Beaconsfield. It is said that on the morrow of the signature of the Treaty of Berlin Bismarck sent for the Turkish representatives and said : ' Well, gentlemen, you ought to be very much pleased ; we have secured you a respite of twenty years ; you have got that period of grace in which to put your house in order. It is probably the last chance the Ottoman Empire will get, and of one thing I 'm pretty sure—you won't take it.' The story may be apocryphal, but it accords well enough with Bismarck's sardonic humour.

Prince Gortschakoff never forgave his pupil for the rupture of the *Dreikaiserbund*. Russia and Germany drifted further apart ; and in 1882 Bismarck formed a fresh diplomatic combination. Italy joined Germany and Austria in the *Triple Alliance* ; and, a year later, the Hohenzollern King of Roumania was introduced into the firm as ' a sleeping partner '. The ' Battenberger' was no favourite at Berlin, but the election of a ' Coburger ' to the Bulgarian throne in 1887 decidedly strengthened Teutonic influence in the Balkans.

Bismarck, however, to the end of his career, regarded Balkan politics as outside the immediate sphere of Berlin. Ten years he devoted to the task of creating a united Germany under the hegemony of Prussia. The next twenty were given to the consolidation of the position he had acquired. But Bismarck's course was nearly run.

In 1888 the direction of German policy passed into other hands. Like his great-great-uncle, George III, the young Emperor William mounted a throne quite determined ' to be king '. In the English executive there was no room for both

George III and the elder Pitt ; Pitt had to go. In the higher command of German politics there was no room for William II and Bismarck ; the pilot was soon dropped.

The young emperor was by no means alone in his anxiety to initiate a new departure in the Near East. The visit to Constantinople in 1889 was the first overt intimation to the diplomatic world of the breach between the young emperor and his veteran Chancellor. The mission of Bismarck was, in the eyes of the younger generation, already accomplished. The past belonged to him, the future to the emperor. ' Bismarck ', wrote one of the younger school, ' merely led us to the threshold of German regeneration.' [1]

The man who more than any one else persuaded the Kaiser to the new enterprise, and in particular to the effusive demonstration of 1889, was Count Hatzfeld, who had been German ambassador to the Sublime Porte in the early eighties. Count Hatzfeld was quick to perceive, during his residence in Turkey, that there was a vacancy at Constantinople. From the days of Suleiman the Magnificent down to the first Napoleonic Empire, France, as we have seen, occupied a unique position at Constantinople. From the beginning of the nineteenth century that position was threatened by England, and from the days of Canning to those of Beaconsfield England was a fairly constant and successful suitor for the *beaux yeux* of the Sultan.

England's popularity at Constantinople did not long survive the conclusion of the Cyprus Convention (1878). It was further impaired by Mr. Gladstone's return to power in 1880.

Mr. Gladstone was the recognized friend not of the Turks but of the ' subject peoples ' ; and his accession to office was signalized by the rectification of the Greek frontier at the

[1] F. Lange, *Reines Deutschtum*, p. 210 (quoted by Andler, *op. cit.*, p. 23).

expense of the Porte in 1881. The occupation of Egypt (1882) was the final blow to a traditional friendship.

The vacancy thus created at Constantinople the young German Emperor determined to fill. The way had been prepared for his advent in characteristic Prussian fashion. Von Moltke had been sent on a mission to Constantinople as far back as 1841, and had formed and expressed very clear views on the situation he found there. Forty years later a military mission was dispatched from Berlin to avert, if possible, the disruption which Moltke had prophesied. The head of the mission was the great soldier-scholar, who, in 1916, laid down his life in the Caucasus. Baron von der Goltz devoted twelve years to the task of reorganizing the Turkish army, and the results of his teaching were brilliantly demonstrated in the brief but decisive war with Greece in 1897. In the wake of Prussian soldiers went German traders and German financiers. A branch of the *Deutsche Bank* of Berlin was established in Constantinople, while German commercial travellers penetrated into every corner of the Ottoman Empire. The contemporary situation was thus diagnosed by a brilliant French journalist : ' Dans ce combat commercial l'Allemagne poursuit l'offensive, l'Angleterre reste sur la défensive, et la France commence à capituler.' Monsieur Gaulis further suggests reasons for the phenomenal success of the German traders : even ambassadors do not deem it beneath their dignity to assist by diplomatic influence the humblest as well as the greatest commercial enterprises ; consular agents abroad keep the manufacturers at home constantly and precisely informed as to demands of customers, and above all the German manufacturer is adaptable and teachable. Instead of attempting to force upon the consumer something which he does not want—' l'article démodé '—he supplies him with the exact article which he does want. And what the Eastern generally does want to-day is something cheap and nasty. The result may be learnt from a conversation with a typical Turk recorded by M. Gaulis:

' Mon grand-père a acheté sa sacoche à un Français ; il l'a payée deux livres ; elle était en cuir. Mon père l'a achetée à un Anglais ; il l'a payée une livre ; elle était en toile cirée. Moi, je l'ai achetée à un Allemand ; je l'ai payée deux medji-diés (huit francs) ; elle est en carton verni.' [1]

If German diplomatists have not disdained to act as commercial agents they have only followed a still more exalted example. The commercial aspect of the question did not escape the shrewd eyes of the emperor in 1889.

The second visit paid by the emperor to the Sultan, in 1898, was even more productive in this respect. But the promotion of the commercial interests of Germany was not its primary object. The moment was chosen with incomparable felicity. No crowned head ever stood more desperately in need of a friend of unimpeachable respectability than did Abdul Hamid in the year 1898.

The Armenian Massacres (1894–8)

For the last four years Christendom had been resounding with the heartrending cries of the Armenian Christians, butchered in their thousands to make a Sultan's holiday. The story of the Armenian massacres has been told by many competent pens. Pamphlets, articles in contemporary reviews, political speeches, and substantial volumes go to make up a vast literature on the subject.[2] Not the least impressive account is that which is to be found in the papers presented to Parliament in 1895 and 1896.[3] Stripped of all exaggeration

---

[1] Gaulis, *La Ruine d'un Empire*, p. 143.

[2] See bibliographical note at the end of this chapter.

[3] Under the head of *Turkey*.

and rhetoric the story is one of the most horrible, and, for the Christian nations, the most humiliating in the long history of the Eastern Question. The present narrative is, however, concerned with it only so far as it reacted upon the diplomatic situation in the Near East, and the relations of the European Powers to the Sultan and to each other.

Some parts of the story are still obviously incomplete; much of it is obscure; the whole of it is difficult and confusing. But the points essential to our present purpose emerge with terrible distinctness.

The Armenian Church claims to be the oldest of all the national churches, having been founded by St. Gregory the Illuminator in the third century. It is not in communion with the Orthodox Greek Church, and its appeals, therefore, have always left the Russians cold; and only since the abandonment of the monophysite heresy in the fifteenth century has a portion of the Armenian Church been accepted as 'Catholic'. Armenia itself is an ill-defined geographical area lying between the Caspian, the Black Sea, the Caucasus, and Kurdistan, partitioned between the Empires of Russia, Turkey, and Persia. But while 'Armenia' has no official geographical existence in the gazetteer of the Ottoman Empire, the Armenians have been for centuries among the most important sections of Turkish society. 'To the Albanians the sword; to the Armenians belongs the pen.' The familiar proverb indicates with sufficient accuracy their characteristic place and function. These 'Christian Jews', as they have been called, are apt, above all other subjects of the Sultan, in all that pertains to money and finance. Bankers, financiers, and merchants in the higher grades of society; money-changers and hucksters in the lower, they have performed a useful function in the Ottoman Empire, and many of them have amassed large fortunes. Wealth acquired by finance has, it would seem, in Turkey as elsewhere, a peculiarly exasperating effect upon those who do not share it, and the Armenian Christians have always excited a considerable amount of odium even in the cosmopolitan society of Constantinople. Still, it is only within the last quarter of a century that their lot has been rendered unbearable.

Three reasons must be held mainly responsible for the peculiar ferocity with which the Armenians were assailed by Abdul Hamid : the unrest among hitherto docile subjects caused by the nationalist movements in Bosnia, Serbia, and Bulgaria ; the intervention of the European Powers ; and, not least, the palpable jealousies and dissensions among those Powers.

The primary motive which animated Abdul Hamid was beyond all question not fanaticism but fear. Greeks, Roumanians, Serbians, and Bulgarians ; one after another they had asserted their independence, and the Ottoman Empire was reduced to a mere shadow of its former self. That these events had caused unrest among the Armenians, even though Armenia was not, like Roumania or Bulgaria, a geographical entity, it would be idle to deny. Abdul Hamid was terrified.

He was also irritated. The Powers had interested themselves in the lot of the Armenians. Article lxi of the Treaty of Berlin ran as follows :

' The Sublime Porte undertakes to carry out, without further delay, the improvements and reforms demanded by local requirements in the provinces inhabited by the Armenians, and to guarantee their security against the Circassians and Kurds.

' It will periodically make known the steps taken to this effect to the Powers, who will superintend their application.'

But if the Powers in general were disposed to interfere, Great Britain, in particular, had imposed a special obligation upon the Sultan, and had herself assumed a peculiar responsibility.

The first Article of the Cyprus Convention contained, it will be remembered, a promise, a condition, and a territorial deposit.

'If', it ran, 'Batoum, Ardahan, Kars, or any of them shall be retained by Russia, and if any attempt shall be made at any future time by Russia to take possession of any further territories of his Imperial Majesty the Sultan in Asia, as fixed by the Definitive Treaty of Peace, England engages to join his Imperial Majesty the Sultan in defending them by force of arms.

'In return, His Imperial Majesty the Sultan promises to England to introduce necessary reforms, to be agreed upon later between the two Powers, into the government, and for the protection, of the Christian and other subjects of the Porte in these territories ; and in order to enable England to make necessary provision for executing her engagement, His Imperial Majesty the Sultan further consents to assign the Island of Cyprus to be occupied and administered by England.'

From 1878 onwards the Sultan lived, therefore, under the perpetual apprehension of intervention, while his Armenian subjects could repose in the comfortable assurance that they were under the special protection of their fellow Christians throughout the world.

Gradually, however, it dawned upon the shrewd Sultan that the apprehension was groundless, while the miserable Armenians were soon to discover that the assurance was not worth the paper upon which it was written.

If the Sultan was frightened, so also was the Tsar, Alexander III. The nihilist spectre was always before his eyes. His father, the emancipator of the serfs, had fallen a victim to a nihilist conspiracy in 1881. Nihilism had shown itself among the Turkish Armenians, and had led to an outbreak, easily suppressed, in 1885. Bulgaria, too, had proved a terrible disappointment to Russia. After being called into being by the Tsar it was manifesting its independence in most disquieting fashion. Instead of opening the way to Constantinop[le?] [Bul]garia, with unaccountable forgetfulness of past favou[rs] actually closing it. 'We don't want an Armenian B[ulgaria,]' said the Russian Chancellor, Prince Lobanoff. If the road to Constantinople is closed, all the more reason for keeping open the roads to Bagdad and Teheran. Nothing could be more inconvenient to the Tsar than a 'nationality' movement in Armenia. The Tsar's disposition was well known at Constantinople, and the Sultan soon drew the inference that, if he chose to work his will upon the Armenians, he had little to fear from St. Petersburg. He had much less to fear from Berlin; while Paris and London were kept apart by Egypt.

Here, then, was an opportunity; and from 1894 to 1896 not a moment was wasted. The Powers should be taught the imprudence of intervening between an Ottoman Sultan and his rightful subjects; the Armenians should learn—or the remnant of them who escaped extermination—that they had better trust to the tender mercies of their own sovereign than confide in the assurances of the European Concert.

His crafty calculations were precisely fulfilled. In the year 1893 there seems to have been some recrudescence, among the Armenians, of the revolutionary propaganda which had been suppressed in 1885. The Kurds, half-publicans, half-police, wholly irregulars, were encouraged to extort more and more taxes from the Armenian highlanders. The Armenians forcibly, and in some cases effectually, resisted their demands. Supported by Turkish regulars the Kurds were then bidden to stamp out the insurrection in blood.

They soon got to work, and the massacre of August, 1894, was the result. Several villages in the Sassoun district were pillaged and burnt, and about 900 people were killed.[1] The

---

[1] The original reports put the numbers at 7,000–8,000; official inquiries reduced them to 900: see Eliot, *op. cit.*, p. 406.

news of these massacres, the extent of which was at first grossly exaggerated, sent a thrill of horror throughout Christendom, and as a result the Sultan was obliged to consent to a Commission of Inquiry, consisting of English, French, and Russian consuls, together with certain Turkish officials. The Commission inquired, but the massacres went on. In the spring of 1895 a scheme of reform was presented to the Sultan, and after alternate pressure and delay was accepted by him in the autumn. The Sultan had, however, some reason to hope that before the reforms could be executed the Armenians would be exterminated. All through the year 1895 the massacres went on, and by December the victims probably numbered at least 50,000,[1] not to mention the thousands who perished from the ravages of disease and from exposure. The massacres were accompanied by deeds of ' the foulest outrage and the most devilish cruelty '.[2] Great Britain laboured assiduously to induce the Concert to intervene, but Russia, for reasons already suggested, resolutely refused, and Great Britain hesitated to act alone. Our responsibility was heavy; that of Russia was still heavier, for she could act directly in Armenia; we could act only at Constantinople, and there only in conjunction with unwilling allies.

Still the massacres went on; whole villages were wiped out; the cry of the victims rose to heaven; the Powers looked on in impotence; the ' red Sultan ' was gleeful, but his appetite for blood was even yet unsated.

In August, 1896, the interest of the scene shifted from Armenia to Constantinople. On the 26th the Armenians of the capital, frenzied by the appeals of their brethren in Armenia, and despairing of help from the Powers, rose in rebellion, and attacked and captured the Ottoman Bank

---

[1] An American estimate put it at 75,000.

[2] The phrase is the Duke of Argyll's, *Our Responsibilities for Turkey*, p. 87.

in Galata. Something desperate must be done to make the world listen. But the recoil upon their own heads was immediate and terrible. Within the next twenty-four hours 6,000 Armenians were bludgeoned to death in the streets of the capital. But though the aggregate was appalling, the Sultan was precise and discriminating in his methods. Only Gregorian Armenians were butchered; hardly a Catholic was touched.[1] In Constantinople the Armenians were the aggressors; the Turks were plainly within their rights in suppressing armed insurrection; the Powers could only, as before, look on; all the cards were in the Sultan's hands; the rubber was his.

Still, his hand was bloodstained. No respectable sovereign could grasp it without loss of self-respect. That consideration did not deter the German Emperor. The more socially isolated the Sultan, the greater his gratitude for a mark of disinterested friendship.

In the midst of the massacres it was forthcoming. On the Sultan's birthday, in 1896, there arrived a present from Berlin. It was carefully selected to demonstrate the intimacy of the relations which subsisted between the two Courts, almost, one might say, the two families; its intrinsic value was small, but the moral consolation which it brought to the recipient must have been inestimable: it consisted of a signed photograph of the emperor and empress surrounded by their sons. That was in 1896. In 1897 came the Turco-Greek War. The success of von der Goltz's pupils in Thessaly afforded a natural excuse for a congratulatory visit on the part of von der Goltz's master to Constantinople.

In 1898 the visit was paid; but it was not confined to the Bosphorus. From Constantinople the German Emperor, accompanied by the Empress, went on to the Holy Land.

The pilgrimage, which was personally conducted by

---

[1] Eliot, *op. cit.*, p. 411.

Messrs. Thos. Cook & Co.,[1] extended from Jaffa to Jerusalem, and from Jerusalem back to Damascus. The avowed purpose of the emperor's visit to the Holy Land was the inauguration of a Protestant Church at Jerusalem. Down to 1886 the Protestant bishop in Palestine was appointed in turn by England and by Prussia, though the bishop was under the jurisdiction of the See of Canterbury. The German Protestants have, however, shown remarkable activity in mission work in Palestine, and the emperor's visit was intended primarily to set the seal of imperial approval upon these activities and to mark the emancipation of the German mission from Anglican control. But the German Emperor is lord not only of Protestants but of Catholics. To the Catholics, therefore, in the Holy Land he also gave proof of his special favour. Nor must the Moslems be ignored. True, he could count few Moslems among his own subjects as yet. But who knows what the future may have in store ? At Jerusalem Protestants and Catholics had claimed attention. But the emperor, as M. Gaulis wittily observed, varied his parts as quickly as he changed his uniforms. At Damascus he was an under-study for the Caliph, and the Mohammedans got their turn. Of all the emperor's speeches, that which he delivered at Damascus, just before quitting the Holy Land, on November 8, 1898, was perhaps the most sensational and the most impudent. It contained these words :
' His Majesty the Sultan Abdul Hamid, and the three hundred million Mohammedans who reverence him as Caliph, may rest assured that at all times the German Emperor will be their

---

[1] ' Des caisses, des malles, des sacs portant l'inscription " Voyage de S.M. l'empereur d'Allemagne à Jérusalem ; Thos. Cook & Co." Deux royautés dans une phrase. Celle de Cook est incontestée en Palestine.' Gaulis, in whose work, *La Ruine d'un Empire*, pp. 156-242, will be found an entertaining and illuminating account by an eye-witness of the Kaiser's pilgrimage.

friend.' Well might those who listened to this audacious utterance hold their breath. Was it intoxication or cool calculation ?

' Ceux qui ont vu, comme moi ', writes M. Gaulis, ' le pélerin et son cortège dans leurs trois avatars successifs : protestant, catholique et musulman, restent un peu abasourdis sur le rivage. Quel est le sens de cette grande habileté qui, voulant faire à chacun sa part, jette un défi aux passions religieuses de l'Orient ? L'Allemagne, nous le savons bien, est venue tard dans la politique orientale. Comme toutes les places y étaient prises elle a jugé qu'elles étaient toutes bonnes à prendre. Elle s'est mise alors à jouer le rôle d'essayiste, tâtant le terrain de tous les côtés, guettant toutes les proies et ouvrant la succession des vivants avec une audace souvent heureuse. Mais ce n'est plus de l'audace, c'est de la candeur, tant le jeu en est transparent, lorsqu'elle offre dans la même quinzaine un hommage à Jésus-Christ et un autre à Saladin, un sanctuaire à l'Eglise évangélique et un autre au pape.'

But if Frenchmen marvelled at the audacity of the performance, other reflections occurred to the applauding Germans. Among those who were present at the banquet at Damascus was Pastor Friedrich Naumann, the author of a work which has to-day made his name famous throughout the world.[1] Side by side with the impressions of the French publicist it is instructive to read those of the German philosopher. Pastor Naumann discerned in the emperor's speech a secret calculation of ' grave and remote possibilities '.

(1) ' It is possible that the Caliph of Constantinople may fall into the hands of the Russians. Then there would perhaps be an Arab Caliph, at Damascus or elsewhere, and it would be advantageous to be known not only as the friend of the Sultan but as the friend of all Mohammedans. The title might give the German Emperor a measure of political power, which might be used to counteract a Russophil Ottoman policy.

[1] *Mitteleuropa*, by Friedrich Naumann (Berlin, 1915; Eng. trans., London, 1916).

(2) ' It is possible that the world war will break out before the disintegration of the Ottoman Empire. Then the Caliph of Constantinople would once more uplift the Standard of a Holy War. The Sick Man would raise himself for the last time to shout to Egypt, the Soudan, East Africa, Persia, Afghanistan, and India " War against England ". . . . It is not unimportant to know who will support him on his bed when he rises to utter this cry.' [1]

The Bagdad-bahn

But the Kaiser had not undertaken a personal mission to the Near East merely to patronize the disciples of various creeds in the Holy Land ; nor even to congratulate his friend Abdul Hamid upon a partial extermination of the Armenians. His sojourn at Constantinople coincided with the concession of the port of Haidar-Pasha to the ' German Company of Anatolian Railways '.

That concession was supremely significant. German diplomacy in the Near East has been from first to last largely ' railway-diplomacy', and not its least important field has been Asia Minor and Mesopotamia. The idea of directing German capital and German emigration towards these regions was of long standing. The distinguished economist, Roscher, suggested as far back as 1848 that Asia Minor would be the natural share of Germany in any partition of the Ottoman Empire. After 1870 the idea became more prevalent and more precisely defined. In 1880 a commercial society was founded in Berlin, with a capital of fifty million marks, to promote the ' penetration ' of Asia Minor. Kiepert, the prince of cartographers, was employed systematically to survey the country. About 1886 Dr. A. Sprenger, the orientalist, and other savants called attention to the favourable opening for German colonization in these regions.

[1] *Asia* (1899) quoted by Andler, *op. cit.*, p. 57.

' The East is the only territory in the world which has not passed under the control of one of the ambitious nations of the globe. Yet it offers the most magnificent field for colonization, and if Germany does not allow this opportunity to escape her, if she seizes this domain before the Cossacks lay hands upon it, she will have secured the best share in the partition of the earth. The German Emperor would have the destinies of Nearer Asia in his power if some hundreds of thousands of armed colonists were cultivating these splendid plains ; he might and would be the guardian of peace for all Asia.' [1]

Ten years later the Pan-German League published a brochure with the suggestive title, *Germany's Claim to the Turkish Inheritance*, and in the editorial manifesto wrote as follows :

' As soon as events shall have brought about the dissolution of Turkey, no power will make any serious objections if the German Empire claims her share of it. This is her right as a World-Power, and she needs such a share far more than the other Great Powers because of the hundreds of thousands of her subjects who emigrate, and whose nationality and economic subsistence she must preserve.' [2]

The field in Asia Minor was open to them alike for commercial penetration and for railway construction. But it was not for lack of warning on the part of clear-sighted Englishmen. The question of establishing a steam route to the Persian Gulf and India by way of Mesopotamia had been again and again raised in this country. In the early forties the fashionable idea was the establishment of steam navigation up the Euphrates ; in 1856 a private company did actually obtain a concession from the Porte for the construction of

[1] A. Sprenger, *Babylonien das reichste Land in der Vorzeit und das lohnendste Kolonisationsfeld für die Gegenwart* (1886). Quoted by Andler, *op. cit.*, p. 40.

[2] Quoted by Andler, *op. cit.*, p. 38. See also Chéradame, *La Question d'Orient*, pp. 5–7.

a line of railway from the mouth of the Syrian Orontes to Koweit, but the scheme was insufficiently supported and never materialized ; a committee of the House of Commons reported favourably upon a similar scheme in 1872, but the report was coldly received in Parliament ; finally, an abortive *Euphrates Valley Association* was formed in 1879 under the presidency of the Duke of Sutherland. But after 1880 attention in this country was concentrated upon Egypt and the Canal route ; not unnaturally, but in so far as it excluded consideration of the alternative possibilities of Asia Minor and Mesopotamia, with very questionable wisdom.[1]

England's indifference was Germany's opportunity. In 1880 an Anglo-Greek syndicate had obtained from the Porte certain rights for railway construction in Asia Minor ; in 1888 all these rights were transferred on much more favourable terms to the *Deutsche Bank* of Berlin and the *Württembergische Vereinsbank* of Stuttgart, and in 1889 the *Ottoman Company of Anatolian Railways* was promoted under the same auspices. Further concessions were obtained between that time and 1902, and in the latter year the convention for the construction of a railway from Constantinople to Bagdad was finally concluded. This railway it need hardly be said was only one link in a much longer chain stretching from Hamburg to Vienna, and thence by way of Buda-Pesth, Belgrade, and Nish to Constantinople, with an ultimate extension from Bagdad to Basra. Thus would Berlin be connected by virtually continuous rail with the Persian Gulf.

It was, and it remains, a great conception worthy of a scientific and systematic people. Should it materialize it will turn the flank of the great Sea-Empire, just as, in the fifteenth

[1] Cf. a most informing article by Mr. D. G. Hogarth, *National Review* vol. xxxix, pp. 462–73 ; and an article in the *Quarterly Review* for October, 1917.

century, Portugal, by the discovery of the Cape route to India, turned the flank of the Ottoman Turks.

That a line should be constructed from the Bosphorus to the Persian Gulf is in the political and social interests of one of the richest regions of the world; it is in the economic interests of mankind. But there are alternative routes from Western Europe to Constantinople.[1] Not all these routes are controlled from Berlin or even from Vienna. Which of them will ultimately be selected? The answer to this question is one of the many which depend upon the issue of the present war.[2]

For the first twenty years of his reign all went well with the policy of the Kaiser in the Near East. But everything depended upon the personal friendship of the Sultan Abdul Hamid, and upon the stability of his throne. In 1908 his throne was threatened; in 1909 it was overturned. The triumph of the Young Turk revolution imposed a serious check upon German policy; but, to the amazement of European diplomacy, the check proved to be only temporary. Enver Pasha quickly succeeded to the place in the circle of imperial friendship vacated by his deposed master. Bosnia and the Herzegovina were definitely annexed by Austria. Bulgaria finally declared her independence. Russia was successfully defied by Germany. Once again the Kaiser was supreme at Constantinople.

It now seemed as if one thing, and one thing only, could interpose a final and effective barrier between *Mitteleuropa* and its ambitions in the Near East—a real union between the Balkan States. In 1912 that miracle was achieved. Again the Kaiser's schemes appeared to be finally frustrated. Again

[1] Cf., for instance, Sir Arthur Evans's exceedingly interesting suggestion of a route via Milan and the Save valley to Constantinople.

[2] Written in 1916.

the check was only temporary. The brilliant success of the Balkan League in 1912 was followed, in 1913, by the disruption of the League and by fratricidal war. Once more had German diplomacy triumphed. But the crowded events of these fateful years must be reserved for treatment in the next chapter.

For further reference: Paul Dehn, *Deutschland und der Orient* (1884), and *Deutschland nach Osten* (1888); Karl Kaeger, *Klein-Asien ein deutsches Kolonisationsfeld* (1892); F. Lange, *Reines Deutschtum* (1904); Paul Rohrbach, *Der deutsche Gedanke in der Welt : die Bagdadbahn*; Sir V. Chirol, *The Middle Eastern Question* (1903); A. Murabet, *Le chemin de fer de Bagdad* (1914); Morris Jastrow, *The War and the Bagdad Railway* (1918); Sir E. Pears, *Life of Abdul Hamid* (1917); Albrecht Wirth, *Türkei, Oesterreich, Deutschland* (1912); Count von Reventlow, *Die auswärtige Politik Deutschlands, 1888–1913* (Berlin); J. L. de Lanessan, *L'Empire Germanique sous Bismarck et Guillaume II*; Bismarck, *Reflections and Reminiscences*; G. W. Prothero, *German Policy before the War* (1916); Klaczko, *Two Chancellors*; André Chéradame, *La Question d'Orient* (1903), and *Le Plan Pangermaniste démasqué* (1916).

For Armenia: Lord Bryce, *Transcaucasia* (1896); E. M. Bliss, *Turkey and the Armenian Atrocities* (1896); W. E. Gladstone, *The Armenian Question* (1905); H. F. B. Lynch, *Armenia : Travels and Studies*, 2 vols. (1901); Saint-Martin, *Mémoire historique et géographique sur l'Arménie* (Paris, 1818).

15

The Macedonian Problem

Habsburg Policy in the Balkans. The Young Turk Revolution

'The history of the last fifty years in South-Eastern Europe is to a great extent the history of the disentanglement of the Slavonic races from Greeks and Turks, and to this is now succeeding the disentanglement of the Slavonic races from one another.'—Sir Charles Eliot.

'La Macédoine est vraiment le fondement de l'Hellade unie et grande, la Macédoine est le boulevard de la liberté grecque, le gage de son avenir.'—Kallostypi (in 1886).

'Macedonia has for two thousand years been the "dumping ground" of different peoples and forms, indeed a perfect ethnographic museum.'— LUIGI VILLARI.

'Voilà un siècle que l'on travaille à résoudre la question d'Orient. Le jour où l'on croira l'avoir résolue l'Europe verra se poser inévitablement la question d'Autriche.'—ALBERT SOREL.

MACEDONIA is the microcosm of the Balkan problem. In Macedonia we can see simultaneously, and in compact and concentrated form, all the different elements which, on a larger scale and in successive phases, have combined to make up the Eastern Question.

There we see in the forefront the Turk; heavy-handed in extortion; in all other matters careless and indifferent; impotent to absorb the various races and creeds; but determined to prevent their fusion. There we see exemplified not only his attitude towards his own subjects, Moslem and Christian, but his relations to the concerted Powers of Europe : there, as elsewhere, we see him ever prodigal of promises but tardy in fulfilment.

The presence of the Turk is, however, the least perplexing of the problems which confront us in Macedonia. The country with its ill-defined boundaries and its kaleidoscopic medley of races is in itself a problem. And the problem has been intensified by the demarcation of the Balkan nations in the last half-century. For Macedonia is a 'no man's land'; or rather it is an all men's land. It is the residuum of the Balkans. Moslems, Jews, Albanians, Bulgars, Serbs, Kutzo-Vlachs, Greeks—all are to be found here cheek by jowl; only the roughest territorial discrimination is possible.

The Greeks have always desired to see Macedonia 'Hellenized', and an Hellenized Macedonia is plainly an indispensable preliminary to the realization of the dream of a revived Hellenic Empire with Constantinople as its capital. Yet to

Macedonia itself the Greeks have, on ethnographic grounds, no overpowering claim. Greeks are numerous on the coast and in most of the towns ; they form a preponderant element in the south-western part of the vilayet of Monastir and in the south of that of Salonica, but they are outnumbered by the Spanish Jews in the city of Salonica, and in the aggregate they are far inferior to the Slavs.

The Greek claim to a Hellenized Macedonia rests partly upon a Byzantine past, and partly upon the possibility of a Byzantine future ; but in the present it is mainly ecclesiastical. 'Hellenism', writes a close observer, 'claims these (Macedonian) peoples, because they were civilized by the " Greek Orthodox " Church. . . . To the Greek Bishops all Macedonians are Greeks because they are by right the tributaries of the Patriarch. True, they are at present in schism, but schism is an offence against the order of the Universe.' [1] This purely ecclesiastical claim is buttressed by a ' spiritual ' claim. Macedonia may not be Hellenic in speech or in race, but its spiritual (or, as the Germans would say, kultural) affinities are, so the Greeks urge, incontestable. Macedonia being Hellenic in spirit must eventually, therefore, form part of the Greater Greece.

But the Greek is not without competitors. The most serious of these are the Bulgarians. The Bulgars are the more detested by the Greeks since their rivalry is of recent date. Down to 1870 all the Bulgarians in Macedonia, as elsewhere, were, according to the official nomenclature of the Ottoman Empire, Greeks. Creed being the only differentia acknowledged by the Turk, all members of the Orthodox Church were in the same category. The establishment of an independent Bulgarian exarchate [2] was the first blow to the Greek monopoly in Macedonia. But although Bulgaria came into existence

[1] H. N. Brailsford, *Macedonia*, pp. 195, 196.   [2] *Supra*, p. 328.

as an ecclesiastical entity in 1870, it was not until 1878 that its existence was acknowledged in a political sense.

The conclusion of the Treaty of San Stefano appeared to deal a death-blow to Hellenic ambitions in Macedonia. Lord Beaconsfield's intervention was a godsend to the Greeks. But the success of the Philippopolis revolution in 1875 and the subsequent union of Eastern Roumelia and Bulgaria again rendered acute the Macedonian situation. The events of 1885 seemed once more to bring within the sphere of practical politics the realization of the dream of the Greater Bulgaria actually defined at San Stefano. For some years after 1885 the Bulgarians entertained the hope that it might be realized. Geologically and geographically [1] Bulgaria is drawn towards the Aegean. So long as Constantinople and the Straits are in hands potentially hostile, a good commercial harbour on the Aegean is essential to the full economic development of Bulgaria.

Ethnographically also her claims are strong. It is perhaps rather too much to say, with a distinguished American authority, that 'the great bulk of the population of Macedonia is Bulgarian',[2] but it is undeniable that Macedonia has, 'by the educational efforts of the Bulgar people, been to a very large extent Bulgarized in its sympathies' in recent years. The people have 'for a quarter of a century been educated as Bulgars; have fought as Bulgars in 1895, 1903, and 1912; were annexed to Bulgaria by the Russians in 1878, and by the Serbs in 1912; were assigned to the Bulgar Church by the Turks in 1872 and 1897; and are to-day, many of them, perhaps most of them, protesting against being treated other than as Bulgars.'[3]

[1] See chap. ii, *supra*.   [2] H. A. Gibbons, *New Map of Europe*, p. 167.
[3] *Nationalism and War in the Near East*, by a Diplomatist (Clarendon Press, 1915).

The policy of Bulgaria in regard to Macedonia has passed through two phases and into a third during the last thirty years. For some years, as was said, it aimed at the realization of the Greater Bulgaria, mapped out at San Stefano. Gradually abandoning this idea as outside the domain of practical politics, the Bulgarians devoted their energies to the emancipation of Macedonia. Their avowed hope was that, as an autonomous principality under a Christian governor, Macedonia, possibly enlarged by the addition of the vilayet of Adrianople, might become a powerful independent State and the nucleus of a Balkan Federation.[1]

Always practical, however, Bulgaria, while surrendering the dream of political annexation, has pursued a policy of peaceful penetration ; perhaps with a view to the ultimate partition which would now seem to be the least unhopeful of the many schemes which have been propounded for the pacification of Macedonia.

Meanwhile, the Bulgarians have incurred the bitter hostility not only of the Turks but of the other Christian races in Macedonia. The Turks here, as elsewhere, have proceeded on the formula : *Divide et impera.* In the south of Macedonia, as Dr. Tatarcheff (not without a strong Bulgarian bias) writes : ' The Turks support the Greek propaganda ; in the north they encourage the Serbian propaganda ; and everywhere they persecute the Bulgarian Church, schools, and nationality.' [2] In the latter task they have undoubtedly derived much assistance from the Greeks, and some perhaps from the Serbians.

The latter have their own claims to substantiate. Ethnographically those claims are incontestable in northern Macedonia ; historically they extend much further. It was from Serbians, not from Greeks or Bulgars, that the greater part

[1] Cf. Tatarcheff, ap. Villari, *Balkan Question*, chap. vi.
[2] *Op. cit.*, p. 171.

of Macedonia was originally conquered by the Ottoman Turks. The historical self-consciousness of the Serbs is not less intense than that of the Greeks. If, therefore, the hold of the Turks upon Macedonia be relaxed, it is to those who represent the empire of Stephan Dushan that, in the Serbian view, the country should revert. But present politics are more potent in Macedonia than past history, and Serbian pressure towards the south is due rather to the denial of access to the Adriatic than to the hope of reviving Dushan's empire. To this point, however, we shall have, in another connexion, to return.

Two other races claim a share in the Macedonian heritage, and though numerically inferior to the rest, are incomparably superior in antiquity. They are the Illyrians, represented by the modern Albanians, who are numerous in the extreme west, and the Thracians, who, as Kutzo-Vlachs or Roumanians, are to be found in scattered ' pockets ' throughout Macedonia, but are nowhere concentrated in any compact mass. The Roumanians claim that their countrymen in this ' all men's land ' number half a million ; less sympathetic analysts give them a fifth of that sum. In any case, Roumania cannot, for obvious geographical reasons, advance any territorial claims in Macedonia, though the unquestionable existence of a Roumanian element in the population might possibly help Roumania, when the time arrives for a final partition of the Balkans, towards a favourable deal with Bulgaria in the Dobrudja.

The rough outline sketch presented above would sufficiently demonstrate the complexity of the Macedonian problem even if it did not contain other factors. But Macedonia is not only the residuum of Balkan races ; it is not only the cockpit of competing Balkan nationalities ; it has been for years the favourite arena for the international rivalries of the great European Powers.

We have seen that international jealousies were largely responsible for the immunity enjoyed by Abdul Hamid in the perpetration of the Armenian massacres, and for the mishandling of Crete; the same cause operated to prolong the agony of Macedonia. Two Powers in particular—Russia and Austria-Hungary—have looked with a jealous eye upon Macedonia; and the other Powers have, in a sense, tacitly admitted the validity of their superior claims. If Russia had been permitted to carry out her plans in 1878 the Macedonian question would have been settled in favour of Bulgaria. At that time Europe was quite unconscious of the existence of a Macedonian problem. Indeed, in the sense in which we have understood it in this chapter, that problem did not exist. The growing self-consciousness of the Balkan nations and the demarcation of their respective frontiers served, if not to create, at least to accentuate and define it. So soon as the problem was defined there would seem to have been only three possible solutions: an autonomous Macedonia under European protection; Turkish reform under European control; or partition between Greece, Bulgaria, Serbia, and Albania. The jealousy of the Powers was effectual to prevent the adoption of either of the first two, and has practically wrecked the third.

Meanwhile, the condition of the Macedonian peoples, to whatever race they might belong, was nothing short of deplorable. For five hundred years the Ottomans had been undisputed lords of Macedonia. They began to plant colonies in Macedonia, even before they attempted the conquest of the Balkan Peninsula. They have been systematically colonizing it afresh since the shrinkage of their empire in Europe. But at no time have Turkish Moslems formed a majority of the population in Macedonia. There, as elsewhere, many of the upper classes apostatized to Mohammedanism, and were rewarded in the usual fashion. Those who refused to do so shared the common lot of the subject Christian populations in other parts of the peninsula.

With the nature of their grievances we have become, in the course of this narrative, only too familiar. There is, indeed, a painful monotony in the tale of Turkish misgovernment. Here, as elsewhere, the toiling peasantry were subject to a cross-fire of exactions, and extortions, and persecutions. They suffered at the hands of the Moslems because they were Christians; they were exposed to the lawless depredations of the brigands, frequently of Albanian race, by whom the country was infested; they had to meet the demands, both regular and irregular, of Moslem beys and official tax-farmers; they could obtain no redress in the courts of law; life, property, honour were all at the mercy of the ruling creed.

For some years after the conclusion of the Treaty of Berlin these things were patiently endured in the hope that the Powers would fulfil the promises of reforms contained in that document. But from 1893 to 1903 there were sporadic insurrections in various parts of Macedonia, organized by the secret revolutionary committees which quickly came into existence as the hope of reform faded. In 1895 Bulgaria stood forth as the avowed champion of the oppressed peasantry of Macedonia. In that year the 'supreme Macedo-Adrianopolitan Committee' was formed at Sofia, and armed bands poured over the Bulgarian frontiers. Bulgarian intervention effected little good, though it served to stimulate a movement in Macedonia itself which had for its object the creation of an autonomous province under Turkish suzerainty.

The outbreak of the 'Three Weeks' War' between Turkey and Greece in 1897 naturally aroused considerable enthusiasm in Macedonia. But the hopes it raised were destined to disappointment, for, in 1898, Austria and Russia concluded an agreement to maintain the *status quo*. In 1899, however, the Macedonian Committee, which was attempting from Sofia to organize a reform movement, addressed a memorial to the Powers in favour of an ' autonomous Macedonia ', with its capital at Salonica, to be placed under a governor-general belonging to the ' predominant nationality '. Nothing came of it, and from 1900 to 1903 Macedonia was in a state of chronic insurrection, which culminated in the autumn of 1903 in general risings in the Monastir district and in Thrace.

Meanwhile, in 1901, a band of brigands, acting, there is no doubt, under the orders of the Sofia Committee, captured Miss Stone, an American missionary, and held her to ransom. The object of the capture was twofold ; money and publicity. In order to obtain Miss Stone's release a very large sum— £16,000—had to be paid to her captors ; while the excitement caused by the outrage made Europe for the first time generally aware that there was a ' Macedonian question '. Having at last realized the existence of a ' problem ', the Powers confided to Austria and Russia the task of solving it. By this time the Porte was becoming seriously alarmed, and in the autumn of 1902 Abdul Hamid himself produced an elaborate scheme of reform, and appointed Hilmi Pasha as inspector-general to supervise its execution. Austria and Russia, which for some years had acted in close concert in Macedonia, were not to be burked in their benevolent intentions, and early in 1903 they presented to the Porte an independent reform programme.

For the moment, however, both schemes were perforce set aside by the outbreak of a serious and elaborately organized insurrection. The money obtained from Miss Stone's ransom had been expended on the purchase of arms and dynamite, and in the spring and summer of 1903 the results were made manifest to the world. The Ottoman Bank at Salonica was blown up ; bombs were placed upon trading vessels, and there was much destruction of both life and property. These outrages alienated European sympathy, and the Sultan got his opportunity. He did not neglect it. Troops, regular and irregular, were let loose upon the hapless peasantry ; more than a hundred villages were totally destroyed by fire, and tens of thousands of the inhabitants were rendered homeless and destitute.

Meanwhile the Tsar Nicholas and the Emperor Francis Joseph met at the castle of Mürzteg, near Vienna, and the two sovereigns sanctioned the immediate initiation of a scheme of reform known as the Mürzteg Programme.

Acting as the ' mandatories ' of Europe they recommended that Hilmi Pasha, the inspector-general of reforms, should be assisted in the work of pacifying Macedonia by two civil assessors, one a Russian and the other an Austrian, and that the gendarmerie should be reorganized and put under the command of a foreign general and a staff of foreign officers. Germany stood ostentatiously aloof, but the other five Powers each took a district and attempted to maintain order within it. Under their well-meant but misdirected efforts Macedonia sank deeper and deeper into the slough of anarchy. The Powers might put pressure upon the Sultan, but ' bands ' of Greeks and Bulgarians made life intolerable for the mass of the population. The civil assessors had no administrative powers, and it soon became plain that much more drastic measures would have to be taken if any good were to be effected.

But long before Europe had made up its mind to effective action a rapid series of dramatic events had revolutionized the whole situation in the Near East.

In 1905 Great Britain, France, Italy, and Germany combined to secure the appointment of an international commission to control Macedonian finance. This touched the Turk on his tenderest spot, and the Sultan showed every disposition to prevent the action of the Powers. But the latter presented a firm front; their combined squadrons occupied Mytilene and sailed through the Dardanelles, and, in December, 1905, the Sultan, at last realizing that they meant business, gave way. The commission did useful work within a limited sphere, but the essential difficulties of the Macedonian situation were untouched. Nor did the Mürzteg Programme solve them more effectually.

Early in 1908 the two parties to that agreement fell out. In January Baron von Aerenthal announced that Austria-Hungary had applied for permission to survey the ground for a line of railway to connect the terminus of the Bosnian railway with the line running from Mitrovitza to Salonica. The implication was obvious, and the announcement created a great sensation. Russia, in particular, regarded it, and naturally, as a denunciation of the *condominium*, which, with Austria-Hungary, she had been commissioned by the Powers to exercise over Macedonia.

Baron von Aerenthal did not question the correctness of the inference. On the contrary, he declared that the 'special task of Austria and Russia [in Macedonia] was at an end'. Plainly, the Dual Monarchy had made up its mind to play its own hand. Momentous events compelled it to play without delay.

In the long history of the Eastern Question there is no period more pregnant with startling developments than the last six months of the year 1908.

On July 24 the 'Committee of Union and Progress'—better known as the 'Young Turks'—effected a bloodless revolution in Constantinople; on October 5 Prince Ferdinand proclaimed the independence of Bulgaria; on the 7th the Emperor Francis Joseph announced the formal annexation of Bosnia and the Herzegovina to the Habsburg Empire; on the 12th the Cretan

Assembly voted the union of the island with the kingdom of Greece. At least two of these developments will demand detailed treatment. The last, as the least complicated, may be disposed of forthwith.

M. Zaimis, who was appointed High Commissioner of Crete in 1907, had speedily reduced the island to order. The protecting Powers, anxious to lay down their invidious task at the earliest moment compatible with its fulfilment, informed M. Zaimis that as soon as an effective native gendarmerie had been organized and the High Commissioner could guarantee the maintenance of order, and more particularly the security of the Moslem population, they would evacuate the island.

In March, 1908, M. Zaimis formally drew the attention of the Powers to the fact that their conditions had been fulfilled. In July the evacuation began. But the news from Bosnia and Bulgaria created intense excitement in Crete, and on October 12, just a week after the Tsar Ferdinand's proclamation at Tirnovo, the Assembly at Canea once more voted the union of the island with the Hellenic kingdom. M. Zaimis happened to be absent on a holiday, and the Assembly therefore appointed a Provisional Government of six members to govern the island in the name of the King of the Hellenes.

The Moslems, in great alarm, thereupon invoked the protection of the British Government; but the latter, while promising protection to the Moslems, declined either to recognize or to repudiate the union. The Young Turk Government at Constantinople contented itself with a formal protest against the dismemberment of the inheritance upon which it had so lately entered. In July, 1909, the protecting Powers finally withdrew their forces from the island, while at the same time they announced that four ships of war would be stationed off Crete in order to guarantee the safety of the Moslem population and to 'safeguard' the rights of the

Ottoman Empire. Those rights were, however, already virtually extinguished, and the Balkan War of 1912 brought the solemn farce to an end.

The circumstances attending the completion of Bulgarian independence demand only brief attention. Prince Ferdinand's move, like that of the Cretan Assembly, was directly attributable to the astonishing success of the Young Turks.

It had long been Ferdinand's ambition to sever the last ties which bound the principality to its suzerain and to assume the ancient title of Tsar of Bulgaria. So long, however, as the Ottoman Empire was manifestly in a condition of decadence there was no immediate necessity for a step likely to arouse the susceptibilities of the Powers which had signed the Treaty of Berlin. The revolution at Constantinople put another aspect on the matter. Ferdinand could no longer afford to postpone the contemplated step. If the Young Turks succeeded in effecting a real reform at Constantinople the opportunity for the declaration of Bulgarian independence might never recur. A slight offered to the Bulgarian representative at Constantinople in September afforded a pretext for his recall, and on October 5 the independence of Bulgaria was proclaimed. The principality was converted into a kingdom, and the king, by a solemn act performed in the Church of the Forty Martyrs in the ancient capital of Tirnovo, assumed the title of Tsar. Two reasons were assigned for the violation of the Berlin Treaty : first that the Bulgarian nation, though practically independent, was 'impeded in its normal and peaceful develop-ment by ties the breaking of which will remove the tension which has arisen between Bulgaria and Turkey' ; and, secondly, that ' Turkey and Bulgaria, free and entirely independent of each other, may exist under conditions which will allow them to strengthen their friendly relations and to devote themselves to peaceful internal development'.

This hypocritical explanation did not tend to mitigate the Sultan's wrath, but the real significance of Ferdinand's action was to the Porte financial rather than political. The new government at Constantinople demanded compensation for the loss of the tribute which Bulgaria had been accustomed to pay. Tsar Ferdinand bluntly refused to provide it ; Turkey and Bulgaria were brought to the brink of war, but Russia stepped in to facilitate a financial composition, and on April 19, 1909, the Turkish Parliament formally recognized the independence of Bulgaria.

Austria-Hungary and the Balkans

Much more serious, alike in its immediate and its remoter consequences, was the action taken by Austria-Hungary in regard to Bosnia and the Herzegovina. So serious, indeed, that this would seem to be the appropriate occasion for a summary analysis of Austro-Hungarian policy in the Near East.

Of all the great European Powers Austria-Hungary is most closely, if not most vitally, concerned in the solution of that problem. England's interest is vital, but remote, and may be deemed to have been secured by the annexation of Egypt and Cyprus, and by her financial control over the Canal. Russia's interest also is vital. On no account must any Power, potentially hostile, be in a position to close the straits against her. But the interests of Austria-Hungary, while not less vital, are even more immediate and direct. For England it is mainly a question of external policy, except in so far as the fate of the European Moslems reacts upon the hopes and fears of British subjects in Egypt and India. For Russia too, apart from the waning idea of Pan-Slavism and from the position of the Orthodox Church, the question is mainly though less exclusively an external one.

For Austria-Hungary the external question is hardly if at

all less vital than it is to Russia, and more vital than it is to
England, while internally the whole position of the Dual
Monarchy may be said, without exaggeration, to depend
upon the form in which the Balkan problem is ultimately
solved. M. Albert Sorel, writing as far back as 1889, exhibited
the prescience of a great publicist no less than the acumen of
a brilliant historian when he predicted, in words which have
lately become familiar, that the moment the Eastern Question
was solved Europe would find itself confronted with an
Austrian question. As a fact, the Habsburgs have deemed it
imprudent to await the final solution of that question before
flinging the Austrian apple of discord into the diplomatic
arena. It becomes necessary, therefore, at this point to define
with some precision the nature and extent of Austro-Hungarian
interests in the problem under consideration.

No words are needed to emphasize the vital importance
to Russia of a free passage through the Bosphorous and the
Dardanelles. Her dominant interest in the future of the
straits is now generally recognized. It is less commonly
realized that the external problem for Austria-Hungary is
almost precisely parallel to that of Russia. Deprive the
Habsburgs of Trieste, Pola, Fiume, and Dalmatia—and her
enemies would do it, if they could, to-morrow—and the
position of Austria-Hungary would be identical with that of
Russia, or worse. The Danube alone would then give them
access to the sea, and with Constantinople in hostile hands the
advantages even of that access would be cancelled.

Trieste is the Liverpool of the Dual Monarchy; Pola its
Portsmouth. If Trieste be adjudged to Italy, and Istria and
Fiume either to Italy or to the new Jugo-Slavia, the naval
and commercial position of Austria-Hungary would indeed
be desperate. But even assuming that there is no dismemberment of the existing Habsburg Empire, her position on the

Adriatic will still be exceedingly precarious. Secure in the possession of Brindisi and Valona, Italy would find little difficulty in barring the access of Austria-Hungary to the Mediterranean. The Straits of Otranto are only forty-one miles broad; small wonder, then, that Albania is regarded with jealous eyes by the statesmen of the Ballplatz.

Italy, however, is not the only potential rival of Austria-Hungary in the Adriatic. Montenegro has already gained access to its waters, though her coast-line is less than thirty miles in extent. If the dreams of a Jugo-Slav Empire are realized even partially, the Greater Serbia, possessed of Dalmatia and absorbing Bosnia—to say nothing of Croatia and part of Istria—would at once neutralize, in considerable degree, the importance of Trieste, Fiume, and Pola.

These considerations enable us to appreciate the significance of the Habsburg monarchy's *Drang nach Süd-Osten*. If egress from the Black Sea and the Adriatic were denied to her, or even rendered precarious, Salonica would become not merely valuable but indispensable to her existence. Hence the persistent and increasing hostility manifested by Austria towards the development of Serbia and the consolidation of the Southern Slavs.

The Habsburgs have, in Bismarck's phrase, been gravitating towards Buda-Pesth ever since the virtual destruction of the Holy Roman Empire in the Thirty Years' War (1618–48). As a fact, gravitation was for many years equally perceptible towards the Adriatic and the Lombard plain. But the new departure in Habsburg policy really dates, as I have attempted to show in another connexion, not from the Treaty of Westphalia but from the Treaty of Prague (1866). When Bismarck turned Austria simultaneously out of Germany and out of Italy, he gave her a violent propulsion towards the south-east. The calculated gift of Bosnia and the Herzegovina, supplemented by the military occupation of the Sanjak of Novi-Bazar, increased the momentum. Novi-Bazar not only formed a wedge between the Slavs of Serbia and those of Montenegro but seemed to invite the Habsburgs towards the Vardar valley and so on to Salonica.

For twenty-five years Serbia appeared to be acquiescent. Had Serbia been in a position at the Congress of Berlin to claim Bosnia, or even Novi-Bazar, Balkan politics would have worn a very different aspect to-day. But Serbia had not yet found her soul, nor even her feet. Her geographical position as defined in 1878 was, as we have seen, a hopeless one. Nor did she lack other troubles. Prince Milan assumed a royal crown in 1882, but his policy was less spirited than his pretensions ; he took his orders from Vienna, a fact which widened the breach between himself and the Queen Natalie, who, being a Russian, had strong Pan-Slavist sympathies. But Queen Natalie had grievances against Milan as a husband no less than as a king, and court scandals at Belgrade did not tend to enhance the reputation of Serbia in European society.

The disastrous war with Bulgaria (1885) still further lowered her in public estimation. The grant of a more liberal constitution in 1888 did little to improve the situation of a country not yet qualified for self-government, and in 1889 King Milan abdicated.

His son, King Alexander, was a child of thirteen at his accession, and though not devoid of will he could not give Serbia what she needed, a strong ruler. In 1893 he suddenly declared himself of age, arrested the regents and ministers, and abrogated the prematurely liberal constitution of 1888. This act, not in itself unwise, threw the country into worse confusion, which was still further increased when in 1900 the headstrong young man married his mother's lady-in-waiting, a beautiful woman but a *divorcée*, and known to be incapable of child-birth. The squalid story reached a tragic conclusion in 1903, when the king, Queen Draga, and the queen's male relations were all murdered at Belgrade with every circumstance of calculated brutality.

This ghastly crime sent a thrill of horror through the courts and countries of Europe.[1] Politically, however, it did not lack justification. Serbia gained immeasurably by the extinction of the decadent Obrenović dynasty, and the reinstatement of the more virile descendants of Karageorgević; the pro-Austrian bias of her policy has been corrected; and under King Peter she has regained self-respect and has resumed the work of national regeneration.

That work was watched with jealous eyes at Vienna, and still more at Buda-Pesth, and not without reason. The development of national self-consciousness among the Southern Slavs seriously menaced the whole structure of the Dual Monarchy. Expelled from Germany in 1866, the Emperor Francis Joseph came to terms with his Magyar subjects in the *Ausgleich* of 1867. Henceforward the domestic administration of Austria and her dependencies was to be entirely separate from that of Hungary; even the two monarchies were to be distinct, but certain matters common to the Austrian Empire and the Hungarian kingdom—foreign policy, army administration, and finance—were committed to a joint body known as the ' Delegations '. But the essential basis of the formal reconciliation thus effected between Germans and Magyars was a common hostility to the third racial element in the Dual Monarchy, the element which outnumbers both Magyars and Germans, that of the Slavs.

---

[1] There is more than a suspicion that the crime was plotted in Vienna and carried out with Austrian connivance ; for Alexander was less in tutelage to Vienna than Milan ; but its ultimate reaction was opposed to Habsburg interests. Cf. *infra*, p. 429.

Out of the 51,000,000 subjects of the Emperor Francis Joseph about 10,000,000 are Magyars—these form a compact mass in Hungary ; about 11,000,000 are German ; about 26,000,000 are Slavs. Of the latter, about 7,000,000 belong to the Serbo-Croatian or Southern Slav branch of the great Slav family.

Since 1867 it has been the fixed policy of the leading statesmen of both Vienna and Buda-Pesth to keep the Slav majority in strict subordination to the German-Magyar minority. The inclusion of Bosnia and Herzegovina, with a compact population of nearly 2,000,000 Slavs, has rendered this policy at once more difficult and, at least in the eyes of the timorous minority, more absolutely imperative. In proportion, however, as Habsburg methods have become more drastic, the annexed provinces have tended to look with more and more approbation upon the Jugo-Slav propaganda emanating from Belgrade. To meet this danger the Austrian Government has promoted schemes for the systematic German colonization of Bosnia in much the same way as Prussia has encouraged colonization in Poland. But neither the steady progress of colonization nor the material benefits unquestionably conferred upon Bosnia by German administration have availed to win the hearts of the Bosnian Serbs, or to repress the growing intimacy between Serajevo and Belgrade.

This fact, too obtrusive to be ignored, has led some of the more thoughtful statesmen of the Ballplatz to advocate a new departure in Habsburg policy. To maintain, in perpetuity, the German-Magyar ascendancy over the Slavs seemed to them an impossibility. But was there any alternative, consistent, of course, with the continued existence of the Habsburg Empire ? Only, it seemed to them, one : to substitute a triple for the dual foundation upon which for half a century the Habsburg Empire had rested ; to bring in the Slav as a third partner in the existing German-Magyar firm.

On one detail of their programme the 'trialists' were not unanimous. Some who favoured 'trialism' in principle wished to include only the Slavs who were already subject to the Dual Monarchy; others, with a firmer grip upon the nationality idea, advocated a bolder and more comprehensive policy. To them it seemed possible to solve by one stroke the most troublesome of the domestic difficulties of the Habsburg Empire and the most dangerous of their external problems. The Jugo-Slav agitation had not, at that time, attained the significance which since 1912 has attached to it. Serbo-Croat unity was then a distant dream. While the nationality sentiment was still comparatively weak, the religious barriers between Orthodox Serbs and Roman Catholic Croats were proportionately formidable. Whether even then the Slavs could have been tempted by generous terms to come in as a third partner in the Habsburg Empire it is impossible to say; but from the Habsburg point of view the experiment was obviously worth making, and its success would have been rightly regarded as a superb political achievement. With Serbia and Montenegro added to Bosnia, and the Herzegovina to Dalmatia and Croatia-Slavonia, the Habsburgs would not only have been dominant in the Adriatic; the valley of the Morava would have been open to them, and Salonica would have been theirs whenever they chose to stretch out their hands and take it. Greece would certainly have protested, and might have fought, but at that time there would have been Crete and Epirus and even western Macedonia to bargain with. Bulgaria might easily have been conciliated by the cession of eastern Macedonia, including, of course, Kavala, and perhaps the vilayet of Adrianople. The Macedonian problem would thus have been solved with complete satisfaction to two out of the three principal claimants, and to the incomparable advantage of the Habsburg Empire.

If it be true that the heir to the throne, the late Archduke
Franz Ferdinand, had identified himself with this large scheme
of policy, it would go far to stamp him as a great statesman ; it would also go far to explain the relentless hostility
with which he was pursued by the party of German-Magyar
ascendancy.

Things seemed to be shaping, in the first years of the present
century, in that direction.   Serbia, distracted by domestic
broils, was in the slough of despond ; a generous offer from the
Habsburgs might well have seemed to patriotic Serbs the
happiest solution of an inextricable tangle.   Austria, on the
other hand, had reached at that moment the zenith of her
position in the Balkans.   The year which witnessed the
palace revolution at Belgrade witnessed also the brilliant
culmination of Habsburg diplomacy in the conclusion of
the Mürzteg agreement.   Russia was on the brink of the
Japanese War.   Great Britain had just emerged with seriously
damaged prestige from the war in South Africa.   The brilliant
diplomacy of King Edward VII had not yet succeeded in
bringing England and France together, still less in laying
the foundations for the Triple Entente between the Western
Powers and Russia.

The moment was exceptionally favourable for a bold coup
on the part of the Habsburgs in the Balkans.   The Mürzteg
agreement seemed almost to imply an international invitation
to attempt it.   But the opportunity was lost.   What were the
forces which were operating against the Trialists ?   At many
of them we can, as yet, only guess.   But there are some indications which are as sinister as they are obscure.   In 1909 a corner
of the curtain was lifted by a *cause célèbre*.   In December of
that year the leaders of the Serbo-Croat Coalition brought
an action for libel against a well-known Austrian historian,
Dr. Friedjung of Vienna.   Dr. Friedjung had accused the

Croatian leaders of being the hirelings of the Serbian Government, but the trial revealed the amazing fact that a false accusation had been based upon forged documents supplied to a distinguished publicist by the Foreign Office. Dr. Friedjung was perhaps the innocent victim of his own nefarious government ; the real culprit was Count Forgach, the Austrian minister at Belgrade, a diplomatist whose ingenuity was rewarded by an important post at the Ballplatz. Incidents of this kind showed to the world the direction of the prevailing wind. The archduke was already beaten. Baron von Aerenthal was in the saddle.

During six critical years (1906–12) the direction of the external policy of the Habsburg Empire lay in the hands of this masterful diplomatist. The extinction of the Obrenović dynasty in Serbia was a considerable though not a fatal blow to Habsburg pretensions. The tragedy itself was one of several indicative of the growth of an anti-Austrian party. The bad feeling between the two States was further accentuated by the economic exclusiveness of the Habsburg Government, which threatened to strangle the incipient trade of Serbia, and in particular to impede the export of swine, upon which its commercial prosperity mainly depended. The friction thus generated culminated in the so-called ' Pig-war ' of 1905–6, which convinced even the most doubting of Serbian politicians that no free economic development was possible for the inland State until she had acquired a coastline either on the Adriatic or on the Aegean. The latter was hardly in sight ; only two alternatives were really open to Serbia. The Albanian coast is with reference to the hinterland of little economic value. Besides, the Albanians are not Serbs ; nor have they ever proved amenable to conquest. Unless, therefore, Serbia were content to resign all hope of attaining the rank even of a third-rate European State, one of two things was essential, if not both.

Either she must have some of the harbours of Dalmatia, pre-eminently a Slav country, or she must obtain access to the Adriatic by union with Bosnia and the Herzegovina.

All hope of the latter solution was extinguished by Aerenthal's abrupt annexation of these Slav provinces in 1908 Austria-Hungary had been in undisputed occupation since 1878, and no reasonable person ever supposed that she would voluntarily relax her hold. But so long as the Treaty of Berlin remained intact, so long as the Habsburg occupation was technically provisional, a glimmer of hope remained to the Pan-Serbians. Aerenthal's action was a declaration of war. In the following year he did indeed throw a sop directly to the Turks, indirectly to the Serbs, by the evacuation of Novi-Bazar. He took to himself great credit for this generosity, and the step was hailed with delight in Serbia. We now know that it was dictated by no consideration for either Turkish or Serbian susceptibilities; it was taken partly to conciliate Italy, the third and most restless member of the Triple Alliance; but mainly because the Austrian general staff had come to the conclusion that the Morava valley offered a more convenient route than the Sanjak to Salonica.

Could Serbia hope to shut and lock both these doors against the intruding Habsburgs? That was the question which agitated every Chancellery in Europe at the opening of the year 1909. In Belgrade the action of Austria-Hungary excited the most profound indignation, and the whole Serbian people, headed by the Crown Prince, clamoured for war. Feeling in Montenegro was hardly less unanimous. The Serbian Government made a formal protest on October 7, and appealed to the Powers for ' justice and protection against this new and flagrant violation, which has been effected unilaterally by *force majeure* to satisfy selfish interests and without regard to the grievous blows thus dealt to the feelings, interests, and rights of the Serbian people '. Finally, in default of the restoration of the *status quo*, they demanded that compensation should be given to Serbia in the Sanjak of Novi-Bazar.

The Powers were not unsympathetic, but urged Serbia to be patient. Upon the most acute of English diplomatists the high-handed action of Austria had made a profound impression. No man in Europe had laboured more assiduously or more skilfully for peace than King Edward VII. Lord Redesdale has recorded the effect produced upon him by the news from the Balkans.

' It was the 8th of Oct. that the King received the news at Balmoral, and no one who was there can forget how terribly he was upset. Never did I see him so moved. . . . The King was indignant. . . . His forecast of the danger which he communicated at the time to me showed him to be possessed of the prevision which marks the statesman. Every word that he uttered that day has come true.' [1]

The peace of Europe depended upon the attitude of Russia. Her Balkan partnership with Austria-Hungary had been dissolved, and in 1907 she had concluded an agreement respecting outstanding difficulties with Great Britain. That agreement virtually completed the Triple Entente, the crown of the diplomacy of King Edward VII. In June, 1908, King Edward and the Tsar Nicholas met at Réval, and a further programme for the pacification of Macedonia was drawn up. Whether the Réval programme would have succeeded in its object any better than the Mürzteg agreement, which it replaced, the Young Turks did not permit Europe to learn. But at least it afforded conclusive evidence that a new era in the relations of Russia and Great Britain had dawned.

In the Balkan question Russia was, of course, profoundly interested. To her the Serbians naturally looked not merely

[1] Lord Redesdale, *Memories*, i. 178-9.

for sympathy but for assistance. Russia, however, was not ready for war. She had not regained her breath after the contest with Japan. And the fact was, of course, well known at Potsdam. All through the autumn and winter (1908-9) Serbia and Montenegro had been feverishly pushing on preparations for the war in which they believed that they would be supported by Russia and Great Britain. Austria, too, was steadily arming. With Turkey she was prepared to come to financial terms : towards Serbia she presented an adamantine front. Towards the end of February, 1909, war seemed inevitable. It was averted not by the British proposal for a conference but by the ' mailed fist ' of Germany. In melodramatic phrase the German Emperor announced that if his august ally were compelled to draw the sword, a knight ' in shining armour ' would be found by his side. At the end of March Russia was plainly informed that if she went to the assistance of Serbia she would have to fight not Austria-Hungary only but Germany as well. Russia, conscious of her unpreparedness, immediately gave way. With that surrender the war of 1914 became inevitable. Germany was intoxicated by her success ; Russia was bitterly resentful. The Serbs were compelled not merely to acquiesce but to promise to shake hands with Austria. The Powers tore up the twenty-fifth Article of the Treaty of Berlin. Turkey accepted £2,200,000 from Austria-Hungary as compensation for the loss of the Serbian provinces, and in April, 1909, formally assented to their alienation. Bulgaria compounded for her tribute by the payment of £5,000,000.[1] Thus were the ' cracks papered over ', and Europe emerged from the most serious international crisis since 1878.

---

[1] Of which Russia provided £1,720,000.

The Turkish Revolution, 1908

We must now return, after this prolonged parenthesis, to the *fons et origo* of the whole commotion. It was, as we saw, the sudden move of the Macedonian ' Committee of Union and Progress ' which set a light to the conflagration, the slow burning down of which we have just witnessed. The fire was not burnt out. The ashes smouldered, to blaze out again more fiercely in 1914.

Few single events in the whole history of the Near Eastern Question have caused a greater sensation or evoked more general or generous enthusiasm than the Turkish revolution of 1908. The Committee which organized it with such complete and amazing success had been in existence for several years, and was itself the descendant of a party which was first formed in Constantinople after the disastrous conclusion of the Greek War of Independence (1830). It was in that year that the High Admiral, Khalil Pasha, said : ' I am convinced that unless we speedily reform ourselves on European lines we must resign ourselves to the necessity of going back to Asia.' [1] Those words indicate the genesis of the Young Turk party, and might have been taken as its motto. To transform the Ottoman Empire for the first time into a modern European State ; to give to Turkey a genuine parliamentary constitution ; to proclaim the principle of religious and intellectual liberty ; to emancipate the press ; to promote intercourse with the progressive nations of the world ; to encourage education ; to promote trade ; to eradicate the last relics of mediaevalism —such was the programme with which the Young Turks astonished and deluded Europe in the summer of 1908.

Composed mainly of young men who had acquired a veneer

---

[1] Driault, p. 135.

of Western—particularly Gallic—ideas, the Committee was originally formed at Geneva in 1891. Thence it transferred its operations to Paris, and, in 1906, established its headquarters at Salonica. Its first object was to secure the army, more particularly the third army corps then stationed in Macedonia. The sporadic outbreaks in the early part of July in Macedonia, the assassination of officers known to be well affected towards the Hamidian régime, indicated the measure of its success. On July 23 the Committee proclaimed at Salonica the Turkish constitution of 1876 and the third army corps prepared to march on Constantinople.

Abdul Hamid, however, rendered the application of force superfluous. He protested that the Committee had merely anticipated the wish dearest to his heart ; he promptly proclaimed the constitution in Constantinople (July 24) ; he summoned a parliament ; he guaranteed personal liberty and equality of rights to all his subjects irrespective of race, creed, or origin ; he abolished the censorship of the press ; and dismissed his army of 40,000 spies.

The Turkish revolution was welcomed with cordiality in all the liberal States of Europe and with peculiar effusiveness in Great Britain. The foreign officers of the Macedonian gendarmerie were recalled ; the International Commission of Finance was discharged. But the brightness of a too brilliant dawn soon faded. The new grand vizier, Kiamil Pasha, was compelled to resign in February. His successor, Hilmi Pasha, the late inspector-general in Macedonia, was replaced in April by Tewfik Pasha. The army, meanwhile, gave signs of grave dissatisfaction. There was unrest, too, in Arabia and Anatolia. The Young Turks soon learnt that the introduction of a European system into an empire essentially Asiatic is less easily accomplished than they had supposed. The Sultan, Abdul Hamid, was even more acutely conscious of this truth, and on

April 13 he felt himself strong enough to effect, with the aid of the army, a counter-revolution.

But his triumph was short-lived. The Young Turkish troops, commanded by Mahmud Shevket, marched from Salonica, and on April 24 entered and occupied Constantinople. On the 27th Abdul Hamid was formally deposed by a unanimous vote of the Turkish National Assembly, and his younger brother was proclaimed Sultan in his room, under the title of Mohammed V. On the 28th the ex-Sultan was deported to Salonica, and interned there. Hilmi Pasha was reappointed grand vizier; the new Sultan expressed his conviction that 'the safety and happiness of the country depend on the constant and serious application of the constitutional régime which is in conformity with the sacred law as with the principles of civilization'.

A new era appeared to have dawned for the Ottoman Empire. It soon became clear, however, that the Young Turks, so far from turning their backs upon the traditions of their race, were Osmanlis first and reformers afterwards. Abdul Hamid's brief triumph had been marked characteristically by fresh massacres of Armenians at Adana and in other parts of Anatolia. His deposition, so far from staying the hands of the assassins, tended rather to strengthen them. An eyewitness of the massacres has declared that in the last fortnight of April, 1909, 30,000 Christians perished in Asia Minor, and that the murderers went unpunished under the new régime.[1]

In Macedonia, as in Asia Minor, the lot of the Christians, so far from being ameliorated by the reformers, became steadily worse. There, as elsewhere, the keynote of Young Turk policy was unrelenting 'Turkification'. The same principle inspired their ecclesiastical policy. At the name of Allah

[1] Gibbons, *op. cit.*, pp. 178 sq.

every knee was to bow. The obeisance was to be enforced by every form of outrage and persecution. 'They treat us', said the Greek Patriarch, 'like dogs. Never under Abdul Hamid or any Sultan have my people suffered as they are suffering now. But we are too strong for them. We refuse to be exterminated.' [1] But the power of the Young Turks was unequal to their ambition ; their deeds, though as brutal as might be wherever they were strong, were less potent than their words. Their denunciation of tyranny was all sound and fury ; in effect it signified nothing. Their promises of reform were empty.

Still, one possibility remained. Enver Pasha and his crew were bent on making Turkey a nation of Turks. One virtue at least the Turk was supposed to possess. He was believed to be a born fighter. True, most of his battles had been won by the Moslemized Christians. But they had fought in the Ottoman name. If the Young Turks could effect but one reform, a real reorganization of the army, their régime might still justify itself.

It was not long before the army was brought to the test. On September 29, 1911, Italy declared war upon the Ottoman Empire. That war opened the latest chapter in the history of the Eastern Question.

For further reference : the *Annual Register*, 1907–10 ; *The Round Table*, 1911 onwards ; *Nationalism and War in the Near East*, by a Diplomatist (Oxford, 1915) ; Sir C. Eliot (as before) ; C. R. Buxton, *Turkey in Revolution*, 1 vol. (London, 1909) ; Sir W. R. Ramsay, *Revolution in Turkey and Constantinople* (London, 1909); H. A. Gibbons, *New Map of Europe* (London, 1915) ; Victor Bérard, *La Révolution Turque* (Paris, 1909), *La Turquie et l'Hellénisme contemporain* (6th ed., Paris, 1911), *La Macédoine* (Paris, 1900), *Pro Macedonia* (Paris, 1904) ; H. N. Brailsford, *Macedonia, its Races and their Future* (London, 1906) ; L. Villari (ed. and others), *The Balkan Question* (London, 1904) ; E. F. Knight, *The Awakening of Turkey* (London,

[1] Gibbons, *op. cit.*, p. 189.

1909); René Pinon, *L'Europe et la Jeune Turquie* (1911); Virginio Gayda, *Modern Austria* (Eng. trans., London, 1915); Louis Léger, *L'Autriche-Hongrie* (Paris, 1879); B. Auerbach, *Les Races et les Nationalités en Autriche-Hongrie* (Paris); R. Charmatz, *Oesterreichs innere Geschichte, 1848–1909*, 2 vols. (Teubner); A. Chéradame, *L'Allemagne, la France, et la question d'Autriche* (Paris), *L'Europe et la question d'Autriche au seuil du XXme siècle* (Paris); G. Drage, *Austria-Hungary*; D. A. Fournier, *Wie wir zu Bosnien kamen* (Vienna, 1909); ' Scotus Viator ' (R. W. Seton-Watson), *The Future of Austria-Hungary* (London, 1907), *Racial Problems in Hungary* (1908); R. W. Seton-Watson, *The Southern Slav Question and the Hapsburg Monarchy* (1911); H. W. Steed, *The Hapsburg Monarchy* (London, 1913).

16

The Balkan League and the Balkan Wars

' The problem now is not how to keep the Turkish Empire permanently in being . . . but how to minimize the shock of its fall, and what to substitute for it.'—Viscount Bryce.

' The War of the Coalition can claim to have been both progressive and epoch-making. The succeeding War of Partition was rather predatory and ended no epoch, though possibly it may have begun one : it is interesting not as a settlement but as a symptom '.—' Diplomatist ', *Nationalism and War in the Near East.*

' The Turks, who have always been strangers in Europe, have shown conspicuous inability to comply with the elementary requirements of European civilization, and have at last failed to maintain that military efficiency which has, from the days when they crossed the Bosphorus, been the sole mainstay of their power and position.'—Lord Cromer.

In October, 1909, the diplomatic world was startled to learn that the Tsar Nicholas was about to pay a ceremonial visit to the King of Italy. The incident proved to be of considerable significance ; it was the prologue to the last act in the drama of the Near East. At that moment Russia was smarting under the humiliation imposed upon her by the Paladin of Potsdam, who in his shining armour stood forth ostentatiously by the side of Austria and Hungary. The poverty not the will of Russia had consented to the annexation of Bosnia and the Herzegovina by Austria-Hungary. Italy, too, regarded with increasing uneasiness the advance of the Habsburgs in the Balkans. Consequently, after 1909, Italy and Russia tended to draw together.

And not only Russia and Italy. Bismarck's constant, and on the whole successful, endeavour was to throw apples of discord among the members of the European family. Thus in 1881 he had tossed Tunis to France, not from any love of France, but because, as he well knew, Italy had long had a reversionary interest in that country. But in 1896 France and Italy concluded a convention which finally closed a long series of disputes arising out of the French protectorate in Tunis.[1]

The same thing was happening in regard to Anglo-French relations. Just as Bismarck had encouraged French pretensions in Tunis in order to keep Italy and France at arm's length, so he had for similar reasons smiled upon the British occupation of Egypt. For more than twenty years that occupation formed the principal obstacle to any cordial understanding between France and Great Britain. But the growing menace of German diplomacy at last brought the two countries together, and in 1904 an Anglo-French agreement was concluded. This agreement finally composed all differences in the Mediterranean : England was to have a free hand in Egypt and France in Morocco.

Tripoli

France had been in undisputed possession of Algeria ever since 1844. Consequently, of all the dominions of the Ottoman Empire on the African shore of the Mediterranean Tripoli alone remained. As far back as 1901 France, in return for

---

[1] Cf. Albin, *Grands Traités politiques*, p. 290.

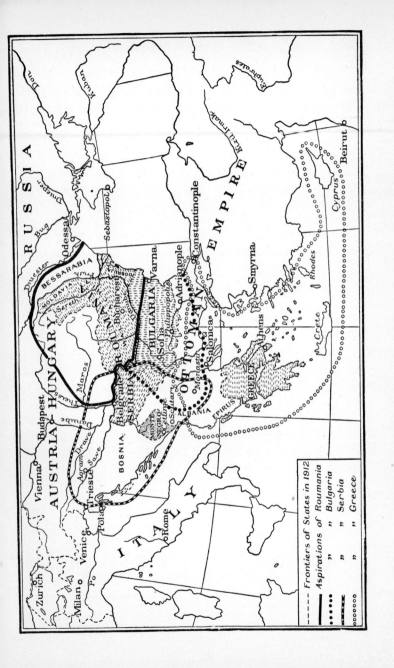

the concessions in regard to Tunis, had agreed to give Italy a free hand in Tripoli; and, from that time onwards, there was a general understanding among the European Chancelleries that when the final liquidation of the Ottoman estates was effected Tripoli would fall to the share of Italy. Her reversionary rights were tacitly recognized in the Anglo-French agreement of 1904, and again at Algeciras in 1906.

Those rights were now menaced from an unexpected quarter. The Kaiser's visit to Tangier in March, 1905, had resulted chiefly in a strengthening of the Anglo-French alliance; the attempted *coup* at Agadir in July, 1911, had a similar effect. But German intervention in the western Mediterranean was merely for demonstration purposes; to assist her 'national credit'; to indicate to the Western Powers that she could not be treated as a *quantité négligeable*—even in fields relatively remote. But the scientific interest which German geologists and archaeologists had lately developed in Tripoli was otherwise interpreted at Rome; and the descent of the *Panther* upon Agadir convinced Italy that, unless she was prepared to forgo for all time her reversionary interests in Tripoli, the hour for claiming them had struck.

For many years past Italy had pursued a policy of economic and commercial penetration in Tripoli, and had pursued it without any obstruction from the Turks. But there, as elsewhere, the revolution of 1908 profoundly modified the situation. The Young Turks were as much in Tripoli as in Macedonia opposed to Christians. At every turn the Italians found themselves thwarted. It might be merely the Moslem fanaticism characteristic of Young Turk policy. But the suspicion deepened that between Moslem fanaticism and Teutonic zeal for scientific research there was more than an accidental connexion. Be this as it might, Italy deemed that the time had come for decisive action.

That action fell, nevertheless, as a bolt from the blue. On September 27, 1911, Italy suddenly presented to Turkey an ultimatum demanding the consent of the Porte to an Italian occupation of Tripoli under the sovereignty of the Sultan, and subject to the payment of an annual tribute. A reply was required within forty-eight hours, but already the Italian transports were on their way to Tripoli, and on September 29 war was declared.

The details of the war do not concern this narrative. It must suffice to say that even in Tripoli Italy had no easy task. She occupied the coast towns of Tripoli, Bengazi, and Derna without difficulty, but against the combined resistance of Turks and Arabs she could make little progress in the interior. The Turks, trusting that the situation would be relieved for them by international complications, obstinately refused to make any concessions to Italy. But between her two allies Germany was in a difficult position. She was indignant that one ally should, without permission from Berlin, have ventured to attack the other ally at Constantinople ; but, on the other hand, she had no wish to throw Italy into the arms of the Triple Entente. Italy, however, was determined to wring consent from the Porte, and in the spring of 1912 her navy attacked at several points ; a couple of Turkish warships were sunk off Beirut ; the forts at the entrance to the Dardanelles were bombarded on April 18 ; Rhodes and the Dodecanese Archipelago were occupied in May. To the bombardment of the Dardanelles Turkey retorted by closing the Straits. This proved highly inconvenient to neutrals, and after a month they were reopened. Throughout the summer the war went languidly on, entailing much expense to Italy, and very little either of expense or even inconvenience to the Turks.

In two ways the war was indeed decidedly advantageous to the policy of the Young Turks. On the one hand, ' by reconciling Turk and Arab in a holy war in Africa, the Tripoli campaign healed for a time the running sore in Arabia which had for years drained the resources of the Empire '.[1] On the other, the naval operations of Italy in the Aegean aroused acute friction between the Italians and the Greeks, whose reversionary interests in the islands were at least as strong as those of Italy upon the African littoral. That friction would be likely to increase, and in any case could not be otherwise than advantageous to the Turk.

But suddenly a new danger threatened him. The Tripoli campaign was still dragging its slow length along, and seemed likely to be protracted for years, when the conflagration blazed up to which the Tripoli War had applied the first match. In view of the more immediate danger the Porte at last came to terms with Italy, and the Treaty of Lausanne was hastily signed at Ouchy on October 18, 1912. The Turks were to withdraw from Tripoli ; Italy from the Aegean islands ; the Khalifal authority of the Sultan in Tripoli was to remain intact ; he was to grant an amnesty and a good administration to the islands ; Italy was to assume responsibility for Tripoli's share of the Ottoman debt. The cession of Tripoli was assumed but *sub silentio*. The withdrawal of the Italian troops from the islands was to be subsequent to and consequent upon the withdrawal of the Turkish troops from Africa. Italy has contended that the latter condition has not been fulfilled, and she remains, therefore, in Rhodes and the Dodecanese. Her continued occupation has not injured the Turks, but it has kept out the Greeks.

On the same day that the Treaty of Lausanne was signed Greece declared war upon the Ottoman Empire. This time she was not alone. The miracle had occurred. The Balkan States had combined against the common enemy. The

[1] *Nationalism and War in the Near East*, p. 159.

circumstances which had conduced to this astonishing and unique event demand investigation.

The Balkan League

The idea of a permanent alliance or even a confederation among the Christian States of the Balkans was frequently canvassed after the Treaty of Berlin. But the aggrandizement of Bulgaria in 1885, and the war which ensued between Bulgaria and Serbia, shattered the hope for many years to come. M. Trikoupis, at that time Prime Minister of Greece, made an effort to revive it in 1891, and with that object paid a visit to Belgrade and Sofia. The Serbian statesmen welcomed his advances, but Stambuloff, who was then supreme in Bulgaria, was deeply committed to the Central Powers and through them to the Porte, and frowned upon the project of a Balkan League.

The real obstacle, however, to an entente between the Balkan Powers arose, as the previous chapter has shown, from their conflicting interests in Macedonia. Bulgaria consistently favoured the policy of autonomy, in the not unreasonable expectation that autonomy would prove to be the prelude to the union of the greater part if not the whole of Macedonia with Bulgaria. Neither Serbia nor Greece could entertain an equally capacious ambition, and from the first, therefore, advocated not autonomy but partition.

Each of the three neighbouring States was genuinely concerned for the unhappy condition of its co-nationals in Macedonia, but the bitter rivalry between them prevented anything approaching to cordial co-operation for a general improvement. The Young Turk revolution brought matters to a head. That revolution, as a close and shrewd observer has said, was ' in fact a last effort of the Moslem minority to retain its ascendancy in the face of growing resistance on the part of subject races and impending European intervention '. The revival of the constitution was little more than an ingenious device for appeasing Liberal sentiment abroad while furnishing a pretext for the abrogation of the historic rights of the Christian nationalities at home. That the subject peoples would combine in defence of their rights, and that their reconciliation would react on the kindred States across the frontier, was not foreseen by the inexperienced but self-confident soldiers and politicians who now directed the destinies of the Turkish Empire.[1]

The triumphant success of the Committee of Union and Progress, so far from improving the condition of Macedonia, served only to accentuate its sufferings. The Bulgarians of the kingdom were deeply stirred by them. They saw with indignation and alarm that the Young Turks were bent upon exterminating such Bulgarians as they could not compel to emigrate. M. Shopoff, the Bulgarian consul-general at Salonica, stated in 1910 that the Bulgarian population had in fifteen years been reduced by twenty-five per cent. ; the number of refugees was becoming a serious problem in Bulgaria, while the terrible massacres at Ishtib and Kotchani, the ' murders, pillaging, tortures, and persecutions ' compelled ' the most peaceful Bulgarian statesmen ' to ask themselves ' if all this was not the result of a deliberate plan on the part of the Young Turks to solve the Macedonian and Thracian problem by clearing those two provinces of their Bulgarian and Christian inhabitants '.[2]

[1] *The Balkan League* : a series of articles contributed to *The Times* in June, 1913, by their ' own correspondent in the Balkan Peninsula '. To these admirable articles I desire to make specific acknowledgement of my obligations. No individual did more than the writer of them to bring into being the League which he so brilliantly chronicled.

[2] Gueshoff, *The Balkan League*, p. 8. The reader may be reminded that M. Gueshoff, Prime Minister of Bulgaria in 1912, was educated at the Owens College (now the Victoria University of), Manchester.

Between 1910 and 1912 there were various indications of some improvement in the mutual relations of the Balkan States. In 1910 the Tsar Ferdinand, the shrewdest of all the Balkan diplomatists, paid a visit to Cettinje to take part, together with the Crown Prince of Serbia and the Crown Prince of Greece, in the celebration of King Nicholas's Jubilee. At Easter, 1911, some three hundred students from the University of Sofia received a cordial welcome at Athens. In April of the same year M. Venizelos made a proposal to Bulgaria for a definite alliance, through the intermediation of Mr. J. D. Bourchier, *The Times* correspondent in the Balkan Peninsula. In May the Greek Patriarch and the Bulgarian Exarch so far forgot their secular animosity as to combine in a protest to the Sultan against the persecution of his Christian subjects. In July the Tsar Ferdinand obtained a revision of the Bulgarian constitution, under which the executive was authorized to conclude secret political treaties without communication to the Legislature. In October M. Gueshoff, Prime Minister of Bulgaria, had an exceedingly confidential interview with M. Milanovanič, the Prime Minister of Serbia.[1] In February, 1912, the several heirs apparent of the Balkan States met at Sofia to celebrate the coming of age of Prince Boris, heir to the Tsardom of Bulgaria.

All these things, the social gatherings patent to the world, the political negotiations conducted in profoundest secrecy, pointed in the same direction, and were designed to one end.

A favourable issue was not long delayed. On March 13, 1912, a definite treaty was signed between the kingdoms of Serbia and Bulgaria. This was in itself a marvel of patient diplomacy. Not since 1878 had the relations between the two States been cordial, nor were their interests or their antagonisms

[1] See Gueshoff, *op. cit.*, pp. 15 sq.

identical. To Serbia, Austria-Hungary was the enemy. The little land-locked State, which yet hoped to become the nucleus of a Jugo-Slav Empire, was in necessary antagonism to the Power which had thrust itself into the heart of the Balkans, and which, while heading the Slavs off from access to the Adriatic, itself wanted to push through Slav lands to the Aegean. Bulgaria, on the other hand, had no special reason for enmity against Vienna or Buda-Pesth. The ' unredeemed ' Bulgarians were subjects not of the Emperor Francis Joseph but of the Ottoman Sultan, and while the antagonisms of the two States differed their mutual interests clashed. To Thrace and eastern Macedonia Serbia could of course make no claim. Bulgaria could not dream of acquiring Old Serbia. But there was a considerable intermediate zone in Macedonia to which both could put forward substantial pretensions. The treaty concluded in March, 1912, reflected these conditions.

By that treaty the two States entered into a defensive alliance ; they mutually guaranteed each other's dominions and engaged to take common action if the interests of either were threatened by the attack of a Great Power upon Turkey ; at the same time they defined their respective claims in Macedonia should a partition be effected : Old Serbia and the Sanjak of Novi-Bazar, that is, all the territory north and west of the Shar Mountains, was to go to Serbia, the territory east of the Rhodope Mountains and the river Struma to Bulgaria ; the intermediate regions of Macedonia ' lying between the Shar Mountains and the Rhodope Mountains, the Archipelago, and the Lake of Ochrida ' were, if possible, to be formed into the autonomous province long desired by Bulgaria ; but if such an organization of this territory appeared to the two parties to be impossible it was to be divided into three zones : Bulgaria was to have the region round Ochrida ; Serbia was to get an additional strip in northern Macedonia, while the unassigned residuum was to be subject to the arbitration of the Tsar of Russia.

In order to give the treaty additional solemnity it was signed not only by the ministers but by the sovereigns of the two States, and at the end of April the Tsar notified his acceptance of the difficult function assigned to him under its provisions. A separate military convention was concluded at Varna on May 29;[1] and a further agreement between the general staffs was signed in June. It is noticeable, however, that there was a marked difference of military opinion as to the 'principal theatre of war', the Bulgarian staff pronouncing, as was natural, for the valley of the Maritza, the Serbians for the Vardar valley.

Two months after the signature of the Serbo-Bulgarian Treaty an arrangement was reached between Greece and Bulgaria (May 10, 1912). It differed in one important respect from that concluded between the latter and Serbia. Between Greeks and Bulgarians nothing was said as to the partition of Macedonia. Further, it was expressly provided that if war broke out between Turkey and Greece on the question of the admission of the Cretan deputies to the Greek Parliament, Bulgaria, not being interested in the question, should be bound only to benevolent neutrality.

There was good reason for this proviso. The Cretan difficulty had become acute, and, indeed, threatened to involve the kingdom in revolution. The accession of the Young Turks had only intensified the confusion in regard to the great Greek island. They were by no means disposed to acquiesce in its alienation from the Ottoman Empire. The Greek Cretans were absolutely determined to unite themselves to the kingdom of Greece. The Powers were impartially anxious to prevent

[1] The full texts of all these important treaties will be found in Appendices to Gueshoff, *op. cit.*

the extermination of the Moslem population by the Greeks, or the Greek population by the Turks, but they were even more concerned to prevent this inflammable island from lighting a wider conflagration. As soon as the foreign contingents had left the island (July, 1909) the Cretans hoisted the Greek flag. A month later the Powers returned and lowered it. The hesitation of King George's Government in the face of these events precipitated a military revolt in Athens, and all but led to the overthrow of the dynasty. The revolt of the army in August was followed by the mutiny of the navy at the Piraeus in September, and the condition of Greece appeared to be desperate.

It was saved by the advent of a great statesman. M. Venizelos had already shown his capacity for leadership in Crete when, in February, 1910, he was summoned to Athens to advise the Military League. Having come to Athens to advise the League he remained to advise the king. In October the League overturned the Dragoumis ministry, and King George invited the Cretan statesman to form a Cabinet. M. Venizelos accepted the difficult task, effected a much-needed revision of the constitution, and propounded an extensive programme of domestic reforms.

But the execution of such a programme predicated peace, internal and external, and in addition a certain basis of financial stability and commercial prosperity.

The Young Turks were quite determined that neither condition should be satisfied. They imposed upon Greek commerce a boycott so strict as all but to reduce to ruin that nation of seafarers and traders. A further obstacle to the commercial development of Greece was interposed by the Young Turks when they declined to sanction the linking-up of the Greek railway system with that of Macedonia. These manifestations of the extreme and persistent hostility of the 'New Moslems', combined with their refusal to acquiesce in the alienation of

Crete, at last drove Greece into the 'impossible' alliance with Bulgaria.

The defensive alliance signed in May was followed in September, as in the case of Serbia, by a detailed military convention. Bulgaria was to supply at least 300,000 men to operate in the vilayets of Kossovo, Monastir, and Salonica. If, however, Serbia should come in, Bulgaria was to be 'allowed to use her forces in Thrace'. Greece was to supply at least 120,000 men ; but the real gain to the alliance was of course the adhesion of the Greek fleet, whose 'chief aim will be to secure naval supremacy over the Aegean Sea, thus interrupting all communications by that route between Asia Minor and European Turkey'. How efficiently Greece performed that part of the common task the immediate sequel will show.

For the crisis was now at hand. It was forced generally by the condition of Macedonia, and in particular by the revolt of the Albanians. In no direction had the Young Turks mishandled the affairs of the empire more egregiously than in regard to Albania. It might, indeed, have been expected that a party which set out with the ideal of 'union and progress' would have dealt sympathetically and successfully with this perennial problem. The Albanian factor, like every other in the complex problem of the Near East, is double-edged, external and internal. On the one hand, Albania is an object of desire to Austria-Hungary, to Italy, and to Greece, to say nothing of Serbia ; on the other, the Albanians, though a source of considerable strength to the personnel of the Ottoman Empire, have never shown themselves susceptible of conquest or absorption. They are, indeed, too far lacking in political integration either to conquer or to be conquered. 'A barbarous country', as Caesar observed long ago, 'is less easily conquered than a civil.' The highland tribesmen of Albania have defied, in turn, every would-be conqueror, by reason not of their strength, but by reason of their weakness. It is easier to kill a lion than a jelly-fish.

The almost incredible fatuity of Young Turk policy promised, however, to give to the Albanians a coherence which they had hitherto lacked, and their successful rising in the spring of 1912, still more the spread of the revolt to Macedonia, precipitated, in more ways than one, the Balkan crisis.

To the rising in northern Albania the Young Turks would probably have paid no more heed than had the Old Turks on a dozen similar occasions, but for the intrusion of a novel phenomenon. The fact that the Turkish troops made common cause with the Albanian insurgents compelled the notice of Constantinople. But there was worse to come. In June the troops at Monastir broke out into mutiny, and demanded the overthrow of the Young Turk ministry. In July the strongest man of the party, the man who had suppressed the counter-revolution in April, 1909, Mahmud Shevket Pasha, the minister of war, resigned, and was replaced by one of the strongest opponents of the Young Turk régime, Nazim Pasha. In August Hilmi Pasha followed Shevket into retirement.

Things were, in the meantime, hastening to a crisis in Macedonia. Both Greece and Serbia were becoming seriously alarmed by the unexpected success achieved by the Albanians, who were now openly demanding the cession to them of the entire vilayets of Monastir and Uskub. Unless, therefore, the Balkan League interposed promptly, Greece and Serbia might find the ground cut from under their feet in Macedonia. Bulgaria was less directly interested than her allies in the pretensions put forward by the Albanians, but she was far more concerned than they in the terrible massacre of Macedonian Bulgars at Kotchana and Berana.

On August 14 a great popular demonstration, representative of all parts of the Bulgarian kingdom, was organized at Sofia to protest against the massacres at Kotchana; to demand immediate autonomy for Macedonia and Thrace, or, in default, immediate war against the Porte. Ten days later a congress, representing the various brotherhoods of the Macedonian and Thracian districts, opened its sessions at Sofia. The resolutions of the congress were identical with those of the popular demonstration. In the midst of the excitement aroused by these meetings there arrived from Cettinje a proposal for immediate action. None of the Balkan States was more whole-hearted in the Balkan cause than Montenegro, and none was so eager for a fight. In April an arrangement had been arrived at between her and Bulgaria; the proposal which now reached Sofia was the outcome of it. On August 26 the die was cast; Bulgaria agreed that in October war should be declared.

While the Turks and the Balkan States were mobilizing, the Powers put out all their efforts to maintain the peace. In September the States of the Balkan League appealed to the Powers to join them in demanding an immediate and radical reform in Macedonia: a Christian governor, a local legislature, and a militia recruited exclusively within the province. The Powers urged concession upon the Porte and patience upon the Balkan League. It was futile to expect either. Nothing but overwhelming pressure exerted at Constantinople could at this moment have averted war. Instead of taking that course the Powers presented an ultimatum simultaneously at Sofia, Belgrade, Athens, and Cettinje. In brief, the Powers will insist upon the reforms adumbrated in the Treaty of Berlin; but the Balkan States must not fight; if they do, the Powers will see that they get nothing by it.

This masterpiece of European diplomacy was presented at the Balkan capitals on October 8, 1912. On the same day King Nicholas of Montenegro declared war at Constantinople. The other three States presented their ultimatum on the 14th.

On the 18th the Porte declared war upon Bulgaria and Serbia ; and on the same day Greece declared war upon the Porte.

The War of the Coalition, October–December, 1912.

Then, as M. Gueshoff writes, ' a miracle took place. . . . Within the brief space of one month the Balkan Alliance demolished the Ottoman Empire, four tiny countries with a population of some 10,000,000 souls defeating a great Power whose inhabitants numbered 25,000,000 '. Each of the allies did its part, though the brunt of the fighting fell upon the Bulgarians.

Bulgaria was, however, from the outset in a false position. Its true political objective was Salonica ; its purpose the emancipation of Macedonia. Military considerations compelled it to make Constantinople its objective, and Thrace its campaigning ground. The greater, therefore, its military success, the more certain its political disappointment.

The success of the Bulgarians in the autumn campaign was, indeed, phenomenal. On October 18 a large and finely equipped army crossed the Thracian frontier under General Savoff. Its first impact with the Turks was on the 22nd at Kirk Kilisse, a position of enormous strength to the north-east of Adrianople. After two days' fighting the Turks fled in panic, and Kirk Kilisse was in the hands of their enemies. Then followed a week of hard fighting, known to history as the Battle of Lule Burgas, and at the end of it the Turks were in full retreat on Constantinople. One Bulgarian army was now in front of the Tchataldja lines, another was investing Adrianople. On November 4, after a campaign of less than a fortnight, the Porte appealed to the Powers for mediation. Bulgaria refused to accept it ; but no progress was, thereafter, made either towards Constantinople or towards the taking of Adrianople. Bulgaria had shot its bolt ; it had won an

astonishing victory over the Turks, but politically had already
lost everything which it had set out to attain. On November 19
orders came from Sofia that the attack upon the Tchataldja
lines must be suspended. What did that order import? Was
it the cholera which had broken out in Constantinople, and
which protected the city from attack more effectually than the
Young Turks? Was it pressure from the Powers? And more
particularly from St. Petersburg? We learn from M. Gueshoff
that M. Sazonoff had wired to Sofia on November 9 that
Serbia must not be allowed to seek any territorial acquisitions
on the Adriatic coast [1]; but M. Gueshoff is silent as to any
orders respecting Bulgarian access to the Bosphorus. The
explanation must be sought elsewhere. Before we seek it we
must turn to the achievements of Serbia.

Hardly less astonishing, though on a smaller scale than
the victories of Bulgaria, were the equally rapid victories of
the Serbs. On October 18 King Peter issued a proclamation
to his troops declaring that the object of the Balkan League
was to secure the welfare and liberty of Macedonia, and
promising that Serbia would bring liberty, fraternity, and
equality to the Christian and Moslem Serbs and Albanians
with whom for thirteen centuries Serbia had had a common
existence. Splendidly did the army vindicate King Peter's
words. The Serbian forces, which were about 150,000 strong,
were divided into three armies. One marched into Novi-Bazar,
and, after a week's stiff fighting, cleared the Turks out of
that no man's land. Having done that a portion of this army
was dispatched down the Drin valley into Albania.

A second army occupied Pristina (October 23), while the
third and main army, under the crown prince, made for
Uskub. The Turks barred the way to the ancient capital
of the Serbs by the occupation of Kumanovo, and there on

[1] Gueshoff, *op. cit.*, p. 63.

the 22nd of October the two armies met. Three days of fierce fighting resulted in a complete victory for the Serbs. At last, on that historic field, the stain of Kossovo was wiped out. Patiently, for five hundred years, the Serbs had waited for the hour of revenge; that it would some day come they had never doubted; at last it was achieved. Two days later the Turks evacuated Uskub, and on October 26 the Serbs entered their ancient capital in triumph. Now came the supreme question. Should they press for the Aegean or the Adriatic? Europe had already announced its decision that under no circumstances should Serbia be allowed to retain any part of the Albanian coast. But was the will of diplomacy to prevail against the intoxicating military successes of the Balkan League?

Forty thousand Serbian troops were sent off to Adrianople to encourage their Bulgarian allies to a more vigorous offensive in Thrace, and help was also sent in Greek vessels to the Montenegrins, who were making slow progress against Scutari. Meanwhile the main body of the Serbs flung themselves upon the Turks at Prilep and thrust them back upon Monastir; from Monastir they drove them in utter confusion upon the guns of the advancing Greeks. The capture of Ochrida followed upon that of Monastir.

Serbia, having thus cleared the Sanjak of Novi-Bazar, Old Serbia, and western Macedonia, now turned its attention to Albania, and, with the aid of the Montenegrins, occupied Alessio and Durazzo before the end of November.

On December 3 the belligerents accepted an armistice proposed to them by the Powers, but from this armistice the Greeks were, at the instance of the League, expressly excluded. The League could not afford to permit the activity of the Greek fleet in the Aegean to be, even temporarily, interrupted.

On land the part played by the Greeks, though from their

own standpoint immensely significant, was, in a military sense, relatively small. They fought an engagement at Elassona on October 19, and they occupied Grevena on the 31st and Prevesa on November 3. Their march towards Salonica was not indeed seriously contested by the Turks. Whether the withdrawal of the latter was due, as was at the time widely believed, to the advice tendered at Constantinople by the German ambassador, or whether the Turks were actuated exclusively by military considerations, cannot with certainty be determined. The Turks offered some resistance at Yenidje on November 3, but they were completely routed, and three days later the Greeks entered Salonica.

If the Turks were indeed animated by a desire to estrange the Bulgarians and the Greeks their manœuvre was only executed just in time. For hardly had the Greek troops occupied Salonica when the Bulgarians arrived at the gates. Only after some demur did the Greeks allow their allies to enter the city, and from the outset they made it abundantly clear not only that they had themselves come to Salonica to stay but that they would permit no divided authority in the city which they claimed exclusively as their own. From the outset a Greek governor-general was in command, and the whole administration was in the hands of Greeks. In order still further to emphasize the situation, the King of the Hellenes and his court transferred themselves to Salonica.

Meanwhile, at sea, the Greek fleet had, from the outset of war, established a complete supremacy : practically all the islands, except Cyprus and those which were actually in the occupation of Italy, passed without resistance into Greek hands. But Greece looked beyond the Aegean to the Adriatic. On December 3 the Greek fleet shelled Avlona, where its appearance caused grave concern both to Italy and to Austria-Hungary. Both Powers firmly intimated to Greece that though she might bombard Avlona she would not be permitted to retain it as a naval base.

Austria-Hungary had already made similar representations to Serbia in respect to the northern Albanian ports. It was obvious, therefore, that the forces of European diplomacy were beginning to operate. But the military situation of the Turks was desperate, and when the armistice was concluded on December 3 the Turks remained in possession only of Constantinople, Adrianople, Janina, and the Albanian Scutari. Outside the walls of those four cities they no longer held a foot of ground in Europe.

The centre of interest was now transferred, however, from the Balkans to London. Ten days after the conclusion of the armistice delegates from the belligerent States met in London. Side by side with the conference of delegates sat a second conference composed of the ambassadors accredited to the court of St. James by the five Great Powers. The latter sat continuously under the presidency of the English Foreign Secretary from December, 1912, down to August, 1913.[1] From the outset the negotiations between the representatives of the Ottoman Turk and those of the Balkan allies were exceedingly difficult, and nothing but the tact and patience of Sir Edward Grey, combined with an occasional plain and strong word in season, could have kept the negotiators together so long.

Turkey held out for the retention of the four cities which at the moment represented all that was left of the Ottoman Empire in Europe : Constantinople, Adrianople, Scutari, and Janina. As to the first there was no dispute ; the main obstacle to peace was presented by the question of Adrianople

[1] The reasons for this arrangement and the course of negotiations were disclosed to the House of Commons by Sir Edward Grey on August 12, 1913, in a speech of great historic importance.—Hansard, vol. lvi, p. 2283.

and Thrace. A secondary difficulty arose from the claim put in by Roumania to a readjustment of the boundaries of the Dobrudja as compensation for her neutrality. By January 22, 1913, both difficulties had been more or less overcome, and Turkey had agreed to accept as the boundary between herself and Bulgaria a line drawn from Midia on the Black Sea to Enos at the mouth of the Maritza on the Aegean, thus surrendering Adrianople.

But Europe was reckoning without the Young Turks. On January 23 Enver Bey, at the head of a military deputation, burst into the chamber where the Council was sitting in Constantinople, denounced the proposal to surrender Adrianople, insisted on the resignation of the grand vizier, Kiamil Pasha, and shot Nazim Pasha the Turkish commander-in-chief.

Enver's *coup d'état* brought the London negotiations to an abrupt conclusion, and on February 1 the Conference broke up. Mahmud Shevket Pasha, the hero of 1909, replaced Kiamil as grand vizier ; but the Young Turks proved themselves quite incapable of redeeming the military situation. It was indeed beyond redemption.

The armistice was denounced by the allies on January 29, and on February 4 the Bulgarians resumed the attack upon Adrianople. Not, however, until March 26 did the great fortress fall, and the Bulgarians had to share the credit of taking it with the Serbians. Meanwhile the Greeks had won a brilliant and resounding victory. On March 6 the great fortress of Janina, the lair of the ' Lion ' and hitherto deemed impregnable, fell to their assault ; the Turkish garrison, 33,000 strong, became prisoners of war, and 200 guns were taken by the victors. The completeness of the Greek victory did not, however, make for harmony among the allies, and it was of sinister import that the day which witnessed the entry of the Greeks into Janina was marked by an encounter of desperate and sanguinary character between Greek and Bulgarian troops near Salonica.

Adrianople and Janina gone, there remained to the Turks, outside the walls of Constantinople, nothing but Scutari in Albania. Already (March 2) the Porte had made a formal request to the Powers for mediation. On the 16th the Balkan League accepted ' in principle ' the proposed mediation of the Powers, but stipulated for the cession of Scutari and all the Aegean islands as well as the payment of an indemnity.

Scutari was indeed the key of the diplomatic situation. Montenegro, the tiny State on whose behalf Mr. Gladstone had evoked so much passionate sympathy in England, was determined to take Scutari whatever the decision of the European Powers. The latter had indeed decided, as far back as December, 1912, that Scutari must remain in the hands of Albania. The latter was to be an autonomous State under a prince selected by the Great Powers, assisted by an international commission of control and a gendarmerie under the command of officers drawn from one of the smaller neutral States.

Whence came this interest in the affairs of Albania ? On the part of Austria and Italy it was no new thing. An autonomous Albania was an essential feature of Count Aerenthal's Balkan policy, and upon this point Austria-Hungary was supported by Italy and Russia. Italy's motives are obvious and have been already explained ; those of Russia are more obscure.

There was, however, another Power supremely interested, though in a different way, in the future of Albania. Nothing which concerned the future position of Austria-Hungary on the Adriatic could be a matter of indifference to Berlin. But Germany had a further interest in the matter. If the argument of the preceding chapter be accepted as sound, little pains are needed to explain the action of Germany. The Young Turk revolution of 1908 had threatened to dissipate the carefully garnered influence of Germany at Constantinople. That danger had, however, been skilfully overcome. Abdul Hamid himself had not been more esteemed at Berlin than was now Enver Bey. Far more serious, however, was the set-back to German ambitions threatened by the formation of the Balkan League. Still more by its rapid and astonishing victories in the autumn of 1912.

Hardly had the League entered upon the path of victory when Serbia received a solemn warning that she would not be permitted to retain any ports upon the Adriatic. This was a cruel blow to her natural ambitions ; but it was something more. It was a diplomatic move of Machiavellian subtlety and skill. If Serbia could be effectually headed off from the Adriatic ; if the eastern boundaries of an autonomous Albania could be drawn on sufficiently generous lines, Serbia would not only be deprived of some of the accessions contemplated in her partition treaty with Bulgaria (March, 1912),[1] but would be compelled to seek access to the sea on the shores of the Aegean instead of the Adriatic. A conflict of interests between Serbia and Bulgaria would almost certainly ensue in Macedonia ; conflict between Serbia and Greece was not improbable. Thus would the solidarity of the Balkan League, by far the most formidable obstacle which had ever intervened between Mitteleuropa and the Mediterranean, be effectively broken. How far this motive did consciously inspire the policy of Germany and Austria-Hungary at this momentous crisis it is not yet possible to say with certainty ; but the subsequent course of events has rendered the inference almost irresistible. In the light of those events, the words of Sir Edward Grey on August 12, 1913, his congratulations upon the achievement of an autonomous Albania, have a ring either of irony or of innocence.

[1] *Supra*, p. 446.

But to return to Scutari. With or without the leave of the Powers Montenegro was determined to have it, and on February 6, 1912, the town was attacked with a force of 50,000 men, of whom Serbia contributed 12,000–14,000. But Scutari resisted every assault and inflicted heavy losses upon its assailants. On March 24 the Montenegrins so far yielded to the representations of the Powers as to allow the civil population to leave the town, but as for the possession of the town and the adjoining territory that was a matter between Montenegro and the Porte, with which the Powers had no right to interfere.

The Powers, however, were not to be denied. On April 4 an international squadron appeared off Antivari and proceeded to blockade the Montenegrin coast between Antivari and the Drin river. Still Montenegro maintained its defiance, and at last, after severe fighting, Scutari was starved into surrender (April 22). The Turkish garrison, under Essad Pasha, was allowed to march out with all the honours of war and to take with them their arms and stores, and on April 26 Prince Danilo, Crown Prince of Montenegro, entered the town in triumph. But his triumph was brief. The Powers insisted that the town should be surrendered to them ; King Nicholas at last yielded, and Scutari was taken over by an international force landed from the warships. The pressure thus put upon Montenegro in the interests of an autonomous Albania had an ugly appearance at the time, and subsequent events did not tend to render it less unattractive. To these events we shall refer presently. Attention must for the moment be concentrated upon Constantinople.

A few days before the fall of Scutari an armistice was concluded between Turkey and the Balkan League, and the next day (April 21) the League agreed to accept unconditionally the mediation of the Powers, but reserved the right to discuss with the Powers the questions as to the frontiers of Thrace and Albania, and the future of the Aegean islands. Negotiations were accordingly reopened in London on May 20, and on the 30th the Treaty of London was signed. Everything beyond the Enos-Midia line and the island of Crete was ceded by the Porte to the Balkan allies, while the question of Albania and of the islands was left in the hands of the Powers.

The European Concert congratulated itself upon a remarkable achievement : the problem which for centuries had confronted Europe had been solved; the clouds which had threatened the peace of Europe had been dissipated; the end of the Ottoman Empire, long foreseen and long dreaded as the certain prelude to Armageddon, had come, and come in the best possible way; young nations of high promise had been brought to the birth; the older nations were united, as never before, in bonds of amity and mutual goodwill. Such was the jubilant tone of contemporary criticism.

Yet in the midst of jubilation there sounded notes of warning and of alarm. Nor were they, unfortunately, without justification. Already ominous signs of profound disagreement between the victors as to the disposal of the spoils were apparent. As to that, nothing whatever had been said in the Treaty of London. Whether the temper which already prevailed at Sofia, Belgrade, and Athens would have permitted interference is very doubtful : the Treaty of London did not attempt it. In effect the belauded treaty had done nothing but affix the common seal of Europe to a deed for the winding-up of the affairs of the Ottoman Empire in Europe. How the assets were to be distributed among the creditors did not concern the official receivers. Yet here lay the real crux of the situation.

The problem was in fact intensified by the sudden collapse of the Ottoman Empire and the unexpected success achieved by each of the allies. The Balkan League might have held together if it had been compelled to fight rather harder for its victory. Greece and Serbia in particular were intoxicated by a success far greater than they could have dared to anticipate. Bulgaria's success had been not less emphatic ; but it had been achieved at greater cost, and in the wrong direction. The Bulgarians were undisputed masters of Thrace ; but it was not for Thrace they had gone to war. The Greeks were in Salonica ; the Serbs in Uskub and Monastir. For the victorious and war-worn Bulgarians the situation was, therefore, peculiarly exasperating.

Bulgaria's exasperation was Germany's opportunity. To fan the fires of Bulgarian jealousy against her allies was not difficult, but Germany spared no effort in the performance of this sinister task. The immediate sequel will demonstrate the measure of her success. Bulgaria and Greece had appointed a joint commission to delimit their frontiers in Macedonia on April 7; it broke up without reaching an agreement on May 9. Roumania, too, was tugging at Bulgaria in regard to a rectification of the frontiers of the Dobrudja. On May 7 an agreement was signed by which Bulgaria assented to the cession of Silistria and its fortifications, together with a strip of the Dobrudja. Notwithstanding this agreement a military convention was concluded between Serbia, Greece, and Roumania, and on May 28 Serbia demanded that the treaty of partition concluded between herself and Bulgaria in March, 1912, should be so amended as to compensate her for the loss of territory due to the formation of an autonomous Albania. The demand was not in itself unreasonable. It was impossible to deny that the formation of an autonomous Albania had profoundly modified the situation, and had modified it to the detriment of Serbia in a way which had not been foreseen by either party to the treaty of March, 1912. On the other hand the demand was peculiarly irritating to Bulgaria, who found herself bowed out of Macedonia by Greece.

The situation was highly critical when, on June 8, the Tsar of Russia offered his services as arbitrator. Taking advantage of the position assigned to and accepted by him in the treaty of March, 1912, the Tsar appealed to the Kings of Serbia and Bulgaria not to 'dim the glory they had earned in common' by a fratricidal war, but to turn to Russia for the settlement of their differences; and, at the same time, he solemnly warned them that 'the State which begins war would be held responsible before the Slav cause', and he reserved to himself 'all liberty as to the attitude which Russia will adopt in regard to the results of such a criminal struggle'.

Serbia accepted the Tsar's offer; but Bulgaria, though not actually declining it, made various conditions; attributed all the blame for the dispute to Serbia, and reminded the Tsar that Russia had long ago acknowledged the right of Bulgaria to protect the Bulgarians of Macedonia.

The War of Partition

Events were plainly hurrying to a catastrophe. Greece had made up its mind to fight Bulgaria, if necessary, for Salonica; Serbia demanded access to the Aegean. 'Bulgaria is washed by two seas and grudges Serbia a single port.' So ran the order of the day issued at Belgrade on July 1. Meanwhile, on June 2, Greece and Serbia concluded an offensive and defensive alliance against Bulgaria for ten years. Serbia was to be allowed to retain Monastir. The Greeks did not like the surrender of a town which they regarded (as did Bulgaria) as their own in reversion, but Venizelos persuaded them to the sacrifice, on the ground that unless they made it they might lose Salonica. Bulgaria, in order to detach Greece from Serbia, offered her the guarantee of Salonica, but M. Venizelos had already given his word to Serbia, and he was not prepared to break it.

On the night of June 29 the rupture occurred. Acting, according to M. Gueshoff,[1] on an order from head-quarters, the Bulgarians attacked their Serbian allies. M. Gueshoff himself describes it as a 'criminal act', but declares that the military authorities were solely responsible for it; that the Cabinet was ignorant that the order had been issued, and that as soon as they learnt of it they begged the Tsar to intervene. We cannot yet test the truth of this statement, but M. Gueshoff is a man of honour, and it is notorious that the army was in a warlike mood. But wherever the fault lay the allies were now at each other's throats; the war of partition had begun.

It lasted only a month; but the record of that month is full both of horror and of interest. The Serbs and Greeks, attacking in turn with great ferocity, drove the Bulgarians before them. Serbia wiped out the stain of Slivnitza; the Greeks, who had not had any real chance for the display of military qualities in the earlier war, more than redeemed the honour tarnished in 1897. In the course of their retreat the Bulgarians inflicted hideous cruelties upon the Greek population of Macedonia; the Greeks, in their advance, retaliated in kind. But the Bulgarians had not only to face Serbs and Greeks. On July 9 Roumania intervened, seized Silistria, and marched on Sofia. Bulgaria could offer no resistance and wisely bowed to the inevitable. Three days later (July 12) the Turks came in, recaptured Adrianople (July 20), and marched towards Tirnovo. Bulgaria had the effrontery to appeal to the Powers against the infraction of the Treaty of London; King Carol of Roumania urged his allies to stay their hands; on July 31 an armistice was concluded, and on August 10 peace was signed at Bucharest.

[1] Gueshoff, *op. cit.*, p. 92.

Bulgaria, the aggressor, was beaten to the earth and could not hope for mercy. By the Treaty of Bucharest she lost to Roumania a large strip of the Dobrudja, including the important fortress of Silistria; she lost also the greater part of Macedonia which she would almost certainly have received under the Tsar's award, and had to content herself with a narrow strip giving access to the Aegean at the inferior port of Dedeagatch. Serbia obtained central Macedonia, including Ochrida and Monastir, Kossovo, and the eastern half of Novi-Bazar; the western half going to Montenegro. Greece obtained Epirus, southern Macedonia, Salonica, and the seaboard as far east as the Mesta, thus including Kavala.

But the cup of Bulgaria's humiliation was not yet full. She had still to settle with the Porte, and peace was not actually signed between them until September 29. The quarrel between the allies put the Ottoman Empire on its feet again. The Turks were indeed restricted to the Enos-Midia line, but lines do not always run straight even in Thrace, and the new line was so drawn as to leave the Ottoman Empire in possession of Adrianople, Demotica, and Kirk Kilisse. Having been compelled to surrender a large part of Macedonia to her allies, Bulgaria now lost Thrace as well. Even the control of the railway leading to her poor acquisition on the Aegean was denied to her.[1] The terms dictated by the Porte were hard, and Bulgaria made an attempt by an appeal to the Powers to evade payment of the bill she had run up. The attempt though natural was futile. The Powers did go so far as to present a joint note to the Porte, urging the fulfilment of the Treaty of London, but the Sultan was well aware that the Powers would never employ force to compel Turkey to satisfy a defeated and discredited Bulgaria, and the joint note was ignored.

---

[1] Gibbons, *op. cit.*, p. 325.

H h

For the loss of Adrianople, Demotica, and Kirk Kilisse, therefore, Bulgaria blamed the Powers in general and England in particular. It was believed at Sofia that England was induced to consent to a variation of the Enos-Midia line by Turkish promises in regard to the Bagdad railway. There was no ground for the suspicion, but it was one of several factors which influenced the decision of Bulgaria in 1915.

We may now briefly summarize the results of the two Balkan Wars. The two wars were estimated to have cost, in money, about £245,000,000, and in killed and wounded, 348,000. The heaviest loss in both categories fell upon Bulgaria, who sacrificed 140,000 men and spent £90,000,000 ; the Turks 100,000 men and £80,000,000 ; the Serbians 70,000 men and £50,000,000 ; while the Greeks, whose gains were by far the most conspicuous, acquired them at the relatively trifling cost of 30,000 men and £25,000,000.

In territory and population Turkey was the only loser. Before the war her European population was estimated to be 6,130,200, and her area 65,350 square miles. Of population she lost 4,239,200, and she was left with only 10,882 square miles of territory. Greece was the largest gainer, increasing her population from 2,666,000 to 4,363,000, and her area from 25,014 to 41,933 square miles. Serbia increased her population from just under three millions to four and a half, and nearly doubled her territory, increasing it from 18,650 to 33,891 square miles. Roumania added 286,000 to a population which was and is the largest in the Balkans, now amounting to about seven and a half millions, and gained 2,687 square miles of territory, entirely, of course, at the expense of Bulgaria. The net gains of Bulgaria were only 125,490 in population and 9,663 square miles ; while Montenegro raised her population from 250,000 to 480,000, and her area from 3,474 to 5,603 square miles.[1]

[1] Robertson and Bartholomew, *Historical Atlas*, p. 24.

The significance of the changes effected in the map of 'Turkey in Europe' cannot, however, be measured solely by statistics.

The settlement effected in the Treaty of Bucharest was neither satisfactory nor complete. Of the recent belligerents Greece had most cause for satisfaction. To the north-east her territorial gains were not only enormous in extent, but of the highest commercial and strategic importance. The acquisition of Salonica was in itself a veritable triumph for the Greek cause, and Greece would have been well advised to be content with it. The insistence upon Kavala, whatever her ethnographic claims may have been, is now recognized as a political blunder. To have conceded Kavala to Bulgaria would have gone some way towards satisfying the legitimate claims of the latter in Macedonia, without in any way imperilling the position of Greece. If Greece had followed the sage advice of Venizelos the concession would have been made. To her undoing she preferred to support the hot-headed demands of the soldiers and the king. On the north-west, Greece acquired the greater part of Epirus, including the great fortress of Janina, but she was still unsatisfied. For many months she continued to urge her claims to portions of southern Albania, assigned by the Powers to the new autonomous State. But to press them would have brought Greece into conflict with Italy. 'Italy', said the Marquis di San Giuliano, 'will even go to the length of war to prevent Greece occupying Valona ; on this point her decision is irrevocable.' [1] On that side Greece, therefore, remained unsatisfied. There remained the question of the islands. Of these, incomparably the most important was, of course, Crete. Crete was definitively assigned to Greece, and on December 14, 1913, it was formally taken over by King Constantine, accompanied by the Crown

[1] Kerofilas, *Venizelos*, p. 155.

Prince and the Prime Minister, M. Venizelos. Thus was one long chapter closed. The question as to the rest of the islands was reserved to the Powers, who ultimately awarded to Greece all the islands of which the Porte could dispose, except Imbros and Tenedos, which were regarded as essential for the safeguarding of the entrance to the Dardanelles, and were, therefore, left to Turkey. The Sporades, including Rhodes, remained in the occupation of Italy. Greece, therefore, had reason for profound satisfaction. Not that even for her the settlement was complete. Some 300,000 Greeks are said to remain under Bulgarian rule in Thrace and eastern Macedonia, while in the Ottoman Empire—mainly, of course, on the Asiatic side of the Straits—Greece still claims some 3,000,000 ' unredeemed ' co-nationals. But no settlement can achieve ethnographic completeness, least of all one which is concerned with the Balkans, and Greece had little cause to quarrel with that of 1913.

Nor had Roumania. In proportion to her sacrifices her gains were considerable, but for the satisfaction of her larger claims the Balkan Wars afforded no opportunity. The ' unredeemed ' Roumanians are the subjects either of Austria-Hungary or of Russia. Transylvania, the Bukovina, and Bessarabia are the provinces to which, in any large settlement on ethnographic lines, Roumania will be able to prefer a strong claim. But the time is not yet.

Of Bulgaria's position in 1913 it is not, at the moment,[1] easy to write with detachment and impartiality. Bulgaria is at present fighting on the side of the enemies of Great Britain. Whether she would be found in those ranks if the diplomacy of the Quadruple Entente, and in particular of England, had been more skilful, is a question which it is not, at the moment, possible to answer. Wherever the fault may

[1] 1916.

lie Bulgaria is to-day in the enemy camp. Moreover, the misfortunes of Bulgaria in 1913 were largely of her own making, not the less so if her shrewd German king was pushed on to the destruction of his country by subtle suggestions from Vienna and Berlin. When the Treaty of London was signed in May fate seemed to hold for Bulgaria the promise of a brilliant future. Despite the secular hostility of the Greeks and the rivalry of the Latins, Bulgaria was then first favourite for the hegemony of the Balkans. The Bulgarians lacked some of the cultural qualifications of their neighbours ; they were the latest comers into Balkan society, but they had given proof of a virile and progressive temper and were advancing rapidly in the arts of both peace and war. Then suddenly, owing, if not solely to their own intemperate folly, then to their inability to resist subtle temptation or to restrain the impatience of their co-nationals, they flung away in a short month the great position secured to them by the patient labours of a generation. Had they but been able to resist provocation and to await the award of the Russian Tsar, the greater part of central as well as eastern Macedonia must have fallen to them. As it was, they got an area relatively circumscribed, with a wretched coast-line bounded by the Mesta, and in Dedeagatch a miserable apology for an Aegean port ; above all they lost the coveted districts of Ochrida and Monastir. The impartial judgement of history will probably incline to the view that in defining so narrowly the share of Bulgaria, Greece and Serbia alike showed short-sightedness and parsimony. Even on the admission of Philhellenists Greece blundered badly in pressing her claims against Bulgaria so far. The latter ought at least to have been allowed a wider outlet on the Aegean littoral with Kavala as a port. Nothing less could reconcile Bulgaria to the retention of Salonica by Greece.

Serbia, too, showed herself lacking in prudent generosity.

But while Greece was without excuse Serbia was not. What was the Serbian case ? It may be stated in the words of the general order issued by King Peter to his troops on the eve of the second war (July 1, 1913). 'The Bulgarians, our allies of yesterday, with whom we fought side by side, whom as true brothers we helped with all our heart, watering their Adrianople with our blood, will not let us take the Macedonian districts that we won at the price of such sacrifices. Bulgaria doubled her territory in our common warfare, and will not let Serbia have land not half the size, neither the birthplace of our hero king, Marco, nor Monastir, where you covered yourself with glory and pursued the last Turkish troops sent against you. Bulgaria is washed by two seas, and grudges Serbia a single port. Serbia and her makers—the Serbian army— cannot and must not permit this.' [1]

The gains of Serbia were, as we have seen, very considerable. The division of Novi-Bazar between herself and Montenegro brought her into immediate contact with the Southern Slavs of the Black Mountains, while the acquisition of Old Serbia and central Macedonia carried her territory southwards towards the Aegean. But Serbia's crucial problem was not solved. She was still a land-locked country ; deprived by the subtle diplomacy of the German Powers of her natural access to the Aegean, and pushed by them into immediate conflict with the Bulgarians, perhaps into ultimate conflict with Greece. Disappointed of her dearest ambition, flushed with victory, duped by interested advice, Serbia can hardly be blamed for having inflicted humiliation upon Bulgaria, and for having yielded to the temptation of unexpected territorial acquisitions.

Montenegro shared both the success and the disappointment of her kinsmen, now for the first time her neighbours.

[1] Gueshoff, *op. cit.*, p. 102.

To Scutari Montenegro could advance no claims consistent with the principles either of nationality or of ecclesiastical affinity. But King Nicholas's disappointment at being deprived of it was acute, and was hardly compensated by the acquisition of the western half of Novi-Bazar. His position as regards seaboard was less desperate than that of Serbia, but he too had an account to settle with the European Concert.

To have kept the harmony of that Concert unbroken was a very remarkable achievement, and the credit of it belongs primarily to the English Foreign Secretary. Whether the harmony was worth the trouble needed to preserve it is an open question. There are those who would have preferred to see it broken, if necessary, at the moment when the German Powers vetoed the access of the Serbs to the Adriatic. It must not, however, be forgotten that this masterpiece of German diplomacy could hardly have been achieved had it not appeared to coincide with the dominant dogma of English policy in the Near East, the principle of nationality. Macedonian autonomy had so long been the watchword of a group of English politicians and publicists that little pains were needed to excite them to enthusiasm on behalf of an autonomous Albania.

Macedonia, as we have seen, was a hard nut to crack. Albania was, in a sense, even harder. That the idea of autonomy was seductive is undeniable. Such a solution offered obvious advantages. It might stifle the incipient pretensions of Italy and Austria-Hungary; it might arrest the inconvenient claims of Greece upon ' northern Epirus '; it might interpose a powerful barrier between the Southern Slavs and the Adriatic; it might, above all, repair the havoc which the formation of the Balkan alliance had wrought in German plans in regard to the Near East. Nor was it the least of its advantages that it could be commended, without excessive explanation of details, by democratic ministers to the progressive democracies of Western Europe.

Of the conditions which really prevailed in Albania little was or is accurately known. But it was decreed that it should be autonomous, and on November 23 Prince William of Wied, a German prince, a Prussian soldier, a nephew of the Queen of Roumania, was selected for the difficult task of ruling over the wild highlanders of Albania. On March 7, 1914, he arrived at Durazzo, where he was welcomed by Essad Pasha, the defender of Scutari, and himself an aspirant to the crown. Prince William of Wied never had a chance of making good in his new principality. The ambitious disloyalty of Essad Pasha; the turbulence of the Albanian tribesmen, among whom there was entire lack of coherence or of unity; the intrigues of more than one interested Power, rendered his position from the first impossible. The prince and his family were compelled to take refuge temporarily on an Italian warship on May 24, and in September they left the country. The government then fell into the hands of a son of the ex-Sultan Abdul Hamid, Bushan Eddin Effendi, who appointed Essad Pasha grand vizier and commander-in-chief. When the European War broke out no central authority existed in Albania. The authority of Essad Pasha was recognized at Durazzo; the Greeks took possession of southern Albania or northern Epirus; the Italians promptly occupied Valona. For the rest there were as many rulers in Albania as there are tribes.

Besides Albania two other questions were left outstanding after the Peace of Bucharest. The settlement of the Aegean islands has already been described. That of Armenia demands a few words. If 'autonomy' be a word to conjure with in regard to Albania, why not also in regard to Armenia? But the former has at least one advantage over the latter. Albania exists as a geographical entity; Armenia does not. Nor is there, as Mr. Hogarth has pointed out, any 'geographical unit of the Ottoman area in which Armenians are the majority. If they cluster more thickly in the vilayets of Angora, Sivas, Erzeroum, Kharput, and Van, i. e. in easternmost Asia Minor, than elsewhere, . . . they are consistently a minority in any large administrative district'.[1] Where, then, as he pertinently asks, is it possible to constitute an autonomous Armenia ? The question remains unanswered. In February, 1914, the Porte agreed to admit to the Ottoman Parliament seventy Armenian deputies, who should be nominated by the Armenian Patriarch, and to carry out various administrative and judicial reforms in the Anatolian vilayets inhabited largely by Armenians. But the outbreak of the European War afforded the Ottoman Government a chance of solving a secular problem by other and more congenial methods. Massacres of Armenian Christians have been frequent in the past ; but the Turks have been obliged to stay their hands by the intervention of the Powers. That interference was no longer to be feared. An unprecedented opportunity presented itself to the Turks. Of that opportunity they are believed to have made full use. A policy of extermination was deliberately adopted, and has been consistently pursued. It is at least simpler than autonomy.

For the conclusion of peace at Bucharest one Power in Europe took special credit to itself. No sooner was it signed than the Emperor William telegraphed to his cousin, King Carol of Roumania, his hearty congratulations upon the successful issue of his 'wise and truly statesmanlike policy'. 'I rejoice', he added, ' at our mutual co-operation in the cause of peace.' Shortly afterwards King Constantine of Greece received at Potsdam, from the emperor's own hands, the bâton of a Field-Marshal in the Prussian army.

[1] *The Balkans*, p. 384.

If the Kaiser had been active in the cause of peace, his august ally at Vienna had done his utmost to enlarge the area of war. On August 9, 1913, the day before the signature of peace at Bucharest, Austria-Hungary communicated to Italy and to Germany ' her intention of taking action against Serbia, and defined such action as defensive, hoping to bring into operation the *casus foederis* of the Triple Alliance '.[1] Italy refused to recognize the proposed aggression of Austria-Hungary against Serbia as a *casus foederis*. Germany also exercised a restraining influence upon her ally, and the attack was consequently postponed ; but only for eleven months. Germany was not quite ready : on November 22, however, M. Jules Cambon, the French ambassador at Berlin, reported that the German Emperor had ceased to be ' the champion of peace against the warlike tendencies of certain parties in Germany, and had come to think that war with France was inevitable '.[2]

France, therefore, would have to be fought : but the eyes of the German Powers, and more particularly of Austria-Hungary, were fixed not upon the west but upon the south-east.

Serbia had committed two unpardonable crimes : she had strengthened the barrier between Austria-Hungary and Salonica ; and she had enormously enhanced her own prestige as the representative of Jugo-Slav aspirations. Serbia, therefore, must be annihilated.

But Serbia did not stand alone. By her side were Greece and Roumania. The association of these three Balkan States appeared to be peculiarly menacing to the Habsburg Empire.

---

[1] Telegram from the Marquis di San Giuliano to Signor Giolitti : quoted by the latter in the Italian Chamber, Dec. 5, 1914 (*Collected Diplomatic Documents*, p. 401).

[2] *Collected Diplomatic Documents*, p. 142.

Greece, firmly planted in Salonica, was a fatal obstacle to the hopes so long cherished by Austria. The prestige acquired by Serbia undoubtedly tended to create unrest among the Slavonic peoples still subject to the Dual Monarchy. And if Jugo-Slav enthusiasm threatened the integrity of the Dual Monarchy upon one side, the ambitions of a Greater Roumania threatened it upon another. The visit of the Tsar Nicholas to Constanza in the spring of 1914 was interpreted in Vienna as a recognition of this fact, and as an indication of a *rapprochement* between St. Petersburg and Bucharest.

If, therefore, the menace presented to 'Central Europe' by the first Balkan League had been effectually dissipated, the menace of a second Balkan League remained. One crumb of consolation the second war had, however, brought to the German Powers : the vitality and power of recuperation manifested by the Ottoman Turk. So long as the Turks remained in Constantinople there was no reason for despair. The key to German policy was to be found upon the shores of the Bosphorus.

Constantinople and Salonica were then the dual objectives of Austro-German ambition. Across the path to both of them lay Belgrade. At all hazards the Power which commanded Belgrade must be crushed.

How was it to be done ? The military problem was, of course, easy of solution ; not so the diplomatic. The time has not yet come for unravelling the tangled skein of events which will render memorable the history of the months which preceded the outbreak of the Great European War in August, 1914. Attention must, however, be drawn, briefly and simply, to certain unquestionable facts which bear directly upon the theme of this book.

On June 12, 1914, the German Emperor, accompanied by Grand Admiral von Tirpitz, visited the Archduke Franz

Ferdinand and his wife, the Duchess of Hohenberg, at their castle of Konopisht in Bohemia. What passed between the august visitor and his hosts must be matter for conjecture. A responsible writer has, however, given currency to a story that the object of the Emperor William's visit was to provide an inheritance for the two sons of the Duchess of Hohenberg, and at the same time to arrange for the eventual absorption of the German lands of the House of Habsburg into the German Empire.[1]

The Archduke Franz Ferdinand was heir to the Dual Monarchy, but his marriage was morganatic, and his children were portionless. Both he and his wife were the objects of incessant intrigue alike at Vienna and at Buda-Pesth, where the archduke was credited with pro-Slav sympathies.

On June 28 the archduke and his wife were assassinated in the streets of the Bosnian capital, Serajevo. None of the usual precautions for the safety of royal visitors had been taken. On the contrary, the police of Serajevo received orders that such precautions were unnecessary, as the military authorities were to be responsible for all arrangements. As the imperial visitors drove from the station a bomb was thrown at the carriage by the son of an Austrian police official. On arriving at the Town Hall the archduke is said to have exclaimed: ' Now I know why Count Tisza advised me to postpone my journey.'[2] Still no precautions were taken to safeguard the archduke, though the town was known to be full of conspirators. On their way from the Town Hall to the hospital, the archduke and his wife were mortally wounded by three shots deliberately fired by a second assassin. It is reported that the archduke, in

[1] Cf. *The Pact of Konopisht*, by H. Wickham Steed, *Nineteenth Century and After*, February, 1916, but other stories are current.

[2] Stated by Mr. Steed on the authority of *The Times* correspondent at Serajevo.

his last moments, exclaimed : ' The fellow will get the Golden Cross of Merit for this.' True or not the story points to a current suspicion. The assassin, though not a Serbian subject, was a Serb, but by whom was he employed ? No steps were taken to punish those who had so grossly neglected the duty of guarding the archduke's person, though the *canaille* of Serajevo were let loose among the Serbs, while the Austrian police stood idly by. The funeral accorded to the archduke served to deepen the mystery attending his death. Prince Arthur of Connaught was appointed to represent King George, but he did not leave London. The German Emperor announced his intention of being present, but when the time came he was indisposed. The funeral of the heir to the Dual Monarchy was ' private '. The satisfaction which prevailed in certain quarters in Vienna and Buda-Pesth was hardly concealed.

Nevertheless, the Serbians were to be chastised for a dastardly crime planned in Belgrade.[1] Accordingly, on July 23, the Austro-Hungarian Government addressed to Serbia the following ultimatum :—

' On the 31st March, 1909, the Servian Minister in Vienna, on the instructions of the Servian Government, made the following declaration to the Imperial and Royal Government :—

' " Servia recognizes that the *fait accompli* regarding Bosnia has not affected her rights, and consequently she will conform to the decisions that the Powers may take in conformity with article 25 of the Treaty of Berlin. In deference to the advice of the Great Powers, Servia undertakes to renounce from now onwards the attitude of protest and opposition which she has adopted with regard to the annexation since last autumn. She undertakes, moreover, to modify the direction

---

[1] The Serbian Government challenged proof, never afforded, of its connivance in the crime. It also pointed out that it had previously offered to arrest the assassins, but the Austrian Government had deprecated the precautionary step.

of her policy with regard to Austria-Hungary and to live in future on good neighbourly terms with the latter."

'The history of recent years, and in particular the painful events of the 28th June last, have shown the existence of a subversive movement with the object of detaching a part of the territories of Austria-Hungary from the Monarchy. The movement, which had its birth under the eye of the Servian Government, has gone so far as to make itself manifest on both sides of the Servian frontier in the shape of acts of terrorism and a series of outrages and murders.

'Far from carrying out the formal undertakings contained in the declaration of the 31st March, 1909, the Royal Servian Government has done nothing to repress these movements. It has permitted the criminal machinations of various societies and associations directed against the Monarchy, and has tolerated unrestrained language on the part of the press, the glorification of the perpetrators of outrages, and the participation of officers and functionaries in subversive agitation. It has permitted an unwholesome propaganda in public instruction; in short, it has permitted all manifestations of a nature to incite the Servian population to hatred of the Monarchy and contempt of its institutions.

'This culpable tolerance of the Royal Servian Government had not ceased at the moment when the events of the 28th June last proved its fatal consequences to the whole world.

'It results from the depositions and confessions of the criminal perpetrators of the outrage of the 28th June that the Serajevo assassinations were planned in Belgrade; that the arms and explosives with which the murderers were provided had been given to them by Servian officers and functionaries belonging to the Narodna Odbrana; and finally, that the passage into Bosnia of the criminals and their arms was organized and effected by the chiefs of the Servian frontier service.

'The above-mentioned results of the magisterial investigation do not permit the Austro-Hungarian Government to pursue any longer the attitude of expectant forbearance which they have maintained for years in face of the machinations hatched in Belgrade, and thence propagated in the territories of the Monarchy. The results, on the contrary, impose on them the duty of putting an end to the intrigues which form a perpetual menace to the tranquillity of the Monarchy.

' To achieve this end the Imperial and Royal Government see themselves compelled to demand from the Royal Servian Government a formal assurance that they condemn this dangerous propaganda against the Monarchy ; in other words, the whole series of tendencies, the ultimate aim of which is to detach from the Monarchy territories belonging to it, and that they undertake to suppress by every means this criminal and terrorist propaganda.

' In order to give a formal character to this undertaking the Royal Servian Government shall publish on the front page of their " Official Journal " of the 13/26 July the following declaration :—

' " The Royal Government of Servia condemn the propaganda directed against Austria-Hungary—i. e., the general tendency of which the final aim is to detach from the Austro-Hungarian Monarchy territories belonging to it, and they sincerely deplore the fatal consequences of these criminal proceedings.

' " The Royal Government regret that Servian officers and functionaries participated in the above-mentioned propaganda and thus compromised the good neighbourly relations to which the Royal Government were solemnly pledged by their declaration of the 31st March, 1909.

' " The Royal Government, who disapprove and repudiate all idea of interfering or attempting to interfere with the destinies of the inhabitants of any part whatsoever of Austria-Hungary, consider it their duty formally to warn officers and functionaries, and the whole population of the kingdom, that henceforward they will proceed with the utmost rigour against persons who may be guilty of such machinations, which they will use all their efforts to anticipate and suppress."

' This declaration shall simultaneously be communicated to the Royal army as an order of the day by His Majesty the King and shall be published in the " Official Bulletin " of the Army.

' The Royal Servian Government further undertake :

' 1. To suppress any publication which incites to hatred and contempt of the Austro-Hungarian Monarchy and the general tendency of which is directed against its territorial integrity;

' 2. To dissolve immediately the society styled " Narodna Odbrana ", to confiscate all its means of propaganda, and to proceed in the same manner against other societies and their branches in Servia which engage in propaganda against the Austro-Hungarian Monarchy. The Royal Government shall take the necessary measures to prevent the societies dissolved from continuing their activity under another name and form;

' 3. To eliminate without delay from public instruction in Servia, both as regards the teaching body and also as regards the methods of instruction, everything that serves, or might serve, to foment the propaganda against Austria-Hungary ;

' 4. To remove from the military service, and from the administration in general, all officers and functionaries guilty of propaganda against the Austro-Hungarian Monarchy whose names and deeds the Austro-Hungarian Government reserve to themselves the right of communicating to the Royal Government ;

' 5. To accept the collaboration in Servia of representatives of the Austro-Hungarian Government for the suppression of the subversive movement directed against the territorial integrity of the Monarchy ;

' 6. To take judicial proceedings against accessories to the plot of the 28th June who are on Servian territory ; delegates of the Austro-Hungarian Government will take part in the investigation relating thereto ;

' 7. To proceed without delay to the arrest of Major Voija Tankositch and of the individual named Milan Ciganovitch, a Servian State employé, who have been compromised by the results of the magisterial inquiry at Serajevo ;

' 8. To prevent by effective measures the co-operation of the Servian authorities in the illicit traffic in arms and explosives across the frontier, to dismiss and punish severely the officials of the frontier service at Schabatz and Ložnica guilty of having assisted the perpetrators of the Serajevo crime by facilitating their passage across the frontier ;

' 9. To furnish the Imperial and Royal Government with explanations regarding the unjustifiable utterances of high Servian officials, both in Servia and abroad, who, notwithstanding their official position, have not hesitated since the crime of the 28th June to express themselves in interviews in terms of hostility to the Austro-Hungarian Government; and, finally,

' 10. To notify the Imperial and Royal Government without delay of the execution of the measures comprised under the preceding heads.

' The Austro-Hungarian Government expect the reply of the Royal Government at the latest by 6 o'clock on Saturday evening, the 25th July.

' A memorandum dealing with the results of the magisterial inquiry at Serajevo with regard to the officials mentioned under heads (7) and (8) is attached to this note.'

Forty-eight hours only were permitted for a reply to this ultimatum, which was communicated, together with an explanatory memorandum, to the Powers, on July 24.

Diplomacy, therefore, had only twenty-four hours in which to work. The Serbian Government did its utmost to avert the war plainly pre-determined by the German Powers. It replied promptly, accepting eight out of the ten principal points and not actually rejecting the other two. No submission could have been more complete and even abject. To complete the evidence of Serbia's conciliatory attitude it is only necessary to recall the fact that she offered to submit the whole question at issue between the two Governments either to the Hague Tribunal or to the Great Powers, which took part in the drawing up of the declaration made by the Serbian Government on the 18th (31st) March, 1909.[1] But nothing could avail to avert war. The German Powers were ready and they struck.

[1] British Diplomatic Correspondence, No. 39, 1914 (*Collected Documents*, p. 31).

BALKAN STATES
1878-1914

English Miles
0   50   100   200

BUKOVINA · RUSSIA

MOLDAVIA

Jassy · BESSARABIA

TRANSYLVANIA

H U N G A R Y

Temesvar

Vulkan P.

Tömös P.

Orsova

1858-1878

Galatz

1878

AUSTRIA

BOSNIA

Serajevo

DALMATIA (AUSTRIA)

HERZEGOVINA

MONTE NEGRO

Cattaro

Cettinje

Belgrade

SERBIA

Nish

Pirot

Uskub

1913

Ochrida

Monastir

ROUMANIA

WALACHIA

Bucharest

Vidin · Rustchuk

Silistria

1913

DOBRUJA

Plevna

BULGARIA

Tirnovo

Sofia

1885

Philippopolis

1913

Burgas

1913

Varna

BLACK SEA

ADRIATIC SEA

Durazzo

Brundisi

1913

ITALY

Valona

Otranto

Corfu

IONIAN

S. Maura

Cephalonia

Zante

ALBANIA

1913

1913

Salonica

AEGEAN SEA

Yanina

1881

Larissa

GREECE

PELOPONNESE

Athens

SEA

Adrianople

1913

Constantinople

OTTOMAN EMPIRE

TROY

Lemnos

Mitylene

Chios

Samos

Smyrna

Crete

Acquisitions of Montenegro 1913
    "   "   Roumania   "
    "   "   Bulgaria   "
    "   "   Serbia   "
    "   "   Greece   "
Ceded to Bulgaria by the Treaty
of London May 30th 1913, retroceded
to Turkey Sept. 29th 1913.
State frontiers
Old   "

From the mass of the diplomatic correspondence two not insignificant, but almost casual, remarks may be unearthed. On July 25, Sir Rennell Rodd, British ambassador at Rome, telegraphed to Sir Edward Grey : ' There is reliable information that Austria intends to seize the Salonica Railway.'[1] On the 29th, the British chargé d'affaires at Constantinople telegraphed : ' I understand that the designs of Austria may extend considerably beyond the Sanjak and a punitive occupation of Serbian territory. I gathered this from a remark let fall by the Austrian ambassador here, who spoke of the deplorable economic situation of Salonica under Greek administration, and of the assistance on which the Austrian army could count from Mussulman population discontented with Serbian rule '.[2]

The old and the new Rome were equally awake to the fact that Austria was looking beyond Serbia to Salonica.

Austria declared war upon Serbia on July 28 ; Germany declared war upon Russia on August 1, and upon France on August 3 ; Germany invaded Belgium on August 4, and on the same day Great Britain declared war on Germany.

Once more the problem of the Near East, still unsolved, apparently insoluble, had involved the world in war.

For further reference : I. E. Gueshoff, *The Balkan League* (Eng. trans., London, 1915 : contains many original documents of first-rate importance) ; C. Kerofilas, *Eleftherios Venizelos* (Eng. trans., London, 1915 : popular but useful) ; *Annual Register* for the years 1912–14 ; *Collected Diplomatic Documents relating to the outbreak of the European War* (London, 1915 : contains British, French, Belgian, Serbian, German, and Austro-Hungarian official correspondence) ; *Nationalism and War in the Near East*, by a Diplomatist (Clarendon Press, 1915) ; J. G. Schurman, *The Balkan Wars, 1912–13* (Clarendon Press, 1915) ; D. J. Cassavetti, *Hellas and the Balkan Wars* ; Jean Pélissier, *Dix Mois de Guerre dans les Balkans* (Oct. 1912– Aug. 1913) (Paris, 1915) ; H. Barby, *Les Victoires Serbes* (Paris, 1915), *L'Epopée Serbe* (Paris, 1915) ; Balcanicus, *La Bulgarie* (with documents)

[1] *Idem,* No. 19.   [2] *Idem,* No. 82.

(Paris, 1915); Songeon, *Histoire de la Bulgare, 485–1913* (Paris, 1914); Gabriel Hanotaux, *La Guerre des Balkans et l'Europe* (Paris, 1914). For the Albanian problem lecture by F. Delaiji in *Les Aspirations autonomistes en Europe* (Paris, 1913).

The contemporary volumes of the *Edinburgh Review*, the *Quarterly*, the *Round Table*, the *Nineteenth Century and After*, the *Fortnightly*, and other Reviews are also of great value for the history of this as of other recent periods.

Epilogue

1914–16

' Le plan pangermaniste constitue la raison unique de la guerre. Il est, en effet, la cause à la fois de sa naissance et de sa prolongation jusqu'à la victoire des Alliés indispensable à la liberté du monde.'—ANDRÉ CHÉRADAME (1916).

' The war comes from the East ; the war is waged for the East ; the war will be decided in the East.'—ERNST JACKH in *Deutsche Politik* (Dec. 22, 1916). (Quoted in *The New Europe*, Feb. 8, 1917.)

THE Great War, initiated by the events which have been narrated in the preceding chapters, still rages without abatement. As these pages go to press the war is nearing the close of its fourth year. Each month that has passed has rendered it more and more clear that the clue to the attack launched in August, 1914, by the Hohenzollern and the Habsburgs upon their unprepared and unoffending neighbours must be sought and will be found in the Balkan Peninsula.

When the storm-cloud burst upon Europe in July, 1914, the minds of men were bewildered by the appalling suddenness of the catastrophe. Opinion as to the origin of the crisis and the scope of the resulting conflict would seem to have passed since those days through three distinct phases. Before the actual outbreak of war, and while diplomacy was still at work, there was a disposition to regard the Serbo-Austrian-Hungarian dispute as merely a fresh manifestation of the secular problem of the Near East. It was hoped that the area of conflict might, by the efforts of diplomacy, be again localized as it had been in 1912–13. That the Central Empires in striking at Serbia were really challenging the whole position of Great Britain in the Near East and in the Farther East was, to say the least, very imperfectly realized even in the most responsible quarters in this country. Why should Great Britain concern herself with the chastisement inflicted by Austria-Hungary upon a nation of assassins and pig-merchants? Such was the thought commonly entertained and not infrequently expressed.

Then came the attack upon Belgium and France. The public mind, incapable of grasping more than one aspect of the question at a time, rushed to the conclusion that the quarrel fastened upon Serbia was merely the occasion, not the cause, of the European War. The Central Empires had found in Serbia a pretext for the attack—long contemplated and prepared for—upon France, Russia, and Great Britain.

Gradually, as men have had time to reflect upon the essential causes of the conflict and to reconstruct the recent past in the light of the present, opinion has hardened into conviction that the assault upon the peasant State of Serbia was not merely the occasion of the world-war, but a revelation of its fundamental cause. That assault was, in fact, the outcome of ambitions which have dominated the mind of the German Emperor, and have dictated the main lines of his diplomacy, ever since his accession to the throne. Bismarck had long ago perceived the gravitation of the Habsburgs towards Buda-Pesth. Just as in 1866, by the niggardly gift of Venice to Italy and the denial of the Greater Venetia, he involved the Habsburgs in perpetual hostility with the Italian Irredentists, so later he attempted to console the Habsburgs for their expulsion from Germany, and at the same time to involve them in perpetual hostility to Russia, by the gift of the Southern Slav provinces of Bosnia and the Herzegovina. That gift suggested to the Habsburgs the idea of opening up a road between Vienna and the Aegean. But the way to Salonica was barred by Belgrade. An independent Serbia, still more a Greater Serbia of which the Southern Slavs had long dreamt, must block the path not only of the Habsburgs to Salonica but of the Hohenzollern to Constantinople. The Jugo-Slavs alone stood between the Central Empires and the realization of their dream of a *Mitteleuropa*, stretching from Hamburg to Constantinople. Nor was Constantinople the ultimate goal. From Constantinople a highway was in building which should carry German traders and German soldiers to the Persian Gulf. Once established on the Persian Gulf what was to hinder a further advance ? The flank of the Great Sea-Power had been turned ; there was no longer any insuperable obstacle between Germany and the dominion of the East.

There were, however, one or two intermediate steps to be taken. Behind the Southern Slavs stood Russia ; Russia, therefore, must be crushed. In close alliance with Russia stood France ; a swift descent upon France, the occupation of Paris, a peace dictated to the French, on sufficiently lenient terms, should precede the annihilation of Russia. True, Great Britain would regard with grave concern a German victory over France ; but what could Great Britain, rendered impotent by domestic dissensions, do to avert it, even if she would ?

Such were the calculations which determined the method and the moment of the world-war. The dominating motives of that war were the realization of the dream of a great Central-European Empire stretching from the German Ocean to the shores of the Bosphorus, and the extension of German influence in those Asiatic lands, of which, for a land-power, Constantinople as of old still holds the key.

If this diagnosis be correct, the successive symptoms which, in the course of the disorder of the last four years, have manifested themselves appear not merely intelligible but inevitable.

Whether by a timely display of force the Turk could have been kept true to his ancient connexion with Great Britain and France; whether by more sagacious diplomacy the hostility of Bulgaria could have been averted, and the co-operation of Greece secured; whether by the military intervention of the Entente Powers the cruel blow could have been warded off from Serbia and Montenegro; whether the Dardanelles expedition was faulty only in execution or radically unsound in conception; whether Roumania came in too tardily or moved too soon, and in a wrong direction: these are questions of high significance, but the time for answering them has not yet come.

Meanwhile, it may be convenient to summarize the events of the last four years, so far as they have reacted upon the problems discussed in the preceding pages.

On the outbreak of the European War (August, 1914) the Porte declared its neutrality—a course which was followed, in October, by Greece, Roumania, and Bulgaria. The allied Powers of Great Britain, France, and Russia gave an assurance to the Sultan that, if the Ottoman Empire maintained its neutrality, the independence and integrity of the Empire would be respected during the war, and provided for at the peace settlement. That many of the most responsible statesmen of the Porte sincerely desired the maintenance of neutrality cannot be doubted; but the forces working in the contrary direction were too powerful. The traditional enmity against Russia; the chance of recovering Egypt and Cyprus from Great Britain; the astute policy which for a quarter of a century Germany had pursued at Constantinople; the German training imparted to the Turkish army; above all, the powerful personality of Enver Bey, who, early in 1914, had been appointed Minister of War—all these things impelled the Porte to embrace the cause of the Central Empires. Nor was it long before Turkey gave unmistakable indications of her real proclivities. In the first week of the war the German cruisers, the *Goeben* and the *Breslau*, having eluded the pursuit of the allied fleet in the Mediterranean, reached the Bosphorus, were purchased by the Porte, and commissioned in the Turkish navy. Great Britain and Russia refused to recognize the transfer as valid, but the Porte took no notice of the protest. Meanwhile, Germany poured money, munitions, and men into Turkey; German officers were placed in command of the forts of the Dardanelles; a German General, Liman Pasha, was appointed Commander-in-Chief of the Turkish army, and on October 28 the Turkish fleet bombarded Odessa and other unfortified ports belonging to Russia on the Black Sea. To the protest made by the ambassadors of the allied Powers the Porte did not reply, and on November 1 the ambassadors demanded their passports and quitted Constantinople. A few days later the Dardanelles forts were bombarded by English and French ships; Akaba in the Red Sea was bombarded by H.M.S. *Minerva*, and on November 5 Cyprus was formally annexed by Great Britain. For the first time Great Britain and the Ottoman Empire were really at war.

Left to themselves the Ottoman Turks might possibly have remained true to their traditional policy; but considerable irritation had been aroused against England by the detention of two powerful battle-ships which were being built in English yards, and the arrival of which at the Bosphorus had been impatiently awaited by a large body of patriotic subscribers. That irritation supplied the spark utilized at the last moment to set fire to the combustible materials which had been steadily accumulated by German foresight at Constantinople.

The German anticipation unquestionably was that by means of the Turkish alliance she would be able to exploit Meso-potamia, to penetrate Persia commercially and politically, to deliver a powerful attack upon the British position in Egypt, and to threaten the hegemony of Great Britain in India. For all these ambitious schemes Constantinople was regarded as an indispensable base.

It cannot be said that all danger in these diverse directions has been dissipated. Nor can it yet be accurately known how serious during the last four years has been the German threat to British world-power. The symptoms change so rapidly that scientific diagnosis is difficult and prognosis impossible. Two things may, however, be said; first, that none of the threatened dangers has thus far actually materialized; secondly, that nevertheless the situation is not wholly reassuring. By the annihilation of Serbia a road has been opened from Berlin to the Bosphorus, and in Constantinople itself German influence is unchallenged. Even more imposing are the results achieved by the treaties concluded by the Central Empires with the Russian Bolsheviks, at Brest Litovsk (March 3, 1918), with the Ukraine (February 9), and with Roumania at Bucharest (May 7). It is not easy, as yet, to see those results in true perspective; but this much is manifest: the work accomplished for Russia by Peter the Great and Catherine II has been cancelled: the windows to the west and south opened by those great rulers have been closed: Russia no longer touches either the Baltic or the Black Sea; her position as a European power is, for the time being, annihilated. The Black Sea has become virtually a German lake. Her vassals and allies command every inch of its shores, and control the entrance to it and the exit from it. It is true that the situation is not one of unrelieved gloom; there are many and striking compensations. The Turco-German attack upon the Suez Canal and upon Egypt has ignominiously failed and a series of momentous victories has established British power in Palestine. The memory of the serious reverse suffered in 1916 by British arms in Mesopotamia has been more than wiped out by the brilliant campaign of 1917; British prestige has been amply vindicated and

British supremacy substantially reasserted in the middle-East. But neither the Suez Canal nor the Euphrates valley possess quite the same significance to-day [1] which attached to them two years ago. The situation at the moment is somewhat obscure, and startling developments are not impossible. Assuming, however, that the power of resistance in Russia and Roumania is for the time being broken, that Germany holds the Ukraine in fee, and that Bulgaria and Turkey are (to put it no lower) in friendly alliance with the Central Empires, it is obvious that *Mitteleuropa* can command alternative routes to the Far East, and to the Middle East, which turn the flank of Egypt and even of Mesopotamia. Clearly there is a new menace, on the one hand, to the security of the north-west frontier of India, on the other to the Powers of the northern Pacific which, though not yet measurable, it were folly to ignore.

In the Balkans, moreover, German influence is predominant. In the autumn of 1914 Austria-Hungary launched a terrific attack upon Serbia, and after four months of sanguinary fighting succeeded (December 2) in capturing Belgrade. But their triumph was short-lived. By an heroic effort the Serbians, three days later, recaptured their capital; the Habsburg assault was repelled, and for the first half of 1915 Serbia enjoyed a respite from the attacks of external enemies. An epidemic of typhus fever in its most virulent form wrought terrible havoc, however, upon an exhausted, ill-fed, and, in certain parts, congested population. From this danger Serbia was rescued by the heroism of English doctors and English nurses, warmly seconded by American and other volunteers. Had the methods of English diplomacy been as energetic and effective as those of English medicine, Serbia might still have escaped the terrible fate in store for her. Judged by results, and as yet

[1] Written in June, 1918.

we have no other materials for judgement, nothing could have been more inept than the efforts of allied and English diplomacy in the Balkans throughout the year 1915.

Italy and the Adriatic

One difficulty that arose cannot, in fairness, be attributed to the diplomacy of England and her allies. It was inherent in the situation. In May, 1915, Italy threw in her lot with the Triple Entente. She had declined in 1914 to regard the Austro-German attack upon their neighbours as a *casus foederis*, and on February 12, 1915, she informed Austria that any further action in the Balkans, on the part of Austria-Hungary, would be regarded by Italy as an unfriendly act. That her action contributed to the respite enjoyed by Serbia cannot be gainsaid: Germany was very anxious to avoid a rupture with Italy, and offered large concessions, of course at the expense of her ally ; but early in May Italy denounced the Triple Alliance, and on May 23 declared war upon Austria-Hungary.

Italy was in fact determined to seize the opportunity for completing the work of the *Risorgimento*, for rectifying her frontier on the side of the Trentino, for securing her naval ascendancy in the Adriatic, and for ' redeeming ' the islands of the Dalmatian archipelago and those districts on the eastern littoral of the Adriatic which had for centuries formed part of the historic Republic of Venice. Her quarrel, therefore, was not primarily with the Hohenzollern, but with the Habsburgs, who since 1797 had been in almost continuous occupation of these portions of the Venetian inheritance.

The pretensions of Italy, however well justified politically and historically, introduced a considerable complication into the diplomatic situation. In particular they aroused grave perturbation among the Southern Slavs and especially in Serbia. In the eastern part of the Istrian Peninsula, and along the whole coast from Fiume to Albania, the population is predominantly Slav. The dream of a Greater Serbia would be frustrated were Italy to acquire the Dalmatian coast and islands. Rather than see Italy established there, the Serbs would prefer to leave Austria-Hungary in occupation. The situation was an embarrassing one for the Triple Entente, and, in the event of their victory, may again become acute. Southern Slav opinion was strongly roused by the rumour which gained credence in May, 1915, that in order to secure the adhesion of Italy the Powers of the Triple Entente had conceded her claims to Northern Dalmatia and several of the islands of the archipelago. Be this as it may, Italy, as we have seen, adhered to the alliance of which Serbia forms an integral part.

For Italy, as for other belligerents, sunshine has alternated with shadow during the last three years. On the whole she somewhat improved her position during the campaign of 1916 ; she tasted triumph in the summer of 1917, but in the autumn of that year it was her fate to learn the bitterness of defeat. Surprised by an Austro-German force at the end of October, the second Italian army was compelled to fall back ; the retreat became a rout ; the rout of the second army involved the retreat of the third, and within three weeks the enemy had captured 2,300 guns and made prisoners 250,000 men.[1] The disaster on the Isonzo may perhaps have rendered the temper of Italy somewhat more amenable to compromise in regard to her territorial claims ; at any rate it was announced in March, 1918, that an agreement had been reached between a representative Italian Committee and the Jugo-Slavs. The agreement is purely unofficial, but, on the part of Italy, it is the work of a Committee formed in Rome for the purpose of promoting joint political action among all the nationalities

---

[1] Since these words were written Italy has gone far to retrieve her position by a brilliant victory on the Piave (June, 1918).

subject to Austro-Hungarian rule, and should it be officially confirmed it will be of the happiest augury for the solution of one of the most obstinate factors in the problem of the Near East. Even an unofficial agreement has been cordially welcomed in Great Britain. That Italy and the Jugo-Slavs should accommodate their differences in the Adriatic and on the Dalmatian coast has been for years one of the most ardent hopes of a nation which is sincerely friendly to both parties. An official agreement would, moreover, relieve an anxiety which has weighed heavily upon the conscience of the Western peoples ever since the conclusion of the Convention, only nominally secret, of April, 1915.[1]

The Dardanelles Expedition

For that Convention there was some excuse. The Triple Entente needed, at the time, all the friends they could muster in south-eastern Europe. In February the world learnt that an English fleet, assisted by a French squadron, was bombarding the forts of the Dardanelles, and high hopes were entertained in the allied countries that the passage of the Straits would be quickly forced. Nothing would have done so much to frustrate German diplomacy in south-eastern Europe as a successful blow at Constantinople. But the hopes aroused by the initiation of the enterprise were not destined to fulfilment. It soon became evident that the navy alone could not achieve the task entrusted to it. Towards the end of April a large force of troops was landed on the Gallipoli Peninsula ; but the end of May came, and there was nothing to show for the loss of nearly 40,000 men. On August 6th a second army, consisting largely of Australians, New Zealanders, and English Territorials, was thrown on to the peninsula. The troops displayed superb courage, but the conditions were impossible ;

[1] See *New Europe*, vol. iv. 45, 52 ; vi. 74 ; vii. 85.

Sir Ian Hamilton, who had commanded, was succeeded by Sir C. C. Munro, to whom was assigned the difficult and ungrateful task of evacuating an untenable position. To the amazement and admiration of the world, a feat deemed almost impossible was accomplished before the end of December, without the loss of a single man. How far the expedition to the Dardanelles may have averted dangers in other directions it is impossible, as yet, to say; but, as regards the accomplishment of its immediate aims, the enterprise was a ghastly though a gallant failure.

The failure was apparent long before it was proclaimed by the abandonment of the attempt. Nor was that failure slow to react upon the situation in the Balkans.

Greece

On the outbreak of the European War Greece had proclaimed its neutrality, though the Premier, Mr. Venizelos, at the same time declared that Greece had treaty obligations in regard to Serbia, and that she intended to fulfil them. But in Greece, as elsewhere in the Near East, opinions if not sympathies were sharply divided. The Greek kingdom owed its existence to the Powers comprising the Triple Entente; the dynasty owed its crown to their nomination; to them the people were tied by every bond of historical gratitude. No one realized this more clearly than Mr. Venizelos, and no one could have shown himself more determined to repay the debt with compound interest. Moreover, Mr. Venizelos believed that the dictates of policy were identical with those of gratitude. The creator of the Balkan League had not abandoned, despite the perfidious conduct of one of his partners, the hope of realizing the dream which had inspired his policy in 1912. The one solution of a secular problem at once feasible in itself and compatible with the claims of nationality was and is a Balkan Federation. A German hegemony in the Balkans, an Ottoman Empire dependent upon Berlin, would dissipate that dream for ever. To Greece, as to the other Balkan States, it was essential that Germany should not be permitted to establish herself permanently on the Bosphorus. If that disaster was to be averted mutual concessions would have to be made, and Venizelos was statesman enough to make them. Early in 1915 he tried to persuade his sovereign to offer Kavala and a slice of ' Greek ' Macedonia to Bulgaria. He was anxious also to co-operate in the attack upon the Dardanelles with allies who had offered to Greece a large territorial concession in the Smyrna district. To neither suggestion would Constantine and his Hohenzollern consort listen. Venizelos consequently resigned.

Policy of the Allies in the Balkans

If Venizelos desired harmony among the Balkan States, so also, and not less ardently, did the allies. Macedonia still remained the crux of the situation. Hohenzollern-Habsburg diplomacy had, as we have seen, thrown oil upon the flames of inter-Balkan rivalries in that region. Bulgaria, the willing cat's-paw of the Central Empires, had in 1913 drawn down upon herself deserved disaster, but that she would permanently acquiesce in the terms imposed upon her by the Treaty of Bucharest [1] was not to be expected. Venizelos was quick to recognize this truth. Had his advice been followed Bulgaria would have gained a better outlet to the Aegean than that afforded by Dedeagatch. Serbia possessed no statesman of the calibre of Venizelos. But the situation of Serbia was in the last degree hazardous, and under the pressure of grim necessity Serbia might have been expected to listen to the voice of prudence. How far that voice reached her ears in the early

[1] *Supra*, p. 465.

summer of 1915 we cannot yet know for certain. Almost anything can be believed of the diplomacy of the Entente at that period, and many things can be asserted on the authority of Sir Edward Carson, who in October resigned his place in the Cabinet as a protest against the Balkan policy of his colleagues.[1] But the time for a full investigation has not yet come, and, in the meantime, it must suffice to record results.

Bulgaria

Not until August, 1915, was Serbia induced to offer such concessions in Macedonia to Bulgaria as might possibly have sufficed, in May, to keep Bulgaria out of the clutches of the Central Empires. In Bulgaria, as elsewhere, opinion was sharply divided. Both groups of Great Powers had their adherents at Sofia. Had the Russian advance been maintained in 1915 ; had the Dardanelles been forced ; had pressure been put by the Entente upon Serbia and Greece to make reasonable concessions in Macedonia, Bulgaria might not have yielded to the seductions of German gold and to the wiles of German diplomacy. But why should a German king of Bulgaria have thrown in his lot with Powers who were apparently heading for military disaster ; whose diplomacy was as inept as their arms were feeble ? What more natural than that when the German avalanche descended upon Serbia in the autumn of 1915 Bulgaria should have co-operated in the discomfiture of a detested rival ?

Yet the Entente built their plans upon the hope, if not the expectation, that Bulgaria might possibly be induced to enter the war on the side of the allies against Turkey.[2] Serbia was anxious to attack Bulgaria in September, while her mobilization

---

[1] Cf. for a powerful indictment of Entente diplomacy : Auguste Gauvain, *L'Affaire Grecque* (Paris, 1917).

[2] Cf. Speech of Sir Edward Grey in House of Commons, Oct. 14, 1915.

was still incomplete. It is generally believed that the allies intervened to restrain the Serbian attack; hoping against hope that a concordat between the Balkan States might still be arrived at. To that hope Serbia was sacrificed.[1]

The Chastisement of Serbia

A great Austro-German army, under the command of Field-Marshal von Mackensen, concentrated upon the Serbian frontier in September, and on the 7th of October it crossed the Danube. Two days later Belgrade surrendered, and for the next few weeks von Mackensen, descending upon the devoted country in overwhelming strength, drove the Serbians before him, until the whole country was in the occupation of the Austro-German forces. The Bulgarians captured Nish on November 5 and effected a junction with the army under von Mackensen; Serbia was annihilated; a remnant of the Serbian army took refuge in the mountains of Montenegro and Albania, while numbers of deported civilians sought the hospitality of the allies. On November 28 Germany officially declared the Balkan campaign to be at an end. For the time being Serbia had ceased to exist as a Balkan State.

Balkan Policy of the Entente Powers

What had the allies done to succour her? On September 28 Sir Edward Grey, from his place in the House of Commons, uttered a grave, though not unfriendly, warning to Bulgaria, and declared that Great Britain was determined, in concert with her allies, to give to her friends in the Balkans all the support in her power in a manner that would be most welcome to them 'without reserve and without qualification'. How was this

---

[1] Cf. *The Times*, Nov. 22, 1915: but for a contrary view cf. Dr. E. J. Dillon — no apologist for English diplomacy—*ap. Fortnightly Review*, Jan., 1916.

solemn promise fulfilled ? Russia was not, at the moment, in a position to afford any effective assistance, but on October 4 she dispatched an ultimatum to Bulgaria, and a few days later declared war upon her. On October 5 the advance guard of an Anglo-French force, under General Sarrail and Sir Bryan Mahon, began to disembark at Salonica. The force was miserably inadequate in numbers and equipment, and it came too late.

King Constantine and Mr. Venizelos

Its arrival precipitated a crisis in Greece. As a result of an appeal to the country in June, King Constantine had been reluctantly compelled to recall Venizelos to power in September. Venizelos was as determined as ever to respect the obligations of Greece towards Serbia, and to throw the weight of Greece into the scale of the allies. But despite his parliamentary majority he was no longer master of the situation. The failure of the Dardanelles expedition, the retreat of Russia, the impending intervention of Bulgaria on the Austro-German side, the exhortations and warnings which followed in rapid succession from Berlin, above all, the knowledge that von Mackensen was preparing to annihilate Serbia, had stiffened the back of King Constantine. Venizelos had asked England and France whether, in the event of a Bulgarian attack upon Serbia, the Western Powers would be prepared to send a force to Salonica to take the place of the Serbian contingent contemplated by the Greco-Serbian treaty. The landing of the Anglo-French force in October was the practical response of the allies to the 'invitation' of Venizelos. Technically, however, the landing looked like a violation of Greek neutrality, and Venizelos was compelled by his master to enter a formal protest against it. But the protest was followed by an announcement that Greece would respect her treaty with Serbia, and would march to her assistance, if she were attacked by Bulgaria. That announcement cost Venizelos his place. He was promptly dismissed by King Constantine, who, flouting the terms of the Constitution, effected what was virtually a monarchical *coup d'état.*

The king's violation of the Hellenic Constitution was the opportunity of the protecting Powers. They failed to seize it, and King Constantine remained master of the situation. From an attitude of neutrality professedly ' benevolent ', he passed rapidly to one of hostility almost openly avowed. That hostility deepened as the year 1916 advanced. On May 25, in accordance with the terms of an agreement secretly concluded between Greece, Germany, and Bulgaria, King Constantine handed over to the Bulgarians Fort Rupel, an important position which commanded the flank of the French army in Salonica. Two months later a whole division of the Greek army was instructed to surrender to the Germans and Bulgarians at Kavala. Kavala itself was occupied by King Constantine's friends, who carried off the Greek division, with all its equipment, to Germany. Nearly the whole of Greek Macedonia was now in the hands of Germany and her allies, and the Greek patriots, led by Venizelos, were reduced to despair. In September a Greek Committee of National Defence was set up at Salonica, in October Venizelos himself arrived there, and his rule was accepted not only in Greek Macedonia, but in Crete and most of the islands. Only in Athens and the western provinces did the King's writ run. The allies impartially recognized both the government of Venizelos and that of King Constantine.

Roumanian Intervention

By this time, however, the Balkan situation had been further complicated by the military intervention of Roumania on the side of the allies. In Roumania, as elsewhere, opinion was, on the outbreak of the war, sharply divided. The sympathies of King Carol were, not unnaturally, with his Hohenzollern kinsmen, and, had he not been, in the strict sense of the term, a constitutional sovereign, his country would have been committed to an Austro-German alliance. Nor was the choice of Roumania quite obviously dictated by her interests. If the coveted districts of Transylvania and the Bukovina were in the hands of the Habsburgs, Russia still kept her hold on Bessarabia. A 'Greater Roumania', corresponding in area to the ethnographical distribution of population, would involve the acquisition of all three provinces. Could Roumania hope, either by diplomacy or by war, to achieve the complete reunion of the Roumanian people ?

In October, 1914, the two strongest pro-German forces in Roumania were removed, almost simultaneously, by death : King Carol himself, and his old friend and confidant Demetrius Sturdza. Roumania had already declared her neutrality, and that neutrality was, for some time, scrupulously observed. The natural affinities of the Roumanians attract them, as we have seen, towards France and Italy, and it was anticipated that Italy's entrance into the war would be speedily followed by that of Roumania. But not until August, 1916, was the anticipation fulfilled. On August 27 Roumania declared war and flung a large force into Transylvania. The Austrian garrisons were overwhelmed, and in a few weeks a considerable part of Transylvania had passed into Roumanian hands. But the success, achieved in defiance of sound strategy, and also, it is said, in complete disregard of warnings addressed to Roumania by her allies, was of brief duration. In September Mackensen invaded the Dobrudja from the south, entered Silistria on September 10, and, though checked for a while on the Rasova-Tuzla line, renewed his advance in October and captured Constanza on the twenty-second.

Meanwhile, a German army, under General von Falkenhayn,

advanced from the west, and on September 26 inflicted a severe defeat upon the Roumanians at the Rothen Thurm pass. The Roumanians, though they fought desperately, were steadily pressed back; at the end of November Mackensen joined hands with Falkenhayn, and on December 6 the German armies occupied Bucharest.

Thus another Balkan State was crushed. Throughout the year 1917 there was little change in the situation. The Central Empires remained in occupation of Roumanian territory up to the line of the Sereth, including, therefore, the Dobrudja and Wallachia, and from this occupied territory Austria-Hungary obtained much-needed supplies of grain. Meanwhile, the Roumanian Government remained established in Jassy, and from its ancient capital the affairs of Moldavia were administered. Into Moldavia the Central Powers made no attempt to penetrate, being content to await events. Nor was it long before their patience was rewarded.

The Russian revolution was of tremendous import to Roumania. Roumania, it is true, had attributed the military disasters which had befallen her in the autumn of 1916 to the supineness, or something worse, of the Government of the Tsar. But whether the accusations of treachery were well founded or not, the military collapse of Russia sealed the fate of Roumania. From no other ally could succour reach her. Perforce, therefore, Roumania was compelled to concur in the suspension of hostilities to which the Russian Bolsheviks and the Central Empires agreed in December, 1917. Roumania, nevertheless, announced that though she agreed to suspend hostilities she would not enter into peace negotiations. But the logic of events proved irresistible; on February 9, 1918, Germany concluded peace with the Ukraine, and on March 5 the preliminaries of a peace were arranged with Roumania. The definitive treaty of peace was signed at Bucharest on May 7.

That the terms of that treaty should be humiliating to the pride and deeply prejudicial to the material interests of Roumania was, under the circumstances, inevitable. A large proportion of her territory was in the actual occupation of the enemy; on one flank was Germany's new vassal state, the Ukraine; on the other Germany's devoted but dependent ally, King Ferdinand of Bulgaria. Consequently Roumania, deserted and indeed attacked by Russia, cut off from all possible means of succour from her Western allies, had no alternative but to accept the terms imposed upon her by the Central Empires. Those terms were the terms of a conqueror *sans phrase*; they embodied in its extremest form the principle of *vae victis*.

Roumania was compelled to surrender the whole of the Dobrudja, except a corner of the Danube delta; Bulgaria regained all that she lost of the Dobrudja in 1913 with a considerable slice added—in fact up to Trajan's wall; the remainder of the province was for the time to be held by the Central allies in condominium. If Bulgaria behaved well, if she paid her debts to Germany and made the required territorial concessions to Germany's ally the Ottoman Sultan, she was eventually to acquire the rest of the Dobrudja; but she was to stand on her hind legs until her master threw the biscuit to her. Nor might she deprive Roumania of commercial access, via Constanza, to the Black Sea. Austria-Hungary, disdaining territorial annexations, obtained nevertheless a substantial frontier rectification demanded by strategical considerations, a rectification which will bring her to the foothills on the eastern and southern slopes of the Carpathians, whence she will have Roumania completely at her mercy. Roumania was to demobilize at once the greater part of her own army, but to maintain at her own expense the allied army of occupation. Her economic resources, and in particular her surplus supplies of grain and oil, were to be at the disposal of her conquerors, who were further to enjoy rights of military transport through Moldavia and Bessarabia to Odessa. By thus providing a corridor to Odessa and Constanza respectively Germany would command two of the most important ports on the Black Sea and would secure alternative routes to the Middle East. 'Roumania', as Herr von Kühlmann lately pointed out, ' is of great importance for us (Germans) as a thoroughfare to the Black Sea and the East in general.' Consequently the interests of Danube shipping ' have been very much considered in the treaty '. Moreover, the railway questions have been ' adjusted in the most comprehensive way ', notably by the leasing of the Czernavoda-Constanza Railway to a German industrial company for a long term, and in addition ' an exclusive right of laying cables on the Roumanian coast has been acquired until 1950.' Thus, as von Kühlmann complacently remarks, ' Germany has secured the possibilities of increased use of the Danube route, unrestricted traffic on the railways, and assured through cable and telegraphic communication,' not to mention ' the necessary guarantees both for securing the fundamental conditions of our commercial intercourse for long years to come, and for making sure that the country (Roumania) shall deliver such cereals and other natural products and oil productions as it is in a position to give.' Other provisions of the treaty secured to the Central Empires pretexts for perpetual interference in the internal concerns of what remains of the independent kingdom of Roumania and the means of playing off race against race and creed against creed.

In view of the cruel terms imposed upon Roumania by this treaty, it is pathetic to recall the high hopes with which that country entered the war less than two years ago. The hour of her destiny, as she believed, had struck. At last she was about to achieve the ethnographical unity of the Rouman race. ' To-day it is given us to assure unshakeably and in its fulness the work momentarily realized by Michael the Brave—the union of the Roumanians on both sides the Carpathians.' Such was King Ferdinand's call to his people on August 27, 1916. To-day Roumania, like Serbia, and with less hope than Serbia of succour from the Western Powers, lies crushed beneath the heel of a pitiless conqueror.

Disastrous to Roumania, destructive of her economic and political independence, deeply humiliating to her pride, the Treaty of Bucharest possesses an even deeper and wider significance. It is accepted and proclaimed in Germany as ' a model of the peace to be imposed on all our enemies.' [1] Those enemies will neglect that warning only at their peril. Almost incredible in its insolence, it is seriously meant. In such measure as Germany has meted out to Roumania will she mete out to all who similarly fall into her power. In August, 1916, Roumania, taking her courage in both hands, reached a momentous decision. Like her Italian kinsmen in 1855 she put her fate to the touch : and the words of Mr. Bratianu, uttered in December, 1917, recall not remotely the famous speech delivered by Cavour under widely differing circumstances in 1856 : ' Whatever our sufferings are to-day . . . we have introduced Roumania's just cause to the conscience of Europe.' The Western Allies will not be so base as to ignore the introduction.

The Allies and Greece

Meanwhile, as regards their immediate aims in the Near East, the Central Empires have already achieved even more than they hoped for. From Belgrade to Constantinople, from Bucharest to the valley of the Vardar, they are in undisputed command of the Balkan Peninsula. Towards the end of November, 1916, a Serbian army, reformed and re-equipped, had the gratification of reoccupying Monastir, and the allies

[1] *Munchener Neueste Nachrichten*, ap. *New Europe*, vii. 87.

still hold a corner of Greek Macedonia. But the German successes in the north-east of the peninsula naturally emboldened their friends in the south-west, and the increasing hostility of the Athenian Government rendered the position of the allies in Salonica exceedingly precarious. The patience with which the vagaries of King Constantine were treated by the allied governments tended to evoke contempt rather than gratitude in Athens. We may not even hazard a conjecture as to the obstacles which impeded the dealings of the allies with the Hellenic Government. Whatever the nature of those obstacles the results were disastrous. We discouraged our friends and put heart into our enemies. King Constantine, obviously playing for time, was allowed to gain it. The attitude of his partisans in Athens towards the allies grew daily more insolent, until it culminated (December 1–2, 1916) in a dastardly attack upon a small Franco-British force which Admiral de Fournet landed at the Piraeus. To the action taken by the admiral there may at the moment have been no alternative ; but many people regarded it as singularly misjudged and as to its results there can unfortunately be no dispute. They are thus summarized by Mr. Venizelos himself. ' The consequence was to release at once the Germanophile propaganda from all restraint on the part of the Venizelist press, from all control by the allies, and from every obstacle that could have stayed its furious excesses. The allies also checked by the blockade the whole movement of exodus to Salonica on the part of those who wished to join us. It is due to their action that a reign of terror was instituted against all Venizelists, who were massacred, plundered, or hunted like wild beasts by the Royalist hordes at whose mercy they found themselves.' [1]

Formally, there was, for a time, some improvement in the relations between King Constantine's government and the

[1] Interview with Dr. R. M. Burrows, ap. *New Europe*, vol. ii, No. 24.

protecting Powers. An apology for the outrage committed upon the Franco-British force was tendered and accepted, and the king consented to withdraw the Greek army from Thessaly, a position which obviously menaced the security of the allied force in Salonica. Essentially, however, the situation was an impossible one. The authority of Mr. Venizelos firmly established at Salonica was, in the spring of 1917, gradually extended to Corfu and other islands. In Athens the king's position was apparently unassailable, and from Athens he maintained a regular correspondence with Berlin. The allies, meanwhile, looked on helplessly, and the hands of Mr. Venizelos were tied by the allies.

Then there occurred two events of profound and far-reaching significance. On March 13, 1917, the revolution broke out in Russia ; on April 6 the United States of America entered the war on the side of the allies. The repercussion of these events was felt throughout the world ; not least powerfully in south-eastern Europe. On May 1 a Congress representative of the Hellenic colonies assembled in Paris passed a resolution in favour of the establishment of a Republic in Greece and called upon the protecting Powers —Great Britain, France, and Russia—to facilitate the summoning of a Constituent Assembly in Athens and to recognize the Republic which such an Assembly would assuredly proclaim. A few days later (May 6) an echo came from Salonica where the National Government demanded the immediate deposition of King Constantine. At last the allies made up their minds to tardy but energetic action. On June 11 they required King Constantine to abdicate, and on the following day the king handed over the Government to his second son Alexander, and with the queen and the crown prince was deported to Switzerland.

The young king, after a futile manifestation of independence, was taught his constitutional position ; he was required to dismiss Mr. Zaimis and to recall Mr. Venizelos, under whose rule Greece once more regained her unity. A few days after the return of Venizelos to Athens the Hellenic Kingdom broke off relations with the Central Empires (June 30, 1917) and definitely took her place in the Grand Alliance. Whether, and if so how far, the stiffening attitude of the Western Powers towards Constantine was attributable to the overthrow of the Tsardom; how far to a fresh infusion of democratic fervour supplied by the adhesion of the United States, are questions which it is natural to ask, but impossible, as yet, to answer. This much, however, is certain. These events, so momentous and all but simultaneous, could not fail to have profoundly affected both the diplomatic and the military situation.

The local situation in Macedonia has not since that time materially altered; but by the collapse of Russia and the treaties which, in consequence of that collapse, the Central Empires have been able to dictate to Russia, to the Ukraine, and above all to Roumania, the situation in the Near East has been, in the large sense, revolutionized. The definition of the problem with which this book was to be concerned has been rendered by recent events conspicuously inadequate.[1] There has entered into the problem a new and most important factor. The place of Russia as the dominant power on the Black Sea has been taken by Germany and her vassals. The advance of Russia was for two hundred years continuous and unbroken. Not merely has that advance been arrested; the fruits of it have been completely obliterated. At the moment Russia counts as little in south-eastern Europe as she did before the accession of Peter the Great, when the Black Sea was still a Turkish lake and Pan-Slavism was as yet unborn. How long this eclipse will continue no man can conjecture. Nor can any one foretell how the future will shape itself in the Near

---

[1] Cf. *supra*, chap. i.

East. But there are one or two features in the situation which may possibly neutralize the German triumph. It is already becoming clear that the interests of Germany are likely to clash with those of her subordinate allies. A broad hint of such a conflict was conveyed by von Kühlmann's recent speech to the Reichstag (June 24, 1918). The disappearance of the Tsar's Government gave rise, as he justly remarked, ' to a whole series of questions in the Caucasus.' One of these was the sphere of influence to be assigned respectively to the Germans and the Turks. The Porte obtained a promise in the Brest-Litovsk Treaty that it should recover the districts which it had lost in 1877–8 to the Russians. But the Porte, having got much, resolved to get more. The Turkish army ' for reasons of safety ' (towards such reasons von Kühlmann ought to be sympathetic) ' pushed the left wing of its advancing army fairly wide into regions which indubitably, according to the Brest-Litovsk Treaty, could not come into question for permanent occupation by Turkey'. Meanwhile, the Turkish advance in the Caucasus has, we learn, ' been stopped ', while General von Kriess has been dispatched on a diplomatic mission to Tiflis in order to obtain a satisfactory insight into the situation in Georgia itself and the ' very confused situation in the Caucasus '. It is easy to conjecture how the confusion, now that the Turkish advance in the Caucasus has been arrested, will be exploited in the interests of Germany.

The uneasy relations between Germany and the Porte in the Caucasus find a parallel in the still more uneasy relations between Turkey and Bulgaria in the Balkans. The Tsar Ferdinand is determined to get, and without delay, the whole of the Dobrudja. But he is not to have it until he has satisfied the Porte in Thrace. This satisfaction he is not, it would seem, prepared to give. So long as the Russian army was in the field, still more when Roumania joined the Entente, Germany's vassals in the Balkans were amenable to reason. With Russia and Roumania both *hors de combat* the respective claims of Bulgaria and Turkey begin to wear a less reconcilable aspect.

Meanwhile, Constantinople itself has, owing to the course of events, become less indispensable to Germany. According to the original project of the Kaiser the Turkish alliance was pivotal. From the Bosphorus he would threaten Egypt and the Canal. Constantinople was all important as a station on the trunk line between Bremen and Basra. The project has miscarried at both points. The British successes in Palestine and Mesopotamia have dissipated the menace to our interests in the Far East. But the admission must be made that the danger has been not so much frustrated as diverted. Fresh possibilities have opened out to Germany. It cannot be pretended that Berlin to Bokhara is quite so attractive a project as Berlin to Basra. The Trans-Caspian line is neither so direct or so convenient as the *Bagdad bahn*. But it is a very tolerable second string. The route via Kieff and Baku runs through a country which is exceptionally rich in grain, oil, and minerals. Nor is it less important strategically than commercially. One of the stations on the trunk road to Bokhara is Merv, whence a branch line runs to the frontier of Afghanistan. A line of communications depending for its continuity upon the goodwill of Poles, Cossacks, and Armenians, to say nothing of the tribes of the Trans-Caspian provinces, cannot be described as perfectly secure ; yet the menace to British India is sufficiently grave.

The Peace Settlement and the Eastern Question

At this point, the argument of the present work must come to an abrupt end; it cannot pretend to reach a conclusion. The problem which this book was designed to unravel appears for the time being more than ever insoluble. All the Balkan

States have been thrown into the witches' cauldron, and what may issue therefrom no man can tell. But the allied governments have, with admirable perspicacity, enunciated principles which, if they be accepted as the basis of a European settlement, must have far-reaching consequences in the lands once subject to the Ottoman Empire. ' No peace ', the allies have declared, ' is possible so long as they have not secured . . . the recognition of the principle of nationalities and of the free existence of small states.' [1] These principles are inconsistent with the continued presence of the Ottoman Turk in Europe. Turkey has forfeited its claim to the protection of the allied Powers. ' A Turkish Government, controlled, subsidized, and supported by Germany, has been guilty of massacres in Armenia and Syria more horrible than any recorded in the history even of those unhappy countries. Evidently the interests of peace and the claims of nationality alike require that Turkish rule over alien races shall if possible be brought to an end.' [2] From the day when the Ottomans first made themselves masters of the Balkan Peninsula down to the present hour their rule has been that of an alien tyrant. They have never even attempted the task of assimilating the subject peoples ; they have been content to establish and to maintain in European lands a military encampment. Depending from the first upon the power of the sword, and upon that alone, they are now destined to perish by the sword. The allied governments are pledged beyond recall to ' the setting free of the populations subject to the bloody tyranny of the Turks ; and the turning out of Europe of the Ottoman Empire as decidedly foreign to Western civilization '.[3]

[1] Allies' Reply to German Peace Overtures, Dec. 31, 1916.
[2] Mr. Balfour's Dispatch to the British Ambassador at Washington. *The Times*, Jan. 18, 1917.
[3] Allies' Reply to President Wilson, Jan. 10, 1917.

The task thus indicated was all but accomplished by the States of the Balkan League in 1912. The formation of that League, and still more the astonishing success achieved by its arms, constituted a serious set-back to the realization of Pan-German hopes in the Near East. At all hazards the unity of the League had to be broken; the remnant of Ottoman Power upon the Bosphorus had to be saved. Both objects were successfully attained by German diplomacy. The Balkan allies were precipitated into a suicidal conflict; the Sultan recovered Adrianople, and the terms of peace were so arranged as to render practically certain an early renewal of the contest between the Balkan States. The German Emperor congratulated his Hohenzollern kinsman in Roumania upon the conclusion of the Treaty of Bucharest. The congratulations were due rather to Berlin. From the first moment of his accession to the throne the Emperor William had spared no pains to bind the Ottoman Sultan in ties of gratitude to himself. Of the 300,000,000 Moslems throughout the world he had proclaimed himself the champion and friend. Their Khalif still reigned at Constantinople. The gate to the East was still guarded by the ally of the Habsburg and the friend of the Hohenzollern.

Not upon these lines can any permanent solution of the Eastern Question be reached. The peoples who were submerged by the oncoming of the Ottoman flood have emerged again as the waters have subsided. If the principles solemnly proclaimed by the allies are to prevail; if the new map of Europe is so drawn as to respect them, the Balkan lands will be divided among the Balkan peoples. But the geographical distribution of those peoples is so complex, the ethnographical demarcation is so disputable, that the mere enunciation of the nationality principle will not suffice to secure a satisfactory settlement. Greeks, Bulgars, Albanians, Roumanians, and

Southern Slavs will have to learn to live side by side in the Balkan Peninsula on terms, if not of precise mathematical equality, at least of mutual forbearance and goodwill.

Otherwise there can be no peace for them or for Europe at large. Ever since the advent of the Turk, the land they conquered has been one of the main battle-grounds of Europe. For at least a century the storm-centre of European politics has lain in the Balkans. The struggle for Hellenic independence; the ambition of Mehemet Ali; the rivalry of Russia and Great Britain at Constantinople; the jealousies of Great Britain and France in Egypt; the inclusion of Jugo-Slavs in the conglomerate Empire of the Habsburgs; the determination of the Hohenzollern to extend Pan-German domination from Berlin to Belgrade, from Belgrade to the Bosphorus, from the Bosphorus to Bagdad, from Bagdad to Basra—these have been the main causes of unrest in Europe from the overthrow of Napoleon to the outbreak of the European War. In an unsolved Eastern Question the origin of that war is to be found. For that secular problem the Peace must propound a solution. Should it fail to do so, the Near East will in the future, as in the past, afford a nidus for international rivalries, and furnish occasions for recurring strife.

For further reference : R. G. D. Laffan, *The Guardians of the Gate* (1918); V. R. Savic, *The Reconstruction of South Eastern Europe*; N. Dacovici, *La Question du Bosphore et les Dardanelles* (1915); C. Phillipson and N. Buxton, *The Question of the Bosphorus*; A. Gauvain, *The Dardanelles* (1917); *L'Affaire Grecque* (1918); E. Venizelos (and others) *Cinq ans d'histoire Grecque, 1912–17* (1917); G. F. Abbott, *Turkey, Greece, and the Great Powers* (1916); A. H. E. Taylor, *The Future of the Southern Slavs* (1917).

II

1917–24

THE preceding paragraphs of this epilogue were written at a moment (the spring of 1918) when everything seemed in doubt—the future of the Balkans, of Europe, of the world. The dream of *Mittel-Europe* had been already partially fulfilled; the Central Empires were dominant in the Balkans; Russia was in process of disintegration; the wonderful work accomplished for her by Peter and Catherine had been cancelled; the windows to the south opened by those far-seeing rulers had again been closed; the Black Sea, once a Turkish and later a Russian lake, had become to all intents and purposes a German lake; Roumania like Serbia had been crushed; Bulgaria and Turkey were vassal states; Constantine, the pro-German King of Greece, had indeed been sent into exile, but Greek politics were a byword for uncertainty, and a German victory would certainly have brought the ascendancy of Venizelos to an end and have led to the recall of Constantine. On the other hand, the brilliant success attained by British arms in Mesopotamia (1917) had dissipated the dream of a through route from Berlin to Basra, while Palestine and Syria, thanks to an unbroken series of victories won against the Turks by Sir Edmund (now Lord) Allenby in the winter of 1917–18, were safe in English hands.

Yet who could say what the summer of 1918 would bring forth? In the West the German attack—the fourth within five months—opened on July 15, and Foch permitted the enemy, for the last time, to cross the Marne; on the 18th, however, the allied commander let loose his reserves and the Germans were driven back with immense slaughter.

Three weeks later the British counter offensive began; a series of operations, almost continuous from August to November, broke into fragments the great military machine of Germany, and on 11th November the terms of an armistice, dictated by the allies, were accepted by the German Government.

Their Balkan allies had already fallen away. The victories in Palestine, Syria, and Mesopotamia had at last convinced the Turks that they had put their money on the wrong horse. The adhesion of Greece to the allied cause had further alarmed the Porte and had turned the military balance in the Balkans in favour of the allies. Within a fortnight of King Constantine's forced abdication (17 June 1917) Venizelos had declared war on Germany, Turkey, and Bulgaria, but matters still tarried on the Salonika front. In June 1918, however, the command was taken over by General Franchet d'Espérey. The arrival of 250,000 Greek troops gave the war-wearied allies fresh confidence, and in September the offensive was opened against Bulgaria. A week's brilliant fighting resulted in the rout of the Bulgarian army, and after a harrying retreat, in which the Serbians played a foremost part, King Ferdinand sued for peace. On 30th September, barely a fortnight after the advance had begun, Bulgaria made an unconditional surrender and handed over her army, her railways, stores, and even her Government into the hands of the allies. On 12th October the Serbians had the satisfaction of occupying their old capital Nish, and by this operation cut the Berlin–Constantinople Railway at a vital point. Constantinople itself was now at the mercy of the allies, and they were on the point of advancing to the attack upon the historic city when the Sultan sued for peace and the armistice of Mudros was concluded (30 October).

What a series of complications might not have been avoided

had the Sultan been more stubborn, the allies less complaisant, and had the intention, so frequently announced, of ' turning the Ottoman ' Turks out of Europe, been literally fulfilled ! As it was, the august allies, vainly imagining that their task in the Near East was accomplished, sat down at Paris to elaborate a covenant for a League of Nations and to draw up the terms to be imposed upon the two chief criminals, the primary disturbers of the world's peace—Germany and Austria-Hungary. Serbia and Roumania were intimately concerned in the winding up of the Habsburg estate, but the Turks had been so hopelessly beaten that the settlement of the Ottoman Empire might without danger, it was supposed, be deferred to a more convenient season. Events were to prove the folly and danger of delay.

It is, however, only fair to the diplomatists to remember that so long as President Wilson retained power, and until the Senate and the people of the United States had made clear their determination to assume no responsibilities in connexion with the world-settlement, the hope was cherished that America would act as the principal liquidator of the Ottoman Empire. ' We cannot ', said Mr. Lloyd George (September 1919), ' settle Turkey till we know what the United States is going to do.' The chief author of the Covenant of the League of Nations would, it was hoped, be able to persuade his countrymen to accept mandates under the League at least for Palestine and Mesopotamia. To those who were familiar with the unbroken traditions of American policy, who realized the hold which the Monroe doctrine still exercised upon the American mind, the hope was from the outset vain, but the old world was reluctant to abandon it, and the reluctance explains the delay in dealing with the problems of the Near East.

Nevertheless the delay was an incalculable misfortune. The core of the Eastern Question, as this book has striven to demon-

strate, is the position of the Ottoman Turk in Europe. Had
a Peace Treaty been concluded early in 1919 the Turk, whose
appeal to the wager of battle had gone decisively against him,
might, without difficulty, have been finally compelled to
retire into Asia. Delay gave him the opportunity to recover
something of military strength, to appeal to Moslem sentiment
in many lands, and, above all, to sow dissensions among the
allies.

Meanwhile, the destiny of the Southern Slavs and of Roumania was decided by the treaties concluded with Austria at
St. Germain (10 September 1919) and with Hungary at
Trianon (4 June 1920). By the acquisition of Bessarabia from
Russia, Roumania attained a long standing and legitimate
ambition, and attained it with the hearty goodwill, nay at
the express desire of the inhabitants.[1] Under Catherine's
partition scheme of 1782 (*supra*, p. 155) Bessarabia was to
have been thrown in with Moldavia and Wallachia into the
independent kingdom of Dacia. Russia, however, obtained
Bessarabia by the Treaty of Bucharest (1812), and, despite
the efforts of the Porte to recover it, retained it at the general
peace settlement of 1815. By the Treaty of Paris (1856)
Southern Bessarabia was ceded to Moldavia, but with not less
ingratitude than impolicy Russia claimed its retrocession at
the Treaty of Berlin (1878).[2] Bismarck was not sorry to see
Russia multiplying enemies in South-Eastern Europe ; Lord
Beaconsfield was unwisely indifferent to the fortunes of a
potential friend. The Great War brought to Roumania an
opportunity, perilous indeed but golden, and she used it with
discretion, and with ultimate advantage to herself.

Not only in regard to Bessarabia. The Principality of
Transylvania has had a chequered history which may be

---

[1] Recognized by the Supreme Council of March 1920. Treaty signed
28 October 1920.   [2] *Supra*, pp. 341, 344.

followed in outline in preceding chapters of this book. Predominantly Roumanian in race, it had, since 1699, been incorporated in the kingdom of Hungary. If, however, the claims of nationality were to be primarily regarded, Roumania's irredentist ambitions could not be denied, and Hungarian Transylvania, together with Austrian Bukovina and half the Banat of Temesvar, passed to her under the several treaties of Peace. By these acquisitions Roumania was more than doubled in size, and emerged from the war with a population of over 17,000,000 (as against about 7,000,000 pre-war) and a territory of 122,282 square miles. But she has difficult problems to face, both internal and external.

Of the external problems, perhaps the most difficult is that presented by her relations with Hungary. The Hungarian Republic of to-day represents only a shrunken fragment of a proud and historic kingdom. Apart from the cession of Transylvania to Roumania she was compelled to cede a large district in the north to Czecho-Slovakia and another in the south to Yugoslavia. Hungary was thus reduced in population to less than eight millions, in area to 35,790 square miles, and to a position in both respects markedly inferior to that of neighbours whom she regards, though unjustifiably, as parvenus. That Hungary deserved condign chastisement at the hands of the victorious allies is undeniable ; whether that chastisement will make for permanent peace in South-Eastern Europe is less certain. Transylvania, in particular, is not ethnically homogeneous. Of the 4,294,000 inhabitants, only 2,310,000 are Roumans ; while the Magyars number 1,475,000. Roumania, therefore, finds herself faced in turn, as was the Habsburg Empire, by an obstinate racial problem. Hardly less difficult are the financial, economic, and agrarian problems which have confronted the short-lived ministries which have successively held office since the war. Nor has Roumania been free from

Bolshevist propaganda. A large measure of agrarian reform has, however, been passed, by which, under a scheme analogous to the Ashbourne-Wyndham schemes of land purchase in Ireland, the bulk of the land will be owned by the peasants who cultivate it. Externally, Roumania has attempted to secure the permanence of the *status quo* by the conclusion of a close alliance with Czecho-Slovakia and Yugoslavia. The close relations existing between this 'Little Entente' and France and Poland respectively would seem to offer to its members a further guarantee for the maintenance of the Peace settlement in Central and South-Eastern Europe. A double dynastic connexion between Roumania and Greece, the only two Balkan States whose interests at no point collide, has been established by the marriage of King George II of Greece with the eldest daughter of the Roumanian House and that of the Crown Prince Carol, heir to the throne of Roumania, with Princess Helen, daughter of the late King Constantine of Greece. These marriages further connect both the Greek and the Roumanian dynasties with the reigning families of Great Britain and Denmark, not to mention the former dynasties of Russia and Prussia. The significance of the matrimonial alliance for the Balkans has, however, been discounted, if not actually cancelled, by recent events in Greece.

The Southern Slavs have reaped the just reward of the high courage and endurance manifested by them from July 1914 to November 1918. The dismemberment of the old Habsburg Empire with its congeries of States and mosaic of nationalities gave the Slavs of Central and South-Eastern Europe their opportunity. They have eagerly embraced it. The new triune kingdom of the Serbs, Slovenes, and Croats represents the union of the southern as Czecho-Slovakia and

Poland represent the triumph of the northern Slavs. Yugo-slavia (as it is conveniently termed) now includes in addition to Serbia and Montenegro, Bosnia and the Herzegovina (definitely annexed by the Habsburgs in 1908), Croatia-Slavonia, parts of Styria, Carinthia, Carniola, and practically the whole of Dalmatia, embracing a population of over 12,000,000 and an area of 96,134 square miles. In one of the darkest hours of their agony in the war (20 July 1917) the Southern Slavs formulated the terms of a draft Constitution known as the Pact of Corfu—the island where their constituent conference took place. The document declared that the State of the Serbs, Croats, and Slovenes would be a free and independent kingdom with indivisible territory and unity of allegiance, under a ' constitutional democratic and parliamentary monarchy under the Karageorgevic dynasty ' ; that the two alphabets Cyrillic and Latin should rank equally in official and general use ; that the Orthodox, Roman Catholic, and Mussulman faiths, 'which are those mainly professed by our nation', should enjoy equal rights and status ; that elections, both for the central legislature and local bodies, should be by universal suffrage and secret ballot ; that a constituent assembly, thus elected, should meet after the conclusion of peace to ratify a Constitution which would then provide ' the source and consummation of all authority and rights by which the life of the whole nation would be regulated '. This document formed the basis of the Constitution which was adopted in June 1921. Montenegro, which was left at the Peace in a position of some ambiguity, was definitely united with Serbia on the death of King Nicholas of Montenegro (1 March 1921).

Second only, among the Balkan States, to Roumania both in area and population, the kingdom of the Serbs, Croats, and Slovenes is confronted by problems not less difficult than those which confront her Latin neighbour. 'Yugoslavia' suggests a more perfect unity than does in fact exist. The new kingdom is not entirely homogeneous either as regards race or religion, and the Croats and Slovenes, though glad to be freed from the yoke of the Magyars, might have preferred a federal rather than a unitary type of Constitution. Moreover, they mainly adhere to the Roman Church, the Serbs are Orthodox, while in Bosnia a considerable portion of the inhabitants—the proportion is generally computed to be one-third—are neither Greek nor Roman, but Turkified Moslems. Nor is there much in common between the big landowners of Bosnia and the democratic peasants of old Serbia. Federalism, therefore, might have corresponded more closely with local conditions than the unity which alone could satisfy the ambition of the Serbs.

The union of the Croats and Slovenes with the Serbs accentuated another difficulty, which proved to be one of the most obstinate of all the territorial problems confronting the Peace Conference. For two full years after the armistice the Adriatic problem remained unsolved; the conflicting claims of Italy and Yugoslavia unreconciled. Italy claimed, quite justly, that the allies should implement the promises contained in the Secret Treaty of London (26 April 1915), which brought Italy into the war. Italy was promised the district of Trentino, the whole of Cisalpine Tyrol up to the Brenner Pass, the city and district of Trieste, the county of Gradisca and Gorizia, the Istrian peninsula up to the Quarnero with Volosca and the Istrian archipelago, the 'province of Dalmatia in its present administrative frontiers', together with nearly all the Adriatic islands (including Lissa), and the retention of Valona and the Dodecanese. The Adriatic coast from Volosca Bay to the northern frontier of Dalmatia, with the ports of Fiume, Spalato, Ragusa, Cattaro, Antivari, Dulcigno, and San Giovanni di Medua, were with several islands assigned to Croatia, Serbia, and Montenegro, its component parts. Fiume was destined to form a bitter bone of contention. Yugoslavia and Italy both claimed it; the latter mainly on sentimental and cultural grounds, the former on the ground of its economic importance to Croatia, to which, by the admission of Italy, the Treaty of London had assigned it.

At the Paris Conference President Wilson hotly championed the Yugoslav cause; England and France, while anxious to reconcile the claims of two staunch allies, felt themselves bound by the terms of the Pact of London, a Pact which as the product of 'secret diplomacy' was to Wilson anathema. Throughout the year 1919 the Adriatic problem continued to give great anxiety to the allied diplomatists, and more than once threatened to break up the Conference. In September 1919 the problem was further complicated by the action of D'Annunzio—one of the most romantic figures in Italy, a great poet and an ardent patriot—who at the head of an enthusiastic band of volunteers occupied Fiume and defied both the Italian and Yugoslav Governments to turn him out. Both the Italians and Yugoslavs were, however, anxious to reach a settlement of a tiresome question, and, after prolonged negotiations, a treaty was, in November 1920, signed at Rapallo. Fiume, together with a narrow strip along the coast north-westwards towards Volosca, was declared independent under the guardianship of the League of Nations. The neutral corridor gave Italy direct access to the independent State.

Sushak, the easterly suburb of Fiume and important as a railway junction, was given to Yugoslavia; Zara and its adjacent islands were assigned to Italy together with the islands of Cherso, Lussin, Lagosta, and Pelagosa, with the adjacent islands and rocks. Lissa, on the other hand, went, with the rest of the islands and Dalmatia, to Yugoslavia. The frontier line between the two States in the north-east was drawn in a sense favourable to Italy, but in such a manner as to leave under the Italian flag some 500,000 Slavs who may give trouble. On the whole, however, a reasonable compromise was reached. With Valona, Lussin, Pola, and Trieste in her own hands, Italy realized her wildest ambition and should be able to dominate the Adriatic. The triune kingdom, on the other hand, obtained ample commercial access to the sea, and provided it does not develop naval ambitions ought to manage to live at peace with Italy.

But D'Annunzio was still in Fiume. He refused to recognize the Treaty of Rapallo, and even dispatched an expedition to Zara in order to prevent the ' surrender ' of Dalmatia. Finally, however (December 1921), he yielded to force applied by the Italian Government, and Fiume was occupied by an Italian detachment. Yet the settlement tarried, and it was not until January 1924 that a definitive agreement was reached between Italy and Yugoslavia. The ' full and entire sovereignty of the Italian kingdom over the city and port of Fiume ' was recognized by the Serb-Croat-Slovene State, while the Italian Government, on its part, recognized ' the full and entire sovereignty of the Serb-Croat-Slovene State over Porto Barros and the delta '. There the matter rests. There are Slavs left under the Italian flag, and Italians under the flag of the triune kingdom. But Italy and Yugoslavia have not merely concluded peace, but have entered into a pact of friendship which should contribute to the tranquillity of South-Eastern Europe.

The position of Bulgaria need not detain us. Deservedly chastised for her perfidy in 1913, she again suffered for her miscalculation in the Great War. Under the Treaty of Neuilly (27 November 1919) she had to surrender the Strum-nitza line and a strip of territory on the north-west frontier to Serbia and Bulgarian Macedonia to Greece. Under the Treaty of Sèvres (10 August 1920) she was further condemned to cede a small portion of Eastern Thrace to Turkey, and the rest of it, with Western Thrace to Greece. Access to Dedeagatch and the Aegean was, however, guaranteed to her. In 1923 Bulgaria succeeded in getting her Indemnity cut down from £90,000,000 to £22,500,000, but her plight remains a sorry one. That Bulgaria has deserved her fate is undeniable, but it does not follow that her successful rivals were wise in making the punishment so severe. By pressing her claim, however just, to Kavala, in 1913, Greece committed what has since been recognized as a grave political blunder. To cut Bulgaria off territorially from the Aegean, as the Peace Treaties did, is to drive her to desperation. The Treaty of Lausanne, by neutralizing the Straits, may do something to mitigate the commercial hardship, but it does little to assuage the political indignity. The peoples on the Black Sea littoral, so far and in proportion as they cherish European aspirations, must have free access to European waters. For four and a half centuries the keys of the gate have been in the keeping of an Asiatic Power encamped on European soil. Had the opportunity given by the fortunes of war been accepted in 1919 the keys would have been entrusted to European custody ; but delay rendered almost insoluble the difficulty of finding a custodian who would enjoy general confidence. Once again the Turks, endowed it would seem by a fairy godmother with at least nine lives, found salvation in the jealousy and disunion of their enemies.

The events which ensued between 1919 and 1923 are, in detail, exceedingly complicated. In broad outline they will readily be mastered by any one who has followed the main argument of this book. That argument has turned largely upon the unique significance of Constantinople in world-politics, and upon the internecine jealousy of the European Powers in regard to the custody of the narrow Straits. Had Russia not committed suicide she would have found herself in a position to demand the fulfilment of a pledge given by her Western allies under the exigencies of war ; the Cross would have supplanted the Crescent at St. Sophia ; the age-long ambition of the Czars would have been achieved ; the Russians would have succeeded the Turks as custodians of the Straits.

The Russian revolution negatived the possibility of that solution of an historic problem. It did not render more easy of adoption another alternative. The Greeks have never surrendered their claim to Byzantium—the seat of the old Greek Empire. But a Greek hegemony in the Eastern Mediterranean was not particularly acceptable to France, the secular friend of the Turks, nor to Italy, heir to the political traditions not only of the Roman Empire, but of the Republics of Venice and Genoa, and always the jealous rival of Greece. Great Britain was sympathetic towards Hellenic aspirations, but while anxious to see St. Sophia restored to the Cross, was uneasy as to the sentiments of her Moslem subjects. If the Greeks could single-handed expel the remnant of Turks from Europe and make good their position in Asia Minor they might rely upon the sympathetic encouragement and upon the friendly diplomatic offices of the British Government, but on nothing more.

What were the practical possibilities of the situation? A brief recital of events may help to answer that question. The Turkish Armistice was signed, as we have seen, on October 30, 1918. At the beginning of February 1919 M. Venizelos, on behalf of Greece, put in a claim to the Smyrna zone. By the agreement signed at St. Jean-de-Maurienne between Great Britain, France, and Italy, the vilayet of Smyrna together with a large part of the coast and even the hinterland of Asia Minor had been provisionally assigned to Italy. In the spring of 1919, however, Italy was making herself disagreeable to the allies about Fiume, and M. Venizelos, seizing the opportunity of Italy's withdrawal from Paris (April 24), obtained the sanction of the allies to a Greek occupation of Smyrna (May 1919).

This occupation, supported by British, French, and American warships, aroused bitter resentment among the Turks, and particularly among the 'Nationalists', a party which was rapidly establishing its supremacy under the vigorous leadership of a brilliant soldier, Mustapha Kemal Pasha. In July 1919 Kemal escaped from Constantinople, proceeded to rouse the Turks in the Anatolian highlands, and established at Angora a rival Government to that of Constantinople. In January 1920 certain Turkish deputies in Constantinople adopted a 'National Pact', which has formed the basis of the Fundamental Law of the new Turkish State.

Meanwhile it became clear that America would accept no mandate or any other specific responsibility for Turkey, and the British Government was officially warned by the Viceroy of India (May 1919) that Moslem feeling was deeply stirred by the prospect of the expulsion of the Turks from Constantinople, and on 18 February 1920 Admiral de Robeck, British High Commissioner at Constantinople, officially announced the fact that 'the allies had decided not to deprive Turkey of Constantinople'.

The terms of a Treaty to be imposed upon Turkey were handed to Tewfik Pasha in May 1920, and the Treaty of Sèvres, which embodied them, was signed on 10th August. Constantinople was to remain under Turkish sovereignty, but, except for a strip of territory assigned to the Turks for the defence of the capital city, Turkey in Europe ceased to exist.

The zone of the Straits and their navigation were to be controlled by an international commission, and contiguous areas were to be demilitarized. Western Thrace and Eastern Thrace up to the Chatalja lines were, as already indicated, assigned to Greece, which was also to have Imbros and Tenedos, and other islands. The Dodecanese were assigned to Italy, but Italy had already agreed to cede them to Greece, with the exception of Rhodes, which was to be retained by Italy, as long as Great Britain retained Cyprus.

The city of Smyrna, with the Ionian hinterland, was to be under Greek administration for five years, at the end of which their future was to be decided by a *plébiscite*. Armenia and Kurdistan were to be independent; and the Turks were to renounce all their rights over Arabia, Palestine, Mesopotamia, Syria, Egypt, Sudan, Cyprus, Tripoli, Tunis, and Morocco. In Arabia the King of the Hejaz was recognized as independent and to have the custody of the Holy Places. It had already been arranged (May 1920) that France should receive the mandate for Syria and Great Britain for Palestine and Mesopotamia. The Treaty recognized the rights of the two principal allies over Egypt, Sudan, the Suez Canal, Cyprus, Tunisia, and Morocco respectively. The Turkish Navy and Air Forces were virtually abolished and the army reduced to 50,000 men, while Turkish taxes were to be controlled by a Commission of Great Britain, France, and Italy.

These terms were admittedly severe, and Turkey had made a strong protest against them, particularly against the cession of Smyrna and its hinterland to Greece, and against the exclusion of the Porte from the Straits Commission. On the latter point the allies gave way; for the rest Turkey was sternly reminded that she had ' entered the war without the shadow of excuse or provocation ', and was ' thereby guilty of peculiar treachery to Powers which for more than half a century had been her steadfast friends'; that in August 1914 those Powers had promised that if Turkey maintained her neutrality throughout the war the allies would guarantee the integrity of the Turkish dominions; that her intervention had involved infinite loss and suffering to humanity, and that in consequence of the savagery directed and organized by the Turkish Government against people to whom it owed protection, the allies were resolved 'to emancipate all areas inhabited by a non-Turkish majority from Turkish rule'.

Brave words; but were the allies in a position to give effect to them? The Treaty of Sèvres was never ratified even by the Turks of Constantinople; still less by Kemal and his 'Nationalist' Government at Angora, who promptly declared that under no circumstances would they accept the terms. In the summer of 1920 it seemed that they might be forced to do so by the brilliant success of the Greek army. Encouraged by the allies and sustained with a British loan, the Greeks attacked and defeated the Nationalist Turks, and on July 8 occupied Brusa—the ancient capital of the Ottomans. Before the end of July the Greeks had also made good their position in Thrace; Adrianople was occupied on the 25th, and on the 26th King Alexander made a triumphal entry into the town. On August 10, as indicated above, the Turks signed the Treaty at Sèvres.

Tewfik Pasha, however, could commit only the Government at Constantinople. The Kemalists at Angora defied alike the allies and the Sultan; and fate smiled on their defiance. In August 1920 M. Venizelos returned to Athens, bringing with him the sheaves of victory, in the shape of the Treaty of Sèvres; but from this moment fortune deserted him. On October 25 the young King Alexander died from the effects of a monkey's bite. The election campaign was already in full swing, but M. Venizelos immediately postponed the dissolution, and procured the appointment as Regent of Admiral Conduriotis, pending the arrival of the late king's younger brother Prince Paul.

Prince Paul further complicated a difficult situation by a formal declaration that he would accept the crown only if 'the Hellenic people were to decide that it did not desire the return of his august father and were to exclude the Crown Prince George from his right of succession'.

The recall of the ex-King Constantine thereupon became the one real issue of the pending election. Nor was the conclusion by any means assured. M. Venizelos, despite his brilliant success at Paris, had lost ground in Greece. His prolonged absence had given his many enemies their chance; he was badly served by his subordinates; many of the best elements in Greek society were against him, and among his noisiest supporters were many of the least respectable. The polls, taken in November, went decisively against him; he immediately left the country, and in December King Constantine was recalled by *plébiscite*, and was enthusiastically welcomed back to Athens.

The situation was, however, not an easy one. The allies declined to recognize King Constantine, while the Turkish Nationalists at Angora adopted the 'National Pact', and demanded the 'security of Constantinople', the union under Turkish sovereignty of all parts of the Empire 'inhabited by an Ottoman Moslem majority', and that a *plébiscite* should be taken in Western Thrace to determine 'its judicial status' (January 1921).

In the hope of reaching a settlement a Conference was called by the Supreme Council in London (February–March 1921), and was attended by representatives of Greece and of both the Turkish Governments. The allies offered a considerable modification of the terms of the Treaty of

Sèvres, but the offer was rejected alike by the Greeks and the Turks. The opportunity of the London Conference was, however, seized both by the French and the Italians to negotiate an agreement with the Kemalist Turks. The result of the French intrigues was the publication (20 October 1921) of the agreement concluded at Angora between M. Franklin-Bouillon, on behalf of France, and Yussuf Kemal Bey, 'Minister for Foreign Affairs of the Government of the Grand National Assembly of Angora'. This meant the recognition by France of the Angora Assembly, as the sovereign authority in Turkey, the abandonment by France of the allies with whom she had been acting in such close co-operation since August 1914, and the conclusion, contrary to the Franco-British Treaty of the 4th September 1914 and to the London Pact of November 1915, of a separate peace with 'Turkey'. Incidentally the French were to obtain valuable commercial concessions, but to the British Government it appeared that France had abandoned its responsibilities for the protection of minorities, and had even jeopardized Great Britain's position in Mesopotamia.[1]

The French Government offered 'explanations', but that the Turkish attitude was materially stiffened by the Angora agreement does not admit of question. And there were other reasons. The Greek offensive in the spring of 1921 was checked, but when renewed at midsummer was more successful; in the autumn, however, the Greek forces suffered a severe reverse, and a section of Greek opinion demanded that an attempt should be made to obtain foreign mediation. By February 1922 it was recognized that the situation of the Greeks was almost desperate, and in that month an allied conference in Paris decided to suggest to both belligerents terms which represented a drastic revision of the Treaty of

[1] Cf. Lord Curzon's Note of 5 November 1921.

Sèvres, in favour of the Turks. The Greeks and the Constantinople Government accepted the suggestions, but the
Kemalists refused to grant an armistice, except on the basis
of an immediate and unconditional evacuation of Anatolia.
Negotiations were consequently suspended, and in August the
allies made yet another attempt to bring the belligerents to
terms. Before the projected conference could meet the Turks
had begun their triumphant advance, the Greek forces were
swept before them into the sea, and Smyrna, delivered over to
massacre and arson, was occupied by the Turks on September 9.
Greek refugees from all parts of Asia Minor fled in panic before
the Turks, and about 1,000,000 of them were fortunate enough
to escape on board Greek and allied ships.

The Greek *débâcle* was complete; their dream of an
Ionian Empire was shattered. Upon disasters abroad there
ensued revolution at home. The troops mutinied in Salonika,
Crete, Chios, and Mytilene, and demanded the abdication of
King Constantine. The king yielded before the storm, left
Athens with his family (27th September), and early in January
1923 died at Palermo. Meanwhile, a serious international
crisis had developed. The victorious army of Angora advanced
towards the Dardanelles, actually entered the neutral zone,
and came within fighting distance of the British garrison at
Chanak on the southern shore. France withdrew her troops;
Italy, who like France had concluded an agreement with the
Turks (April 1922), made it clear that in the event of war no
help was to be expected from her; Great Britain alone stood
firm. Reinforcements of ships and men were hurriedly dispatched to the Dardanelles; the British Dominions and the
three Balkan Powers were invited ' to take part in the defence
of the zones ', and the Turks were bluntly informed that they
would not be allowed to cross into Europe.

That war was averted, though narrowly, was due partly to

the firmness of the British Government at home, and not less to the admirable tact and temper of Sir Charles Harington, the allied commander-in-chief at Constantinople. Negotiations between the Kemalists and Greece and the allies were opened early in October at Mudania, and on the 11th an armistice was signed. The Turks were to guarantee the ' Freedom of the Straits '; the allies undertook that Greece should immediately evacuate Eastern Thrace, which was to be temporarily occupied by the allies.

In November the allied signatories to the Treaty of Sèvres met in conference at Lausanne with the representatives of the new Turkish State. Between the armistice of Mudania and the opening of the Lausanne Conference an event of great historic interest, albeit of small practical significance, had taken place. On 1 November 1922 the Grand National Assembly at Angora issued an edict that the office of Sultan had ceased to exist, and that the office of Caliph should henceforward be filled by election from among the princes of the House of Osman. In brief, Constantinople was to be ' Vaticanized '. On 4 November Rafat Pasha took over the administration of Constantinople in the name of the Angora Government ; on the same day, the Grand Vizier, Tewfik Pasha, resigned into the hands of the Sultan the trust confided to him and his colleagues, and on the 17th the last of the Ottoman Sultans left Constantinople on board a British warship.

A great chapter in modern history was thus brought to an abrupt and inglorious close.

On November 18 Prince Abdul-Mejid, cousin to the ex-Sultan Mohammed VI, and the eldest prince in male descent of the House of Osman, was elected Caliph ; but in March 1924 the Caliphate itself was abolished by the Grand National Assembly, and the Caliph with his family sent into exile.

Meanwhile, Angora had been formally declared, by the National Assembly, to be the Turkish capital (13th October 1923), and on the 29th, by the same authority, Turkey had been proclaimed as a Republic, with Mustapha Kemal Pasha as its first President.

Greece reached the same goal, though by a more devious route, in March 1924. On the second abdication of King Constantine the crown passed to his eldest son, who ascended a perilous throne as George II. Such authority as survived in the unhappy country was, however, vested in a group of military dictators of advanced republican views. Certain of the ex-ministers and military chiefs who were held to be specially responsible for the *débâcle* in Asia Minor were summarily tried by court martial, and despite the protest of the British Minister at Athens, M. Gounaris and five others were executed; while the ex-king's brother, Prince Andrew, charged with military disobedience, was banished for life. These events led to the severance of diplomatic relations between Great Britain and Greece.

At the Lausanne Conference M. Venizelos patriotically consented to represent his country, and, as will be seen presently, obtained for it the best terms possible under circumstances so disastrously altered. Internally, however, the situation was chaotic, and, in August 1923, was rendered still more desperate by the quarrel with Italy which ensued upon the murder of General Tellini (26th August) and other Italian Commissioners who were engaged upon the task of delimiting the Graeco-Albanian frontier. Italy immediately demanded full apologies, an inquiry *in loco* into the circumstances of the murder to be conducted by an Italian officer, and an indemnity of 50,000,000 Italian lire to be paid within five days. To certain of the conditions Greece demurred as inconsistent with its sovereignty and honour. Whereupon the Italians bombarded Corfu, killed and wounded a considerable number of Greek and Armenian refugees, and occupied the island. Greece thereupon appealed to the League of Nations. Signor Mussolini, on behalf of Italy, refused the arbitration of the League, but accepted the mediation of the Conference of Ambassadors, which virtually conceded to Italy almost everything that she had demanded. Accordingly, Italy (September 27) evacuated Corfu, and an incident which at one moment threatened a renewal of the European conflagration was fortunately closed.

Meanwhile, Greece was torn by factions, Royalist, military, republican; plots were followed by counterplots, until in December his countrymen turned again to M. Venizelos and besought him once more to save his country. King George II and his consort were requested to leave the country, and retired to Roumania, while the Regency was vested in Admiral Conduriotis. M. Venizelos, though broken in health, gallantly responded to the call, and returned to Greece in the first days of the New Year (1924). He was immediately elected President of the National Assembly, and assumed office as Prime Minister. But the task confronting the great statesman demanded the fullest vigour of body and spirit ; M. Venizelos, after a brave but brief effort, found himself unequal to it, and consequently resigned office on February 4, and a month later left Athens and Greece.

Though professedly a republican, M. Venizelos might, not for the first time, have preserved the monarchy and saved the State. His departure was the final blow to a cause already desperate, and on 25th March 1924 a Republic was, subject to the taking of a *plébiscite*, proclaimed. The *plébiscite* was taken on 13th April 1924, and of those who voted 68 per cent. declared in favour of a Republic, which was accordingly confirmed.

Having seen the establishment of Republics both in Greece, where the soil might be thought congenial, and in Turkey, where every tradition pointed to monarchy if not to autocracy, we must now revert to the proceedings in the Peace Conference which opened on 20th November 1923 at Lausanne.

For more than two months the European diplomatists, under the skilled and patient presidency of the Marquess Curzon of Kedleston, the British Foreign Minister, laboured to formulate terms which might provide a durable, if not a permanent solution of the problem of the Near East. But the circumstances were none too favourable. The Turk has for two centuries ingeniously contrived to evade the worst consequences of almost unbroken defeat. Could he now be expected to forgo the fruits of a victory as dramatic as it was complete ? Nor was the success of the new Turkey confined to the battle-field. In sure reliance upon the traditional hatred of Italy for Greece, and the recurrent jealousy between France and England, the Turk took up and successfully sustained at Lausanne a tone lofty to the verge of insolence. Nevertheless, by the end of January 1923 terms had been all but agreed upon, when Ismet Pasha, the chief representative of Turkey, demanded further delay, and at the fifty-ninth minute of the eleventh hour refused to sign the Treaty, and the diplomatists dispersed.

Undeterred, however, by this unexpected fiasco, the diplomatists reassembled on 23rd April 1923, under the presidency of Sir Horace Rumbold, who since 1920 had been British High Commissioner and ambassador designate at Constantinople. After another three months of assiduous labour the Treaty of Lausanne was signed on 24th July 1923. A month later (23rd August) it was ratified by the Assembly at Angora. On the same day the British troops, which had been in continuous occupation since the armistice, began the evacuation of Constantinople. A finer example of British discipline and morale there has never been than that afforded by the occupation and evacuation of Constantinople. What Turkey, and England, and Europe owed in this, and in even larger matters, to the perfect temper and tact of Sir Charles Harington, the allied commander-in-chief, it is not yet possible to estimate; but history may tell.

We must be content to summarize the main points embodied in the Treaty of Lausanne. The Greeks had, of course, to pay the penalty for over-vaulting ambition and disastrous defeat. That Great Britain must accept some responsibility, if not for the defeat, at least for the ill-grounded pride which preceded and in some sense prepared it, is unfortunately true. The only excuse for the encouragement given to Greece is that the British Government were assured by the most competent military advice available that the Greek army was fully equal to the task it had essayed. The advice might well have been justified had the Greek commanders exhibited ordinary skill and prudence in the actual conduct of the campaign. As it was, their incompetence was equalled only by their self-confidence.

The extent of the disaster was naturally reflected in the terms which Turkey unexpectedly found itself in a position to dictate. Greece lost to Turkey Eastern Thrace, with Adrianople and the islands of Imbros and Tenedos, but with these exceptions retained the rest of the Turkish islands in the Aegean and Western Thrace only up to the Maritza. Italy retained the Dodecanese. Turkey surrendered all claims upon Egypt, the Sudan, Cyprus, Syria, Palestine, Mesopotamia, and the rest of Arabia, but retained in full sovereignty Smyrna and the remainder of the Anatolian peninsula. The problem of minorities, racial and religious, had been to a large extent solved by the simple method of extermination, but, for the rest, the Treaty provided for a compulsory interchange of Greek Moslems and Turks of the Orthodox Church, excepting only the Greeks of Constantinople and the Turks of Western Thrace, who were permitted to remain in their respective homes. Otherwise the rights of minorities were confirmed by the Turks, as promised in the National Pact of Angora, on the same lines as those accepted by Poland, Czecho-Slovakia, and other sovereign States. There remained two other questions: the one concerned the control and navigation of the Straits; the other the position of foreign traders in Turkey. On the latter point the New Turks were as sensitive as foreigners were anxious. The fact that ever since the sixteenth century foreigners in Turkey had under the ' Capitulations' enjoyed special privileges was plainly indicative of the inferior status of the Ottoman Empire and of the mistrust of Oriental justice not unnaturally entertained by Europeans. That mistrust has never been dispelled, and if the Turk wants to enjoy in fullest extent the advantages of financial and commercial association with Europe he must needs submit to some sacrifice of international dignity. But in 1924 his mood was haughty, and pride successfully asserted itself against self-interest. The contention was bitter and protracted, but in the event the Capitulations were abolished; foreigners, therefore, trading in Turkey must take their chance of Turkish law and Oriental justice, though for a period of seven years they are to be exempt from any taxes or disabilities which are not equally imposed upon Turkish subjects. As regards the famous waterway, the Turk is, inevitably under the circumstances, to remain at Constantinople under specific and stringent guarantees from the signatory Powers, and to be allowed to maintain a garrison therein, but the Straits are to be neutralized, and free passage for foreign warships and aircraft as well as merchant ships, subject to a reasonable limitation of numbers, is guaranteed to the States of the world, and on both coasts demilitarized and unfortified zones are to be created under the guarantee of the League of Nations.

That the Treaty represents a conspicuous triumph for the Turkish National State and a corresponding humiliation for those upon whom the victorious Turks virtually imposed it, cannot be denied. Yet it has been argued with some plausibility that, despite all its obvious imperfections, the Treaty of Lausanne is likely to inaugurate a more lasting settlement not only than the Treaty of Sèvres, but than the Treaties of Versailles, St. Germain, Trianon, and Neuilly. This contention, at first sight wholly paradoxical, rests upon the argument that, unlike the latter Treaties, the Treaty of Lausanne represents ' an agreement between the principal parties concerned, in which each had to make sacrifices and bear disappointments, but none was subjected to impossible commitments or intolerable humiliations '.[1]

A question at this point obtrudes itself : How far was the Treaty of Lausanne consistent with the more important declarations made by statesmen of the allied nations, during the progress of the war? On 10th November 1914 Mr. Lloyd George had spoken of the Turks as ' a human cancer, a creeping agony in the flesh of the lands which they misgovern, rotting every fibre of life ', and had rejoiced that the Turk was to be ' called to a final account for his long record of infamy against humanity '. If the Lausanne Treaty can hardly be described as a ' final account ', still less did it fulfil the intention of the allies as announced in the Balfour Note to President Wilson (18th December 1916). That Note referred to one of the allied war aims as the ' setting free of the populations subject to the bloody tyranny of the Turks, and the turning out of Europe of the Ottoman Empire as decidedly foreign to Western

[1] Temperley (ed.), *A History of the Peace Conference of Paris*, vi. 115.

civilization'. The collapse of Russia and the repudiation by the Soviet Government of all the annexationist ambitions of the Tsarist Government had, of course, entirely altered the situation of the allies *vis-à-vis* Russia. There could no longer be any question of fulfilling the engagements of 1915, under which Great Britain and France had assented to the complete realization of Russia's hopes in relation to Constantinople and the Straits. Indeed on 5th January 1918 Mr. Lloyd George had specifically denied that we were ' fighting to deprive Turkey of its capital, or of the rich and renowned lands of Asia Minor and Thrace, which are predominantly Turkish in race . . . While we do not challenge the maintenance of the Turkish Empire in the homelands of the Turkish race, with its capital at Constantinople—the passage between the Mediterranean and the Black Sea being internationalized and neutralized —Arabia, Armenia, Mesopotamia, Syria, and Palestine are in our judgement entitled to a recognition of their separate national conditions', and could not be restored ' to their former sovereignty '.

President Wilson's declaration was less precise. The twelfth of his ' Fourteen Points ' (8th January 1918) ran as follows : ' The Turkish portions of the present Ottoman Empire should be assured a secure sovereignty, but the other nationalities which are now under Turkish rule should be assured an undoubted security of life and an absolutely unmolested opportunity of autonomous development, and the Dardanelles should be permanently opened as a free passage to the ships and commerce of all nations under international guarantees.'

Neither with President Wilson's nor with Mr. Lloyd George's later definition of war aims was the Treaty of Lausanne inconsistent ; with Mr. Balfour's it plainly was ; but Mr. Balfour's Note was published some months before the Russian revolution.

That event compelled the Western Allies to reconsider the situation in the Near East, and to readjust their war aims. Consequently, there was no attempt, even at Sèvres, to complete the process, already so far advanced, of turning the Turk ' bag and baggage out of Europe '. Still less at Lausanne. The Greek *débâcle* in 1922 dissipated the dream of a revived Byzantine Empire, with its capital once more on the Bosphorus. Nor was the internationalization of a city with the traditions and situation of Constantinople a practical proposition. *Faute de mieux* the Turk had to stay ; and the problem of the Near East, the intricacies of which it has been the purpose of this book to unravel, remains to that extent unsolved.

The advent of the Turk in Europe was the origin of the Eastern Question, in its modern phase. His military encampment in the Balkans at once propounded the problem and delayed its solution. The Turk conquered the Balkan kingdoms, but made no attempt to absorb or assimilate the Balkan peoples. For four hundred years these peoples were lost to view, buried beneath the superincumbent mass of Asiatic conquerors ; but they lived ; and as the Turkish rule weakened and degenerated they once again re-emerged and reasserted their national identity. Step by step the Turk was driven back ; his European territory was gradually circumscribed, until by 1914 it had all but reached the vanishing point. His choice of sides in the Great War seemed—at any rate to those who never doubted the ultimate triumph of the allies—to promise its final extinction. It was not to be. Neither the War nor the Peace has provided the hoped-for solution of a problem, which for nearly five centuries has confronted and baffled succeeding generations of European diplomatists. It would wholly accord with the paradox of Turkish history if the ultimate solution were to come not from the ingenuity and wisdom of the West, but from the inextinguishable vitality of the Turk himself; not from London or Paris, nor even from Constantinople, but from Angora; from a Turkey which, for the first time in the history of the Ottomans, aspires to be a nation-state, with ideals not merely military but political; from a Turkey which cutting itself adrift from the miasma and corruptions of Constantinople, from the enervating softness of the shores of the Hellespont, looks to reinvigoration of body and mind from the bleak and bracing uplands of Anatolia, from renewed contact with the earlier homes of the Ottoman race.

The omens would seem at the moment to point that way; yet the historian who should venture to predict the future of the Turk would prove himself incompetent to draw the only irrefutable inference from the story of the past. That inference is writ large over the pages of this book. It may be summarily stated thus: The Turk has been consistent only in inconsistency; by the ostentation of simplicity he has confounded the wise, and in his weakness has found strength.

III

1924–39

THIS book was written during the World War. When it was published (1917), the War had reached a critical stage and peace was not yet in sight. An epilogue to the Second Edition (1918) brought the book up to date, but even then it was uncertain whether the War might not be prolonged for at least another year. In the event, the resistance of Germany and her allies suddenly collapsed, and on 11 November the terms of an Armistice, dictated by the allies, were accepted by the German Government.

To the Third Edition (1924) a second epilogue was added summarizing the events in the Near East down to the conclusion of the Treaty signed at Lausanne on 24 July 1923. The future in South-eastern Europe could still only be dimly discerned, and the second epilogue concluded consequently on a cautious note.

That the post-War history of the 'Eastern Question' has profoundly disappointed hopes and even expectations, it were futile to deny. If, during the war, one belief was more firmly held than another, it was that the Peace settlement would provide a satisfactory and perhaps permanent solution of a problem which had perplexed Europe for nearly five centuries. The *fons et origo* of that problem, in its modern phase, may be discerned in the advent of the Ottoman Turks into Europe in the fourteenth century, and in their conquest during the fifteenth and sixteenth centuries of the Balkan Peninsula, the Aegean Islands, Syria, Egypt, and the northern coast of Africa.[1] Suleiman 'the Magnificent' (1520–66) ruled over 50,000,000 people, and his

[1] See *supra*, chaps. i–v.

empire extended from Buda to Basra, from the Caspian to the Western Mediterranean.

The decadence of the Ottoman Empire, gradual in the seventeenth and eighteenth centuries, was rapid in the nineteenth. In 1817 it counted (in Europe) more than 19,000,000 subjects, and extended over an area of 218,600 square miles. By 1878 the population had been halved (9,600,000) and its territory reduced to 129,500 square miles. After the Balkan Wars (1913) its population was reduced to 1,891,000 and its territory to 10,882 square miles. It was confidently expected that the European War would eliminate the last remnant of Ottoman power. By the autumn of 1918 the allies had not only conquered Palestine, Syria, and Mesopotamia but were masters of the Balkan Peninsula, and their advance on Constantinople itself was averted only by the conclusion of the Armistice of Mudros (30 October 1918). Had the Armistice been promptly followed by a definitive Peace, almost any terms would have been accepted by a broken and dispirited Turkey. But the allies procrastinated; not until August 1920 was the Treaty of Sèvres signed.[1] That Treaty was never ratified by the Sultan, though he was left in possession of Constantinople, with a minimum of circumjacent territory. Still less was it accepted by the rival Turkish Government which Kemal Pasha had already established at Angora in the Anatolian highlands. Its terms, therefore, are merely of academic interest.

The dramatic events which revolutionized the whole situation in the Near East have been summarized in the preceding epilogue. That epilogue carried the story down to the conclusion of the Treaty of Lausanne which was signed on 24 July 1923, and was ratified a month later by the Turkish National Assembly at Angora. In the Treaty of Sèvres the allies had dictated terms to a conquered Turkey. At Lausanne the Turks

[1] See *supra*, p. 527.

were again in the saddle, and only the firmness of Lord Curzon averted the further humiliation of the allies. As things turned out the expulsion of the Greeks from Asia Minor proved a blessing in disguise to Greece.

Greece

Greece emerged from the Peace Conference in Paris laden with spoils which she had not earned. The high character and compelling eloquence of Venizelos laid upon the allied statesmen, particularly upon Mr. Lloyd George, a spell which they were powerless to resist. They refused to listen to the warnings of their military and naval advisers, to Foch and Sir Henry Wilson, Lord Beatty and Marshal Badoglio, and gave Venizelos almost everything that he asked for. The services rendered by the great Greek statesman to the allied cause had, indeed, been of inestimable value. The Macedonian offensive in 1918 was brilliantly organized, and both in a military and diplomatic sense crowned the allied effort in the Balkans. The Bulgarians collapsed, and thus the link between Germany and Turkey was finally severed. What could the allies in Paris refuse to the statesman who had made such a contribution to the final victory? The supreme prize of Byzantium did indeed elude his grasp. Under the Treaty of London (1915) Constantinople had been promised to Czarist Russia. In 1919 Russia had forfeited all claims upon the allies. Great Britain, though anxious to see San Sofia restored to the Orthodox Church, could not wholly ignore the susceptibilities of her Moslem subjects; France and Italy were much less sympathetic towards Hellenic aspirations. As a result, Constantinople, with a minimum amount of circumjacent territory, was even in 1920, under the Treaty of Lausanne, left in the hands of the Sultan; Turkey also recovered Eastern Thrace, Adrianople, the islands of Imbros and Tenedos.[1]

[1] See *supra*, p. 533.

Thus, as Count Sforza has truly said, Europe was constrained to consent 'to the re-entry into Constantinople and Eastern Thrace of the Ankara Government; in short, to the triumphant return of the Turks into Europe, under the leadership of the same Mustapha Kemal whom, at the beginning of 1919, the British agents in Constantinople had planned to arrest and confine in Malta'.[1]

There remained the problem of Asia Minor. There had been, prior to 1922, in the coast towns and the immediate hinterland, more than a million people of the Greek race, wealthy merchants, bankers, shopkeepers, and carpet-makers in Smyrna, and widely scattered over the upland country, cultivators of rice, tobacco, and vines. Kemal's triumphant advance swept them all before it. The Turks occupied Smyrna on September 9; the Greeks who were not slaughtered by the Turks escaped on board Greek and allied ships.

Where were they to go? In Western Thrace and Macedonia there was a large number of Moslems, Greeks, and Turks. Here was a basis for compromise, and on 30 January 1923 a Convention was concluded between Greece and Turkey. It was agreed that there should take place a compulsory exchange of Turkish nationals of the Greek Orthodox religion, established in Turkish territory, and of Greek nationals of the Moslem religion, established in Greek territory. Greek inhabitants of Constantinople and Moslems in Western Thrace were alone excepted from this arrangement. Elaborate machinery was set up, and though immense difficulties in detail were naturally encountered, these were gradually overcome, thanks to the tact and skill of Venizelos and Ismet Pasha, and by 1932 the vast process of interchange and migration was accomplished. There is still a Greek minority in Turkish territory and a Turkish minority in Greece, but both minorities are less discontented

[1] Sforza, *European Dictatorships*, p. 201.

with their lot than other minorities in the Balkans. Heart-rending were the sufferings of the migrants; no fewer than 2,000,000 people were actually transferred from one jurisdiction to the other. In addition some 1,500,000 Greeks from Asia Minor found new homes in Attica and Macedonia. Between Piraeus and Athens a new satellite town has come into existence, and an immense impetus has been given to Greek industry—notably carpet-making—in Athens, Salonika, Volo, and Kavalla, while large areas of land have been brought under profitable cultivation in Macedonia. No less than 88 per cent. of the inhabitants of that disturbed and debatable province are now Greek. Thus economic prosperity has done something to compensate Greece for political humiliation.

Not that Greece achieved stability. On the contrary, revolution has followed revolution. After the Greek débâcle in Asia Minor King Constantine, who in December 1920, amid exuberant enthusiasm, had been recalled to his throne, was for a second time expelled (27 September) and died at Palermo in the following January. He was replaced by his son George II, who occupied an uneasy throne until 1924, when he was given indefinite 'leave of absence' and a Republic was again declared. Venizelos returned to Athens in January 1924, but held office only for a month, after which he retired as a private citizen to his native Crete. The brief dictatorship established by a successful soldier, General Pangalos, in 1926 was of such brief duration as hardly to deserve mention except as illustrative of the general instability of Government in Greece. In 1928 Venizelos reappeared. Politics was as the breath of his nostrils. He again became Prime Minister (for the fifth time) in July 1928; a General Election in August gave him a magnificent majority, and for four years he ruled Greece with eminent success. Old sores were so far healed as to enable him to conclude a Pact of Friendship with Italy, as well as to reach an agreement with Yugoslavia on the thorny question of the Free Zone at Salonika. More wonderful still, Venizelos concluded a Treaty of Friendship and Arbitration with the Turks for which the way had been prepared by a personal visit he had paid to the Ghazi at Angora (1830). The economic crisis of 1932 hit Greece very hard; she defaulted on her debt, and Venizelos resigned, though only to resume office again in a few days.

The Greek Royalists were, however, gradually gathering strength; the General Election gave Venizelos a very narrow majority; and the Royalists formed a minority government only to yield place again to Venizelos. But although he again became Prime Minister, he lost caste by his association with General Plastiras, who attempted to establish a dictatorship. A determined attempt was made on the Prime Minister's life, and though he escaped unhurt, his wife and chauffeur were wounded, and a member of his bodyguard was killed. Venizelos's part was nearly played. Completely worn out by his tempestuous life, and lacking as ever in circumspection, he allowed himself to be involved in rebellion in 1935, fled the country, and was condemned to death in his absence. A plebiscite taken in November 1935 decided in favour of a restoration of the monarchy, and after an exile of twelve years, spent largely in England, King George II was restored to the throne. He promptly issued an amnesty, in which Venizelos was included, but the old statesman never returned to Greece and died in Paris in March 1936. The Greek monarchy is, by tradition and in theory, 'Constitutional', the régime is Parliamentary. But fond as the Greeks are of debating, parliamentary government, despite repeated attempts to plant it, has never really taken root in Greece. Consequently the country was not greatly perturbed when, under the menace of Communism, General Metaxas, a powerful minister, carried out a *coup d'état*, suspended Parliament, and established a monarchical dictatorship.

Whether, after long years of turmoil, and many sudden turns in the wheel of fortune, the monarchy will be able to establish stability in Greece is a question which prudent men will decline to answer. But this at least can be said. Greece is more homogeneous in race, culture, and creed than either Roumania or Yugoslavia; it has great strategic advantages over Bulgaria; the Pact of 1933 should ensure its friendship with Turkey, while the Balkan Pact of 1934 gave to both those countries, as well as to Yugoslavia and Roumania, a guarantee of 'the territorial order now established in the Balkans'. What that guarantee is worth only the future can disclose: but unless King George II should imitate his father's folly—a most improbable event—his country can count upon the traditional friendship and support of Great Britain.[1]

Roumania

From Greece we pass to Roumania. Territorially Roumania was, as we have seen, the greatest gainer of all Balkan States by the World War. What she gained in territory, however, she lost in homogeneity.[2] Her population of 7,897,311 (1915) had in 1935 exceeded 19,000,000. The production of an ethnographic map of the Balkans has always defied the ingenuity of geographers. Consequently the application of the fashionable doctrine of nationality has presented to diplomatists a problem beyond their skill to solve. Modern Roumania affords a signal illustration of the difficulty. Less than half her present population is contained in the old kingdom. At least 25 per cent. of all the present inhabitants of Roumania are aliens in race and sympathies; 750,000 of the latter are Germans or 'Saxons', as they are locally distinguished. The danger to be apprehended

[1] As these pages go to press (November 1939) the conclusion is announced of a Pact of Friendship and Non-aggression between Greece and Italy.

[2] See *supra*, p. 517.

from the latter has been accentuated by the absorption of Austria and Czechoslovakia into the German Reich, which, unless prevented by the intervention of Russia, will be able to threaten the economic and political independence of Roumania even more directly than before.

Hungary has never acquiesced in the loss of Transylvania, nor have the Magyars, forming some 25 per cent of the population of that Province, ever renounced the hope of reunion with their co-nationals in Hungary. As to Bessarabia, the Russian Soviet has never recognized its union with Roumania, though it has seemingly acquiesced in its detachment from Russia. But, 'beyond the Dniester', as a special correspondent of *The Times* (2 June 1939) has truly said, 'Russia has hitherto remained aloof, enrapt and enigmatic. Even now that she is emerging from her fastness Roumania is hesitant to accept her, finding her odious in her creed and perfidious in her history'.

About Bulgaria's attitude in regard to Southern Dobrudja there is no ambiguity. Bulgaria is still exceedingly sore about Roumania's continued occupation. That unattractive but highly debatable region is said to contain no fewer than seventeen nationalities. The Roumanians contribute the largest element (over 40 per cent.), the Bulgars come next with 24 per cent., but there are also a good many Turks, Turkish-speaking Gagauzes, and Tartars, not to mention Germans, Frenchmen, Russians, and Poles.

The collapse of the Little Entente has weakened the international position of Roumania, but she has found compensation in the protective guarantee of Great Britain and France, and even more immediately in the formation of the Balkan Pact (1934). From that Pact Bulgaria has hitherto (1939) held obstinately aloof. Her adherence is much to be desired. Nothing would more effectively contribute to the internal tranquillity and external security of the Balkans.

Economically, Roumania is the most important of the Balkan States. She is, indeed, dependent for egress to the Mediterranean on the goodwill of the guardians of the Straits, and her railway system requires development, but she has immense domestic resources. She is rich in minerals and her oil-fields are among the most extensive in the world. Her vineyards yield a harvest which makes excellent wine, while the soil of Transylvania, Bessarabia, and Roumania proper is exceptionally suitable for the cultivation of wheat and other cereals.

In regard to government the recent history of Roumania differs little from that of her neighbours. Technically, the monarchy is 'Constitutional', but, as elsewhere in the Balkans, Parliamentary Government has never taken root, and ever since the fall of M. Titulescu (1936), King Carol has been the real ruler of the country and been compelled to establish a monarchical dictatorship. As the King has the reputation of being both shrewd and clever, there is a hope that he may overcome the difficulties, external and internal, with which his country is confronted. But the future is obscure.

Yugoslavia

It is hardly less obscure in Yugoslavia. Like Roumania the newly created Triune Kingdom of Yugoslavia attempted to establish Parliamentary institutions among peoples but recently united under a single government, and entirely lacking in the experience and traditions essential to the successful working of representative democracy. The attempt was predestined to failure. The constituent peoples of the Triune Kingdom all profess, doubtless with sincerity, great admiration for the Western Democracies. But they will have to serve a long apprenticeship before they can safely imitate them. In 1928 M. Raditch, the leader of the Croat peasant party, was shot by a Montenegrin deputy during a parliamentary debate. The

Croat party thereupon withdrew from Parliament, and King Alexander suspended the Parliamentary Constitution and declared a Royal Dictatorship.

Two years later the Parliamentary Constitution was formally re-established, but in appearance rather than reality. Racial passions were again revealed by the assassination of King Alexander in 1934, and though Prince Paul, as Regent, has done his utmost to appease them, he has only partially succeeded. The existing situation is thus graphically described by the Balkan correspondent of *The Times*:

'Yugoslavia is a cauldron of conflicting historical and cultural traditions. The Angelus is rung throughout Catholic Croatia and Slovenia; the muezzin calls the believers to prayer from the minarets of Bosnia and Herzegovina, while in Serbia the Orthodox Church with its Oriental atmosphere remains the unchallenged guardian of the national culture. The Venetians left their mark in Dalmatia . . . the cities of Croatia and Slovenia are typically Austro-Hungarian; the towns of Serbia and Bosnia still bear the marks of the Turk.'

Racially and linguistically the Serbs and the Croatians are closely akin; in all else they are not merely apart, but bitterly opposed to each other. A federal solution of the difficulty has frequently been suggested, and by many friends, both of Serbs and Croats, is strongly favoured. But the conditions which make for success in federalism are as rare as those demanded by Representative Democracy, and though it is common ground that the administration in Yugoslavia is over-centralized, it is doubtful whether the federal principle could be successfully applied.

The outstanding obstacle is creed. To 6,500,000 Orthodox Serbs, 3,500,000 Roman Catholic Croats are bitterly opposed. It is probably true that 'other important communities, such as the 1,000,000 Roman Catholic Slovenes and the 600,000

Bosnian Moslems, would have little difficulty in fitting themselves into a system which both Serbs and Croats considered to be feasible'.[1] But that system has not yet been discovered.

Apart from the domestic situation another consideration obtrudes itself. In 1918 the Southern Slavs hoped that they had achieved not only national unity but national independence. If the one is menaced can they preserve the other?

The absorption of Austria into the German Reich in 1938 and the annexation of Albania to Italy in 1939 greatly diminished the security of Yugoslavia. Still more serious for her was the annihilation of Czechoslovakia (1939), which supplied the keystone of the arch of the Little Entente. Like Roumania, Yugoslavia has its Magyar and German minorities. Wedged in between the two great Axis Powers, with Hungary, Roumania, and Bulgaria, none too friendly, hanging on her flanks, the strategic position of Yugoslavia is conspicuously precarious.

Albania

The Italian annexation of Albania has made it worse. Of the position of the Albanian mountaineers a good deal has already been said.[2] Ever since the advent of the Turk Albania has held a unique place in Balkan affairs.

Of late years, particularly since the dissipation of the dreams of Habsburgs and Hohenzollerns, Albania has been of special importance in relation to the ambitions of Italy. In 1912 the Powers were congratulating themselves upon having untied one of the many knots in the Balkan problem by the creation of an 'autonomous Albania'. Prince William of Wied, a German Prince, was selected for the difficult task of ruling the autonomous Province, but his rule lasted exactly six months, and during the World War there were as many rulers in Albania as there are tribes. In 1918 a Provisional Government was set up

[1] *The Times*, 16 February 1935.   [2] See Index: Albania.

under the military protection of Italy, but after a succession of 'revolutions' Albania was (1925) proclaimed a Republic, and Ahmed Bay Zogu was elected as its first President. In 1928 a Constituent Assembly transformed the Republic into a democratic monarchy and offered the Crown to the President, who accepted it and assumed the title of King Zog I. King Zog rapidly carried through a series of far-reaching reforms. Under the new agrarian laws, a portion of the land of the larger landowners was expropriated, and a still larger portion was left in their hands only on condition that they shared the expenses of cultivation with their tenants. An agricultural bank was set up, and a road-making scheme was drafted, but tardily put into execution. New penal and civil codes were introduced, and elective councils were set up in each of the 189 Communes into which the country was re-divided, with a view to the break-up of the tribal economy and the improvement of administrative efficiency. For the newly established Cadet Corps Italian instructors were imported, as well as for the technical colleges in four of the most important towns. In the latter case the instructors are actually paid by the Italian Government, and are naturally responsible to their paymasters.

In this and in many other ways the Italians gradually increased their stranglehold upon this little State, with only one million inhabitants, mostly hardy mountaineers, adhering to three different creeds. The Roman Catholics are predominant in the north, the Orthodox in the south, and there are also, especially in the central district, a good many Moslems. The penetration of the Italians, economic, cultural, and political, has in the last few years widened and deepened. On Good Friday (1939) Italy suddenly swooped down upon the country, and occupied it with 100,000 troops. King Zog, with his Consort, the Countess Geraldine Apponyi, to whom he had been married hardly a year, fled the country, and the Italians by a lavish distribution of largesse, and still more lavish promises of similar favours to come, have achieved an easy, if superficial, popularity. At the moment (August 1939) Albania is reported to be basking in the sun of prosperity, but that nothing has yet been done to develop the natural resources of the country, or to carry out works designed for the permanent improvement of economic conditions.

Strategically, the annexation of Albania is immensely important for Italy. The straits of Otranto are only some forty miles wide. Brindisi and Valona hold the keys of the Adriatic. Fiume, Cattaro, Durazzo, Scutari—what does their possession, so eagerly desired, so long denied to her, now avail to Yugoslavia? The Adriatic is an Italian lake.

Bulgaria

Bulgaria, once the favoured pawn of Russia; rent in twain by Lord Beaconsfield at Berlin in 1878; reunited without protest from the Powers in 1885, and encouraged—not least by England—to strengthen her position in every way as the most effective barrier to the advance of Russia towards Constantinople.[1] Since 1912 Bulgaria has fallen on evil days. The misfortunes she suffered in the Balkan Wars were accentuated in the settlement which followed the Great War. Bulgaria, the victim of the miscalculations of her Czar, 'Foxy' Ferdinand, neither deserved nor obtained any consideration at the hands of the allies. Nevertheless, it is arguable that on the long view Venizelos overreached himself in regard to Bulgaria as he did in regard to Turkey.

Access to the Aegean is admittedly important, not to say vital, to Bulgaria. As regards economic access, it was secured to her even under the Treaty of Neuilly. Article 48 of that Treaty said: 'The Principal Allied and Associated Powers

[1] See *supra*, p. 355.

undertake to ensure the economic outlet of Bulgaria to the Aegean Sea.' Partisans of Bulgaria complain that the undertaking was not fulfilled. Greece has, in fact, always been willing to implement the promise of the Treaty had not Bulgaria based upon it a larger claim. What Bulgaria wants—not unnaturally —is not merely economic but territorial access to the Aegean. That claim, so far as it was based upon the Treaty of Neuilly, was specifically repudiated by Lord Curzon at the Lausanne Conference (24 November 1922). 'The creation of an autonomous area at Dedeagatch or of a Bulgarian property there, was never contemplated by the Treaty of Neuilly.'[1] Yet even if claims based upon that Treaty cannot be sustained, generosity might well be the best policy for Greece.

In respect of government, Bulgaria has exhibited no greater consistency than her neighbours. Technically, the monarchy is parliamentary, but the establishment of the Hitler dictatorship in Germany was quickly followed by suspension of the Bulgarian Sobranjé (1934). In March 1938, however, a General Election called the Legislative Body once more into being. Constitutionally unstable and socially restless Bulgaria has not proved at all an accommodating neighbour. She might, on her part, argue that it is rather for her neighbours to accommodate her, since they have all in these latter days gained territory at her expense. Between Sofia and Belgrade there is traditional rivalry, which was accentuated when in 1919 Bulgaria had to surrender to Yugoslavia the Strumnitza line and a strip of territory on her north-west frontier. The tenacity with which Roumania clings to the Southern Dobrudja—justified as her tenacity may be by history, geography, ethnology, and policy—must perpetuate friction on that side, while the assignment of Bulgarian Macedonia to Greece inflicted real injury upon Bulgaria. Italy has not neglected to accentuate discord in the Balkans, and

[1] See Sir Charles Petrie's letter to *The Times*, July 1939.

on the whole it is not surprising that all efforts to draw Bulgaria into the Balkan Entente should hitherto have been unavailing. In January 1937 she did indeed conclude an agreement with Yugoslavia, and in July with the Balkan Entente. But to join it she has persistently refused.

The New Turkey

Much the most important development of the Eastern Question since 1923 has still to be considered. The Turkish revival is, indeed, an event of European significance, and demands more detailed treatment.

The revival has been due, in exceptional measure, to one man of outstanding genius. Of all the great men thrown up by the World War and its sequelae, Mustapha Kemal was perhaps the greatest. He has brought into being a nation and on the basis of that nation he has created an entirely new State. The son of a contractor in a small way of business Kemal was born at Salonika in 1881. His father died young and Kemal, like all great men, owed everything to his mother, an Albanian woman of strong character. Well educated, Kemal joined the army and had just taken a staff course when an incautiously manifested interest in politics led to his arrest on a charge of conspiracy. The charge was not proved, but the young cadet was transferred to Syria where he founded a Liberty Society among the younger officers. Having seen service in Macedonia he joined the Union and Progress Party, but a quarrel with Enver Bey kept him out of the inner councils of the Party. The quarrel was accentuated rather than appeased when he joined Enver's staff in the Tripoli campaign, and it was not until the outbreak of the Great War that Kemal got his chance.

He opposed Turkey's entry into the War, but nevertheless was appointed, early in 1915, to the command of a Division in the army commanded by Marshal Liman von Sanders in the

Gallipoli campaign. For the Turkish success in that campaign Kemal was largely responsible, but his brilliant services only increased the jealousy and dislike of Enver Bey, who ultimately removed him from his command. In June 1918, however, he accepted the command of the Seventh Army in Palestine, though he was powerless to avert the defeat of the Turkish forces at the hands of General Allenby.

On 15 May 1919 a Greek army, supported by the warships of Great Britain, France, and the United States, occupied Smyrna. That was the day of fate, both for Greece and Turkey. 'Greece', writes Count Sforza, 'was doomed on the very day Athens went mad with patriotic joy at the news that the Hellenic flag had been planted on the walls of Smyrna.'[1] The Turks heard the news with the bitterest indignation. That the Greek, so long serviceable in many capacities to the Turk, but always despised by his employer, should have dared to plant his flag in the chief city of Asia Minor, was to every Turkish patriot an unforgivable affront.

Kemal's moment had come. Four days after the landing of the Greeks at Smyrna Kemal left Constantinople for Samsun, having been appointed Inspector-General of the Turkish forces in Eastern Anatolia. The brilliant soldier promptly proved himself to be a statesman of the highest capacity. His activities alarmed the Porte: he was ordered to return to Constantinople, and on his refusal was outlawed. All orders emanating from Constantinople he henceforward ignored. Kemal could appeal to a new spirit evoked among the Turks by the Greek landing at Smyrna. That event, as Sir Harry Luke well says, 'restored to the Turks the vitality which seemed to have gone for ever, infused into them a patriotism probably more real than any which the War had been able to evoke and created the spirit of Turkish patriotism at the expense of the Allies'.[2]

---

[1] *Op. cit.*, p. 198. [2] *The Making of Modern Turkey*, p. 169.

That spirit Kemal worked assiduously to foster. His work was assisted by the allied occupation of Constantinople (16 March 1920), and still more by the signature of the Treaty of Sèvres (10 August), which was promptly repudiated by the Kemalists. Meanwhile, in July 1919, a National Assembly met on Kemal's summons at Erzeroum, and in the following December a Conference was held at Sivas where Kemal and his friends drew up the 'National Pact'. From Sivas the head-quarters of the Kemalist Government were transferred to Angora. Angora was at that time a wretched little town situated in the Anatolian highlands, 215 miles from Con-stantinople, and was surrounded by treeless desert and mos-quito-haunted marshes.

In April 1920 the Grand National Assembly was inaugurated at Angora and Kemal was elected its President.

The Greeks, however, were in occupation of Anatolia, and after defeating the Nationalist Turks in a brilliant campaign in the summer of 1920 they occupied Brusa, the ancient capital of the Ottomans. But the tide turned in 1921. France and Italy came to terms with the Angora Government; Kemal, appointed Commander-in-Chief of the Turkish army, not only arrested the Greek advance on Angora, but took the offensive against them and, after a brilliant campaign, which earned him his title of Ghazi, swept the whole of the Greek forces into the sea.

The Kemalist Turks, flushed with their victory over the despised Greeks, not only occupied Smyrna but advanced to-wards the Dardanelles and threatened the British garrison which, from Chanak, held the southern shore of the Dardanelles. That war was not renewed between Great Britain, deserted by her French and Italian allies, and the Turks, was due primarily to the combined tact and firmness of Sir Charles Harington, the Allied Commander in Constantinople. An Armistice was concluded between the Greeks and the Turks at Mudania (October 1922) and the Treaty of Lausanne was signed in July 1923.

Meanwhile, the Grand National Assembly at Angora issued an edict that the office of Sultan had ceased to exist (1 November 1922), and on 17 November Mohammed VI, the last of the Ottoman Sultans, fled from Constantinople on board H.M.S. *Malaya.* On 13 October 1923 Angora was formally declared to be the Turkish capital, and a week later Turkey was proclaimed a Republic and Mustapha Kemal Pasha its President. No single act in the Ghazi's career was more courageous or more characteristic than the cutting adrift from Constantinople. Thus did the Turk throw off, as Sir Harry Luke has well said, 'the Byzantine vestments—perhaps shackles would be a truer term, by which he had been encumbered for centuries . . . to find himself again, as he hopes, the simpler more natural Turanian who emerged from the plains and plateaux of Central Asia'. Constantinople had always been 'Rum, something non-national, something supernational, something Imperial which would impose its character on the people whose capital it was, rather than receive the impress of its owners'.[1]

Something of all this was doubtless in the mind of 'the new Constantine' (as he has been happily called); but between the new Constantine and the old there was this striking difference— a difference accentuated by the transference of the capital. The Byzantine Emperor transmitted to the Ottoman Sultan— with much else—that close association between Church and State which was a characteristic feature of both Empires.

Kemal dissolved the association. After the abolition of the Sultanate Prince Abdul-Mejid, cousin to the late Sultan, was elected Caliph; but in March 1924 the Caliphate itself was abolished by the Grand National Assembly; all the members of

[1] *Modern Turkey*, pp. 234, 209–11.

the house of Osman were banished and their property con-
fiscated. Shortly afterwards all the Moslem Clerical Schools
were abolished and, in 1925, all the Religious Houses and Holy
Tombs were closed; all Religious Orders were abolished; and
the wearing of distinctive clerical dress in public was forbidden.
Religious worship was not interdicted, but the Islamic religion
was disestablished and the State was definitely laicized. Later
on (1934) San Sophia, venerated by Christians for centuries as
a Holy Shrine and later by Moslems as one of the stateliest of
Mosques, was converted into a national museum.

Nothing could more effectively illustrate the truly radical
nature of Kemal's reforms and the thoroughness of his methods
than his efforts to impose a wholly new type of culture upon the
new nation he has created on Asiatic soil. When he took office
95 per cent. of the people were illiterate, and the written
language of educated people has been truly described as 'more a
design than a written language'. 'In the printing houses men
worked before innumerable cases of characters and signs. To
read a word correctly it was necessary to have heard it spoken
by one's mother. Kemal insisted that it was essential to get
rid of 'these difficult characters which had constricted the
people's minds as by an iron band for centuries'.[1] Nothing was
neglected to bring the new Turkey abreast of other progressive
nations. The international calendar figures and metric system
were adopted, and the Latin was substituted for the Arabic
alphabet. On 1 December 1928 all the newspapers came out
printed in Latin characters. Popular schools were opened for
instruction in the Latin alphabet. 'In a few years', said Kemal,
'every one will have learned the new characters. Our nation
will show that it is in step with the civilized world as much in
its language as in its intelligence.' In order to hasten the process

---

[1] *Cf.* 'Modern Turkey', a series of valuable articles contributed to *The
Daily Telegraph* (December 1933).

Kemal himself travelled round the villages with a blackboard and chalk. A great impulse was also given to technical education, and a university, with a medical school, a law school, and an agricultural institute has been established at Angora. The Turkish language itself was purified by the excision of Arabic and Persian words; a Linguistic Study Society was formed; and an Association of Historical Studies was established in order to undertake researches into Turkish history, with a view to breaking down the barrier between Turks and non-Moslems and establishing their racial consanguinity with other civilized peoples. The Ghazi himself set an example of persistence in good works. On Sunday, 16 October 1927, he began a speech designed to summarize historical events since his landing at Samsun in May 1919. The speech broke all records. For six successive days the Ghazi spoke for seven hours a day, concluding his speech only on Friday, 21 October. The speech was subsequently published in book form, running to 543 pages.[1]

Nor was Kemal's reforming zeal confined to education and culture in the narrower sense. He revolutionized the sartorial habits both of men and women. The men were compelled to abandon the fez, originally adopted to facilitate Moslem ritual and allow the worshipper to touch the ground with his forehead, and to adopt the 'bowler' and the 'Homburg hat' in the Western mode. The women were deprived of their veils. Not, however, without compensation.

'You cannot', said the Ghazi to a sympathetic Englishwoman, 'have a true democracy such as we intend to build up with half the country in bondage. Besides, women have got to take their share in the terrific work of building up this country. Harems, veils, fezzes, lattice windows, separation of the sexes, polygamy, and all the nonsense of a retrograde civilization have got to

---

[1] It is summarized by Sir T. Waugh, *Turkey Yesterday, To-day, and To-morrow*, pp. 201–64.

go. Women are growing to be men's companions and equals
with equal opportunities in education and work, and the
nation is going to be built on the solid foundation of a home
and not a harem.'[1]

The Ghazi has been as good as his word. Polygamy was
abolished; women were admitted to all educational facilities
and to the liberal professions, and finally to the parliamentary
franchise and to parliament itself on the same terms as men.
All men and women became qualified as voters at twenty-
three and a candidate for Parliament at thirty-one. The only
restriction on a woman's candidature is a clause prohibiting the
wife of a Deputy from standing. At the General Election of
1935, seventeen women, having been previously passed by the
three chiefs of the People's Party, its President, Ghazi Mustapha
Atatürk, General Ismet Inönü, and Rejeb Peker, its Secretary
General, were elected. Of these sixteen were town-bred and
highly educated; the seventeenth is an Anatolian peasant, an
illiterate farm worker and the mother of five children. She
had, however, already been prominent in local affairs and had
attracted the attention of the Ghazi himself as a woman of
exceptional native intelligence. At his invitation she stood for
Parliament.

Of all the domestic reforms carried out by Kemal the
emancipation of, women is perhaps the most revolutionary.
But there were many others. In the domain of law and order
Kemal introduced a Civil Code modelled on that of Switzerland,
a Penal Code adapted from that of Italy, and a Commercial
Code answering to the entirely independent position of the
New Turkey. More difficult still, he has made the whole
country safe for the wayfarer. The tribute paid by the Saxon
Chronicle to our own Henry I has been earned by Kemal's
enforcement of order. 'A good man he was and all men stood

[1] Grace Ellison: ap. *Daily Telegraph* (Oct. 28, 1933).

in awe of him; no man durst misdo against another in his time.
. . . Whoso bare his burden of gold and silver no man durst do
him aught but good.' Public security has been greatly assisted
by the development of means of communication. The State
has acquired almost all the railway lines constructed and owned
by foreign companies, and, in addition, has built new lines at
the rate of about 125 miles a year, and at an expenditure of
some £T.200,000,000 without recourse to borrowing abroad.

In the sphere of finance wonders have been accomplished:
the budget is balanced; salaries and pensions are punctually
paid; taxation, though still heavy, is more equitably distributed,
and a stop has been put to the gross abuses connected in old
days with the collection of the revenue. As regards the public
debt, an arrangement has been concluded with the old bond-
holders of the Ottoman public debt, and the interest payments
on that and the new debt of the Republic are punctually paid.
The internal currency has been put on a sound basis; an
Exchange Control Department has been set on foot to prevent
currency speculation; an Agricultural Credit Corporation was
established in 1929, and a Central Bank in 1930. Banks for
industry and mining, and for dealing with mortgages, had
previously been established. But with all their help the process
of industrialization was slow. The inhibition of the Treaty
of Lausanne having expired, a high protective tariff was imposed
in 1929, and an impulse was thus given to manufacturing
industry; many factories were built, and in 1934 a 'Five Year
Plan' was started; foreign experts were imported and Turkish
youths were sent abroad to study technical processes. Considerable progress can now be registered, but the results have,
as a whole, hardly answered expectations. Smyrna retains its
high reputation for carpet-weaving; several sugar-beet factories
have been built, with the result that Turkey has no further
need of imported sugar; efforts have been made to make her

self-supporting in regard to cotton and other textiles, and clearing agreements have been made with several countries in order to avert an adverse balance of trade. Turkish exports, however, are still almost entirely confined to raw materials, tobacco, gums, raisins, figs, and the like. The forests are now scientifically exploited, and the production of coal, iron, and other minerals gives promise of considerable wealth for the country. As far as possible industry is being taught to rely on raw materials produced at home. It was authoritatively reported in 1938 that the first 'Five Year Plan', which had cost £10,000,000, was practically completed.

Nor has the Ghazi ignored the truth that it is 'men not walls [even tariff walls] that make cities'. It has been estimated that Turkey could comfortably support forty to fifty million people. Its population, according to the census of 1935, is 16,200,694 which shows an increase of 23 per cent. since the census of 1927, but gives only 35 to the square mile as compared with 124 in Greece, 140 in Yugoslavia, 145 in Roumania, 150 in Bulgaria, and 360 in Italy. There has been a certain amount of immigration of Turks, notably from Greece, Macedonia, and the Dobrudja, but any large increase in population must, as the Ghazi realized, be effected by increased security of life and property, by industrialization, and above all by improvements in sanitation and public health, in the nutrition of mothers and infants, and so forth. Already Angora and its neighbourhood have, by the draining of the marshland, been cleared of the scourge of malaria, water-supply has been improved, and a strenuous effort has been made to eliminate zymotic diseases; but much still remains to be done in this respect. The new President, Ismet Inönü, may be trusted to do it.

In respect of Government Turkey almost defies classification. In form it is a Parliamentary Republic with an elective President, a single-chamber Legislature elected quadrennially by adult suffrage, and an Executive nominally responsible to Parliament (*Kamutay*). The latest revision of the Constitution (1937) reaffirmed the principles of the Republican People's Party, namely, nationalism, democracy, dynamism (or adaptation to circumstances), laicism, and 'etatism' or state ownership or control of the principal means of communications, industry, mines, and public utility services. By amendments adopted in that year the clause guaranteeing private property was amended to permit the expropriation of large properties to enable peasants to be settled as owners on the soil, while another amendment excluded from the guarantee of religious liberty certain sects which were suspected of performing their rites at secret meetings.

How far the realities of administration correspond with the terms of the written Constitution it is not easy to say. Two things, however, are certain. First, that Kemal Atatürk has from the first exercised dictatorial authority, and secondly, that his dictatorship differed in motive and to some extent in practice from the dictatorships established in Russia, Italy, and Germany. Kemal's motive, stated in a word, was 'educative'. His object was to prepare his country for the day when the Government might become in fact, as it is in theory, 'Constitutional', when the President might act on the advice of ministers really responsible, not to him, but to Parliament. But no one knew better than the first President of the Turkish Republic that his country was a long way from being ready for that development.

Meanwhile, his dictatorship was eminently benevolent, and amazingly successful. Nor did he fail to establish his claim to be a genius by his infinite capacity to attend to small things as well as great. Observing the waste of working hours involved in the conflicting claims of different creeds to a day of worship, he ordained that for all alike Sunday should be the day of rest, with Saturday afternoon as the universal holiday. In order to eradicate from the New Turkey all traces of the Ottoman régime all decorations were forbidden, and all titles such as 'Pasha', 'Bey', 'Effendi' were abolished (1934), and every one had to take a surname. Thus Ismet Pasha assumed a place name, Inönü, the name of the scene of one of his great victories. Kemal himself took the name of Atatürk, Chief or 'Father' (*Ata*) Turk.

Finally, Kemal gave to the foreign policy of Turkey a new orientation. During the last days of the Ottoman Empire Germany had succeeded to the place at Constantinople so long occupied by France and Great Britain. When the Turkish Republic was established it was to Moscow, not Berlin, that it looked for sympathy and help. For ten or twelve years the U.S.S.R. was the sheet anchor of Turkish diplomacy, and Kemal was not unmindful of the debt which he owed to Soviet support. In 1919 Great Britain was the archenemy. England had supported the enterprise of the Greeks in Anatolia; the English plenipotentiary had treated with hauteur Ismet Pasha at Lausanne; to English intrigues in general, and to Lawrence 'of Arabia' in particular, Turkey attributed the restlessness of the Kurds and most of the other troubles on her Asiatic frontiers. Then came the dispute with Great Britain about the Mosul oil-fields, involving the question of the frontier between Turkey and Iraq, then administered under Mandate by Great Britain. The Mandate was happily terminated in 1932 when Iraq took its place as an independent State in the League of Nations. Turkey was also elected to the League in the same year (18 July 1932) and proved itself a most loyal member of it. The League provisionally awarded the Mosul district to Iraq, and Turkey was persuaded to enter into direct negotiations on the question with Great Britain. As a result an agreement was reached under the terms of which both parties accepted the frontier suggested by the League. That agreement, and still more the friendly negotiations which preceded its conclusion, paved the way towards improved relations between the Turkish Republic and Great Britain.

Meanwhile, the Ghazi, becoming increasingly suspicious of the designs of Italy in the Eastern Mediterranean and of Germany in the Balkans, decided to enter into closer relations with his immediate neighbours. To the visit of M. Venizelos to Angora reference has already been made. The result was the conclusion, in 1933, of an alliance with Greece. That was the beginning of greater things. A Conference met at Angora which drafted the statutes of a Balkan Pact concluded between Greece, Turkey, Yugoslavia, and Roumania on 9 February 1934. That Pact gave to the consignatories a guarantee of the 'territorial order now established in the Balkans'. Bulgaria was not a party to that Pact: it held as stubbornly aloof from this Pact, as it did from the Little Entente. But at long last, in 1938, thanks to the tactful diplomacy of King Boris and the persistent pressure of events, Bulgaria did go so far as to come to an agreement with Turkey.

The Balkan Pact of 1934 had in the meantime been followed by the conclusion of an agreement between Turkey, Iraq, Iran, and Afghanistan, known as the Pact of Saadabad (1936). The effect of this was to guarantee Turkey and its Asiatic neighbours against the troublesome activities of the Kurdish mountaineers, to which they were all more or less, but Turkey more particularly, exposed.

The same year witnessed a still more important triumph for the diplomacy of the Ghazi. The Straits Convention was, indeed, the crown of Kemal's diplomatic activities. On 11 April 1936 Turkey made a formal application to the signatories of the Treaty of Lausanne for permission to refortify the Dardanelles, the Sea of Marmora, and the Bosphorus. A similar request was made to the League of Nations that the case of Turkey should be brought before the League under the terms of the Covenant, which in Article XIX provided for the revision of treaties which have become inapplicable, and for the consideration of international conditions, the continuation of which might endanger peace. Whatever the issue might be, high commendation was evidently due to the Turkish Government for having adopted the correct procedure instead of following the bad example of unilateral denunciation set by Germany. Nor was that commendation withheld. On the contrary, it was cordially expressed on all sides when the Conference opened towards the end of June at Montreux. Particularly cordial was the tribute paid on behalf of Roumania by M. Titulescu who, observing that if the Straits were the heart of Turkey they were the lungs of Roumania, pertinently added that if the one country which had adopted the correct procedure were denied what she wanted, a serious blow would be struck at the cause of the peaceful revision of treaties by mutual consent.

The Straits Convention attached to the Treaty of Lausanne (1923) provided for the demilitarization of the Straits of the Dardanelles and the Bosphorus, together with the islands in the Sea of Marmora (except Emir Ali Island), and the islands near the entrance of the Dardanelles, of which Samothrace and Lemnos are Greek, and Imbros, Tenedos, and the Rabbit Islands are Turkish. In those areas no permanent fortifications, no naval base, nor any military equipment were to be maintained, and the armed forces stationed there were to be limited to the police and gendarmes required for the maintenance of order. The Straits were to be open, with complete freedom of navigation for all vessels, and the observance of the Convention was to be superintended by a Straits Commission under the League of Nations. A similar 'Convention respecting the Thracian frontier' was also attached to the Treaty of Lausanne. This demilitarized a zone some 9½ miles in depth on each side of the common frontier of Turkey and Bulgaria, and Turkey and Greece.

The Turkish case for revision was stated moderately and convincingly. It pointed to the fact, deplorable but indisputable, that since Turkey signed the restrictive clauses of the Straits Convention world conditions had entirely changed. In 1923 'Europe was progressing towards disarmament, and the political organization of Europe was to be based solely on the unchanging principle of law embodied in international engagements'. By 1936 the countries of Europe had started on a race in armaments and the prestige and power of the League of Nations were lamentably waning. In 1923 Turkey relied not only on the guarantee afforded by Article X of the League Covenant, but on the further assurance, given her by Article XVIII of the Straits Convention, that 'the United Kingdom, France, Italy, and Japan would co-jointly undertake by all the means decided upon for that purpose by the League Council the defence of the Straits if threatened'. Of what value, Turkey pertinently asked, is that assurance when of the four Powers Japan has withdrawn from the League and Italy has openly flouted its authority. Meanwhile, the situation in the Mediterranean had become precarious, and 'political crises had made it clear that the present machinery for collective guarantees is too slow in coming into operation'.

Under these circumstances Turkey felt herself constrained to take measures to ensure her own safety. She reminded the Powers and the League that

'she had followed a policy of peace and understanding necessarily imposing heavy sacrifices and had shown a spirit of conciliation and loyalty to her engagements. She was therefore entitled to claim the security she had always ensured to others.

But circumstances had rendered inoperative clauses drawn up in good faith and the issue at stake was the existence of Turkey herself. Hence the request for negotiation and a new agreement for a new régime under conditions of security and the constant development of navigation between the Mediterranean and the Black Sea.'

The plea was in truth irresistible. Great Britain, France, Greece, Russia, Bulgaria, Yugoslavia, Rumania, Italy, and Japan were accordingly invited to meet the representatives of Turkey at a Conference which opened at Montreux on 22 June 1936. The issues involved were exceedingly complex, and the discussions had hardly begun before it became manifest that there was a real conflict of principles and interests between some of the Great Powers represented at the Conference. This was notably true of the conflict between Russia and Great Britain about the navigation of the Straits. As to the re-militarization demanded by Turkey, there was practically no division of opinion, the universal feeling being (as one correspondent pithily put it) that 'Turkey should be gracefully conceded that which she cannot be denied'. Accordingly, the new Convention virtually conceded to Turkey, with much elaboration of detail, all that she had claimed. Thus, despite her defeat in the World War, despite the loss of almost the whole of her European possessions, Turkey became more completely mistress in her own house, and more particularly of the approaches thereto, than at any time since the Treaty of Kutschuk-Kainardji dictated to her by Russia in 1774.

It was not, however, between Russia and Turkey that the area of conflict now lay. On the contrary there was a shrewd suspicion at Montreux that the new proposals as to the navigation of the Straits were the outcome of close collaboration between the two Powers which, ever since 1919, had been friends if not allies. But ever since the day when Russia imposed on

Turkey the Treaty of Unkiar-Skelessi (1833), Great Britain and Russia had been in conflict on this question.

Russia's claim at Montreux was, crudely stated, that her ships should be allowed free egress from the Black Sea, while ingress into the Black Sea should, for other Powers, be severely restricted. As to the rights of merchant ships there was practically no dispute. Nor as to the position of warships during a war in which Turkey was a belligerent. In this case Turkey would obviously open or close the Straits as suited her. But what if Turkey were neutral? The conflict between Great Britain and Russia became acute. Japan was hotly opposed to the Russian claim; France and Roumania, on the whole, supported it; Great Britain was all for reciprocity, complete 'freedom of the seas'. To concede the Russian claim would, she contended, convert the Black Sea into a Russian lake or (as a journalist more picturesquely phrased it) to present Russia with 'a secure funk-hole for the Russian fleet and a base for forays into the Mediterranean, against which an enemy Power would be debarred from redress by its Treaty obligations'. M. Litvinoff maintained the Soviet claim with persistence and ability; the dispute threatened to end in a deadlock. Turkey, however, pressed for a prompt decision, and on 20 July the new Straits Convention was signed. The Russians obtained free egress for their warships in peace-time; Great Britain secured more favourable conditions for commercial shipping passing through the Straits. The Convention was signed by all the nine Powers represented at the Conference. Italy had not attended it, and refused to adhere to the Convention, but gave it her adherence after the conclusion of the Anglo-Italian Agreement (2 May 1938). Lord Stanley, speaking for Great Britain, said at the final sitting of the Conference: 'The Agreement which we have signed has an importance far beyond the limits of its own terms, for it shows to the world that mutually satisfactory results can be obtained by compliance with the usual practices of international relations.'

The general result was an unmistakable triumph for Turkey, and a complete justification of the methods pursued by Kemal Atatürk. How happily those methods contrasted with Herr Hitler's it were superfluous to insist. By adopting a procedure, correct and constitutional, without making an enemy or alienating a friend, the Turk had attained an object at least as important to him as that attained by Germany in the Rhineland, in Austria, and in Czechoslovakia by the flagrant violation of international agreements.

The Thracian Convention naturally shared the fate of the Straits Convention. Turkey and Greece were thus freed from the restrictions which provided for the demilitarization of their European frontiers.

The Montreux Convention had a further and somewhat paradoxical result. It marked the loosening of the ties between Russia and Turkey and the beginning of the *redintegratio amoris* between Turkey and Great Britain. It was noticed that the speech in which the Turkish President opened Parliament in 1938 omitted, for the first time, any mention of Turco-Soviet friendship. To the growing friction between the two friends several things contributed. Russia mistrusted the increasing intimacy between Turkey and her neighbours revealed in the Balkan and Asiatic Pacts, and in the welcome given in the Turkish Press to the agreement between Italy and Yugoslavia (March 1937). Still more did the U.S.S.R. mistrust the settlement of the dispute between Turkey and France about Alexandretta; but most menacing of all, in Russian eyes, was the renewal of the historic friendship between Turkey and Great Britain.[1]

[1] This Agreement was embodied in *The Treaty of Mutual Assistance* signed between Great Britain, France, and Turkey at Angora on 19 October 1939.

Turkey had already given proofs of her wish to follow the lead given by Great Britain to the League of Nations: she joined in the 'Sanctions' directed against Italy's policy in Abyssinia; she adhered to the Anti-Piracy Agreement respecting the Mediterranean, concluded at Nyon (14 September 1937); most significant of all she signed an agreement with Great Britain (12 May 1939). The two Governments recognized the imperative necessity of taking all measures possible for maintaining the security of the Balkan States and undertook to co-operate effectively in the event of war in the Eastern Mediterranean. Before the Anglo-Turkish Agreement was concluded the amazing career of Kemel Atatürk had been cut short by his death at the age of fifty-seven (10 November 1938).

Kemal will unquestionably occupy a unique place in the history of his country; and in the category of Dictatorships. His contribution to Turkish history has been demonstrated in preceding paragraphs; it is well summarized by Sir Harry Luke as follows:

'The old Ottoman Empire has been thrown into a crucible in which its Turkish core has been separated from the non-Turkish elements . . . to emerge small indeed, but compact, refined. The new Turkey has relaxed its hold on the Arab countries, it has . . . achieved racial homogeneity . . . it has rejected the

The Treaty constitutes a mutual guarantee against aggression in the Mediterranean area on the part of any European Power. Russia is expressly excluded from the terms of the Treaty, but it provides for the intervention of Turkey should Great Britain or France be compelled to implement in arms the guarantee given by them to Greece and/or Roumania. The Treaty though purely defensive is plainly an act of far-reaching diplomatic importance, and (as Mr. Chamberlain said in announcing its signature to the House of Commons) it is 'no temporary arrangement to meet a pressing emergency but is a solid testimony of the determination of the three Governments concerned to pursue a long-term policy of collaboration'. For text of Treaty cf. Cmd. 6123.

religion of Arabia . . . abandoned the political and spiritual leadership of the Mohammedan world. . . .'[1]

As regards Kemal's place among post-War dictators it may be premature to anticipate the verdict of history. But even Count Sforza, a robust Liberal, both in letters and in politics, makes an exception in Kemal's favour, and he makes it on two grounds: that his dictatorship was 'involuntary' and has aimed at 'making autocrats and dictators impossible in the self-government of a renovated free nation', and that he has remained faithful to the policy of 'renunciation of any Osmanli idea of domination over non-Turkish peoples'. 'He has dared', adds Count Sforza, 'to do what no dictatorship has ever done—to cut down or renounce the noisy and rhetorical legacies which the empty prestige policy of the previous régime had bequeathed to him.'[2]

The personal character of the man was extraordinarily complex and full of contradictions. Estimates are consequently various and confusing. One fine character sketch described him as the 'Cromwell of the Near East'.[3] As a soldier he may indeed be compared with the man who was never beaten. As a ruler he may well rank with the few dictators who, like Cromwell, accepted the responsibilities of a position which they knew to be imposed upon them by temporary necessities, and with a view to preparing the peoples they respectively ruled for the enjoyment of a wider liberty in the future. In one respect, however, the parallelism between Kemal and Cromwell breaks down. Cromwell was, in every sense of the word, a stern Puritan—in creed, in character, and in life. Kemal was simply unable to understand, still less to conform to, the ordinary conventions of morality. Very superstitious, as men devoid

[1] *Modern Turkey*, p. 224.
[2] *European Dictatorships*, p. 204.
[3] *The Times*, 16 Nov. 1937.

of 'belief' often are, he was purely materialistic in outlook. Though his charm of manner was, when he chose to exhibit it, irresistible, he was heartless, cynical, and cruel. Yet, withal, a man to whom history will assuredly ascribe the rare quality of greatness.

The one thing a Dictator cannot do, it has been generally affirmed, is to provide his country with a successor. Atatürk, unique in this as in all else, undoubtedly intended that General Ismet İnönü should succeed him, and on 11 November 1938 Ismet was unanimously elected by the Assembly as second President of the Turkish Republic. Every preparation for the change over had, doubtless, been made; Kemal had for some time been in the grip of an incurable disease; his successor was ready to hand. Nevertheless, the complete tranquillity and order with which the transition took place was, considering the circumstances, nothing less than astonishing.

Like his predecessor, Ismet is a great soldier: but he is like him in nothing else. To Kemal, passionate, impulsive, and impatient of details, Ismet, cautious, precise, painstaking, and imperturbable, presents the strongest contrast imaginable. For some fourteen years the two men had worked in complete harmony, each supplying the qualities the other lacked. Having won military fame by his victory over the Greeks at İnönü, Ismet showed to equal advantage in diplomacy when he wrestled with England, France, and Greece at Lausanne (1923). From 1925 to 1937 Ismet was continuously in office as Prime Minister and in the reforms carried out by his chief he had a large share. In 1937, however, he was incontinently dismissed. The reasons for the sudden rupture between the two friends have never been explained. A cruel and abrupt dismissal it appeared to be: it left Atatürk (it is said) broken-hearted, and Ismet deeply hurt, yet unfailing in loyalty to his chief. During the twelve months which elapsed between his dismissal and his election as President Ismet kept entirely aloof from politics, and gave no sign (at any rate in public) of resentment or even disappointment. The reward of virtue was not long withheld. Ismet Inönü has now been in office for a year.

Neither in domestic nor in foreign policy is there any indication of a break between the late and the present régime. The recent signature of the agreement with Great Britain has set the seal upon the policy initiated by Atatürk. At home a fresh impulse has been given, but without any change of direction, to industrial development and to reforming activity in many fields, while in the constitutional sphere Ismet has renewed an experiment which, when attempted by Atatürk, in 1930, was the reverse of successful. A dictator who would fain prepare his country for Parliamentary Government is faced with a dilemma. To the success of that system party organization is essential. With dictatorship, however, more than one party is incompatible. Conscious of the dilemma Atatürk attempted to create a Liberal Opposition in the Assembly. The experiment failed. Ismet is renewing it on somewhat different lines. It will be watched with interest by all who believe that the supreme test of the success of a Dictatorship is whether it does or does not make the people ready for its supersession; whether, in a word, it is constructive and educative, or merely destructive. Our own Tudor dictators reacted successfully to the test. Effectively if unconsciously they gave to the new middle classes a training in local administration which prepared them to take upon themselves, under the Stuarts, greater responsibilities. The circumstances of England and Turkey are not, of course, parallel. The Tudors merely gave a temporary check to a constitutional development which had been in progress for centuries. Before Queen Elizabeth died it was already clear that Parliament was ready to resume it: under the Stuarts they resumed it with effect. The Turks have had no similar discipline or training. Consequently it would be disastrous for them if constitutional development should be too rapid. Long years must elapse before they can be ready for self-government as the Anglo-Saxon peoples understand it. But in a few short years by the genius of one man an amazing revolution has been effected, in the structure of the State, and in the social habits and the cultural outlook of the people. That extraordinary achievement gives ground for hope that the period of apprenticeship may be shortened, and that a democracy of the western type may, in the fullness of time, at last take root in Asiatic soil.

The core of the Eastern Question, as treated in this book, has been provided by the Turks. The modern phase of that immemorial problem opened with the advent of the Ottomans in Europe in the fourteenth century. One aspect of it has evidently closed with the transference of the Turkish capital from Istanbul to Angora, with the creation of a modern State, and the birth of a new Nation in the bracing atmosphere of Anatolia. Other factors in that problem, as defined in preceding chapters of this book, still obstinately await solution.

For further reference:

GENERAL

Sir J. A. R. MARRIOTT, *History of Europe, 1815–1936.* 1937.

F. LEE BENNS, *Europe since 1914.* 1930.

Count CARLO SFORZA, *Europe and Europeans.* 1936.

R. B. MOWAT, *A History of European Diplomacy.* 1927.

A. J. TOYNBEE, *Survey of International Affairs, 1920–1923.* 1925.

A. J. TOYNBEE, *Survey of International Affairs.* (Annual.)

G. M. GATHORNE-HARDY, *International Affairs, 1920–1934.* 1934.

E. L. HASLUCK, *Foreign Affairs, 1919–1937.* 1938.

The Annual Register. (Annual.)

The Statesman's Year Book. (Annual.)

THE EASTERN QUESTION AND THE BALKANS

H. H. CUMMING, *Franco-British Rivalry in the Post-War Near East*. 1938.

Sir R. W. GRAVES, *Storm Centres of the Near East, 1879–1929*. 1933.

R. MACHRAY, *The Little Entente*. 1929.

P. G. MOSELY, *Russian Diplomacy and the Opening of the Eastern Question* 1931

Royal Institute of International Affairs, *South-Eastern Europe*. 1939.

J. S. ROUCEK, *The Politics of the Balkans*. 1939.

B. H. SUMNER, *Russia and the Balkans*. 1937.

TURKEY

JACQUES BAINVILLE, *Les Dictateurs*. 1937.

L. BROAD and L. RUSSELL, *The Way of the Dictators*. 1935.

H. EDIB, *Turkey Faces West*. 1930.

GRACE ELLISON, *An Englishwoman in Angora*. 1923.

GRACE ELLISON, *Turkey To-day*. 1928.

H. FROEMBGEN, *Kemal Ataturk*, translated by K. KIRKNESS. 1937.

T. L. JARMAN, *Turkey*. (Modern States Series.) 1935.

A. VON KRAL, *Kamâl Atatürk's Land*, translated by K. BENTON. 1938.

Sir H. LUKE, *The Making of Modern Turkey*. 1936.

Sir J. A. R. MARRIOTT, *Dictatorship and Democracy*. 1935.

W. MILLER, *The Ottoman Empire and its Successors, 1801–1927*. 1934.

D. VON MICKNACH, *Mustapha Kemal between Europe and Asia*, translated by J. LINTON. 1931.

Official Text of the *Straits (Montreux) Convention* (1936). Cmd. 5551.

Official Text of the *Treaty of Lausanne* (1923). Cmd. 1929.

Official Text of the *Anglo-French-Turkish Agreement* (1936). Cmd. 6123.

S. RONART, *Turkey To-day*, translated by J. M. GREENWOOD. 1938.

Count CARLO SFORZA, *European Dictatorships*. 1932.

SIRDAR IKBAL ALI SHAH, *Kamal Maker of Modern Turkey*. 1934.

A. J. TOYNBEE and K. P. KIRKWOOD, *Turkey*. (The Modern World.) 1926.

The New Turkey (reprinted from *The Times*). 1938.

Sir A. T. WAUGH, *Turkey Yesterday, To-day, and Tomorrow*. 1930.

W. W. WHITE, *The Process of Change in the Ottoman Empire*. 1937.

GREECE

S. B. CHESTER, *Life of Venizelos*. 1921.

G. B. EDDY, *Greece and Greek Refugees*. 1931.

C. KEROFILAS, *Eleftherios Venizelos: his Life and Work*, translated by B. BAIRSTOW. 1915.

J. Mavrogordato, *Modern Greece, 1800–1931.* 1931.

W. Miller, *Greece.* (The Modern World.) 1928.

W. Miller, *A History of the Greek People, 1821–1921.* 1922.

ROUMANIA

N. Bañesca, *Historical Survey of the Rumanian People.* 1926.

J. Clerk, *Politics and Political Parties in Roumania.* 1936.

J. Howath, *Transylvania and the History of the Rumanians.* 1935.

N. Iorga, *History of Rumania,* translated by J. McCabe. 1925.

J. S. Roucek, *Contemporary Roumania and her problems.* 1932.

R. W. Seton-Watson, *A History of the Roumanians.* 1934.

YUGOSLAVIA

C. A. Beard and G. Radin, *The Balkan Pivot: Yugoslavia.* 1929.

J. Buchan (ed.), *Yugo-Slavia.* 1923.

G. Ellison, *Yugoslavia.* 1935.

L. Marcovitch (ed.), *Serbia and Europe, 1914–1920.* 1921.

S. T. Patterson, *Yugoslavia.* 1936.

BULGARIA

G. C. Logio, *Bulgaria.* 1936.

HUNGARY

C. A. Macartney, *Hungary.* (The Modern World.) 1934.

C. A. Macartney, *Hungary and her Successors, 1919–1937.* 1937.

O. Rutter, *Regent of Hungary.* 1939.

O. Zasck, *The History of Hungary.* 1939.

ALBANIA

J. Swire, *Albania.* 1929.

J. Swire, *King Zog's Albania.* 1937.

APPENDIX A

LIST OF OTTOMAN RULERS

Othman I	1288–1326
Orkhan	1326–1359
Murad I (Amurath)	1359–1389
Bayezid I	1389–1402
Interregnum and Civil War . . .	1402–1413
Mohammed I	1413–1421
Murad II	1421–1451
Mohammed II	1451–1481
Bayezid II	1481–1512
Selim I	1512–1520
Suleiman I (Solyman the Magnificent) .	1520–1566
Selim II (the ' Sot ') . . .	1566–1574
Murad III	1574–1595
Mohammed III	1595–1603
Ahmed I	1603–1617
Mustapha I	1617–1618
Othman II	1618–1622
Mustapha [1]	1622–1623
Murad IV	1623–1640
Ibrahim	1640–1648
Mohammed IV	1648–1687
Suleiman II	1687–1691
Ahmed II	1691–1695
Mustapha II	1695–1703
Ahmed III	1703–1730
Mahmud I	1730–1754
Othman III	1754–1757
Mustapha III	1757–1773
Abdul Hamid I	1773–1789

[1] Sometimes omitted from the list.

Selim III	. . . . . .	1789–1807
Mustapha IV	. . . . . .	1807–1808
Mahmud II	. . . . . .	1808–1839
Abdul Medjid	. . . . . .	1839–1861
Abdul Aziz	. . . . . .	1861–1876
Murad V	. . . . . .	1876
Abdul Hamid II	. . . . .	1876–1909
Mohammed V	. . . . . .	1909–

APPENDIX B

SHRINKAGE OF THE OTTOMAN EMPIRE IN EUROPE DURING THE LAST HUNDRED YEARS

	Area sq. miles.	Population.
1817	218,600	19,660,000
1857 (after Treaty of Paris) . .	193,600	17,400,000
1878 (after Treaty of Berlin) . .	129,500	9,600,000
1914 (after the Balkan Wars) . .	10,882	1,891,000

APPENDIX C

REIGNING DYNASTIES IN THE BALKANS

GREECE (SCHLESWIG-HOLSTEIN-SONDERBURG-GLÜCKSBURG)

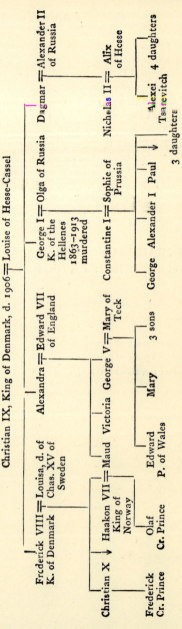

Christian IX, King of Denmark, d. 1906 = Louise of Hesse-Cassel

(To illustrate the dynastic connexions of the reigning Greek House.)

MONTENEGRO

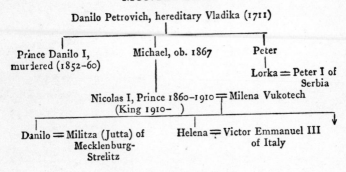

Danilo Petrovich, hereditary Vladika (1711)

Prince Danilo I, murdered (1852–60)

Michael, ob. 1867

Peter

Lorka = Peter I of Serbia

Nicolas I, Prince 1860–1910 = Milena Vukotech
(King 1910–)

Danilo = Militza (Jutta) of Mecklenburg-Strelitz

Helena = Victor Emmanuel III of Italy

SERBIA (OBRENOVIĆ)

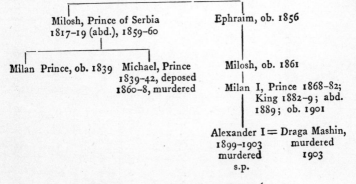

Milosh, Prince of Serbia 1817–19 (abd.), 1859–60

Ephraim, ob. 1856

Milan Prince, ob. 1839

Michael, Prince 1839–42, deposed 1860–8, murdered

Milosh, ob. 1861

Milan I, Prince 1868–82; King 1882–9; abd. 1889; ob. 1901

Alexander I = Draga Mashin, 1899–1903 murdered murdered 1903 s.p.

SERBIA (KARAGEORGEVIĆ)

George Petrovich (Kara George), murdered 1817

Alexander I, Prince 1842–59, deposed, ob. 1885

Peter I, = Lorka of Montenegro
King 1903

George
Denounced rights 1909

Alexander

BULGARIA (SAXE-COBURG AND GOTHA)

Clementina, daughter of Louis Philippe, King of France = Augustus, Prince of Saxe-Coburg and Gotha, ob. 1881

Ferdinand I (Prince of Bulgaria 1887, King 1908), 1887– == (1) Mary Louisa of Bourbon-Parma / (2) Eleonora of Reuss

Boris   Cyril →

ROUMANIA (HOHENZOLLERN-SIGMARINGEN)

Charles Anthony, Prince of Hohenzollern-Sig., ob. 1885 = Josephine of Baden

Charles I, Prince of Roumania 1866, King 1881–1914, ob. s.p. = Elizabeth of Wied (Carmen Sylva)

Leopold, Prince of Hohenzollern, ob. 1905 = Antonia, d. of Maria II of Portugal

William, P. of Hohenzollern

Ferdinand I = Maria, d. of Alfred, Duke of Edinburgh, 1914–

Charles   Nicholas →

INDEX

Abbas I, 245.

Abdul Aziz, Sultan, 311, 312, 325.

Abdul Hamid I, Sultan, 158, 161.

Abdul Hamid II, Sultan, 18, 25, 77, 325, 331, 358, 362, 387, 395, 397–8, 401, 402, 404, 414, 416–18, 421, 434–6, 459.

Abdul Mejid, Sultan, 238, 249, 310, 311.

Abdul-Mejid, Prince, 559.

Abdullah Pasha, 231.

Abercromby, Sir Ralph, 172.

Aberdeen, 4th Earl of, 247, 248, 252, 257, 260, 261, 265, 310.

Aboukir: *see* Battles.

Acre, 241; siege of, (1799) 170, (1832) 231, (1840) 243.

Adana, 234, 237, 435.

Aden, 92, 99; occupied by England (1839), 239.

Adrianople, 44, 47, 122, 330, 335, 427, 452, 454, 456, 465, 466; fall of (1913), 457, 528; recaptured (1913), 464; Ottoman capital, 64. *See* Battles *and* Treaties.

Adriatic, the, 19, 21, 27, 28, 31, 166, 174, 175, 190, 191, 198, 204, 391, 429, 430, 446, 453–5, 458, 471, 492–4; problem of, 389 seq., 521–3.

Aegean, the, 3, 4, 9, 19, 30, 31, 36, 46, 47, 82, 85, 113, 391, 446, 454, 455, 459, 463, 470, 496.

— Islands, 84, 95, 200, 458, 461.

Aerenthal, Baron von, 418, 429, 430, 458.

Afghanistan, 177.

Agadir, 440.

Ahmed I, Sultan, 107.

Ahmed II, Sultan, 108.

Ahmed III, Sultan, 108, 133.

Aix-la-Chapelle, Peace of (1748), 143.

Akaba, 489.

Akerman, 162. *See* Treaties.

Alaeddin, Seljukian Sultan, 43, 100.

Albania, 15, 16, 27, 48, 60, 80–2, 115, 187, 204, 207, 228, 342, 423, 449, 450, 454, 458–62, 471, 472.

'Albanian Gap', 27, 28, 31.

Albanians, 413, 429.

Alberoni, Cardinal, 6, 141.

Albert, Prince, of Saxe-Coburg (the Prince Consort), 247, 298, 310.

Aleppo, 232, 234.

Alessio, 27, 454.

Alexander I, Tsar, 6, 7, 10, 173, 184, 186, 187, 189, 195, 196, 206, 207, 212, 246, 275, 291, 292.

Alexander II, Tsar, 272, 281.

Alexander III, Tsar, 352, 358, 361, 398.

Alexander, King of Greece, 507–8.

Alexander I of Serbia, 314, 424–5.

Alexander of Battenberg, Prince of Bulgaria, 351, 352, 353, 354, 356–9.

Alexandria, 22–4, 169, 176, 229, 230, 238, 243; fall of (1806), 227. *See* Battles.

Algeciras, 440.

Algiers, 92, 95, 97, 226, 438.

Ali Pasha, of Janina, 178, 203, 204, 207, 226.

Allenby, General, Lord, 514, 557.

Alma: *see* Battles.

Amastris, 83.

Amiens: *see* Treaties.

Anatolia, 3, 83, 434, 435, 473.

Ancona, 82.

Andrassy Note, 323, 324.

Andrew II of Hungary, 58.

Andronicus III, 60.

Anglo-French Agreement, 440.

Angora: *see* Battles.

—, City of, 530, 559.